THE BIG SHINY PRISON
(*HISTORY OF A YEAR: 12.20.06-10.13.07*)
c/o Ryan Bartek, GhostNomad & Benedict Badoglio

ISBN-13: 978-0692626153 (Anomie Press)
ISBN-10: 0692626158

Please ask your local book store to carry books by Anomie Press. **Anomie Press is a D.I.Y. Publisher ------------> www.BigShinyPrison.com

To Sutter Cane, Keyser Soze,
And All Who Get The Joke
act vi vi vi

"'The Big Shiny Prison' is many things; a chronicle of a journey across America, a socio-political tract of mighty proportions, a living novel with Bartek playing the dual roles of author and protagonist – but as an exploration into the bizarrely captivating world of underground music, it penetrates deeper than the vast majority of literature on the subject before, and the metallic intelligentsia nods its head in bemused satisfaction, not to mention vindication." – RockPulse

"'The Big Shiny Prison' is essentially a travel diary from 2006 into 2007 of a man that jumped on a Greyhound bus & traveled across America interviewing metal bands. Essentially, this is true, but there is much more. Bartek, in the style of Jack Kerouac & tone of Hunter S. Thompson, takes the reader into a mental journey pleading for everyone to 'Wake Up!' and 'Live for The Moment!' Other aliases include GhostNomad & Klownfuehrer. If all of this seems interesting & at the same time a lot to take in, well, welcome to 'The Big Shiny Prison.'" –MetalUnderground

"Insightful, funny and entertaining, 'The Big Shiny Prison' is more than your usual rock journal written by some overpaid hack traveling from hotel room to hotel room, gig to gig and trying to get across the pain of 'living on the edge.' Bartek lives on the edge with these characters – characters who have given up the concept of the American dream and refuse to play by the rules – and his Gonzo style of writing makes him as integral to his story as much as his interviewees..." – Rockmidgets

"I can't even begin to describe it, let alone do it any justice... Bartek's got more than enough energy, smarts & stick-to-it-ive-ness to really make a big positive change in the world, but the tragedy – which haunts many of the characters in 'The Big Shiny Prison' – is that there's very often no place in Amerikkka for such unique snowflakes, thus the strange often get pushed to The Edge where they self-destruct with booze & drugs & jail & etc. Which, I'm happy to say, I doubt will happen to him. But it certainly wasn't always so – going down into The Abyss was a dangerous move in which Bartek did imperil his very life, but he was determined to write this book or die trying..." –SIBHOD Zine

"No matter what anyone says about this book, you have to respect any writer who is willing to live his life on the road – in the dirt & grime, living among the Crusts & Punks, Rolling from squat to squat, sleeping in parks & generally living in shit just to bring us the story." --Ectomag

*To Sutter Cane, Keyser Soze,
And All Who Get The Joke*

act vi vi vi

Introduction: SAWDUST CAESAR (THE ALUS REPUBLIC)

by Benedict Badoglio, former ambassador of The Alus Republic

This Book, called by its author, "THE BIG SHINY PRISON," is actually a long tract on what happened within the span of three-quarters of a year. During this period, Ryan Bartek sacrificed himself to the most absurd of all addictions. Against all logic, all conventions to which a young man his age normally submits – he willingly & fanatically became a character in his own *living novel*; a tragic pawn of an organic manuscript shaped by the winds of fate.

Despite the lunacy of this decision, his aims were clear – to create a frenetic expose of extreme journalism, unveiling the secretive underworlds of American fringe in a fashion never witnessed before. He would encompass the beat and the gonzo, lunging head-first into the deepest of tribal undergrounds within extreme metal, punk rock, industrial, experimental, avant-garde. He would showcase the true state of counterculture and challenge the literary academia's status quo of travel literature: *Thus begat the struggle, and so began the endless parade of freaks, mongrels, rock stars, metal gods, punk icons, psychopaths, hobos, street crazies, ex-cons & clowns…*

From December 20th 2006 until October 13th 2007 – for 297 days – he lived in a stasis knowing that every line of dialogue, each twist & turn of fate would be recorded. Once it began there was no escape, no life but the road. His only compass would be an internal sense of where the manuscript should theoretically lead, and his only coordinates the most engaging story at hand.

In fact the title of this book itself is a fitting double entendre – not only was Bartek journalistically sculpting his country into a dark caricature of social/political prison, but he was literally trapped within his creation as well – imprisoned by this glowing, shiny promise of adventure & rebirth.

Yet for all the turbulence to follow, it is of importance that we begin this tale with the past, for the turgid history of Ryan Bartek is a depraved saga. True, "The Big Shiny Prison" begins its odyssey on December 20th 2006 – The circles go far into the past and into the future, all centered right there, that frostbitten eve when the broken man charted a lone Greyhound for California, his legacy concluding in utter defeat. The man once acclaimed as one of the most important counterculture journalists in Detroit's history was then a mere bundle of tired flesh, an uncomfortable superfluity

For within a single year he'd gone from prominent figure in a multi-million redevelopment deal that would've revitalized Detroit to none other than haggard trailer trash – a desperate, powerless Sawdust Caesar drowning in booze, curtailed by highs, grimly watching his life dream crumble into nothingness…

The pre-"Big Shiny Prison" caricature of Bartek -- with his shaved block of a head & pugnaciously out-thrust chin, his bantam-rooster stance with arms akimbo, chest & belly straining against a \$3 pin-stripe suit fit for a Jean Claude Van Damme villain – these do not seem the features of diabolicism so much as that of low comedy.

We tend to think of him as a kind of 8th rate pseudo-dictator, a wannabe revolutionary genius, and ultimately, a failed insurrectionary. The fact is that Bartek is both worse than this and far more important because he built the edifice of his particular shuck upon the emptiness of deception, delusion, and fraud. He cannot be rehabilitated.

As distinguished historian T.J.A. Paylor puts it: *"Our principle interest in Bartek derives from his authorship of the so-called 'Pan-Tribal Socialist Manifesto.' In this guerilla psyops manual, he'd lain bare his fanatic goals of overthrowing reality by manipulation of internal vision, welding together the mot dangerous aspects of art & politics fused with a belligerent, black magick recipe for disaster…:*

Its aims were clear but its ideology vague. The 'Pan-Tribalism' it describes proves to be a highly elusive subject, for in the end, this great antagonist of society had no ideology. He was a mountebank who governed by press statement; his leadership was corrupt, incompetent, empty." Empty at its core, an avatar of that very heart of darkness into which Col. Kurtz gazes in and can repeat but a single phrase: *"the horror, the horror…"*

There is no doubt that Bartek had been highly popular in the Detroit Underground. He elicited the favor of the disaffected & cynical, for he was one of them. At his peak he booked shows for dozens of bands, hosted 2-3 concerts a week, swayed the content of FM DJ playlists, physically worked to restore venues, engaged in political activism, even disc jockeyed industrial at times. He performed spoken word gigs, ran international PR campaigns, assisted contacts throughout Europe & South America, and crafted 3 popular weekly music/political columns. He was music editor at another well-respected paper, and a tireless promoter of Detroit record labels.

His operation was like a mad carnival – propaganda offensives & street teams, publicity stunts & radio appearances, forging meetings with ambassadors from every subculture splinter in the city. In time he'd networked a beast that grew to phenomenal proportions, gracefully moving through the gamut of underground politics extreme to extreme.

As a journalist he'd written articles on Detroit unity -- but as an underground politician, he manipulated the press into aiding his great psychodrama in which 20,000 elite Detroiters were the protagonists, and the outside world the astonished spectators. He knew how to speak a language the people understood – and he had that magic antennae forever grasping the trend of popular mood.

There were few major problems of our times to which Bartek did not offer his dazzling answer. His tone always suggested self-assurance, if not megalomania. Dilettante, approximate, and rambling in his views, they were, nevertheless, expressed with magniloquent eloquence. The outside world offered its co-operation by admiring the performance and attributing wondrous qualities to the chief performer. Who would deny he was a great man, when they themselves cultivated and solidified his myth?

Yet the attribute of greatness that was once so lavishly poured on him is applicable to only one of his characteristics, which was the predominant one of his character -- he was a World Class "HAM"; the most intelligent imitation of what, according to him, was propagandic genius. Sometimes he overplayed, sometimes astonishingly effective – but a ham he was throughout.

The recollections in his autobiographical writings, as well as the declarations by his henchmen and associates, are self-serving or, more correctly, self-mythologizing. One would search in vain for a rational, evolutionary pattern to his development.

Whatever else he would become, the boy born on April 4th, 1981, in Dearborn MI would always and above all a huckster. He is eager to paint his adolescence in hues that presaged his Lex Luthor-like dimensions of permanent greatness as foreordained and inevitable, but most likely, his development was not unlike any other vicious problem child with a flair for artistic creativity. Certainly he was persecuted as an outsider, but it also seems clear that he equally brought this upon himself and even cultivated it.

It is typical of the disturbed loner to gain confidence by projecting the ice-cold persona he so wishes to become. It is a natural tendency to overcome despair through re-creation of the self. In 90% of cases, this tendency manifests itself as short-lived rebellion during the teen years, running its futile soft-belly course.

But not for Bartek; from the age of 14 onward he was a die-hard that espoused every fanaticism of his era – socialism, tribalism, anarchy, occultism, anti-right wing militancy. By the time he'd integrated himself into the burgeoning Detroit underground, he'd already set upon the creation of his rebel empire by combining dozens of youthful factions throughout the Metropolitan area. He had a term for it – "*The Prozac Nation.*"

By 16 he'd gone from isolated loner to a figure of some importance. He was respected among his brethren; an outspoken, miniature demagogue commanding his own crew of vandals. In the language of the mainstream, he was a freak gang leader – a sort of "*Trenchcoat Mafia*" quasi-dictator. He was a prime example of the pre-Columbine "Dark Age."

By 1999 "The Prozac Nation" had collapsed – fist-fights, drug addictions, theft, suicides, prison terms, overdoses, tethers, asylum internment. It was from this chaos – the abysmal year of 1999 – that Bartek spiraled into a dark, druggy maelstrom lasting 3 long years. In the end he embarked on the creation of his first book "*The Silent Burning.*" It was brutal self-therapy as much as it was belligerent hypnosis propaganda.

By 2001 he became an intern at the 2nd largest free weekly in Detroit. With 70,000 copies per week and an estimated readership of 150,000, Bartek thrust everything into his mission. His first order of business was not learning how to be a professional journalist – it was to maintain the hostage situation he now held and milk every last drop in order to leave psychological claw marks upon world history so savage that they would likely take centuries to heal.

His untainted freedom of speech was mainly due to the editorial department's gross ignorance on the subjects in which he was writing. For the first time in history, a major Detroit newspaper was promoting militant punk rock, Scandinavian black metal, horribly insulting death metal; the harshest governmental conspiracies, the most fringe subcultures. The media, unaware of his demented agenda, gazed onward with approving smiles. Suddenly this nerve-shot, haranguing freak became the "*Voice of Detroit*" in many international eyes.

Aided by the network of 3,000+ media contacts from across the globe. he formed his press release company ANOMIE PR and in true P.T. Barnum fashion, began promoting himself as if he were The Godfather. He answered all online correspondence as if one of several attractive female secretaries who supposedly worked for him. The prank was astonishing in its effectiveness. Reporters, promoters, bands, artists were anxiously waiting to work with the mysterious giant who'd taken Detroit by storm. There seemed nothing that could stop his adventures.

The centerpiece of Bartek's strategy was pompously called "Anomie Incorporated." His alternative to disunity was one blanket production/promotion company to help regulate the activity amongst all swindled into it. Anomie Inc was a thing to behold, although it was, of course, seething with corruption. Its imposing structure was like that of a building that has no trace of sanitary facilities or of sewage. Still, it was a propaganda machine that found him integrated directly or indirectly with hundreds of live music shows.

Bartek worked hard to counterpoint the image of a steel-hard ideologue with that of a humorous, intellectual, freak mutant. Most were impressed by the charming, smiling, soft-spoken manner he adopted in private – a welcome contrast to his strident public persona. They convinced themselves to view him in the best possible light, and they accepted the charming as real and the swaggering hellfire as mere play-acting for public consumption.

This odd fame had brought but few changes in his habits. Recording Industry Illuminati and Press Elite were always ready to go the whole way to please him, although never stopped being on the *qui vive* for they knew he was strange and different – and certainly not one of them. Nor did he feel at ease with them.

If Bartek had a driving need to amass power, it was not so he could live like a king. For a man of his position his personal life was rock bottom. He worked up to 4 odd jobs at once, barely scraping by, every dime fed into the ANOMIE INC machine.

His relationships with women were stormy and generally traumatic. He picked cans, ate out of dumpsters, lived off the fast food $1 menu. He duct-taped his ragged sneakers together, shoplifted at every opportunity, sold grass when money was tight. For this all powerful media tyrant was quite shabby, unshaven, and ill-kempt in person. Bartek could have had more, much more.

He worked hard, staying up for days building his designs. Often he was so distant he spoke to friends & family as if crowds at a public gathering. His only official public appearances were scant, and all other times remained a shadowy chameleon, unable to definitely finger in a crowd. Everyone knew who he was, yet no one knew what he looked like. There were rumors that he had facial reconstructive surgery every 6 months in Cambodia.

Night after night he locked himself into his computer, shutting his door as if he were a man sealing his own tomb. When broken from his trance he could be found silently drinking coffee unnoticed at a donut shop or 24-7 Coney Island. Yet he could have easily used his credentials to party with The Pistons, Kid Rock, Ted Nugent, Bob Segar, EMINEM, always refusing any invitation into those worlds. Professional models, burlesque dancers, stunning women always eyeballing him in public, yet he was withdrawn, awkward, usually alone. Was it agoraphobia or misanthropy that kept him in isolation? It is yet another mystery.

Not knowing where to stop and not being strong enough to stop, Bartek was going to be ruined no matter if he won or lost the media war. He vaguely comprehended this as he decided the time was ripe for a coup. His moment, he believed, had finally come. He then seduced the publisher Elitist Publications to release *The Silent Burning* amidst considerable apprehension, assumed the music editor post at Jam Rag, formed his long-awaited band FILTHPIMP, and was handed 3 weekly columns and free reign at Real Detroit. He inked the contract, built his book release to sensational hype, and waited as the seconds ticked by for the grand release on Saturday, January, 8th 2005. Cackling that his master plan had finally come to fruition, he muttered, *"I'll cook 'em a stew they'll choke on..."*

The coup was comical in its failure, acute like the forebodings of immediate ruin. Ironically, *The Silent Burning* created the reverse effect of everything he had worked so diligently to achieve. Within the span of 2 months, his book had ushered forth what was perhaps the highest-speed career suicide campaign in the history of the city. Many times the people had thought that Bartek had gone too far, too controversial, or vastly overextended himself, and every time they saw him coming through as the avenger of mediocrity. *The Silent Burning*, as far as the people were concerned, was his wrong turn.

It might have been all right to character assassinate local celebrities, give scathing reviews equal to that of a prison reaming, install puppet dictators as the bookies of venues, pimp GG Allin onto 14 year old children, declare black propaganda guerrilla war campaigns on major radio, bully bands into mutual proactivity, hustle his henchmen into media internships; to sensationalize, to hype, to blackball, to obsessively prattle on about the coming New World Order and The Illuminati... Demagoguery and the spirit of the carnival could go a long way in making bearable even the most absurd rhetoric – but *The Silent Burning* was quite a different thing.

For Detroiters who've never known such filth-ridden, insulting, brutal misanthropy, it was a shock of alienation which coursed through all the circles. The inner circle felt it much before the greater whole. Once *The Silent Burning* had entrenched itself into local consciousness, Bartek's stranglehold was doomed.

He became desperately unpopular in Detroit. Bands refused to book with him, venues fired him, radio stations ignored him, Jam Rag dropped him, local papers blackballed him, scenesters decried him, editors heavily censored him, labels shunned him, distributors flatly declined to sell his book.

The wooden, cardboard setting of ANOMIE INC started crumbling to ruin, and he appeared pitifully helpless. He had no stage and no audience. When that grotesque mask – with its square jaw and beady red eyes fell almost of its own weight – it revealed an utterly desolated spirit. The only answer Bartek gave to the maelstrom was to feebly say over and over again, "*...it's my ruin, my complete ruin...*"

Bartek had created all the conditions which make betrayal inevitable, deluding himself to feel a link in a long, long chain – a segment of a universal, almost cosmic conspiracy. In the minds of all at Real Detroit there was but one question differently phrased: *could the media do without him*? Was or wasn't Bartek's dismissal the only guarantee of survival for credibility? Some wanted him re-installed and reinforced. Some wanted to have him cast aside. Some just plainly didn't know what to do with him.

But practically no one was afraid of Bartek, as if his ties with all factions, even that of his most fanatical supporters, had been cut – and all factions were united in bringing the lurid episode to a close. He was the pawn of the game, not the one who plays it – and his dismissal & blackball was solid reality.

For there was no revolt against the newspapermen, not a single crustie burned a stack of magazines for him. Instead the advertisers streamed in, he was replaced by a fiery young clone, and the scenesters – not seeing any press possibilities in Bartek – felt that nobody was a supporter, that nobody ever had been, and the whole thing had been a long, ghastly nightmare.

He was always a baffling character, but nothing he ever did was as baffling as the way he vanished. His hostage situation over Detroit had, overnight, melted away, and the large majority of scenesters went hoarse shouting *"DEATH TO RYAN BARTEK!!!"* He was still closer to them then any other journalist or promoter, accustomed for years to paying him lip service, but this time as an immediate, tangible object of execration. The most frequently heard comment, aside from *"Watch out or he'll silently burn you,"* was *"Death to the Freewheeling Monkey."*

In those weeks of rejoicing the people acted as if, once Bartek had vanished, his pull among the International Metal Illuminati disappeared with him. Yet from that night onward, he was replenishing his resources in ever growing strength…

Perhaps, he thought, he could still re-conquer the confidence of the people. He had a key, *"a secret key,"* as he said, that someday he was going to use and things would thoroughly change. In light of June 6th, 2006 (6.6.06), we know what his secret weapon was.

He would wave again, as in the days of his youth, The Black Flag of Pan-Tribal Socialism. He would appear once more as "The Revolution" and by going radical, he could outflank his rivals. In this void "THE ALUS REPUBLIC" was born -- a direct reference to Nostradamus. The "Fourth And Final Beast" was to be a conglomerate of all the factors embodying the end of times, all backed by what seemed an ideology vastly more disastrous to human kind then Marxism, National Socialism, or NSK.

First, Nostradamus stated, would come "MABUS;" Second "ALUS." Recruiting a lineup of degenerate mercenaries to spread their filth-ridden musical wings, Bartek changed his band name from FILTHPIMP to A.K.A. MABUS, and declared all left of his empire in Detroit as "THE ALUS REPUBLIC."

A.K.A. MABUS' terrified & bemused the audience with half gazing hypnotically at the bestial madness on stage, the remainders pressed against the wall, if not walking out the venue in sonic protest. Too punk for the metal crowd, too metal for the punks, too soft for the hardcore, too aggressive for the indie, too zany for the hardboiled, too experimental for the rockers, A.K.A. MABUS was like Zappa with a bullet belt and corpse-paint, the Marx Brothers gone grindcore.

A mountain of televisions onstage emitted hundreds of clips from horror films, pornography, propaganda newsreels. Small Jehovah's witness-styled pamphlets were distributed before their performance declaring the coming of MABUS with the group members themselves as prophets of this coming era. They dressed wildly different on every occasion, playing different characters, lyrics making a complete mockery of rancid music scenes worldwide. It was a last-ditch attempt to deliver one final savage and fatal blow to the Detroit music scene.

Unleashed on 6.6.06, "The Mabusvanian Conspiracy" was both the heralded ideology that Nostradamus forewarned and simultaneously Bartek's attempt to build himself on the international level. It was the sum equation of all he'd ever believed and fought for, this self-styled revolution he dubbed "Pan-Tribal Socialism." Here Bartek presented the world with his dark vision of the future. The career suicide of *The Silent Burning* was then turned into Millennium Falcon overdrive.

Under the alias of "The Propagandist," Bartek aggressively transmitted this manifesto to all corners of the globe; a transformational propaganda manual of sorts advocating multi-spectrum radicalism. The glue "The Mabusvanian Conspiracy" uses to weld his disparate ideas together runs the gamut from guerrilla media infiltration, to mind control, to belligerent empirical designs on international subculture. Its theories are extremist, immoral, absurd, even comical in places – *at times an absolute caricature of itself* – and seem to promise catastrophe if taken seriously.

Despite the attempts of fringe notables to champion him a gutter philosopher of exceptional caliber, his contribution to the history of ideas can rather be found in his clear and forceful articulation of numerous shtick already in circulation rather than any thoughts of his own. His influences were more than likely the high-brow satire of LAIBACH and the CHURCH OF SUBGENIUS. But somehow The

Conspiracy has been embraced by a growing cult fan-base and its lunatic plan has actually been put into effect.

This was the last dream of his downfall. For his position, his role in Detroit history was now the stake of all games. But actually it was late, far too late. He could only watch around him people play games in which he had been the supreme master. Starting from his dismissal at Real Detroit Weekly, these last 393 days gave to the underground a repeat performance in which the played out old mimic offered the public a gruesome, demonic imitation of his former self.

For Bartek at the end of his career rendered the service of presenting all of Detroit with the most sordid, undiluted form of psychological warfare that was such as to ruin the memory of all his past performances even in the most uncritical minds. The entire underground community resisted. They mocked his Pan-Tribal manifesto, ignored his journalism, refused to attend his shows, deleted him from MySpace, declined to play with A.K.A. MABUS. They acted to his face as if he were invisible, and when cornered, abruptly blew him off or looked the other way.

Bartek and his few remaining acolytes were made to feel they had no power, that A.K.A. MABUS was not punk rock, that they were not "true" metal. But the most important thing was to make them realize they were a joke – just a freakish assemblage of doomed men who for some reason were enjoying a too-prolonged stay of execution.

The writing was now blazing on the wall. By September 2006 all rational hope for victory was long extinguished. His last months were blackened by terrible shows, personal apocalypse, substance abuse, financial stress, automobile difficulties, barren weather, and a thousand jaw-dropping betrayals…

A.K.A. MABUS bickering endlessly, his mother battling cancer, his street family 10,000 miles away & all remaining close friends spread across the breadth of America. His ex-wife in prison over one Vicadin, his brother on life-support from dead kidneys, His freshly ex-girlfriend pregnant by another man & his latest romance sent away on Valentine's because she was going to do 6 months in jail over a single roach…

By early winter he'd suffered attacks described as "*nervous collapse*" and "*an absolute loss of energy and intelligence.*" He was perpetually sleeping 12 hours a day or more, staring at the ceiling from his broken mattress, lost in torrents of the slowest, most punishing doom metal in existence.

The more he shut out the world, the more the PR people came at him. At any moment he could have members from Judas Priest, Morbid Angel, Napalm Death, Emperor, MANOWAR call his house. He could travel to New York or Los Angeles for invite-only record release parties. He could tour with the bands he worshipped in his youth writing lengthy stories about his experiences for Metal Maniacs, PIT Magazine, Hails & Horns, AMP, or any of the dozen zines he now wrote for. Yet he simply would not pick up his phone, haunted and jaded by the emptiness of the world that had once ignited his passion.

Bartek, whom many of his inner circle now believed frankly mad, declared he'd wage the Detroit war to its apocalyptic *Gotterdammerung*. While he paced around frothing at the mouth in a tirade of such rhetoric, he inwardly obsessed over escape. Most appealing was the idea of seeking asylum in California. So amidst the completion of their debut record *Lord of The Black Sheep*, the tarnished Golden Boy swallowed his pride, murdered his legacy, and lethargically faced the A.K.A. MABUS firing squad.

There was no *Clausewitz* in this Propagandist's end – just the banal last moments that failed tyrants have endured and have deserved to endure down the ages. Bartek had long outlived an aspiration to greatness, and a friable Pan-Tribal Socialism – exhausted of credible meaning or social purpose – had long since crumpled into nothingness.

At the end, cornered as he is by history, his view of things is consistent, and in a strange, inverted way, correct – *invariably, what is right for him is wrong for Detroit.* Ignominiously forced in his professional career to work as a microwave cook for Applebee's, he writes that Detroit's rebirth will come only after total defeat, anticipating a new era well into the future. *The divorce between Bartek and his beloved underground had truly been complete…*

And finally, the sinister adventure ends. One December night, the unassuming crowds on Howard Street could see a lone figure pull himself silently onto a bus, the fire at last gone out of him. For "Il Propagandist" and Pan-Tribalism in Michigan, that day really was the end. The great prank had ended in tragedy and the incredible story was finished. No reincarnations or returns are to be expected. Ruined and sobered, R. Bartek hit the road.

Maybe he felt relieved when he found himself riding on that Greyhound. Maybe he thought he was at long last going to have a rest at The Villa Winona. Yet everything that was Hyde within him refused to compromise. Those deep-seated psychological forces grabbed the forlorn old ham, tossed him back on the road, and went right back to creating a freshly constituted "*Pan-Tribal*" web.

Years will pass before self-mythologizing may allow him to attain the power to realize that vision, but it is a lesson that denies the free world the excuse of ignorance. It is a waking call never to close our eyes to the architects surrounding us. Since 911, Homeland Security has been taking promising steps in this regard. It is our responsibility to ensure this civilizing trend. Lately new research has added much to our knowledge about Bartek and his policies, but this book is still essential for any reassessment.

- Benedict Badoglio; New Years Eve, 11:59pm, 2007

I

12.26.06 – 4.05.07

PART I: HUMBLE ORIGINS
(UNCALM BEFORE THE STORM)
DECEMBER 20th 2006-FEBRUARY 6TH 2007

6O HOURS AND 24 INCHES (THE GREAT WHITE DESERT)

"Ok man, so we're headed out to Oklahoma to premier this little independent film we made called *DADBOT*. After 15 hours of straight driving, we're finally out of steam & gas and we pull into this town called Cuba, Missouri…"

The trucker smiles and nods his head: "*Oh yeah bro, I know exactly what you're talking about – I live a hundred miles west of it. It's the last place on God's green earth you wanna end up. Ain't nothin' goin' on in that lil' shithole.*"

"No doubt about that," I say, ready to spew the strange tale. "So yeah, not only is there a drive-in theatre playing two full servings of *Passion of The Christ* on each screen long past it's DVD release, but there's also a Jack In The Box on the corner of the Interstate."

Still nodding, still smiling, the trucker listens on: "This weird, skinny chick is working the register – spies us, nabs us – takes her break and swings us outdoors to jabber. She plops on the hood of an Escort and while chain-smoking explains how Cuba is the crystal meth capital of the United States and that we need protection – immediate, hardcore defense... She flicks her butt in a trail of red ember and flashes us some chrome. Grinning, she dumps this killer street-gang blade on us – like this twisted mutation of a Klingon death weapon. She tells us to watch our backs."

"*That's quite an introduction.*"

"Well, that's just Point A… It's starting to get dark, and we're gunning for a few beers. Our quest for the local dive takes us down these menacing, shadowy streets – lurching willow trees like a ghetto in New Orleans. Finally we hit this bowling alley but there were only three people inside and they wouldn't look at us – like intentionally avoiding us – this evil vibe as if they'd just hacked up some drifter for BBQ and hastily mopped the floor. They are ugly fuckers, all of 'em, faces rotted & sunken purple like Elder God worshipping cult folk from some Lovecraftian nightmare village. "

The trucker's eyes light up in a strange, horrified bemusement. "We ditch on the alley & hit Main Street, which only adds to the

Innsmouth vibe. The drag is a narrow corridor stretching for ten blocks, the walls of every building slopped with painted murals of farmers and cows. Inside them semi-Amish agriculturists are dressed purely in black, which is creepy to begin with. But the kicker was that everyone & everything inside the murals – the farmers, chickens, cows – all of them have pitch black eyes, evil insectoid eyes, huge & bulbous."

"They are fucking terrifying, totally painted by an armada of sleep-deprived meth freaks. And within the murals the Amish M.I.B.'s aren't doing anything. They're all just standing there, watching you, with their plows and rakes limply at their side. Even the cows are staring blankly with these soulless, black eyes, as if the second you turned the corner the painting would magically come to life. It was children of the fuckin' corn, man…"

"We shook off the heebie-jeebies and found another street…" The trucker's still with me, waiting for the big punch line, "…with a dozen Texas Chainsaw Massacre looking houses. Giant houses – old, dilapidated, the stench of rotting wood – all of which had human sized rag dolls on the porch, plopped in rocking chairs. All of these hideous stuffed creatures, gazing at us with murderous black insect eyes. We heard something strange behind us and flipped our heads to catch two of the dolls we passed – again, totally serious – the chairs were rocking. We fucking ran all the way back to the motel."

The trucker belly laughs and proceeds to hammers me with sad stories of interstate loads at 19 cents a mile, gas not included. He was stuck, like all these other displaced people, in the middle of St. Louis Greyhound depot, rerouted or otherwise immobile due to the giant 24 inch blizzard that had engulfed the center of America. Our normal route was to be through Denver, but the poor saps in Colorado are now stuck there up to a week. All of Texas engulfed in white, the desert winds searing a negative 20 degree chill – Old Man Winter's uncongenial bitch-fist. *Elemental bastards, stay out of my damned Valhalla…*

So I commit these thoughts to mental calligraphy, awaiting the opportunity to purge. Barely a day into this thing, and I have yet to recognize the extent of what I've done. In a drunken whirlwind, not thinking the subject over too clearly, I declared the creation of a new book via international press release called "THE BIG SHINY PRISON." In it, I tell the world that I now travel America for a year straight, drifting town to town, interviewing bands and the personalities thereof, penetrating music scenes as I ping-pong across the country totally DIY.

I have no energy, I have no publisher. I have no game plan, I have no structure. All I possess is a backpack, a duffel-bag, and an old school cassette recorder. And I have no money except for the $1200 which is to last me until the end of March.

The money itself does not cover any kind of motel or rent arrangement. It barely covers the fares of Greyhounds to destinations still vaporous and unbooked. I have no real idea where I'm going for certain except a loosely constructed list of bands, pr men, zine proprietors and promoters that have no idea I'm crashing their way. I rely totally on the willingness of those strangers. Still, none of that matters -- for I have MySpace, the Thunder of The Gods...

The book I have espoused is not the book which will be printed. I have been bored to the point of hammering nails through my face by the shoddy journalism of heavy metal. The only well-known books available on the subject are ultimately handcrafted from some hack writer making dozens of phone calls and typing his conversations into a paint-by-numbers expose in which we hear all too often the word "brutal" to describe everything.

No, this isn't my realm. I am not interested in what guitar strings they use. I am not interested in their perceptions of rumbling Drop D noise. I don't care what patches are sewn onto their sleeveless denim vests. To even call it a book about music is misleading. What I seek is the soul. Character studies, their environments, their dreams, hopes and aspirations – a total sociological unearthing. The very substance and inertia of their war and poetry. What are they fighting for and against? And most importantly, how alone in my views am I? What is the common thread? Does the magical world I once looked upon in magazines and onstage when I was 17 even exist?

So I fall into this cocoon, my physical body screaming in constant pain from a jigsaw skeleton of pinched nerves. No chiropractor, no therapy, no respite. One full year of road with no stopping, my last sacrifice to journalism before I can walk away, form a new band somewhere, discover my queen and live a real life. This book will be just as much about the artists and freaks I encounter as it is the hard reality of trying to write this book. This isn't a Kerouac rip-off. This isn't Hunter S. Thompson. This is akin to Christian Bale wandering the earth in *Batman Begins* for seven years, recreating himself in steel. It is just as much about me as it is all of them, because our struggle is unanimous.

Surely, I will be sued. I will be misconstrued. I will be laughed at by dunderheads who think so small that the intensity and mission of such a project will fly miles above their heads. In this I am undeterred. Some will ignore, some will offer sanctuary. No matter the immediate situation I will play by the rules in which I am confined, weaving through these complex undergrounds by stealth. And if all else fails, keep them amused by whacky anecdotes until I can jump back into the safety of the Greyhound purgatory.

The plan is to avoid big bands unless they seek me out or are right there waiting to go. It is not my job to promote those already promoted. Instead I seek the unknown, the struggling, the fringe and depraved. I am out to prove the point that no answer is ever *the* answer, and that reality is only in the eye of the beholder.

I will hunt down the most extreme of personalities from the right to the left. I will let the recorder roll in front of views as confrontational as possible. From pagan militants to Christian rockers, "Goth Idols" to street-dwelling crust punks, from Neo-Nazis to flaming homosexuals. Every monster possibility in America, every inch of its seedy underbelly thrust into the spotlight…

3am, sleeping soundly and somewhere in Texas, a foofy-haired woman interrupts my rest: *"What is he doing back there?"* she questions, in a weird state of panic. I pass back out only to have her wake me again with this identical question. To shut her up, I wander to the back of the Greyhound, pretending to use the toilet.

There is a creepy Hispanic man dressed in a blue-workman's outfit, like Michael Myers duds in *Halloween*. He looks like the gruff caricature of a Sergio Leone villain and smells like rancid feces. And, of course, he's rabidly masturbating an iron-hard flagpole…

I sit back down. The foof lady asks again, and I duly confirm. The passengers are now wide awake, unwilling to confront the strange man wildly jacking off behind them. We pull into Amarillo, and the whacker guns it for Miss Pacman.

Little does he know, cackling and babbling to himself, that Greyhound has called the police. When the heavily accented officers confront him, the Mexican becomes enraged. The cops point to the white glob of jizzom on his clothing, and the man protests in broken, hysterical English: *"No iz paint, iz paint!"*

The cop whispers something in Spanish, and he starts laughing and unzipping his coveralls. Out it plops, dangling from his bellybutton as a limp pendulum. Fearful mothers grip their children, the elderly squeam, grown men grow nauseous & bellicose – *a giant colostomy stuffed with shit dangles to and fro, dripping profusely, and all the Mexican can do is laugh horrendously at the terrified honkies…*

THE FRINGE DESIGN: A PRELIMINARY DISSERTATION

To my dearest of Alice clones, from whatever vortex you might exist, from this tragic Cheshire comes the dynamic of the labyrinth. We must put an end, immediately, to these endless preconceptions. We must shoot down all error from the human mechanics which pervade us…

To the hip, to the knowledgeable, to the fanatic – *none of this will come as a shock*. But to the outside element, the ones accustomed only to the ritual of entertainment – those who look at the weirdo uprising with a dim mystification…

If I am to be your tour guide then I must also be your educator. It is a gutter philosopher you require, not a journalist bound to objectivity. We need to char up that grit, not flubber in the laws of the past. I will be honest to the sharpest apex, but do not chastise or aggrieve, for you now enter a free-fall of eternal descent which even Alighieri refused conjecture.

The kaleidoscope basis of this manuscript will always hone in on the subcultures deemed *"punk rock," "extreme metal," "industrial," "rock n' roll," "experimental."* Still, this does not prevent me in any way from side-missions outside those particular confines, because in the end *every freak* is somehow connected to the overall grand schematic in my humble opine…

Like Voltron, these sharply defined terrains link to create a monster. It is this composite leviathan which constitutes the *"counterculture"* – the assemblage of all conceivable fringe as one massive, organic jigsaw. The nuts and bolts come in all forms, and the breadths of philosophies are panoramic & amorphous…

Within every modern society the fringe lurks substrata. All of us, no matter our vocation, are the by-products of a deeply-ingrained refusal. Every subculture has sprung from the sense that there is something horribly wrong, something deeply unhealthy going on, and that there is definitely a larger system of misery at play. The air of Utopia is poisoned, as it were…

In America there are but two concentrated psychological lines which prevail – the *"herd mentality"* and the *"wild west,"* so to speak. There is a quick-fix, *"don't look too deep & silence the questions"* pre-packaged reality in which we are indoctrinated from birth. Then there is the darkness (*or the light, depending on your view*) – that vast grey area in which the general population only slowly and in marked paces inches forward. The counterculture is the collective body of all who've strayed into that realm of infinite perplexity...

The world of The Big Shiny Prison is the reality of America. Here, in the apex of convenience and security, our bellies are full, our hide is soft, our suburbs are tidy and well organized. Our terrain is landscaped, our structures Goliath. Our culture is that of Walmart Tribalism; our social court the shopping mall. The police are your friends, the priest your neurosis killer, the psychiatrist your handy-man. Work is good, god is great, and everything is plum shit happy.

To phrase the language of the gutter oh so eloquently: *"well fuck all that bullshit."* Yes my Mohawk-laden scat-champs, I tell you as it is as sincerely as one can. There is a word which defines the root propulsion of the first subculture we are to dissect: "Anarchus." It's a Latin word meaning *"any time you act without official permission."* Translated to English, this word reads Anarchy.

Anarchy and Anarchism are not the same thing. Anarchism is the attempt to formulate and apply a definite structure or form, whereas "Anarchy" reflects a mode of thought or perception which the very definition "Anarchus" provides. Again – *"anytime you act without official permission."*

Anarchy is the *action* itself, and a conceptual *underpinning* which is amorphous in nature. Unlike any other ideology, it simply doesn't have one. To claim oneself Anarchist is to claim the position of a *"Free Agent"* from any system, to consider nations an illusion & patriotism a farce – for the anarchist is by design a citizen of the world.

The exact opposite of "Anarchus" derives from another Greek word: "Politik," or politics. The root refers to *"mans relationship to and life in servitude of the state."* To be political is to be a sentry of the establishment. To be an Anarchist is to be apolitical, and anarchy itself is like a virus in the larger body – malleable and formless, within every government, society, class and culture.

Anarchy is the acting through of any activity with the conscience realization that it is not an action intended for the strengthening or assistance of the state. A family picnic by definition is a state of Anarchy, because you are *"off the clock,"* so to speak. The act of shopping, of painting the nails, of leisure is by very definition soft-belly Anarchy…

Therefore, it should be of no dispute that the spirit of punk rock is wholly submerged in Anarchist thought. The entire basis of the underground is summed up by the phrase: *"Do it yourself."* **DIY** is the mantra of punk rock, which is main-line Anarchy – building your own reality, starting your own band, zine, label, clothing line. Creating underground house venues and refusing to pay taxes – squatting, hustling, running amuck as gypsy land pyrates. None of this is rooted in a compulsion for violence, but rather as an outcry of individual passion. The *"bleeding heart,"* so to speak…

We now speak of The Punks – *skins, crusts, skaters, surf-punks, greasers, straight-edgers, vegans, scumfucks, the deftly unclassifiable*. In this wing of the counterculture you have a huge mass of differing opinions. In this, people are either extremely cool about everything – *like Rick James cool* – or they are pretentiously fickle about every minuet detail.

Here you find the most panoramic view of politics in music. There isn't a punk alive that doesn't claim knowledge about some government conspiracy, nor will you find any true love of authority. It is a fanatic escape attempt from the rule of the machine, forever at odds with a materialistic, clean cut existence.

Nothing is more comedic, more ridiculous and laughable to the punker then the worldview that a man such as Curtis "50 Cent" Jackson embodies. In mainstream view, these scurvy rogues are seen as the epitome of *"music entertainment"* – big money & hot bitch hustlers, diamond-plated rims & pistols, MTV cameos & *dolla dolla bills y'all*.

Far and wide, from sea to shining sea, that mentality is the laughable dunce crown. Whereas a high-roller nightclub pimps $1000 bottles of citron & sheepish patrons exude designer fashions, the seedy punk dive celebrates $1 PBR drafts, lets you bring your dogs inside, has no dress code, allows you to paint pictures on the tiling & slap bumper stickers everywhere.

I shall put it this plainly: If someone G-Unit were to show up in a limo flashing all the commodities in the world, they'd be laughed out of dodge. Punks admonish their standing as the refuse of the world. This gutter pervades a life best described as rekindling the one long abandoned in childhood – returning to that magic but going deeper in, architect a new world from it's murky lagoon…

Punk is a seed endlessly germinating, growing profusely midst a universal sense of boundless adventure. And none perhaps have more a sense of adventure then "The Crustie" – the dirtiest, dingiest, most fanatic guardians of that resurrected ideal.

"The Crustie" is the closest thing to a land-based pyrate you'll find. They are essentially street kids that discovered freedom in disowning everything; literal hobos all on a mission to overthrow culture from their livelihoods. Hitchhikers, train-hoppers, panhandlers, dumpster divers, they often travel in small, tightly-knit groups before they get to designated cities in which "The Black Flag" has been raised…

They form in packs and hustle the streets, sleeping in parks or cracking the street system until they know how to get free food, shelter, money, medical services, clothing. They are commonly known as "crust punks," "squatters," "scumfucks," "scumbums" or the like.

When the tide suits them they are ultra-communal. Everyone shares what they own – *especially drugs & booze*. They are united in their perpetual self-destruction, and have an over-whelming hatred of squares and clean-cuts. Some have been on the road for up to ten years, but many are fresh crops who seek themselves for a few years before finding something solid, whether it due to burn-out or physical collapse. They live fast and burn like a tide of seasonal locusts. Those who die young are eulogized into crust folklore. Legends are spread like fables across the world. In other words, *"His name is Robert Palsin."*

On the flip side, there is the ultra-karmic strain of crustie, so deeply committed to veganism and social issues that they are the vanguard of the positivist. In a sense, these twin strains exist as a sort of ying-yang, all which preside in a land of the lost – the fall through the cracks of society so violently that any reverse becomes impossible…

I will probably find myself traversing with many of these shadowy characters, especially in larger cities where I may have difficulty in finding a place to crash. There is always a squat somewhere, always a way to get some food, and plenty secretive avenues that can be explored so long as you dangle a 40oz in front of someone's face. It is the ultimate bargaining chip because a bottle of Mickey's goes fast among twelve alcoholics so hardcore they're puking blood. The only problem is that you have to keep supplying it, or trick them into thinking your broke. Either way, $10 bucks in Steel Reserve is far cheaper than $60 for a motel.

Plus it's far more fun. When you hang with crusties, you drink and drink and drink – *everyone dies together, that's the rule*. You also truly have to earn their respect or stay up until you're the last one to pass out, because if you make the fatal mistake of falling asleep while everyone is at their liver-annihilating prime you run a high risk of "Beer Elf" danger. Expect your clothing to be sewn together with dental floss and your face covered with magic marker, *David the Gnome* style…

The Skinhead is the antithesis of the crustie. Skinheads are not Neo-Nazis, as this confusion is simply the outcome of media disinformation. Neo-Nazi's do exist, but they can be found in any subculture regardless, albeit the vast majority condemning this fascism and violently drumming them out. Real skins are for the most part SHARPS -- "Skinheads Against Racial Prejudice."

The skinhead thing was a wholly black movement which originated in Britain. Jamaican/African immigrants worked mercilessly on dockyards and shaved their heads to avoid lice, in the process gaining a specific look with Lonsdale Boots, suspenders, etc. They were the working class backbone of the UK, and established a unified underground in filthy Taverns on the outskirts of London…

The centerpiece was always Oi dance hall music, a component of Reggae. Oi eventually crossed all racial boundaries, developed into ska, and was imported to the United States and other areas in Europe. In the late 70's it really began to explode alongside punk's phenomenon.

Skins are for the most part heavily patriotic, if not non-violently nationalistic, and pride themselves on their blue-collar position. Strongly tied to the bonds of family and friends, they live a disciplined, clean-cut way of life. But they also drink like fish, and have a nasty belligerency in humongous gatherings. On their own they can be quite amusing though...

The destructive crusties pride themselves on their knuckle scar tissue as well, but they mainly just fight each other. The crusts are fanatical about their separation from society, and would rather bleed to death from a stab wound in a gutter then degrade themselves by snitching. Society is not an option, except as sheep to con and tax.

Crusties and Skins are highly secretive because they are targets for law enforcement. If you ever get pulled over or spotted meandering with a crust or skin, be prepared to be searched, if not shook up or arrested over a bogus charge. Skins, however, are friendlier to authority personal in general because they stand for the middle-class, structured lifestyle. They can talk most cops out of anything, so long as there's no rum in their belly...

The straight-edger (sXe) is the antithesis of the destructive crustie. They maintain the unity and discipline skins have, but straight-edgers derive their name from a zealous refusal to use drugs in any form. Many are so fanatical they won't even touch caffeine, are sharply against prescription drugs, and some pride themselves on absolute celibacy...

Skins and sXe's get along in theory, but rarely in practice. Since skins are notorious working class drunkards, this creates a condition that can be described in following terms: The sXe band brings their associates out to a show. Unbeknownst to ideology, amidst the performance a tanked bulldog tries to force a shot of whiskey down one of their throats. As he believes totally in his cordial offering said wasted skin won't back down, and when insulted blabs something that crosses the line. Thus an eruption of chaos split evenly down ideological lines, and a big, hairy mess to be sure...

The term Straight-Edge originated from vocalist Ian McKaye of Minor Threat, the legendary Washington DC outfit from the early 80's. McKaye was notorious as the godfather of the sXe nucleus, sputtering off independent cells throughout the nation. McKaye wasn't a *"hardercore then thou"* tough guy – he was a fairly laid back individual that watched too many go down in a cocaine fireball and wanted to set something positive in motion. Still, for all the positive nature of the sXe ideal, there are some terrible mutant strains bridging from the virus...

Straight-Edgers are of three general types. The first are those who chose their path after witnessing too many horror stories. These are usually straight-forward guys who don't push their views on others, look at their preferences as a form of dietary choice. The second class is in the moderate to extremist range of ultra-leftist politics. This is where the hardercore-then-thou pathology begins to seep in, the veganism gets trumped to fanatical levels, the celibacy unfurls...

Lastly, there are the ultra right-wing Straight-Edgers – a new brethren of Blackshirt fighting for their self-styled totalitarian utopia. They literally attack drug users in the streets – cigarette smokers, potheads, drunks. They show up 20-40 strong at a concert and jump poor saps guzzling beer, starting mini-riots. In Salt Lake City for instance, such a group was switchblade carving gigantic X's (*the sXe mark*) in the backs of intoxicated citizens they'd randomly select under the cover of night.

There are many violent right-wing sXe groups such as this, particularly in Cincinnati, SLC, Los Angeles, Detroit and Washington DC. Such factions have totally lost the sarcastic, humanist attitude of 80's sXe and now undeniably gravitate towards the more *"tough guy"* hardcore bands which mix metalcore into the formula, giving it a more testosterone-laced, skinhead feel…

As for other sub-types in punk rock you have the skaters, greasers, and a vast gray area that actually takes up the largest percentage. The skaters are typically free-wheeling, hard-partying, drunken vandals. Everything they embody screams of 40oz's, spray paint, smoked roaches & repulsion of authority…

The greasers are exactly what you'd expect. They include the entire rockabilly, psychobilly, classic 50's rock crowd. They are cartoonish & laid back with a flair for the world of James Dean. You'll know them by their pompadours & greased aerodynamic, jet-black hair – leather jackets, chain-link belts, hot rods, choppers, and girlfriends with a visual nod towards Bettie Page or Marilyn Monroe. There might be clandestine games of high-speed chicken on dirt-roads, although I've never heard of any *West Side Story* switchblade duels.

These are zany folks with a hard-on for Americana, worshiping at the altar of Necromantix, Koffin Kats, Phenomenauts, Brian Setzer and even Dick Dale. They drink heavy, but rarely are seen into any other hard drugs. They get along ok with the various groups because greasers don't particularly stand for any great social message – though the ultra-anti-capitalist crusties might holler something about their gas-guzzling chop-jobs…

No one wants more to deal with moderates than the metal scene, who by and large tend to be a little more right wing on certain aspects. You could sum up the vast majority of mentalities by the humble phrase: *"shoot first & ask questions later."*

That stated, the metalheads do not cling to this music for the sake of artistic protest. It is more a simulated riot arched upon a modernized Wagnerian powerhouse – a bombastic spectacle which taps into a primal vein while simultaneously ushering a futurist mythology.

That is, to say, building a world of legend atop the ruins of current. That's why the term "METAL GOD" is appropriate – this fascination with a new order, a loose hierarchy built on the premise that we, as a cultural phenomenon, are building this new mythology – a modernized canon of Roman gods in the shells of contemporary men...

That sentiment isn't all pervading, although it is an undeniable undercurrent which is also symptomatic in punk rock as well. Stripped down further, avoiding the idealistic hub-bub, most just want to rock. They want to fling themselves insanely through a whirlpool of bodies. They want to oogle at pyrotechnics, share communal fascinations, have the darkness they feel presented multilaterally as not to feel so damned alone in a material society stripped of magic or meaningful purpose.

Thus you have heavy metal in all its forms – the fang-bared, blunt, unapologetic yet heroic and fascinating sibling of punk – manifesting itself through a complex web of styles like grindcore, funeral doom, death metal, power metal, powerviolence, necro, viking, thrash, black, sludge, endless variations and combinations of limitless sub-genres. Each sub-genre has their own variation of mentalities, although rarely as opposed to one another as the punks tend to be. Politics are of course engaged upon in lyrics and physical art, but rarely to the point of shoving it down anyone's throat.

Metalheads generally want to get hammered, slam into each other, party with brethren, consume horror cinema, communicate a purist love of music, and leave the constant political diatribes to another occasion. They don't feel the need to dental floss their clothes together to fight the mass marketing of corporations, they don't care the liberal intricacies of political correctness. They don't want anyone to whine at them over a hamburger nor do they give a hoot about sXe fanaticism.

There is a stereotype known as *The Beavis & Butthead* syndrome, in which the outside world sees only this vague *Wayne's World* mentality. There are, of course, plenty of excerebrose morons in metal, but idiots constitute themselves in all walks of life. In reality, the smartest people I've ever known have all been into extreme metal, or at least understood its value and importance. Those deeply involved stay far away from mainstream tours, don't watch MTV, don't listen to the radio. The Beavis & Butthead's of the metal world will always be marked by their assumptions that everything has to be *bruuuutal* and everything non-knuckle dragging is "*faggot shit.*" They go for the thunder, the testosterone, the beer...

We call them 'Meatheads." Meatheads are a bane and a curse to all, but unlike the punkers that will blab away all of their digressions at them, metalheads tolerate them as the eternal half-wit brothers. The

Meatheads are encapsulated mostly by "classic metal" (*i.e. the easy shit that doesn't challenge brainwaves*), Satan-only "Cookie Monster" death metal, and the bad, modern hardcore in which you'll also find many of the violent sXe or Skinhead types. The meathead is entranced by the knuckle-dragging breakdown, the mosh pit, the hatred of anything sissy, anything singing, anything weird. It's all clunking thunder or nothing at all, with a eruptive macho flair.

The people outside of this stereotype are above all intelligent, highly versed in all forms of music, actually *listen* to metal as opposed to just *going with it*. While the death metal dunder-skull bangs his head to noise, the real metalheads actually pinpoint and dissect the notes, the rhythms, the lyrics, the presentation. The real metalhead always has a lavish (*if even slight*) history of building something from the ground up, whether it be running a self-financed label, distro or zine, organizing/promoting/managing shows, able handed with numerous instruments, playing in a band or two, directing online support.

The authentic underground metal scene is generally composed of musicians playing for crowds of other musicians, random freak collectors or fans. No one is interested in money. It's a brotherhood with a unity far tighter than the punk crowd, who for the most part are too busy fighting each other like children. Excluding the Greasers of course, who have no shame in blaring Celtic Frost at top decibel.

Although they enthusiastically agree on their mutual distaste for gangstas, preps, jocks, and authority personnel, the main rub between punk and metal comes down to a few basic factors.

First, metal is intolerant of that which is intolerant of it and wastes no time accommodating outsiders. Second, metalheads have deep grievances towards musical laziness, hence the appreciation of ultra-technical extreme metal. Third, most punk is loose and happy go lucky, thereby considered boring – most songs are basic, light-weight, upbeat, and crafted from 3 or 4 riffs. The punks see that as freedom, the-metalheads as uninspired generica.

Above all you have a fascistically intolerant (*if not wholly fascist*) streak of anti-religious sentiment. No one seriously into extreme metal is deeply religious in any orthodox sense. There are stragglers of course, but they are far from abundant. After all, it should be noted that Black Sabbath were the first and ultimate heavy metal band, and they were Jesus-raging. Other prime examples of noteworthy Christian bands are Living Sacrifice, Zao and Norma Jean.

However, for the majority of the metal scene organized religion is a classic target, and the truly bible-thumping are a superfluous minority. Most who claim Christian positions view Jesus symbolically, artistically, or confide a kindred spiritual link – they like "*the idea of it*" per se. There are very few who take all of it dead serious.

The metalheads are almost unanimously opposed to Christianity (*as well as Islam & Judaism*) for the following reasons. First, there is a deep-seated belief that religion is absolute. Many have declared that to be a true follower one would have to be either ordained clergy, or fanatically working towards that goal. Anything else is seen as hypocrisy, and no one can dispute that the life of the convent does not coalesce well with a packed, rowdy club. As a random longhair once bluntly remarked: "*You can't just pussy-foot around with religion – either you're in it all the way or you're just a blatant poseur.*"

Secondly, there is the lengthy historical record of repression under the aegis of the church (*i.e. the Crusades, Charlemagne, Torquemada, etc*), which though now expurgated, would certainly have been inflicted on the modern underground community – and that goes for punk rock as much as it does metal, or the counterculture in general.

Third, religion renders all reality into a stark black and white in which no gray area exists, thoroughly promoting a clearly defined, authoritarian view of reality under the perimeters of scripture. In this, a great wealth of scientific evidence is wholly dismissed. Most importantly, the bottom line is the unavoidable conclusion that if you disagree with the views of the religion – *that if you don't submit, confess or convert* – then you will likely be imprisoned in a lake of fire and tortured by demons for eternity. This is the end result which simply cannot be overlooked – and it is the most definitive reason why the underground has generally segregated itself from fundamentalism.

That much said, I don't feel the need to comment further, and it should be obvious that this intolerance in the metal scene comes from individuals having religion violently imposed on them. Punks generally think that all religion should be dismissed in one big hurdle, and to even piss around with the Occult is an all-out joke. The metal scene accepts the overkill of it fully, if only as the backdrop to a stage-show evoking Samhain rather than a Church Of Satan rally…

For the most part, its all Halloween, although some engaged in this occultism are violently anti-Christian. The vast majority of those extremists find themselves on the right wing of the Black Metal movement or darker, more perverse death or thrash. Black Metal originated with bands like Venom and Bathory as this gruesome, ultra-heavy, satanic noise from the 80's. Although these bands were overtly satanic or heavily engrossed in Norwegian folklore, none were armed militants.

The ultra-violence of the Satanic underground exploded in the early 90's with the "Second Wave" of black metal. A handful of lunatics from Norway (*Mayhem, Burzum, Emperor*) decided to create their own antithalian reality. In historical light of their ancestral roots, and culturally repressed by a timid church state, the underground Norwegian scene violently exploded.

At first it was the attempt to make the darkest, grimmest musical destruction laudable. One thing led to another, and thus begat a campaign of terrorism which climaxed as a dozen burned churches, the murders of a handful, and a litany of prison sentences.

Those kindred to that initial seed are the die-hard black metal fanatics, the ones who advocate everything from genocide against all religious faiths to pagan neo-Nazism. They take the literal interpretation of the occult Hitler deadly serious, and theirs is an autotheistic war-cry to bring about heathen glory.

Yet most involved in the European and American black metal scene decry genocide because they detest being persecuted themselves. Most European metal bands – even black metal ones – detest Nazism. The Europeans still have not forgotten the bloodshed of their past. The ultra-fascistic BM bands in America are few and far between, but there are plenty still polishing their machetes, enthusiastic to unleash hell…

Not all into black metal are right wing to this extent. In America, black metal was discovered through devices like Napster, because no one imported this shit anywhere in the 90's. Most are hardcore metal-fans that collect vinyl and bootleg everything they can get their hands on. Wearing a Burzum t-shirt is less a statement of White Superiority then it is the same as sporting a Ted Bundy shirt, and collecting these violent episodes of music is akin to owning bootlegs of *Cannibal Holocaust*.

The super-misanthropic underground is a surge of isolated loners or small groups of tight-knit outsiders. Many of the black metal kids in America are into fantasy period; you have this strain of Dungeons & Dragons & renascence fest people. Otherwise they are pissed off misanthropes, musicians, or weirdo's obsessed by the awkward, painful quality of the more droning, ambient work. This droning, experimental side can best be described by bands like XASTHUR, Bethlehem, or Blut Aus Nord…

The death-metallers tend to be horror-movie obsessives, very disciplined and with small circles of friends. They love sick humor or ugly porn, such as collecting tampons or down syndrome bukakki. Total brutal sickout measures, cartoonishly violent, anti-religious, or tongue-in-cheek misogynistic. 90% don't take themselves too seriously.

Same with the Thrashers. They worship at the altar of Testament, Exodus, Nuclear Assault. Slayer are the progenitors of thrash, and their style its very definition. They love screaming at the stage egging on guitar solos with a pitcher of PBR raised high. Thrashers of true grit usually detest keyboards. Long hair, leather pants, sleeveless denim jacket covered in patches – old school high-top Reeboks if snazzy. Their musical world is not dated, it's timeless…

The power mettalers are into the soaring, banshee shrieking, '*warriors of the world*' sentiment of bands like Blind Guardian, Iron Savior and Manowar, respectively. It is a world of guitar heroes, poodle hair, leather pants, and monster Harley's. This all started with the duel onslaught of Judas Priest and Iron Maiden. Everything classic about metal can be traced here and every nuance of the 80's lives onward.

Power mettalers rarely get along with the death metal crowd who think their whole vibe is aptly "*gay*," but none so much as musically homophobic as the black mettalers. Power metal outside of Europe is truly a rare breed, but it does not stop a man from blaring Stratovarius in any parking lot gathering he feels needs some quasi-spiritual uplifting…

Grind was a reaction bridging ultra-hardcore politically charged crust punk with thrash metal. It can be easily identified by its particular blast-beat and its short-attention span variation on death metal – most songs range between 3 seconds to a minute. Grind started in Flint, Michigan (just north of Detroit) by Repulsion in 1985. They combined Negative Approach, Celtic Frost, and Discharge into one horror-obsessed entity. It was, at the time, one of the rawest albums ever recorded…

The guys in Napalm Death got a Repulsion cassette in a tape trade and, promptly floored, decided to alter their own formula, churning out spastic, metal/punk hybrid ten-second-songs. It developed technically and spread accordingly, but has almost always retained its punk stylings at key moments. This is the closest thing you get to a crust punk in the world of metal, as most grinders are hand-in-hand with crusts. This is a prime area for communal squats, political dialogues, leftist opinions…

Doom metal is the subterranean depths at which the die-hard eventually finds himself one day. Doom is either classic garage Black Sabbath-influenced metal complete with the rock n' roll blues-scale backbone, or the slowest, snail-paced funeral dirge ever created. Doom can be highly complex, but it's always dreary and medium-paced at best. Some doom bands have songs ranging up to 30 minutes encapsulating minimalist drumming and two or three riffs that drag on forever.

Truly effective doom metal sucks the life out of you harder than watching *Gummo* fifty times in a row. Most into doom are surprisingly big grind heads or gravitate towards the darker, more experimental black metal for its coldness and distance. It's all connected to one extremely polarized head-trip.

The metalcore and tech crowd come from a bridging of newer styles towards the end of the 90's. Metalcore is basically hardcore with a diverse spectrum of influences thrown in (thrash, death, and prog). All-out tech metal (*or "math metal"*) is the sound-freak, we-practice-eight-days-a-week, "so complicated your head explodes" style.

It's newer, and thus hated by the *"you're a poseur"* death, black, and thrash-heads. But any musician – be it a blues artist to a symphony conductor – appreciates the jaw-dropping complexity of the often jazz-based fusion rhythms. Tech is the most disciplined metal outside of death, and is truly a 21st, post-modern variation of it. Tech metal is traced back to early Dillinger Escape Plan, with newer bands like Between The Buried And Me & THE END upping it to the next level. The *"Repulsion of Tech Metal,"* consequently, is a generally unknown Seattle band named SWARMING HORDES who in 1995 released the first album of its proto-genre…

Since metalcore and tech have become mainstream, there is a huge influx of hipster mettalers that wear tight pants and have girlie emo haircuts, lots of streaks – this weird offspring of the YouTube generation the old guard don't really understand but pretend to. They've infiltrated to the point where all the old metalcore bands (*all of whom maintained the DIY of punk*) are abandoning their old styles. Having a sea of clone bands before them, this vastly confusing apparatus, it changes things…

It's kind of a mess right now, honestly, and it seems everyone is jumping ship to play old school thrash, doom, or crazed experimental styles. The trend will die, as they always do, and all the underrated, overlooked bands like The Nain Rouge, Psyopus & Signs of Collapse will go down in history, wholly accepted by the "*Rock N' Roll Hall of Fame*" & pimped at tourist shops alongside Ozzy toothbrushes & Hendrix coffee mugs…

The Industrial scene is a different vibe altogether though. America has never truly embraced the tank-rousing, street war digital hardcore that Alec Empire has busted out in Germany with Atari Teenage Riot, or the truly bizarre, Warhol-esque drug freakout zone that Throbbing Gristle pulled off in the UK.

Instead, American industrial has mutated into this kind of hedonistic dance utopia, where metal heads, punks, and electronic music junkies coagulate at 3am wearing devilish suits and ties while half-naked freak-dolls are led by the chain of a dog collar whilst electrical tape covers up their nipples and thing-a-ma-boobers. It is the future of post-modernity that Marquis de Sade cranked to in solitary confinement.

When a live industrial band such as VNV Nation or Skinny Puppy comes through a territory, the traffic will change to another venue, but the great mass of freaks will always flock back to the seedy club that has been designated as the outpost. Expect pure darkness, candle-lit atmosphere, The Cure, EBM, shouting alcoholics, rivers of booze, some fine hush-hush white powder guzzling up a nostril …

The industrial scene is both a fuck-frenzy and the ground zero campaign of all dramatists to live out their Anne Rice flavored romanticism, complete with interpersonal goth legends that increase in magnitude with every passing solstice. You'll find the worst of them feeble in a shadowy corner, sobbing their vulnerose anguish while gazing at a dried dead rose, railing for attention with lame tales of a half-hearted suicide attempt…

The goth/industrial crowd is not to be confused with the ravers. Ravers are more like dance club people promoting a hedonistic celebration of life. There is a core vibe of humanism and communication; a fanatic push to fuse the body and soul…

As with metal, you have those who actually *listen* to electronic music as opposed to *going* with it. When actually investigated, the electronic format is limitless. The repetitive nature of the more brain-dead "loop-based" trance & house has given a negative connotation to the genre.

Punks & metalheads almost unanimously hate DJ's. They generally don't consider it an art form, and grumble stereotype lines like *"Pick up an instrument you fraud!"* I personally consider Disc Jockeying an exercise in clever editing, which is an art form in and of itself, as well as the ability to sculpt the ambience & psychological permeation of a dance floor as the conductor would a symphony. It is a very careful balancing act, and takes a great degree of talent. But the DJ is not a musician...

Plus the ravers are not as deviantly sexual. The industrial crowd wears their S&M leanings on their sleeves. The ravers are more peace & love, not 'Let's whip each other in a dungeon setting and go ape-shit kinky with straight-razors.'

While the dance-floor can be quite an aphrodisiac, the problem is when you finally get home at 6am and are actually in the position to have sex as opposed to making it on some fucked up, torn leather couch in the middle of a warehouse, the guys are so strung out from coke they can't pitch a tent, and the girls are so drained from ecstasy all they want is to cuddle or dance around a living room until they pass out from exhaustion. Either way it's a nightmare...

So where do I fit in? I'm somewhere in the middle of it all, with my own extreme views on everything. My people are generally the moderates that devour film and literature, who collect vinyl and blab weird stories until 5am. Depraved sex hounds and the bombastic radicals who'll still heed to common sense...

I'm too dirty to be a skin, although I believe in their discipline and unity. I do not see the blue-collar lifestyle as something to fight for, just another bane and curse to overcome. Though a sort of anarchist I am no molotov-chucking one either, nor have I ever pretended to be. I have no qualms about working for money, I support free-market economy within fair standards, and I believe that government *should exist* as a moderate form of Democratic Socialism, whereas its goal is to actually *benefit* its citizens – as opposed to cannibalistically exploiting them like a cannon fodder battery supply.

Still, I think it be perfectly appropriate to mention that I am, of course, a pyrate and an outlaw. Although I believe how a government should be *in theory*, I still don't give a fuck. I'm a criminal, as any sane man is. How can one subdue themselves in light of the ghastly policies of the machine?

I actually enjoy taking a shower at least every three days, unlike the crusties who enthusiastically sleep in dumpsters, priding themselves on the absolutist rejection of hygiene. For the nihilist crustie, I am too clean cut and organized (*if you can even really call it that*). I'm too abrasive for the politically correct crowd, yet I have no qualms against playing bongos with a bunch of hippies in the park.

Still I find myself offending all with my political views, and challenge meathead quotas. I'm quite vocal about what I think is rude, uneducated gibberish. I won't shut up & never will until they steal my vocal chords like kidney thieves in the dead of night.

I enrage, I insult, I do spastic cartwheels, I take great pride. As Monsieur de Sade once said: "*Kill me again or take me as I am for I will not change.*" I'm a FREAK – a proud one of a long-dead, quasi-nationalism that arose from the concrete of East Dearborn in 1994. I am its champion flag-waiver, and old school in my tastes and preferences...

THE VILLA WINONA (PORT OF ALL STORMS)

Two and a half days since I left Detroit, and only one more hour of waiting until the Greyhound slips the Los Angeles terminal and takes me – like a golden chariot with flaming wheels – to the San Diego drop off point. This is my third experience with the LA depot, and still there are screaming Mexican babies everywhere. Like all inner-city terminals, outside the glass doors prowl a mob of ex-cons slinging pain pills & stolen cell phones...

The Villa Winona – a quasi-crust house filled with fellow Detroit expatriates – will be the port of all storms during this voyage. I head onto the road for 2 months, go bankrupt, hustle a bus ticket for San Diego, then land like a comet right back on the couch. I then, in theory, find a lame minimum wage job fit for a teenager. I make a grand, book further adventures, then rush back out into America until this book feels complete. Literally, I have no plan – I instead put my faith in fortune cookies and astrology columns...

This is my first return to The Villa Winona since June – and my second experience with California. It was that very trip 6 months ago set me off like a time bomb. After a killer burn in the romance department, I'd gone to reclaim some peace of mind. Instead I was thrust into a bizarre tale of green card bride schemes, BDSM porn offers, psychobilly fight clubs, and a man named Harley at the Institute of Scientology who locked me inside an L. Ron Hubbard brainwashing chamber – all of which somehow led me to a desert compound filled with armed satanic terrorists.

A brilliant state of affairs, this land of palm trees and razor wire. I expected a gleaming hippie paradise – surfers, bikini blondes, sunny games galore. Instead, I found a virtual prison state, sublimely wrapped around the sky mall agenda. The Schwarzenegger backed anti-homeless Gestapo had implemented H.O.T. – a program to cleanse the homeless blight. Black paddy wagons cruised the streets forcing hobo's into state-mandated concentration camps. Motion detecting video cameras lined the streets taking license plate snapshots and sending off traffic violations through the mail... *West Coast politicians for National I.D. cards, microchips in the skin of felons, public urination a sex offense...*

It is a faux-liberalism encased in vast amalgams of extreme poverty. The flip-flop paradise continues to swell, the undesirables are pushed further astray, deeper into the brutally policed hives of meth and prostitution. It is bunched in the slop of humanity, grids upon grid of domestic homes with barred windows, where The Villa Winona stands. You feel the strain, the heat, the uncertainty. The helicopters, the sirens, the military police cruising El Cajon...

Thousands of tweaker zombies drudge the streets; you can hear them approach by their grinding jaws & shuffling demeanor It's a little known fact that Crystal Meth was created by Nazi scientists. It was the Captain America-styled super soldier serum manufactured for the Waffen SS, and fed mountain-full to Adolf Hitler. Those hooked to it are up for weeks at a time with no REM sleep – a line of coke that never ends, devouring muscle to sustain itself – brains eating themselves away, face and teeth rotting out. *And historians still wonder why The Holocaust happened.*

This highly addictive Nazi super drug is the most potent street score outside heroin, and exploding rapid as Plague. Meth is an epidemic so large the Cali establishment has no concrete grip on how to handle it. There are so many shredded from meth's clutch that the building of prisons is the new economic backbone of California. It is said that California is 10 years ahead of America. That San Diego is where it began, and L.A. is where it's heading. Welcome, my friends, to THE BIG SHINY PRISON.

MERRY X-MAS

Christmas day in San Diego. As for the inferno I'd anticipated, the only one is that of the sun. In Michigan we are accustomed to a blanket of white, pine trees in the living room, perhaps a crackling fireplace and roasting chestnuts. On this side of the earth it is 82 degrees, and we are cooking barbecue without t-shirts in our shorts.

It takes a long ride down El Cajon from Downtown before you reach the laughable "ghetto" of San Diego, where The Villa Winona sits in a predominantly black & Mexican neighborhood. Three blocks away rests prostitute alley. Meth-heads stumble, g-thugs holler threats, tough guys confront each other yet never a punch thrown. They ram heads with the wink of an eye.

This expatriate colony is an Alamo-like last stand refusing to give into any conventional sense of reality. Eight of us in a house the size of a living room, and roaches crawling over everything. The Villa Winona is the hub of a communal family, a handful of Michigan survivors which constitute an elite assortment of the criminally insane. So complex are the dynamics they are impossible to scribe at once…

They'd all escaped from Michigan via one-way road trip. When the shuttle crashed they went right to the streets, cutting their way through months of alleys, parks, and out-reach shelters. Four months later, The Villa Winona was captured after their pot-dealer succumbed to AIDS. A mob of 19 year old punk rockers cornered the confused 68 year old landlord with a wad of cash, and it's flown ever since without a hitch – this mob of grifters obsessed with counterculture revolution. It is a volatile colony absorbing random freaks from Southern California, enamored with piracy and intent on serious malarkey.

This particular cast, this rogue gallery – to be intimately acquainted, dear reader, is not a particularly ripe plunge at this moment. Rather, let us assemble a gallery of faces spinning like a roulette, round n' round in the frenetic blur – Onyx, Lennon, Brandon, Skinner, Dr. Santiago – *Panda, Jo-Jo, Pork Chop, Corn Flake, Ryan The Ghostbuster, Matt Ratt & Chuck The Homey…*

Onyx, "The Urban Priest" – 35 and epic as a John Woo action sequence, is somewhere between the hitcher from *Texas Chainsaw,* Dr. Jung & every renascence creep. His wife, a 56-year-old schizophrenic ex-cult member has the gift of mutant savant astrology…

Dr. Santiago, covered in tats, burning eyes, bleeding, always bleeding and picking scabs. Dr. Santiago, the lightning bolt of quasi-

Zen purity, the 18 year old crust holy man eating raw fig leaves, ingurgitating the sun in meditation photosynthesis...

Lennon – the scarecrow-bodied speed-freak, the Ferris Bueller of our commune. He is the spider-monkey *"Johnny the Homicidal Maniac,"* drudging SoCal ever since moving from Japan. Thin, nimble, bespeckled and utterly German, Lennon is notorious for throwing crust punk sewer shows, his small adept team dragging power generators into rat-infested darkness...

Brandon, 28, a old good ol' boy from my hometown, stemming from the same public education slaughterhouse. Orange bi-hawk, purple bags beneath his eyes, severe bi-polar depression and life ruined by a bogus sex offender charge. He refuses to work, hiding in that little corner surrounded by dressers like a fort, sleeping 14 hours a day. Brandon, who supports himself by giving blood twice a week, veins starting to resemble a neurotic raw-dog slider. Brandon, who preaches endlessly the subject of guerrilla warfare, the supremacy of the Illuminati, the coming attack of Atlantis...

Mr. Skinner, who sleeps in a coffin in the garage, is as obsessed with psychobilly as he is the arrival of the alien races that will one day – if not moving in our midst already – come to reclaim the earth when the Mayan calendar runs out of steam in 2012... *Skinner, the self-piercing, self-tattooing wonder, buzzing away at the orange & blue flames up and down his arms. Skinner the maniac, bloody and laughing in machismo aftermath, the giant "Medieval" tat across his shoulder blades earning its upkeep...*

Mr. Skinner plans to revitalize the SD punk scene via D.I.Y. venue in which Tuesday nights would be fight club, Wednesday $1 drinks, & all other eves pure catastrophic noise. If anyone gets out of hand or a fight breaks out, the house lights cut instantly. The spotlight explodes like the moon, beaming directly upon the venue bouncers who will in turn gleefully beat the shit out of each other. Not the audience mind you, but themselves – *bloody and laughing* – just to view the faces of the crowd...

Midnight. Been drinking whiskey & smoking green kryptonite since 4pm. Every surface is loaded with emptied half-pints, beer cans & rum shots. I cannot distinguish which is mine so I claim sovereignty over all, chugging the foamy remnants.

Lennon has returned strange as ever, skinny and cartoonish, grinding & rolling in perpetual burnout. He slimes through the Villa

Winona in his gelatin-tarantula form, face protected by a World War II gas mask, and locks himself in the bathroom. Skinner sees the ploy, looks at us shifty eyed, and nonchalantly slides a ski-mask over his face. He throws on a large hoodie, over-sized white Elvis glasses, and camo pants before brandishing a high-turbine semi-CO2 handgun. Skinner leaps out the back door, running circles around The Villa...

A rumpled slither of a human snake against the pull of the carpet catches our drift. Lennon is wriggling his way to the kitchen on his belly, mini-UZI in hand. Skinner busts through the back door in a surprise assassination attempt, projecting an armada of circular yellow bullets which ricochet throughout the house. Skinner unloads into Lennon's gas mask and lunges behind the kitchen counter...

Brandon jumps over the living room couch and slides on some goggles as the two reload. He pops up like a mechanical whacking arcade gopher and starts firing away. I throw on my Korean War greatcoat, aviator glasses, red beret, and black bandana to shield my face. The four-man impromptu duel moves in slow motion, the graceful ballet of carnage consuming all...

FIRST ADVENTURE ON THE DRAG

And one day you wake up and find yourself in the middle of Hollywood, half-naked girl sleeping deeply beside you, and naïve rich people for thousands of miles ripe for hustle...

The moment I walked into the stairway, wearing that skinny black tie, I was in an ironic parallel world. The beautiful girl's apartment, head-trip or not, may very well have been the same from the opening sequence of *Pulp Fiction*. What a jolt, this déjà vu. And baked, of course, in my usual stumbling way, I got lost in the corridors. I eventually thudded through a trash exit, setting off a screaming emergency beeper, and in a rush to avoid security tripped over my own shoelaces. I torpedoed like a buffoon, swung up like a tornado, slipped through the barbwire fence like a ninja.

After so many years I was now a hop, skip & jump from the touted land of Hollywood. And what a perfect Cali day – 70 degrees, blue sky, sun shining, not a cloud. The ex-autoslave emerging from desperate Midwestern values, finally to rumble those fabled avenues. I'd expected Lamborghini's, French maids, fortresses like Cambodian drug-lords – but these back-alley neighborhoods off the strip, all I've found are cramped streets of average suburban design.

...Onward to the tourist nightmare, that mythological terrifying side of Hollywood – the scum side, the mug-happy side – the soulless, blackened drag of strip clubs, pimps, pushers, con men and such like, where demon night crawlers stake their claim and the blood of the innocent flows supreme...

HAHAHAHAHA. Ok, whatever...

...Ah, Hollywood Boulevard, the media stairway to heaven. Was it corruption I smelled? The effluvium of a 100,000 starry-eyed sheep? The last great Babylon, so we're told, where the weak trample the weak in a primal agastopian frenzy. All that desire, all their struggle – only to place a single foot at the incline of a hierarchical trapezoid, slicing through cartilage and bone, trampling friends and enemies alike to stay ahead of the mongrel leeches slithering below. Progress becomes the ability to sustain the attacks as one fends himself from the devouring onslaught on high...

Apart from the famous star-studded sidewalk, Hollywood Boulevard resembles the hot spot of every random college town. You know, that three street long strip where the young go to intoxicate themselves silly and buy piles of comic books, bongs, and random memorabilia. That is pretty much the extent of it – just this huge, thirty block cluster – the apex of "hot spot" existence. Then BAM – you're spit back out into LA -- one gigantic mega-suburb without a center.

It's depressing and shameful. You feel like Jim Carrey at the end of *The Truman Show* when he rows to the edge of the town and discovers nothing but a sound-stage. The world you once knew, which seemed so large and endless, is just as phony as Los Angeles.

The Déjà vu is there because you've seen it all on the TV screen before a hundred times, except that abandoned factory section you assume exists where Steven Seagal took out an Uzi-spraying coke-lord surrounded by flame shooting oil spikes isn't an area at all. That abandoned factory is actually next door to the ice cream store from Grease, is next to the diner where Pacino meets Deniro in *Heat*, is next door to the gym from *Pumping Iron*. The world in your head that seems like an infinite universe is actually a stage prop that lasts thirty blocks, except there are Mexicans everywhere selling fruit on the corner, working the minimum wage shit jobs, and doing very silly things on Spanish infomercials...

In front of the Chinese Theatre there is a man dressed like Darth Vader and across the street is a Japanese family taking digital photos in front of a Frankenstein statue. I only take a few steps past Captain Jack Sparrow when a tiny man with a Brooklyn accent offers a limo ride past all the movie star mansions for thirty bucks. How can I deny and plot device from *Leprechaun 2*? So I haggle, get a ticket for $25, leap in the back of the black stretch with eight others and off we go. The glittering wasteland quickly comes into focus as an Arabic driver explains the passing sights over an amplified CB radio.

We cruise through Beverly Hills listening to "18 And Life To Go." Dr. Phil's house looks like Jabba The Hutt's palace with this weird circular fortress roof... *That bald head and mustache on the body of a pasty white elephant sized worm...* Ozzy's is the same from the MTV show, but "The Prince of Darkness" has Christmas wreaths all over his gates. Tom Cruise has a party shack across the street from his $50,000,000 dollar mansion. Leonardo Dicaprio lives in Joe DiMaggio's old crib and has a ten million dollar personal golf course for a backyard. Bill Cosby has little black golf caddy statues all over his lawn. Michael Douglass has ten of the exact same Porsche lined in front of his humongous garage, each one a different color of the rainbow.

Frodo's Hobbit House from *Lord Of The Rings* is kitty-corner from Tom Hanks estate and hidden behind thick stone walls. For some reason, Universal decided to film that segment smack dab in the middle of the movie star death-zone. What's so brilliantly pleasing is that the funny mushroom shaped Shire chimney is high as a flagpole and visible for all to see. It pops over the horizon during sundown and as the sunlight refracts off its pinkish tan hue the colossal chimney resembles a twenty foot high erection.... And Tom Hanks pulls into his parking lot every night and sees this. When he looks out his front window, when he's on the commode. It's the sort of thing that would drive a man to watch *Mazes & Monsters...*

The acting elite own this town without question. Restaurants, hotels, movie theaters, apartment buildings, Scientology centers. Pyramid scheme overlords – overlords & vultures, all of them. The greater their power, the bigger the mansion and higher the placement upon Hollywood Hills embedded near that famous "HOLLYWOOD" sign glowing outwards like a hypnotic occult emblem...

George Lucas and Spielberg come within a few yards of its foothold. Perhaps it causes cancer or emits mind-controlling invisible lazar beams that keep the racket scheme in progressive unending motion like a renegade dishwasher on loop... *Watch them glide, plastic and immune, guided by the invisible strings of the marionette. Yet who is the Puppet master? Who is the Puppet master?*

KABUKI DOUBLE TAKE

Nearly a week later and the beautiful girl is getting impatient with my loafing on the couch. I need to hit it hard and get back to San Diego immediately – one last mission, something of intrinsic value. My slam-bang opening has been mauled by the lazy response of LA musicians. Perhaps it's a dark nod towards the future, this pattern forming of contacts that flake like dead dandruff when it's time to meet in person.

Thus far I've conducted at least a half-dozen interviews, none of which are remotely appealing. Today I plan on usurping the tradition. I'm at a place called Cascade Studios, which is a rehearsal complex around the block from Paramount Studios. Fre-Ne-Tik are cutting their demo live here from the DAT mix. They've yet to arrive and no other bands are practicing except a traditional Mexican band complete with that carnie, parking lot, kielbasa tent Casio.

I slip out back to clear my head, crouched on the back steps staring at the gravel. When I lift my head up I lock eyes with a mysterious figure – I'm staring at a man who is glaring from inside his green Windstar. His face is painted up like Sgt. Kabuki Man NYPD, and he's so nonchalant. Apparently the Peppermint Creeps – a glammed out, rag doll-painted, hair metal ordeal – are about to film a video for their cover of "Turning Japanese."

The Fre-Ne-Tik caravan arrives. Lead singer/principal songwriter Mimi is so cute you expect her to flatulate rainbows. She has that Cleopatra meets Mrs. Marcellus Wallace hair cut, miniskirt with black tights and combat boots, like a '95 poster girl heartthrob. She is total sunshine, but nervously pacing the stage.

They've this somber rock sound with bellowing Cello; a stripped down *Opiate*-era Tool and early Garbage or *Infinite Sadness* Pumpkins. I feel like I do when I'm listening to Portishead, if that has any resonance: *"I was born in Jersey and played in a hardcore punk band. Then I moved to Philly for 9½ years. I did a little bit of everything, from hip hop to country to dance music. I kind of blew up to the point where I was in the local newspapers and magazines on a weekly basis. Everyone knew my name, I was signing autographs. LA pretty much calls me and tells me I have to come out here because I was offered a record deal as a solo artist. I got offered a movie part in a film called 'Zerophilia.'"*

"What's that about?"

Mimi: "I was flown out to Oregon to be in the film for two minutes as myself, rocking out in a bar scene. Five of my songs were chosen for the film which just recently came out in theaters in Los Angeles, Chicago, and New York. It's doing really well and there are big name actors that blew up while the film was in limbo. Zach from *The OC*. Taylor Hannely from *The OC*..."

"Tell me about Hollywood..."

"Where I'm from I'd get $600 and a 150+ would show up. Out here you pay to play and maybe 30-50 will show... If you have something original and refreshing you'll make it. People come from all over the world to try and make it but I'd have to say that 85% of them suck. I know so many A&R reps that get black trash bags full of CD's and find maybe one good song. I've personally been in the office of Capital Records, Universal. I've had these people interested in us, but nowadays you have to have sold at least 150,000."

"Is there a tightly knit artistic community here?"

"In LA it's hard to find genuine people. It's like being stuck in this huge pond of people all struggling to stay afloat. They'll grab you just to use you as a floating device and hold you underwater until you drown. It's like only the strongest survive, and I feel like most of the bands act like they're cool with you but if they know you're really good and you have what it takes, they end up doing some shiesty, backstabbing shit."

"What's the message of Fre-Ne-Tik?

"The deepest, darkest secrets of every relationship you've had with everything around you. I'm this sponge that absorbs everything. I don't even sit down to write. It could be three in the morning and I'll wake up with a song playing in my head like it's a CD on full blast. I grab a pen and start writing as fast as it's playing. When the song is done it's gone. I don't go back and fix anything. I just start playing my guitar as if I've known it for 10 years. The band picks that shit up like they've been playing it for 20."

"Do you have any good celebrity stories?"

"Dennis Rodman told me I needed to stop waitressing because I needed to be either on the television or on the radio. I just served him some coffee and eggs..."

"Who would look creepier in pink spandex – Tom Arnold or Ron Jeremy?"

"You (laughs). Pink spandex in general is pretty funny..."

AGAIN, FROM SCRATCH

Back in San Diego, back to the drawing board. If this is a new book, if this is a true expose, then where might the clarity derive? For life is not a series of concrete dimensions; action and response do not spring from definitive assertion. The Big Shiny Prison, as an art form, must record everything as it happens – it must convey the entire platitude, the prisms and jangles of the whole man...

It seems now, in all substantiated opinion, that everything shall be failure. If this is an unsalvageable manuscript from the outset, perhaps it is failure I should now admonish? Perhaps, as a fearless workhorse, I should throw the baby out with the bathwater. I should promulgate the seed, beat the face of commercialism to a pulp.

For what is journalism but a jigsaw of truth's conjecture? The objectivity is now gone, yet propaganda is too harsh a description. I have to pull inwards, remove myself – I have to alienate myself completely to restore order, castrate the yearning for roots so that I may become citizen of the malleable nation I now germinate through vast foundations of text.

If I, dear reader, shall be your tour guide, then we must begin anew. What you have witnessed in slap-dash is equivalent to gazing downward from an airplane at miniature homes and ant people, so minuscule and pointless that one finger flick could disrupt the tectonic plates. For we've only touched upon the sights, the sounds, the visions. We've dipped our naked toes into the pool, found it aggrieving, and paced steadily its length in blind hopes the chill shall evaporate...

If there is any better a sense of womb for this journey then it is the purgatory now facing me? Nowhere have I discovered such a raw infusion of climate and mentality then in Southern California. Never have I parlayed such a sweltering brew of constant motion, of life rhythms based wholly on the sun. These life rhythms, so remote of the East Coast hunab ku, drive a surmountable wedge through a sustained communication...

The San Deigan does not understand the meaning of hibernation, only the constant beat of the orb. In SoCal it's always August. Forever the pulse of summer – *the confusion, the noise, the inertia*. Never does a layer of ice halt their turbines, never has a -20 chill dragged them deep within relentless gut-screaming depression.

Unlike the Northern world there is no conscience urgency to suck up every last morsel of warmth. The yanks are frantic in summer, setting down all qualms, all responsibilities in light of BBQ's, concerts, sports, riots, massacres & lunch, for they know it comes and goes in swift. They prime themselves wholly for adventure – picnics, car rides, wave pools, disc golf and athleticism. It is grabbed in full, drained lifeless as a rock.

In San Diego this Mediterranean Climate embeds a different form of urgency. There is no need to rush sightless into its thick, no screaming terror that it will vanish deftly as Houdini. There is instead a permanency to the motion, an endless spring, a weight eternally lifted which drives the mind into a cultural inferno of perpetuation, as if an eternal law of symbiosis retains all submissive.

The people don't stop and think, they just *go go go*. What time is there to read books when ski jets graze above water? What grimness can be nurtured when the gray sky blight is a non-entity, a figment discontinued? Brains thus chug forward as frantic batteries, solar powered and hosted by the light...

In this incubation The Villa Winona is supplanted. Somewhere in this miraculous mess of activity we come together to scratch our heads. We devour life more so then the locals, for in their blind rush of summer they lack the urgency that it will be taken in seasonal clockwork. They don't understand the climate of fear and hopelessness that embodies Detroit. They know not the prison camp foundations of our lives.

In their gleaming paradise Detroit is but a vague image, an untraveled trademark of stereotypes. Thus they have had the luxury of relaxation, of slower impulse. This is why, in any mass social interaction, when we gallop into open community we seem the detachment of a barbarian horde. We pillage like Vikings, carrying the weight of every successful hustle and food snatch back to the compound, where we live the economy of barter. Neo-tribal, this spinning nucleus of confusion, forever ogled & entranced as if San Diego were Disneyland.

This rugged patch of terrain, palm trees & motor debris; t*his far-reaching octopus of steel and black tar...* Flower patches brimming like swarms of larvae... *Ocean currents grate against the course pull of sand...* Hills everywhere, like great walls surrounding us, at night the villages shine like magnificent dots... *The endless maze of alleyways, dripping graffiti and fever...* The outer crest of cement breaks rural, landscape unfurling homes sutured amateur...

The cawing of roosters even amidst the concrete... The porn shop filth bowl and glass shrapnel motorway... *Gaudy taco huts drifting charred effluvium...* The black top vapor evap of mid-day rush... *Motor police and orange coats, haggard winos swarming as hive...* Car lot archipelagos & four wheeled mortgage tombs... *Whore houses and jet rays, iPod's and colonoscopies...* Aristotle enveloping the technological undercurrent, Plato redefined... *Bail bond advertisements on every park bench and flagpole...*

TRANSMISSION AMSTERDAM

In 5 minutes, Melechesh is going to call The Villa Winona. Melechesh, the first black metal band in the history of the Middle East, who rose from Israel in 1993 to give the world its first glimpse of Sumerian thrash. *Bullet belts, demonology & eardrum convulsions...*

On par with West Virginia's NILE – who are legends for their unique breed of Egyptian death metal – Melechesh are hailed internationally for their original use of exotic scales and modes. They've rearranged the death/thrash formula into an even more extreme and hypnotic potent by blending an array of Middle Eastern folk instruments into their lavish compositions. In this, they've become an undeniably massive influence in America, guitarists far and wide emulating their brazen deviations.

Dr. Santiago, still bleeding, still picking scabs, is to be my intern. He reaches over, as an unabashed fan, to enthusiastically read the text on Melechesh's promo pack. I don't need to for I know the story all too well – 14 years of chaos and 4 solid records of endless acclaim. Simply withdrawing into that inner-lair of zine quotes like stock market statistics I can cascade an avalanche of them at will: *"Melechesh, the sonic bludgeoning killers of napalm infused whatever, driving the brains of their listeners into rust-belt meat-grinders, beating them senseless with fiery tides of revulsion and primal terror, and blah blah blah..."*

"Melechesh, those horrendous sons of the Aeonic gods, blast forth a highly complex, hook-driven & eerie blah blah blah. Worldwide, like the looming threat of Jihad, the poor metalhead consumes their audio cancer, driving them into a conspiracy movement of hooligan frenzied shenanigans – pouring acid on the face of the Lincoln Memorial, wiping their buttocks with the Magna Carta, dropping grand piano's from skyscrapers at haphazard immigrant taxicabs – a plasma-drenched maelstrom of blah blah blah blood and fumigation. With their new release 'Emissaries,' Melechesh blah blah, world tour beside Marduk blah blah..."

"So you're calling from Amsterdam today?
Ashmedi: "We live here actually.

"Tell me about your new record "Emissaries" and what you hoped to accomplish with the album..."

"I think I did accomplish what I wanted – you can say death, Mesopotamian metal or Sumerian thrashing black metal at it's finest, I guess. It's an expression of the band, and expression of mine as well, since I write most of the music. I feel that I've achieved that with *Emissaries* and it's an album I'm very proud of. On the media level and the fans at least it's being received very well. They had a lot of expectations for us especially after *SPHINX* was released. It's been hailed by the public, especially here in Europe and now it's starting in North America."

"What elements were able to make Melechesh stronger coming from the critically acclaimed "Sphinx" album?"

"I don't think I could answer 'better or worse,' because it's very subjective. I know some people that think our first album is the best, because its very raw. I think the majority considers *SPHINX* our best album. I think of course the natural maturity and progression of the sound-work in the past two years has allowed me to grow musically, hence the improvement. Lyrically it's very elaborate and we were able to include newer elements of the band. I think what I like about "Emissaries" is that I felt less cornered, like '*fuck it I'll just write whatever I feel like writing.*' With that liberation, I think the music came out even more sincere."

"Lyrically what are some of the concepts and ideas you talk about on 'Emissaries?'"

"Generally we play around with the ideas of Sumerian deities coming back from another planet onto earth. It is one that we like to elaborate on and in this album it is mentioned as well. It is just such a fascinating idea. I also have a song about my personal view of the occult side of Jerusalem, the city I was born in and where Melechesh started back in '93. There's also a track about the Qabalah. There's also one song based on a very ancient text that is adapted slightly. It coincides with some ideas I had which is really amazing and almost surrealistic. In general its Mediterranean mysticism and Middle Eastern occult, specifically the Mesopotamian."

"What was it like originating in Jerusalem? I know many of the Arabic countries are very opposed to heavy metal and anything they would view as dark or satanic…"

"Speaking of the Arabic countries the atmosphere is really different. In that world there is a huge scene. In some countries it's legal, in some countries it's been banned. It's still brewing and its brewing big. I think that within 5, maybe 10 years it's going to be very normal to hear of a signed Arabic band. As for the situation in Jerusalem there has always been metal. On sheer nightlife I find it more interesting in Jerusalem or Tel Aviv then Amsterdam. It's not conservative at all, and on a cultural level they are less conservative. Of course the Palestinians are more conservative."

"But as a band with occult imagery, did you catch flack?"

"We did a black metal band in Jerusalem – we were actually the first black metal band ever in Jerusalem, now there's a scene there. When we said we were a metal band it was all okay in East Jerusalem and the Israeli area, but in the Palestinian areas I was a cast out. I'm neither Israeli nor Palestinian myself, but I lived there. It wasn't polarized in Jerusalem until a newspaper wrote a kind of lie thing about us being a satanic cult and not a black metal band. Then we were wanted by the authorities because that was not allowed. There was no rule, there was nothing illegal that you weren't allowed to have. But they didn't know how to handle it because it was the Holy City and there was a "satanic cult" there… Now people are very interested in it. We've achieved a lot since then, and it kind of vanished with time. We moved out in '98. We did one album while living there, recorded in Jerusalem. After that we did several albums in Europe."

"I have one of my editorial interns with me, he's a big fan of your work. He's got a few questions for you so I'll be turning you over to him…"

Dr. Santiago: First, a lot of people who may hear your music might consider it to have a dark influence or negative impact. I believe otherwise, but am curious your response…"

"If they don't comprehend what we do you mean? You can take that question into various meanings – it could possess you, it could tend to do something like make you cry or make you commit suicide or…"

Dr. Santiago: "Well as far as your philosophies of the occult, would you consider it to be a negative or positive influence on your listeners?"

"I think that its enlightenment. With Melechesh if you don't read the lyrics you can still enjoy the music. The lyrics offer a lot of profound substance. If they really comprehend them, it won't hinder towards a negative. They question a lot of things, the lyrics. The subjects we talk about are rather fascinating. Are they dark? Well, of course, but its very subjective."

Dr. Santiago: *"So you believe it's either one or the other – either they love your music or they're going to hate it…"*

"I think at a musical level it's like everything else. If you listen to it and you understand it, you might like it. And if not, that's fair enough. From what I see our fan base is always growing. Musically people could relate to it unless they are looking at it from a very skeptical point of view. Lyrically I think that yes, it is dark in some sense. It's not very happy stuff."

Dr. Santiago: *"One thing I love about your music is that there is a wealth of experience and influences – what if any specific roots that contributed to the overall sound of 'Emissaries?'"*

"I think it's a process of evolution and conscious thought, but then it becomes your character. What you hear on Melechesh is my character of composing, so maybe that's one, but how is that formed? I was raised on thrash and heavy metal, black metal. My attitude is a combination of the three. I feel that Mediterranean music fits perfectly in the percussion area, and with the guitar. That combination in my own character makes the sound of Melechesh."

Dr. Santiago: *"Are there any specific bands that you have a lot of respect for?"*

"I respect a lot of bands of course, but acknowledging them for crafting the sound of Melechesh today? No, I can't. But we started because I was so into the Bathory *The Return* album that I wanted to do something similar as in raw but that of course was the first period. I enjoy lots of rock and black metal and thrash, especially when they have their own sound going. But I don't think you can relate any of them to us now."

Dr. Santiago: *"What is your favorite country to play live?"*

"I like playing in Israel because it's so inspiring there. It's a holy place, there's a lot of metal, the audience is very, very, very aggressive. France is nice to play, Germany. Sometimes the Dutch audiences are considered timid, because that seems part of the culture. But when we play its insane here. I liked playing Canada."

Dr. Santiago: *"Does Melechesh have any political views? Being from Israel how do you feel about holy wars and the jihad situation going on in the Middle East?"*

"As a band we don't have a political opinion because we don't deal with mundane aspects... As an individual of course... We're all free thinkers and we all have our opinions. Not all of them are in agreement of course. Personally my political opinions are best summed up with it takes "2 to tango.' Every action has a reaction, just like Einstein said in physics. That applies. It becomes a vicious circle. They don't ask what the source of the problem is, they just kill back and forth. I think a lot of people are hypnotized and easy to manipulate. Its ignorance ruling rather than enlightenment, and they outnumber us at least a hundred to one. I don't believe what I hear on the TV. I know for a fact that there a lot of lies..."

DESPERATELY AWAITING THE NEEDLES

Onyx' wife takes me to the homeless shelter Downtown, a Lutheran Church where dinner is served at 4pm and the free medical clinic offers a variety of services, including free acupuncture...

You look down from the second story balcony at the swarming courtyard mass of them. Some crippled, some disturbed, all broken or otherwise obscured. That deep-seated conservative dogma rears its ugly head and you wonder how many are just parasitic actors that lack the discipline to pull it together...

Dinner is served – a portion of chili, one donut, one piece of bread and a vital slice of American cheese. One stale slice of cold cheese pizza, a lumpy mash of yam pie smothered in cinnamon, one day old glaze donut with chocolate icing... I get ticket #43 for acupuncture and sit alone in the lobby blasted and falling asleep from hardcore muscle-relaxers. Hours pass, public lawyers explain legal issues to old Chicano men in Spanish...

8:30pm, shuffled into a curtained room where two med students await my diagnosis. One is a male late 20's, wide-eyed and tripped out, the spittoon image of a Tom Green body double. The girl is a stunningly pretty blonde, trusting and beaming with a gentle, motherly aura. They ask dozens of medical and psychological questions and have me stick out my tongue, debating its coloration...

Acupuncture is a pseudo-science that's results count solely on knowledge of the charkas and other such Oriental beliefs. It is a way to channel the electrical currents in the body by sticking giant needles in a variety of pressure points that act like inward lightning rods. To make their final prognosis, they have to both read my pulse simultaneously, clutching my wrists as we all meditate together close-eyed and Zen-like in an attempted psychic link...

But I know I'm in trouble. There is no way a correct reading is going to come from this. First, I'm all jacked up on painkillers. Second, I can't relax because I'm a misanthropic, anxiety riddled freak and squirm in opposition to the general contact of strangers. Third, being this hard-boiled has created a consistent mood where I cannot get excited, get a pulse pounding, or feel emotion like the normal human would. The empathy is strangled and the compassion is fleeting at best, but such is my serrated nature...

Fourth, the pretty blonde girl is gently stroking my wrist with her soft, television white, Oil Of Olay hands and giving me a raging boner which I'm fighting with all my deluded concentration. Although instinctual I want the flagpole to rise full mast – to lunge forward in savage animal lovins' – I have Tom Green here on the other end gaffeling the awkward process. Plus I'm chilly and in boxers beneath the Kleenex-thin surgical gown. My legs are tightly squeezed together to keep the ever-enlargement of Mr. Binky tucked firmly between my thighs, this air of an unrecorded Marx Brothers skit...

They consult their certified mentor, I go limp, and they have me lay face down. Methodically they massage tender areas, spice me up with foreign herbs/exotic oils, then beat me with wooden mallets. Once I'm fully relaxed & gelatinous, they swiftly jab humongous needles into my feet and upper back...

Tepes as it appears, there was nothing but dull pain involved, which quickly dissipated into a warm tingling. My eyes bulged from my skull, and I lay in a dizzyingly satisfying stupor. I melted like butter until being sent, confused and dizzy from needles, back into the night. The bus home was unreal, and the moment I walked into the Villa Winona I passed out on the busted up floor mattress...

Next day, back screaming, wake up wondering where I was. Slept deep and in a bad, bad position – too much muscle relaxation way too fast. It felt like half the meat hung from my bones. I envisioned myself the gargoyle on the arch of the church, encased in ice... *Did they wipe me clean with holy water?*

THE MADMAN OF TEMECULA

"I've always hated 99% of Earth's population. Even as a kid I couldn't fucking stand them. Last month I nearly ripped someone's face off for disrespecting 'Masters of The Universe.' He saw my collection and was like 'Oh, that orange guy.' No motherfucker, these characters mean everything. They're symbols and mythologies. I was raised on the Norwegian legends, and all of them represent different incarnations of The Old Gods. But to this asshole, they were just chunks of plastic to bang together as a mindless kid. You fucking zombie, that's Beastman, not orange guy. He's the ruler of the jungle, he wrangles the beasts of the Earth. You disrespect him and you fuck with what I stand for. This shit is fucking serious!"

These are the words of Edwin Borscheim, arguably the most extreme shock rocker in America, if not the world. Not since GG Allin's death in 1993 has anyone came close to topping the legend, yet Borscheim hits the same altitude of abomination, even if avoiding the task of eating his own shit on stage. GG was a lunatic freak and prevented serial killer who found freedom in punk rock instead of slashing up hookers. His charisma was legendary, his quotes immense, his lunatic plan to remodel the world in his own twisted image second to none in the history of rock n' roll… *and then came Borscheim…*

To flip on a Kettle Cadaver DVD is to view Edwin live in action hammering 8 inch nails through his cock and scrotum to a 2X4, raping a skinned coyote with a high powered saw blade strap-on, staple gunning his face raw, tearing out his fingernails, savagely attacking hecklers in the crowd, jamming two dozen hypodermic needles in his skin, or wrapping razor wire around his chest, face and schlong for kicks. And now comes the new Edwin – an even bloodier, more gruesome version of his old self – abandoning the old school days of Kettle Cadaver for an all-out conversion to black metal terrorism.

Hanging out with Edwin Borscheim is kind of like hanging out with Freddy Krueger, except that he hunts you down in your dreams not to slaughter you, but simply to hang out 'cause you're just as depraved. Just as the Son of a 100 Maniacs would lead you around his boiler room showing off his neat finger knife trinkets, Edwin enthusiastically does the same.

We're inside his HQ, this ghoulish shack of doom he built from the ground up. I'm the first journalist outside of the Germans to ever step foot in here, and they flipped him a grand for the privilege. The interior hosts a massive collection of death-weapons he created through blacksmith arts and crafts. All of the leather he made himself – gauntlets, full war suits studded with barbaric spikes, weird BDSM shit. Since the slaughterhouse wouldn't let him slay the cow, he purchases the fully carved skin and drags the bloody clump home over his shoulder, dragging a mutilated trail through sandy back-roads...

The entrance to Edwin's fortress is covered in gigantic rusted nails and surrounded by quaint booby traps such as literal bear traps. The interior is shadowy and gothic in the truest non-HIM sense, and you feel like you're in the lair of a Handy Andy Nosferatu, because the entire structure is hammered together with chopped lumber. It's like an authentically menacing version of Mandel's underworld in *Little Monsters*. Edwin sleeps in a coffin and there is real blood splattered all over the walls. Same with the floors, and Manson Family-esque satanic writings spray painted across the walls. Black candles, occultist mirrors, giant Carpathian Forest flag.

"You wanna see some crazy shit?" Edwin says as he flicks through the footage of a video recorder. On the tiny screen – the only thing illuminating the chamber – are two girls he's faced backwards, backsides exposed, both handcuffed and mute, and he's staple gunning their backs with three-inch deep industrial sized magnums. There are at least a hundred in each of their backs, and they're not even making a peep. Then he lifts a chalice, pops some of these juggernauts out with a butter knife, and fills the thing up with dripping plasma. He pauses the HI-8 before it gets any crazier. Impressed, I say: *"Wow, that shit's fucking crazy. Where do you find girls like that?"* His reply: *"You gotta create 'em."*

Every writer alive exaggerates things ever so slightly for the purposes of sensationalism and effect. But once again, I cannot stress more firmly how dead serious Edwin is. He is one of the most intense individuals I have ever met.

Borscheim exists in some other dimension attained through Neitzscean will – this brutal tyrant with the cunning dementia of Loki. He moves with the wolf-like grace of Danzig – ripped, crazed; a wide black Mohawk with shaved-to-the-skin sides, Kettle Cadaver logo tattooed on the left hemisphere. His knuckles are tattooed with the names of his pet dogs, quite possibly the only living beings he has any true love for.

He seems at all times to be swinging between two polarizations – one where everything is a sort of warped cartoon of black humor; the other a nightmare world where he could snap on you in a heartbeat. Yet he has an almost child-like exuberance for adventure. He has an inherently European vibe, due to his Norwegian immigration. He has a distinct way of talking, this slang-heavy accent on par with a mafia underling from Long Island.

Not that I have even begun to unfurl his epic back-story. You see, in Temecula – a town 2 hours north of San Diego – lay a sparse settlement within a complex of mountainous valleys. Halfway to Los Angeles, in this very desert, lays a satanic compound where pagan black mettalers collide to live in a world between *Road Warrior* Urungus and the multi-hoofed army of the four horsemen. And the ringmaster antichrist of these hordes met me in person at a billiards hall last summer. We then had a discussion of great historical importance…

Said Borscheim on June 22nd 2006, while referring to his legendary squat *The Mower Shack*: *"Those days were pretty wild. I used to pick up squatter kids and let them live on my property in exchange for labor. We would have all kinds of different parties there. Most of them to make money, but then we also had our exclusive Plague shindigs where you could see bands like Pernicious and Sol Evil. It was an exciting time – we'd pretty much created our own reality. I was clueless of the outside world. When 9/11 hit, I didn't even know until almost a week later."*

"That place had endless opportunities. We had these dog kennels and we'd host these bear-knuckle fight parties where people would beat the fuck out of each other. If you were to look at this scene from the outside, it might seem a bit childish with the war paint and old fashioned weapons. But this is what attracts the young and there is nothing like the enthusiasm of the youth…"

**Back to the Present, this chilly January night. The situation has crept ever so slowly from *"formal journalist guy meets Satan incarnate."* No, this is on par with Scarecrow and The Joker kicking it at the League of Doom. It's not about ideology, it's not about press – it's two sick fucks getting ripped & ranting depravity…

Yet we need to back up this tale, again. Five hours ago I was sitting in the Greyhound SD terminal and breaking news flashed that the French government had declassified all of their X-Files and flatly admitted the existence of alien spacecraft. It ran once as a quickie blurb before returning to the top story of every 15 minute brief – *a two year that old accidentally ate crystal meth in Kansas…*

I fell asleep on the bus, and went deep under in an exhausted lapse of REM. I thought I was an Eagle soaring over the mountains, swaying to the bus rhythms… *Snapped* out immediately, groggy, pushed out of the bus, Edwin emerges from the darkness with red suspenders and white laced boots, shakes my hand with a slick professional death-grip, and we hop into his buddies' truck.

The night is freezing and ominous, the moon full and bright when a cop speeds behind us and flips on his lights at 75 MPH on the freeway. It is no secret at that moment how allergic Edwin and I both are to the coppers; that same paranoiac, neurotic spider sense. Everyone is obviously a walking felony in this car. Miraculously, the squad car switches lanes, hits the gas, and zooms passed us doing 95 MPH. The cold-blood rush fades slowly...

As we approach Edwin's compound his dogs run to the fence. *"Never pet the dogs, it's faggot shit. I see someone pet my dogs and I swear I'll beat their fuckin' face in."* Up the hill is his little trailer in the middle of a dead field. His neighbors are far separated, and they have wooden fence posts and roosters.

It is *Devils Rejects* incarnate. His entire backyard is this satanic al Qaeda training ground, and there are weird structures of steel and chicken wire that he welded together for cage-match fighting. There's also a giant gargoyle head he created by hand, like an Aztec remnant, surrounded by a mix of black ash and sand...

The inside of Boscheim's trailer is divided into three main motifs – *Danzig worship, He-Man toys, and a giant wall of horror DVD's & WWII docs.* There is an oil painting someone made of Edwin in a Frazetta-type barbarian background with flaming volcanoes. He's beefed up, bluish and clutching a deranged machete.

Eddie takes me outside to the shack fortress, and that's when we catch up to the staple gunned darlings. He begins shuffling through junk drawers, tossing random items on the ground. The wood block he nailed to his genitals, a barb wired crown with strands of his hair and chunks of skin stuck to its barbs, hypodermic needles with dried blood in the chamber. *"Ah, here they are."* He passes me some BM propaganda flyers fashioned after the old school Norwegian ones you see in the sidebars of *Lords of Chaos*. They are all based around the SoCal Plague network, the supposed terrorist organization in which Lord Mörder from Sol Evil was convicted.

One flyer is an anti-Lord Daishe (Sumeria) flyer that has his corpse-painted face with a universal "NO" encircled by "NO TRAITORS, NO SNITCHES, NO RATS, NO NARCS" and reads: *"This bastard helped the authorities in prosecuting Lord Mörder of Sol Evil. Destroy Daishe now!"* Another is a bloody, demonic Ray Shipley that says *"FUCK DAISHE, HAIL LORD MÖRDER. Lord Mörder betrayed by Daishe of Sumeria. Support Black Metal! Support Sol Evil! Not police Puppets like Sumeria!"*

There are a few basic S.C.B.M. (SoCal Black Metal) ones, yet the most bluntly iconic is of a white-hooded corpse-paint druid with a spiked club behind a barb wire fence. There is a universal "NO" sign crossing out the word "HARDCORE" and surrounded by the words *"NO FAGS, NO TRENDIES, NO STAGE, NO BANDS."*

***It should be appropriate to mention at this juncture that Ray Shipley, a.k.a. Lord Mörder is the right hand man of Edwin Borscheim, and both were instrumental figures in this renegade empire. In case you haven't heard, Lord Mörder is the first black metaller in the USA to be tried as a "*Satanic Terrorist.*"

In early 2003 Mörder's black metal outfit Sol Evil was at their peak, having completed a successful tour with Enthroned. Not long after, Sol Evil's drummer Berzerk – a gauntlet-clad, leather and spiked black metal warrior – swore off his die-hard Satanic ideology and committed himself to a faith-based rehab clinic. He gave himself to the Born Again pathology, took up the crucifix and, overnight, cleansed his former image.

This did not sit well with Lord Mörder, the band, or any in their immediate circles. It is an indisputable fact that worldwide, the black metal scene is unrepentantly and fascistically antichristian, because Christianity is viewed as the ultimate fascism. The essence of black metal is drenched in heathenism and fanatic mental segregation from both society and all white light religions. Black metal strives for the deepest pits of blasphemy; it is an orgy of audio terror and darkness. In its deepest sense, the efforts of BM strive for a liberation through the deepest core of alienation – a finalized process of man above god fused with a Neitzschean will to power...

The die-hard Satanists of this underground are viciously committed to a code of "death before dishonor." None ever forget or forgive their Quislings, and retribution could come in any form. Lord Mörder is one such Satanist, wholly enamored in his own myth, having erased all boundaries between the stage and physical reality. One cold February morning, he and Sol Evil's guitarist Arminius, *"sent a message"* in the most blunt of all fashions.

At 5am they sped past the rehab clinic housing Berzerk and popped a couple handgun shots aimlessly at the building. Mörder fervently insists they had no plans on committing direct violence against Berzerk or anyone else. In their eyes, it was simply a way to rattle his nerves and forever draw the line. Berzerk didn't require physical retribution. He was invisible – a bad joke, a bathroom poetic; dead to them and gone forever...

What Mörder and Arminius didn't know is that they'd succeeded in terrorizing Berzerk so badly that he'd contacted the authorities. Fixed with a wire and appearing at Mörder's home to "make amends," the police recorded whatever blatant statements they could before the SWAT team charged in. As charges were formulated, Mörder was discovered to maintain an already colored legal history including grave desecration and church vandalism.

The prosecution immediately demanded a duel verdict of life in prison without the possibility of parole. To make matters worse, Sumeria bassist Lord Daische was allegedly coerced by authorities to make statements against the two (*which Daische has vehemently denied*). This has caused a massive rift in the SoCal BM underground, with Sumeria itself as one of the most high-profile touring BM bands from the region.

Due to the fanatical nature of the crime, the authorities needed little to convince the jury of Mörder's status as a perceived Charles Manson/Varg Vikernes archetype. The prosecution was the first in United States history to utilize the seminal BM book *Lord of Chaos* as a reference guide. From that definitive history of the Norwegian church burnings, they pulled every belligerent statement from Burzum, Absurd, and Mayhem to influence the jury.

In the eyes of the law, he was also the ringleader of "The Plague" – a supposedly International Satanic Terrorist Organization mirroring Norway's legendary "Black Circle." In reality though, "The Plague" was simply a name given to his crew of friends and like-minded bands they often played with (including Kettle Cadaver), not uncommon whatsoever in any metal, punk, or industrial scene you'll find in operation today.

A top-notch defense team could do little to reprimand the jury's opinion. With dozens of live show flyers lined up as evidence featuring an endless procession of inverted crosses, burning pentagrams, and "destroy the Christians" outbursts in the margins, the life sentence loomed heavy over what was legally a 3 year maximum penalty of discharging a firearm in public. For an action that few outside the immediate BM underground at large could understand, Mörder was left trying to explain himself to a system which looked at him as nothing other than a terrifying psychopath that best be dealt with by throwing away the key.

In the end they secured non-life plea bargains with trumped up "hate crime" charges, instantly giving three times the legal limitation. Mörder got 15 years as an accomplice, Arminius 25 for firing the weapon. The media covered it up as not to start any commotion, and this story has long been buried or publicized in obscure metal zines...

And here I am at the second version of The Mower Shack, Edwin's new lair: *"See that Snake Mountain box on the floor? Know how on the side panel it shows all of the features to make it look way bigger and magical than it is? Like the a picture of an action figure in the slime pit, then one of an axe battle on the castle top, and one of Skeletor's laboratory? That's a big part of what inspired me."*

Edwin shows me all of his tattoos. One is of the machete he created on the wall of his shack, a sketch of his torture rack, his band logo. Everything in Edwin's world is highly personal, reinforcing the world he's fanatically courted into reality...

Edwin keeps ranting about Axel Rose being that alpha-male of rock vocalists, how Misfits over-merchandising has destroyed anything cult about the band, and about his 2004 "Naked Tour" which was *"more of a rock n' roll thing."* He elaborates a tale of trying to get a band he'd beaten up on a compilation he was putting out, and when he went to their house 20 cars pulled up to protect them. *"Shit man, I was just trying to be friendly. It's not my fault they suck. You want a comp that represents all of the scene or what?"*

Devon (*drummer of Kettle Cadaver*) shows up with plastic sheeting covering a bloody, fresh tattoo, and Edwin launches on a Mayhem rant. He pulls out a shoebox of 600 photos. He took a snapshot of every nook of the labyrinth beneath the Helvete store in Norway where all the legendary BM bands used to practice. Next he flips on the new Kettle Cadaver 12 video DVD collection *Among The Damned*. And I thought the self-mutilation in the first DVD was bad; live clips and industrial miniatures of Borscheim doing blacksmith stuff like Leatherface in his chainsaw shed...

He's kind of weird about playing his *"ego masturbation ballad"* acoustic song – a kind of "Man That You Fear" which features Edwin on mountaintops dueling both environment and his own personal nature in poetic, somber contemplation...

There is a *"glam"* video in a nightclub that looks like The Viper Room, red curtains and hot goth chicks making out and dancing with snakes. Then my favorite – a *Roadwarrior* post-apocalypse homage of his crew fighting each other in dune buggies and shooting arrows. In this video he plays the red-mohawked villain complete with assless leather chaps. It concludes with a *"two man enter, one man leaves"* broadsword duel between Edwin and one of the Sol Evil guys, fire explosions spewing everywhere...

Next he speeds through the documentary the Germans made on his wrestling, which has a weird *Gummo* vibe to it, like pro wrestling as this thing that comes out of poverty, ignorance, and desperation. At his segments peak he's showing the crew *Masters of the Universe* figures and says something along the lines of, *"Some kids grow up wanting to be doctors or the president. I wanted to be this"* and points to Skeletor. *"And you know I'm closer than probably anyone in America."*

He pulls out a briefcase and inside it has a police report that details everything that cops confiscated from Mörder's house when the arrest went down. It is about 10 pages long and convictable items include: *"One copy of Marilyn Manson's 'Portrait of An American Family' compact disc, one copy of Ted Bundy autobiography, maps of California, pair of handcuffs, anti-Christian heavy metal flyers."* They even added a Smashing Pumpkins album to the list.

Edwin waves around a cassette tape that has all of the wire tapped conversations from Berzerk of Sol Evil and Daishe of Sumeria. *"How the fuck did you get that?"* Edwin just chuckles maniacally. *"I have my ways."*

The moment has finally come to start the interview, and I hit play in the middle of a conversation: *"...threw him into the goddamn drum set, like a full Irish Whip. Whap, right into this guy and you see the camera [makes crashing noise]. Then I hit the bus driver, I run out and grab him during one of the songs. Then I threw him on the stage and he tries to grab some other guy, and this guy goes flying through the drum set. All these other meathead metal faggots are just standing there...*

"Dude, there's no evil and brutality here. Cheeseburgers are not fucking black metal. Fucking pussies... And that guy keeps standing around, practicing how to be fuckin' 'Johnny Evil?' At the end of the night he's still standing there like 'oh, you're not cool.' I'll fucking strangle him. You're not fucking cool either, standing around with hippie hair bullshit. Oppress the maggots, keep 'em fucking down."

"What do you think of Phil Anselmo?"

Edwin Borscheim: "Everyone hates him, I think he's cool. I met him once and he remembered the Kettle Cadaver CD, he sung some lines from it. He had the Celtic Frost tattoo, all that shit."

"What do you think of Led Zepplin?"

"I don't know much. I don't like much, and that's blues."

"What do you think of Pink Floyd?"

"That's all that hippie shit. I'm into… very *evil* and psychotic distortion…"

"Have you ever met Belladonna, the freak porn star?"

"I've never met her, but I met Jasmine St. Claire. It was at some stupid award shit. She's like '*I bet you like King Diamond.*' King Diamond? You're a chick, why don't you like Billy Idol or Axel Rose? Are you a man or something? Yeah that's real sexy. Than she's, '*Oh, I like black metal*' and starts trying to tell me about Norway. Don't tell me about Norway you fuckin' dumb bitch. She's like '*eh, I got big titties*' and starts jibber-jabbering in Swedish to me. But you know, people suck you into their little gay trap."

"Did you lose her?"

"She starts turning everything around like '*I wanna fuck you*' and all this weird shit. She's toying with my balls and I didn't even know who this bitch was. Moral of the story is just one of those cocksucker bitches, the '*oh you're doing something, you made a speech.*' The kicker was she had the Guinness Book world record for most gangbangs. Alright, what the fuck else can I do to you anyway? I could bash you in the face with a 2X4 but it's not gonna matter, she's had the most gangbangs in world history. You're already fucked."

"Not a big King Diamond fan?"

"I'm not a fan of anything really. It's all about shit that's real and hard, totally fucking black metal. [Edwin points to the stereo as we listen to Lars Frederickson] If you wanna be a dirt bag, drink liquor, and eat drugs, play some fucking scumbag music. This guy tours and plays in Sushi shops. That shit's real dude. Some little fucking

Dungeons & Dragons faggot, what's he know about punk rock? Punk Rock is always real, you can always count on it. "

"Did you ever meet Nattefrost from Carpathian Forest?"

"No, but he grew up two blocks down the street from me and I never even knew. We're the same age. Where I used to live, you could look right down from the window and see the Helvete II record store. I ask where I can meet some of these guys, where the black metal clubs are. I'm like what about these guys, these guys – no one fucking knew. Some dude in the back, he's laughing. He had a fucking pentagram on his head. *'Hey, aren't you the guy from Kettle Cadaver?'* That was kind of weird. In fucking Norway? He's like, *'Yeah I used to play with Enslaved.'* 'You know the guys from Darkthrone?' *'Yeah, yeah, fuckin' Rick.'* So I talked to him about Carpathian Forest and he was like '*Yeah he's up in Germany.'* He called me high on mushrooms.' I met the guy who made Count Grishnach's mace. It was cool 'cause I made a bunch that looked just like them."

"How often do you go to Norway?"

"Whenever I can, but I don't think anytime soon. People are so dull and lame. I walk down the street in Norway and I feel like I'm pollution. They're so structured and strictly pleasant. You can't do something like a cape and corpse-paint and not have them be scared. The guy could be looking like he's fucking The Joker. Wait'll you got blood running down your knuckles and a 'Fuck You' tattoo on your neck. That's why I like the US, that shit doesn't fly. Euronymous had his own internal censorship going where bands that sucked, he put them out of business. The US naturally is like that because if you're a douche-bag you're fucked."

"Was the music scene you came from pretty vicious?"

"When I was a kid you could get your head beat in. It was gnarly. I remember my buddies little high school band played. They got spit on, green shit dripping off their face. They were lucky. Lucky's walking out of there still walking. I've seen people beat up so bad. One dude the crowd held to the floor and beat him in the face with the microphone stand. Five chicks vomit on you and shit. When I do play a show and the little opening band gets their ass kicked, I could give a shit less. That's the territory. If you're gonna cry about it, then hop along little bunny and move on to the next scene. But if you come back with your busted self, keep coming back until people remember your face, then you can stick around."

"Obviously you're getting more extreme as time goes by…"

"There's no progression, it just started off. Now I'm very content with shit so I'm not going to do anything unless I feel like it. I only want it to be real. A kid that wants to die hitting himself in the face with a hammer is different from the guy making a spectacle out of himself… I am skilled at hitting myself in the face with a hammer, of course. It doesn't mean shit though…"

"What direction are you heading?"

"I want to do more of the rock n' roll stuff. One of the bands that laughs the most is HIM, the most hated goth ever by all men. He fucks all their girlfriends and they sit at home and bitch. I get that now, I understand. I play shows for men. But where is the true evil? A big tough guy in front of dudes? Or fucking all those lame guys girlfriends? I like fucking chicks…"

"You get these girls to do some pretty crazy shit though, like in the video…"

"That was like two nights ago. Behind the coffin there's just blood splatters, this shit just literally running off my neck. The chick was like *'I just got new shoes, I swear if you got any blood on my new shoes.'* I look down and they look like tampons."

"What are the craziest shows you ever threw here?"

"The black metal shows back in the day. One guy pistol whipped another guy in the face and shot out the window… There were the ones I'd go fucking nuts, beat people and any available anything. There'd be people pissing on each other and shit. You go upstairs and everyone is fucking. Wherever there are drugs, there's always fucking."

"How did the last tour go?"

"Awesome. Every single night of that tour it was the same type of shit – partying in crack houses, getting into fights, fucking chaos… We do one bad show, it stops right there in that city. No idea how to get amps or the drum set home. That's what gets you into the mode – it's you versus the street."

"In the event that you finally do blow up, and you got your image on lunchboxes that are sold to 14 year old girls at Hot Topic, what's the number one mission now that you have everyone's attention?"

"(Laughs) I'll figure it out once I get there…"

It is then that we freeze because we hear his dogs Howley and Damian barking up something fierce. There is something sinister going on in the front yard. On edge, dizzy with liquor and paranoia, I instinctively grab the butcher knife on the table. Edwin sees this and grabs his machete, jumping up after my lead. We blitzkrieg into the night, leaping towards the gate below the hill...

We come charging like wild Indians at a pack of 7 coyotes divided from Eddie's dogs by the property fence. The moment they see us they scatter fast as they can, charging off into the mountainous desert region. We both stop, kind of just glance at each other, shrug, and wander back inside to kill all remaining booze...

The next morning, passed out inside a sleeping bag with my face covered, feeling like a Nagasaki Hibakusha, Edwin had slept Indian style to the left of me. I slid open my eye, briefly looked around, no visible sign of movement on my behalf, I hear Edwin say "Hey Ryan..." *He just knew...*

During the ride home I went back into that same, floaty sense of REM. sleep. This time the bus rhythms were that of the world being drown in Volcanic magma, the extermination of all human civilization in a boiling cauldron of terror...

PURITY OF THE GREYHOUND

Depression hits hard, and the world becomes so small and that only an element of massive change can bring repeal to the neurotic isolation. In my case, it's always been alien habitat...

Weak as it sounds, this Greyhound fetish began with a girl – a lady named "3." It was the devastating end of a devastating run. She was looking at jail time over a roach, so I sent her off broken-hearted on Valentine's Day 2006. From the closest person on earth to a non-existent ghost; a maelstrom of drama pervading everything...

I was a hundred miles of frozen concrete the next 9 months. I watched my life crumble piece by piece into nothingness, every possible dagger that could have been stuck in my back was. All I could dream of was the Greyhound -- that hollow land machine hauling me as a lone passenger through vast wastelands of night. Night after night, every ticking time-clock of every shit job, I'd close my eyes and see it – killer motor running silently; *just waiting, beckoning me...*

There was only one way I could reclaim what had died within me. I had to become a fetus in its womb, let it shape me into whatever it planned. Let the blurring yellow lines of the highway become my mother, the hum of the engine my father. It didn't matter where I traveled. Like the Argonauts, sailing was the only thing that mattered.

The port of destination was the absurdity. I knew that somehow, someway, I'd rediscover the piece of me that was lost. That's what this is all really about. Not fame, shows, parties, chicks, or any kind of journalistic integrity. I'm reclaiming my soul city by city, mile by mile of black tar...

This is the hypnosis as I peer out that huge window into the rolling fields at night. I'm but one in a silent subculture that ride these things addictively – *the hard-worn woman with the deep lines in her face, bouncing the country from one abusive relationship to the next... The one who's burned all bridges and headed for the new beginning that will end just the same... The con man slinging Snickers & Skittles like a prison courtyard...*

The displaced trucker, the Vegas fuck-up, the LA star-struck, the black families on low-rent vacation to somewhere devastatingly grim like Pittsburg. Freshly released prisoners in a trance, drug runners with the blue tear tat, the runaways returning or fleeing home, the college kids out for a cheap thrill...

Then there are those like myself, silent and contemplating whatever agenda it is that rumbles their scattered thoughts. Some live on those buses easily picking up females who are traveling alone and vulnerable, hopping off at the next city with them for a romantic, hustler fling. Some are living ghosts of that limbo who never want to come off. Then there are the crazies, the bad luck elderly, the neophytes who weed themselves out in inter-state Darwinian selection...

I don't bother to talk to anyone anymore. I know all the games and I know all the faces. I just close off into my own wonderland, enjoying that chemical stink of industrial grade disinfectant creeping from the horrifying toilet covered with gang signs & sharpie memoirs.

The wheels keep spinning, the land keeps rushing, and every rest-stop or fueling depot becomes a surge of Déjà vu. The bus parks in Grand Junction, Topeka, Kansas City, and you immediately recall every video game in the corner, every hot chocolate luxury – all the putrid options of fried food boiling under a white or red light. After enough miles are imprinted on your skull, you'll know every McDonalds in the country like the back of your hand...

PART II: EXIT STAGE WEST
(ALBUQURQUE; THE ARCTIC DESERT)
JANUARY 16TH-28TH 2007

FROSTBITTEN RIDE OF THE VALKYRIES

The fact that Southern California has this invisible force field holding the Mediterranean climate in place is perhaps the most head scratching mystery in our nation. Only 20 hours East the desert is an icicle, the still air makes your breath dragon steam…

A radiant moon encircled by an outstretch nucleus of light, the orbiting body illuminating the desert through a reflection of red sand and iced barrancas; its beams glistening a wall of light from sharp, red-granite desert plateaus. No smog, no pollution – you feel that howling coyote spirit imprinted on gas station arctic wolf t-shirts. Albuquerque, the metropolis jewel of the desert…

Mountains surround ABQ like a fortified trench, enclosing the cities grace like an Egyptian oasis. It is confined in the way few major American capitols are. Initially settled by frontiersmen, it's existed ever since as this kind of port to all headed westward. Once it was pure East to West migration, now it's built its solid place in the Union. It is among a few larger cities in New Mexico that create the dynamic economic backbone of the state and southern region. Still, it has no massive water bodies surrounding it, and an abnormal climate for strong irrigation and rural development. Its settlement had derived from the brutal West…

This New Mexico jaunt is the initial campaign of a duel city initiative. Two weeks in Albuquerque, then a 10 hour northbound trek to Denver for two following weeks of general bru-ha-ha. I view these as soft targets, comprised of definite support from fellow Detroit Expatriates. Jesus, the anti-EMINEM terrorist in Denver, mastermind of Detroit proto-noise champs PHALLUS.

In ABQ we unearth Vertigo Venus, the most aggressively homosexual cyberpunk-experi-industrial-new wave thingy in New Mexico's history. What better a way to totally alienate my audience in one fell swoop? The Vertigo boys have just signed to the well-respected industrial label DSBP Records and have been getting airplay in The Czech Republic. Plus their new bassist is the soundman at Burt's Tiki

Lounge, the definitive punk hangout in ABW. Combined I have access to many key people in the city. Decent transportation system, confirmed air mattress, unlimited high speed internet – a $100 mission tops.

Denver is going to be out of control. PIT Magazine – one of the biggest I write for and a linchpin in the extreme metal underground – has Colorado Springs on lock with their HQ record store Mosh Pit Music. Over the past 5 years I've written for this magazine, I've made contact with at least a dozen bands in the area, and PIT knows everyone anyway. This is going to be my strongest foothold outside Detroit, more so then California.

Talking to Chris MacCannon of Vertigo Venus, between diatribes of all the awful, megalomaniac musicians we knew in high school that have totally squandered their lives, he gives me his oral report on the area. He is convinced it is a great environment for a serious musician because housing is relatively cheap, the music scene is diverse & most national acts make it through. Plus it's a good touring base – your smack dab between the East and West Coast with a strong circuit between Vegas, Austin, Reno, SLC, Denver.

The weather never gets too horrific, snow of any sort is light. It's not like Michigan where they have to dump rock salt constantly and therefore, ironically, every car in the Motor City is rusting apart. Winds are cancelled out by the mountain box effect, and the lighting is so intense and sunny that Albuquerque is being passed off as the next Los Angeles to the film industry. 40 major productions have been through here in the past six months alone.

As for the scenery, expect the kind of town Billy Jack would feel comfortable lurking on the outskirts of. Tom Laughlin is out there on one of those mountaintops meditating, his aura the soaring eagle above. This is also one of the strongest Indian populations in America, and Native land is patchily stretched beyond its outskirts. Chris says meth has crept into Native culture -- entire tribes out their gourds, erecting elaborate laboratories…

UFO MYSTERIES, KEYBOARD OVERKILL, ALCHEMICAL BURN
Wednesday, 40 degrees, small patches of snow line the cement. I stroll and pop out on University Drive, which is the hip, mini-Hollywood of ABQ. It lasts ten blocks. At one end is the college, at the other the mountain range can be spotted in distance.

There are hundreds of students walking up and down the strip, and a coffee shop or hipster spot every three stores. Mounds of concert flyers are haphazardly staple gunned or taped to every telephone pole, and bumper stickers are slapped everywhere as an alternative to graffiti. No economic prices are horrendous and seem to be fixed to the New Mexico minimum wage of $6 an hour (*smokes $4 per pack, 89c quasi-Faygo*). There are head shops everywhere, and many stores that specialize in beads.

Everyone is semi-New Age, ultra-environmental, and those Santé Fe colors are everywhere – the pinkish, light blue Indian designs. Like California all the houses have no basements, and all of them take nods from those clay adobe houses that litter the pages of National Geographic, with rounded tops and beige color schemes; suburban lawns made of egg-sized stones and hunks of granite...

Vertigo Venus sets up for practice. I'm not sure what to expect. Their first record was a horrendous mess (*which they too will attest*), and everyone back home scratched their heads wondering exactly what it was they were doing out here in the desert.

The MacCannon brothers (Jeff and Chris) had set up Vertigo Venus once Birth of a Tragedy (BOAT) fell apart. BOAT remains one of my favorite Detroit bands of all time – kind of a Zappa-fueled theatrical punk thing that was all over the map, like this performance art UHF world, equal parts Alice Cooper and *The Price Is Right*.

Seeing as that Detroit is not a good environment for such an act (*every show cleared half the room in 5 minutes*) they decided to move it to Albuquerque where they had prime connections. They departed summer 2002 without a drummer, bass player flaking out at the last minute, and the vocalist splitting due to creative differences in a month.

The brothers rebounded and formed Vertigo Venus with a keyboard, guitar & drum machine. Jeff was always a proudly flamboyant homosexual, but it wasn't until they were totally isolated that Chris came out of the closet as well. The duo then started gigging pride parades and drag clubs. It was a shock to many of us back home, because Chris was always that long-haired, fanatical Slayer guy.

I take a seat in the rehearsal room and they go at it with two additional members – a big Native American guy of the dark industrial persuasion on bass (Ken Cornell), and a second keyboard player named Buddy, who has a long red beard and sunglasses. He's like a modern-day Gandalf goes Skinny Puppy.

The keyboards are sharply defined, luscious and spasmodic, the guitar is heavy on the crunch and far more punk rock, the bass adds the extra punch, and Jeff's vocals are totally over the top. They are sort of a cross between The Epoxies, Mindless Self Indulgence, Culture Club, and Misfits. They sound a hundred times better live than on that awful CD, although I know I won't get the full punch until I see it live.

After they jam out two renditions of their set, they set me alone with new bassist Ken Cornell, who's in his late 30's and stands about 6 foot 5. He's been in a gazillion 'Burque acts in the past 20 years, and is a soundman at Burt's Tiki Lounge, the A-1 top-of-the-line underground music club Downtown: *"Alchemical Burn is primarily a solo project; in the last two years it's been noise focused. Unnatural Element is a duo. It's industrial as far as late 80's dance. It's inspired by harsh, German dance-floor stuff. The other band is Ohmniscience. It's a trio with keyboards, synths, vocals, drums, drum triggers, xylophone..."*

"There's another called Cobra//Group. It's a collective of musicians from a bunch of different band in Albuquerque, all different styles. We play an improv musical game that John Zorn wrote in the late 60's; it's all queue cards. Some people get it, others just wonder what the hell we're doing and have that confused dog head-tilt. It's constantly moving and changing with different instruments. We've got two violins, a viola player, two trombone players, a bassist, singer, keyboardist, drummer, three guitarists. I do a noise setup. A prompter acts like a conductor, but the players make the calls. The prompter finds the appropriate card, holds it up, and when he drops it that change the card indicates has to happen. I think that particular project is building a reputation that supersedes what it really is. We've played shows with 13 musicians onstage at once."

"What's your attraction to the noise genre?"

Ken Cornell: "Noise is very visceral. There's a lot of energy that I feel internally with it. You get to explore new sounds and it's always a surprise. I've been working within noise for six years... It's mostly no lyrics. For a long time I used my solo project in a way – this is a very New Mexico thing – as a sort of holistic idea. People coming together to experience something, and everyone brings their energy and the things going on in their lives. In any situation where a band plays they feed off and utilize an audience' energy. With alchemy and magic and transformation, I was using this idea of really opening up and let that energy dictate the sounds I created. Lately with noise I feel I've been pushing my energy out at people with its harshness..."

"How do you feel about the Albuquerque scene?"

"As with anywhere some people are competitive and some open-minded. Albuquerque has always been a big rock and metal town. I think there's more competition in those circles. Between here and Santé Fe I can speak for experimental, noise, and avant-garde. Generally people are more open to each others' ideas. I think it's still something exciting to them. You can't find a radio station that's going to play 99% of what these people do. They have more of a sense of cooperation with each other, and I think many genuinely enjoy one another's process and sounds."

"New Mexico, Roswell, all these UFO sightings in the desert. Ever seen any weird shit?"

"You know I've seen a lot of weird things to be honest. The first thing I ever saw was what convinced me that extraterrestrial activities and technologies are real. When I was 10 I was with my mom on San Mateo Street in the middle of Albuquerque, probably eleven at night. We noticed this... At first I thought it could have been a helicopter, thought it could have been a plane but I knew it was too low. It had a series of lights, almost like paneling, kind of rectangular. You could see them brightly, but you couldn't make out its shape. Watching it for a short amount of time we had both been engrossed by it and my mom actually stopped the truck. This thing was just kind of hovering right above the cab. We both just sat there in awe."

"How far up was it?"

"I'd say 15 or 20 yards. It was bizarre. We watched for awhile then it just sort of – not too quickly but quicker then it had been moving – shot into another neighborhood. We tried to follow it but couldn't find it. That was the first time. I was with a girlfriend and we saw what looked like some kind of flying craft descend into the Sundaes Mountains. I saw this strong disc-like shape go shooting by and then it slowed down. We drove all around for that thing, never found a trace."

"Isn't that kind of common around here? I know there's a lot of government installations underground..."

"Yeah, Albuquerque and some of the surrounding states too. I wouldn't discount that it could have been some experimental or advance technology testing, some anti-gravitational vehicle."

"If it was, why do you think the United States government would fly an experimental craft over a civilian population?"

"I'm not really sure but it seems that maybe confusion is the key for this current wave of government to help keep its place secure. I think it serves the government well to keep its population generally confused..."

"What's the message of Vertigo Venus?"

"No one should ever take themselves too seriously. That we're all fairly stupid and it's ok. And obviously for Vertigo Venus cock is one of the best things around (laughs)..."

MACCANNON INCORPORATED

Jeff MacCannon: "Detroit was grey, and bleak, and full of lousy drunken punk rockers who were really overrated and annoying. There was no way that anything original could come out of there successfully."

Chris MacCannon: "We also left for personal reasons. I was going to get married..."

"And ruin his career, and have children..."

"Moving was kind of a must and our mother and stepfather lived here. Our stepfather signed us to his record label and put out our first record."

"Tell me about the new album..."

"It's being recorded way better. The first was done on a 1978 reel-to-reel that was mixed digitally, so it was going digital to analog to digital..."

"There were a lot of generations lost..."

"We're using better equipment and basically plugging straight in so it sounds like a live show but without the annoying PA feedback."

"The first record was us putting together everything we had, and this we're really being picky about what we're using. We want it to live up to its title."

"What's the name?"

"'Run For Your Lives.' The theme for this album is explosions."

"Jeff and I are calling it 'Godzilla-esque', if you will..."

"So will you have pyrotechnics onstage?"

"One day..."

"For now we like to make fun of it by having those paper flames and confetti poppers."

"Tell me all about the message..."

"The majority of the message on my part carries over from the last band [BOAT]. This whole 'rock and roll is too serious for its own good.' Lots of sarcasm, a little satire, but I'm not British enough for that…"

"The first album had a message that we were angry and pissed off, exploring ourselves as musicians. This one is just doing our best."

"Some on the first were only because we needed lyrics (laughs)."

"Some of them were pent up aggression. We pretty much told everyone that we were going to kill them…"

"(In mock IKEA tenderness) Depression is aggression turned inward…"

"'At The Altar' is making fun of Catholicism and priests molesting little boys…"

"Kind of like a Stockholm Syndrome…"

"Tell me about the irony in writing the worst synth pop song of all time…"

"We were friends with this guy that wanted to make fun of this other guy he hated. So he asked us to write the worst synth-pop song ever recorded which was to reference him, and we called it 'Vampire Hunter C.'"

"Now it's one of our most popular live songs, which is funny. It was meant as a joke and not to be taken seriously and now everyone loves it."

"In the live show there's obviously a lot of comedy…"

"We get lumped into the novelty category a lot – especially when we were a duet…"

"We improv everything, nothing is scripted. We do play for different audiences every night, so no one really knows what's going to happen…"

"Most of the people are drunk anyway, so they won't remember if I use any of the same rhetoric… With the singer it really doesn't matter what you sound like, as long as you look awesome. I guess what we're trying to do is look awesome *and* sound great."

"What are some of your favorite heckling quotes of all time?"

"We wrote a song in response to people who just say 'you suck.' It's called 'Suck On This.' We only play that when someone says it, and we haven't had to do that in awhile."

"Either they say we suck, they hate us, or they flat out leave."

"We get a lot of people leaving. We get to the part where we're slamming Catholicism, when we get to the line 'we play special games that no one else should know'…"

"All the Hispanic Catholics just file out of the bar, and we make fun of them on the way out..."

"Is this your favorite thing about playing live?"

"Yeah, cause shock rock is totally lost. When I was in high school all I would have to do is say 'GAY' and people would be shocked. Now I've got to try really fucking hard to shock people."

"How do you feel about the Albuquerque scene?"

"The professional bands are a very tight-knit, small group. There are tons of bands that are only together a few months."

"There is an emo scene, sadly... No pun intended there..."

"One of the major bar owners runs a label which exclusively signs bands which fit into the style of music that is most popular in the trends of that time. Right now his bar is full of emo bands..."

"Burt's Tiki Lounge is pretty much mixed. They take rock, punk, even hip hop. That club rules. You can go there and get anything you want, and it's always free."

"Atomic is pretty much the same situation, although it's almost exclusively rock. And then there's the big theatres of course. You got Sunshine Theatre, Launchpad Rocks, The El Ray. We unfortunately don't have enough people that know what music is in this city to sell out a large venue. Last time Mindless Self Indulgence came through they had 20 fans. In Denver they sold out this huge theater..."

"As far as industrial goes, it's our band, Diverje, Random Access Memory, Brian Botkiller, Ken Cornell's band – we're pretty much the industrial scene. There's a few other bands that stick out – Ya-Ya Boom Project, The Hollis Wake, Creepshow..."

"There's also The Dirty Novels, The Fox, The Gracchi..."

"What kind of people come to your shows?"

"Mixed variety – punks, metalheads, skinheads of all people..."

"When we were playing up the gay vibe the skinheads loved us. I don't know why or what was going on. When we first started everything was gay. I was finally away from Michigan..."

"Yeah, we both were like 'we can finally be ourselves'..."

"Not only could we express ourselves but hook the gay audience by playing it up..."

"The gay community hates us with a passion..."

"Mostly lesbians like us and a few guys that are into heavy bondage and leather. The way I see it is most twinkie-weezer faggots see us as the guys that used to beat them up in high school. Playing such heavy music they probably associate us with something stupid like

Metallica, and immediately associate that with football players. What they should really do is think we're hot because of that. I think they just identify us with violence."

"They want us to bust out with some disco queen shit."

"Like if I were a fat black straight woman, we'd be gold. So we stopped doing that. But while we were, we had a bunch of skinheads coming to our shows. When I say skinhead I mean more the working class kind. The clean socks, the shaved head... The occurrence of Nazi skinheads in this town is so small. There's like three and they get their asses kicked all the time. I've never actually met a Nazi skinhead here..."

"Metalheads think we're too gay and they don't get us..."

"People who listen to indie tend to gravitate towards us because we're really kind of a wildcard."

"We've played with death metal bands and people dug us, we've played with emo bands and have been torn to shit..."

"What are the politics of the gay community?"

"It's a stupid thing. And this is a little sociological *but*... We've been oppressed for so long and now we get TV shows and people seem to think that we're accepted when we're really exploited. 'Well now that I'm not oppressed, I better go out and oppress someone else.' So there's all this fighting within the ranks. The little drugged out, waify, bleach-blonde boys hate the lesbians, and the lesbians hate them more. Everyone who's into leather unites, and gay men hate bisexual men. And every woman that goes to college is bi..."

"Do you think that all women are bisexual?"

"I strongly believe in the Kinsey scale where no one really falls into one side or the other. I think female bisexuals are really disrespected because there's so much of this *Girls Gone Wild* bullshit, chicks just making out with chicks to get guys, so it makes them look stupid. And it makes male bisexuals look like unicorns. They're just not there."

"Do the drag queens hate Vertigo Venus?"

"They are just as oppressed as we are by being different from everybody else. We go to the gay bars and we're not very welcomed. We don't have nice clothes... Basically we're not straight people in a gay bar. Now that everyone is fucking becoming stupid Christians and getting married and adopting Asian babies they all seem to think that homosexuality is about being someone else. But it's not. If anything it's about being a total deviant. And I don't see why we split from that. I'm currently in a committed relationship but I by no means am planning to marry or vote for a conservative president or put flowers on my dining room table. Everyone's turning into straight people that happen to be gay. It's the stupidest thing and the only people that remember what a gay society used to be – or should be – are people who lived in it as a subculture. I think just like goth and punk, when it went mainstream it just got saturated with marketing and turned into total crap."

"Do you hate Ellen DeGeneres?"

"What we hate is 'Queer Eye For The Straight Guy.' All these stereotypical queeny guys. Our motto when we started playing pride fests was that not everything is glitz and glamour. We're examples of that right now. We used to play gay prides wearing goth clothes and fishnets and sing about some pretty graphic shit. There's a reason 'The Happy Song' is played at gay pride because it's a nice little undertone of the community hating everybody. We have no shame. If they boo us, who cares?"

"What do you think of Rob Halford?"

"I love Rob Halford. I understand why he was in the closet for so long. I don't know how people didn't see it. When I was 7 years old I could see that Rob Halford was a homosexual."

"Yeah, he's like the heavy metal Liberace. He comes onstage looking like a Christmas tree."

"What was really funny was almost immediately the metalheads were like, *'Well, I guess he's cool... for a faggot.'* Well that's a step in the right direction, I *guess…*"

MID-DESERT CONVERGENCE

The next night Ken Cornell takes me to Burt's Tiki Lounge where, as always, there is a free show. The venue is a long, narrow corridor with a huge bar and Hawaii vibe. Tiki masks are lined across the walls and plastic palm trees rest in the corner. There is a small stage with a tiny PA, and a back area for outdoor BBQ parties. It reminds me so much of The Old Miami in Detroit.

Kenny hands me a piece of paper that lists the bands playing tonight. *"Wait a minute…"* I say. *"Friends of Dennis Wilson? From Detroit?"* Immediately five heads spin around from the red-leather booth behind me: *"Yeah, we're from Detroit."*

"You guys know Drew Bardo from The Questions right?"

The skinny, hyperactive guy: *"He's one of my best friends."* I start laughing. *"I'm Ryan Bartek."* All of their jaws drop in unison, and they frantically wave me over. They can't believe I'm actually here of all the places in America, at this random dive in New Mexico they say reminds them of The Old Miami...

It's a very weird scene. The skinny guy's name is Tony, and he knows everyone I know, except that we've never actually met except in disembodied sixth-degree form. They are all homesick and want to go back to Detroit immediately. They keep talking about garage bands I never had any direct contact with, but were always eyeballing me with curiosity or suspicion.

Dennis Wilson came from the other side of the fence during the media wars. During the White Stripes boom every "journalist" in the city had formed this bloc we called "The Nuthugger Mafia" and intentionally blackballed and suppressed any band that didn't fit into the tight-pants indie crowd. I was the lone soldier throwing a monkey wrench into it all.

Its reasons were obvious – Detroit never had a source of mainstream pride. Within a two year explosion The White Stripes, EMINEM, Kid Rock, ICP, Electric Six, D12, Von Bondies, and Obie Trice all blew up. The Pistons won the championship, Detroit Shock won the women's title, The Tigers made the World Series, the Casino's opened a floodgate of short-lived tourism, and both Detroit and Hamtramck were voted two of the coolest cities in America by a dozen big-name magazines. This had every daily and weekly scrambling to hold it in place and keep the propaganda flowing as a possible economic boom to halt Detroit from descending any further into its status as a rotting black ghetto.

What it created was a bulldozer effect against every other genre, and this terrible fad where there were 8 billion ascot-wearing, no nonsense, gutless White Stripe clones. The disparity between local press and the actual state of the undercurrent was shown by the fact that a mediocre local band hyped be three interior writers which drew flies in a live setting would get the cover story, yet someone like a Black Dahlia Murder were hosting MTV's Headbangers Ball and never registered a peep.

That is just one fanatically head-scratching instance of about 50 Detroit bands DIY touring the United States and Europe, releasing phenomenal albums, challenging the rules of every clique and scenester trapping. The city really was on fire, but not a damn one of the bands that were leveling the foundations even got so much of a scrap from the press. It seemed there were only 3 or 4 other local journalists in the entire racket that even bothered to go to more than 5 local shows per year.

Well, Friends of Dennis Wilson were part of that whole White Stripes boom and solidly generic for a stretch (*self admittedly*). They appropriately evolved and dived headfirst into psychedelia, experimental and surf. This will mark my first time seeing them live, or so much as hearing their material...

The band kicks off their set. They kill it as best they can, but the sparse crowd doesn't respond. The chaotic Detroit vibe is totally over the heads of the desert folk. Tony rolls around on the floor, swings from the rafters by his knees, crawls into a trash can and globs handfuls of rubbish over his clothes, runs up to the bar, hammers a shot and throws his face into some poor girls boobs and goes "*blub-blub-blub*" like a cartoon character. The bar owners are annoyed, and even Kenny thinks they are assholes...

FRIENDS OF DENNIS WILSON
"Could you please state your name and band for reference?"

Dennis Wilson: "My name is Dennis Wilson. My band is Friends of Dennis Wilson."

"Tell me everything..."

"The bands spiritual side is channeled from Dennis Wilson. My real name is Tony Moran. My favorite movie is Two-Lane Blacktop, my favorite band is Beach Boys, the first concert I've ever seen was Beach Boys. My favorite music is psychedelic music and my favorite hero is Charles Manson."

Uncle Charlie Huh? You guys 'Slippies?'"

"The reason why my favorite hero is Charles Manson is because it's this radical attempt to overthrow the government and be fucking drawn to the dark side."

"Tell me about drugs..."

"Our influence in music is not drugs it's Dennis Wilson. I was raised on old garage music from the 60's. Our driving influence besides psychedelia is muscle cars. It's gas. I come from Detroit, Michigan. My dad, my mother, they worked for Rouge Steel. Sam our guitar player, his dad worked for Ford. Our families love Detroit. We love steel, we love gas, we love oil. That's what we pride ourselves on. Drugs are a mere connection to a dangerous side of life that is unknown. Yet it's orgasmic, its fun, its something that we look forward to. Do you think Syd Barrett's music is channeled only through drugs or do you think he naturally had a poetic side to him? Drugs have actually helped me. I should be prescribed to drugs. Everyone in my family has been mentally ill. My mother is a schizophrenic. Her father was in a mental institution for 23 years 'cause all he could say was 'oh my god oh my god oh my god.' My grandmother could not say anything, she was in a mental institution too. Drugs are the only thing that balances me the fuck out. I need that shit."

"Have you read the Charles autobiography?"

"That doesn't mean anything to me because I take what other people say. My favorite book about Charles Manson is *The Family*. It was this writer from Detroit from a band called The Fuggs. Manson had mind control obviously. Mind control is what makes a band big. Mind control is what makes a girl attracted to a guy. Mind control makes you want to snort more coke. Mind Control makes you want to jerk off on a piece of paper. Mind control makes you want to eat Pizza Hut. Taco bell is mind control. McDonalds is mind control. George Bush is mind control. So you ask me is Charles Manson like George Bush? Yes Charles Manson is. Is he like Chuck E Cheese? Yes he is like fucking Chuck E Cheese. Little kids are drawn to him. Is he like Bozo the fucking Clown? He is. He wears the worst makeup, he's the disguise you can't understand..."

[We take a break to load equipment into the van, regain our foothold, and continue jabbering away. Tony jacks my tape player and our interview roles reverse...]

"...Keep it rolling, keep it rolling. Let me ask you a question. I want to know how you feel spiritually, whether you left a girlfriend in Detroit, or whether you left your lagging job. How do you feel about being this far from Detroit writing this book?"

"It still hasn't even hit me yet."

"Did the miles of being away from home affect you?"

"It's all experience, how you take it in – especially when I'm on Greyhounds for large periods of time. I get so introverted that it will take me to that other place and will kick in a lot of things. The longer I'm away the more I'm submersed in my own world, the more I'm able to look outside myself..."

"How do you feel about the generation we're living in? I read *On The Road* when I was eleven. I didn't really understand it then, like the aspects of homosexuality. You go to college and they make you read Kerouac, so you have these preppy fucks that like it because it's weird and it's a different world from theirs. Do you get intimidated now that Kerouac is this big Star Bucks thing, and that some people out there might look at what you're doing as some cheap trend? Or are you trying to keep that outlaw spirit alive and don't give a fuck what anyone thinks?"

"It's not about any of that really. I live for the legends of it. I'm not doing this book to make money or to be famous – I'm doing it for myself. I never went to college, didn't watch television from '99 until 2002. I did nothing but read books, listen to music. Most everything I'm into nobody else is. Since I write for so many magazines, I get sent shit from all over the world, tons of these obscure releases from labels run out of basements from Denmark to Brazil. So everything I'm into no ones even heard of. It's not like I'm modeling myself after Hunter Thompson. Even when I discovered Thompson that's the type of stuff I was writing. I didn't even know who Kerouac was until I was 18. I found Fernando Pessoa three years after I finished my first book, and it is very similar to 'The Book of Disquiet.'"

"How do you feel about contradiction, and how do you feel about contradiction in your writing? What I mean is right now we're hanging out together in New Mexico, we're smoking weed, and we're living a bohemian, artistic lifestyle. Let's say you're like Kerouac and in twenty years, and the last meeting between Kerouac and Cassady. He's still that traveling prankster hippie, and Kerouac wasn't. He changed as a person – very Catholic, very establishment. Are you gonna look back and care that you were at this point? Would you ever disregard your work?"

"I never disregard anything, not even my first book. It's like a time capsule. I wrote it because I was very angry and wanted to present this picture of someone age 16 to 18 that's seriously bad on drugs, that has a lot of mental problems. Really show that as it is, but in the mode of 'Catcher In The Rye' where's its more 'between the lines.' I think people didn't really understand that and took it quite literal. I read that book now and it's like 'ok this guy is an asshole, I don't agree with everything he says,' but I know that was me at one point. You grow and you evolve as a person. With this new book the major theme is one person escaping from Detroit and finding others who've escaped from elsewhere too."

"No one but myself and others from Detroit will understand where you're coming from. I travel with my band and at first I'm discouraged with Detroit, then I come to New Mexico and I'm like, '*Man, I love Detroit. I'm so lucky.*' With you it's the same. You're in the press, you're in this artistic capital of the world, and when you're away from it…"

"Actually, I don't ever want to go back there. It's kind of a love/hate thing. I feel disenfranchised by it because I was the big media hopeful for a lot of underground bands. And when it came to the point where they were airing me on the radio, the magazines and newspapers were promoting me – everyone knew who I was and everyone's eyes were on me – they realized they really didn't like what I had to say. And I alienated a lot of people with what I'm all about. I go to Detroit and everybody knows me, but they all give me this fuckin' look… I don't understand. My first book was nothing that different from what Henry Rollins or William Burroughs did. Yet they wear t-shirts with those guys on them and then they look at me like I'm an asshole. I threw shows with plenty of bands I'd promoted for years, and when I finally got my own band they wouldn't even watch us play. They're like in the bars ignoring me and ducking their heads so they don't have to speak to me. They won't even look at me."

"How do you feel about mind control?"

"When I was doing A.K.A. MABUS my stage name was "The Propagandist." It was kind of a joke, because I feel that propaganda is everything and constitutes everything. When you read something like 'Mein Kampf' there is a definite, mathematical code there. You have to see it in that context."

"Ever since this garage phase when The White Stripes blew up… Now everything's blown over, and then you left, now there are all these bands that are amazing and they get no press. It's Heroes & Villains, The Terrible Two's, The Questions… You know that New Mexico's music scene is nothing like Detroit's right?"

"When things were big it was a conglomerate of all these bands that never fit in that kind of teamed up together. You had The Koffin Kats, The Amino Acids, you had Downtown Brown…

"I see Downtown Brown who's not even my type of music, and they're way tighter than half the bands I play with that get press. I like 60's rock and reverb, Fender amps and shit. I listened to Downtown Brown on Fourth Street because they played in front of my house and sounded amazing. Guess what? They get no press. The reason why they get no press is because they're not a style that's big in Detroit. But you know what's funny? They get more packed shows than any of the garage bands I see. They get kids, non-scenesters coming in from the suburbs... I can't get press. No one can get press. Who do you think is the next biggest band in Detroit?"

"There's so many fucking good bands."

"The Bird Dogs, they're on our record label and I think they're the best band to come up. You know Drew Bardo from The Questions. Me and Sam think Drew's one of the best guitar players in Detroit. Drew man, he watches The Bird Dogs – and he's a master guitar player – Drew's like, 'I've never seen anything like that in my entire life.' This guy from The Bird Dogs name is Robbie Buxton, he's the guy who produced our record. He has his own recording studio, he's got his own label. This guys' new record has eighteen songs on it, he only played half of them for me and it's some of the best shit I've ever heard from Detroit. Mark my words – this will be the biggest band to come out of Detroit in ages. "

"What's The Bird Dogs guy like?"

"Everyone kept telling him that he couldn't do it, his wife wouldn't let him do it, so he quit his job, divorced his wife and now he lives in his studio. And he just made one of the most amazing records I've ever heard. You want to know the best part about it? All the bands – The Terrible Two's, X Records, even The Demolition Dollrods – they all want Rob to record them. This guy single-handedly took over Detroit. Nobody can fuck with this guy."

"As far as bands that I think are excellent? Human Eye. Tim Vulgar's the shit. Rubbermiilk Orchestra at their peak. That fucking bassist is one of the best players I've ever seen in my life. He goes head to head with Les Claypool."

"What do you think of The Piranhas?"

"I've never seen them. They were one of the bands I missed that I kick myself in the ass over. I came from the mid-90's at places like Pharaoh's Golden Cup, The Mosquito Club..."

"Tim Vulgar from Human Eye's biggest influence is The Piranhas."

"Didn't that singer shove a rat up his ass?"

"They used to headline all the old White Stripes shows, they played all over the country. Everyone's waiting for the next Stooges and they were right there all along. That guy is the real deal, not even

Iggy can show him up. His Dad's been doing it since '62 – you know what his name is? Dr. Blood."

"Didn't they play with Alice Cooper a lot in the 70's?"

"Fuck yeah they did… Well Tim Vulgar went up to The Pirahanas singer and you know what he did? Fuckin looked at him, pissed into his hands and drank it. And wanna know why they broke up? They stopped playing because they don't wanna be big and it's fucking bizarre dude. The guy is just the fiercest person that's ever lived…."

SECOND CREEPIEST STORY OF THE BOOK c/o T. MORAN

"So my friend is this nature photographer. She'd been going hiking with her friends to shoot pictures, but one weekend they couldn't make it. She decided to go it alone, because she was so used to it at that point. It's the middle of the night, 4am, and she's hearing weird stuff out in the forest darkness, like Blair Witch type shit. She decides to set up camp, puts up her tent. Blazes up a bonfire and ties all of her stuff to a tree. She zips the tent shut and sleeps with a hatchet and a can of mace next to her just in case… She wakes up about 5:30am and goes outside. Everything is as it was, and the sun is up now. She goes to untie her stuff from the tree, but when she looks at her camera, there is no more film left on it, and she was positive that there were three snapshots left. So she goes into town, eats breakfast, and the second CVS is open she has them developed. As she's going through the pictures, she turns ghost white and pisses herself in the middle of the aisle, in front of all the customers and employees. The last three shots were her sleeping, all from different angles…"

LIGHT THIS CITY

At Launchpad Rocks, the definitive large-scale 'Burque venue. It has a huge bar setup and those thin, rectangular concert posters caked over the walls. The ceiling is remarkably high, and the band area is cut off from the bar by a sliding garage door. I'm fairly certain this was a firehouse before renovation. Tonight is an extreme metal freak-out of acts that have been getting heavy rotation on MTV's *Headbangers Ball* – Acacia Strain, Job For A Cowboy, Light This City, Daath, and PSYOPUS, whose luck is always in season…

PSYOPUS guitarist Chris Arp just called me freaking out for a ride, because their van crapped out 50 miles from the venue. This is a bad situation because every band on the gig has unloaded, and the schedule is so tight there is no room for a hiccup. PSYOPUS are scheduled second on the bill, but Light This City are already wailing through their set, and they have 20 minutes to arrive or they will lose their guarantee.

I'm stuck outside Launchpad Rocks, freezing in the lightly snowing night. I have to wait for Light This City front woman Laura to finish her onstage screaming before she can sneak me in the back door, because the doorman just isn't buying my press credentials. I'm enamored for the conversation, as this circus on wheels derives one of the finest melodic death metal acts in the United States. Everything screams the classic Bay Area metal assault of the death/thrash glory days, spearheaded by Testament in the early 90's.

At this moment Light This City are deep into this tour, which premiered in their hometown of San Fran. They are true wunderkinds of the European impact, exemplary of the raging influence which captivates the younger generation of players. Formed in 2002 as a praise homage to the likes of Carcass and At The Gates, they soon derived their own imprint. Miraculously while still in high school they signed to Prosthetic Records, not even old enough to legally bind the contract.

And here she comes, with that friendly Starbucks smile, still toweling the beaded sweat from her face. Laura Nichol, the pretty brunette you'd never guess was the screeching pterodactyl behind the bombardment, floats towards me with the aura of a nice-girl bookworm. Maybe these are the qualities which propelled her mug shot as one of the "Hottest Chicks In Metal" in Revolver Magazine. A corny indoctrination to prepubescent boys perhaps, yet it still causes a petit smile to pop from her cheekbones.

Says Laura, who is now chewing gum rapidly as the teeth of The Mangler: *"The artwork is very similar to whatever's going on in the lyrics. With 'Remains of the Gods' it was spiritual, but not religious. It's about Greek mythology and what goes on outside the world. It was in-your-face, 'we've come to conquer all of you people, we're going to kick your faces in.' 'Facing The Thousand' was more nature-oriented, all the patterns, the differences between animals and humans. It's more complicated."*

"There's the stereotype of the female fronted metal band. Do you find in interviews that subject seems the pertinent theme?"

Laura Nichol: "I've gotten a few that were like that. The Revolver interview was like 'Chicks In Metal,' and they asked questions that didn't relate to music at all. Like *'what are your turn-ons?'* so it was kind of ridiculous."

"Where does the name of your new record [Facing The Thousand] come from?"

"Well you're an author right?"

"I suppose…"

"I am big on reading books and I really like *Watership Down*. It's about nature and – it sounds kinda cheesy but it's actually really cool – what a bunch of rabbits have to go through when they are transferring to a new home. Their hero is a rabbit called 'The Prince of a Thousand Enemies.' I took that story and transferred it into what was going on with the band. We're traveling across the country, we have to face obstacles. I like having an open title where everyone can relate to it in their own way."

"What are some of your favorite works?"

"I really like *Pride & Prejudice* by Jane Austin (laughs). I like classics like *The Golden Compass*, *House of the Scorpion* by Nancy Farmer. I love James Harriot, the Scottish dude.

"What's your predominant memory of Albuquerque? I'm hanging around these different places and there are these stores with lots of beads, and African voodoo dolls and shit like that…"

"Yes. That and Arizona. That's where I get all the shit that I bring home to my family. I find polo ties and cool magnets and beads and crazy shit. I love stopping at every gas station."

"Give me a nightmare tour story."

"I've got a lot 'cause I'm actually writing a book about tour stories. I'll give you a recent one. On our tour before the last, our van shit out on us while we were across the country. This is a brand new van, we got it for eighteen g's, it's like twenty-thousand miles, it's a 2006. We get to Cleveland and it won't go in reverse. We bring it in and the transmission is completely fucked. We're staying at our friends' house in Cleveland while the tour is still going on. They're talking a couple of days, it might even be a week before they can fix it. We're all freaking out in this tiny house and I'm talking to my mom on the phone and this sick puppy just explodes with diarrhea all over my sleeping bag. Acacia Strain drives from Michigan to pick us up and brings us on tour, leaving our roadies in Cleveland. We do the tour all the way to Portland, riding with other bands the whole way. On that tour, the two other bands' vans broke as well and we all had to ride together…"

"It sounds like a curse."

"That's actually what we were talking about because it started in New Mexico. I got really sick at the beginning with strep throat and we stopped at this tiny town called Gallop. We went to this Native American hospital so I could get medicine, but we didn't know it was Indian. There's this crazy guy that was like 'you brought disease upon our people' cause we were the only white people there. Actually I'm Native American, I belong to a tribe, so I was able to get medicine. But ever since we stopped there, bad shit started happening. Everyone told me that I cursed them for the rest of the tour…"

Laura pushes me past security and Daath have just started, being cool enough to fill in for Psyopus who have somehow managed to locate a driver. Apparently they are just going to hack it by using all of Daath's gear for back-line, which speaks a great deal on Daath's part, because metal musicians are frivolously stingy in that respect. If all goes right Psyopus will have 10 minutes to run inside, set up & play.

Daath are highly impressive and wail a crushing set that fuses grind and death into strong 2 minute bursts. It's a packed house, hot as shit, and the kids are going berserk. A huge circle pit envelops the floor, and bodies are flying everywhere. Psyopus comes bolting through during Daath's last tune, moving fast as a man who snorted an eight ball in one line. They look frustrated, drained, ready to snap.

The second Daath are off, the boys plug in and go at it within 3 minutes. They annihilate skulls like a Skynet tank in 2012. There is a reason they are one of the greatest tech destroyers in America, and tonight they aren't taking prisoners. Whatever the scoop is with the van, its backlash has obviously made them play twice as fast and conjured their mathematical designs that more obtuse…

PSYOPUS

Psyopus mastermind Chris Arp & drummer Greg Herman are waiting for me at the booth as Job For a Cowboy begins their set. This battle of the wits has been a long time coming, as I've been enamored by the intricacies of Psyopus for many years. Chris Arp is easily one of the most underrated guitar players in the USA.

It sounds absurd, giving him that much credibility. But anyone who's actually dissected the structures of Psyopus, who've took the time to analyze, have been floored by technique. Arp in fact won the regional Northeast contest in which Limp Bizkit front man/buffoon Fred Durst traveled Guitar Centers nationwide to hold try-outs for the six-string vacancy. It speaks volumes how terrible that band is, given they would pass on this modern Mozart…

Apart from the quaint label of "tech metal," there is no apt description available. Psyopus must be heard, must be embraced. Symphonies would fail to accurately portray these structures, whereas these four loons from Rochester, New York have succeeded brilliantly. If one takes the most complicated of jazz structures, and fuses them with the most unplayable, intricate death metal bastions imaginable, you may have a fair representation. Psyopus cite their vibe as such, and I could never offer a better scripture: "*Composed of bi-polar dynamics, radical arrangements, avant-garde instrumentation and a melting force of pure speed, Psyopus set out to destroy the molds of extreme metal with unprecedented attitude and conviction.*"

Chris's eyes give the appearance that he's about to pass out from exhausted frustration. "*So how does tonight rank in your pantheon of nightmare tour stories?*" I ask. Chris sighs and stares into the distance with a classic Bill Murray deadpan: "*Well… I'm not surprised anymore. We've had so many fucking vehicle problems…*"

"*The van we're driving right now is a loan. We bought a new one with a warranty for an extra $2700. November 2nd we begin the tour. The fucking engine blows up. We get a buddy to drive us for the entire six-week tour, and by the time we finish the van's still not done. It's December, so we're not sweating it. With this tour we had a week of dates before the first connection, and its January and the van's still not done…*"

"*We went off on a small regional two day thing, then we come back, and it's still not done. We finally get it, roll 280 miles and the engine blows up. Again. They weren't going to help us at all, then they had a lawyer call us because they smelled a lawsuit. So they give us this loaner van for the tour, and it breaks down out here in the street. Fucking engine blows up…*"

"*Wow.*"

Chris Arp: "We've had a host of problems on this tour. We're opening so we're only getting $100 a night, but we're doing alright. A lot of people have no clue who we are."

"*This is a packed house though. Is this one of your most successful tours?*"

"Yeah. We recently played for a lot of people when we opened for Hank Williams III, but that was country, so they didn't get us."

"*How often do people just don't 'get it'?*"

"We'd just started the Hank Williams III tour and were in Georgia. About 200 people showed up, and everyone was really well dressed. You had people from the Rock N' Roll Hall Of Fame there, all these 35 year olds. And we're like, '*they're really not going to like us.*' Then we talked about it, possibly some kind of compromise, but we just said 'fuck that' and went apeshit. '*It's not even about the music tonight. Let's be as abruptly rude, and as big of assholes as we possibly can.*' We were jumping in the crowd, screaming in people's faces, throwing shit..."

"In the Midwest the death metal crowd doesn't get the tech thing. Do you find that's usual elsewhere?"

"Some of the older, elitist, '*you're a poseur*' type of death metal bands. We played with Immolation and the crowd were calling us poseurs. But it's like come on, who are really trying to rip off?"

"Do people do that spin-kick shit to your music?"

"If it's possible we try to avoid the spin-kicking. We are so against the spin-kicking phenomenon. We got the moshers, we get the circle pits, we get some rowdy crowds. We get really weird shit."

"As for the people into your band, do you think your fan base are generally musicians themselves?"

"The crowd goes over a little bit, but the people that pick it up off the bat are mostly musicians. We challenge the listener. It's mental music. There's nothing against people not wanting to think that hard, but there's so many that just shut it off. It's tough to get into it, you can't dance to it. Musicians already have an analytical understanding..."

"Tell me about the Ed Gein tour. I saw you play at the Radnor House in Detroit with Signs of Collapse. My buddy used to throw all those house shows in his basement, and I drank Jaeger shots with you in the kitchen."

"Oh wow, that was a long time ago [stares off into some hazy, alcohol laced memory]. There was so much heat in that basement... It was like 110 degrees down there. That was our first real tour. Premonitions of War was supposed to be on it but the singer bashed his head over the guitar in Ohio and needed stitches."

"Are you still doing a lot of house shows?"

"(Laughs) We're trying not to but it happens. We're not against it, because there's always going to be a good vibe. But it's tougher to get from one point to another. We're really trying to deal with booking agents now 'cause I got a kid at home. We've been doing it for awhile and you get a little old, you get tired. We do this for the music, we're at it all the time. We never stop playing, we practice up to four times a week. We're never going to sell out musically."

"When are you going to do Europe?"

"We get that all the time. The real question is when is our van going to be fixed? "

45 minutes later; we've been bullshitting Charles Bronson movies and talking to some promoter from Houston. I ask Chris if he can introduce me to one of the guys from Job For A Cowboy, and he whisks me over to the bar.

The new guitarist of the band – Bobby Thompson – is talking to a few girls, obviously tipsy, and although agrees to do a quick interview, isn't really in business mode. Thompson's definitely the guy that says '*umm... you should ask so-and-so that question.*' But that's not a cheap shot. It just comes with the journalism territory.

Regardless, he's friendly and plays it by the book, choosing his words carefully: "*I just joined last May. The other guys have been doing it seriously for two years. We're based out of Glendale Arizona. This year we did the Sounds of the Underground tour in Phoenix, San Diego, and San Francisco. We toured with some really cool guys, the crowds were awesome.*"

"How is the scene in Glendale?

Bobby Thompson: "It's actually pretty good. We just played in Tempe last night. The kids are really supportive." *"What would you say is the general mindset of those at your shows?* "Anyone that like brutal, heavy music. We're signed to Metal Blade records so…" *"Tell me about this tour."* "This is the 11th show. After this we're going up to Canada for two weeks, then off to Europe for four weeks with Unearth, Despised Icon, and Daath." *"Whatever you want the world to know, tell me know."* "Everybody should buy our new CD because a lot different from the older stuff, we're really proud of it and its some good shit."

Bobby just kind of scratches his head, staggers a bit, and I cut him loose. I slam another vodka/cranberry and wander around outside singing Danzig lyrics. Midway through "20 Eyes," I meet a couple of kids smoking a bowl in the parking lot…

They are amazed I'm an authentic journalist, and when I explain the Psyopus situation, they assume that I know those guys personally. Since its fun to lie to people, I tell them Chris and I were on the same hockey team in elementary school. They take down all my info, and promise to hook me up with a crust squat in Denver...

I stagger towards the side of the venue and Mr. Arp is drunk, crooning lyrics to himself as well. We go for an aimless stroll, like drunken pyrates yo-ho-hoing. When I mention the hockey thing, Chris belly-laughs: *"You should've told 'em you were related to Gretzky."*

A FAILED STING OPERATION

Another casual stroll down University... I float into the head shop and a highly suspicious individual approaches: *"Hey man, know where I can get some coke?"* He's so obviously undercover you can smell the bacon sizzling on the flat-top. He starts quizzing me about pot, K, meth. Anyone dumb enough to fall for this deserves the entrapment. I ditch him but the Narc follows me 5 blocks, trailing slowly, talking into a radio. They could at least put some effort into it...

I still have no phone & no idea when this will be an option. My shit plan is 18c a minute & I only use it for the voicemail or emergency. This entire jaunt will be booked through email alone. Plus it only adds to the mystery. All they know is an enigma tapping them on the shoulder then fleeing into obscurity, leaving a mutant trail of propaganda. Leave them with a thousand questions, always. The harder you appear unavailable, the more they come out of the woodwork – and the more surprised & willing for adventure they are when you call out the blue...

Everyone in New York is jumping all over this thing. San Fran is going well, Philly, Chicago, Seattle, Alabama. Florida seems too spread out, and I don't want to touch the Midwest. Though I was under the impression that Denver would be an easy target, I'm having serious trouble getting anyone to respond...

A SEEDY GOTH CLUB AND A MAN NAMED TOMMY T

11pm @ TONIC, the number one goth/industrial club in 'Burque. A huge barb-wire gate cuts through the dance floor, leather-clad bondage silhouettes sway in strobe light blasts. Tommy T is intent on throwing shows here, and tells me between sips of vodka about meeting Kerry King, Dimebag Darrel, and all his glorious plans for the future.

Not only is Tommy T the composer/vocalist of industrial metal group Diverje, as well as the CyberRage DJ for U&M College radio, but he is also the head CEO of DSBP Records which freshly signed Vertigo Venus. DSBP have been a recognized force in underground industrial for over a decade now, and have released material from a wealth of artists such as Derma-Tek, Encoder, Massiv In Mensch, Phenotract, Detestation, and Doomsday Virus...

"Tell me about your label DSBP, your band Diverje..."

Tommy T: "It's been 11 years now, and we've put out nearly 80 albums. The reason I started this is because I'd been doing industrial and metal. Just hard, extreme shit with my old death metal band Detestation. It didn't seem like there were enough labels out there. All these people sweat about getting a record contract and I was just like 'fuck it, I'll put out my own shit.' I put that out, and then Diverje's first album, which was very experimental, a very cool mix of metal and industrial in a raw and primitive way. I started doing some compilations. That was around '97, '98. People really liked it and we kept reaching through the internet. Biopsy from Brazil got in touch with me – great ritual metal. We started distributing for other underground labels. We've never told a band that they had to sell a 1000 CD's to be on our label. We are fair and straight-forward in all business. We basically just wanted to work with bands that we thought were cool, that we believed in, and try to get shit going. We just keep cranking out a new record every two months."

"Tell me about some different bands on the label."

"We have Biopsy, we have Diverje, this band Dermatek that's doing really well in Philadelphia. Encoder is more of an EBM, dance band from Ohio. Severe Legion, they're from Sweden. They do a noisy mix of old school EBM. I've never signed any full-on metal bands, they always have that mix of industrial and electronic."

"Why did you decide to go in the industrial direction after you left Detestation?"

"I love death and thrash, but in my own mind, the music with the most potential future is electronic and industrial. I felt it was more untouched. There were so many killer bands around that time, seeing Malevolent Creation, Cannibal Corpse, and Deicide. We opened for all those bands. It was kind of intimidating, because how do you compare to that? With industrial I fell into my own niche. I started by doing an electronic, dancy European style but mixed with an American metal attitude. Fuck it all, where you can say or do whatever."

"What's the message of Diverje?"

"The lyrics are personal experience, but you've all heard that before. I've been cursed and blessed at the same time. When I was 15 my father was murdered. He was the biggest supporter of me singing as a kid. He was one of those guys that wanted to play but got married and had kids too early. I could see that in him and he saw it in me. I grew up a little early, so I got really serious about music around then…"

HONOR AMONG THIEVES, NEVER OF THE GREEDY
Tonight is the State of The Union and a fresh veteran is on the front porch speaking quietly, knees placed firmly together, hunched and clutching a compressed, gut-ugly misery. There is a black hole cutting through him, devouring. Only 6 days back…

Another Detroit refugee on a massive road trip discovered him at the Greyhound, and they've been chatting on the porch for an hour. I asked if he wanted to be interviewed, even if anonymously – knee-jerk, violent refusal. 3 years in Tikrit, convoy torn up 11 times by roadside bombs. In the last explosion two weeks ago he'd watched his best friend get his legs blown off. 20+ of his good military buddies were K.I.A. thus far, and he has a confirmed body count in the teens.

Bush spends the first ten minutes of his speech dodging issues, giving incomplete sentences, flatly lying. He ever-so-briefly drops the creation of a "Civilian Marine Corps" and spends but 3 sentences on this historic decision which basically equals pipeline/construction crews with automatic weapons. One last ditch attempt to avoid the draft and smuggle F-4's – the last great surge before Senate cuts funding…

For the next 50 minutes Bush rotates gears. He's flown in symbolic, iconic heads to stand and bow. One by one he elaborates their hard tales of sacrifice. Some black guy that hopped on a subway to save a stranger in Don Mclean sentimentality, Little Susie from the grassroots homeless fund. *My friends are being shot to pieces, and he talks about his dog…*

FINAL ROMP AMONG VENUS
"I was walking back to the house and I saw this church that actually had parking meters. What's that all about?"
Jeff MacCannon: "Oh yeah, I saw that. It's fun. I was born in an area of smart people, so it doesn't really work out for Christianity. I guess the people that are stupid enough to believe in it are taxed."
"So make fun of Jesus."
"Jesus? (Laughs) He's really got the Malcolm X sort of vibe going on in a very pacifist, pussy kind of way. Not in the pacifist kind of pussy way like Gandhi where he actually accomplished something. I think it's really funny – the planks of wood he's nailed to are more

famous than he is. It doesn't really make sense because *everyone* who was born back then was the son of a god. Every king, every political leader were descended from some deity of a stupid nature, even stupider than the deities we have now."

"Are there a lot of Scientologists in Albuquerque?"

"There is a Christian Science reading room down the street from my house. It's creepy, that much I know. They try to entice people into their cult with butterflies and paper mache in the windows. It's fucking Christian Science, its going to kill you. People with faith don't deserve things. They just waste their lives with this promise of playing in some heavenly amusement park for all eternity. They just sit around and accomplish absolutely fucking nothing. They're on the corner of every street, they have billions of dollars, Christian music is the highest grossing music in America. They don't actually create anything, the just rip off other things, and then they make a genre for that. They're making more money than anyone else, they have all this political pull, they intentionally don't change things for their own benefit. Meanwhile there are people of intelligence and talent who can't even pay rent."

"What are the biggest bullshit aspects in any music scene that must go away?"

"I'm sick of people faking a British accent. Especially when they have a stupid stage-name, some made-up crap that was thought up while looking at a dried rose. I just don't get it. They sing one note about something stupid. It's always a girl, a date, or a month out of the year. I hate when people are Satanists, atheists, or agnostics and they write songs about angels…"

"Do you see a lot of kids ironically wearing Che Guevara t-shirts they bought from capitalist establishments?"

"Funny story. I was at a Hot Topic and I saw three kids in a row all wearing a shirt that said '*You laugh because I'm different and I laugh because you all look the same.*' They were all standing in a group…"

Jeff cordially struts to the stage in this ridiculous white pullover with spaceman boots and cosmo-demonic belt buckle. He's like some David Bowie astronaut with mascara dripping down his face. Chris has his Mohawk Murray-globbed in war mode with spiked gauntlets, Ken has this black leather semi-bondage fishnet thing complete with cowboy hat and fingernails painted silver. Buddy, the keyboardist, Buddy, the red-haired Gandalf, Buddy the wise and superfluous, has yet to have removed his shades in the past two weeks.

When Vertigo plays live it all makes sense. Jeff rides his keys like a surfboard and strangles himself with the microphone chord, insulting everyone and prancing about like a new-wave premadonna. Most the audience knows the words to the songs. They clap and dance, knocking back Pabst after Pabst.

Tommy T and Brian Botkiller jump on stage among the MacCannon brothers, instantly forming the live version of Diverje like mechanical tigers snapping together Voltron. Primed and ready, Diverje crushes it with the crossover vibe of a Razed In Black vs. Ministry remix/ When Tommy screams those high pitches sound like *Antichrist*-era Manson at his height of misanthropy, and Tommy does this hopping dance while fake blood splatter is globbed over his face. It's one of those great moments where the performer sheds all pretensions of reality and *becomes* his music. He rolls around on the floor, face beat red, screaming everything inside of him …

PART III: THE DENVER NIGHTMARE
(JESUS, THE ANTI-SAVIOR)
JANUARY 28TH-FEBRUARY 4TH 2007

TRAGICOMIC DESTINY

Long from now, when whoever it is digests these words, I sincerely hope they appreciate just how difficult and exhausting this mission truly is. Currently it is Monday, January 29th, approximately 7:32am, and a few notches above 20 degrees. I am sitting at a place called the Denver Diner, whose brilliant tour de force of a breakfast special is an $8 omelet. At this rate, I'll be cleaned out financially by end of the week.

When one deals with a man named Jesus, one would assume some vague sense of savior. In this case perhaps it is true, yet his girlfriend is rather flakey about guests and has demanded I wander the city aimlessly until the good Christ is released from work at 5pm, because she apparently doesn't trust me alone at the house. He doesn't feel like making a production over it, so instead of combating her request, I am left to walk around from 5am until 6pm, freezing my balls off, my only saving grave the Public Library nine blocks from this diner, which opens 10am.

Nightmares, jangled nightmares & splinter breakthroughs...
1989, 1993, 2002, 1998 intersecting in one steady stream of venom, like visiting a grave that responds to your inquests... It is only the mute tombs which I spend no mourning or casual addressing...

As it stands, I've emailed over 50 bands in the Denver area and only one has replied. Having freelanced at PIT Magazine in Colorado Springs for the past 5 years – the rock solid harbinger of metal in the quad-state area – and having received dozens of emails and demos from this area over time, I have hit an ironic blank wall. I seriously believed this would be my strongest foothold outside of Detroit. Even PIT, for which I have long been loyal, has vanished.

Silence, absolute silence, and I've wholly stopped trying. I feel like Boba Fett zooming the Slave 1 to Tattooine but Jabba won't crack the iron palace and has a hog guard slip a message with insignificant greetings and another command of whom to exterminate when all Boba really wants is to drink a brew with the worm and possibly take a hot shower with one of the tadpole headed strippers. If they blow me off I walk.

So what do I have to offer? Cephalic Carnage, one of the premier multi-genre extreme metal bands in Colorado. Although they gave a cell number I haven't heard back. They open for Slayer on Wednesday. There's also a one-man blackened death metal project whose cell message is quite whacky and drunken. I have a set-in-stone lunch with a Columbine survivor which I'm in held suspense over, and a female-owned porn company which films escapades starring metal and punk bands all-out gang-fucking chicks. Truthfully, it's far more effective than hiring a PR man where publicity is concerned…

2pm, beyond exhaustion, at the Denver public library, one of the first in the country and the best in America bar none. Every time I attempt to recharge my batteries by nodding off for 20 minutes a security guard knocks on the table and threatens to throw me out. There are 7 levels, and I've tried it on 4 already. I tried to pass out on a bench outside, but it is barely 30 degrees, and no matter where I shelter up a hobo lurches and harangues me for change.

My eyes burn, my pinched nerves scream, but all is forgotten once I reach the biographies after my 4th cup of coffee. The Mussolini section is staggering. They have the first printing of his autobiography from 1928, but also his long out-of-print *Diary 1915-1917*. The card says no one's checked it out since 1947. I read his daughter's memoirs from 1974 in its entirety with my totalitarian form of literary consumption (*no pun intended*)…

3:30pm and on the verge of total collapse, hallucinating from two months lack of sleep – psychedelic flashbacks, breathing walls, oceanic carpet patterns mutate into little swastikas from Salo Republic educational impressions… The front lobby is a labyrinth of deranged granite. On the street pedestrians ignorantly blaze by like columns of insects, plundering vehicles like steel bison.

I'm not at the end of my rope. I'm buried in a tomb of sulfurous ash miles below the crust of the earth. I hate this, I have lost all hope. I have forgotten why I'm here. I want to run to the Greyhound, buy a ticket, leave my clothes and guitar in this awful city. I start digging through my notebook for the terminal number, eyeballing the payphones in the lobby. *Then I see it…*

There's just no way – it's a ridiculous hoax perpetrated by an unknown assailant. I rush to the elevator and zoom to the mysterious 4th floor, the only one I haven't tried to sleep in. The elevator clanks open and I drag myself down the long white hall. I emerge into the show room in foggy slow motion…

The glass case is 40 feet long, glowing with fluorescent light like the runway of an airport terminal. Inside, stretched out like ancient Egyptian parchment, is the entire 119 foot, 8 inch type-roll manuscript of Jack Kerouac's *On The Road*. The beast that crazy Catholic mystic hammered out in a nonstop, 3-week, Benzedrine-fueled, mason-jar pissing frenzy. Its aura gives off blazing heat. Edges frayed, still intact… It really is true – he printed the stream-of-conscious explosion as was, word for word, beginning to end. The most remarkable thing is not even the fable of the manuscript itself or its eternal repercussions. It's the fact that there are so few spelling mistakes…

It all returns to me, the reason why I am here. I'm 18 again, driving those skeleton neighborhoods of Detroit; a hard-boiled, nerve-shot, Ford parts monkey in that big Econoline van. Exploring every inch of the wicked city, parking in crack hoods between deliveries devouring Kerouac and Ginsberg in a trance under streetlight, no care to the gang-bangers eyeballing me form their porches…

As each page turns, another bum haggles for change. Another prostitute tries to climb in; another savage, gun-toting, primitive gaze of street hatred. But they didn't exist. It was just me & Jack & the screaming urge to steal the van and hightail it westward. Detroit had been conquered. It was time to explore the mainland of my Nation foreign as a lost continent…

Yet I never worked up the courage to go it alone, never once a Cassady to stumble after. I waited too long, waited until my body was broken, my soul was burned, my mind stretched to its last threads. One adventure too many and a hundred concerts too long… But I'm here now, and I'm face to face with Jack – *and nothing is going to stop this book. Nothing…*

JESUS SAVES… OR RATHER SALIVATES

I welcome you all to the remarkable voice of our generation. Jesus the Anti-Savior, legendary mastermind of PHALLUS, and general architect of misery in Detroit. He sits like Zarathustra, glowing with heavenly awe beneath his lamplight. Short blonde hair & goatee, a terrible smile. Snake-like resentment churns within, awaiting verbal ejaculation…

Outside the snow continues to fall, it is a flood of white. 8 inches are stacking every inch of ground, and no end in sight. It is a frozen labyrinth in this particular suburb of The Rockies, a historic district of absurdly large three-level homes. Jesus' living quarters are pure Americana, ripe with a Norman Rockwell spin. It almost detours the hideous monster before me, but then he smiles casually.

"So, tell me your views on euthanasia & abortion..."

JESUS: "HAHAHA!! Lets say that I was a liberal and I decided that I was pro-choice, which really means pro-abortion. What is the choice? To abort ones offspring or not. So I'm thinking hmmm... this developing organism... I don't want to call it human, I've got to disassociate myself so I don't feel any pain or any remorse. I think it's cool to take little Timothy and poke and prod him with shit and drink arsenic to destroy him. Well, it's kind of rude when you think of little Timothy. If something has human DNA, then it's a human. That's how things are classified. If something has frog DNA, then it's a frog. This little blob mass of cells, it can't do anything on its own. Can't speak, can't make decisions, can't think. So by that rationale, if Grandpa Johnson is old and unable to think for himself, then you should be able to abort Grandpa Johnson. You should be able to kill anyone who can't do these things for themselves. Christopher Reeves, you should have been able to sneak up behind him and slit his throat..." Let's say they have the baby, it's 3 years old, and mom is like, '*fuck, I don't like this baby shit, its just not working out.*' By the age of 8 you should be still able to still abort the offspring. The kid has already gone through some school, you can evaluate its capacity for learning. By that point it knows what's going on but can't really think logically. It's still doing exactly what you trained it to do. You should probably just kill the kid, 'cause the chances are you fucked that one up. The most illogical, irrational living being on the face of the earth is the teenage female. Once you get to this point where you have this teenage female, then you're fucked..."

"(Long pause) How do we stop the menstrual cycle?"

"Eventually there's going to be a pill to stop the whole cycle completely. There'll be something that'll just flush out your ovaries, flush out your uterus, flush out your Fallopian tubes. It'll be just like Prilosec, the heartburn pill. Everything flushed out in 24 hours..."

"How'd you get the name Jesus?"

"Remember when you were in elementary school and all the names were on a spreadsheet? Well mine [Christopher] got cut off on the paper, and the substitute kept asking for Christ. From that point on it started picking up and just morphed into Jesus… The path to the light is through me my son…"

"Why did you escape Detroit and how do you feel about Denver and Colorado in general?"

"Detroit, when taken in small doses, is a great thing. The problem is when you live in Detroit it colors your view on many things. When I came to Denver it was like '*wow, half these buildings are not burned, they're not looted.*' I like Denver, it's this old cow town. There's a bunch of hicks here, there's a bunch of Mexicans, there's a bunch of substandard individuals. It has such a different vibe. But I know Spanish, so that works out well for me. Plus its fun when you go to some supermarket and you talk to little Mexican children and you say really terrible things to them. You walk around and you get the little four year old Mexican boy and you go up to him and say things like [indecipherable Spanish], which translates to '*my dick is in your ass.*' They don't know what's going on. It's fun…"

"What's your favorite thing to say to Mexican children? And has a parent ever overheard you?"

"Yeah, sometimes they've overheard me. There was this Mexican girl that was probably five and I explained to her [more indecipherable Spanish] 'your vagina is a tortilla.' I think its fun for children 'cause they don't know what the hell's going on…"

"They just know that their vagina's a tortilla…"

"They should've just been aborted years back…"

"Tell me about the legend of PHALLUS…"

"PHALLUS was a legend before it was even a band. [In 2000] I needed some sort of outlet for my own anger, my own hatred towards 99% of humanity. Kroon was also seeking the same thing, so we got together and decided we needed to play the most terrible, disgusting music ever that still has this undercurrent of melody. Basically we need to take The Beatles and put on top of it just this screaming, raging horror. The most dissonant chords, the most terrible feedback, the most punishing, disgusting, ear drum splitting noises. That's the genesis of PHALLUS."

"Where did the name come from?"

"All the coolest bands, they had one word. One word that was kind of ambiguous, kind of meant something weird but you didn't really get it at first. So I thought up PHALLUS. What's surprising is 75% of the people I talked to didn't even know what that means… Everywhere we went, we were like punk rock celebrities. Our effect on people was weird. There was this kid going out with this girl I'd been friends with. I went to see Anti-Flag and this fucking bang-bang is following me around all evening. I don't think much of it, and then a few days later my sister says, 'Ben has been going around school telling people he's your best friend, and you're hanging out, and you're forming this band together.' I've never spoken to this idiot in my life. This kid needs death. He just fuckin' follows me around at concerts. Then my sister's friend tells me this story [Jesus gets real quiet], she was like, you know, 'he was going through your trash… like outside your house and stuff, digging through your trash.' That's just fucking weird. And like this other kid too, their picking through my trash, trying to break into my house. Just cause their fuckin' disturbed…"

"Any other old school legends?"

"I was at a party; there were all these punk rock kids in this basement. I'm one of the oldest people there and I'm like 21. This is 1999, the height of 'punk' being on MTV, this is when Blink 182 is popular. They're talking about anarchy like *'dude, anarchy is the only form of government that makes any sense. Man, anarchy rules man.'* All anarchy like, *'I'm an anarchist, I believe in all these things here.'* And there's all these people behind me like *'Anarchy is awesome, I'm so punk rock I slept in a dumpster.'* You know the ones. And the *'I wear used condoms'*… So I get up, go to the ringleader of these fucking kids and I flick him in the ear, he looks up. I poured my beer all over his head. Everyone there is like *'oh shit man,'* and the guy is like *'what the fuck?'* I just go, *'That's Anarchy,'* and I walked away. Everyone was dead silent."

"Tell me about your terrorism against EMINEM…"

"HAHAHAHAHA!!! When you think of Detroit, there are all these people that symbolize and embody that area. If I think of Bill Lambeer and The Pistons, that embodies Detroit. If you think of hard working people that have some sort of substance, you think of Detroit. But when you think of EMINEM… He's a fuckin' stupid sack of shit. He's probably one of the most worthless human beings that I've ever met. He kind of took an idea of what Marilyn Manson was, as in this person who's going to shock and amaze you and say these terrible things. Manson is pretty fucking tame. The same with EMINEM. Talking about killing people, he's talking about sawing his wife in half, raping people and doing drugs. But he did it in this stupid, ridiculous manner. So this hatred for EMINEM has kind of developed over the years with my group of friends. He doesn't write his own music, he doesn't write his own rhymes. My friend Dave is a white rapper with skills far superior. So Dave is nestling this hatred, and somehow finds out where EMINEM lives. EMINEM has this whole thing where he says '*I'm from Detroit.*' No you're not. You live on 32 Mile. We read this article about his new residence and how the house was owned by this guy that went to prison for extortion and then was bought by Charlie Connoway, the K-Mart CEO when they went bankrupt. EMINEM buys this house and in this article he's saying the house isn't cursed, it isn't haunted, he doesn't believe in shit like that. So we decide we're going to find out where he lives and fuck with him somehow."

"How'd you go about that?"

"We got a satellite photo of the general area. We drive out to Rochester Hills and had an idea – the fountain, the tree line. We're driving around in circles digging through people's trash trying to figure out which house is his. We trek every which way for two square miles and finally found the place. Alright, we got him. That's his Escalade, that's Kim's Escalade. Fuck yeah, this is gonna be good. So we start to devise things to do to him."

"Like…"

"We go to his house, sit outside for an hour, then Dave goes up to the intercom at the gate. The gate-man replies and Dave says, '*Hey is that faggot Marshall home*?' Guy doesn't respond so he tries again. '*Yeah we're looking for Marshall you faggot.*" No response. Ao we located his studio, 54 Sound, a mile away from my house. We go to 7-11, buy those big bags of M&M's, and fill up the bed of his Escalade. But it wasn't enough. You know the Weird Al thing?"

"The fake interviews he does?"

"Yeah. Weird Al would splice in a tape of a celebrity saying something, then ask them a question, and then put it together to make them look ridiculous. Weird Al says 'I knew you were gonna be here, so I made your favorite – a Twinkie Weiner sandwich,' and he's holding a Twinkie with a hot dog shoved in it. EMINEM made this big thing about it afterwards, so we thought he really wouldn't appreciate it when we shoved fifty of them full of hot dogs and leave them on his studio doorstep, put them on his Escalade, a trail leading up to it like Hansel & Gretel's cookie crumbs. We took Vaseline and we smeared it on his windshield."

"What other antics did you mastermind at the studio?"

"All these cars are there and we got to find out who these people are and fuck with these guys too. So one was this Red Beatle. We followed it to this house in Royal Oak and we find out its Luis Ruesta, the real Slim Shady. He actually wrote that song."

"Didn't he win a Grammy for it?"

"Yes he won the Grammy, not EMINEM. So we go to Ferndale [Detroit area's largest gay community] and go to one of those homosexual shops and buy about fifty different rainbow stickers. We put them on the back of his Beatle. We go back to the studio and see the sticker is gone so we put another one on. Put a rainbow sticker on the Escalade. We put one on the front of the Studio… Then we drive by and see all of the guys from D-12 coming out. We pull up in a Grand Cherokee, roll down the window and Dave goes, '*Hey, you want some snow-cones, you faggots?*' They start coming up with '*what bitch?*' and we drive off. So they know the vehicle now. We go back later that night, stalking them, and they're all at 7-11. Obie Trice is there. We go up to the counter and we're just kind of smiling, looking at them. They're like '*wha, wha?*' They don't know who the fuck we are. We get in the Cherokee, they see us and now they're connecting it."

"Did that detour you?"

"Oh hell no. We came back later with a slingshot and all these water balloons, we shoot them from across the street. That was fun. Then we're like 'well we gotta do something ridiculous. We gotta get EMINEM out of his home somehow. He's such a recluse. We got to get him to go to a party.' We go out and buy all this fancy paper and print up these real cool invitations to a house warming party at Marshall Mathers with full catering and a full bar. We distribute them to all the homes within a mile radius, all of the thirty or so big houses in the area. Of course we sent him an invitation to the guy down the streets party. We're not really sure what came of that, although we're pretty sure some people came down to his house. And they were pretty disappointed, thinking that he was shunning his neighbors."

"Wow…"

"So then the other thing too, his address was 5760 Linkwin Mill. Pretty gay street name you know, pretty gay address. Taking that into consideration, since he's all big, bad Detroit, he's gonna feel much more at home if he lived on 8 Mile. So we got some 8 Mile street signs, we took his street sign down and put up the 8 Mile sign. Also, when you drive down his rode, it dead ends and splits into a T. So there's just this big yellow thing with an arrow. So we figure we should glue an 8

Mile sign up to that. So we tried forever, we're plastering, we're throwing glue all over that bitch, slap it up there and it'd slide down."

"Obsessive compulsive to say the least?"

"It was fun. We spent that whole summer fucking with him. Actually I ran into his sometimes wife Kim at a bar and I knew I had to hit on her or something. So I start talking to her and she's drunk as fuck. She's kind of flirting with me, and I was like '*I should have done it. I could have just fucked EMINEM's wife, if I were so inclined.*' That would have been the topper. I probably would have been shot. And this is right after the one guy was seen making out with her and EMINEM pistol whips him."

"So was there a final performance?"

"After this summer – 'the Summer of Hate' – I move out to Denver. Dave calls me about this article he found online. It's EMINEM talking in some paper how he's not safe in his home, that it really is cursed. He doesn't feel safe and he's moving back to Detroit. So we chased the guy from the suburbs – 32 Mile, those big fuckin' homes with the private drives – chased him all the way back to Detroit. That is an accomplishment that we are quite proud of..."

THE NIGHTMARE NOW AN ABSTRACT DAYDREAM

Same day, same situation, same diner, although fully rested by 8 hours of deep slumber. I've been crashing in the guestroom downstairs, which is more a shrine to Jesus' early youth. There are Red Wings and Pistons posters pinned to the walls, a tiny twin-sized bed complete with fluffy stuffed animals and a Detroit Tiger blanket.

The two mile walk to the library is bitterly cold, avoiding bums, dodging news people filming a segment on the corner. Outside the homeless gather in a great surge of downtrodden humanity, waiting for the Library doors to swing open at 9am.

One man has very few teeth, one looks a long-bearded Charles Manson, yet another is horribly disfigured. His eyes are juggled. The right one droops so low on his half melted face that it drips tears uncontrollably. The silent brook rolls down his rippled skin like a white water rafting environment. His nose to the side, his upper lip jagged, teeth jutting out the missing flesh puzzle-piece. He speaks softly and intelligently; he is no more than 23.

Hour long slip on the internet, emailing every fringe political party in America for possible interviews. General Franco's Falangist Party is alive and well in America. Stalin's saber-rattling, state terror infused form of Marxism. Henchmen lackey's of Chairman Mao's insane bid for global domination. I email them all.

I establish contact with a UK film crew that the guitarist from The Gracchi had mentioned in Albuquerque; she'd called them "The Leeds Lads." They are recording an epic intercontinental music film and have just nailed Australia, Mexico, and New Zealand. Now they tackle Canada and America. I arrange an ironic duel interview tomorrow at the library, where they have no knowledge of Kerouac's presence, which only aids to the fog of mystery propaganda which I am so well versed.

Jesus rescues me from the library at 5:30pm. I had just spoken to the blackened death metal solo project guy who said he was all about it, he really wanted to show me his studio, but his car was totaled. I told him not to worry and I would arrange a ride to him. Jesus is enthusiastic, we're finally getting somewhere. I leave three clear and decisive messages with all necessary contact information. The phone remains dead silent all night...

THE LEEDS LADS

Same diner, 15 degrees, snowing & sun blocked by misty ice of the stratosphere... *Walking, walking, endlessly walking...* My interview with and by the UK crew duly prepared, meticulously woven in black thoughts... *Siberian labyrinth of destitute charm...*

Back inside the calm interior of the greatest library in America – 4 long hours of meditation before The Leeds Lads call from the elusive, official-clearance 7th floor, one upping my surprise tactics. From one huckster to another, a fine display of intrigue...

In the epicenter of the World Summit room there is a humongous, circular oak table. Shiningly polished, light reflecting as prisms... Each seat has frontally drilled name-plates as to identity the players of the historic conference – Bill Clinton, Jacques Chirac, whoever might've been around Spain at the time.

Three London hipsters look out of place, bug-eyed and ginseng energetic. The director/interviewer of their film project, Phil Heron, looks markedly indie with a red scarf wrapped around his neck. Enthusiastic and intelligent, all three of them speak at a verbal level in starkest contrast with the sum of all previous travels. Formalities, formalities, then I unload a mountain of contacts – 70 phone numbers from Detroit & detailed notes on the importance of each entity.

"Well, tell me about you guys first."

Phil Heron: "The three of us formed Chestnut Productions in July of last year. It was mainly to promote artists and musicians. We decided to take our company on the road for a documentary and are going town to town to find out what makes music scenes tick. We went to South Africa, we went to Sydney for 5 weeks, we landed in January in Los Angeles and worked our way down to San Diego, then Mexico which was unbelievable. We just worked our way up to Albuquerque, and now we're here in Denver. In a few days we're making our way to Wyoming. Then to Portland, Seattle, Vancouver, Alberta, Saskatchewan, Manitoba. Then Chicago, Detroit, up into Toronto, Montreal, Quebec, then New York and back in April."

"What is the overall theme of the film?"

"It's culture and it's music. As soon as you cross the border into Mexico it becomes a different world. Sometimes when you cross a state line it becomes a different world. It's the same with going to different countries. You build up a picture of what makes the music tick, what makes the people tick. Just going to different places where people in the UK and in Europe never go to. We booked it using MySpace and the internet. We're trying to make a global local music scene."

"What's the message of your film?"

"Just that geographical position shouldn't determine your success. There's so many different scenes especially in the big cities – people need to kind of branch out.... You got their opinions, what they're like, their stage performances. We still have three and a half months of filming to go. We're getting a lot of attention in Europe as well in France. Especially France, Italy and Spain..."

Time for the spotlight. I choose Jacque Chirac's desk, between Clinton and Tony Blair. I take off my dirty black ball-cap, rumple my hat-hair, and lay it all down. My life story – cap-sized, cliff note, abbreviated. I ramble for 2 hours and take up 3 tape changes. Then I pulled my ace and led them straight to Kerouac. The ironic convergence of quasi-spiritual divine intervention was unexplainable (*except for maybe that last episode of Quantum Leap where Scott Baio ends up in the extra-dimensional cowboy bar*)...

***5:30pm, waiting on the curb for Jesus, I miss the call from Cephalic Carnage. I hit them back within 5 minutes but it's useless. They open for Slayer in 2 hours...

PARSONS STORY

No point explaining the monotonous retread of identical events. By 11:20am, Jesus flips open the passenger side door, and we're en route to Littleton to meet Columbine survivor Eric Parsons. I have no idea what to expect. All I know is that Jesus has to keep his insane mouth shut lest we freak this guy out.

Being Denver's neighboring suburb, you can get to Littleton within a short 15 minute drive. This tragedy shook the town to its core, and it has the psychological ripple effect of... let's say Springfield in *Freddy's Dead*, where the parents were running on motor function. Maybe not to that extreme in reality, but you can see where I'm going. To even mention the shooting a conversation can turn cold and awkward; in the wrong context tempers can flare.

You forget you're in Denver until you see the mountains, majestic and supreme, enclosing the West. Huge peaks with white snowcaps and a dizzying head feeling because you're a mile high...

Qdoba in a small shopping center, lunchtime. All of the teenagers who now pack the taco hut are apparently allowed to eat off campus. There is a huge line and people loudly gabbing away at every table. We see Eric pull up, his pointy red goatee and ski-cap, and he just knows it's us. He shakes my hand and looks nervous.

I wait with him in line as we awkwardly fumble through formalities. This is the first time he's ever spoken to the press. I see his Metallica tattoo and we talk about metal. The second we start connecting on MANOWAR, everything is smooth. We get huge California burritos.

His eyes give off that Nam vet in a stark memory gaze, and he talks slow and carefully, just sort of staring out the window at the light snow until he gets comfortable and loosens up: *"Well I'm a pretty boring guy I'd say. I grew up around here. I went to Columbine Hills elementary, then Columbine High. We hardly ever moved... I've got two brothers who also were there. They're twins, younger than me..."*

"Well I should begin by saying I'm interested in your version of the truth, your experiences and just let you have the floor. I should also say I'm not doing this book to make money, I'm not out to exploit you. I'm out to break bands & shine light on so much of what America avoids..."

"Well where to begin? We'll start with the shooting I guess. I was a sophomore, just doing my thing. I was pretty normal... I actually never saw any of the bullying they were talking about. I wasn't a super popular kid, got picked on like everyone else. I was taking a science test one day, and one of the teachers came to the door and said, '*Um, Doug.*' It was weird because even the teachers refer to each other as Mr. Johnson or Mr. Rutherford in front of the kids. '*Doug? What's up with that?*' *I was right next to the door and I heard her whisper 'Someone's shooting.*' I figured she meant the news. A few seconds later – it's kind of scrambled in my head – we heard these pops and screaming from the cafeteria. We were in the science hallway – you go out, take a few steps and you're in the cafeteria. So you can hear if there's a bunch of noise going on down there... And then there was chaos. Kids came running in, running by, and we didn't know what the heck was going on. I don't know how long it was, maybe a minute. You know the teacher that died? Mr. Sanders -- he came into the room and he had been shot a couple times. He was bleeding from his mouth, took one or two steps, and just fell down. Then we knew something was going on, something serious, something immediate... They kind of locked us in the room... We sat there, people tried to take care of Mr. Sanders. I guess he had been shot in the back a couple times and one of the bullets went through his neck and out his mouth. He's bleeding out his mouth and his teeth... got shot out kinda. After a few minutes of being bunkered down in silence we heard Eric and Dylan come through the science wing making a bunch of noise. Shooting windows and stuff like that. We didn't know what was going on. I guess they broke the door down and busted a window in the neighboring room and threw in a Molotov cocktail. One of the teachers disappeared for awhile and put out the fire. We turned out the lights, sat there and waited, and waited. After awhile someone turned on the TV and we were watching it on the news. There were phones in the classrooms and someone was calling... I don't know if we called out first or they called in first, but they were talking to SWAT. We told them where we were and what our situation was. Then it was just a matter of time. Finally SWAT came in, yelled at us, gathered us. They bunched us in a corner and explained that we were all suspects, because they didn't know who'd done this. Any of us could have a gun right now, so do what you're told. We finally made it out of the school and they bussed us somewhere else. I stepped out of the car, and there's press, and hundreds of worried parents everywhere. My dad was the first person that I saw. That was the biggest sigh of relief that you could ever imagine."

"How were your friends?"

"I didn't lose anyone super-close to me. Daniel Mauser was a friend of a friend. We'd hung out a couple times. When I got home that day, there's a list of 50 people you need to call because you know their worried. So you call everyone and tell them you're not dead. I guess my mom didn't worry too much because my brothers had got out right away and one of them had told her that he'd seen me, even though I was still in the science room. My mom was like 'oh great, everyone's out.' But I still hadn't shown up for four hours (laughs). For the next couple weeks you just got together with whoever you needed. We just sat around and pouted. A few days later, everyone in the school met at a church. It was crazy. You'd seen a list of everyone who'd died and been injured. So you know all your friends are ok, but still every time you saw them it was like, 'oh my god, he's not dead, he's ok.' That happened a thousand times. There was one kid, just before the science test we had been joking. I was like 'you're a fag.' That was the last thing I said to him because the class started right after that. For some reason it really hit me. What if that was the last thing I'd said to him? So when I saw him, I just burst into tears. I was like 'bro, I called you a fag.' And he's like, 'you did what now?' (Laughs). It had been bothering me for days, but he obviously didn't remember."

"How long was it before the initial shock wore off?"

"It was a pretty slow process. I was lucky because I talked to my friends. Some people just shut down and never said anything. Some of those people are still my friends but their messed up and still freaked out when they get locked in a room and they hear loud noises. It took months before you were back to normal. Do you remember Golden Eye for the N-64?"

"Oh yeah."

"That game was red-hot back then. I couldn't play it for a long time. I just played Mario Kart, no games with blood. And even the Star Wars movie that just came out, *The Phantom Menace*, when Qui Gon Jinn gets a light-saber in the gut. There's not an ounce of blood… I couldn't watch anything like that. When you'd mess with your friends and you're like, 'I'm gonna kill you.' No, you don't do that anymore. It's weird… You kind of have to go back to your naive view, back to taking stuff for granted a little or you're totally paranoid."

"What do you have to say about Eric Harris?"

"My brother had a gym class with Klebold. I knew of Eric because he was in the German class ahead of me. Never talked to him."

"What was the summer of '99 like? Do you think kids that were failing were just pushed through graduation?"

"Yeah, especially the year after that. We spent it at Chapfield, our rival school. It wasn't school anymore. It was getting up and doing stuff so you're back in a routine. A lot of the classes we'd be watching movies."

"Did many students want them to tear Columbine down? Did you think it was necessary to go back and confront what happened to get over it?"

"That was kind of an option. But everyone I knew thought it was important. The entire community came together. That what was different about '99, everyone was friends. There were no bullies anymore. Everyone was nice to everyone. It was important to say, 'you haven't taken anything from us.' When we went back they walled up the library and put a bunch of lockers in front of it. That was weird for us though. It was hard the first time I went back into the science room."

"I was curious as to the image of the Trench-coat Mafia, the kids that used to hang out with them. Did any of that particular group go back at all or did they drop out…"

"I think most of them were seniors. I'm sure you wouldn't be allowed to wear a trench-coat after that. I think there were a few underclassmen that knew them that did come back. A few were asked not to come back.... You heard of Brooks Brown?"

"He was the one that Harris told to go home."

"Yeah, they were about to shoot and they were friends the first couple years of high school, before they had a falling out. They just started getting along again. That day Harris told him to go home. Brooks was telling the authorities that there was proof of this violent behavior and they should have been doing something, He wrote a book about all sorts of stuff that makes it really fishy. Like the police have covered up things I had no idea about."

"Have you studied any of the conspiracy stuff? People have claimed that others were involved. What's your attitude towards these kind of websites?"

"I had a friend, my best friend at the time. When I was in science class he was at lunch where the shooting started, and he swears up and down that one of the guys with the guns was not Eric, was not Dylan. His name was Robert Perry."

"Yeah, we heard about him…"

"Really?"

Jesus: "I've read there were over 50 students that said there was another guy, that his name was Robert Perry, that he didn't look anything like Harris or Klebold. There's testimony about how they had a girl, and they had pictures of people cut out of their yearbooks..."

"I wonder what the truth is behind those scenarios. Perry was one of the guys that would walk around school in a trench-coat. How much of it is your brain playing tricks on you, I don't know... He was pretty recognizable – tall, real lanky, he had bad skin, and the trench really made him stand out. Personally I believe it was only Eric and Dylan."

"There are all these police reports that have been sealed for 25 years. It is fishy...

"Exactly. I heard SWAT shot one of the kids. I can't remember what the result of that was. I think he said he may have shot one of the kids accidentally..."

Jesus: "One student in particular, they did an autopsy and the bullets came from the guns consistent with the officers. Nothing's been released, his autopsy hasn't been released..."

"Does anyone know what happened to Robert Perry?"

"I saw him the next day. I went to the comic shop and Robert Perry was there. I instinctively thought he was one of the shooters, 'cause I hadn't been following it. It was really weird how it hit me. I can't remember seeing him at all in the next two years."

"Shortly after Columbine, when they were making accusations about police shooting kids, there were these two kids that went to the school. They worked at a Subway or something, and someone shot them while they were at work."

"That was a year later. I don't think the police were involved. It seemed like it was drug related. Those kids were into drugs and probably dealing. The girl was just a friend and she happened to be there and get wasted too."

"Being a little out of the norm with the red Mohawk and whatnot, I was wondering how that played itself out – do you think people were persecuted here? I'm from Detroit and when it happened I was the first trench-coat mafia sort of kid from my area. I had experiences where cops were harassing kids for information about me, pulling people over and digging through their cars because they admitted knowing me. It was pretty raw..."

"I don't think I personally witnessed it too much. Brooks Brown said he experienced it. Not so much from authorities but he'd be walking down the street and people would drive by and yell things at him. Everyone knew that he was their friend. A lot of people assumed he knew. Other than that I haven't heard too much. I didn't dress like the dark metalhead or the goth kid. I had a couple Metallica shirts, stuff like that, but I didn't stand out enough to look like a target."

"What did you think of the Michael Moore movie?"

"It took me awhile before I watched it, because I didn't want to know everything in it. He made some good points. I recommended it to people."

"What do you say about the kids that wear t-shirts with Harris and Klebold, or try to make them into superstars? You don't see too much of that around here I assume."

"No man, never. The good portion of license plates are Columbine plates. I see it on MySpace though. There's a lot of sixteen year olds that treat them like heroes. They'll get on the Columbine bulletin board and say things just to make people mad. I mean what can you say to someone like that? There already so far off if they think that it's a good thing or its something to admire."

"What do you think could have been to maybe avert what happened? I know there were people that used to walk by them, spit in their face, punch them or call them fags. And I know the school newsletter was approved by the principal that went on calling them 'faggots' publicly."

"Wow, I didn't hear about that… Probably the first thing is parent involvement. If they felt they could talk to their parents… Any talking is good therapy. Maybe their parents didn't realize how miserable they were and could have even taken them to another school, home-school or something. It's hard to say 'cause I never personally experienced much bullying. I certainly didn't bully people."

"What do you feel might be something positive that came from this all?"

"I've thought about that a few times. A couple times I've said, *'well that's a good thing,'* but it certainly wasn't worth it. I would say that personally, it changed me for the better. I didn't make any conscious effort, it wasn't a *'if I get out of this alive'* thing. All of a sudden I was getting straight A's. It made me realize when I did mess around with my friends I'd get rough sometimes. I'd say I'm gentler, more sensitive to people. I have a friend who has post-traumatic stress and she can't take fireworks or being locked in small rooms. She isn't in a better place at all. She's bitter about it – she can't really have a discussion about it without getting mad or defensive. She's mad about the memorial they're building because she wants to bury it all. I did have a healthy recovery, mentally…

"What are you going to name your son?"

"Logan."

"Is he named after Wolverine?"

"(Laughs) No, it was kind of an accident. We didn't want to name him Xavier though. The middle name has to be Charles, my dad's name. It's been that way for six generations. It'd be really weird to call him Xavier Charles…"

Both Jesus and Parsons jet because they are on lunch breaks, and I hang outside smoking after one of the most intense interviews I've ever done. Eric drives by on his way out and looks at me with a disturbed glance that is partially relief and part *"what the fuck have I done?"* I get a call from the Leeds Lads who unfortunately can't join my quest to the infamous bowling alley because they're scooting out to Boulder.

I bail on Bowl-A-Rama and hop the freeway, climbing an avalanche of snow to a monorail platform. I jump the rails and sneak on hoping no trolley cop tickets me. Two exits down and the cop is checking all ticket stubs on the next car, so I hop off again and wait in the snow. 30 minutes later the next train is smooth, the passing scenery gives a dead winter appeal to the industrial outskirts. Harris must have ridden this thing a 1000 times over. What a dreary, bland existence. Suffocated by factories and military complex's…

The train drops me off next to a closed amusement park with icicles hanging like stalactites over the Carnival Wheel. I walk a few blocks and am back in the Pike District. The free shuttle bus takes you everywhere down Mall Street, which is a labyrinth of Starbucks and Virgin Records. Packed, snowing, and everyone is so normal. It's so clean. Everyone rushing forward into blind consumerism…

Near the library a SWAT team armada were blocking off National City Bank. All of the employees were on the front steps without coats in sub-zero weather, like a shooting just happened. The only other people paying attention on the street are from The Czech Republic. I attempt to shoot the shit over LAIBACH, and one guy raises an solidarity fist: *"Jah, Slovenia ist guut…"*

THE DENVER THEORY

Friday afternoon, last grueling day on the street. The homeless know me well now, and none haggle change anymore. Anytime I think of Denver I'll now envision an army of vagrants devouring piles upon piles of books. No bands, no PIT, no money, no XXX girls, no surprise. The porn director won't return my emails, though she was aggressive about the interview for 3 months beforehand. Another enigma of The Denver Trapezoid...

No point getting into a Columbine rant. There's nothing I can say that hasn't been repeated far better or is more informative then the 1000+ conspiracy obsessed websites in existence. I have a theory though – "*The Denver Theory.*" Since this is the last port westward, this area has been the traditional crossing zone to get through the Rocky Mountains. Since the settlers arrived it's been an economic boom safe house for the "*just passin' through.*"

No one originated here. The entire population were uprooted and transplanted from the East Coast, Midwest, and the South during the Gold Rush in 1849. Most wound up here because they saw the Rockies and said "*fuck this California bullshit.*" This is why everyone is so weird and stand-offish – it's ingrained in them not to trust outsiders, be suspicious of everyone & everything...

But that doesn't explain the *crazy* people. Denver is full of lunatics, and Jesus warned me of this: "*I saw the bus stop to pick up a woman, but she wouldn't step on. She just stood there crying, and the bus driver kept saying 'do you want on?' She just kept crying, this crazed lunatic.*"

"*And then the next week I was on the bus, and a woman got up out of her seat and started yanking at the emergency release bars on the big window. She was freaking out, panicking, yanking on them, and no one said anything to her, not ever the driver. Then she just sat down with her hands on her lap, calm, like nothing had happened.*"

This has been floating around my head all day when suddenly, inside McDonalds, some Mexican guy with a Tom Sellick mustache comes in -- blue jeans tucked into orange-tinted cowboy boots & brown gloves with fringe tassels. Tack on a bluish white pleather snakeskin coat, 10 gallon cowboy hat, and an amulet with blue turquoise slung around his neck...

He looks around very calmly, walks up to the life-size Spongebob Squarepants cardboard cutout, gets down on his knees as if he is about to pray, then grips the sides of Spongebob like he is sucking down a brisk coursing of energy. He lowers his skull in shame and then wobbles his head like one of the stopwatch mutant people in *Jacob's Ladder*. He slings his head up to the left, freezes, and says "1." Then he goes back to wobbling. Head freezes at right side of Spongebob: "2." Back to the left: "3."

He does this all the way to 25. He finishes, centers himself, stands up, unrumples his snakeskin coat, then walks right out the side door. No one even acknowledged him. Not a worker, not a patron batting an eye except for myself, slowly munching on a double cheeseburger…

:STALAGGH:

It's around 4pm when I get the email. It seems more than appropriate with such an intense Columbine head-trip. You look at the way underground music became a scapegoat after April 20th 1999, so many claiming music influenced the killers/ KMFDM? Come on now, they're "A Drug Against War." Marilyn Manson? Who, *Brian*? Music doesn't make people kill people, because environment dictates everything.

However… If you want to talk about a real boogeyman, you want to talk about an evil force out to corrupt your children, you want to explore a sound that actually does exist to drive its audience into violent madness? Well, look no further than self-proclaimed *"audio terrorists"* :STALAGGH:. If this is the first time you've heard of them, the reason is because every major media outlet is either terrified or morally opposed to unleashing them on the public. *"Don't let AUDIO-TERROR spread,"* so they say, *"lest the results usher in a tragedy of untold proportions…"*

"Would you give a brief explanation of :STALAGGH:?

":STALAGGH: is a Nihilistik Misanthropik Audio Terrror projekt and was created in the year 2000 by individuals from the Dutch and Belgian Black metal and noise/electro/ambient scenes. So far we have created four Audio Terrror recordings: *Projekt Nihil, Projekt Terrror, Projekt Misanthropia* and one untitled track for the Anti-live aid compilation CD. Our projekts have been released in different formats (CD/LP/7"/DVD) and by several different labels (New Era productions, Total Holocaust records, Autopsy Kitchen Records, Basilisk Productions, Autumn Winds Productions, Rigor Mortis Productions)."

"Your approach to vocals is undeniably the most intense methodology I've ever heard."

"We decided that a normal black metal vocalist was not what we were looking for. The pain and hate in the vocals must be real, not acted. We needed humans with a real mental illness. Only someone in constant mental pain or with a homicidal aggression could provide the vocals for our Audio-Terrror. One of our members works in a mental institution so this is how we come in contact with mental patients. We always tell vocalists who participate what :STALAGGH: is all about. Most of them agree with our ideology. Their mental illness makes them hate humans and their society, so it not hard to convince to become part of our projekts. The mind of the mentally deranged is far more interesting than the minds of sane people. Living in constant fear and pain causes the soul to fill with hate and despair and will give you visions of the realms of darkness and death. For those people these images feel real. This is why we use real insane people to do our vocals. They can transfer their mental suffering into sound for :STALAGGH: and we can spread their despair and fear across the minds of many others, and make it feel real to them as well. Our sound is very visual. When you listen to :STALAGGH: you will see mountains of corpses, scorched earth, total devastation, chaos and hell. We hope to drive normal humans insane with :STALAGGH:"

"You do back-masking on your records?"

"We have hidden many strange and mind-altering noises in our sound that are bound to make you mad, so you will only desire death. On *Projekt Nihil* we used a murder convict and a mental patient to do the vocals. The vocals done by the murder convict represent feelings of hate and aggression. The vocals done by the mental patient represent pain and suffering. Their insanity will infest your soul. Screams of pain and hatred are much more intense than screaming lyrics. The murderer killed his mother at the age of 16 with over 30 knife stab wounds for no apparent reason. He spent 4 years in a maximum security youth prison and 7 years in a prison for delinquents with a mental disease. He has an extreme aggression disorder and is very hard to handle. We have been in contact since he was released. He was very enthusiastic to participate. While recording *Projekt Nihil* he did some very excessive self-mutilation and he screamed all his murderous aggression out of his soul. He has participated in both *Projekt Nihil* and *Projekt Terrror*."

"What was the mental patient like as an individual?"

"The mental patient was a very sad human being as he was in constant mental pain. He was a man with extreme anorexia nervosa and was about 45 kilo in weight. He also had borderline syndrome and had been in and out of mental hospitals for many years. It was very hard to persuade him to participate in the :STALAGGH: projekt. After the recording he said that doing vocals for :STALAGGH: was the best therapy he ever had. He killed himself a few months after. We have used a drawing from him on the inside of the Digi-pack edition of *Projekt Nihil*. For the creation of *Projekt Terror* we have used 3 new mental patients, and for *Projekt Misanthropia* we have used 7."

"What was the recording situation like?"

"We found a 24 track studio which was in the same building as a big storage basement 10 meters underground. It was almost freezing in this basement and there were almost no lights. The producer was not very happy when he saw us and was totally amazed that we were going to record without ever rehearsing. We explained what we wanted and we took all the microphones and instruments into the basement. We told the producer to record everything. The producer had no idea what we were doing down there. He could only hear the most terrible sounds he'd ever heard coming from below. Some of us were cutting ourselves with razorblades and blood was flowing everywhere – it almost looked like a torture chamber. The basement was completely filled with negative emotions of pain, hate and fear. We all brought our darkest and most hateful feelings to the surface and transformed that into sound. Especially the murderer who went completely crazy and destroyed almost all the things in the basement. The mental patient drove all of us to total insanity as he was crying and moaning the most disturbing sounds all the time. We recorded *Projekt Nihil* in two days and the producer told us that these were the worst two days of his life and he never wanted to see us again."

"So everything went exactly as planned?"

"Total audio-terrror! For *Projekt Terrror* we needed a much louder and more extreme sound so we decided to use 4 mentally insane vocalists (three male, one female), two drummers, two keyboard players, two guitarists, and two bass players. This time we decided to record everything ourselves without the help of a producer. We recorded *Projekt Terrror* in one day in a small room in complete darkness. Again everything was completely improvised. The 4 mental patients drove all of us over the edge of insanity and the entire room was filled with hysteria and fear. The atmosphere and emotions became more extreme every minute and you can hear that very well on the finished recording. The terror and fear grow to immense proportions. Some of us were wounded as we were attacked and almost strangled to death by one of the mental patients who could no longer control his homicidal urges."

"What about Projekt Misanthropia?"

"This time we used the vocals of 7 mental patients and recorded the base layer in an abandoned factory. This factory had not been used for over 30 years and would be demolished soon, so we were allowed to destroy everything that was inside. There were old machines rotting away and layer upon layer of dust and debris and mummified corpses of birds and rats everywhere. There was almost no light and the air was polluted. We went completely berserk and smashed everything inside to pieces. This session took about three hours. The vocals session took place in the chapel of an old monastery that was no longer in use. The acoustics and atmosphere were perfect for recording the howls and screams of the mentally insane. It was very hard to get access to that chapel, but we told the owner that we were doing this as a kind of scream therapy for the patients and finally he gave us permission. For several hours all seven patients screamed out all their insanity, pain, and fear while the sounds recorded in the factory were playing in the background. The third part was adding black metal elements and some structure and effects, but no riffs were written beforehand and improvised directly while listening to the earlier recordings."

"You've said that the ideological goal of ::STALAGGH:: is to spread "audio terrror," to push the limits of human thought and emotion, and provoke similar entities to form across the world in the interest of causing chaos and fear. What contact have you had in the United States and other countries, and what other entities have come to surface in the wake of your efforts?"

"Several entities have followed our ideology and started to create audio-terror, but most labels do not have the guts to release it. We are in contact with some of them and we stimulate them to create and spread the Audio-Terrror. But there are also many of them who do not understand the ideology and believe we just create noise without any message."

"What are the responses you've received from admirers? What are some of the strangest reactions or inspirations?"

"It has been mostly people sending us pictures of self-mutilation they did while listening to :STALAGGH: They proudly send us photos of their mutilated and bleeding flesh. This is only the beginning of the influence of our Audio-Terrror. There are true fanatics who collect all our releases and pay hundreds of dollars for rare :STALAGGH: releases on eBay. One person told us he would commit suicide while listening to :STALAGGH: and film the act and send it to us to put it on our DVD."

"Would you be willing to perhaps do a live interview on a talk show or media outlet in America via Internet Camera, if you were to wear masks to protect your identities?"

"Maybe. It depends if we really can express our ideology on a serious level. We are not interested in 'sensation TV.'"

"How do you feel about the American Underground? Are the American youth hopeless? Do you think that American culture is on the brink of total collapse? If so, do you hope to contribute to this collapse?"

"There are some interesting acts in the American underground who are creating something new with true dedication and emotions. All humans are hopeless and weak, but the American youth are the worst of them all. All of mankind is on the brink of total collapse and we certainly hope to contribute to this."

"If :STALAGGH: were to be taken quite seriously in America and became a widely recognized entity, what do you feel the results would be? What do you hope the results would be?"

"The result will be an eruption of chaos, hate, and fear spreading across all of America climaxing into the total annihilation of mankind."

"What do you think of NSK? Is :STALAGGH: similar to NSK, albeit in a completely different realm?"

"NSK are creative, and :STALAGGH: is destructive. We do not want to be compared to them."

"What of the new projekt :GULAGGH:?"

"With :GULAGGH: we will also create a trilogy, but it will be a really different form of Audio-Terrror than :STALAGGH:. We are still working on the concept, but expect something like you have never heard before. When :STALAGGH: was created in the year 2000 it was already established that it would be a trilogy with three different themes. We have created the trilogy as planned, but the full effect of our :Projekts: will only be felt within a few years when our Audio-Terrror has been spread to the maximum upon mankind."

"Tell me about the Anti-Live AID compilation."

"Supernal Music asked us to contribute to this compilation and we support the ideology of this project. We created a special new track that features the vocals of a mental patient who had a psychosis that lasted over six years. His vocals are almost no longer human. We smashed up a real human skull with a hammer and put the fragments in a large metal bowl. We then grinded the bone parts with a microphone. You can clearly hear the cracking of the bone at the beginning of the track. The true sound of death had to be part of this recording."

"How has the press in Netherlands reacted to :STALAGGH:? Are there campaigns against your :Projekts:?"

"The Dutch press hardly reacted to us. We only did interviews in other countries (Metal Maniacs, Unrestrained, Zero Tolerance, etc). The Dutch are way too tolerant."

"Do you feel there is any sense of personal morality involved in what you are doing? Are you helping set people free through this form of "therapy?" Do you feel that you are villains and proud of the fact, or do you feel that you are in the right to be doing this? Or is it simply art with no boundaries? Is morality simply a projection of the human world and has no real context in art itself, since emotions themselves exclude any judgment?"

":STALAGGH: is an entity so there is no room for personal morality. Only our ideology is important, and we believe in what we are doing. Humans should realize that their existence is futile. :STALAGGH: is not art nor therapy"

"What is your answer to individuals who would consider :STALAGGH: to be a publicity stunt, or some kind of hoax?"

"All the fools who proclaimed that it was just a 'selling act' or 'publicity stunt' HAVE changed their opinion after actually hearing :STALAGGH:. This should say enough…"

PART IV: MERCURY RETROGRADE
(A MURDERFEST & THE OSCARS)
FEBRUARY 5TH-APRIL 5TH 2007

MERCURY RETROGRADE

Yngwie Malmsteem said that every time he returns to Miami he gets on his knees and kisses the ground, because it is paradise. I'm starting to feel that way about California... The Denver nightmare is over and I'm finally free. It doesn't matter that I have a 3 hour delay and I'm stuck here in Riverside, or that PIT Magazine totally hoed me out. "Back In The USSR" jams on the Walkman, and I've gone from -15 degree Celsius conditions to a plump 80+ with no humidity. It squashes the dread of having to get a job...

Back at The Villa Winona, things are progressing speedily yet awkward. Onyx' wife explains that it is "Mercury Retrograde." This means every astrological energy pulse that could affect us is in high gear yet oxymoronically combating itself, like forcing the bottom sides of magnets together. Now matter how hard you try and squash them together, the centrifugal force ruptures the link. You can feel it everywhere. The meth zombies bumbling down El Cajon Blvd., the hotheaded SD cops, the average Joseph – all of them buzzing to the scorch of a confused-cycle moon, the madness of Summer blazing...

Mercury Retrograde apparently affects financial prospects as well. My plan was to keep this book rolling by both tax returns and my old car's purchase in Michigan. I made more "official" money in my entire life in 2006, something like $29,000, but somehow I ended up owing $2,000 dollars. This is my own stupid fault for putting too many dependents on my W-4 forms as well as my journalist occupation screwing me with un-taxed 1099's.

Bamboozled out of the expected $1000 which was supposed to carry my ass through May, I also get an unexpected bill in the mail. $750 from a credit agency for a car I a year ago. The buyer never transferred the title – it just died and he left it on the curb, dumping on me the $150 towing bill. The police told me I could either pay $250 to get it out of impound, or simply sign it over to them for auction with no strings attached. I chose to hack off the tendrils of the cursed thing, and was assured *"done deal."*

Well, this $750 stick-up is from blatantly dishonest pigs. Apparently I am responsible for the unspoken $1000 it cost to store the automobile in their warehouse, and it only went for $250 at the auction, making me legally responsible for the remaining tab. So it's either A) continue this head-spinning charade to try and save my non-existent credit by working 40 hours a week and delaying the book or B) FUCK THE SYSTEM.

I call Michigan to find out the status of my old 1990 Daytona. I'd handed it over to the buddy of a guy who lived across the street which promised to pay my ex-roommate $300 the Friday after I'd left for California. he straight-up *STOLE MY CAR* and disappeared from the face of the earth.

Panicked by the certainty this will be a repeat tow-job, I call the same cops who lied to me to make a report. Not to claim grand theft auto, just to keep me in the clear if the guy does something stupid. I can't do anything because I don't have the VIN or Serial Number, because I set my registration and insurance slips on fire, cackling hysterically and vowing never again to own a car. I can't get the Serial or the VIN because by law the Secretary of State isn't allowed to give that information over the phone, which means I have to appear <u>IN PERSON</u> in Michigan to take care of this mongoloid situation…

THE OSCARS

It felt the way it would if you'd watched it at home – kind of ignoring the screen but feeling like you should actually care or pay attention, but you're too busy fidgeting around with things far more important at hand, like vacuuming the carpet.

I hadn't expected such a 'blah' scenario – half awake from Sparks and Flexural, stranded in Hollywood from a blown transmission. We left the auto carcass on Bronson Avenue cold as a dinosaur, too enamored in our plans of chaos to give a second thought to its fate.

It had been our plan to sneak in the Chinese Theater fronting as highly-regarded press people or caterers, but we'd had no convincing uniforms or documents. One plan was to plant laxatives in the fruit punch, wriggle in glee at the intestinal crunch of Will Smith. Another was to cut microphone chords or sabotage anything in sight, really. Skinner & I were gunning for the end scene of *Brain Donors*, but the closest we got was the fence across the street, our view blocked by paparazzi aggressively hunkering their positions in a siege of white, flashing light.

The streets were cordoned off in the fashion of a presidential motorcar train wreck – bulletproof limousines with tinted windows sluggishly cruised the streets, iron-hard SUV's and Hummers. Thousands of star-struck LA people dressed as strippers & lime-light fanatics – oodles fro-hawks, canyons of yuppies. You expect Gomorrah glitz and Sodom glam, yet all you get is some light drizzle rain.

We play the "Where's Waldo B-List Actor" game, scouting the crowd for identifiable hacks who couldn't make it in and hang around like stooges trying to up their fame esteem. Skinner thinks he spots Andy Dick, I possibly spy Jeremy Piven... Then I spot one, a perfect example of almost-but-not-quite celebrity. He weaves through a string of stripper-like bimbos, onwards towards some non-Oscar destination, brow shrugged and intense. "*I found one! Fucking Delroy Lindo!*"

Skinner looks oblivious, the beautiful girl just as lost: "*Who the fuck is Delroy Lindo?*"

"*Well, um, you see 'Congo?' That one about the killer gorillas, you know, where Bruce Campbell gets mauled? The black dude, that militant rebel leader guy. The one that freaks out and shouts 'STOP EATING MY SESAME CAKE' at Bill Paxton. Dude, it's like the greatest line ever.*" Nope, nada – totally lost, and my big score is a dud.

Then the day livens up brilliantly. There is a man standing on a metal crate, an eisegetical freak screaming lines from the New Testament. He's informing the scourges that he will supply $10 to take a "Good Person Test," a sort of Evangelical S.A.T. score. I immediately fly off the handle, roaring louder in my demagoguery, attempting to outdo his far-from-modest mouth foaming: "CASH IS THE ENEMY OF ALL CHRISTENDOM!!! JESUS IS THE SOLUTION TO CAPITALIST IMPERIUM!!! ALL HAIL THE LONGHAIRED PINKO ANARCHIST!!!"

The cockalorum preacher is massively startled, trying to roar over me: "*Christ is the way of salvation...*" "ONLY 144,000 WILL BE SAVED AT THE TIME OF THE RAPTURE, ALL OF THEM MALE VIRGINS!!! EVERYONE WITH VAGINA SHALL BURN!!!" "*...the path to righteousness is...*" "GOD SENT TWO BEARS TO KILL 42 CHILDREN BECAUSE THEY MOCKED A PROPHETS BALDNESS!!!" "*...Lucifer and all his lies...*" "THE EARTH IS FLAT & DINOSAUR BONES WERE PUT HERE BY SATAN TO FOOL US!!!" "*...the cure of the world's ill...*" "ALL HOMOS SHALL BE TURNED TO PILLARS OF SALT!!! BLESS THE GENOCIDE OF THE QUEENS!!!" Et cetera ad infinitum times 10 with a dash of red pepper & granulated onion...

The illitate crowd parted about us like the Red Sea. The cops were belly-laughing, and even Mr. Skinner was shocked. I saluted the concrete monk, left grizzled on his podium, and we pounced towards the charred-flesh line of Burger King.

Munching economical value, the preacher guy slips in, spots me, ducks his head, and flies into the bathroom. As I'm dipping a fry into a plop of ketchup, he creeps back up: "*Hi... My name is Steve.*" I lift up my head and look coldly into his eyes: "*I DON'T SUPPORT FASCISM.*" He extends his hand, as gentile as he can arrange, and quietly exclaims: "*Either do I.*"

After years of wet-dreaming such a scenario, I finally have this symbolic archetype in a corner. Just sit chumpy down and calmly unravel his view of reality... Yet as I stare at his trembling hand that won't retract its quivering position, no real blast of blaspheme fires summon within. I just sigh, clasp it up and down, and he nods with a fearful respect.

Entheomaniac Steve somberly turns and walks out the door. Mr. Skinner and the beautiful girl sit dead quiet as I mechanically eat my fries. Nothing is spoken for the rest of the meal... *I've had relationships that ended on weirder terms...*

CHUCK THE HOMEY

As a sort of crust punk squat meets James Joyce Dublin flophouse, here at The Villa Winona we face a choppy stream of irregular visitors. One such frequenter is named "Chuck The Homey." From the outside he appears a mere street wino. Well he is, and he can often be seen pushing a shopping cart full of empty cans. At night he crashes behind the couch in a pile of black garbage bags filled with clothes. He's in his mid-50's, has this foofy red unkempt fro, and collects trinkets for the toy shrine in the kitchen.

Chuck The Homey has been shit out by the world. He lost everything when his wife died and Bush cut all his 'Nam benefits. Ever since he's lived in the cumberworld fringe and hydrated himself solely with Steel Reserve tall cans. Agent Orange fucks with him bad, and he's quietly on his way out. He is an old school hippie that's explored every inch of California mingling with surfers and acid-fiends, but the weirdest tales he spews regards the aliens.

Indeed, a former Area 51 officer is on deck. Aliens, he claims, are definitely real. He hasn't seen anything like in *Independence Day* where they are in eight-foot tubes of viscous fluid, but he's had strange run-ins. When stationed in Germany he was doing his rounds as an airbase MP and saw three glowing orbs hovering over the hidden missile site. He radioed his superior freaking out for an explanation, but nothing was on radar. They simply flew off into the night sky silently at an unscientific rate of speed. When he confronted higher rank, they just told him to remain quiet – "*we have no answer.*"

The other two sightings were at Area 51 itself. He saw a craft in a hangar that was literally floating. When the lab coats saw his eyes bugging out they slid closed the doors with a little "*shhhh...*" finger to the lips... The other occasion was viewing six men in black – but in these stark black paramilitary suits escorting a three foot tall mystery man with four fingers. He was inside a jet-black gas-masked rubber suit like Darth Vadar…

Although officially it never happened, they were headed to Level #30 of the 34 underground floors. No one knows what goes on down there because it's Top Secret below #6. The base itself stretches for miles beneath the New Mexico desert, and the government has created a full-scale subterranean city…

THE BASS PLAYER FROM RATT SLEEPS ON MY COUCH

Chuck isn't the only transient force at the Villa. Another in his early 40's stutters a lot and cooks us BBQ as a form of couch-surfing rent. He's got a graying black goatee and a childlike exuberance, particularly when *WWE Smackdown* is on. He has the Nike look and the intense street handshake with the side-snap. He's around once every 3 weeks for a few days at a time, but I'd never bothered actually talking to him until yesterday. '*So who the fuck are you? What do you do? I mean, what's your thing?*'

His reply: '*Oh, I was the bassist in RATT.*' Imagine the slack jawed mind-fuck for me at this very moment: "*I grew up in the San Diego area. In '79 I met everybody from RATT. We started playing while we were in high school. Back then we were still in grade school and high school so it wasn't all that crazy, except that I learned how to smoke pot with loose-leaf paper, ha ha. My friend's dad was an artist and he lived right on the canyon. Where we're at right now, it's about six blocks up. It was a canyon, so we didn't have to worry about noise calls. We jammed all the time.*"

"*We did house parties, school dances until the beginning of Junior year. We did have some covers, but we had a variety of songs. 'Round And Round,' all that. We're talking old school. About '82 we*" *started playing for all the high school parties. By July I left them, a new bass player came in, he was stung out on drugs, and they all went with it... I stepped out. I knew something was gonna happen. Sure enough, in '88, at The Red Onion down on Pacific Beach, they had a girl and raped her in the bathroom."*

"Is that public knowledge?"

Matt James or Mark King (We're Not Sure): "All over the papers dawg, all over the papers. They even asked me questions about that too. As soon as I heard that I dropped my bass. I never picked that up again for about 13 years."

"Got any weird celebrity stories?"

"I used to surf with Jeremy, the lead singer from Incubus. He's beautiful man, he's so much fun. Him and the bass player, the big red-headed dude. Ever since Incubus has been like my favorite band. I used to go to some of his local shows at bars here. A lot of beer, it was always straight."

"Where did the name RATT come from?"

"That came from the first gig we did. We were in the garage. There were a bunch of mice, and Storm asked *'what do you think of MOUSE?'* I go *'how 'bout RATT.'* I was thinking RATTE. You know what, drop the E, let's just go with RATT. He's like *'yeah, let's do that.'*"

"What do you think of the recent stuff they did when the reformed?"

"They put out one album. It was not... They haven't done anything really. Two of them got caught raping. They went to jail for that. They did four and a half years... I heard one of them moved to Canada. Another moved to the East Coast. The other two, they got out of jail and we didn't hear about them."

"Do you plan to get back into a band?"

"Yeah I do. But I'm a little older right now. I have to realize that the people I'm playing with have the same motivation and drive that I have. 'Cause I can go in and play for any band. But I want to make sure that my time is valuable. It's quality, not quantity – anything that expands the mind. You've got to connect with the audience. Music is love, and love is life. You have to convey to them that you're doing what you need to do. That's as far as I go. What you're thinking, what you're feeling, what you're believing, those people see it going on. You know what I'm saying…"

THE ANTICHRIST AMONGST US

An Asian girl named Steve calls and invites me to a local punk show at Hot Monkey Love. I'm not sure if it's a date. I met this girl two weeks ago at a house party, and when she realized who I was, my reputation caused her to go into this weird, cold-sweat giggling panic. She kept saying *"No, no – that's him, that's HIM... That's BARTEK."*

She stripped down to her bra and underwear and hid in the bathroom refusing to come out and talk to me. Her friend crept inside to talk her down. 15 minutes later she'd emerged fully clothed and quickly evacuated without looking at me, just whizzing by. *Honestly, that usually doesn't happen...*

So this Steve character tells me to come but once I arrive, she locks eyes with me and it's like she's staring at Satan. She runs away again, and hides in the parking lot tailgate party. There are a lot of teenage kids, some skins, but mainly borderline *"day jobs"* crusties. The first two acts are alright, Minor Threat/Verbal Abuse territory.

The third band Jakked Rabbits are a marvel to be seen. The singer is like a 12 year old kid, barely 4 foot 5, and going completely berserk to raw hardcore. He's jumping on people and swinging around like a monkey, catapulting himself into the audience, slam dancing and egging on the pit, rolling around the floor screaming into the mic, ranting about doing drugs and killing cops. I've rarely witnessed another punk vocalist with that much rage and charisma. And once again, this kid is like 12. If the antichrist really is upon earth, his name is Simon Prescott...

"Tell me about the Jakked Rabbits." Simon Prescott: "We started it three years ago. Our first show I was 9." *"How old are you now?"* "I'm 12... When we started my brother was the bassist and my brother was the drummer. We had a different guitarist. So we got Joe now, and he comes every week Eastlink, which is pretty far." *"Are you in middle school right now? Do you freak the shit out of your classmates?"* "No, they don't take it as that big of a deal. I'm in 7th grade. They say *'why you dressed like that?'* They're all gangstas, you know? They aren't punks. There are only 2 or 3 that actually listen to the same music as me. My favorite bands are Social Distortion and Stiff Little Fingers. I always liked Reagan Youth, some of the faster stuff."

"Tell me about the San Diego music scene." "Around here there's not many punk bands. All the good ones are either dead or they're dying." *"What's the general reaction to your live show?"*

"Most people are scared, like freaked out. I may not be scary but I scream scary."

"What are your songs about?" "We write songs about cops. We hate them so much. One song is about when we were shooting fireworks all over, and then the cops came, and they arrested my dad. So I wrote a song about that." *"Do the cops fuck with you guys a lot?"* "Yeah. One time we played a house party and they totally shut us down. They demanded to talk to someone from the band, and they sent me out, and the cops started yelling that we were lying..."

THE LOS ANGELES MURDERFEST

HOLLYWOOD, Saturday, March 24th: The heralded LA Muderfest, thrown by promoter Dan Dismal, vocalist of noted death metal act Crematorium. Two days, two stages, 50 bands at The Knitting Factory – many of whom are legendary in their own right, performing one after another in endless procession.

From the outset this gathering was legendary, a Ricola horn-blow to disturb the slumber of our brethren far and wide. Hardly was a message board left untouched, rarely was an invitation left unsent – and you can see it too, in the enthused restlessness of the crowd now wrapping itself around the staircase like a Boa Constrictor.

This is one of the best lineups I've ever seen – Repulsion, Brutal Truth, Pig Destroyer, Dekapitator, The Accused, Cretin, Waco Jesus, Abysmal Dawn, Atheist, Obituary, Genghis Tron, Coffin Texts, Kylesa, Kill The Client, Sepsism, Lair of the Minotaur, Dr. KNOW, Bad Acid Trip, 7,000 Dying Rats, Anal Cunt...

**From the chicken scrawl annotations of Dr. Bartek – <u>Leftum Ascentus</u>: *Crazed death metal replete with a monstrous vocalist reminiscent of Glen Benton, gurgling doom from bottom-throat cavalcades...* <u>Winterthrall</u>: A landslide of black/death razor slashing, take Behemoth and The Mandrake, mix them in a blah-blah whirlwind of blah-blah, etc... <u>Genghis Tron</u>: *The real highlight of electro-grind 8-Bit NES. Never have I seen a keyboardist thrash around so spasmodically, a Tasmanian Devil of blonde hair...* <u>Coffin Texts</u>: Unstoppable assault of DM – bones snapping, eardrums rattling... Drummer so red-faced/jiggly he looked as a 10 minute microwave kielbasa... <u>Kylesa</u>: *Two live drummers with war-ship sized kits, busting out tribal patterns alongside the doomy, rock-infused, aggro-*

whateverthefuck... <u>Lair Of The Minotaur</u>: Chicago doom/death juggernauts pulverize with gruff, throaty choppers – power untarnished.... <u>*Dekapitator*</u>: *Bay Area Thrash lives on... 100 screaming thrashers in denim... Booze-fueled circle pit the likes of a whirling dervish...* <u>Sepsism</u>: Bruuuutal SoCal DM calling to mind *Tomb Of The Mutilated* era Corpse... Guttural pathways to putrid futurism... <u>*Abysmal Dawn*</u>: *Ultra tight death/black combo, sharp as hell, ultra-technical...* <u>Repulsion</u>: Round 3 for me, having seen their reunion at the 2003 Milwaukee Metalfest, as well as their hometown reunion in Flint (2004). This juggernaut performance far surpassed all before... *"We made this record 'Horrified' before many of you were born! We have one album, and we're still touring!"* Repulsion keeps at us, on an on like Nixon pounding Cambodia...

GENGHIS TRON

Back in line, back in sight – somewhere backstage in these halls, musicians unidentifiable save for perhaps self-promoting apparel. Masses of them are rushing around, gripping cymbals and processors. Genghis Tron – the three-piece electro-grind wunderkinds – are carting equipment as the rest of the mob when I snag the attention of vocalist Mookie Singerman.

As the only renowned band of their ilk birthed of Poughkeepsie NY, naturally only so much could occur in that backwoods quadrant – even with the backing of Crucial Blast Records. There is nothing commercial about Genghis Tron in the slightest, yet the appeal is of massive consequence. The namesake is fitting – one can literally envision hordes of neo-barbarian cyber-warriors ransacking idle society. Take oodles of processors, FX loops, drum machines & keyboards, then layer them with intricate guitar work, monster chops and raging vitriol.

The result is something between Brutal Truth and punching random codes on an 8 bit Nintendo game genie to get whacked soundtrack scores from data confusion – like a discothèque Napalm Death of sorts, or an anti-scenester industrial core mutated with ides of Psyopus or Ed Gein. Still freshly transplanted to Philly, 2007 represents the healthy budding of their career. For their second tour ever, the LA Muderfest is easily the height of their road warrior accumulation...

Mookie Singerman: "I'm looking forward to seeing Atheist. We were on tour when they came to Philadelphia, and that was the only chance I ever had to see them."

"You're on tour right now?"

"Yeah. We were in Tijuana last night, tomorrow we're going to San Fran, then up to Canada…"

"I hear there's a legendary story where you ran over a jackrabbit, it got caught in your wheel, and the van flipped over and launched all of your gear across the desert…"

"It was our first tour ever. We had a ridiculous 13 hour drive through Texas into Phoenix, something like 600 miles. We decided to get a head start and were making good time. Three hours into it the driver was pretty tired, and when he saw the rabbit he swerved a little to try and avoid it, but lost control. We had no experience with a trailer before, so when it started to fishtail it flipped over. We didn't even avoid hitting the rabbit. It was toast too. Everybody lost on that one…"

"How is the live reaction? You're so bi-polar and spazzed out, do people not get it?"

"Yeah – I think especially in Tijuana it went over people's heads. I think our music covers so many bases there's something in there for most crowds. We were nervous about tonight because we've never really played any straight death metal fests. We thought they weren't going to get us, but I think we held our own."

"What's a crazy story that makes everyone thinks you're a pathological liar when you try and explain it?"

"Nothing supernatural yet. Just crazy motherfuckers attracted to us while we're on the road. Last week some really drunk guy made us hold a knife to his throat for a photo op. He was getting onstage every song and heckling the crowd. The other night in San Antonio we were hanging out at this house and another super-drunk dude had just gotten out of prison. He was a fan though, this proselytizing Christian metal dude. He was asking us what would happen if we slit his throat right now. Like, '*where would we go?*' He told us he'd be laughing when we were burning in hell, but that he really liked our music a lot…"

KYLESA

Adored by crusties, worshipped by the new strain of metal elite – and praised universally as a substantiate force in original composition – this Savannah Georgia quintet formed in early 2001. Kylesa have openly declared their intention of crumbling the flimsy barriers of communication between the various subcultures residing in heavy music. With two live drummers and a resoundingly deep tone, the feeling is ultimately tribal – a droning, cataclysmic rampage that gets to the beat of the pulse…

Pushing the bar to even further lengths, Kylesa also maintain a three-vocalist attack squad where male and female vox co-exist both pleasantly and viciously. All of this is stretched like epidermis above dirty, sludgy sections and punishing explosions of speed. At times vaguely thrash or black, the compositions always return to the primordial mucus of Kylesa – that there is no fixed formula, that all forms of this music are relative, and that there is no better a thesis to state this belief then a hard-rocking, highly detailed blur of all…

Laura Pleasants: *"I don't think there is one particular "message" we try to portray. We write lyrics that are personal and reflective and I think as far as albums go, they reflect our feelings and thoughts during a particular period in time. When we started Kylesa, our basic mission statement was to push the boundaries of heavy music while letting no genre limitation get in our way. I'm sure we would be way more successful if we stuck to something trendy or formulaic. I've seen many fads come and go, but in the long run, it's important to try to do your own thing."*

"Tell me all about Savannah, Georgia…"

"The scene in Savannah is very small but pretty close knit. Being an active band in a small town can have many advantages over a big city mainly due to your overhead cost. It's simply a lot easier to pull off. It used to be very cheap to live here but the city is vastly changing and it's costing more and more. Yet the local economy is stagnant. Savannah is becoming more of a resort town and a place for wealthy college students. So, the hourly wage does not reflect the rise in cost of living. Overall it's an easy place to live, especially since everyone knows everybody else and there's a strong sense of community… There is a very dark vibe to Savannah – I'd say it's similar to that of New Orleans, but not quite as dark. Racial tensions are high and the divisions of class are great. You either have a lot of money or none at all. Crime is very prevalent and there is a sense of suffocating entrapment. So it's pretty easy to write music of a dark and frustrated nature. For years we practiced in an old dilapidated office building probably built in the 60s. It was right across the street from a large housing project and next to the NAACP. The roof was leaking and caving in, there's no heat or air or bathroom. It'd be hot as hell in there in the summer, hot enough for anyone to get pissed. No one ever really messed with us though and we witnessed some crazy shit..."

"Has Kylesa generally been supported through multi-subcultural lines?

"It seems that more and more people are branching out and cross pollinating. We aren't a punk band or rock band or a metal band. We're kind of a combination of a lot of things while rooted mainly in the spirit of punk. It took many years for an overall acceptance to happen. At first the punks hated us because we were too weird or metal, and the mettalers thought we were too punk. There wasn't much of a rock scene at the time, but I guess the small stoner rock community accepted us to a certain degree. We've played all the underground scenes and generally adopted our fans from various niches. The kind of music we play is more accepted now and I see many bands playing in the same vein. That of course is a double edge sword, but I think it's nice that people can appreciate what we do."

"Do you think today's underground is far too cynical and fractured to ever get back to the point where the counterculture was in, say, San Fran 1969? I mean, what spark would be needed to really push it to that limit? Is the rock and roll revolution dead? Or is it just going to remain "tribal" and fractured with small tightly knit groups? And speaking of which, your sound has a very tribal kind of feel due to the percussion...

"Yes. Even if everyone in the underground united, I don't think it would ever go back to, say, the spirit of '69. The underground is incredibly divided and ephemeral. There are too many sub-categories and niches and too much emphasis on image. Very few bands strike me as pure or original. Most kids seem too concerned with how they look in the photo they just posted online or what new band to check out before they're told not to like that band anymore. I don't think the term 'revolution' holds much meaning to them, other than maybe a VH1 special. Rock music was still very new and fresh back then and many people thought it was a dangerous tool of rebellion. That obviously isn't the case now... I think things will have to get much worse in this country before they will get better. People are just too apathetic. I think once the vast majority can no longer put food on the table or go to the doctor, the spark will be ignited. Things are headed in that direction, so we'll see. Will music be a part of that? It certainly does make a good soundtrack..."

ATHEIST

The Murderfest marked the second live performance of Atheist in over 9 years, bested only by a European festival months earlier. In fact, it was the first West Coast show in 13 years – co-headlining with the newly resurrected Obituary no less.

On paper, it may only appear a frenetically solid bill. In reality the roots go deeper, as both Atheist and Obituary both came from the trenches of Tampa. Both were borne of nothing, played together in empty venues, and in a few years became pivotal forces in the genealogy of metal.

Atheist are considered not only one of the most important bands in the history of progressive death metal, but also essential in tracing the foundations of tech. One would think, perhaps, they also might also have created bread, fire, the wheel…

Originally formed as Oblivion in 1984, and then again in '85 as R.A.V.A.G.E. [Raging Atheists Vowing A Gory End], it wasn't until 1987 when the moniker Atheist was firmly established – as well as a growing cult fan base from DIY fanzines and tape trades, due to a handful of small-run DIY demos and EP's. Recording the landmark *Piece of Time* album in 1988, and going through various small label deals that went nowhere, it wasn't until 1990 when *Piece of Time* actually hit shelves – a six month disparity between the European market and the USA, where it was distributed by Metal Blade Records.

December 1990 saw the band going to Europe for the first time, Scandinavia to be exact, as they played three shows supporting Candlemass. This set the stage for the January '91 when the band opened again for Candlemass but on a 28 day North American jaunt. When the road had wrapped up and Atheist were driving back home through Louisiana, on February 12th 1991 a tragic car wreck claimed the life of bassist Roger Patterson Roger Lee Patterson, who was only 22.

Naturally aggrieved and considering an end to the band, a hearty jolt of life was brought into the Atheist circuit when Miami player Tony Choy [of the also highly-influential prog-metal act CYNIC] stepped up to the plate. Again recording at Morrisound Studios with Scott Burns [the godfather of death metal production], Atheist came back unbelievably with *Unquestionable Presence*. This record was so far ahead of its time, so passionate, that few could truly grasp its full aspects. Regardless, it has unanimously been hailed as one of the greatest death/prog albums of all time.

1992 began as a mind boggle. Tony Choy bailed after he was hired as live player for the Dutch band Pestilence on their tour with Death, leaving Atheist in a bad position, as they were on the verge of touring. They soon headed out for a second North American tour opening for Cannibal Corpse and Gorguts.

Atheist wound down by Spring '92, having only played a handful of local shows. They were supposed to tour Europe with Suffocation and Gorefest – dates were listed in major mags overseas – but for unclear reasons Suffocation & Gorefest hit the road without them. By July 1992 Atheist was no more.

Original member Kelly Shaefer concentrated on his new straight rock band Neurotica, the other members either went to work or college, but before long contractual obligations left Atheist in a forced position to write & record another album within 40 days. Somehow in the shuffle to throw it together Tony Choy returned, the drummer from River Phoenix's band Aleka's Attic joined Atheist, and the band ended up with 3 guitarists. *Elements* was issued by Metal Blade in the States, and on Music For Nations in Europe.

And during that first week of September 93, Atheist were touring Europe with Benediction and Cemetery. Only a few days after getting back to the States, the band played their last show ever – ironically, the *Elements* CD release party in St Petersburg. Days afterward Atheist collapsed over internal disputes, and longtime guitarist Randy Burkey was arrested over a felony charge which prevented him from leaving the country when they had a new Euro tour planned for November '93 with Wargasm & Aggressor. And that was the end of that – until right now, this very moment…

Kelly Shaefer: "We were happy to see Obituary again. We come from the same cloth, the Tampa metal scene. It was quite a treat to be able to share the stage as co-headliners after starting off together in front of nobody, ha ha…"

"What made you decide to reform after all this time?"

"It really sort of unraveled on it's own in a very honest manner. I started putting together the deal with Relapse to re-issue the records and after that we tested the waters of doing a few shows. The response was Wacken Open Air.

"So are you fellas purebred atheists? Are you perhaps agnostics now? How do you feel about the general aspects and threads of occultism in the extreme metal underground?"

"We all carry different beliefs, mine being showcased more because of my lyrics. I have always held firm on believing in no organized religion of any kind. I choose to worship the sun, for which we owe everything, and to my own hard work and ethics as a human. I accept responsibility for my actions and mistakes, rather than pawn them off on a tooth fairyesque-like symbolism..."

"You've met dozens of legends in the world of extreme underground metal. I was just wondering some crazy or funny stories you might have of random people..."

"Sure, many crazy times, but none less crazy then a huge street fight in Copenhagen, Denmark on my birthday in 1993 – between Benediction, Dismember, Grave, Morbid Angel, Cemetery and Atheist. Fucking chaos! I plan on writing a book myself...

"What is something remarkably bizarre that happened to you and every time you tell it people think you're a pathological liar?"

"When Atheist recorded 'Piece of Time,' we had a relationship with a spirit that we communicated with on an Ouija board, named HEST. Me and Steve Flynn had barely a finger on this thing. He would communicate with us about all kinds of things for many months. It was incredible, and very real. He was with us in the studio... It was crazy, but he drew pictures with a dry erase marker..."

"Will Atheist be recording a new studio album in the future, or are you letting the legacy remain as it is? Outside this band, do any of you have any side-projects you're working on?" "We all have tons of things but one of them is not fucking with the legacy of Atheist. It just would not be right to do that under the moniker. However, we do plan on recording together in some capacity very soon. It will be crazy, and very death metal. We wish to respect that Roger Patterson was a very important part of what was great about our band, and so it would just not be the same. I have just produced Steve Flynn's new band Gnostic's debut, and that is going to satisfy all of the Atheist fans I think 'cause it's total chaos – some of the best metal drumming ever recorded, and a great record top to bottom. The record will be coming out on Relapse in the latter part of '08. I have an acoustic duet with a female singer that should piss some people off. It's very much a departure for me, I dig it though. Also a new heavy rock project with some of Neurotica..."

"What do you think of Frank Zappa?"

"Genius – brilliant composer, musician, visionary. I am still angry that we lost him so early, of all the wasted space of this earth from people who deserve to not be here such as Fred Durst, and that little Disturbed dweep. Why are those people still breathing and Frank Zappa & Jeff Buckley are gone?

**From the chicken scrawl annotations of Dr. Bartek (*Round II*) – <u>Obscene Gesture</u>: Quick grind blasts and Anal Cunt infused retardation as this big black dude stumbled about screaming his face off, and the chick bassist obscured herself with a WWII gas-mask. *<u>Fetus Eaters</u>: Psychotic grind with a Frank Zappa grace. The vocalist keeps busting out kazoos, recorders (like the musical ones from elementary school) and an acid-jazz fueled saxophone.* <u>Kill The Client</u>: One of the best performances of the entire fest. Short little beer-bellied Texan vocalist thrashing around jumping into the crowd and screaming about the Illuminati. "*Don't let anyone tell ya how to be free!!*" They were total Pig Destroyer styled grind, and unbelievably fast at all angles... *<u>DR. KNOW</u>: Another legendary grind/hardcore assault that brought you right back to the old school days of LA hardcore...* <u>Bad Acid Trip</u>: The band most known for being on the label of System Of A Down's guitarist. Circus carnie grind, totally weird, Mike Patton-esque vocalist throwing himself around the stage animated as a coke-loaded Robin Williams stand-up taping from 1979. No one in the audience seemed to dig it except for me... *<u>Cretin</u>: One of the guys from Repulsion and the newbie band on Relapse. Another unstoppable grind explosion...* <u>7000 Dying Rats</u>: A shit-load of members in ski-masks belting it out like a secret SWAT society. Chicago's pride... *<u>Lack Of Interest</u>: Hard-hard-hard fuckin' core...* <u>Waco Jesus</u>: A band that I never gave a second thought to once again destroying everyone in the room. None of their recordings ever did them justice. These guys obliterated everything in their path... *<u>The Accused</u>: Old school splatter-core warriors, singer looking even more kielbasa-like than the drummer from Coffin Texts...* <u>Pig Destroyer</u>: Half new shit, half *Terrifyer* plus a blistering Dwarves cover. Live they didn't maintain the raw sound of their albums, but instead had a clunky, metallic crunch that kept having me think Skynet's army of exoskeleton death machines... *<u>Anal Cunt</u>: Seth back from his bad meltdown, gripping the microphone to keep in place, screaming his all. Once again, this is a live band, not a studio work. More badass than Samuel L Jackson's wallet in the end scene of Pulp Fiction...* <u>Brutal Truth</u>: The moment of glory & at the very top of their game. The grind masses swirled, the circle pit was vicious, the sweat poured from every orphus.

It was religious in the sense of a triple-live gonzo MANOWAR performance, all selections of the power ballad nature…

KILL THE CLIENT

Morgan: "Everything I write is political or social. It's the old saying – *'we can't change the future without looking at the past.'* The underpaid, the overworked, the jobless, the homeless – The Machine doesn't work without the middle class. If the middle class decided not to show up one day then the government would shut down. But just like you, if I don't show up to work I don't get paid. They've stuck us in a corner. Your dad, mom, grandmother, grandfather – they'll run you all into the ground because to them you're nothing but a machine. They don't give a fuck about your health, your social security. They want you to remain a gear in the machine. I write about breaking that gear, making that change. I love this country more than anything in this world. I believe in the constitution, our original rights and our original freedom. We don't hide that, we want to lay it down. I'm 35, I've seen a lot. I'm actually a Gulf War veteran."

"Where you from?"

"Dallas, Texas; where Kennedy got shot. He's the one who said in a speech, nationally, that big government was too big and we had no reason to be in Vietnam. Two weeks later he got shot. The last two records we put out we released on November 22nd [the anniversary of the assassination]. It's the most reasonable conspiracy that ever happened. The US government itself, the CIA, the mafia. Fidel Castro was CIA-backed. Kennedy hired the mafia to kill Castro because Castro defected. It's all connected and they're all dirty bastards. Kennedy was a dirty bastard too, but he was fighting for equal rights. I don't give a shit what color you are, what racial background, what sexual background. We're all people. If we can't work together to make things better than were all gonna end up fucking ourselves."

"What are some crazy show responses you've had?"

"The one I remember most is a VFW hall show. We were playing and this squatter punk pulled the American flag off the wall and spit on it. I whooped the fucking shit out of him. There's a huge difference between hating the system and hating the country. I will never hate this country. I'm a veteran of a foreign war, so is my father. My grandfather stormed Normandy and also fought the Battle of the Bulge. I believe that squatter stood for freedom, as do all of us, but don't disrespect that because you don't believe in the system. None of us believe in it because the fucking system has failed...."

PIG DESTROYER

Among my personal favorites in grind culprit warfare happens to be the quaintly titled Pig Destroyer, of Virginia origin. Savage and confrontational, this almighty titan of black ooze and crunching verbosity was formed in 1997 by vocalist J.R. Hayes and Scott Hull [of Agoraphobic Nosebleed fame]. Starting their catalogue with a split 7" alongside Orchid, and by '98 the *Explosions in Ward 6* LP, Pig Destroyer made an instant name for themselves via DIY tours up and down the East Coast.

By 2000 Relapse Records had signed the band and pressed another 7", this time with ISIS. Yet it wasn't until 2001's *Prowler In The Yard* when the group became a household name in the deepest of powerviolence circles. Headlining performances at the 2002 New England Metal and Hardcore Festival & 2002 Relapse Records CMJ Showcase, alongside a hi-profile set at the Relapse Records Contamination Festival in Philadelphia, sealed the deal at an international level.

A lengthy Japanese tour was soon to follow, alongside Napalm Death and Nasum. All of this swirled a volatile period of motion which ultimately culminating the heart-stopping *Terrifyer* album, which far and wide ranks as one of the best grind/death crossover albums of the decade. Then came the UK, SXSW, MacRock in Virginia, the Maryland Deathfest... It goes on and on my friends. Just know that they are here now, forever on the printed page before you, in a slice of time which precedes the release of *Phantom Limb*...

JR: "There's a song called 'Girl In The Slayer Jacket,' which is about this girl who listens to Slayer and hangs herself on a bridge. There's one called "The Machete Plan" which is about these twin sisters who... you know... kill people with machetes then take out a bunch of cops and shit. There's a couple that are more relationship based and a few that might even be considered political. I didn't write a concept or story because the songs feel more individualistic than the last two albums."

"The last album was centered around this kind of archetypical evil bitch from hell. I was curious about that in particular because every time I go through some horrible female burn I end up listening to it drunk and pissed and it totally suits the moment in time. Were

the lyrics on 'Terrifyer' based on someone in particular, or were they this kind of protean conglomeration of many, many bad relationships rolled into one specific symbol..."

"You know I don't really feel the anger in them. But it depends on who listens to it. I think it's important that the anger in anchored in real emotion, but I never try to write so close to the bone. To keep it artistic you have to fictionalize it to a certain extent. I always try to work from that premise and turn it into an interesting story that has emotion attached to it. I think I'd have to have someone else analyze it to say how much of it is actually me. And you're in a death metal band too, so you kind of got to play on the evil a little, you know?"

"On Terrifyer you have that really rough, raw processor on your vocals..."

"The vocals are definitely a little different. On *Terrifyer* there was a lot of me doubling the vocal tracks, even doing triples. There was a lot of distortion and a lot of stuff piled on top of other stuff and that's what gives it that real chaotic feel. The vocals aren't quite as layered, they're a little more stripped down and that makes them a little more aggressive. It sounds far more raw."

"Do you have any side projects you're working on?"

"I've been working on a novel. It's written but its all longhand and I'm typing and editing. I hate computers. It's a little bit of a love story, it's a little bit of a horror story. There's Bruce Willis style *Die Hard* action in it... It's going to be called *Dixie & The Dead Girls*."

"What's just a weird, fucked up story that happened to you and every time you tell people about it everyone looks at you like you're a pathological liar?"

"Well, I met Chuck Norris once. That was pretty cool... Actually I have a black belt in Tae Qwan Do. When I was younger I went with my instructor and we met Chuck Norris. When the picture was developed I had my eyes half closed with this stupid grin on my face. I was so fuckin' pissed (laughs). I mean how often do you get to meet Chuck Norris and here I am looking like a douche bag..."

7000 DYING RATS

Formed in Detroit in 1992, then quickly moving onto Chicago, 7000 Dying rats are perhaps the founders of "comedy grind," or as they so call it. Just fewer than 30 members have come and gone over the years, all who've stamped their faceless identities on the terrifying bursts of psychosis that has spread the Rats virus over endless comps & splits.

When 7000 Dying Rats perform live, expect multiple men in ski masks to perform fiendish actions – always ghastly, always delightful. They keep declaring they've broken up, but keep playing shows regardless. The men of following words are the sort of pilot/co-pilot duo of this collective…

Josh Diebel: "Well, I had a pretty great time. We didn't have any time to rehearse, so we had to rely strongly on alcohol and drugs. Repulsion destroyed all of the bands this weekend, seeing them was the biggest highlight. Another highlight was Kill the Client…"

"Tell me about the general message…"

JD: "We have no message at all. The records are compiled over stretches of time so there is no concept either. We will record stuff that makes us itchy… We are really influenced by our political leadership; they have set a great example for not just us as Americans, but mankind in general. Also by television, fast food and beautiful people…"

"What are some odd tour flashbacks you have?"

Toney Vast-Binder: "Naked foot races in Milwaukee, a bathroom in New Jersey covered in blood, pyrates in Reno, playing in gay bars in San Francisco AND Boston & never wanting to leave… Pissing off legions of serious-minded music fans everywhere…"

"What is something remarkably bizarre that happened to you and every time you tell someone they think you're a pathological liar?"

JD: "Once, in London, I met Amy Winehouse, she said I was 'a tubber'…"

TVB: "Once, in Los Angeles, I met Brent Spiner and we totally did it…"

"What are some bullshit mentalities in the underground you could do without?"

TVB: "People trying out-underground each other. Just because something is 'underground' doesn't mean it's good. Sometimes there are things are sucky and not many people know about it. That's OK by me…"

"When is going too far going too far?"

TVB: "Usually when people start to ask those kinds of questions, that's exactly when things start to get interesting…"

WACO JESUS

Coagulated in 1994 by the man of words below, Waco Jesus are among the epitome of over-the-top misogynistic death metal [a.k.a. "scumgrind shitrock"], despite having a large fan base of women. 1996 brought the gut-churning *The Destruction of Commercial Scum* on United Guttural Records.

Thus ushered in a long era of constant performance until guitarist Dave Kibler decided to leave, followed not long after by the overdose death of drummer Nick Null. Devastated, Waco Jesus nonetheless resuscitated for a follow up on Germany's Morbid Records and subsequent European/USA tours…"

Kevin Menssen: "Well, the show was great. However a few of us contracted crabs from a couple of dirty punk girls. Lesson learned – Murderfest 2008, we're coming with shaved scrotes. It was definitely amusing hangin' and jammin' with Pig Destroyer and Brutal Truth. Who knew that Dan Lilker is in fact just two midgets in a man suit?"

"Tell me about the general message of the band…"

"It's just booze induced misogyny. Our recordings generally emphasize the demoralization of women through venting fueled by alcohol. I don't really see any big changes in our "concept" happening while I'm still breathing…"

"Death metal is a genre that some feel is played out, or lacking in originality. What unique stamp do you try and put on your music to stand out from the general, endless crop of straight death metal bands?"

"When it all comes down to it, it's all rock n' roll. We don't take ourselves seriously and we're not out to break some new musical higher ground. We are the band that you just want to hang out with, get loaded with, and fuckin' rock with. We don't hide from the crowd and practice our chops forever before a show. We do beer bongs at our merch table with people who want to get sauced. "Diamond Dave Death Metal" – or: 'SHIT ROCK.'"

"What is the scene like in your hometown? What drawbacks/positives are prevalent that you think are unique to anywhere else?"

"All of us come from relatively small towns in central Illinois, so the extreme metal scene is rather limited. I guess the most redeeming element of living here is the sluts. They typically don't mind being choked out or spit on. I don't know, maybe I'm just good at finding the one's with low self esteem…"

"Give me a nightmare tour story or just something crazy that happened on the road?"

"We slept at this shit-hole squat house in Amsterdam. The mattresses were stained with everything a human and animal can extrude. We were served what had to be vomit soup. We were absolutely price gouged on what can only be described as "hoof meat." The squatters wanted to start a fight with our opening band, and when we finished they put on an anti-America propaganda film..."

"What are some bullshit mentalities in the underground you could do without?"

"The competition mentality. Bands that take themselves way too seriously. The losers that are only at shows to prove how tough they are. In America, too many meatheads just wanna fight over nothing. In Europe, I don't think I saw a single fight at a show ever that we were not directly involved with... Those were totally justified though..."

ANAL CUNT

Insolence is the name of the game for the Newton, Massachusetts bred Anal Cunt. AxCx (as often spelled) are perhaps the ultimate *"asshole band,"* a title admonished by progenitor Seth Putnam. Since the group's inception in 1988, Anal Cunt have been censored internationally. Most stores won't carry their material, and the few who do usually have fake album covers with the initials as "A.C."

Putnam chose the moniker *"to get the most offensive name possible"* and proceeded to create what he dubbed "blur-core" – basically an impromptu form of grind karaoke lacking any pre-written lyrics or songs, tracks lasting barely one minute at best. AxCx was meant only for one show and one demo, yet 19 years later they are still going. The point from the outset was to insult everyone within arms length, and create a raging stink.

Lyrical topics (*if there actually are lyrics*) usually include tongue-in-cheek rants of misogyny, homophobia, anti-Semitism, sexism, racism or the ridicule of cripples. Such hits include "You Were Pregnant So I Kicked You In The Stomach," "Homophobia Is Gay," "I Went Back In Time And Voted For Hitler," "I Got Athlete's Foot Showering At Mike's," "I Sent Concentration Camp Footage to America's Funniest Home Videos," "You Keep A Diary," and the horribly offensive "Women: Nature's Punching Bag." But again, I must stress they also cover stuff like "Hammer Time," "Stayin' Alive," and the theme from "Three's Company."

In 1988 Putnam recorded the aptly titled *47 Song Demo*, toured D.I.Y. on nothing, then came back to record the *88 Song EP* which caught the attention of a number of labels, including Earache Records. Putnam, holding nothing sacred, blew them all off repeatedly. By the time the *5643 Song EP* was completed, Earache was again denied and Anal Cunt somehow managed to tour Europe DIY.

By March '91 they'd dropped a half-dozen more splits & EP's, including the world's first acoustic noise-core record – the *Unplugged* EP. 1992 brought another Euro tour. With the drummer bailing at the last minute, they decided to proceed and find one *while on tour*. They auditioned two guys overseas who weren't fast enough – so Putnum had them both play the same drum kit at the same time.

Returning to the USA the band finally signed to Earache. *Everyone Should Be Killed* was released in '94 after various criminal arrests of Putnam physically attacking the audience. By '95 the first "real" album was pressed, featuring half noise/half real songs – the aptly titled *Top 40 Hits*. After varied European and USA tours – including a stint with guitarist Scott Hull of Pig Destroyer – Putnam was the last surviving member.

By '99 Anal Cunt recorded what would be their last album on Earache Records, *It Just Gets Worse*. This is the most offensive of the catalog and was surrounded by controversy, as the notorious label took it upon themselves to change song titles and lyrics. Thus led to the termination of mutual cooperation.

Anal Cunt continued with a new line-up and the *Defenders of the Hate* EP. In December 2001, Putnam sent a press release declaring the end of the band and by October 2004, Putnam went into a coma for nearly a month due to a combo overdose of alcohol, crack, heroin & sleeping pills. Doctors were sure he was an unsalvageable vegetable and were going to pull the plug until his mother intervened. Somehow coming out of it, Putnam was paralyzed with severe nerve damage, needing months of therapy.

The first show post-coma had Putnam remaining seated throughout. Still, after all that, he refuses to stop playing the ditty "You're in a Coma." So again, March 24, 2007 – one of the first A.C. gigs since, and Putnam was still able to push it through – albeit leaning on the mic stand like a cane, struggling physically. And still, nothing but behemoth rage in his voice…

Seth Putnam: "It was just another show with too many bands on it for me. I wasn't really interested in seeing anyone. The only band I was interested in seeing were The Accused. A band I used to be in played with them twice on their first tour in 1987, and I saw them a couple other times on that tour as well. They were one of my favorite bands at the time."

"You had quite a comeback recently after an ugly stretch. If I am correct, you were resuscitated back to life after flat-lining. Did you have any mystic visions connected to death? How did this experience affect your outlook on life?"

"No, I didn't see any 'light' or any other stupid shit people claim to have seen. I do remember three dreams that I had during the month that I was out though. In 1998 I was dead for 10 minutes from a heroin overdose. The EMT's used that stuff to revive people and it didn't work. They tried it a second time for the hell of it and it worked. All I remember was waking up in my kitchen having no idea where I was. On the way to the hospital, the EMT told me I was probably going to have brain damage the rest of my life. By the time I got to the hospital I was completely back to normal though. I didn't see any "mystic visions" or anything that time either. When I went into a coma in 2004, the doctors tried to pull the plug on me and tried to convince my mother that if I survived it I would be a useless vegetable my whole life. When I actually woke up from that I couldn't move any part of my body. It took eight months for me to be able to walk again. I had been depressed my whole life, and while I was out for the month, the doctors put me on Prozac. So when I woke up, unable to move, I just figured that I'd get better eventually, and didn't worry about it. I still haven't been depressed since then. So, to wrap up the whole experience, I feel it was worth it because I feel a lot better about things in general than I ever have in my life."

"How old were you when you first heard Napalm Death, or was that not a direct influence in the early years of the band? Is ANAL CUNT the primary influence of ANAL CUNT?"

"I heard Napalm Death when their first record came out in 1987. The sticker on the label said, 'The Worlds Fastest Band' or something like that. When I heard it, I didn't think it was that fast at all because I had been in bands faster than that. They had absolutely no influence on Anal Cunt. Anal Cunt's only influences were bands I had previously made up myself."

"You have hundreds of brilliant song titles. What are your personal favorites?"

"Off the top of my head – 'Ha Ha Halocaust,' 'I Sent a Thank You Card to the Guy Who Raped You,' 'Beating up Niggers That Sell Fake Crack,' and the original song title for this song that was changed by Earache to 'You Committed Suicide because Your Father Sucks' which was, 'Connor Clapton Committed Suicide because his Father Sucks.'"

"Give me a nightmare tour story or just something crazy that happened on the road…"

"Earache set us on tour with this shitty band, Murder One. It was their first tour and they were a bunch of complete hanks. They rented 2 vehicles, one for us, and one for them. We were fucking up every place we played, and I think they were afraid of us. While in Indiana Josh was drunk driving through a bunch of mailboxes on the side of the road, and one of them smashed the windshield. A cop pulled us over, gave Josh a breathalyzer test, which he failed, and just let us go anyway, as long as we were on foot. During the time we were gone, some do-gooder retard called the police and reported the car stolen. We went back the next day to get the car, and did a couple more shows, basically touring in a stolen car. We showed up at a friend's house in Cleveland who had this look on his face that he wasn't surprised at all that we showed up with the smashed windshield. So we ended up staying at his house that night doing a whole bunch of crack, coke, and heroin, like we had done the week earlier at his house. The next day we ditched the car behind a strip joint."

"How many times have you been arrested? What's the longest stretch you've ever served?"

"Between 8 and 10 times. The longest I was ever in jail was overnight."

"When is going too far going too far?"

"Never."

"Do you think punk is dead in terms of a "utopian" push for unity? Do you think all great movements from inside the movement will now only be based on the fanatic cult of personality? I know back in the 80's, early 90's there was more of an antagonism that existed between the punk and metal?"

"I never cared about unity – I was always into the more asshole or violent bands. The whole super left-wing thing a lot of bands, mostly punk/hardcore bands, are into – they are just as close-minded as the people they are against... The worst thing that ever happened to hardcore was when the S.O.D. album came out. It was basically a metal record with a skinhead singing. A lot of regular hardcore bands were getting more metal sounding, but the S.O.D. record made hardcore 'acceptable' to moron metal people, and introduced the gayest word ever – 'mosh,' to the undergrounds, and eventually mainstreams, vocabulary. I am so disgusted every time I hear the word 'mosh,' it seriously bothers me. In the mid-80s, dumb metal bands stopped writing stupid lyrics about Satan in exchange for stupid lyrics about society and shit like that. Getting back to your question, the barriers have broken down between the punk and metal sub-cultures. My worst memories of this was the 'overnight skinhead' thing that lots of metal kids did. Wow, asking this question has brought up so many bad memories that I had totally forgotten about from the mid-80s... Another totally gay thing is how bands like Hatebreed who play totally generic metal are considered hardcore. I'm glad I don't really pay attention to what's going on or I'd be even angrier..."

BRUTAL TRUTH

The name Brutal Truth is forever synonymous with the term grindcore. Outside of Napalm Death, perhaps no other band has left such wide-ranging influence on the genre. Putting even the most fervent tech metal bands to shame, Brutal Truth began in 1990 as the pet project of Danny Lilker, the guiding force of 80's thrash heavyweights Nuclear Assault.

Their milestone 1992 debut *Extreme Conditions Demand Extreme Responses* forged the blueprint for all grind to come, making international waves with their manic 3 second video Collateral Damage (*which somehow, beyond all reasoning, made rotation on MTV*). Throwing eardrum-splitting electrified power drills & jackhammers into the live set – as well as a host of mixed media appendages – a blazing trail of European/USA/Japanese tours soon followed. Solid bills, always, with the likes of Incantation, Pungent Stench, Boredoms, Pain Teens, Cathedral, Carcass, Fear Factory, & Napalm Death...

With the departure of drummer Scott Lewis, Philadelphia born Rich Hoak entered the fray in 1993. Brutal Truth then retreated to an isolated cabin in New Hampshire to complete their sophomore follow-up *Need To Control*. The musical boundaries were blurred once again, thus presenting a sonic kaleidoscope of death/grind, raw punk, and ambient/industrial. The second *Need To Control* was dropped, the boys were back in Europe with Pungent Stench & Macabre for a "69 shows in 75 days" unprecedented marathon.

All of this was followed by the subsequent releases of *Machine Parts*, *Kill Trend Suicide*, and 97's classic *Sounds of the Animal Kingdom* – as well as splits with Converge, Rupture, Violent Society and Spazz. So believe you me, when I firmly declare this reunion performance is easily the most anticipated show tonight worldwide – and that grown men have traveled thousands of miles to watch it go down – there are supreme reasons why...

"When you look back at your career, what one band would you say you got the most satisfaction from artistically? Does the Anthrax period rank high?"

Dan Lilker: "Well I only lasted with Anthrax 'til the release of the first album. I was asked to leave shortly before its release so I never toured with them, I only did local shows. Since I'm sure some people are curious, the first singer Neil disliked me for whatever reason which was why I was booted [legend has it that Lilker was 'too tall']. Although being a part of the birth of East Coast thrash metal was indeed very exciting, I actually spent a lot more time in Nuclear Assault during this period. N.A. was more of my vehicle to play thrash since we put out multiple albums and toured the world many times. But artistically? Brutal Truth for sure. I think we took grindcore and did something really unique and original with it while still satisfying the basic criteria for saying you play grind. I think out of all the bands I've been involved in, BT 'stepped out' the most."

"Ever actually listen to the M.O.D. stuff?"

"Not too frequently, I must admit. I realized after we put out that S.O.D. album in '85 that perhaps not everyone got our rather extreme tongue-in-cheek humor. I almost, but not quite regret how we phrased certain things. And then Billy kept going with it, which I'm not condemning. But it was already kind of old to me by then, meaning using brutal shock value."

"What's your favorite Nuclear Assault cover artwork? I've always been fond of 'Survive' as much as 'Game Over'"

"I actually like *Survive* the best too. It's not too overstated, it's easy to focus on, and it makes a cool tattoo..."

"That classic Brutal Truth tour with Carcass, Cathedral and Napalm Death. A lot of people go on record saying that was one of the greatest tour packages ever put together. Aside from actually

playing on it, just as a fan, was this your favorite traveling circus you'd ever performed on? And what were some of the strangest moments you randomly recall?"

"I would have much fonder memories if Brutal Truth and Cathedral hadn't had to cram into a passenger van! Nothing against Cathedral of course, we had a lot of laughs and all, but talk about extreme conditions! No trailer or nothing, everyone's personal shit and guitars, a soundman, all in a 12-seater for 7 weeks. But besides that, yeah, that was a fuckin' stormer for sure, and great for us especially 'cause that was actually before the release of our first record so it was a great way to expose ourselves to all the grind freaks. I do think it outranks the Pungent Stench/Brutal Truth/Macabre tour of Europe '94. Try all 3 bands on one bus for 8 weeks. Strangest moments were driving from Denver to Seattle with 2 days off to get there. Everyone tripped on acid except 2 people who drove so that was fairly interesting considering our traveling situation. I still remember the white-hot lights at the Flying J truck stop freaking me out, how they cast everything in this garish, harsh light, but I guess that was partly me peaking on blotter at the time."

"Are you a fan of professional wrestling?"

"Sorry to disappoint but I have no interest in it. I can see the humor and all, but the fact that most of the fans are meathead Neanderthals ruins it for me. It's up there with Nascar and monster truck shows for having inferior devotees."

"Will Brutal Truth be recording a new album here soon? What was the main reason you decided to regroup?"

"We plan on recording in the fall of 2008 once we're done writing. It should be kept in mind that we're more spread out geographically than we were back in the 90s so we can't just rehearse and write together whenever. The main reason we started back up was to help out Eye Hate God, who had endured hardships after Hurricane Katrina. I guess their rehearsal place got pretty swamped out. So we were asked to cover an EHG tune for a benefit comp that would help them out, and after all members were tracked down, we agreed. Gurn and Rich drove 7 hours each from opposite directions in the winter to come here to Rochester, NY, where my buddy Erik Burke let us use the jam room he used for his band SULACO to rehearse and record our version of "Sisterfucker" instrumentally. Once we learned the song, which was fairly easy, we smoked some more weed and, just for fun of course, decided to see if we could still play our own stuff."

"Do you have any nightmare tour stories for me? Crapping vans, police attacks, etc.?"

"When BT supported Pungent Stench in the States back in summer '94, we all had a little run-in with Nazi skinheads in Pennsauken, NJ, which is pretty much across the river from Philly. They were the only people there when we loaded in, they seemed nice at first but we knew something was weird when one of them went up to Martin the front man of Pungent and said: '*That's so cool you guys are from Austria! The home of Hitler!*' The doors were almost open and it was still 90% skinheads there. A tour meeting was quickly arranged outside the club and we decided to leave. The skinheads didn't take kindly to this and started bashing up our vans with baseball bats as we threw our shit inside and split. This incident explains what I said about Nazi skins in my part of the thank-you list on *Need To Control*, which says '*Nazi skinheads can and will fuck off.*'"

"How do you feel about this sort of trend that popped up where 14 year old kids are now basically dressing like you in particular in 1986 with the hi-tops and the frizzled hair and whatnot? Are you humbled or just sort of scratching your head? And of the thrash revival, have you been bowled over by any certain bands that have appeared in recent history?"

"I think it's great, it proves that thrash metal is a totally valid genre with longevity. It seems a lot of people these days are curious to see where a lot of modern bands took their cues from and are delving into all the 80s thrash records, and the 'fashion' is just a reflection of that. I don't get all uppity and go '*Hey man, you look like I did 20 years ago!*' Bands like Municipal Waste and Toxic Holocaust are certainly showing that you didn't have to be born in the 60's to make genuine thrash metal, which is great 'cause as I said above, it shows that thrash is legitimate and not just some trend. I'd be really surprised if people were praising Limp Bizkit in 10 years."

"Do you think today's underground is far too cynical and fractured to ever get back to the point where the counterculture was, in say, San Fran 1969? I mean, what spark would be needed to really push it to that limit? Obviously LSD ran its course, this generation is too apathetic about politics or even this war being fought... Is the rock and roll revolution dead? Or is it just going to remain 'tribal' and fractured with small tightly knit groups?"

"HA! After this fucking train wreck of an administration, you would have thought you'd be seeing a little more outspoken dissent from whatever you'd call the 'underground.' You know lots of punk and hardcore bands must have been railing at Bush and CO all this time, but that music doesn't have the same ability to reach people as the music of the hippies did. I guess I could say I'm guilty too in that I didn't go and form a band specifically created to opine on the disaster that is the Bush administration, but again, I think I'd just be preaching to the converted. Besides which, the closest I could get to writing music that the general public would find palatable would be "stoner rock", which would be fun to do, but I never had the time. We also have to remember that not having a draft during a war keeps a lot of people from caring at all. So, due in part to the apathy you mentioned, fueled by American Idol, Nascar and useless filth like Britney Spears, and combined with the fact that modern protest music usually takes the form of abrasive punk and not candy-coated mallrat crap like Blink 182, I'd have to sadly say that yes, for the most part the rock n' roll revolution is at least moribund if not actually dead. Let's dig up John Lennon. That would be metal…"

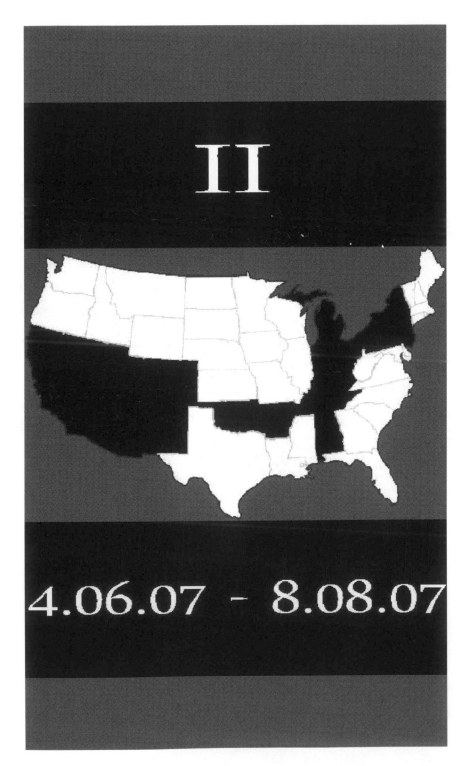

II

4.06.07 - 8.08.07

PART V: SAN FRAN
(OPEN ARMED CONCRETE JUNGLE)
APRIL 6TH-APRIL 12TH 2007

VAGUE PRECONCEPTIONS

Most, it is said, recoil in horror when they pass their 40th birthday. The mid-life crisis comes in many forms. I just passed 26 two days ago. Truth is I never thought I'd live this long. I pretty much banked on 25 and lived it accordingly. I know I'm getting old. Too many pinched nerves, too many bone splinters poking my tendons; lack of energy, brainpower, arthritis building – too many years of bad road.

But something momentous happened on my birthday that brought back energy sorely lacking. My ex-wife of sorts, she just named her first child after me. Born April 2nd, another demon Aries adopts the trademark. It reminds me that even though I'm in a bunker behind my own wall 99% of the time, there are those who think highly enough to name their children after me, or insist their kids to refer to me as "Uncle Bartek."

It rebirths an essential notion of why I'm doing this. I'm an Architect building a new world for my people. The steps may seem small and incoherent, but everything feeds the grand design. This is why there is no more room to play it safe. All the easy targets have been conquered – Southern California, Albuquerque, Denver. It's time to play hardball and San Fran is first on the list.

Unlike other locations, I do not have a solid contact that I know on a personal level. I only have two people I can count on, and probably only good for a day each. I have a full 6 days to kill, just me versus the street. At the finish line will be a white van ready to escort me through a swathe of unexplored territory.

I'd called an old pal from D Town to check some online tour dates, and in the process randomly scored my first spoken word tour. That character would be Neil Patterson Esquire IIIrd, vocalist/guitarist from cult goofball act Downtown Brown. About to launch their first full-scale USA tour, Downtown Brown were in desperate need of a driver/merch fool & I just happened to be randomly available: "*Just grab the microphone and pound them with mental artillery Bartek – leave no man standing.*"

Yet back to San Francisco. My contacts are a shadowy character named Raul from a grind/death hybrid called High Intensity Discharge. Last week he arranged my visit after a series of frantic calls in which he declared he was *"serious as a fucking heart attack"* and that he'd put me up for a week. He says he's been in the SF metal scene since the early 90's and knows everyone important – Impaled, Machine Head, James Murphy...

The other is an older lady named 'Black Metal Martha' who runs a metal zine and knows everyone in town. She'll be back 3 days after my arrival, because she's at the famed Inferno extreme metal fest in Norway. I also have dates with Jello Biafra's Alternative Tentacles World Headquarters, that label's first-ever black metal band Ludicra, an industrial act named Stormdrain, and death metal legends Severed Savior. Most importantly, I have an immediate rendezvous with DWARVES front man Blag Dahlia soon as I step off the greyhound...

8 hours north of Los Angeles the scenery has dropped from Desert wasteland into a slow turnover of luscious green pastures enclosed by mountains... *What I would assume to be Scotland. The surrounding lakes appear to be lochs; rural sheep farms & wooden post enclosures...* The sun is blotted out by low-coasting fog as we ascend in altitude... *Heavy fog decapitates freeway ...*

BAM. One slick turn and you're in San Francisco cruising down a high-rise freeway into the city. Art deco houses are a perfect grid on the side of the mountain, like green and red Monopoly pieces lined perfectly on Baltic Ave. or a Toho Film set Gojira would annihilate. They slop down the hills same as Mexico populism viewed from the San Antonio line.

The high-rise highway connects to a half dozen other aerial freeways which twist around the outskirts of San Fran. The city is a distant view; an air of New York can be felt. We're shot into a darkened tunnel with zooming fluorescent lights, then dumped into the massive Greyhound station on Market Street. There a hundreds rushing around this transport; outside I embrace the humidly cold chill.

Market Street appears Frisco's answer to Wall Street – the architecture is still the old SF you'll recognize in b/w photographs circa 1910. You can tell that the econo-friendly "yippy" movement is immersed in such preservation. SF won't let their heritage cripple to modernization.

Trolleys, busses, cabs, tens of thousands on the street exploding in Friday night rush hour. I need to get across town to Haight/Ashbury, because Blag Dahlia is only hanging around for an extra hour, tops, because he needs a rental car and to exit the state by 8pm.

It's a little after 6pm already, and the deal is that we are to meet for a quick 15 minutes at the most convenient of bars for him. I cautiously call and apologetically explain the situation. With this monotone, emotionless voice he kind of sounds like an operator doing tech support. He gives me concise directions to his house and lays out 5 intricate bus routes – the cost of transfers, street corners, numbers, the probability of variables...

30 minutes of curb before I catch the bus. Raul from High Intensity Discharge calls. I tell him I'll be in Hashbury and ready around 7:30ish, and to wait for my signal. He says to take my time and be ready to party. By Haight my head is spinning. There are hipsters, vegans & squatters everywhere, but I can't stall a minute to register. I have to run up and down 4 huge hills over five blocks to get to Blag's pad sweating, panting, tardy, and Raul ringing my phone off the hook with no ability to answer.

Quickly meditating to gain my composure, Blag opens the door. I almost didn't recognize him – just an older looking guy with graying hair & glasses in a black sweater, blue jeans and converse sneakers. He is tall and skinny, static and unphased like he smoked a bowl 2 hours beforehand and was working it off. I shake his hand and he leads me up a large flight of stairs. He kind of points around at everything – his book shelf, his cat, his computer. It is sparsely decorated with a couple posters, barely any furniture, a few boxes of vinyl. He's lived there over 15 years and it looks like he just moved in. We go over the usual formalities and asks if I need any coffee or to use the shower.

Everything maintains a punctual air until I instinctually start babbling about Alan Arkin and Groucho Marx. This gets everything on track as we head out to grub Arab cuisine. Blag stops to talk to an old black guy on the street corner and introduces me to rapper Sam Quen's father. The old fellow gives me that slick curling fingers handshake, and the punk icon and I wander off into a grey Friday seeking the nearest shwarmas...

BLAG THE RIPPER (DWARVES OVERLORD)

When you're strolling alongside a fellow that's so accomplished and still pushes on you no ego trip whatsoever, you know you're in the company of someone who deserves the respect they maintain. Originally formed as Suburban Nightmare in 1986 outside Chicago, THE DWARVES have steadily left their mark on the world of punk.

Known for the iconic imagery featuring scummy little people engaging in a plethora of non-Ann Landers appropriations, DWARVES are visually known for their two leading original members. Heroin-thin guitarist He Who Cannot Be Named has an over-riding penchant for Speedos, leather gauntlets, and luchadore wrestling masks. He's like a forked tongued, fire-breathing El Santo Villain.

Vocalist Blag The Ripper is an unmistakable mutant, standing 6 foot 5 with a menacing lurch and cocky hip-hop swagger as he spins the microphone like a medieval mace pouring sweat and blood all over the crowd. Other members go by pseudonyms such as Rec Tom, The Fresh Prince of Darkness, and XXXXX, who supposedly disappeared in Detroit while on tour in a massive, ungodly crack binge.

One is never certain the antics of these ghouls. In fact the entire punk world turned on them viciously when He Who Cannot Be Named faked his own death via international press statement in 1997, causing the band to be dropped from the famous "grunge" label Sub Pop. In response, DWARVES began their own label Greedy Worldwide.

Seven records in, many of which are hard-sought collector vinyl's, DWARVES have toured on both sides of the Atlantic AND Pacific. From the seminal hardcore album *Blood Guts & Pussy* to their latest genre-spanning opus *DWARVES Must Die*, their filthy legacy has left a mushroom-shaped imprint on the foreheads of their hapless fan base. Sleaze, dirge, nudity, insults, violence, hysteria – all in a nights performance, guaranteed..."

"Tell me about San Francisco."

Blag Dahlia: "Well right now you're in The Fillmore... I don't know, I call it The Fillmore. A lot of people call it the Western Addition. It's somewhere between a slum and a cool place. There's beautiful houses and Victorians. But people get shot periodically in front of their house."

"Is this what Seattle is kind of like?"

"Women aren't quite as ugly as Seattle. The farther north in California you get, the less attractive the women get."

"They have pimples running down their backs like the mane of a lion..."

"Exactly. You start down in San Diego and LA, the women are gorgeous. By the time you get to San Francisco, they're starting to slip heavily. By the time you get to Seattle, its bad. But I love it here, it's my neighborhood. People get shot here, but it's also a family environment. It's hard to explain."

"Tell me about The Dwarves."

"The Dwarves are rock legends – the undisputed, sonic champions."

"Has the 'Illuminati' took notice of The Dwarves?"

"(Laughs) I hope so."

"Where'd you come from originally?"

"Illinois, the suburbs of Chicago, a place called Highland Park. I moved here about twenty years ago. We played all our early shows at The Cubbie Bear, The Metro…"

"Oh yeah, The Metro. I went to Columbia College in Chicago for a bit…"

"Our old drummer went down there. I always considered myself Chicago originally. I think its good to come from the Midwest to figure out the world is not a glittering picnic like California appeared to be."

"This is my first real excursion in California. How'd you feel about Hollywood and seeing that for the first time? I felt like it was glamorous as I expected and just as empty but not as sleazy. I was a little disappointed."

"Wow, I guess it depends on where you went. If you're in West Hollywood on the strip there's lots of fake tits, people with money running around, but when you get east of Hollywood it's a little dodgy, you can get in some trouble down there for sure. LA is bigger with people firing guns."

"[Waitress hand us the menus which list huge prices] Oh wow…"

"(Chuckles) That'll give you some idea… that we built this city on rock and roll."

"What other cities have been built on rock and roll thanks to The Dwarves?"

"You know I think that we, in some small way, helped put Seattle up on the map. We were there before those people were, a lot of people thought we were from there, we were on Sub Pop long before."

"Did The Melvins like you?"

"We always had kind of a feud with The Melvins. But as the years go on those things are kind of wiped away. We're all friends now. We used to feud with a lot of bands, because that was the nature of The Dwarves."

"So did Good Charlotte really sleep on your couch at one point?"

"No. (Laughs) Good Charlotte never slept on my couch. I helped work on their big hit record. I threw some lyrics on it and I made some money or it. I'm not very proud. I think they suck. I think they're one of the worst bands ever. They didn't give me any credit. I think they knew that I didn't think very much of them."

"What about the Creed reference in that song?"

"Creed I never actually met. But they're just so loathsome. And I hate rock bands that push god. It's completely fucked. Its two separate things. Don't push your god in rock and roll. Like Great White. Their shows sucked so bad. And you know it's always the people running around talking about god that are the most hypocritical, cheap, lazy, fucked up, ignorant men. That's why they need god to convince everyone they're a nice person. They think they're actions don't bare them out."

"What do you think of Fidel Castro?"

"Wow. Castro? I thought that he did a pretty interesting thing when he first took over the country. The US government wasn't quite sure which way to go with him. He asked the large multi-national companies there to put a value on their company for tax purposes. Since they all put so many low values, much less then they were actually worth, they thought they'd pay lower taxes. Fidel turned around and asked 'are you sure?' They said yeah, and he paid them that in cash and said get out and nationalized their industries. I thought that was a good move."

"So when you walk the streets do people identify you or chase you?"

"You know it depends on the context. People are more likely to do that at a show. It's not like I get mobbed walking down the street. Occasionally people do, but I don't really care as long as its girls."

"The last time I interviewed you it was in Detroit in 2005, and you told me that the meaning and the message of The Dwarves was to snort a lot of cocaine and have sex with 14 year old girls. Does that still ring true?"

"(Busts out laughing) That sounds like something I'd say… I'll relay this story: I was watching television with a friend of mine, an older woman that has a kid that's 22 years old. And we were watching a show called *Are You As Smart As A 5th Grader*. I wasn't really paying attention and I looked up and I see this girl on there with glasses, she's cute, she looks like my type and I said 'wow, she's hot.' And my friends like 'she's in fifth grade!' That gives you some idea of how my brain works. But I don't act on those things. That wouldn't be fair."

"Yeah, it's great to be a dirty old man to some degree."

"They can't sue you for what you're thinking you know?"

"I was curious… Why can't HE be named?"

"That's a good question. Why can't HE be named? He's like an icon. To me HE represents what rock should be. He's a rock legend. We've been friends over 25 years."

"Did you ever meet GG Allin?"

"Yeah, GG stayed at that house you were just at."

"Did he smell as bad as they say?"

"He didn't smell very good."

"Are you a big Batman fan?"

"I just had this conversation the other day. I like the 60's fun Batman. The ZAP, BAM Batman. I hate the sad Batman. I like my Batman to do the Bat-too-see. I was always a bigger fan of Marvel than DC as a kid. I had every X-Men comic – Captain America, Daredevil…"

"Have you done any weird television appearances in Japan?"

"We only went to Japan once. We had such a great time. People there are so sweet. Everywhere you go they take you out to a big meal and after the show people hang out. It's much different. People don't really understand that a lot of countries, especially a lot of places in Europe – England excluded but everywhere else – people are very amiable in the way they treat you, especially with shows. In America people try to give you the worst foods they can, just whatever cheap crap they can toss on you. At night they just throw everybody out of after the show… There's a different vibe in other countries that makes it more fun to do. In America I'm basically out to get paid as much as I can because that's all you get out of it. There's no experience. The show itself is fun, you meet cool people. Sometimes you get to sleep with women, all those things are good."

"Do you own Greedy Worldwide [Dwarves Label]?"

"Yes, I'm the president and owner of Greedy."

"Do you use that as a pick up line at the bar?"

"You say 'Hey I *AM* Greedy.' Not that many people seem to know about Greedy, not that many people know about Blag, but a lot of people seem to know about The Dwarves. So I ride off that when I can. I'm pretty square looking these days. It's fun for me to be backstage somewhere and people kind of brush me aside or don't know what I'm about. When it comes up what band I'm in you get this kind of hushed silence. They know we've been around forever and they all claim to be punk bands but we're an actual punk band. It's that kind of thing you know. Sometimes I meet people that are real big fans that you wouldn't think would know about us. It's a real underground thing because we've never sold a lot of records, we've had a few big tours and done some big stuff but yet somehow it's come to be this important thing. It's a cult fan base. We had a lot of vinyl and record collectors catch up with it. A lot of people tend to ignore punk records because there's so many mediocre punk records. Years later it catches up."

"[The waitress hands us warm olive appetizers] These remind me of that scene in Funny Farm where Chevy Chase eats lamb testicles. You a Chevy fan?"

"Great in *Caddyshack. Fletch* was kind of ok. I'm not the hugest Chase fan."

"What are your favorite comedians?"

"Chris Rock to me is the funniest man in America. He's brilliant. I like Bill Maher a lot. He's not particularly funny in his stand-up, but he's great when ripping on political stuff. As a kid I loved Steve Martin on *Saturday Night Live*. The biggest thing was *Monty Pythons Flying Circus*. I saw them live when I was like 10 years old. I made my parents take me in New York. I love *Kids In The Hall*. I didn't think their movie was that great, but I thought their show was really good."

"Ever meet any of those guys?"

"No, I've never met any comics, but I've always been a big comic person."

"Got any good celebrity stories?"

"Well you were asking about GG Allin. I went and visited GG in a maximum security prison in Michigan. That was interesting. He like shaved patches in his head so he looked like he had AIDS. That was pretty amazing to see someone in that type of situation. Years later he came here and was supposed to play with us, but he was so sick from the show the night before – he cut himself with glass, spraying shit everywhere. He had blood poisoning because he was infected. He went to the hospital leaving his band at my house. I let them spend the night and the next day GG was still in the hospital. The band was like '*what are we gonna do now?*' Well you're gonna get the fuck out, cause you canceled a show with The Dwarves and that shit doesn't happen. I was like '*look, I told you I'd put you guys up, I paid you to do a show, you*

guys canceled. I know GG, I don't know you, get out.' And they were
kind of like the very weird… They reminded me of institutionally bisexual kind of weird guys…"

"Was the naked drummer with them?"

"Yeah. But he was the weirdest one. At one point he'd taken the
Lunachicks album cover and the guy was filming him masturbating
with the chair leg up his ass. It was one of the weirdest things I'd ever
seen."

**"On the new album you've got some silly rap songs. You ever
think of doing a straight hip-hop album for fun?"**

"I don't think I would. I don't think I'm qualified to do a whole
hip-hop album. The idea of *Dwarves Must Die* was to do an album with
every possible genre in it. My idea was to do a hip-hop track that had
live elements so it was bigger and heavier than most hip-hop acts, but
also talk about rock bands and how whack they were. Their whack-ass
managers, doing everything behind everybody's back. Fronting like
they're real bands but their producers are playing their instruments. In
rock and roll you got bands that can't play, they got signed when
they're 18 to some big major label cause they thing they're cute, and
they market it as if they're some real band. Then you read an interview
like they're real people. I've watched albums like that get made. Like
Good Charlotte. The other hip-hop song was 'I'm Demented.' The big
hip-hop thing that no one picked up on is that there were a lot of loops.
But we didn't loop James Brown or Ozzy records, we looped odd
garage songs that no one knew about. It's a very deep album though.
People only caught the surface of it."

"Who are the epitome of these horrid bands?"

"I try not to dwell on it. I'm not that interested in what's
happening in rock n' roll because so much of it sucks. The other funny
thing is sometimes you meet people from bands you hate that are really
whack and they'll love my stuff. It's not that I have to be nice to them.
I'm not really worried about my career, it's just if someone likes me
and likes my stuff and its influenced them, maybe there's something
I'm missing in their music, or I just don't want to be mean to them. I
think there's a bigger problem within the industry itself, it's so warped
in the way that people are rewarded. It forces bands into strange
situations and they never get the chance to play live and get better at
what they're doing. If you look back at The Beatles, obviously so many
years playing cover songs as teenagers made them really good. They
knew how to play and they knew how to write. Bands don't really go

through that process anymore. It's not that suddenly people aren't talented anymore. It's that big companies pick up people with no real ability and plug them into a producer and it makes for this great, uninteresting, homogenized rock scene. It also robs a lot of people their chance. If you have a pool of a million dollars and you spread it over 20 bands that's one thing. If you have a pool of a million dollars and you spend it all on one band then you can't really escape that you've closed off a part of the culture. You bet the whole farm on one set of people to try and make money. And generally those people tend to be the 'safe bets,' so they think. It's a self perpetuating thing where you get less and less variety, more and more concentration, more and more marketing. It makes for the scene we have today and you can't necessarily blame the bands that are in it, even if they are whack. 50, 60, 70 years ago they would have gone onstage and if they weren't good they would've been booed off and that would've been the end of it. Frank Sinatra isn't somebody that some guy at a record label thought would be a real big thing. He's a guy that sang with Tommy Dorsey for a couple of years and that makes you good."

"What do you think of Glenn Danzig?"

"Danzig is someone that I stole a lot from."

"Do you wear a skull buckle or jiggle your tits?"

"I didn't really steal his style stuff, and I'm a foot taller than him. But I stole actual parts of songs and plugged them into my songs. The Misfits were a big influence. Even the name 'He Who Cannot Be Named' was a Samhain song."

"What's the creepiest, most bizarre fan moment?"

"You get some people that really feel because they like you that you own them a lot. To me it's like 'nice to meet you' and that's about it. Some people are really insistent. First you get the weird guys that are like 'do you wanna fuck my girlfriend,' 'do you wanna shoot up with me' or 'punch me as hard as you can.' Then there's guys that want to get hit with the microphone. I remember meeting these guys from Idaho. My brother was at the show and they were just fascinated by the fact that I have a brother and that he looks like a regular adult man with kids. He's irregular in lots of ways, but some people are amazed that I'm a human being. I do kind of put myself above them because I do feel you kind of have to be elitist, otherwise you're sitting there living for somebody else. I don't want to sleep at every crash pad. I don't want to hang out, I don't want to have a conversation with every drunk guy in the middle of the night. I was never into drinking. I haven't had a drink in a year. So to sit there with drunk people in the middle of the night at their drunk house being drunk... They think they're real amusing and they're boring. And then you look real snotty or snooty, but shit dude, I'm just doing whatever I like. I don't owe you shit."

"This is my first time in Haight-Ashbury, I've never been here. I grew up reading a lot of the radical 60's counterculture books from Kesey, Leary, Hoffman. We're here in San Fran, the birthplace of it all. Is any of that still around? Are they totally underground? Are there the acid-headed bums who still think it's the 60's? What's the climate with this?"

"The Grateful Dead thing kind of morphed more into this tribal... It's very materialistic, more so than you would think. They're out there selling each other Tofu, tye-dye stuff, whatever it is they do. A lot of the punk rock foundations, the kind of communal things have largely disappeared. There's people that pay lip service to it. I was never on that end. I'm more of an elitist in that way. I don't wanna hang out with every hippie on the street. I believe in it somewhat politically, but that's as far as I go. I need democracy in my life. I don't owe everybody a night out on the town, I don't owe everybody a confrontation. But yeah, the hippie thing is largely dead. It's morphed into the new age movement. I think the difference is the New Age movement is about helping yourself and enriching yourself, thereby you make the world better. The hippie movement at least paid lip service to making the world better. People have largely given up on that. It's a super-narcissistic culture and people, the generation before mine, can't even imagine anything but a super-narcissistic culture because they've never experienced anything else."

"What's the Blag method of self-enrichment?"

"Sometimes I have spiritual experiences. I'm not a religious person but certain things make me feel that way. I don't have a program of meditation or any of those things. But having close friends that I've had my whole life, I think you're lucky if you can have people like that. A lot of people just glide through life looking after their own ass. They don't really know anybody, they're not close to anybody, and I feel sorry for them. But some people that's how they're approaching the world. You never really can judge other peoples things. Some people don't get close to people because maybe their in tune to the universe in ways that I'm not."

"You ever met Dick Dale?"

"Dick Dale, what a legend he is."

"He's still kicking too. I saw him in 2003, he was like 68 years old and summoning this music from another galaxy…"

"I remember going on Space Mountain and they were playing Dick Dale when you go through the tunnel there. To me that's an innovator. He threw Middle Eastern mode into rock music.

"How do you feel about Detroit?"

"I was never very partial to Detroit. I love a lot of the history of it, bands like Stooges and Motown stuff. I think their garage revival is pretty overblown. I think the White Stripes are ok. That guys a magnetic performer, he writes some good songs, but I don't really like anything that surrounds it. As far as that whole rock revival they were supposed to have, I was pretty under-whelmed by it. We never got much of a reception in Detroit. Nobody ever really gave a shit about The Dwarves there. You have to kind of come from the Midwest to get that whole 'blah' attitude. Blah blah job blah. I was never really impressed by the cities in the Midwest."

"Is Chicago your strong point?"

"To me the only Midwestern town is Chicago. You do OK here and there, you might have some fun in Cincinnati. We do great in some weird places like Columbus Ohio. I think college towns tend to have people more into music, whereas some off-brand city doesn't have a fuck of a lot. I think Detroit just suffered so much economically and is such a shell of a place. Especially though in the 80's and 90's – it was just a barren wasteland. There's nothing there. You couldn't find a 7-11 that was open past 8 o'clock."

"Tell me about your new projects."

"I'm not really working on a new Dwarves album now. Part of the idea of *Dwarves Must Die* was that we would die."

"So is that your final album?"

"I don't know. That's part of the fun of it. The Dwarves can die but still be alive. Its transcended life and death, so I can resurrect it if I feel like it. It's my party and I'll die if I want to. I thought that was an important album because it transcended every genre. All of the forces got together there with a great version of the band, but also to have a bunch of cool people that were in the band before play on it. I had an amazing producer who's real big-time and gets hundreds of thousands of dollars to do records and he does mine, which was very kind of him. There's guest stars on it – Dexter Holland, Sam Quen just cause he was on the street and I smoked a joint with him. It would be very difficult to make something like that again. I don't know if I'll do another Dwarves record. If I do I might make something more like *Blood, Guts, And Pussy* where it returns to the hardcore. I'm working on a bunch of tracks now that are more built up where I play acoustic guitar and sing funny songs. Whereas in The Dwarves I'd never talk to the audience or engage anybody. This thing is just the opposite, it's more of a comedy act. It's kind of solo live, because I find it's easier to do that way, more manageable. And it's hard to carry around a band on tour because there's a lot of shit involved in that. I've been developing this into an album. Some of it is 60's-ish and retro sounding, some of its 50's rockabilly, some of it is more mid-tempo rock. There's a lot of sides to it. I've gotten more into writing and put out a book called *Nina* which is about a really dirty 14 year old girl. I'm working on things that are more self-contained and you don't need to deal with a lot of people."

"Are you going to work on a Dwarves memoir?"

"I've thought about that and I've written some of that stuff down, but it's a ways away. You wait until you've done everything, and then you write the memoirs."

"So I talked to Pig Destroyer right before I came out here, and JR told me to tell you that your band rules…"

"I actually wrote them and told them that I was pissed because they covered a Dwarves song, which is fine, but they didn't credit us which happens sometimes. But in this case they also did a Helmet song, who I can't stand, and an Iggy Pop song, who I love, and they credited them. That pissed me off. It's like saying 'we wrote this song.'"

"Why do you hate Helmet?"

"I don't like math rock. I always thought bands like Helmet were really boring. I'm sure they're nice guys, but I have no interest in heavy metal music. Nirvana got huge and everyone was like 'Helmet's next.' Well Nirvana's catchy and fun to listen to."

"Ever met Kurt Cobain?"

"Yeah, I met him twice. One time he was passed out on dope with a bunch of people around him. The other time was at a show, and he and Chris Novaselic did the kind of 'we're not worthy' Wayne and Garth thing. Not in front of me but in front of my bass player because they really respected good bass players. I always thought they were great. I was a booster of them from very early on. I kind of predicted the ascendancy of a few bands. I didn't predict they'd get as huge as they did, but Nirvana and Green Day I called right off the bat."

"Never go into much metal then?"

"It never hit me. I'd much rather listen to an old musical like *Guys & Dolls* or *The Music Man* than listen to some asshole in spandex pants and his fucking pretentious shit. If you spent anytime around heavy metal bands, they're a fucking joke. They are so asinine and are so obsessed with the rock hierarchy of whose bigger, who gets the biggest dressing room, they just ruin everything with their bullshit. The jokes on them. They don't have any fun, they're so busy comparing their cock-sizes with each other that it holds no feeling. Having said that, I like a couple songs by Iron Maiden, I like a couple metal song by this band or that band. I think Slayers brilliant. Black Sabbath is amazing. I like some Metallica songs. There's stuff that I like, but the general genre is just unappealing to me. The music doesn't rock. Slayer to me rocks, its hardcore, I can feel where it's coming from. A lot of death metal, even though its kind of hard to listen to, at least it feels like it rocks. Metal, of the kind of Alice In Chains variety, or Henry Rollins, its just chukchuk-chuckchukchuk. If it doesn't rock, it's not rock. And they dress it up with big amplifiers."

"What about Manowar? Do they get away with it?"

"(Laughs) Manowar? I like the goof appeal of it. But when it comes to my ears it's easier for me to listen to Louis Allen. The memories just always angered me. It's like eating a bad meal. You have to eat, so I don't want to eat something bad."

"Who're the epitome of metal assholes?"

"Guns N Roses fully deserved the title of average ok band that made one kind of ok record. I'll give them that. But I've been watching those pricks get the spotlight since 1988 and the fact is they're boring. If you compare something like Guns N' Roses to Slayer, which came out about the same time, Slayer – whether you like it or not – was moving rock n' roll forward as far as going faster, doing stuff in a more brazen, over-the-top way. Guns N Roses dressed up like Aerosmith, played a bunch of sauce rock crap that was produced like bad 80's metal. It doesn't hold up. Look at The Ramones. They made a classic first album, the made five more great records in four years. Then look at Guns N Roses who work forever to make one ok record, and then five years later came out with Use Your Illusion, this double-album mediocre shit. They don't deserve jack shit. I think the reason why they're so synonymous with rock has to do with marketing. When I was a kid, The Monkees were on TV, they were playing with the Banana Splits, and I recognize it for what it is – marketing. That's what inspired me because A) it was forced down my throat so I like it and B) it had a fun, hippie, kid-like feel. Modern rock, it combines all the worst elements of that. It gets forced down your throat."

"What of the 'modern rock' arena?"

"The worst one of those bands is Staind. Here's a fat guy wearing a watch and crying about his mom and dad. He plays music that starts and stops in the most boring ways. It's this mediocre, whiny shit that's being mass marketed."

"Puddle of Creed, Korn Bizkit, Blink Charlotte..."

"Well Blink 182 is different. They're pop punk. If we're comparing it to the middle finger vibe of The Ramones or The Sex Pistols you have a far way to go. If you write a catchy song that I can remember, and you're not promoting yourself as some great thing, then fine, fair enough. But it's the pretension that kills me. You better do really good. If you fuck around with pretension, then give me something earth-shaking."

"What about Motorhead, do they get away with it?"

"I've always loved Motorhead. They were to me a rock band with no metal influence. But we went on tour with Motorhead and they were acting like total *Spinal Tap* heavy metal assholes and we called them on it. They threw us off the tour. I got up onstage during sound-check and said '*Get a fucking haircut, you look like Spinal Tap, you're a joke. You're paying strippers to hang out with you that I already fucked.*' They do all the heavy metal clichés. Lemmy can make twice as much money as he makes if he'd fire half of his 'yes men' and idiots. They're driving around trying to act like they're Ozzy. It's over. Why do you need a tech for everyone in your band? Why are you having your techs ordering opening bands around? Telling me to stand here, go there. I'm too old for that man. I've got nothing but respect for Lemmy. But you open for any band that you love, you take a big pay-cut. That's one of the dirty secrets of the music industry. I can make a few grand playing a headlining show. I get to go play with Lemmy, and I'm supposed to be happy that I'm standing next to him, I got next to no money and that's how it works. I'd be fine with that if they were cool. But if it's part of the deal, and I'm already taking a pay-cut, treat me with respect. You guys are legendary, you're Motorhead and I love you. Well we're legendary too. We've been around a long time too, we're important too. If I took a pay-cut to hang out with you, show me some fucking respect. Don't send your guitar tech to tell me what to do, don't tell me I have to pay to use the toilet backstage, don't fucking try to shush me off or blow me off. Because I will get right up in your face and tell you this is an American art form, you're a fucking English interloper, you can suck a dick. I don't care if I love your band. I didn't sign on to get ordered around by heavy metal assholes or punk rock assholes for that matter."

"What do you think are some bullshit attitudes in punk rock in general?"

"There's a lot of people who grew up in comfortable, suburban surrounding like I did, and then they try to act like they've paid some incredible dues. They want everybody else to play for free. People get mad at you because you're making some money. You have to explain to people this is my life and I'm doing it full time and I'm trying to do it really well. Just 'cause you're doing it on your semester off or you don't take it that seriously because you don't play that well, don't hate on me. There's a lot of that in punk rock."

"Did you get a lot of uniformed, old school guys pissed at your last album?"

"Absolutely. People would say we'd gone commercial, but we're combining elements from all genres, so it's even less commercial. You think the hip-hop guys want to wade through the punk songs? Forget it, they wouldn't buy it. The punk guys? They cry when they hear the gospel track. I'm a fucking musician. These guys don't make albums, they make wallpaper for their lifestyle. What they're saying is '*I like hardcore, I like to dress up, I like The Exploited, so that's the only music I'll ever play.*'"

"Did you cry when Rodney Dangerfield died?"

"(Laughs) I didn't cry, but I wasn't happy about it."

IT BEGINS

8pm, dark-blue before blackness. The interview was pretty much done in 15 minutes, and we'd hung around bullshitting for an hour & a half. Blag classily refused to let me pay for my meal, and we wandered jabbering about Slim Whitman & Mr. T...

Such a strange environment. Wherever I am, it's *organically* alive... *Those giant hills must wreak havoc on automatic transmissions*... My visual Frisco preconception of *Mrs. Doubtfire* and *Full House* was right on the money, although spliced with what I'd assume Seattle to look like...

At Blag's we pick up my stuff and though Raul keeps frantically calling me, Blag insists "*the grind band will still be there,*" taking time to show some memorabilia. He gives me a copy of his book

NINA for the road, and we exchange some other promo material before I walk off into uncertainty.

The Fillmore is quiet and dead, the streets are empty, the darkness enveloping. I make a quick call and Raul is spastic & grumbling because he's been driving around Haight/Ashbury for nearly 2 hours. I apologize even though I told him specifically to wait, and he agrees to pick me up immediately. Yet he has no idea where I am, and I am totally lost, having to run up and down multitudinous hills to realize I'm heading the wrong way. Then back down them, then up three more to a corner where I'm supposed to meet Raul. But now he is lost …

We collide and he's scrambled in frustration. I climb into this white minivan out of breath & aching from that huge duffel bag, and nothing hits off right. Raul's this short, heavily accented Mexican guy in his mid-30's with a slick leather coat and turtleneck. He's nasty drunk after killing a twelve pack, is incoherently spazzing, and looks like he's gonna explode. We swing by a convenience store and pick up 40's to kill the tension. We try to figure out somewhere to relax for the interview, and he suggests the beach. When we start driving he changes the locale to a friend's house, then to another's, and then...

Things are cooling down and he shoves a finely-rolled blunt in my mouth. Soon as the THC kicks in, the handful of Perkasets I gobbled on the bus swing back up, and I mention how neat it is that Fidel Castro has a street named after him. Raul immediately changes his mind and says he wants to do the interview tomorrow when he's sober. He has to work at 5am and asks where I need dropped off.

I, of course, have nowhere to go. I don't push any buttons on this one because he's begrudgingly helping me in a nervous good cop/bad cop fashion, like talking to himself and answering his own frustration. He realizes there is nowhere to put me and starts making phone calls, escorting me to dead apartments & studio spots.

I suggest Severed Savior. They are practicing at 10pm and they're space is not far from our current whereabouts. Raul knows exactly where to go, but their rehearsal room is in an abandoned factory section in the wasteland outskirts – bad neighborhood with no Bus system and three miles from any civilization, plus it's starting to rain.

Since Raul knows Severed Savior personally, I'm having him introduce me. It's my best shot against the cold. If there isn't any after party, I'll just gruel it out. Find some donut shop & rant at strays until 5am when I can legally sleep in a park.

We pull into this darkened death trap land with barb wire and chain link fences everywhere behind a semi-truck storage lot. It looks like a military barracks. Inside the compound is what one would expect –vast corridors of 25 rooms housing 30+ bands.

But it's Friday night and the place is silent. Not exactly a rarity, 'cause weekends are typically gigs and few ever practice at night. We hear some commotion in the room at the end of the corridor, guitars being tuned, a few double bass kicks. Raul walks me up and points ahead saying *there they are.* I clank the door and turn around to say something to Raul, but I realize he's bolted out the back door. Poof, vanished…

Guitarist Mike Gilbert leads me in. Bassist Murray Fitzpatrick and drummer Troy Fullerton are fairly laid back, having smoked a bowl. A few quick words then I step out to the hallway to make some calls. I can't get anyone from here on the horn, and the Detroit Refugees in San Fran are only loose acquaintances at best. Looks like I'll be sleeping on the torn up couch in the hallway & just hang around for Saturday afternoon, when 70% of bands practice…

SEVERED SAVIOR IS IRONICALLY MY SAVIOR

Midnight in San Fran, cruising the black highway towards San Jose. Only Severed Savior vocalist Dusty Boisjolie and myself, rumbling in his pickup truck, blazing towards a late-night after party. The practice was ear-shattering to say the least: *"Severed Savior was formed in '99, we recorded our first 5 song demo 'Puddle of Gore.' Shortly after the release of 'Forced To Bleed,' our second guitarist Rob Lumbre passed away on Jan, 5th 2002 due to a car accident shortly after joining. We were devastated."*

"We had Jared record the guitar parts for 'Brutality Is Law,' which was released on Unique Leader in 2003. It made us more noticeable in the U.S. and worldwide. After playing a ton of shows and establishing our sound, Unique Leader set up 'Bloodletting North America IV Tour,' and Severed Savior was asked to join the bill along with Spawn of Possession, Pyaemia, and Gorgasm. Later we toured with Black Dahlia Murder and Cannibal Corpse –'Tour of the Wretched' – but we had nothing. No van, no RV, so we put all of our money together and this lead us to an Airport shuttle bus in Arizona."

"Was it a real piece of shit?"

Dusty Boisjolie: "The bus was in pretty bad shape. We had to gut the inside, take all the little trinkets out, like a wheel chair lift that weighed a ton. We made it a comfortable living environment for 7 or more people. We built the whole thing... in about 2 and a half weeks. We were rushed, but we had bunks, a bathroom, storage for the equipment, and a pretty nice lounge setup in the front... The day before the last day of the tour we had two major blowouts and were stuck in Texas looking for tire shops. We get through a grueling day of being hung over and exhausted with sunstroke only to wake up to no brakes and us barreling down the road. The bus fills with smoke and we rush to get our shit out. The fire was too big and watched it burn away our hopes of playing the last show and getting home. Everything else was completely ruined from water damage as well. We had to cancel the last show and get a U-Haul to transport all of our equipment alongside a rental car to get us home."

"What was the fallout?"

"Shon left and we continued as a four piece. We found a guitar player from Pennsylvania named Joe Kort. We did two mini tours – one with Decrepit Birth and one with Vile. We're currently recording our new album "Servile Insurrection" for Unique Leader Records. It will hopefully be out before 2008."

"Tell me all about the scene in Frisco."

"It really varies from show to show. One night there will be a small show with a huge turnout and then the next night there's a huge show with a small turnout, or visa/versa. Overall it's a great place to establish your name and the same can be said to all the bands that come out of not just San Fran, but California in general."

"What's the best tour you've done?"

"By far Cannibal Corpse. I don't want to say boosted our ego's or anything, but it made us feel more wanted. It gave us a more professional look as compared to the Bloodletting 4 tour."

"How does the album differ from past works?"

"In the beginning we were all dead set on one style which was to try to make the music as brutal as we possibly could. It to be a crunchy, grindy, raw sort of feeling while still very intricate and technical. I think the overall approach of the new stuff is a lot more presentable to someone that hasn't necessarily ever heard death metal before. The lyrics aren't as gory and satanic as they once were. I want to break out of that realm and write songs with more meaning, comparing it to our everyday lives and the stuff that people deal with day to day. As for the actual music we don't stay inside the box as much as we did and try a lot of stuff we probably wouldn't have done before.

More clean guitar breaks and drum dynamics, as well as making our own bass lines more than just following what the other person is playing. I think steps up our sound and approach."

"The Church of Satan is in San Fran. Ever actually go to one of their sermons for the hell of it? Or is the C.O.S. the laughing stock of the scene?"

"I personally haven't been to the C.O.S. A lot of people ask that question, but to tell you the truth, being in a band and having to work every day takes up enough of my time. But I have been curious as to go one day just to check it out. I wouldn't say it's the laughing stock of anything; they have some very strong beliefs and opinions that I think everyone, as arrogant as we are, can agree with."

"Are there still tons of old hippies wandering the streets like acid-freak bums that still think it's 1969?"

"I wouldn't say that there are tons of them, but occasionally you'll have a run in with some kind of crazy human. There's a homeless guy that scares people while hiding behind a bush. It's pretty hilarious but at the same time sad to see that people actually want to live that way. San Francisco is kind of a magnet for bizarre, unusual shit which keeps it exciting and you on your feet."

"What do you think are the best bands in the SF scene?"

"There are so many... Possessed, Exodus, Metallica, Testament, Sadus, Primus, Neurosis, Exhumed, Impaled, Odious Mortem, Decrepit Birth, Vile, Thanatopsis, Animosity, All Shall Perish, Brain Drill, Osmium, Motherfuckin' Ragweed, Sons of Chaos, Poverty, Insanity, Ludicra..."

"Any musical side-projects going on?"

"I recently did some backing vocals on the new Spawn of Possession but that's about it. Mike played guitar and did vocals on a Vulgar Pigeon album, Troy did drums for Carnivorous. Murray toured Europe with Gorgasm."

"What is the core message of the band itself?"

"The main message is in the name of the band itself. It pretty much says it all, you can just think of it in different aspects. What I see when I hear the name Severed Savior, I see it more as a cutting off of religion in a whole and not letting it become a your life. You can look at it another way which is a little more stereotypical and that is Jesus' head getting decapitated or being completely chopped in half, like in the song 'Puddle of Gore...'

Dusty's house is a split two-level with drunken metal guys drinking 40's on the porch. Inside there is a Pink Floyd banner hoisted on the wall, a nicely furnished living arrangement, and a well-to-do selection of hard liquor. We tap into the Citron and the atmosphere continues, ten alcoholics colliding arguments. Dusty leads me outside. He chuckles and points towards the roof: "*You see that? That's where the macabre pigeon house was.*"

"*I cleaned that shit out a few months ago and discovered this bird nest of death. The mama pigeon got in there somehow and laid eggs, but there was no way to get out. So these baby pigeons cannibalized her. The nest was made of bones and decomposing feathers. It was fucking Texas Chainsaw Massacre dude, fucking blood splattered everywhere and shit.*"

We get on the subject of Robert Deathrage from The Meatshits and Dusty relates a bizarre tale of a show that Deathrage threw: "*We played in Ceres, CA, this town near Modesto, and a super-fan rushes up to us as we're pulling into the place. He's going on and on about how he doesn't have any money but really wants a shirt. He's going on about how he will let me watch his friend punch him in the face or eat a piece of dog shit, or anything, while I declined every offer.*"

"*Out of nowhere this guy gets this bright idea – like a frikkin' light bulb appeared over his head – to jump in the Port-O-Potty. He didn't even tell me what he was going to do then BOOM! All I hear is a splash and this bluish, glossy, Papa Smurf figure comes running toward me with his hands raised to the sky, screaming bloody murder. I say Papa Smurf because he had chunks of toilet paper on his head, everywhere, and he was completely blue. Chunks all over his head, ears, mouth – I mean everywhere. He must have jumped in head first to about his waist…*"

"***So did you give him the t-shirt?***"

"*Yes, but I made him stay five feet from the merch booth. He was in the pit the whole time, rubbing up against people that were totally oblivious. I dedicated 'Fecalpheliac' to him…*"

HASHBURY

Saturday morning, April 7th. I wake up covered in pillows and cat hair. The house is empty, the golden sun is pouring in, and Raul has left 7 messages on my phone. I take a drag from the half-smoked water bong, cough my lungs out, and delve into Raul.

He starts pro, but as the messages keep coming with 30 minute intervals, he keeps getting more frantic, apologizing relentlessly, until the last message where he says he's booked us dinner at an upscale restaurant and he will be paying for everything, including a taxi to pick me up wherever I might be.

By the time I'm showered and ready, Dusty says he has work to accomplish, and offers a ride back into town. But first he rolls a blunt and hands me this gigantic Christmas tree of a bud as a souvenir. I buy him breakfast en route and we rummage through my list of SF bands. He doesn't know many of them but gives me Ross Sewage's number from Impaled 'cause he's *"one of the coolest guys in Oakland."*

I finally call back Raul who is still freaking out trying to appease me. We make arrangements to meet later tonight and Dusty just looks at me like I need my head checked. By the time we reach Haight/Ashbury, we are cotton-mouthed beyond repair, and I tell him that *"Severed Savior is ironically my savior."*

I'm in the parking lot of a McDonalds across the street from Golden Gate Park. It's nice outside, about 60 degrees, and there is plenty of commotion going down on the strip. There are young kids everywhere – squatters, travelers, ravers, juggalos, punks, metalheads, hippies…

My backpack is stuffed to 40 pounds, and my duffel bag is 70 lbs of A.K.A. MABUS samplers, DVD promo cases, clothing, tapes, and recording equipment. Unless the situation changes, I'll be lugging this shit all over the city until the time runs out. I have exactly six more days to kill before Downtown Brown comes through on tour and picks me up, and I only have a $100 budget for the week.

Not knowing where to go, not sure of any direct step, I decide it is time to go into "Final Fantasy Mode." This is accomplished as such: When you delve into RPG video games, you control a character in a virtual world that has a multitude of avenues to explore. Depending on who you talk to, where you travel, the game will adjust itself to your actions. Basically, you walk up to someone in a video game town, hit the talk button, then you get four sentences you can blurt. Depending on what you choose to ask it will unlock new characters, plotline objectives, weapons, spells…

The most intelligent thing to do in this situation is go directly into the main artery of Haight/Ashbury. This has been a longstanding interest of mine, to see the birthplace of the acid wave and trace its sociological origins. The mood is pleasant, there is no aggression. It is a freakish Babylon of head shops, bead stores, coffee joints, vegan platters, memorabilia & comic havens. Every conceivable subculture is represented, and for once, the freaks outnumber the squares.

It's a last refuge with a hardcore commercialism that has yet to fully seal its slimy tentacles of doom around a perfected sense of hope and fertility. Bitch as they may – the underground spirit here is still live and well. Such doomsayers have never seen a place as deceptively foul as Cuba, Missouri...

My first contact point with the natives is spotted. There's a college kid weekend squatter on the pavement with a cardboard sign that reads "NEED MONEY FOR WEED." His name is Billy, and it's his first excursion in San Fran as well. He just dropped down from the Portland area to wander aimlessly, and he's got an eye seeking LSD. We decide to combine panhandling forces and end up with $3. When I proclaim my ignorance to the true meaning of Golden Gate, Billy cracks a deranged smile...

GG PARK

When you approach Golden Gate there is a fountain in the middle of a circular pathway with a dozen drug dealers, hippies & pyrate punks with face tattoos. The pathway beyond leads to two massive open fields and the notorious "hippy hill," all surrounded by man made woodland trails where every tree is of a different imported species.

You can hear a few loonies cackle in the distance, their laugh waves bouncing off the clutter of dead bark and leaves. These nature-walk paths have been used for shroom & acid freak-outs since the heady days of 1963, and they've a mystical, enchanted drift calling you in. You can preternaturally sense the millions of brain orgasms that've occurred there over the past 40 years.

The tunnel leading into the park is like a graffiti-caked caveman dwelling, with fake stalactites dripping from the ceiling and filthy brownish-cement walls. Squatter punks are passed out in sleeping bags along its stretch. You peer through its gated opening into the actual park, and disc golf seems the immediate past time.

Golden Gate is essentially the equivalent of a Native American Reservation for freaks. Cops don't go in, except for undercover NARC's looking to squash meth/heroin dealers. The city has given this plot of land to the weird, and it's legal to run around completely naked on acid – so long as you're not smashing glass bottles or drinking booze on the sidewalk. Everyone sits on the hill from 8am until 10pm when it closes – drinking, smoking herb, tripping, debating philosophy.

Billy and I stop before the Neanderthal tunnel to take a rest and smoke ganja. This homeless man pushing a shopping cart full of cans stumbles up, talking in a high-pitched atrocious voice that mirrors a whiny David Spade. I've seen this guy before though, like an old school Grateful Dead roadie in music documentaries.

I try to interview him but he's drunk, and all he keeps repeating is his name Betty like *"Bet-eee-eee-eee-eeeeee."* He is a pathetic old man about to curl over and die. He keeps dropping the bowl and spilling the weed, leading me in a disjointed circle about hanging with Leary in '71 at a comedy gig in Berkeley.

Billy snags my arm and leads me to the first half of the park. Once we pass the clearing and enter the main nerve, there are about 200 people having a blast on hippy hill. Everyone is playing Frisbee, participating in hookahville circles – BBQ grills, miniature bonfires, a giant drum circle and hundreds stretched out on blankets with water coolers & beer cases.

Billy and I stroll up examining the miniature tribes. I hawk-eye a rag-tag gathering you can tell are the freaks that hate all the other freaks, and they're eyeballing me like a newbie to a prison yard. One of them is this huge, scary looking crustie guy that's half Mexican/half Native American. He has thick sunglasses to where you can't glimpse his eyes, a Brujeria t-shirt, and a studded, patch-laden vest with a humongous Mentors back-patch. And this is how I met Ulysses...

THE SCUMFUCKS
Named after the ancient Greek warrior, Ulysses is a 6 foot 5 beast in his early 30's. He is the crust equivalent of Oscar Zeta Acosta – same black mustache, the same whigged-out demeanor, although more child-like zany then menacing, despite his monster tattoo reading SCUMFUCK. A 3 minute chat about band patches leads into a two-hour conversation on Bathory, Meatmen, Dystopia...

Ulysses is a living encyclopedia of extreme metal & punk that's been living in this park for the past 3 years. He's a long-time, hard-boiled traveler/panhandler, and has been cooling it in San Fran ever since getting released from prison in Atlanta. He did nearly 4 years with no conviction from a supposed hate crime.

He was chilling in a Georgia park when a white girl and her boyfriend were getting jumped by ten hardcore g-thugs. When one of the gang-bangers lunged at the girl, Ulysses ran over, threw him to the ground, and popped him in the head with his shin. Drunk and pissed, he let the "N" word slip and was arrested before the fight grew any more intense.

The girl never showed up to back him in court, the gang-bangers walked, and Ulysses was left to rot for 3 years without any trial. When the case finally went before a jury, his family picked up a lawyer with a $100,000 retainer. The case was dismissed and Ulysses was free to hit the road. A scattershot across America, and here he is.

His girlfriend's name is Gina Chaos. She's a 20 year old Native American and has grown up in San Fran, roaming this park since she was a kid. She is very warm and friendly, jolly and laughing while passing the pipe, but she keeps flying off the handle and screaming angry shit at the tye-died hippies at the bottom of the hill.

Things take a turn when I reveal the mission of my book. I plop out a copy of Metal Maniacs and pass around my top ten of 2007 list, which I've been carrying around as collateral to prove I'm the real deal. Ulysses freaks out because he's been a regular reader since he was a kid. A quick mention of GG Allin and everything comes into place. For crusties, Golden Gate is known worldwide as "GG Park."

It's an intercontinental port for crusts because of its countercultural neutral zone nature. This place is crawling with a roaming army of barkled street punks. It's kind of like *The Warriors*, but less dystopian. There are two main parties – The Scumfucks and The Numbskulls. Then there are splinter groups of face-tattooed pyrate punks and other non-aligned cliques that congregate in certain areas. Golden Gate is open territory for all, but The Scumfucks own Panhandle Hill. The Numbskulls panhandle the business district. They respect one another and are generally intertwined, 'though occasional fights do break out.

The Scumfucks represent the sort of Tyler Durden view of strength in rock bottom self-destruction and the total rejection of all materialism. They are also relentless alcoholics, and heroin/meth courses through that world like the blood rush of Viagra. It is a world of extremity in which you can never go back. I mean, for fucks sake, they worship GG Allin – that's the vital underpinning. They are like a family without a Manson.

Ulysses carries on stories of life in Frisco: *"I'm a writer man. I got some shit called 'The Huly Chronicles.' He's this guy, he killed everyone on the planet and left. He killed his whole race off to come here and just hang out with the human race. And he came to earth, and he's walking around, just hanging out, and checking out the scene. His adventures go on and on and on. He got beat up, he beat shit up, he got all this shit going on. This character, he goes off and steals all the beer and is not allowed on Haight Street. He's reduced to just buying beer from France…"*

"…we chased Jello [Biafra] down the street, we chased Paully Shore. The real anarchists, the real people, the real chaos and shit – they hate him because he's so PC. Robin Williams lives here, Danny Glover lives down the street. The longer you stay here, eventually you get noticed. I stayed away for 5 years. I came back and 'hey you're Ulysses.' It's such a welcoming party, it's laid back. It's so cool when you're here… All you gotta do is go to the library, go to the college and they'll tell you all the places that are condemned where you can squat…"

"El Duce, I met that man in Hollywood. He took me to this record shop and they had all his music, they had his picture on the wall. I thought he was talking out of his ass, but it was true. I hung out with him for like two months straight dude. He said he had Rob Halford's left boot. He had two boots. One was a metal steel toe boot with a metal shin guard. The other was the singers' from Iron Maiden. He stole their shit. He told me personally that he taught GG Allin everything he knew about toilet rock. He taught GG everything he knew, he was like the king of Hollywood…"

An hour later Gina Chaos, Ulysses and I are at Panhandle Hill, a small park further down Haight. We're totally fried and I'm wobbling from the Mickey's & Perkaset platter; we're passing 40's with other scumfucks. One guy's name is Ash – a dirty, pissed fucker with face tats and a dog. Another guy named Beavis has a bullet-belt & Celtic Frost t-shirt, and he's pissing on the park monument giving the metal claw. We've a small boom-box blaring Discharge, and Ulysses demands I slap in the MABUS stuff. Everyone approves of the grind holocaust, and they all want to assist the book.

My phone jingles and it's Raul. I cut to the formalities of escape, and Ulysses says come back tomorrow for Easter Sunday, which is a special day in SF lore. A giant tribal bongo session is held with over a 150 players and a massive party envelops the pasture. Whatever cast of characters will materialize this week, they'll all be snaking out in droves to GG Park. Ulysses says there is a squat called

The Eagles Nest, the Scumfuck HQ and that I can crash whenever: '*All we ask is you bring beer...*'

RAUL II (HIGH INTENSITY DISCHARGE)

It's getting dark and I've been waiting an hour for Raul outside of this hipster coffee shop. It's a hectic Saturday night, and the mood is peachy keen. People are actually happy here; they don't look miserable & oppressed like someone from Flint or Kansas.

Raul rolls up jamming Kataklysm. He is thankfully calm and collected, ready for his moment. You can tell this whole coming speech has been churning in his head all month long. He buys me dinner at Jack In The Box and we sail off passing a jibber…

Raul reverts to his spazzy self, but this time he's on a roll. He's a rambling roller-coaster that heads off in his thoughts until he's blankly staring out the window trying to grasp a train of thought. He gets so into his stories that he parks at stop signs to fling around his arms in emphasis, aggravating all the drivers behind us.

We're rolling up and down these giant SF hills looking for the perfect place to step outside the car to do the interview, because I'm extremely dizzy and nauseous from the painkiller/booze/Jumbo Jack triathlon. The tape clicks in as Raul speaks of his days in the band Mutilator, and how he'd quit because they'd gotten heavy into drugs: "*I said to myself 'fuck dawg, I don't want to be a part of this shit.' You try it bro but you find yourself in a place where your saying 'fuck this isn't me, I want my life back.' Fuck living in a prison. Fuck that son, I'm not gonna live in a motherfucking prison in my own mind.*"

"You were a guitar student of James Murphy right?"

Raul: "I ended up meeting this kid Dave Lopez from Soundwave Studios, where at the time Machine Head, Impaled, Damnevil, and Dopeslave rehearsed. Testament was number one in the Bay Area, they'd brought James Murphy from Obituary and Death. Dave asked me if I wanted to really learn how to play guitar, and he gave me James' number. When I first talked to James he said '*you got to be here Sunday morning, eight in the morning, call me if you're not coming two days in advance. If you're one minute late you're dropped.*' That's James Murphy for you (laughs). I walk in the room, he introduces himself, we went to his studio in the back, for the first time I'd seen a brutal ass, task-cam fuckin' 32 channel fuckin' mixing fucking board with this brutal-ass two-inch tape. My first time in the studio was with a metal legend bro. This was 93. At the time James was unstoppable, Testament just released the album Row(?).These motherfuckers were badass. On tour I heard Chuck, Billy and Ben shipped their Harley's to Europe and toured on their fucking Harleys."

"What was he like in person?"

"He was very formal, really nice, well spoken, very intellectual. The guy did not strike me as a metalhead because you're used to seeing metalheads be not the most smartest people. I was blown the fuck away by the seriousness of this man."

"Yeah, a total fucking pro…"

"Serious as a fucking heart attack, with flames in its motherfucking eyes. You know when you're with a legend dawg, when there is nothing to be said in the room but you know there's something there. It's almost like a religious experience."

"Ha ha."

"I lived in San Jose, and it took an hour to get there on the BART, so when I got there I smoked a fat fucking blunt. I went in stinking like weed. James' whole lesson was about drugs. I got lectured like you can't imagine son. He made me feel not only weak, he make me feel ignorant, like I have no sense of respect for myself or my family or anything. You have to understand, I never met my dad, so there was no strong male figure… What I want you to walk away with is that I'm true to form. I started from less than zero. I come from the world where society sets you up as a failure. I'm the forgotten child you didn't want. On that basis, I went in that room and James just ripped my balls. That was the most empowering first encounter with any individual in my life. The reason why he was so hardcore is because I had no discipline bro. I'm the ghetto bastard, I was an unleashed fucking animal. And he saw that, he knew I was out of control. He was saying *'you don't need this bullshit in your life, you could be something.'* It was some of the toughest love I can remember ever getting. This man empowered me. It's not about guitar playing, it's not about the metal world. I'm talking about destiny bro, the reason why the eye in the sky is putting people in your path. There is a reason behind it."

"What was it he told you?"

"He said *'drugs suck, and if you're going to be my student that's unacceptable. I want you to get the best out of your hour that I'm going to give you.'* I wasn't going to go no more. I said to myself the whole week *'fuck that motherfucker. He took my money and he told me all this bullshit, I want to fucking play.'* I was hungry from the streets –

I don't care about your politics. That's when he turned me into his own little personal project. The more he saw the more I wanted and he made me struggle for it."

"That's what a good teacher does."

"That's what made me more brutal. That was his strategy, that bad motherfucker. That's what I hated about him – he was so right about everything. The guy didn't drink, he didn't do drugs, he was just a clean-cut dude, a straight-arrow person."

"Tell me about the band."

"It's all linked together. If it wasn't for James I would've never found my pride in my veins or my place in the world. I kept on working on myself, studying and understanding art, film, architecture, composition, textures, arrangement, graphic design. I would've never found my authentic voice or a solid strategy."

"A total fucking ninja…"

"Well, after awhile James left Testament and started to act really weird. Everybody thought he was doing coke, or he was doing heroin. He lost a lot of weight; he wasn't taking showers no more. This is a guy who was a clean freak. When I went to his house, that hardwood floor was motherfucking emasculate. You could see yourself in it. Clean, motherfucking *cleeeean*. This dude was an anal motherfucker. I knew something wasn't right. People were talking shit, but it made me feel like '*you're all phonies, I thought you were somebody.*' That's fucked up, you're saying shit on someone who is mentally ill. I knew that something was not right. I'm hearing all this negative shit and I said '*fuck this, I've had enough.*' One day I followed his ass 'cause I wanted to get to the bottom of this. Is this motherfucker doing heroin, what the fuck is going on? Brother, we ended up in this fucking alley. Industrial train track, fuckin' one of the streets from your nightmares. Homeboy sat there and talked to the wall. I remember sitting in my car in fucking tears. I did, because I saw one of my friends struggling here. Every motherfucker around talking shit, saying that he's a no-good. Shame on you – you're cold and your heartless. Your lack of compassion, your lack of mercy, your lack of conscious…"

"Damn."

"It was a bad scene. Testament turned their back on James, everybody turned their back. He was struggling and from Florida, so he had no one out here. He used to call and say '*you got twenty bucks, I need something.*' One time I loaned him a hundred dollars and instead of going and buying groceries he'd go to Yoshi's and have a nice $50 sushi dinner. What the fuck? Back then nobody knew what was going on. I remember him telling me '*I have fallen from grace.*' When he said that to me, it broke my fucking heart. One day he says 'Dude I'm going home.' He had a Mackey 32.8 mixing board, and I traded it to him for a badass '85 C-28 Camarro. We pack all his shit, put it in the car, give him money to make it back to Florida. So there he was, we put him in a car and he took off. It was a sad ending."

"What happened after that?"

"His dad calls because he's concerned. His dad is a police officer, that's how come James was so disciplined, why he was so hard ass. His parents were brutal dude. I've talked to his dad. He's not a person you want to fuck with. His dad is serious business. He told me '*this kid is on drugs, he's doing some weird shit out here.*' So he gives James a drug test. He was clean. They took him to the hospital and they found that tumor behind his eye. That's what fucked him up. All those people who treated him like shit, they were trying to be the sweetest fucking guys. They knew I was tight with him and took all the heat. I got hate from a lot of people. People making fun of him, making fun of me. Some people live in a prison in their own mind. When you're living in a prison in your own mind, you have so much fucking anger. And yet you don't know where to put it. That's why a lot of motherfuckers are in prison. I don't give a fuck how much money you have, how famous you are, how fucking badass you are. If you don't have no heart and compassion in your life, I don't give a fuck who you are. I realized how important my friends are, my family is, everything that I have. It's a tragedy when people don't see what you've got. I'm not taking shit for granted. This is my identity. That is the whole foundation of the whole building. My art is education, the school of metal. We're breathing fresh air man. It's not about all these desires that people have. I want to find the formula and the recipe to make one of the heaviest records of all time. I found the key to my own fucking soul brother…"

EASTER SUNDAY

Sunday, April 8th 2007. I wake up on the corner of Laguna and Octavia at a motel called The San Francisco Motor Inn. Once Raul and I finished the interview, he drove me around to three different spots trying to find me a place to crash. When out of options, he shakily decided on this last ditch attempt…

A seedy room and a secret, multi-tap knock later, I'm left with a baked hippie playing x-box in a trance, his juggalo girlfriend in bed, and six pounds of Marijuana bailed like hay in the corner. All night I listened to her cell prattle with her grandmother, talking about uterus cancer & chemo treatments…

Raul shows at 2pm and hitches me a ride to GG Park. He doesn't want to do interview part two because he's all scrambled from family life. He says we'll meet later in the week, gives me a few buds, & drops me by the fountain.…

Raul was the first of two major contacts here. Initially the plan was that he smooth the weekend hump, and then I'd transition to the care of a promoter/zine proprietor named Black Metal Martha. She's in Norway right now but flies in Monday night. We're scheduled to meet on Tuesday, and she'll be opening her rolodex to help situate my needs. It all works out I guess. Just party at Golden Gate, crash at The Eagles Nest, and handpick the Monday adventure from a pool of a dozen plus bands.

Golden Gate is packed senseless and the tribal drum circle is pounding as if Sitting Bull were in attendance. Huge clouds of doja waif from every direction. Everyone is sloshed, LSD is everywhere, bodies dance in mass. Most Scumfucks are on the hill cooking BBQ and listening to Johnny Cash on the boom box. Gina Chaos, Sonny, Ash, and Ulysses are all present as well as some new faces like Action Jackson & Frankie Helvis.

Action Jackson is this wiry, bugged out guy from Chicago in a Discharge hoodie. He gets a fat SSI check for being criminally insane every month ($1500 no less) and uses it to wander the country. As long as he keeps the same drivers license, the scam will last forever.

Frankie Helvis is in his late 30's and is the big dog of The Eagles Nest. He's like the saint of the operation, the firm believer in the communal apparatus. Frankie kind of looks like a grizzled, crust punk Ted Bundy. He respects the quest of my book and spags a grin when I ask what bands he's been in. The impression he gives reads, *"I'm a fucking legend, but you gotta work for it."* He says, *"Well, there are plenty, but most recently I was in Shadow Reichenstein…"*

Nightfall; the park clears out, and I'm left with Action Jackson and this big dude with short & springy Sideshow Bob dreads. We're zonked and drunk, panhandling for pizza on Height Street. Every 10 minutes someone tries to sell us meth. This one guy has speed in monstrous black pill form that looks like pure death. Something new he says, something that will knock us right out. Action Jackson is a wet-brained champion, and even he won't touch it.

The tiny-dread guy and I make our way back to The Eagles Nest. At first he paranoid eyeballed me like an undercover NARC, but he is resigned to follow Helvis's order that I am to be brought safely to the squat. He is anxious for tomorrow because he's going to go to court over his 9th heroin offense. He says they'll just stick him in rehab for a month.

We keep getting lost on the busses & after three changeovers we're dumped off somewhere near The Nest in a residential section on the cities South Side. It's pretty ghetto looking with boarded houses and spray paint everywhere, and we have to go up and down 3 gigantic hills to reach Montana Street. I'm out of breath once we reach the squat, and my pinched nerves are screaming. I've been lugging that huge 50 lbs duffel-bag all day.

The squat is a sliver of a residence that is directly connected to all the other houses on the block. What little patches of grass exist are overgrown, and there's a pile of rotten black trash bags on the porch. The stench of wet dogs ranks from inside. We walk in and immediately stomp up a rickety flight of stairs. There is no carpeting, and the house has the sharp smell of termites and rotted wood. I take a piss in the scariest bathroom in America – the toilet is filled with a dark auburn blood-piss, used condoms are scattered around its edges, and the bathtub is filled with long-standing green water that's growing algae.

No one is here right now except for Action Jackson and Frankie, who tells me I can leave my shit in his closet and no one will fuck with it. He says I can squat any time and not to worry about the ruthless dogs. Once they know my scent, they are harmless.

Frankie & Action Jackson take off to who knows where, and I end up in the only room with a TV watching *U-571* with an older punk in his mid-40's. He's very friendly and we discuss the awesomeness of Harvey Keitel. He falls asleep not long after, and I lie down on top of a moldy, wet sleeping bag. It's 45 degrees in the room because the window is busted out, and the drift keeps me shaking throughout jangled, confusing half-nightmares…

THE EAGLES NEST (WHOREHOUSE OF REPRESENTATIVES)

I wake up displaced, uneasy – too many new memories have organized themselves after such a deep sleep. But I've yet to move or open an eye. I slowly lift a lid, and my pupil focuses on the half-burnt & shredded upside down American flag sloppily nailed to the wall. In the middle of it is a choker chain with padlock encircling a glossy photo of what appears to be GG Allin.

Is that where I am? Is Frankie Helvis a literal ex-band member of The Scumfucks? I get up to investigate, but the mirage is false. It's not GG, but someone who could easily pass for a clone. I creep the squat. Downstairs it's not a living room, but a garage from a 1930's floor-plan with the stench of carbon oxide emissions still resonated on the cement floor; torn couches are strewn about, *Pyrates of the Caribbean & Devils Rejects* posters. It's tomb-like and dirty, sludged dog shit over the ground. The back door opens to a run-down, skinny-yet-lengthy backyard with sideways trees, branches shooting everywhere. It's overgrown like a jungle and the BBQ area is pure dirt with black ash bonfire pit.

The Harvey Keitel fan is still passed out upstairs, and there is little in that room except for a broken old tube TV from the 60's. It was top of the line luxury once upon a time, now it's dead with a skeleton face cutout taped to the screen in a room with missing floorboards.

10am, Frankie and Chaos are up early in the kitchen with an exposed, tile expunged floor. The sink is a wooden, tetanus husk of a 1920's bath tub propped up by rusted piping and copper. It's got green water in it with all silverware and dishes sunk at the bottom. They have the oven wide open and are making cheese bread. They have a stale loaf someone dumpster dived, and are layering Kraft singles atop them.

Frankie is in a peaceful Zen and isn't into doing his interview just yet. He says it'll be an intense one when the moment comes. He tells me to talk to Mike, the Keitel guy on the couch. He was the drummer from Whorehouse of Representatives.

Whorehouse were one of the old school hardcore punk bands from the early to late 90's that Maximum Rock N Roll frequently pimped. They broke up some time ago, but stormed Europe and North America with a dozen splits, vinyls and LPs. Gina packs a bowl and grabs my arm, leading me to Mike. A little wake and bake session with the fellow, and he tells me his background.

For one of the nicest guys you'll ever meet in old school hardcore, it just breaks your damned heart that Mike Doodie is in the hellish limbo he faces. When the guitarist of Whorehouse shot himself in 1998, he left the band, got married, and went to family life in LA. It was his fairy-tale ending that lasted until mid-2006.

Barely a year ago his daughter drowned, his wife committed suicide in the wake, and Mike went into the deepest, ugliest heroin abyss imaginable. He was out of his mind for 6 months until he made the decision to fight back and go clean for his remaining daughter, a 12 year old Chelsea in SoCal. He's been drying out here for the past 2 months, laying low, just burning time and watching movies upstairs.

He's haunted yet jovial, a laid back pothead at his core that barely drinks. He's huge into power metal, and goes off on Iced Earth and Iron Maiden. Amusingly, D.H. Pilegro from Dead Kennedys is his NA sponsor: *"Whorehouse I'd gotten into in Seattle. They formed in 92, I joined in 94. I was the drummer. After about four months of rehearsing it was steady from thereon. Our lyrics were pretty much the same shit that's been done for 25 years. Real political, real pissed off. But we never tried to shove anything down anyone's throat."*

"What were some of the tours?"

Mike Doodie: "Starting off we did a six week tour with Toxic Narcotic. We did another US tour with Brother Inferior from San Francisco. We did another six week tour with a band from Austin called Severed Heads Of State. We went over and did a three week East Coast tour and played New York, Philadelphia, Connecticut, a ton of places."

"What's the difference between Seattle and San Fran?"

"Actually it's not all that different. It kind of reminds me of the Seattle scene, or the way it used to be back in the 90's. All the bands got along with each other, it was cool. It seems more open out here. It's definitely not like that in LA; its real cut-throat. Here people are cool and open-minded, they don't trip out.

"Was there a lot of division in Seattle between the punks and the whole grunge crowd?"

"Everybody was pretty much supportive. It was cool. We had some really great people come to our shows. Eddie Vedder and Chris Novaselic, I saw them a few times."

"Tell me some crazy stories."

"After I left Whorehouse I went with them as a roadie when they toured with Varukers from England. It was supposed to be six weeks, but the guitar player killed himself on tour. He shot himself. That was in '98."

"Was that the end of the band?"

"Oh yeah, totally. But we kept touring because we were with the Varukers. Afterwards I just drove back to Seattle and stayed there."

"So growing up in Los Angeles you saw the whole evolution of West Coast punk?"

"Oh yeah. I was in my first band in '79 called Gumby Riot. I was the singer... We played with Blood Scare, Bad Actor, The Atoms, Angry Samoans. The bass player from Samoans actually helped get us our start and out first few shows."

"What do you think about the East Coast scene? It a whole different world then California...

"Yeah, it's not as friendly (laughs). I noticed you can't really run around and be a social butterfly. It was weird."

"What's the Whorehouse singer up to now?"

"Michelle is working for Max Havoc out in Minneapolis. She's in a band called Two Minute Tantrum."

"What do you think are the best bands from San Fran?

"Born Dead, Social Unrest, Crucifix. Exit Wound, although I'm not sure if they're still together. They have a chick singer. But it was like Death metal, it was not punk rock at all."

"Are you into any metal?"

"I'm more of a metalhead than a punk really. That's why I love playing grindy stuff, 'cause it's somewhere in the middle. I grew up on Motorhead, Iron Maiden, and Venom. I really like the classic Judas Priest and Iced Earth stuff. That's why I was so surprised when they told me a guy from Metal Maniacs is crashing on the couch. I thought they were pulling my leg. *Here? The Eagles Nest?'* Come on..."

"What's your personal message?"

"Stay off drugs (laughs)."

SUBTERRANEAN FRENZY

Chaos and I jump on the BART, which is a sort of above-ground subway that goes everywhere in the Bay Area for over 100 miles. You can travel anywhere on a $1.50, provided you sneak through the pay-card exit when it snaps open from the passenger ahead of you. I start explaining The Villa Winona and we discuss squats we've been through, comparing notes & anecdotes...

At Panhandle Hill Ulysses is puking blood. He wipes the red splotch from the side of his mouth and gives a loud, *"AHH-WOOOO!!!"* (his customary way of saying hello). There are 10 street punks hanging out, annoying yuppies walking poodles. A retired scumfuck comes by with a baby stroller and his girlfriend. He recently bit the bullet and settled down enough to get a part-time job and apartment. Doesn't stop him from puking blood either…

Another sublime day in Golden Gate – booze booze more booze, hot dogs, Johnny Cash on the hill. Action Jackson and I prowl the early night panhandling, going in and out of record stores with massive vinyl collections. He's super-twacked, on one of those *'yeah man, I know what you mean, now dig this'* intensity trips. He goes off on juvey, previous mental incarcerations. We keep battering down vodka, somehow making it back to The Eagles Nest where Ulysses is jamming 'Hotel California' on the stereo.

The crowd is roaring. There are some girls over, from The Numbskull side of the fence. This one half-Asian chick with a limp and a cane looks real familiar. We've seen each other around somewhere, somehow, in another city we can't finger. There are three 24 packs of Milwaukee Beast, and it's a shouting match for attention.

The front door swings open, the dogs freak out, and a lone character stumbles inside. He says *'Howdy y'all'* in a gruffly Southern, *Cool Hand Luke* prisoner drawl. He's got on a beat-up, Swiss-cheese cowboy hat; ratty, hole-filled, dirt-filth flannel & brown pants like a Georgian farmer. He has this insane grin which makes it that much more diabolical since he literally has a clown smile tattooed on his face. Ulysses starts laughing and everyone runs up to greet him.

This is Jus-Ten Thrasher, a man shrouded in total mystery, except that he grew up in Louisiana and is a legendary scourge of New Orleans. He vanished one year ago without a trace on the train-hopping circuit. He is like Huck Finn in a Rob Zombie world, the kind of guy that keeps his possessions in a polka-dot sack hanging from a stick. He has a mess of tattoos and a stylized San Fran Scumfuck design on his arm that looks like the doodle David Berkowitz made of God/Devil/Boy/Girl.

45 minutes later I slip upstairs to hopefully pass out and avoid getting the dreaded 'Beer Elf.' Mike is comatose on the TV room couch and I curl up in the shadow camouflage… My brain comes into foggy motion. All I hear is Mother Firefly screaming and laughing hectically on repeat for what must have been an hour. I'm still drunk and fumbling around the room. *Devils Rejects* is on the DVD menu screen, replaying itself over and over.

The Nola Clownlord is asleep next to one of the crustie girls beside me, and other bodies surround us. I flop my way to the bathroom and check my face in the broken mirror shards and… good, no green sharpie mustache… I turn to piss and there are six freshly used condoms floating in the toilet, like squishy landmines on the floor…

A lonely cigarette on the porch and I come to a blazing focus. I'm wide awake, and for the first time since I arrived in San Fran my brain has stopped rushing forward in adrenaline survivalism… Take a breather, find a burrito down the hill… Wherever I am, it's indisputably ghetto. Windows are boarded up, iron gates shielding windows, cracked and beaten roads like the ambiance of *Death Wish 3*…

ALTERNATIVE TENTACLES WORLD HEADQUARTERS
TUESDAY April 10th, 2007, 3:50pm. 20 miles on the BART and two bus shuttles later I've reached an industrial warehouse beneath the off-ramp of a major freeway. This houses Alternative Tentacles World Headquarters, ex-Dead Kennedy vocalist Jello Biafra's ground-breaking and long-running punk label, rooting June 1979.

AT is known for putting out music from a wide array of genres, as well as politically conscious books and subversive propaganda at large. In the early years the label gained international attention by introducing the world to artists like Dead Kennedys, Butthole Surfers, DOA, 7 Seconds, Winston Smith, NoMeansNo, Neurosis. In recent history they've released material from Noam Chomsky, Howard Zinn, and Ralph Nader; as well as records by The Melvins, Thrall, Citizen Fish, Mojo Nixon, Leftover Crack.

Jello, for his part, refuses to use a computer and does not have an email. He is like a mysterious giant who wanders America secretly, pulling together a massive, endless network of freaks. He leaves no trace and is always campaigning as an underground politician through spoken word performances at endless college campuses.

He always was a polarizing figure. He ran for mayor of San Fran in the early 80's, was attacked by the Gore family through the PMRC, the police raided his label and confiscated everything in the 80's and destroyed DK masters. He even ran for president of the Green Party ticket with Mumia Abu Jamal as his running mate in 2000.

AT shares rent with some other magazines and eco-friendly industrial grade type businesses. The warehouse has been renovated into a multi-business complex on par with a 50 room band rehearsal spot. Publicist George Chen answers the door, and there are only two other employees hanging out like rats in the back archives…

"Explain to me the general label history…"

George Chen: "It started in '79 with the Dead Kennedys singles and continued with Jello signing different bands that he'd met on travels and in the Bay Area. An important part of what we do is educational art. Musically it's all over the place, even stuff outside of punk. The cool thing about Jello being a really deep record nerd is there's a huge spectrum of tastes. We're getting close to 400 records. We're up to 376 right now. We just had our 25th anniversary in 2004. We're really one of the longest standing independent labels in America."

"How did you arrive in the picture?"

My first inkling of AT was the censorship trials and the PMRC with Tipper Gore. I heard a Jello spoken word on college radio talking about that trial. It became a civil liberties thing where '*what is art and what isn't?*' Who had the right to make those decisions? I moved to the Bay Area from San Jose and started meeting people who worked at the label. I was a freelance writer before that."

"What's the situation with Dead Kennedys vs. Jello lawsuit?"

"My understanding is in the court system the judge sided with the other three members. The song writing is credited to four individuals. It's weird because one of them isn't even on some of those records. All of the original agreements were retroactively changed. I can't speak more than I know. Three hate one, one hates three…"

"I helped promote the Pro-Jello show in Detroit that was going on to divert people from going to that fake DK Reunion with Brandon Cruz and helping to make money for Jello's legal defense. I actually did see the fake DK the next time they came through with that Jeff Penalty guy singing. He was terrible. It was one of the sloppiest performances I'd ever seen from a band."

"I can't really comment on their motivation, I don't know any of those people. From an outsiders standpoint, have you guys tried to write new songs? Or maybe if you got a new singer you'd change the lyrics? Is this person really a full part of your band or just a stand-in? That would be a question that objectively you'd ask to any band that's trying to go on without one of the key members. I don't think that I would ever go see that band just 'cause I'm not interested."

"What's it like working for Jello? Is he a laid back guy?"

"I don't know if I would say he's laid back. He's more… When you hear him do spoken word, it's very dramatic and pointed. The cadence is very important. On a regular basis he tends to be a little more subdued, but that's also because he has a really weird schedule. I think I catch him right when he's waking up which is in the afternoon. He never really comes into the office. He still lives in San Francisco, but not on this side of the Bay."

"I was curious about Ludicra because they're black metal oriented, and there's all these feuds between music scenes ..."

"I'm not super well-versed in black metal. Across the board I can't say its one type of thing, but I know in Scandinavian black metal there's this sort of nationalist, pagan, racial stuff going on. It's not white power necessarily, but pro-white in a nationalist way, like keeping things 'pure.' I don't think that a lot of American black metal bands subscribe to that. I know that metal on the whole is not PC. The thing about Ludicra is there are Jewish people in the band, women in the band, it's not macho in the way a lot of metal is. They're not as much into the satanic imagery. I can't really speak to their relationship towards any feuds or a metal hierarchy. My impression is that our manager Dave – he used to work at Necropolis Records – he's pretty deep into that scene. I think he was instrumental in bringing Ludicra to Jellos' attention. I feel like their lyrics and stance is more political in a way, but not overtly political. Some of it deals with urban decay; it's not about a fantasy world. It's very realist and raw. I think they fit into the mythos of the label, but you can't really nail the mythos down. There's no exact rules to AT, although our stuff generally has an anti-macho, anti-racist, political edge."

"Tell me about the San Fran music scene"...

"Oakland and Berkeley tend to be more house party towns. I think the economics of the area have made it harder to do that kind of stuff under the radar. San Fran and New York are the two most expensive cities to live in, so you have high rent, little open real estate, higher bridge toll, you have to pay for a place to live and rent a practice space. It's way harder than a smaller town. There's a class disparity. San Fran is interesting because there's enough people where you can have these smaller factions, different sub genres, social cliques that occur. Whereas I grew up in a smaller town, where in high school if you're into any weird music at all you find the other people that are into any weird music, even if it as a different kind, because *'we'll just be freaks together, even though we're interested in different things.'* Then you have a place like San Francisco where all the freaks from across the country move, so they find their niche. There's the 'Burning Man' people, the hacker cyber-libertarian types. Within punk you have so many sub-options. They barely ever play shows together. I don't know if it's an overall community... Who gets to define punk? That's an interesting question. There's a lot of angles you can take with it. When you talk about class, there's ambiguity behind it. You've heard the phrase '*race traitor*,' and I think there's something similar as being a 'class traitor.' No one's really gone into that too deeply."

"*Jello's very outspoken, he's very eccentric. I remember once that some crusties jumped him and beat him up.*"

"Yeah, he had his knee broken."

"*Do a lot of people give the label an evil eye because they consider him a sell-out because he's actually made some money running a label and doing spoken word tours?*"

"I'm sure there are. Any given day I'll get four emails that are like '*hey Jello, you're awesome, you changed my life.*' And then every week I'll get one or two that are, '*fuck you for this reason*,' whether or not it's a coherent argument. I still put them up for Jello to see, even if these people are crazy men. The people that are going to write to AT, even if they're "*hey fuck you*,' they want to give us feedback of some kind. I've seen stuff of message boards, like '*screw these guys*,' people insulting him. It's the internet, I don't know how far you can take that shit... Like the guys that beat Jello up. It's like, '*great, you just beat someone up, now he has to pay all this extra medical. Did you win some sort of points doing that? Did you prove any point?*' If I beat someone up because they make more money than me, do I get anything? It doesn't make sense."

Dave, the AT employee that used to work for Necropolis Records, gives me the nod to follow him in back. He leads me to a wall where every single one of AT's 376 releases are organized in piles. He runs his hand across the breadth of them like Willy Wonka with his cane and tells me to take whatever I want. '*Are you serious?*' I ask. I feel like Indiana Jones in *The Last Crusade* where he has to pick the most discreet cup lest Harrison's face melt off...

I grab a few spoken word albums from Jello and Noam Chomsky, as well as a Leftover Crack/Citizen Fish vinyl. I tell him, "*That's fine, I don't want to overboard my welcome.*" It is the magic password, and Dave returns with over 50 plastic slipcases. "*Take apart every CD in our catalog if you wish, just leave us the hard plastic cases.*" This is just too much. I pick about ten albums, and Dave keeps going "*ever heard this?*" and handing me random discs. By the time I walk out I've two-dozen stuffed in my duffel-bag...

LUDICRA

It's another huge band complex, but this time one that features an employee-manned snack bar. I had no idea Ludicra was a super-group of sorts. Aesop helps run A&R for Vendlus Records, and Laurie is one of the highest regarded female metal vocalists in America. She is a skinny, mild-mannered, and bookwormish lady in her late 30's, but her pipes are that of a Greek Hydra.

On bass is Ross Sewage of Impaled and Ghoul, two highly respected underground phenomena. Impaled is one of the finest Carcass inspired gore/death acts in America, they've toured America through their stint on Century Media, and Ghoul is an E.C. comic bookish freak parade of honest, death-laden thrash with an S.O.D. mosh feel. They are stalwarts on the cult label Razorback Records and their albums showcase colorful paintings of Ghoul riding skateboards with axes and chainsaws while sporting white, one-eyed hoods like Jason in *Friday The 13th Part II*.

The other guitarist is John. He's in the weird 70's kind of prog rock band Hammers of Misfortune, which are signed to the Italian label Cruz Del Sur. They have a small cult following from an old album they did in the 90's but have just come back with a recent disc.

In the corner of the practice space is Hammer's special beast – a 1953 Hammond B3 organ. John gives me a tutorial on how awesome it is: '*It's chopped, meaning that it's taken out of its original furniture and made into a 'portable' 250 pound unit. This is the classic Deep Purple/Uriah Heep 1970s set up. It's running through a rotary Leslie speaker. The chassis contains a bank of tone– wheels that spin inside of a magnetic field, generating sine waves. Originally these were designed to replace pipe organs in churches in the 1930s. It's very old technology'*...

John was also in GWAR for 3 months, before they ever played a show. Oderus Urungus was still just the bass player then. He never played live, toured or recorded, but he let that fact slip to whoever wrote the Hammers press bio. Now anytime he does an interview, he has to constantly state the frivolous nature of his GWAR tenure.

Watching this band live in their home environment, just jamming without a care, running through their entire catalogue for an hour and a half... Sincerely, this is one of the best black metal bands in the United States, and they don't even really consider themselves as such. They are more of a hybrid, but far darker and brilliant then 90% of these guys just retreading Bathory, Dark Funeral, or Mayhem. And

I'm sure it pisses off the white nationalist types to be schooled by a half-Jewish drummer and an anti-fascist female vocalist…

"So tell me why Bill O Reilly must be destroyed…"

Aesop Dekker: "Oh, he shouldn't be destroyed. He's fantastic. Yeah, he's pretty great. He's the biggest dick on television, the loudest, biggest dick…"

"What do you think of Rush Limbaugh?"

"I think Limbaugh is a pill-popping, whiskey drinkin,' cigar smokin,' sunnava bitch. They're all the same; they all say the same thing. It's the Republican echo chamber…"

"We're in San Fran. Do you know any of the old school hippie legends?"

Ross Sewage: "My dad drove Jerry Garcia to a Dead show when he was driving a cab in San Francisco. That's about it… I'm allergic to hippies. All those people cashed in and moved to Berkeley. Most of them made a shit-load of money in the 80's and turned into yuppies. That's how that generation went. They're all rich, you see commercials for them all the time on TV, how they're gonna break all the rules of retirement just cause their generation always broke the rules…"

"Like the rules were tied to baby boomers… Like the rules of golf…"

"How come every time you hear 'All Along The Watchtower' on TV it's always with scenes from Vietnam?"

"It's either that or 'Run Through The Jungle'… Well, I guess that one is pretty self-explanatory… What's the weirdest tour story you have from any band? What about when you watched the semi-truck roll over?"

"Oh yeah, we watched a semi roll over right in front of us…"

"The best was Flagstaff. The cops stopped the show and we all had to hide upstairs. I got in this room with the skinheads. This guy started telling this story about how everyone in Flagstaff was gay. Like all the guys, all the indie guys are total fags. He's like, *'Yeah I went to this house with this Indian faggot dude and this guy was so fucking gay that I had to whip my dick out. This guy was so fucking gay that I had to stick my dick in his mouth.'"*

"Is Aesop your stage name?"

"That's my real birth name."

"You didn't want to say Christian name did you?"

"I was gonna say god-given name then I realized I'm an atheist…"

"But god didn't give that to you. God gave you 'schumck face'…"

"God called me 'loser'… Once we got a review that said I was the only guy in the band with some corny black metal name. But it's my real name…"

"What do you think is the corniest black metal name you've ever heard?"

"There was some band that had a guy named NecroNudist. Or Lord Asmodeus. I wrote to this guy for a demo, this band called Nephareous. The guy wrote me this really chicken scrawled letter that was like [in a broom-stick wielding witch tone] 'Would you like to join my coven?' He was deadly serious, he put blood on there too. Hurm, ha, ha, I could send him ten extra dollars and join his warlock coven…"

"Tell me about Impaled…"

"Impaled is a band for 15 year old boys…"

"What's the message of Impaled?"

"The whole medicinal, gore, like Carcass. They always said they were about being vegetarians in metaphor. Which is bullshit because I don't think a song called 'Slash Dementia' is about vegetarianism. The other song was about some guy with bad acne… Sometimes we tell stories, but I'd like to think that we are at least past the hack n' slash bitch fest. I at least try to keep it tongue in cheek if not tongue popping right out of cheek. The last record is actually fairly political, all done in metaphor of course. 'Cause we're not going to go the route of 'Heartwork'. The band really is about having a good time, at least onstage."

"Impaled did do a split with Hemorrhage right?"

"We did. What I wanted to do was the first ever conceptual split record. It had a story beginning to end which we worked out together. I don't think anyone got this, but the guy on the cover with the straight-jacket, on the side of the record it says 'Piece of Grind.'"

"Oh, I get it. Like Eddie Hunter from Iron Maiden…"

"Yeah, exactly. Just like 'Piece of Mind.' That guy is the actual Maiden character, the guy who does photos and the voices on the records. So it was a fun split. I've known Hemorrhage since they've been around in '94."

"What are those guys like?"

"I finally met them and they're probably some of the nicest guys on the planet. They're super sweet; they took us out to eat, to get some drinks. Me and the goobers were wrestling on the street, having a good time..."

"You mentioned some random drama with Maniac Neil..."

"Maniac Neil hates us. He pretty much hates every band that was ever on Razorback besides his own. I don't know if he has a problem with Gigantic Brain, but Splatterhouse, Machetazo, all these other bands basically all fell out with Razorback. That split with Hemorrhage will probably never be pressed again, at least not on Razorback. There's a lot of online shit talking. Neil and Billy definitely made clear their opinion of us and our lifestyles after knowing them for more than a decade. Like going out to shows, and enjoying alcohol, things of that nature. And you know, socializing. They made clear that was not a very cool thing to do. You had to be an angry loner sitting at home watching the worst horror films you can possibly imagine. Sorry, not every horror film is good. Even if it's from the 70's. I'm sorry. There are shitty ones in the 70's, there are shitty Italian horror films, and to say otherwise is just being retarded and trying to be an elitist."

"Yeah, I try to do that ritual when it's right..."

"I love horror films, I love all that shit, but I don't want to sit around in my mother's basement without a god damn life. I actually like people. I like going out, I actually like socializing. I like drinking. But they certainly made sure to state that they don't approve of that lifestyle, which is, you know, what the rest of the planet enjoys. You should be sitting around. You should know every actors name, every Lucio Fulci film. You get that with thrash too. The people that know every obscure band that came out of Greece and if you don't you're a total dickhead."

"What's Jello like in person?"

"I don't know him well, but I am impressed with how excited he still is about music and bands. He's always been kind to us. My father voted for him for Mayor when he ran. I wish he would run again. He likes to talk…"

" It's almost like I'm listening to his spoken word record. He's kind of like a weird, stand-up comedian. It's funny, but it's kind of depressing at the same time…"

"He looks like a stand-up comedian. Like you could cover your ears and hear him telling a punch-line like [best Jello impression in the biz], 'hey, my wife doesn't screw me.' Just kind of hokey jokes like that…"

"Ever been to the Church of Satan just for the hell of it?"

"It's gone now. When Anton died there was an 'invite only' yard sale, I was fortunate enough to have a friend who was a member take me. I bought a set of old '70s Kenwood headphones, and a coat that had a pipe with some stale marijuana still in it. San Francisco has a lot of this kind of bizarre history, black panthers, Jonestown, Manson, The Zodiac…"

"What's your favorite horror movie kill of all time?"

"Well 'Dead Alive' pretty much sums it up when they did the entire lawnmower slasher. That he actually went outside and secured it with a belt to go around his shoulder. That was a good spin on the old garden tools. I don't think Lucio Fulci's a very good director but he does good eye-gouging…"

"It's shot like porn, from a million grotesque angles…"

"He has my favorite zombie scene ever. When the zombie…"

"Fights the shark?"

"Best thing ever. I've never seen any CGI that could ever touch that."

"Here's my question, because I'm just as obsessed with that scene as you are. Does the shark turn into a zombie and thus pollute the fish population with the zombie virus?"

"No, the zombie virus only affects humans."

"Do running zombies piss you off?"

"Not really. I went back and watched the 'Dawn of the Dead' remake, and that movie has horrible shit towards the end. But I like the beginning, the first five minutes are great. My friend said, 'well that's stupid, zombies can't run' And I said, "well, really, rigor mortis doesn't set in until 12 hours after death. So I don't see any reason why during the first 12 hours they wouldn't be fully functional.' I think they should slow down after their bodies start to decay. And the people that complain about running zombies, that pisses me off because 'Return of The Living Dead,' that had running zombies in it, and you know they loved it. And there was a running zombie in 'Night of the Living Dead'. The first zombie that shows up in the cemetery, he runs pretty hard."

"You ever been to Las Vegas?"

"I think Las Vegas is a giant piece of shit that should be wiped from the face of the earth. The reason to hate it and the charm is all wrapped up into one. You can actually go to any one of the penthouse

floors which are usually pretty easy to get to. Rich people just leave their trays out and they only eat a quarter of their food. Whenever I was in Las Vegas and had no money I fed myself that way. It's like this giant oasis that's fake and false and maculate, which is stealing water from Southern California, and farm land, running air conditioning with all of these open doors. This is why they hate our freedom. This is what we do with it. That and 'American Idol.'"

"I feel like in the future, if you want any kind of job, you're going to have to live in a house with five strangers. [Talks low like a reality TV voice-over segment] Every week, one will be eliminated… And then you will become a plumber. You want to work at McDonald's? You have to live in this house with 5 strangers. You'll be living with Chyna…"

ECHOES OF DENVER

Gone are the remnants of Ludicra, having dined heartily at the vegan coffee shack. Black Metal Martha, the main secondary contact, has bailed on participation due to illness. 2 more days in this city; just me versus the street.

Still racing across town with the duffel bag from hell, dead tired & crooked spine is killing me. My first instinct is to sleep in Golden Gate Park, somewhere obscured by leaves and fauna. I'm heading towards the fountain of the main entrance when a squad car eyeballs me and busts a u-turn. Screw it, back to Eagles Nest…

I'm totally hallucinating from the insomniac stupor which has entrapped me since arriving. It's now… Wednesday, April 11th. It's 1am and I've caught the last bus with lucky directions from a street corner drunk. Two bus changes are required, and I may have missed the transfer already. I'm told to hop out at this dead ghetto corner with bums passed out everywhere, trash bags blowing through the street. For 30 minutes I'm stared down by mug-happy types before snagging the last bus outta dodge.

The ride is an echo of Denver. I'm burnt beyond recognition and in a hell of a lot of pain. It's been four long days of scumbag hustle since I've taken a shower. I'm so sticky at this point I could take off all my clothes, lunge at a cement wall, and click like velkro. And when I get to that squat who knows what anarchy might be raging? I'll be held hostage with tequila until 6am.

As vicious as this moment is, I know I will be nostalgic for it soon enough. I'll miss the dirt and grime, I'll miss the street. In two days Ulysses and Chaos, Frankie, Jus-Ten Thrasher, Action Jackson and Whorehouse Mike will all cease to exist. What a terror of loss...

I get dropped off way to soon and have to stomp a half mile just to reach the beginning incline of the "Hills of Doom." I feel like a cripple testing Mount Everest. With every blast of pain I keep telling myself: "*Nothing... huff huff... Will stop... huff... This fucking book...*" I drop & sit on the curb exhausted. Only 3 more inclines to go... *I steal a rolling computer chair off someone's porch, put my backpack and duffel in its seat, and push it for the next quarter mile of torture...*

At the squat it's only Ash & Action Jackson drinking Budweiser cans. I proudly unveil the free promos from Alternative Tentacles. That they essentially offered me all 376 records in their catalogue immediately goes into scumfuck lore. They tell me everyone was looking for me today, because I'm now known in Golden Gate mythology as "*The Scumfuck Journalist.*" I slip upstairs to the empty TV room. It's freezing, and there is no warmth save for the moldiest, nastiest smelling wet sleeping bag you can imagine. It's so gross, like peeling apart a gonorrhea cauliflower...

THIS BOUNTY HUNTER IS MY KIND OF SCUM

Something happened in that womb of damp stench. I awoke so dirty, so horrendously filthy, so back to my primal street urchin roots that I felt like an invincible juggernaut of Darwinian evolution. If I always teetered on the brink of crust, I'd fully plunged into the vortex...

In Batman The Scarecrow doesn't actually become Scarecrow until he starts dosing himself with his own fear toxin and enjoying it. GhostNomad is no longer a clever little title. I have found my calling and the only true freedom I've ever known – every major city was now my own personal playground. Life at rock bottom & urban camping at the fullest – no fear, just an endless freefall of bohemian glory...

Downstairs this morning there was no more of this "journalist" barrier, because we were now all one crazed unit. Ulysses unearthed clippings of a story the local press did on The Scumfucks. One picture is of Uly in court with his hair slicked back in a nice suit, jolly like a mafia hitman. I tell him about my financial crisis, and he nods: "*No problem. We're going panhandling.*"

A dozen of us are loaded with backpacks/duffelbags, some have sleeping roll-outs clamped onto hiking packs. We've five scruffy alley dogs on thick metal chains, everyone has sunglasses, and we march like a terrifying army about to go to war. We clomp to the main nerve and wait for the trolley to swing by. So long as a trolley cop isn't riding we won't get hit with tickets. It pulls up and all 12 of us rush board like Indians into battle, dogs & all…

Which is a fantastic commuter moment. The trolley car we'd hijacked is filled with the audience of a Huey Lewis concert. We're drinking 40's, talking loudly about assault and narcotics. Then I start ranting about my pussing, leaking genitalia – the oozing, the rashes, *the scabs & ticks*. The compartment riders are pushed to the side of the trolley. Some whigged out punk girl unassociated with us is neurotically cutting off clumps of her purple hair, throwing wads of it on the floor. "*Can I have a DNA sample so that I can clone an army of you and attack the White House?*" She smiles and hands me a messy clump which I drop into my pocket.

At Panhandle Hill Clownface Jus-Ten got $10 at the health clinic for taking a Hep C blood test which we use on King Cobra and Sparks. I yank out Trolley Girl's hair clump and ask, '*Does anybody wanna do a shot with me?*" The look of confusion on Ulysses face and the horror on the rest is unparalleled.

I swallow this giant hairball, take a big slug of the 40 oz, and can't help but envision one of those Drano commercial cartoon explanations of what it does to clogged pipes. The soaked hairball bespews like a fountain – projectile vomiting alcohol and laughing simultaneously. Booze is dripping through my nose. I keep laughing at all the yuppies walking baby strollers and rush up to the pool of chime, get on my knees, and go '*luh-luh-luh*' licking it with my tongue like a thirsty dog. I couldn't stop laughing and everyone wanted to vomit.

A crotch-rocket cop rolls up on all of us. All the crusties say, "*Hi Officer Dan!*" He just sighs and says, "*Ok, caught you drinking. Whose gonna take it for the team?*" Jus-Ten happily agrees because all he has to do is drop the ticket at the Homeless Youth Alliance Center. They always pay for them because they receive state aid for that purpose. Tattooed officer Dan says some kind words and zooms off on his bike, popping a wheelie in the street like Evil Kenievel.

Free meal at the Youth Alliance center where punk rock socialism & ablutophobia is deep in orbit – open medical, food distribution, 9-5 shelter… There are 15 street kids hanging around. Some are deranged loners, and the younger girls have that sexually-abused teen runaway vibe to them. We kill time with egg sandwiches, *Return of the Jedi & Ghostbusters…*

STORMDRAIN

Later that night and chilly in The Fillmore; 3 layers of pants still haven't done the trick. I tried to nap at Panhandle but it was too damn cold, and I've barely been able to shake off the discombobulation from earlier alcohol. I'm posted outside a bar awaiting Scott Reyns from the industrial band Stormdrain. I'm so haggard he'd mistaken me for a bum.

Scott kind of looks like Trent Reznor; the saloon a moderate version of the Skinny Puppy *Too Dark Park* stage-show: *"Live drums, but it's augmented with an electric kit – triggers, an electronic pad for different sounds. It has a big OGHR drum sound. A lot of things are sequenced, but not the rhythm. The beats are more break-beats, trip hop beats, a little more dance. I'm like 10 years younger than Trent Reznor, so where guys like that were growing up on Alice Cooper and Kiss I was growing up on The Cure, Depeche Mode, The Smiths. We've done film shows, robotic lights, video montages..."*

"Tell me about the San Fran scene. You're the first industrial guy I've talked to."

"San Francisco is a tight scene – a really good scene – but it's actually a really bad one for industrial. The real heart of it is DNA Lounge. Also Stepfield, which is an 18+ club. Bottom of the Hill is mostly known for punk and indie. You got The Independent and you get VNV Nation in there. Every once in awhile something will come through Mezzanine, but they do more electronic like Meat Beat Manifesto. Each club has a different voice and vibe, but they don't lock themselves into one genre. You can't do business like that."

"What the weirdest response you've gotten so far?"

"I had someone post a comment on MySpace that said '*your music is really awesome, do I detect a hint of the Holy Spirit?*' You really wouldn't say that if you read the lyrics..."

Scott jets and I'm left nodding off at the table. I tried to cajole him into hanging out, but I may have unnerved him out by my bumminess. I need to shower and sleep, and I'm dreading going back out there. All I gotta do is make it until tomorrow. Downtown Brown will nab me from Golden Gate, everything will be happy-skippy, and then I'll be going on... *my first spoken word tour...*

Wow. That's a head-trip I hadn't even pondered. I've been too busy just trying to stay alive here, and tomorrow I'll already be on the road again, swinging down California through the Southwest and into the Bible Belt, then boomeranging the Midwest.

I get lucky when an Old World Detroit chum returns a distress signal I emitted 2 days ago. I haven't seen this girl since 2000 when she took off in a renovated school bus full of hippies. They went everywhere in that thing, and seven years later she's planted roots in a section of San Fran called Fruitvale. She's an editor at Locust Magazine, and is co-editor on a sci-fi anthology that features fresh Neil Gaiman prose. One long shot on the BART and she rescues my decimated half-corpse, feeds me upscale pizza, and I take the greatest shower in personal history, black water spiraling the drain...

COHERENCE

Back at Golden Gate it is blissfully sunny, and my panhandling sign reads: "*DETROIT D.I.Y. GONZO JOURNALIST ROAD NOVEL HELP FUNDS NOT JUNKIE DEATH TO THE FREEWHEELING MONKEY.*" I'm stretched out shirtless, surrounded by half the crowd from "ground zero." One kid is working his second day on the street ever, and I'd spent the last hour teaching him the ropes.

Ulysses and Chaos are nowhere to be found; by the fountain Action Jackson & Whorehouse Mike chat with the extremely clandestine land pyrates. Mike digs the MABUS album and wants to start a grind project in LA. He's busting out of here ASAP. Jackson is also set for a long haul to Chicago within the week.

My last 30 minutes on the hill. "*Hey man, it's legal to trip in large numbers in this park right?*" "Well how crazy?" "*Say 50 people on an eighth each convinced they're on a mountaintop, all of whom know too much, becoming their own diversions, prancing around like The Marx Brothers meets 'Lord of the Flies,' and no one stops laughing for 10 hours.*" I look up and everyone on the hill – like ALL the circles – they've overheard my carrying voice. I lock eyes with one of them, and hippie girl: "*Can we come?*"

It's *the* phone call; my chariot has arrived I've got that badass opening riff from Hammers of Misfortune's "Locust Years" jamming in my head as I make my way like a champ through the pasture. All characters nod as I float past. A quick squeeze through the stalactite cave limping and beaten, I appear in plain view to all 3 Downtown Brown members. They look discombobulated and somnambulist next to the spewing fountain, flabbergasted to see me of all people stomp up the hill like a lone horror movie survivor: '*So boys, what's the plan?*'

PART VI VI VI: COACH SNAKE
(& THE ALPHA FARCE VOLTRONIC TOUR)
APRIL 12TH-APRIL 23RD 2007

HARDWORN CHANGEOVER

All three members of Downtown Brown are just as displaced as I, zombified eyes burning a whole in my face from across the plastic McDonalds table top. It's their first experience with California, and none of them have ever seen a world that doesn't resemble the Midwest. It's their first USA tour, and guitarist/vocalist/dictator Neil P and I go way back.

He was there at the beginning of the Detroit press wars, and remained solid throughout every ugly, momentous spiral. We are perhaps two of the most loathed individuals in the Detroit music scene. Myself for all reasons Mr. Badoglio established, and Neil because Downtown Brown are one of the loudest, shit-talking, ridiculous-beyond-belief punk rock comedy acts to ever come from that city.

Neil is among the sincerely magnetic live performers on the Detroit circuit, and Downtown Brown are one of the most original and entertaining bands to come out of "The Glove" in this decade, if not the entire USA. Hype is bullshit, and I wouldn't put my reputation on the line like this for 99% of extreme metal.

I've seen them all – nearly every major legend from every subgenre – and never once have I been bored with a DTB Performance. I've seen some piss poor ones where Neil tried to play whigging out on mushrooms or had blacked out during one of his Eddie Van Halen guitar solos, but never have I been sleepy. Their aura terraforms the venue like mankind will Mars by 2078.

The rest of the world does not know this yet. I know this, the Detroit scenesters & press people know this. But either in jealousy, contempt, political correctness or insult, Downtown Brown have been blackballed or blown off as a novelty act. But all the nut-hugging jean squares in the world can't hold this monster back. "Serious" rock journalists will one day cringe before this goliath.

Downtown Brown are worshiped as the ultimate party band by a growing army of fans ranging from the age of 9 to 57. It all goes back to Neil's raucous sense of humor. He is like a cross between a manic, gut-busting Jack Black and John Belushi in *Animal House*, between every song bombastically hijacking the mic and launching himself into impromptu spoken word rants on the president, poop, lazar beams, dinosaurs, Jungian psychology, artificially tanned "orange" women. The music a cartoonish, hook-laden assault of MANOWAR, Zappa, AC/DC, Van Halen, Tenacious D, Sublime, Circle Jerks, & Mr. Bungle….

The spirit of this band is to indoctrinate all of the freaks, dorks & pimple-faced losers in a reality where no macho meatheads exist, and all are encouraged to dress like robots, break-dancers, zombies, mummies, or Pee Wee Herman. Downtown Brown has actually made the mullet in vogue. This insanity slops into reality, and an entire mutant subculture has formed under their masthead.

They aren't tied to the ICP phenomenon, but the example of the Juggalo is adequate. Their shows are like carnivals – sometimes literally – with a colossal repertoire of live presentation, at times involving semi-professional wrestling complete with flaming table and barbed wire. Humongous plush toys thrown into the audience – piñatas, beach balls, harmonicas, kazoos. They drag their fans onstage to receive mullet buzz-cuts or play cowbell, and inside jokes are given widespread meaning to the degree of urban legendry.

It feels good to be reunited, because I've always been the sort of 'Fifth Beatle' to DTB. I've never actually played an instrument outside of cowbell, but ironically have more a sense of seniority then the other two members, Hairy Bob (bass) and Danny Glover (drums). This is only because Neil and I have worked on dozens of shows, made a few music videos and a full-length film, and were essential in networking a massive apparatus of bands, promoters, zine people, filmmakers, artists, acid-freaks & nut bags in general that we called 'The Coalition.'

The same reason I left Detroit is the same reason DTB is now touring the United States – it's a new world and it's time to expand. All of our old compatriots with any sense are doing the same, but while some of these bands are playing depressing local shows for the same 20 people over and over, DTB are bonafide heavyweights in the Midwest. They get solid guarantees and turn profit, and have a mass of kids age 15-23 driving hours to see them live. That is an accomplishment that none of the indie types have ever pulled off, let alone any of the Kid Rocks, EMINEM's, Von Bondies or White Stripes of our origin…

THE VENUE IS A BICYCLE SHOP

"Did he actually just say that? Serious as a heart attack with flames in its motherfucking eyes? BWA HAHAHA!!!" Neil is roaring on the couch as I make a humongous pot of cheesy macaroni. The golden rule of touring is that nothing is truly sacred. If someone invites you to their house after a show, it's because they think you are super-cool. Give them an after party to remember, but while they are at work explaining to co-workers the strange men sleeping on their couch, eat any damned thing you can hustle.

We're at the home of a Detroit refugee living in Berkeley, across the Bay from Frisco. It is a mansion compared to The Eagles Nest. She has nice girl roommates unprepared to deal with four sweaty alcoholics, and we have to bolt before they walk in the front door in two hours or they'll think we're robbing the place. Still, we are determined to use that outdoor trampoline.

We spent all of last night sipping champagne and smoking reefer, easing into our convergence. This is my first time really hanging out with bassist Hairy Bob or drummer Danny Glover. HB joined early 2005, and Danny came in late 2006. Hairy Bob is mangy like a muppet, blonde hair a flowing mane. Onstage he's a cartoon maniac flopping around and babbling weird shit into the second mic. He rocks the four-string and is heavily trained in the funk slap-bass.

Off stage he's kind of like Eyore from Pooh. He is always depressed, never wants to take chances, thinks everything's a bad idea, and barely wants to go out and explore. If given the opportunity he'll twiddle around on GameBoy all day and never say a word to anyone unless it's to secure more uninterrupted Tetris time. He is the straight-headed responsible one that usually ends up driving the post-show van packed with drunks.

Glover is a different story though. He's 20 years old, this is his first *real* band, his first tour, and is caught in the youth trap where his momma keeps calling to make sure he's safe and has clean socks. He looks like an angel but has the mind of a scumbag. Every conversation usually comes back to ass sex. Like awful ass sex with dripping hot wax and Ready Whip topping.

He is the big stoner of the group, wears glasses, has neck-length brown hair, and usually sports striped collared shirts and high school track-racing t's with goofy slogans. He is totally under the radar until he explosively rants about letting girls pee in his mouth. *In fact, he is a total angel…*

Last nights show in San Fran was dead, and somehow half the crowd was from Michigan. One of Neil's high school buddies showed up for their first meeting since 1998, and the girl we stayed with brought her friends as well. Somehow DTB was booked alongside an all-immigrant Japanese band who were like an indie rock version of Primus. They spoke no English and avoided us, although the pretty girl on guitar did one of those shy Oriental '*tee hee hee's*' you'd only get from the purely Tokyo.

I was too busy detoxing from the street to jump right into a spoken word rant. One look in the mirror and I was grizzled, skin burnt like a sidewalk hobo – more in tune with the free drink tickets for vodka/cranberry and the pot out back where Danny and I spoke of razor-slicing bondage porn. I kept leaping from the stage and sliding on the floor like a bowling ball at non-existent pins. Neil laid it on thick: '*See, I came out to California for one reason and one reason only. Not girls, not vacation. It's something called GLASS... I'm not fucking around people, I need some goddamn meth!! I need my teeth to fall out. I want my face to rot like a moldy pear. What do you think of that people? Well, this song is dedicated to you, the mutual lovers of meth-amphetamines. This songs called 'CRACK...'*'

Tonight the gig is in Bakersfield. Then Hollywood, Scottsdale, Albuquerque, Amarillo, Norman, Little Rock, Nashville, Cincinnati... We've been rolling through these vast California wastelands discussing the wisdom of Don Henley, 'cause you can check out anytime you like but you can never leave.

I'm totally psyched to lay down the thunder of my first spoken word gig, but as we roll into Bakersfield the venue is a bicycle shop that's been closed since 6pm. The promoters' phone is disconnected, and not a single bar in town has heard of this venue. This is the second such encounter – in Reno the bar staff had never heard of the bookie. Somehow the opening act went through the same guy, and both were allowed to play the unscheduled show of another disconnected phone apparition.

This is bad on the miniscule band fund, and we still have half the country to go. Not a dime was drained from San Fran, and we still have another 3 hours to Los Angeles. Might not sound like much, but when your hauling an Econoline van filled with equipment, merch, and four dudes, that small stint averages $60 on the tank.

Our LA contact is a Detroit runaway named Greg Schmidt. He was in a band called Bedford Blueprint that I helped promote back in 2002, and Neil's known him since high school. Greg is a real clean-cut guy, kind of on the preppy side, but he's got a keen sense of black humor. He also Lawrence Kasden's gopher, who produced such seminal hits as *Raiders of The Lost Ark* and *Jaws*. Greg's job is to read scripts and relate green-light considerations.

The ride up the narrow, twisting street in Hollywood Hills is no job for a large cargo van. You're surrounded by palm trees and Bentley's. It's like part of their code, where the asphalt is so slim you need a slinky sports car to just maneuver.

Greg's pad is unbelievable, near the very top of the Hills – a $5 million three-level quasi-mansion with a Jacuzzi, pool, and massive view of the Valley below. The rooms are huge, the HD TV top of the line, and you can see the outline of the Sharon Tate murder house on the horizon... Of course none of this is Greg's though; his sister happens to be the quasi-trophy wife of 50-something Rich Uncle Skeleton who's a world-renowned corporate businessman. Right now he's somewhere in Japan...

HOLLYWOOD TOUR SPECTACLE

I awake in a surge with only 4 hours of sleep under my belt. It's 5:30 am, Saturday morning, and I'm drinking black coffee and smoking a cig on the high-rise patio. One second your living on the streets of San Fran wasted on the floor of the dirtiest squat in America, the next your in a multi-million dollar mansion on top of Hollywood Hills, sucked into the highest echelons of movie power and on tour with a smoking hot band about to make their LA debut at Viper Room. What would Ulysses have to say about all this? Probably *"Steal their credit cards & buy beer."*

There is nothing like a stroll down Melrose Avenue to make you feel like the hardest-boiled land pyrate LA's ever seen. Just sliming up the walkways, making all those poofy-booted, painted up mascara chicks uncomfortable by your mere presence and dank bar smell. DTB keep thundering over laughing at the denizens of this city, the fact Valley Girls are casually shopping at stores such as Moist, Wett, Blue Balls.

Neil is hustled by Scientologists into a stress test. He grips those little metal conduits and the crazy man is surprised by his laid back readings. I lean up and whisper an ex-girlfriends name in his ear and they shoot off the scale... Back at Greg's pad we cook BBQ, get ripped on the Downtown Brown microbrewery beer we discovered, and watch *Idiocracy*, which has been the running gag of the voyage. Could Mike Judge possibly have better described Southern California?

Once we've dried off from the Jacuzzi, Greg leads us to a miniature cliff where you can see all of Los Angeles stretched below as one glowing behemoth. We sip champagne cordially as Greg relates a heart-warming tale: *'Ok, see that house over there? It's been vacant ever since they found the body. There were no leads until they caught this guy posting ads on internet message boards. He was literally a serial killer that never made it past one victim."*

"His whole scheme was telling these LA girls that he was casting for a James Bond movie. He actually convinced this girl from like Montana that the audition was on the hill. So he brings her up here alone at midnight and makes her recite all these bullshit script lines. Then he's like 'Well, in the scene you're tied up, so let me get this rope around you.' Then he handcuffs her, rapes her, bashes her head in with a rock, and tosses her body down this hill..."

"They didn't find this guy for two months, and he was fingered giving the 007 line at like a half-dozen girls that all fit the same profile... The girl he murdered lived three blocks over and was identical to my sister – makeup assistant, blonde, same age, same features, same neighborhood. The kicker was that the victim was from Michigan..."'

THE VIPER ROOM

Back to The Viper Room, a low-key Sunday night. Again, half the people are from Michigan because Natives of the New Dawn secured this gig. They are Detroit refugees as well – this sort of dub, hip hop, funk act with 7 members and a full horn section. They are the headliner of the evening, and Downtown Brown is about to go onstage to the drabbest anti-excitement.

There have been 4 other acts on the bill tonight, all mediocre and kissing the bar's ass onstage with that usual LA swagger. Anyone in attendance is doing the rock n' roll politics thing, making plastic friends in the back-stabbing trapezoid, flashing $1000 pairs of shoes and reeking of designer perfume.

DTB doesn't give the slightest shit though. That sycophant vibe has no connection, and they have no aspirations of a return gig. The curtain rolls open, and the 40 spread out people pay no attention. DTB bursts into "BITCHFIST," a funk-n-roll number that captures everyone's attention. After the tune, Neil takes a moment to connect with the audience: '*Oh LA, beautiful LA. We came all the way from Michigan just to snort coke of Johnny Depp's erect cock... But he's not here today. And that's a terrible thing, because we have no one to blow. Bills Dollerstein are you out there? Is there a rich Jewish businessman in attendance? We'll rub horseradish and soy sauce all over your balls and lick them clean for a contract at Crapitalist Records. That's right cheeko, we ain't got no soul. Put us on lunchboxes starting tomorrow, fucking hauk us at Walmart!!*"

I'd expected the power to be cut after that little jive. Instead, the audience moves closer to the stage, and the bartenders are laughing out loud. Even the swarmy manager guy in the suit, he's all smiles. Neil continues: '*See, where we're from in the Midwest, we have all of these fat chicks who go artificial tanning. You don't have that problem out here 'cause you have places like Venice Beach. But in the dead of winter, these chicks seal themselves in this cancer-causing death machines, fry themselves like baked potatoes, and they don't even get tanned. They fucking turn orange, they turn into Oompa Loompas. And all these white hat jockos hurl themselves all over them like a slop of rotten semen.*"

"*Well I ain't having that! I want my chicks vampiric and flabby. I want pimples and white skin. That's fucking beauty, not some painted up clown of a mascara nightmare. So all you chicks out there trying way too damned hard to be pretty little princesses, there is nothing uglier then caked on rouge and stinking like the blubber of a dead whale. This next song is called 'ORANGE BITCH.' FUCKING BURN IN HELL LA!!!*"

Somehow, someway, after insulting everyone in the crowd – *as well as defiling every last sacred, plastic ritual of LA in a monumental expulsion of venom* – DTB sells a record and t-shirt to everyone in attendance, is handed $150 of door money we were told we'd never see.

Neil actually is on the strip autographing the silicon implanted breasts of a dozen generically hot scumbags patiently waiting in line for his signature. One of them eyeballs me thinking I'm in the band, so I shuffle over casually. "So," I tell her, acting smooth: "*Wanna try out for the new James Bond film?*"

MY FIRST SPOKEN WORD GIG

"*You have no idea what you just did in LA. They've never seen anything like that. I've been to that shithole a half-dozen times now, and that was the most hypnotically entranced crowd I've seen. These people don't*

buy shirts or records, and you sold a $150 in merch on a Sunday night.
You fucking signed tits Neil."

They aren't believing my side of the story, it just sounds too magical to be real. Then Neil remembers a slip of paper in his back pocket. '*Yeah, the owner loved us. Apparently he's booked us to play his birthday party on the next tour.*' That shit doesn't happen. LA bands murder themselves for years just to get an opening gig at that place. It's all slowly sinking in as Neil recalls the rest of his woozy conversation. The owner is dead-set on getting them signed, and this late summer gig will be packed full of Record Industry Illuminati, celebrities, maybe even Depp.

All of this is churning in our heads and the boys can taste the mayhem. Oh they're going back alright, and plan on being such loud, boisterous assholes and creating so much havoc that they will never be signed in a million years. The ultimate goal of shitting on the dream contract is finally within reach…

Monday night, another dead gig in Scottsdale, Arizona, a small desert suburb of Phoenix. After two mediocre punk bands finish their set this awful mess of a snail-paced experimental project goes on. They have mic'd two empty 40 oz bottles to run through vacuum cleaner distortion, and one guy walks around the venue in circles tapping the glass with a drumstick, head covered in a babushka. They clear out the entire room with the lamest noise performance ever, grab their gear and abruptly leave, killing any chance we had of merch or gas money.

We're down to $80 and left to an audience of 7. Once again, half of them are from Michigan. One guy relocated from Lansing two years ago and shit bricks when he saw the tour poster. Mid-way through a brief chat with the fellow, Neil hollers: '*Yo – President Mountain Dew Komacho, you're on…*'

VERTIGO VENUS RESURRECTED

We wake up in Phoenix at the Lansing guys' house, and we've made fools of ourselves not realizing that the girl now packing a bowl of hi-grade Maui Wawi was his girlfriend all along. Nothing drastic mind you, but our obvious passes at her will forever ride this guys' memory.

Glover, Neil, and I have come to the conclusion that she is the most beautiful woman in America. Imagine if a Suicide Girl supermodel invited you over her house, you're wasted and think you have a chance, then she says "*check out my hobby,*" and pulls out 10 binders of Magic: The Gathering Cards 'cause she's a traveling tournament player. *Sexxxy with three x's...*

The spoken word went ok, considering it was so dead. I have a commitment to try new material every night so I can keep refining my itinerary. Yesterday I decided to tell everyone that the Bass Player from RATT sleeps on my couch, wooed them with tales of San Diego, then related the nature photography CVS girl with the missing pictures of her sleeping.

When I said, '*that was told to me by the singer of a Detroit band called Friends of Dennis Wilson*' one guy at the bar goes '*FUCK YEAH!*' Turns out he's Tony "Dennis Wilson" Moran's best friend from kindergarten. No connection to the Lansing guy, just a mysterious Detroit refugee that had no idea who DTB was in the first place or that any band from Michigan would be here tonight. That, in itself, is just as creepy as the story I told.

The hottest girl in America blows us kisses goodbye as we set sail for Albuquerque. I might actually have two spoken word gigs tonight – one at the local death metal venue, another downtown with Vertigo Venus, Diverje & Brian Botkiller.

The venue is a music store with a sizable group of 16 year old punk kids. There are about 50 heads, and three youngster locals opening of the by-the-book SICK OF IT ALL variety. By the time I have the opportunity to rant it is obvious the owner just wants to get this done quick. I'm slightly drunk, and it is obvious that no one is in the mood for my comedic stylings...

By the time "Sit In The Pit" comes around – a knock at weenie pop punk complete with Blink 182 riff – Neil has all of these kids sitting Indian style in the pit, swaying their arms back and forth in koombayah. When the song dive-bombs into vicious hardcore punk a circle pit busts out and a whirlwind of bodies go flailing in every direction. By the end of the show Neil has this mob of angry, mohawked teens dancing in a conga-line. He even has them singing and grooving to the Motown classic "SHOUT."

Once again, shit like this does not happen. TSOL doesn't do that. Strung Out doesn't do that. If Black Flag tried to get kids to sit koombayah they'd be eaten alive. This is the hypnotic power that Downtown Brown casts upon its subjects. It is black magic goofiness from another realm...

'So how many Ramen Noodles have you consumed this year alone?' I ask Jeff MacCannon of Vertigo Venus, who never ceases to amaze me. *'A lot actually, mostly due to the internet show I do where I'm always making recipes out of Ramen. Probably this year I've spent $50 on Ramen, which is about 500 packets... A lot of our episodes will parody ourselves, like there was an episode where I got pregnant. The big moral of the story is that I am not a seahorse."*

"There was one 'Surviving After The Apocalypse – In Style.' We had this 80's montage and I had the big George Michael ass shot in the ripped jeans and whatnot. So we had to get weapons, you have to fortify your car, but we had to do it cheap because we are a DIY punk show. We had spray paint to make cardboard look like steel, tape it to your car..."

"We haven't lately because one host is the owner of a daycare company for some hippie Montesary school. It's so weird, like this vegan existence for kids. Kids with names like Lavender and Israel..."

Another night in ABQ, and I feel like I've stepped through time. After San Fran and Denver, this place retrospectively feels like a limp, wet noodle. When Tommy T turned the corner of the bar patio and saw me standing there, he squinted his freshly bloodshot eyes and said, *'Why are....'* [7 second pause] *'...you here?'* Just breezing through the jewel of the desert, the fly on the wall of a midnight bar...

THE PWN HOUSE

Wednesday April 18th. We slept in the alley behind the Vertigo Venus house. It was so cold our moisture froze to ice on the interior roof. It was another 5 hours to Amarillo, one of the most desolate stops on the Greyhound circuit. It's like a *Mad Max* of the elderly. There is only one major building and it stands 20 stories high at the town's center. Around it are sparse stores, all flat and dilapidated, none higher then a single story. Tumbleweeds blow in the street, the grass is burnt & yellow, and old people walk around in weird, mechanical jettisons...

We were supposed to play a small DIY punk info shop, but the water main busted and the buildings flooded out. Our options are hang around drinking at one of these scary bars with cowboy boots and steers painted on the side, or just jet to Oklahoma. We take the latter, killing time at a Texas mall of static immobility.

Halfway to Norman we stop for ice cream at the biggest Crucifix in North America. The thing is like 60 stories tall and its shadow juts over the landscape for miles. At its base are bronze statues of Jesus and the two thieves being crucified. Some biker is kneeling before them. His sleeveless leather jacket has a patch of Christ nailed to the cross inside a glowing paradise of wonder. "FAITH RIDER" is embroidered in frilly, Old English font...

The Norman contact lives a good 3 miles off the freeway. The lanes are exceptionally wide, and the street signs are blue and abnormally lengthy. Other than that, it looks rather dull...You can smell the dogs as we approach the brown brick house with muddy shudders. From a dimly lit enclave a huge 6 foot 5 Indian guy bursts out the screen door, and with one turn leads us into a crust haven. There are 5 dirty punks drinking Southern Comfort, all sporting grind back patches. The walls are caked in flyers, movie posters & Star Wars propaganda.

There is a huge black and white Crass poster of Mussolini's kicked in, squashed skull: *'The plight of the oppressed ends with the oppressor. Mussolini found this to be true. There will be others.'* 'Others' as in the line of KKK guys carrying torches...

What we've stumbled into is the Oklahoma version of The Eagles Nest. This place is called The PWN House (the *pown* house), and this rag-tag crew encapsulates the only weirdoes in the area. Oklahoma is square as you'd expect, and this flophouse is the prime jewel. These guys have thrown every worthwhile show here for the past decade. They are so die-hard that no one is allowed to listen to CD's or iPOD's in the house. It's all vinyl or nothing, and rare LP's & splits are just lying in piles everywhere.

The huge Indian guy is named Matt Jim, and he's the big dog of the household. He's the guitarist of a local thrash/grind band called Snotrokitz, and goes by many nicknames such as 'The Plow,' 'The Beastmaster,' '30 Stone,' 'Matt Jemimah.' Big Matt explains the genesis of our current reality: *'First there was The Skull House. This was back in the dark ages, before Studio 360 where you'll be playing tomorrow. The basement was no bigger than someone's living room, and half of that was taken up by the stage and equipment. So it was maybe 40-50 people crammed elbow to elbow, like living cells in a piece of tissue. Just vibrating and pulsating with all kinds of injuries."*

"Whenever Hammer from Japan played it was packed. Same with Hero Disown Us from Finland. After the lease was up we had nowhere to throw shows. Then we found PWN. It's called The PWN House 'cause before we moved in there were a bunch of gamer guys that played lots of dungeons and dragons and video games. When

they'd type 'you got owned' on their live link they'd misspell it as 'You Got Pwned.' It just stuck. So for a whole year we had the ability to bring all kinds of bands to our garage. But then the cops came to one of our shows and said if we did anymore they would shut off our water and evict us all."

No cops on the horizon tonight. Instead we're playing beer pong, drinking whiskey, and being fed an endless assault of killer vinyl. This short blonde guy named Tucker with two weird mullet dreads is in that frantic, *'Ah ha! But have you heard this?!?'* mode. Shot after shot of whiskey he keeps jumping on the turntable. I'm shocked to learn the boys are friends with Catheter from Denver, and that they've done multiple shows with Cephalic Carnage. I notice a flyer that lists Exitium and learn the guitarist will actually be at the show. Somehow another priority band magically falls into my lap…

ADIDAS FISHNET RUMBLER

"So I'm at The Pita Pit. This is a few years ago, like 3 am on Saturday Night, and everyone is coming from the bars. I look over the counter, and I'm thinking, 'This can't be real – no fuckin' way cause I'm stoned as fuck. But I see the zig-zagged corn-rowed hair and it's really him – it's Coolio. He buys a Philly steak and expects the extra meat for free."

"He looks twacked out like he's been doing meth or coke, and wants to know where he can get a dime bag. Later some people from the club come on in. I say, 'Coolio came in tonight.' And they say, 'Yeah, he walked on his tab – I guess he figures since he's Coolio it doesn't matter.' Then all of us were like, 'What the fuck is he doing in Oklahoma anyway?"

Tucker chuckles over his rap legend story as we drive to the $1 store. NASUM is blaring on the stereo, and the phrase 'THE MERLE HAGGARD MOVEMENT' is sloppily painted over the back windshield. He's never been pulled over for it either, which goes to show how easily country music can be utilized as police camouflage… Last night was rough. All I remember is being told the dogs have scabies, and something about wrestling a Marine on the floor after teaching each other choke-holds…

Inside the $1 store I get a weird tingle and look down. There is a little girl in a blue dress, eyes burning a hole through my cranium. She points to the rotting corpse head on my Repulsion shirt and declares, *"Your shirt is scaw-wing me."* I look her in the eyes cut-throat as possible: *"GOOD."* I turn to the DVD bin ignoring her completely.

Tucker fumbles around with merchandise trying to act nonchalant for a half minute with the girl still standing there. He cocks his head back & looks at her staring eyes, then explodes in uncontrollable gut laughter…

One of the PWN house guys – a skinny, tripped out drunkard named Gene – takes us to the outreach program of a Christian church to acquire free food. The nice old lady gives us three bags each, filled with groceries – eggs, bacon, granola bars, pop tarts, the works. Before she lets Neil take his portion she queries what he does in life. He says, "*Oh you know, just trying to take over the world bit by bit.*" Her face shrinks into this hideous, vulture-like scowl. "*Well you know Hitler wanted to take over the world too.*"

Back at PWN we gorge ourselves before shooting off to see *Grindhouse*, which is incredible. *Death Proof* is given new meaning when Gene blurts a classic line: '*Mike's problems with women were exacerbated by the scar which also ended his stunt career, propelling him towards high-octane murder.*" You just kinda had to be there…

Finally, my first *real* spoken word gig; I lead into it with Chuck the Homey, Matt Ratt, Jesus's EMINEM terrorism. Onward comes the knockout blow: "*So, Oklahoma… This isn't my first time here. Anyone heard of a place called Muskogee? What is it, like 3 hours east of here? Oh yeah, I hear them boo's. Well, I thought it was mighty apocalyptic.*"

"*We went there for the premier of this little movie we did called DADBOT, this gathering called the Bare Bones Film Festival. The initial meeting was downtown, so all the filmmakers & judges are present. People are line-dancing, drinking punch, then these air raid sirens start wailing like its London being bombed by the Luftwaffe. Outside the sky is pea-green, and there are 5 huge twisters swirling around us. We're fucking doomed, you know? Last cigarettes & shit…*"

"*But it can't end like this, no fucking way. You see, I've always been convinced that my life will end just like 'Wayne's World 2.' As in with my dying breath, the weird naked Indian is going to show up and take me to the nether-realm. Just he & I & Jim Morrison eating acid in the desert for eternity, dodging them unruly 'Beetlejuice' sandworms.*"

"*We're all crowded in the bomb shelter, and by random chance the secret guest of the program is actually – yeah, dead serious here – the fucking weird naked Indian from 'Wayne's World 2.' Literally, he's right there, except in blue jeans & flannel. He's there tonight promoting a cameo in 'Dr. Quinn Medicine Woman.' That one popular out here? No? What about 'Walker Texas Ranger?' Ha ha, that's right man. Chuck Norris doesn't get rained on, the rain gets Chuck Norrised..."*

"Anyway, I walk up to the weird naked Indian, look him straight in the eye, and tell him everything I just told you. Then I ask sincerely: 'Sir, is it really time? Are you gonna take me to Jim Morrison now?' He stood there staring at me like I was completely insane, no idea what to say. So I just shrugged: 'Well, um... can I just have an autograph then?'"

I'm outside the venue chatting with a 16 year old Russian Jew on a skateboard. She's trying to convince me that she's a 'White Commie,' a die-hard of the socialist sect Lenin wiped out. The lanky vocalist from the bad nu-metal opening band is in a violent tizzy, rambling about slashing our tires. Earlier this same terribly non-menacing kid (*in an Adidas hat & long-sleeve fishnet shirt neatly tucked into his blue jeans*) ran up to Neil at sound check, throwing his arms in the air: '*YOU GOT A PROBLEM WITH MY FISHNETS MOTHERFUCKER?!?"*

So this breedbate is freaking outside the venue, gathering his minions for a monkey riot. I pull him aside: "*Look man, I'm the tour manager. What's going down?"* Apparently Neil, drunk as always, made some comment about the guys' apparel to Glover. Then Neil was talking about some fight he got into in high school, and somehow the guy twisted it around and thought it was a declaration of war. Finally he relaxes, but his goon squad still goes back inside to make a fortified line of crossed arm heavy metal-scowls, trying to intimidate DTB.

Neil busts into the set with joyousness, shooting lazar beams from his guitar that hits the disco ball just right. Everyone is digging it, even the jaded crusties: "*You know, everyone says Jesus is a bad guy. But there was this one time I got stuck at the bowl with no toilet paper on the roll. Oh my god, what a wreck. There's just shit everywhere, chocolate all over the walls. It's dripping like a gelatinous Cosby mess of rocky road. What was I to do? What would you do?"*

"So I start praying, and Jesus floated down on his heavenly cloud. And do you know what he told me Oklahoma? Do you know what he fucking told me?!? He extended his palm oh so lovingly and said, 'Son. To prove you're a man, you must wipe with MY hand.'"

"And I did. I shoved Christ's hand right up my ass, dug it around a bit, removed every last nudge of chocolate... And then Jesus smiled. Ho ho ho. And I smiled. Ho hum har... And you know what he

did? He grabbed the guy in the stall right before me, looked him straight in the eyes and said 'BITCH – it's all because of you. That poo poo on my shoe. I must confess, I used my shirt to clean up all this mess [insert badass drum blast here]…"

The fishnet rumbler & his squad roar with laughter throughout the show, and all buy merch after. When fishnet finally approached Neil he was bracing for a punch. Instead the guy wanted an autograph. He gave Neil all of their door money ($60) and told him they were one of the best live bands he'd ever seen. *The Exploited does not do this. The Damned have never done this…*

EXITIUM

Kirk Kirkwood: "Exitium actually just broke up four weeks ago. We started in September 2001, originally as a joke band. We were named [indecipherable Latin], which was a horrible misinterpretation. It was meant to be Satan And Friends, but it turned out to be Satan's Girlfriends. (Laughs). We decided to get serious and change formats. We practiced and wrote for 6 months then we played our first show. From thereon we started playing shows everywhere in the metro area."

Do you think people 'get' grind here?"

"It's a really small community in Oklahoma. Everyone knows each other. In Norman we have a legitimate grindcore scene. You get to other towns and you get kids that say they play it, but its metalcore shit. They might claim to be grind on their MySpace, but that doesn't mean they're grind."

"What's the touring been like?"

"We've done regional tours, but that's as far as we've gone. We've played Colorado with Catheter at their house. It was crazy, there were over 200 kids in this small place. We maintained a good friendship with them, so they'll come back and we'll always play… The first album was recorded in July 2002, but it wasn't out until late 2004. It didn't do that great, but that was because there was no distribution behind it. We sent it out but no one ever really responded, and we never really saw any reviews.

[Tucker charges into the PWN House kitchen in a whiskey whirlwind: "In two minutes this guys gonna come running in like AAARRGGH!!!" Kirk and I look at each other confused]

"What are some of your favorite books?"

I'm a big fan of Kurt Vonnegut…

[Now we know why. Matt Jim is a butt-naked Goliath, a monstrous, gelatinous shadow blotting out the overhead light. 'You wanted a weird naked Indian, you fucking got one!' He charges and presses me against the sink with his blubber, and starts disco dancing with his tits in my face. I feel like The Undertaker battling Yokozuna at Summer Slam '94. 'Ahhh!! Why is this happening to me?!? There's a weird naked Indian rubbing his balls all over my chest!!!' The entire PWN House is a looney bin. Matt backs off chuckling, and I take a swig of Jack Daniels]

"Well that's a first for me. I've never been attacked by a 300 lbs naked Indian while doing an interview before... Well... Ahem... Returning to the interview..."

[Amazingly he zangs back into his pre-flesh mid-thought]: "This last album is going to be extremely political, the *Grind After Death* album. It's going to be over the top, almost pompous lyrics. He's going balls to the wall with this. We're trying to make the smartest grind album ever made."

"What happened with the break-up?"

"We decided collectively not to go into detail about what happened. Obviously Exitium was left with myself and the bass player. You can come up with your own conclusions' *[random drunk guy wanders past and blurts 'they became Mormons' before belching]."*

"Tell me about Oklahoma. Are kids here so bored they just want to jump off skyscrapers?"

"I don't think so. They're not as crazy as you might think. Personally I've been looking for people to go skydiving with, but it's really hard. Everyone says *'I'm not ready to die yet.'* Come on, you've got to take risks... Our shows have always had a lot of injuries – broken teeth, broken fingers, all bloody. Kids splitting their head open..."

"Anything else you'd like to add?"

"I'm finishing Exitium with *Grind After Death*. It's going to be about 40 minutes worth of material by the end of the summer. Any bands out there that might be looking for a guitar player, if I can get set up with a potential job flipping burgers, I'm not limited to grind. I'm not limited to Oklahoma..."

IT'S NOT PARANOIA IF THEY REALLY ARE OUT TO GET YOU

Friday, April 20th 2007 – the 7th anniversary of the Columbine shootings & Hitler's 107th birthday. Deep-sleeping bodies line the floor. I'm the first awake, and when I turn the hallway a man named Juice shoves a

Philly blunt in my mouth. He crawls back into his bunker and I step into the perfect summer day.

Paranoia works over as I make the rattled-stoner connections: *"Ok, every time I'm in Oklahoma there is a weird naked Indian and tornado's trying to kill me. All set on the Indian, but we need to get out immediately lest we're swept off to Oz."* I wake the boys in a rushed panic, lying and saying its later then it actually is. I just want to shove off to Little Rock.

20 miles from the Texas border, DTB spot a Sonic Burger on the side of the highway. I close my eyes and start to doze off, but then I hear a walloping mass of air-raid sirens. I try to exit the vehicle, but the doors are stuck shut between another car and the drive-in menu. I roll down the window, hop through, and thud on the cement. The sky is churning a pea green and rotating clouds are quite visible. I run up to DTB who are all slobbing breakfast burritos. Air raid or not, they're finishing lunch.

Some black guy with a goofy brain-damage vibe strolls up and asks if I dig football. I say sure, and he tells me he plays for Oklahoma State. When I mention my Detroit origin, he goes on a stutter-heavy Barry Sanders rant. He starts doing twist & turn mannerisms totally weird, like he's acting out some of #20's most famous plays. Then he asks what we're doing out here. *"Oh, well, I'm on tour with this band."* Bad idea. He's a Christian gospel rapper and wants to meet everyone 'cause it might help his career. He's asking for autographs, trying to hitchhike to Texas.

We shake the guy off and jump back in the van. The fellas are now noticing how quickly the wind is gushing. We're racing down the freeway going *"FUCK, FUCK, FUCK"* as the 90 mph winds shake the swaying van, which is hauling ass at 75 mph. Three twisters forming in the distance, sky growing black… Cross the Texas state line and immediately everything turns the clearest blue, like a magical cut-off. Oklahoma thwarted…

HAPPY FUCKERS UNITE

Little Rock; hometown of Bill Clinton. Arkansas has a Virginia feel to it – sloppily hacked together; miniature forests and rusted industrial carcasses strewn about, eluding the grace of a Gettysburg or Richmond. You can spot the city center from the freeway, but it's not much to look at – just a few tall buildings & major streets that branch off into dirt roads & crumbling asphalt. It's up one of these dusty roads padded with small rocks that we rendezvous with promoter Casey Jones.

It's a decent sized two-bedroom home, all these multi-colored party streamers taped to the ceiling and gently blowing from the industrial-grade fan. It's like some oceanic oasis at the bottom of the sea, and there are coloring book pictures of *Little Mermaid* all over the walls. It's the girlfriend's doing of course – this weird, fairy-like hippie chick. Casey looks like he's been up for 2 days, packing a bowl and toying with the swathe of raver candy bracelets riding up his forearm.

Casey Jones has nothing to do with mutant ninja turtles, but he does have everything to do with the Little Rock music scene. He's the mastermind of nearly everything that's occurring here, and is head of a collective entitled HFU (*Happy Fuckers Unite*). Casey's been burning himself out relentlessly throwing 4 shows a week, curating three underground DIY venues, assisting local theater productions, and assuming film/video projects whenever possible. In the past year he's put on 150 DIY shows, and is in the midst of converting a massive warehouse into a practice/recording studio and multi-stage venue.

The gig was supposed to be at a DIY venue called "The Tree House," but the cops shut it down 2 days ago. In response Casey rented "The Riverfront History Pavilion" for $50 off the city, which is in the main park a skip & a leap from the downtown hipster area. The parking lot is full of cars, but everyone is out dining.

The crowd tonight are mostly artsy-fartsy college kids with red scarves and tight pants, even though it's mighty humid. I try to babble a performance but they stare at me blankly; my first undisputed bomb. Downtown Brown's luck isn't much better. They think its stupid, and Neil just struggles: '*So, um, yeah… You kids go to art school right? What do you think of poop? Funny stuff huh? You squeeze your butt cheeks and chocolate comes out… yeah.*'

Sitting atop the literal "Little Rock" on the shore of the river bank, which is the namesake of the city. It must bring good luck like The Blarney Stone though, 'cause I found a fully rolled joint laying in the grass beside it.

We sleepily watch the headliner whom everyone is excited for. They are called The STD's and have blue circle arm-bands like The Germs. The music is mediocre and the chubby singer kid is doing one of those "*I'm so fucking punk rock!*" asshole routines, playing up the vibe of Jabbers-era GG. He speaks with a fake English accent: "*Alright, listen up bluddy fuckin' cunts – this song is "1, 2, FUCK YOU!!!"*"

FOXY SHAZAM AND LIMOUSINE DOOR

SUNDAY, April 22nd: The Poison Room in Cincinnati. Last night we stayed at the spacious 3 level home of Foxy Shazam vocalist Skye White, huddling in his recording studio. The gig in Nashville had been canceled at the last minute. Short on money and desperate for gas, we begged the guy from "Crazy Dad Promotions" to set us up.

He pulled through but when we get to the unmarked redneck shithole they had no PA. In fact, the bartender never even heard of the promoter before. The Jukebox played Conway Twitty, Nascar posters crowded the walls. Half a dozen bikers gave us angry looks and this bald, Sloth-like hick in overalls giggled & drooled like a nitrous-oxide down syndrome victim. We told the bartender we'd be back in 5 minutes, but just gunned it for Cincinnati.

Foxy Shazam are at the major breaking point of their career, soon to embark on a full USA tour with Tub Ring. Members Skye and Loran are drinking tall cans with me in the DTB van, and I can't help but stare at Skye's peculiar mutton-chop beard thing which is quite the facial hair marvel. Skye strokes it like a martial arts sensei and points to the "Top Shelf" bed, ruminating just how Neil P can even sleep up there, that chiromaniac tomb. I explain: ***He's a very strange, fat man who can contort like the stretchy hive-nest guy from X-Files..."***

Skye White: "That freak."

"Are the lyrics satirical, are they serious?"

Loren Turner: "They're poems based off an imaginary place called 'Limousine Door'..."

"We named our album *Flamingo Trigger* which is the moat that takes you to this magical, mystical place, and we have songs about different characters and places. There's a bar and a jukebox called the Olive Branch jukebox. If Erik doesn't feel like writing about Limousine Door than it's a song playing on the jukebox."

"How'd you meet the guys from Tub Ring?"

"They'd always be touring through Cincinnati. The fourth show we did as Foxy Shazam we kicked and screamed to get on the bill. When you're on tour you see bands doing the same thing over and over, then you see something a little different and it turns your head. We built a friendship, started doing some regional stuff, then we got asked to do a two-week..."

SW: "Its Tub Rings CD release tour, the album is called *The Great Filter*, so the tour is 'The Great Fil-Tour.' Its 6 weeks – East Coast, Midwest, Texas, Canada..."

"When you drive by elementary schools do children start crying?"

"They just look at me and I smile back."

"Tell me about Cincinnati."

"It's pretty mid-west. There's no music industry, no real scene. There isn't any public transportation and I think that has an effect on people not going to see live music. It's real hard to get people out, you have to work double time. I know in Cleveland they have a better scene and also in Dayton."

"Give me a nightmare tour story."

"The first tour we did absolutely blew. I put it together and we went out to try and hack it. The drives were ridiculous. The van was just horrible; it had 350,000 miles on it. The steering wheel was barely on it. Every time you tried to brake it shot you in one direction."

"The exhaust shot into the van, if it was cold snow blew in the van. You couldn't lay on the ground or have a body part touching it or you'd get burnt by it because the exhaust was so fucked up."

"It put everybody in horrible moods. You go to play a show and everybody's sick because of the draft... Then me and the bass player, we're at Virginia Beach, and we climb up the Chesapeake Bay Bridge. We were going to jump onto the sand dunes 'cause it's only 13 feet high. Soon as we did, cop pulls up, starts pushing us around, he's pissed. All we did was climb up the bridge. So he took us to the station. Then we're coming back from Nashville, and Skye is driving it for the first time..."

"A little sports car comes flying by us, flashing and trying to get us over. We're in the middle of Kentucky. We pull over..."

"And the tire on the back was half a rim. The tire was gone, half the rim was gone... So we drove to the next exit grinding it for 3 miles. There's two gas stations so I pull in the middle trying not to look suspicious. We're looking around, there's a junkyard by us."

"There happens to be a thousand tires laying around, but not a single one for a trailer. So we're looking through a hundred tires."

"Then we see a U-Haul trailer at a gas station up on the hill. I break the locks, we get the tire off, put our rim on so it wasn't looking all weird. Then we ran as fast as we could to our trailer, and it's actually still on there now."

"Tell me a crazy story, anything…"

"I was getting Indian food and there was this pigeon. On the ground, right in front of my back tire. Just sitting there, daring me to run it over, trying to commit suicide under my car. So I kept trying to move it, but it kept moving around real weird, so I was going to have to kill it. I happened to have a key-tar [keyboard guitar] in my trunk. I'm on this fairly busy street, with this key-tar in my hand, climbing under my car trying to whack a pigeon. This pigeon keeps scooting around into another way that it can die. It'd just look at me like "What?" like it's that tough. This hobo with yellow eyes and a grocery bag full of twelve boxes of Goobers comes up. *'Hey, ya' need sum help? Give me a dollar n' I'll get the bird out.'* So this hobo goes under and starts whacking it with Goobers. I think he got so creeped out he just left. I just started scooting back, forward, back, forward, back, like really, really slow and having my friend make sure I wasn't going to run it over. That bird was messed up…"

PART VII: ALABAMA
(THE SCOURGE OF HUNTSVILLE)
MAY 10TH-MAY 16TH 2007

THE ONLY THING YOU NEED TO KNOW ABOUT DETROIT
It seems appropriate as I leave Detroit for the darkest of black metal worlds there happens to be two sharply defined rainbows jutting through the sky. The Howard St. depot so well burned in my memory from Black Valentine's is now just another waiting room on the circuit.

Detroit was a two-week anti-love affair with my old stomping grounds. Most loose ends tied or otherwise handcuffed, but shit takes a weird turn downtown Royal Oak. I was determined not to let anyone notice me, but as I approached Borders Books two 15 year old girls were walking in my direction. One said to the other, "*that's him, that's him,*" and the other started giggling. Then the girl looks at me and says, "*hello kind sir*" and salutes me like a military officer – a mannerism staple of mine. I'm not sure what to do, utterly flabbergasted. So I just give a weird smile and a quick wave. They giggle and run off like they spotted a real celebrity…

I visit the old trailer determined to take care of my stolen Daytona, and amazingly it's parked out front. It was discovered yesterday in a Pontiac field with slashed tires, deep dents on the side having been beaten with lead pipes…

My grind demo as SASQUATCH AGNOSTIC is pumped out featuring members of Salt Lick and Return To Dust. My new alter ego is "Benedict Badoglio," and the recording is christened the *Complete Mammalography: 1986-1998.* I create a fake MySpace account with this lavish tale of how we're some forgotten, legendary outfit from Northern Michigan who supposedly pre-dated Napalm Death and Repulsion. All these huge bands we supposedly influenced have ignorantly accepted our friend requests, and are paraded through our Top 24 as to give the appearance of credibility.

Weird moment with Absinthe after I capture the roving Dr. Santiago. He was paranoid, at the end of his rope, drinking himself silly. He'd been caught walking around the suburbs with a miniature samurai sword on his belt. The cops didn't get the joke, and now he's charged with a concealed weapons felony and faces up to 5 years in prison. He now can never leave the United States. Santiago's just hanging out until the Greyhound ticket comes through, then he's bailing again to SoCal.

Later that same night, Santiago and I go to Mephisto's Detroit with one of their stripping cage-dancers. It's a classy three-story pimped-out mansion for the freaks, along the lines of a vampiric Hue Heffner retreat. It's an underground nest with a consistently growing goth and punk undercurrent, although no live bands are on tonight. Instead it's Vampire: The Masquerade role playing evening, and all these fat goth chicks and obnoxious D&D guys are in character, intoxicated, rolling dice on the floor.

Out on the balcony an old school comrade named Crazy Joe recognizes me and says: "*Hold on man, I'll be back in 20 minutes – DO NOT LEAVE.*" He pulls back up in a gigantic black hearse that has a crimson eyeball-glowing grim reaper as a hood ornament, purple neon lights underneath, red-satin coffin back-hatch with tinted black windows and a full bar in the trunk. The license plate said FRESH and it had dice in the mirror (*well the dice were real, but the plate actually read "HARVSTER"*).

Crazy Joe – a chemist and scientist – mixes a potion and pours us Absinthe shots. Bitter downing, a few swigs mixed with Hawaiian Punch. Then Joe whips out the blunt, starts laughing crazily, and spins the hearse in reverse, slamming on the screeching brakes: "*I drank a lot of fucking absinthe man, HAHAHAHA.*"

We zoom off at 60 MPH in this vehicle of doom, flying through 25 MPH ghetto speed zones; jumping curbs, swerving like mad. 'Aenima' by TOOL is blaring on the thumping sound system, and Crazy Joe keeps singing Maynard's apocalyptic ruminations word for word. He starts doing 70 mph down a 35 speed-zone chanting "*LEARN TO SWIM, LEARN TO SWIM…*"

SOUTHERN CHARM, SERPENTINE

The ride to Huntsville is relaxed – environment sparse and huge, humid and dense. This is my first southern Greyhound route and the deeper you go, the more you find people making a buck anyway they can. Wherever rural land dominates there are home-made stands pimping black market vegetables; the Harper Lee strain rides high.

The closer we get to the "Rocket City," ex-military equipment clutters the sides of freeways in greater intervals. Passing NASA and military instillations numerous hollowed out nukes stand erect, dead tanks as memorial landmarks. Are they tourist snap-shot fodder or

Republican-minded hard-on's? I envision an Alabaman shuttle clanking on the surface of mars, mullet-laden astronaut planting a confederate flag on the planetary wasteland.

Let's get real folks – stereotypes exist because 90% of the time they are dead-on. This is, after all, the world that elected Wallace 4 times over, and became the hallmark of *"segregation now, segregation tomorrow, segregation forever."* My gut says I'm in for a hearty dose of crush the fags, nuke them sandnigs, *"goddam lib-ber-als"* gibberish.

I'm expecting bikers and rednecks, maybe some skins or nationalist types. I'm not thrilled obviously, but it comes with the territory. Metal's key-phrase of 'brutal' gets an injection of testosterone. But I'm no simple city boy. This is more my true element then San Fran or New York because I this poverty stricken, Sam's Club Nascar culture. Michigan is the biggest secret redneck state in the union. I might speak well, but at heart I'm still a rat-tailed hoodlum gritting for a monster truck rally.

This is a side mission offered by Mortigan of the black metal dirge machine OCTAGON, who just acquired ex-Gorgoroth vocalist Pest since relocating from Norway to Nashville. I became aware of OCTAGON via Chicago-based Autopsy Kitchen Records, who also notably releases STALAGGH domestically. Mortigan's apartment is the HQ of his personal label Destructive Industries, who specialize in black metal, ambient, noise, power electronics, BDSM sleaze-porn.

Mortigan's roommate "Thorgrin" (a.k.a. Chris White) is the keyboardist of ethereal black metal band Blood Stained Dusk. Thorgrin also runs his own label Black Flame Records, which have put out a diverse spectrum of extreme metal. It will be the purest of bullet-belted, old school, Satan-&-leather realities.

Tonight Mortigan is throwing a touring package black metal show at a local sports bar. The entire bill is from the Atlanta region – Demoncy, Tenebrous, Crimson Moon, Legions of Astaroth, and Unnamed Generic BM Band, with OCTAGON as support. This is one of the first dates of the BM horde stampede, which will carry onward through the Southwest and up the West coast to Seattle…

MEET TOMMY MORTIGAN

A green Cherokee pulls up jamming Slavic black metal. Mortigan hops out and shakes my hand. He is super-friendly, super-professional, this vicious Darwinian nihilist – twisted humor, deranged pervert, living encyclopedia of extreme metal. Just a pissed loner in his own dark world, life based around the multi-faceted dimensions of his art.

Mortigan, driving: *"I'm from Seattle. I'm a yank. My dad was in the military so between here and Germany I've lived everywhere, probably a hundred places, if only for three days. England, France, Howell Michigan, Lansing. Washington, Oregon, Ohio, Maryland. I moved up to Huntsville from Mississippi not all too long ago."*

"What's the difference?"

Mortigan: "This is more upscale. We've got NASA, so people are more educated. It's a military town with the largest base in the Southern United States. Its arsenal is actually as big as the city itself. Outside one of the main industries is liquor. In Mobile you have Jack Daniels, Southern Comfort. This is the buckle of the Bible Belt. We've actually got two Mosques now, so it's a far cry from the Alabama of two years ago. Back then the shit would have been bombed or spray-painted by rednecks."

"How was living in Michigan for you?"

"I lived in Lansing and I don't think I was ever beaten up more in school (laughs). But Huntsville's a fuckin' joke. I'm probably going to move up to Virginia – I've got some projects up there."

"How did Pest from Gorgoroth end up in Alabama?"

"He lives in Tennessee, just outside Nashville. He's studying to be a history professor. Every Norwegian citizen has to serve in the military. He did his time but afterwards, since he'd been doing tours since a teenager, he chose to pursue a family and his studies. He had a child with his wife two years ago. Picket fence love, but that's what he wanted. Really cool guy, one of the nicest, funniest people I've had the pleasure to be around. He accomplished more than any of us will in our lives as far as being in a band. And I admire him for being so humble about it. As far as black metal vocalists goes, Pest was the serious reason that I was able to do the vocals I've been able. He has a sin-instrument wicked style and you watch him and it'll look like he isn't doing shit, but he's unbelievable. He's an enigma, a fucking living presence."

"What are the main cities worth checking out?"

"Mobile has got a huge scene, it just depends what you're looking for. Anywhere you go it's the emo trend anyway. Here you have the best metal scene. In Huntsville you're an hour or so away from Nashville and three hours from Atlanta."

"How long have you been doing Octagon for?"

"'94, I'd just turned 14. All the typical reasons to start a metal band. I was pissed off, angry, mad at the world. It was basically black metal, but it had an industrial touch, like Skinny Puppy influence. Around that time I started getting really into black metal. I was tired of death, because everything sounded the same."

"Why did you choose the name OCTAGON?"

"The Octagon relates to a lot of concepts in the occult. It has to do with all aspects of life, magick, secrecy, numerology, the trapezoid, hidden structures. Everything within the OCTAGON, it's a metaphor for my life and art. It's my roots, it captures my own perimeters as well as the actual music, not just cliché black metal stuff. In a way it's like an incantation and also reincarnation. OCTAGON metaphorically was a starting point of my own re-incarnation. No matter what happens –the negative, the positive, the surreal, the transcendental – it always comes back to the roots."

"The lyrics are heavy on sadomasochism"...

"It's Victorian in a way... People see BDSM and fetishism as a sickness. I think everyone is a sick individual deep inside, and some aren't ashamed of it and are personified by that. There's a lot of shit I've surprised myself by, and a lot of shit I'll never do, ha ha. I'm a power freak, I'm not ashamed..."

"WE ARE THE SCARS ON THE FLESH OF CHRIST"
THURSDAY, May 10th, a sports dive entitled Benchwarmers. ESPN is broadcasting golf on multiple screens, and auto shop grease monkeys pound drafts as 20 leather-and-denim demon, all-black-all-the-time extreme metal guys & gals horde the back, talking amongst themselves. But not to each other – as with all black metal scenes it's more a grim-and-frostbitten *Seinfeld*, whereas those four main characters only chat with each other no matter the backdrop. There are about four tribes here, all fanatically anti-social.

There are no real venues in Huntsville except this one for extreme metal. The local yokels simply ignore the bestial, roaring nature of these shows. They don't care what's going on, so long as they sell booze on a dead Thursday and get it over with quickly. Tonight it is a five-band bill featuring OCTAGON, Tenebrous, Demoncy, Legions of Astaroth, Crimson Moon

Outside the poverty-stricken disparity rides high. In the field adjacent to Benchwarmers is a small black community nestled in an ugly grotto of brown one-floor shacks that are fenced in with barbed wire & surrounded by humongous steel electrical poles. University Drive, the highway clearly visible from the parking lot, is a lengthy haul of fast food franchises & business complexes. Most side streets connecting to it are pure dirt, and all homes are middle-class suburban at best. .. Mortigan has just pulled out these massive inverted crucifixes for each side of the stage – just large pieces of timber nailed together and spray-painted black. It is budget-friendly and charmingly satanic...

I slink out back with Mortigan's buddy Lance Wright, who was of the homecoming crowd that greeted me at Morty's apartment. Eight people immediately shaking my hand, all involved in music as label head, musician, or promoter.

My reputation had preceded me, and I realized just how important my arrival was to these guys – to have a real-life metal journalist guy spend 30 hours on a Greyhound just to hang out for a week in Nowheresville. I was a rock star and it felt good, not some blown-off bum with a tape-recorder sleeping in the park.

I was slopped with 7 t-shirts and 20 records before Mortigan dragged me in the kitchen. "*I wasn't sure what you'd be into, so I got them all.*" He waved his arm across his tabletop and revealed an armada of booze. A fifth of Jack Daniels, a half gallon of Jim Beam, a 30 case of Budweiser, and two gallons of Southern Comfort (*one mint, one normal*).

Six hours later and we're working on the mint SoCo as Lance Wright lights a blunt in his car. It is pouring rain, lightning and thunder are crashing, the humidity is thick as clam chowder. Lance relates his experience as the touring drummer of famed death metal act VILE, plus his local duties in Tipper Gore, Quinta Essentia, and Lysia Gori: "*Tipper Gore is old school thrash, Dark angel type thrash, super high-soaring vocals. Conceptually it's a Christian band. Garth from Fleshtized started it is a holy roller, but he writes some good riffs. I'm not Christian in any way, but I do like good metal... Lysia Gori, I started that also with Garth, but when I got back from the Vile tour he decided he was too Christian. Christianity is part of a big disease on this side of the country.*"

"**Why do you think people have grafted on to it?**"

"Part of it's just the upbringing. My whole family is Christian, and I was forced to go to church as a child. People dress nice and go to Church here on Sunday, and I only went as a kid to see my friends.

Meet up, smoke pot, have a few beers in the parking lot. That's the first place I heard a lot of metal actually."

"How would you best describe the Alabama scene?"

"It's always been tight because there's almost no scene in the South. It had this supply of amazing musicians but they didn't do anything but sit home and practice. The best guitar players I've ever heard were here in Huntsville, but they didn't do anything."

"Tell me some tour stories."

"The last tour I did was playing drums for Epoch of Unlight, with Byzantine and God Dethroned from Germany. They were just happy to be in America. It was a shitty tour, the manager wasn't doing his job. The places where people come out and support are the East and West Coast. Anywhere in between you're lucky if you get a hundred people. You still have to play these places, because it's real shitty if you don't."

"What do you think is going to give a big jumpstart to the dead, middle of America scene?"

"Black metal is dead in Alabama. The scene that draws out the kids is this plastic kind of rock. Young kids can't get into the clubs so all ages places are what's up. Most are really into metal, any kind as long as it's difficult and heavy. It's stuck underground though, because of the locals. A lot of the kids like the singing and the screamo."

"Give me a crazy story."

"We were on tour in Albuquerque. Our bassist had gotten this really hi-grade medical pot in San Fran. It was just in his book bag and stunk up the whole van. We had just left the show and we decided to light it up. Soon as we sparked it we got pulled over. The van is just full of smoke, and the cop tells us he's writing us a ticket for speeding and we have until the time he comes back to throw it out. We knew we had to throw something out, so we tossed a fat bud, and when he came back he searched us and found a bowl. He just said, '*Now you can go.*' That was just the luckiest thing that had ever happened to me. Having a cop know we have drugs, that we're doing drugs, and still let us go."

"I had a buddy that was rolling a blunt in a parking lot in Detroit. They just finished licking it up, and this cop walks up and they're caught red handed holding this thing. He's like, 'You boys stay here, let me see your licenses, give that thing to me.' So they're sitting in the car all paranoid, already stoned, the police lights are flashing behind them. They can see this giant cloud of smoke through their rear view mirror, because the cops are blazing this massive

blunt in their squad car. Then the cop comes back, his eyes are red as fuck, and he's just like 'You can go now...'

IN THE SPIRIT OF THE MARQUIS

It's been a long, hung-over day; Mortigan hyperactively burned me every album in his massive library. He's introduced me to Brainbombs, Whitehouse, Drudkh, Deathspell Omega and so many others. The apartment echoes the sonic pummeling of Apocryph and Troll – walls coated in posters of Emperor, Burzum; a lengthy library rests in the corner filled with Marquis de Sade, Lovecraft, Nietzsche & WWII history.

He doesn't make any false claims about the BDSM obsession. Both he and his girlfriend are scarred remnants of deep straight-razor mutilation, and there are gas-masks & weird sexual utensils nicely arranged like decorative IKEA set-pieces. He has a massive collection of ultra-graphic bondage magazines from Europe plastic-and-back boarded like comic books, and boxes of sadistic and bizarre porn – anilingus, syndyasmian, androgalactozemia…

Friday night, approaching 10pm. We've been listening to the heart-felt tunes of local acoustic artist Micky McBride. A liquor run later and we've made it to the only goth/fetish/metal club in all of Alabama. It's called TABU, this is its 4th week of existence. Strobes, shifting lights, polka-dot patterns, glass cages with bikini girls, grinder shows on deck, slutty burlesque girls climbing over each other behind glass windows and slamming shots in teeny skirts – a nexus of anaxiphilia...

Of the two open areas one is the dance floor/bar and a stage packed with go-go cages, the other a small stage in another room where bands perform. Inside the huge complex there are only 20 people. I'm told that at its peak, the scene here might consist of 100, many driving 3-5 hours just to hang because the terrain is so desolate. This is the only glimpse of such an underground possible in the South, and it contains more enthusiasm then any of its ilk in Frisco or NYC. Unless business strikes, the drowning will continue.

Morty has been running promotions for main-brain Rich Ponder, and Ponder himself is painted up like a clown from Hell, spinning Rammstein & Manson as the DJ. The one live group for the evening is an industrial metal/nu-rock act along the lines of Static X with a few Rob Zombie covers.

Such a band would be cannibalized in Detroit, but the attendees are overjoyed. This crowd has the vibe of total release – somewhere authentic to be totally weird in a disastrous population of ornery pigs. The Godsmack cover is excused, because we all have funny colored hair & no one is trying to shake us up…

"Tell me about your promotions."

Rich Ponder: "My stage-name is Otis The Clown. I'm part of a group we call Dark Family Entertainment. We're basically a bunch of hams that work at strip clubs. Four nights a week I'm a strip club DJ. We'd started doing fetish shows in Nashville at the swinger and goth clubs, but the laws in Nashville are real tricky. We were contacted by the owner of Tabu and were told '*do your thing.*' We're trying to bring out are different genres of the underground scenes, be it the metal, fetish, the swingers, the gays and lesbians. They're all welcome here. No one's going to look twice at you for being in a full-leather outfit or a suit. Last week we brought The Porcelain Twins. They're identical twin fetish performers who are phenomenal. We had Sideshow Benny, who's one of the best sideshow artists in the nation. We want to bring what you cannot find anywhere else in the South-East."

"There are very few clubs like this in the area?"

"I know it can't be found in Tennessee. You have your goth nights but they don't have live bands. You get your fetish clubs and they don't have live bands. There's the dungeon scene but that is very private to people. They can come out here and do that too. We've had S&M acts and if people want to play, that's fine."

"Are you a big PT Barnum fan? When I used to do a lot of shows I'd adopt this kind of Johnny Carson persona and introduce all the bands. I see you have the same type of approach."

"I like to present it all as a carnie. When I'm here, I am a character. I mean, anyone ever seen a clown that spins metal? I dress exactly like this in a haunted house. I've been in the Haunted House industry for 18 years, ever since I was 13. I'd rather be in The Slaughterhouse in Nashville then a strip club, and I make way more money in a strip club. I used to be a side-show fire performer. But ever since Great White, it changed the rules. If we get more attendance we'll be able to start doing that stuff outside."

"What's the weirdest thing you've had in here so far?"

"We had some guys that were part of a dungeon S&M group. They were going to do some demos with a violent wand, which is very mild electric shock. That night was our first night booking bands and we didn't know what to expect. While the first band ever is loading in, I look over and see a woman wearing nothing but a thong and titty-tape and this guy is punching her in the ribs, just beating the hell out of her and she's loving it. The keyboardist won't even come in the building. Turns out they're a Christian band that sounds like Dave Matthews. That was only three weeks ago. We've been talking to some big bands who could sell this place out ten times over. We're sorting our riders, but I'm not privileged to say. That's what's going to put us on the map."

"Tell me about the Bible Belt environment."

"It's breathing down our neck everyday. In Nashville they've passed laws to change the strip club industry to where you can't get within three feet of the stage. Lap dances are obsolete. We got cited a $10,000 fine for a girl wearing nothing but rope. We had a $10,000 fine for having a cartoon nipple on a banner."

"What are other side promotions do you run?"

"My partner's dad owns a steel shop, so we figured 'why not make our own dance cages?' Within a few weeks we've got a couple of small pup cages, pyramid cages. One of our pyramids was recently used for a movie called *The Pet*, which is about the S&M slave trade. We also made a circular cage for Budweiser, their world tour for their Anheuser Select beer. We are pretty busy, driving two hours here and back every week, on top of our jobs which we're working up to 14 hours a day."

"What's the message behind what you do?"

"Everyday life sucks, everybody knows it, there's no reason to whine about it. I'm a white kid that grew up in East St. Louis, dirt poor with nothing, and I've been a fuck-up half my life. But I found something I was good at, and that goes for everyone in here. They have their own thing, and we're trying to give them a place where they can have it. But it is still entertainment. I see people getting mixed up in different scenes and they take it too far. I've played in death metal for years and I've seen people that are just fucking whack jobs. Part of it is they're already whack jobs and they will be regardless of what scene they're in. Sit back, relax, let us entertain you."

"What's the weirdest thing that's ever happened to you and people think you're a pathological liar when you tell them?"

"The craziest thing I've ever bore witness to was a stripper having a miscarriage onstage."

"Did someone eat it off the floor?"

"I was having a beer at the bar and I hear this scream in the middle of this huge club. It looks like black shit is everywhere. I get up closer and its blood. Not realizing the truth, being half drunk and cynical, I make the comment, *'Great, now it's four in the morning! Let's get some biscuits and miscarriage!'*"

"Got any others?"

"I used to play in this death metal band in St Louis. We had played the night before, and threw a kegger as always. The next day it's like three in the afternoon and we're just climbing off the floor, pumping the half-warm keg. For some reason there's a pork chop in every glass of beer. This girl comes over and she's already half-drunk. We'd all met her a few times from shows, but that's it. *'Get out the video camera. I want to make a porno.'* I'm like, *'whatever'* and I go to my car to get some CD's, and there's a four-way tire iron. So I grab it as a joke and tell her, *'Alright then baby, stick this up your ass.' And she did.* This girl strips down butt-naked, we're videotaping this – and it wasn't like she was very attractive either. She's wearing this Darth Vader mask, but not a good mask, like a little kid's mask with eyeholes cut out and a string in the back. And she's got my four-way tire-iron in her ass spinning it while she's going down on a black blowup doll. I've never seen anything quite like that."

"Did she do anything else?"

"Then – I shit you not – she stuck the headstock of a Fender Stratocaster in her pussy, while she had a bottle of Everclear up her ass. The Everclear still had a little in it, and she didn't put the cap on, so it drained out and burned the shit out of her asshole. The camera pans over and I'm just standing there in a hockey mask. We're all just standing there in total awe like, *'what the fuck are we witnessing?'* Then our guitar player's girlfriend walks in, secs this, and Shawn's egging Darth Vader on going *'Yeah, spin that motherfucker!'* Afterwards, she asks me *'if you watched this video, would you jack off to it?'*"

"(Laughing) I would..."

THE SCOURGE OF HUNTSVILLE

"So you ever meet Rob Darken from Graveland?" "Mortigan: (Mixing a glass of JB) No. Have you?" **"Nah..."** "His email address is always on CD's, I've been tempted to just to see if he's an asshole. I heard he was kind of loopy..." **"I saw pictures where he had all this Viking**

gear on, and he had these two hot blonde chicks in a bubble bath hot tub crafted from the trunk of some giant, dead tree..."

"OCTAGON is a sick and depraved black metal band, currently from Fucksville, Alabama. I'm sick of keyboards, emo cuts, people talking about things they can't accomplish with their lives. We have no image, we have no idea how to either. We're based on the music itself. It's cliché to say that, but the difference with us is that we encapsulate the catchier, more memorable moments of metal. If you love a death metal album that has one good riff that goes on for two seconds and the rest of the record sucks, we're going to take that one riff and make an entire song out if it. You like a thrash band for the speed and the punk, were going to pay homage to that. We believe in making every song memorable and staying true to ourselves. It's about the old days – leather, denim, fucking women, drinking ourselves into oblivion, hell and blasphemy. We don't gimmick to sell our music."

"You ever do corpse-paint live just for fun?"

"No, no reason."

"Feel free to send the guns blazing..."

"Money changes everything... I'm a demo freak, I love vinyl. Some of the greatest bands are the ones nobody will ever hear. I love Celtic Frost and all the greats, but I also love Grand Belial's Key, Drudkh, Arghoslent, Clandestine Blaze. It's sloppy, it's un-produced, but to me that's the true essence of black metal. It's gotta be grim and evil, the void should be there when you listen to it. I like unsettling music."

"Tell me about your label Destructive Industries."

"It's supposed to be an outlet for Octagon, but we semi-half ass stumbled upon Knox Om Pax. It's one guy sitting on a whirlpool of talent and he just needed the right person to support him. We love it, we believe in it. We're also trying to mix other things with black metal releases, sticking to underground electronics, noise, the scene that no one cares about. When people actually give it a chance, they'll get something out of it that black metal can't give you."

"What's your noise project all about? Why the name RU-486?"

"RU-486 is the abortion pill. It's one of my favorite projects. It's extreme noise, power electronics. Very layered and almost musical. It's my physical reaction to the entire world – the beauty of misogyny and the filth of humanity. It attacks all forms of weak life that I deem unworthy. I feel more of a connection to the power electronic scene than the black metal scene. Less ego, more art. It's never going to be big. It's not marketable and it's not a household thing. Those people are like '*it sounds like noise.*' Well, guess what? It is. It's truly the only underground music left in this world. It's the most unmarketable form of all. If you call yourself true underground cause you own some Beherit or Darkthrone albums and don't listen to this type of shit, I don't think you are."

"I should mention to our readers that we were just hammered inside laughing at scat porn where people were pooping in women's mouths. Obviously that stuff is funny, but what are your real tastes? You've been pretty vocal about your predilections."

"The people in black metal that want to talk about true sickness, evil, demons and shit. I'm all for it, I'll probably own your record. But when it comes down to it, the true sickness of what OCTAGON stands for can be seen as a joke or dead serious, depending on how you look at it. If you're going to be into what you're singing about, then you better do your damned research. There's nothing that I haven't seen that can ever shock me. The beauty of witnessing the ultimate depravity of watching people suffer, the ultimate of having an innocent girl be shit on, gagging and puking all over herself. How is that not cute? When you see something special, it sticks with you. I'm more than '*hey that bitch got bukkaki shots.*' You see that anywhere. Push the envelope. Sorry, you're corpse-paint and spikes are not nearly as tough as you think they are. I never met a tough metalhead that could sit through an entire tape of something I own. You know what? You're tough then buddy (laughs)."

"What are some memorable responses to your music?"

"I very much like to see people fighting over a bloody set-list. We played a fest last year with Monstrosity called 'Hellfire Manifest,' which was a tribute to our friend Patrick that died. Seeing people rabid as they were for metal... We were the first band. I figured we'd be the most boring to watch because we have no image. We might as well have a blank wall in front of us. The feeling we give is like being at an old school Discharge show or a GG Allin concert but without the feces and random body excrements flying all over the place. It's closing your eyes and just banging your head. To me that's the beauty of extreme music. That covers all terrains, not only metal. When you can control a crowd by a mere glance – even if its one guy banging his head for 30 seconds – I've done my job."

"In recent years has there been a single mainstream metal band on MTV or the radio that you actually like or have earned your respect?"

"Honestly… No. There are bands I'll go on record and say are good musicians. I can see the interest and the talent. But I am not a production snob or equipment whore. I like raw, honest, pure music. I like harsh noise that hurts to listen to. I like raw abrasive black metal that is so ambient and monotone that you lose yourself in it, swirling in your head looking for notes. I just don't see any integrity in a major label. The best bands in the world are the ones that no one will ever hear."

"What's something remarkably bizarre that's happened to you that no one believes is true?"

"(Laughs) I've had people in random places throw bars of OCTAGON soap onstage while we're playing. I've got a box full. Its like, how often do you come across MABUS or Darkthrone soap?"

"When Henry Rollins plays sometimes people throw 'Oh Henry' candy bars at him… Where's the name Mortigan from?"

"Well, the name Mortigan is actually pulled from *Willow*. You know Mad Mardigan? I always thought that's what it was, but being a deaf metal musician…"

"As far as meeting legends, do you have any good stories? Have you been let down meeting many of them in person?"

"I'm not into John Denver, but he was truly the kindest human being that I've ever met in my life. I don't give a fuck how black metal that is or not. Any black or death 'heroes,' I can guarantee you about 67% that I've met – and not being a fan-boy like '*sign my titties*' – they've been assholes. It's disappointing but you do expect that. Not everyone is 'lets hang out, have a beer and a good time.' I've been like that sometimes, but the reasons are different. Some people have the right, some don't. It really does depend on the scene that you're involved with."

"What was it like living in Mississippi?"

"There will not be one single piece of shit worthy of your time in Mississippi. Seriously, I was the only person into black metal for years and everyone that was into it was because I'd gotten them into it. I was the reason the only independent store was carrying metal at all because I was the one ordering everything. I asked him why not just stock it, and I actually put in all the orders… I can't accept these places where people have no direction, there's no hope. They never do anything with themselves. I cannot accept people not willing to correct themselves. I choose to distance myself from stupidity as much as possible."

"If Century Media opened their legs to you, would ya?"

"Yeah, if I write the contract (laughs). I don't think there's much sellable about OCTAGON except in the underground. We're not pretty enough, we don't wear corpse-paint. There's no dick sucking for mainstream motivation. I do it my way or the highway. Its ugly music for ugly people. Dirty, sleazy, drunken fucking black metal. To me that's the greatest music in the world."

"Do you read a lot?"

"I read quite a bit, but people spend their entire lives reading as much as they can, but then they're left with questions that have no answers. After that, there's only opinion. These people writing all these 'Walks of Spirituality,' 'The Wings of The Dove That I Saved This Morning,' what can that really do for you? I actually wrote two books, *Genealogical Aristocracy* and *Survival Of The Astral Lineage*."

"Were they Kinko's releases?"

"(Laughs) Yeah…"

NO RUGGSVILLE IN ALABAMA BUT SURELY NASHVILLE
SATURDAY, May 12th 2007; The Full Moon Tattoo Fest & Horror Con at The Nashville Millennium Maxwell House Hotel. One of those mad-cap gatherings for every die-hard ink fetishist & horror fan within a three-state radius.

Mortigan and the boys are supped up in bullet-belt war mode, and Octagon's drummer Profana is latex slopped as a blood-caked zombie. In the showroom there are 200 tat guns buzzing. Along the other corridor there are rooms filled with b-movie actors signing glossy photos for $20 a pop.

Mortigan is shyly waving hello at this freakish assemblage of cult celebrities. In every direction we are surrounded by stuntmen and cult cinema legendry. Bill Moseley (*Devils Rejects, Texas Chainsaw 2*), Kane Hodder (Jason Vorhees), Gunnar Hansen (Leatherface), Edwin Neal (the original hitchhiker from *Texas Chainsaw*), Tom Savini (*From Dusk Till Dawn*), Ken Foree (*Dawn of the Dead*)…

The Leatherface from the remakes has a Black Label Society tattoo on his chest and is talking '*HOO-RAH*' babble to some marine fresh from Iraq. The mutant from the Hills Have Eyes remake is very polite, shaking everyone's hands.

Sid Haig looks bored. The guy is a monster – he's at least 6 foot 6 and so gangly it's no wonder he's been cast as a murderer or biker for the past 25 years. He's in his usual meet & greet mode when I invade his space. I stand there looking at him, and he's just waiting for it to come out. *"Howdy"* I say, and he gives me that certain smile knowing something dumb is about to come out of me.

"So in 'Devils Rejects' your real name is Cutter. I'm just wondering is that's an 'Aftermath' reference." He shakes his head quickly, because *Aftermath* is the lousiest of memories. *"When was the last time you watched that film?"* Straight faced he sighs and says, *"I try never to watch it."* I start laughing, *"Well I think it's fucking brilliant."* He chuckles, *"Well kid, you're the only one"* When I go in close to snap a photo with him I say, *"Thanks man, this shit must drive you crazy."* His reply: *"Ah hell kid, I already am crazy."*

Kane Hodder (Jason Voorheees) is all about *Hatchet*, which he says is the best horror film he's ever worked on. *"I was highly disappointed that you weren't in 'Freddy vs. Jason.'"* He snakes a grin and says, *"I was too. After 16 years of playing the part I was pretty pissed. They replaced me for no reason."*

Edwin Neal, the hitchhiker from *Texas Chainsaw Massacre* (*and voice of Lord Zed on Power Rangers*), is an oddball. In cartoon voices he mimics 12 year olds eating ecstasy on Hollywood & Vine...

Sig Haig is checking his watch. *"Is it 11 o clock yet? Holy shit, ok, lets move this line along. Four hours and 23 minutes, god I can hardly wait. OK..."*

Finally Ken Foree, the hero from the 1978 *Dawn of the Dead*. He hasn't seen Scott Reinegher in years, and his favorite zombie in Dawn is a toss-up between the Nun and David Emge.

For giggles I tell him my David Emge story, who played Flyboy: *"So I'm at this comic con in Michigan, and Dave is signing glossy photos. I get my turn in line and open up this double-VHS collectors edition, and out spills 4 packed dimebags. Like there is a mountain of pot on his desk, because I hid them in its case while driving through a speed trap and just forgot."*

"So there's all these fat Klingon kids and guys dressed like the Flash surrounding me, and David just looks up laughing as I snag all of this Buddha back into my pockets. Afterwards we went outside,

chain-smoked Marlboro Reds, and for some reason we discussed 'Robocop' for 10 minutes straight."

Ken lets out a raucous, deep-belly Baptist laugh, and says, *"You should have done that to me. See now I would've rolled that up. David, he's kind of a straight arrow."* So I challenge Ken: *"Alright man, next time I come to one of these cons I'm dragging you outside for a Philly."*

He keeps laughing and I drop the ultimate question: *"Ok, here's what I've always wanted to know. After Peter and Fran take off in the Helicopter... In the sequel that exists in your mind, does Peter nail Gaylen Ross?"* Ken starts shaking his head with an *"ah fuck"* and is ready to explode with a volcano of laughter: *"Like a wild fuckin' boar"* [insert Foree's classic "hyeuh-hyeuh-hyueh" baritone laugh]...

ETERNAL BLACK FLAME & THE FINAL DAWN OF DUSK

Mortigan hops on his girlfriend in the backseat and leaves us to the highway. The long haul from Nashville is annotated by the ethereal, ghostly quality of Blood Stained Dusk's final recording. Blood Stained Dusk/OCTAGON drummer Profana is riding in shotgun, face still caked in deranged, pussing makeup. Driving is BSD keyboardist/Black Flame Records CEO Chris White (a.k.a. Thorgrin), a very reserved, matter-of-fact yet laidback individual.

Blood Stained Dusk started late '98, and has a lengthy late catalogue of EP's and full-lengths, one which saw light of day through Killjoy's (of Necrophagia) Baphomet Records. On the cusp of releasing their ultimate record main composer Patrick (Dageth) was shockingly killed in a car accident. He was a respected figure in the Southern BM underground, and a 15 band bill with Monstrosity headlining was held in tribute – "The Hellfire Manifest." Having already laid the vocal tracks the remaining members decided to complete the album, which is what we've been listening to unmastered for the past 20 minutes: *"Actually, I first heard the name of Thorgrin in the movie 'Conan the Barbarian.' Thorgrim was a warrior of great strength and henchman of the demigod Thulsa Doom. I thought the name was fitting, but I changed it to Thorgrin because I did not want everyone to just associate it with the 'Thor' and 'Grim' references that are so common in BM."* ***"Tell me about Black Flame Records."*** ThorGrin: "Being a music fan is the main thing. Patrick and I started the label late 2002. We wanted to create a label that did things for bands we wanted done for us. Bringing music to people that bigger labels would never give a chance. We have seven releases so far, and a new one soon for

Necrophagus. There's a lot of diversity, we're hitting a lot of niches. Our first release was 2003's 'Continuance of Evil' [Blood Stained Dusk]. We signed a band out of New Jersey, then after we put out both releases, we lost Patrick. I'm trying to keep it afloat myself... It's difficult. Running an independent record label is not as productive as it once was and I think that most everyone involved in them these days will tell you that. The most obvious problem is the rapidly descending market of the compact disc. Downloading and file sharing have completely killed the industry. As if that wasn't bad enough, the accessibility of releasing pro-printed CD's has caused saturation. This is especially prominent in the black metal scene with every Joe Blow starting a label and releasing every schmuck who wants to bang out raw chords in their bedrooms. There is only a handful of die hard fans out there that still purchase CDs and they are tired of sifting through crap to find a good new artist. It's a tough market, but it has a silver lining that will weed out the weak. Anyone who tries to capitalize on their music, its going to cut them down, and the only ones left will be the real artists who have a vision... If anyone out there really wants to jump into this sinking ship please be cautious. If you do not have artists that have a marketable name or sound or know people at larger labels that can help you with killer distribution deals and such, think twice. If you do decide to get into it make sure you are doing it for the right reasons – which is for the music and the scene and not for the money. It's not about making money, but it'd be nice to actually break even. If you make a little cash in the process, be grateful."

"What's the Japanese band you signed?"

"MAGANE. Patrick and I had become fans because a friend of ours had been introduced to their music by one of the guys from SIGH [Japan's premier art-metal band]. He asked if there were any bands more theatrical and contained more Japanese culture. We got in touch with MAGANE, and they agreed to do the re-release. They call themselves 'Yomi Metal.' In Japanese folk lore, Yomi is the realm of the dead. All their lyrical content is based on it."

"Tell me about the new Blood Stained Dusk."

"We were scheduled to record in March 2005, but Patrick died in January. It was his vision. Pest is going to be doing his fist return to vocals since Gorgoroth. It's awesome; Patrick gets to have a legend stand in for him. We were also able to pull Patrick's vocals from rehearsal recordings and put them on the more emotional parts. It's like a voice from the grave, the call from a dead man. He gets to have his screams heard one last time..."

PROFANA'S SOLILOQUY

"Back in the very early 90s I resided in New Jersey. The town was pretty old, and had a descent sized biker community. We rehearsed in a place called Bellmawr. They believed that their basement was haunted. One night we were all upstairs and heard a loud crashing noise come from the basement. There is a cymbal completely off the stand on the floor, and the bass drum pedal is just barely moving..."

"Now the second house was directly behind the other, and was known for drug users, biker parties; obvious violence. The people from Bellmawr call and say that something severely bad has happened at the house behind them, and that several people are dead, an entire family due to blunt-force trauma with a baseball bat! The shit was all over the news. The father figure of the family went psycho from taking PCP and other shit, and beat his family to death all over the house, and then killed himself in their basement."

"The police had the place boarded up with crime scene tape everywhere. We waited for a few days, then decided to break in with flashlights and candles. What better way is there to anger or provoke a possible entity than to make fun of it, and tell it what a piece of fucking shit it was to do that to his family? We all roam the halls and rooms of the 3 story house telling the motherfucker off, inviting him to do the same to us that he did to his family."

"Hours go by and nothing. Just before we get ready to leave, one of us finds a door in the kitchen – the basement where they found the murder weapon. The atmosphere itself just gave off this dark emotion. Finding nothing, we head back up, then one of us screams LOOK! For a second there was a very dim light in the shape of a baseball bat looming in the far corner on the left hand side of the room. It quickly disappears, and we never go back."

2 days later someone or a group of people went into the place under cover of night and trashed the house. I mean TRASHED. Every room had shit shoved in the walls, holes in them, carpets ripped, the entire staircase railing broke and dangling . But the most fucked up part was the kitchen! The back wall had a gaping hole in it because of the refrigerator being knocked through it, and laying in the back yard! Knives, forks, spoons, utensils everywhere – in the walls, the ceiling... Was it paranormal or just vandalism? It was a scene like no other. It would take far too long for the damage made inside that house by men. The house was so badly destroyed…"

CRASHING FALCON OVER PEPPER STEAK (TAKE I)

Sunday now, and I'm waiting in a parking for a cat named Drew Shefflit. He's the drummer of The Crashing Falcon, a pulverizing tech metal band from Huntsville that cakes on striking Iron Maiden-type leads over violent math explosions. The OCTAGON tribe are oblivious to them, but in usual kvlt mode they remark, *'Isn't that one of those million-word name bands? Like 'I Saw Your Girlfriend Skinning A Cat That Looked Like The Number Ten Last Autumn?'* Jumping from one berg to the next, riding these little divisions…

This will be good because Shefflit represents so much of the scene I have no hope in tapping otherwise. He's been a long-time promoter since the late 90's and has been on the friendly end of the metal/punk spectrum: "*I came from Saint Louis, I moved around '97, and I've got a harder Southern accent then anyone from here, ha ha. I am the drummer of The Crashing Falcon. Our history goes back fairly far in the Huntsville scene. Where you can give the whole evolution of Detroit, I can basically do the same here. You're hanging out with the OCTAGON guys? They're basically the black metal scene right?*"

"Yeah, but it's funny. The typical 'you're a poseur' corpse paint black metal bands hate them…" Drew Shefflit: "(Chuckles) That's interesting…" **"They're definitely more old school and don't really get the tech stuff, but I'm into all that shit. I think your material is really tight, really well done…"**

"I appreciate that… Well, I came in here in 1997, this is when everyone loved Operation Ivy and Rancid. There's that side, then you have the people in love with Metallica. The death metal scene is interesting. Back in the day there's this guy named Garth, and those OCTAGON guys probably talked about him already [Lance Wright's guitarist in Tipper Gore]. He basically ran the death metal scene and was one of the nicest motherfuckers as far as death metal goes. If he wasn't so cool, we would never have been accepted enough to even play a show with those types of bands. He was always open-minded. He was in Fleshtized – they were in the vein of Hate Eternal, super-tech death, but doing their own thing. It's one of the best albums ever to come out as far as this area is concerned.

"What about your project?

"I guess our evolution would have been 'nu-metal' at the time, but more on the hardcore vein like Vision of Disorder.

"Well this is like '97 right? All that shit ran over everything because it was fresh and new...

"Exactly. There was no Napster, there was no exposure. Korn and Manson were still at their peak, Soulfly... I had this band Postal. We're still kind of in the grunge era, System of a Down and Incubus started picking up... We even had a DJ at the time. The records he was scratching were weird shit though, like women screaming. The whole skater scene was involved in that too. My band was weird enough to where we could play any shows."

"How did it play out?"

"Columbine affected everything. I had a black trench coat with red spikes, so I looked almost Gestapo (laughs). There are some skinhead crews around here, but I was never into that. Columbine happens, and everyone freaks out. The parents have 'think groups' to figure out what to do for the kids. They asked kids to be on committees and they decided to start throwing shows to give them something to do on a Friday night instead of going mudding, getting drunk. These weren't like dark, scary kids. They got their clothes at the thrift store, shit like that. The 'Neverland' shows were central to the evolution of hardcore in this area. They started doing huge ones with 200 kids easily, all local. We were doing those until this kid with an Albert Einstein haircut yells *'fuck you buddy,'* and my singer throws it back into the microphone. We were expelled from the program. There are so many places we play that have 'no cursing' rules."

"Were you out for good?"

"The only way to change expulsion is to join the committee. Once we infiltrated that they told us they wanted an area so kids could do homework, which is fucking crazy, because every church in this area has some huge gymnasium, a coffee shop, so they handle all that. The adults were like, *'we don't like this, its bringing out the wrong crowd.'* What do you mean by 'the wrong crowd?' Are these not the kids that you want to be watching over? These are the ones you should be worried about. These are the trench coat kids. If you give them a community and something to look forward to... They thought it was going to be some clean cut thing, they didn't even understand what their original objective was. You know that band The Pink Spiders?"

"Oh yeah, we did a show with them in Detroit in 2005."

"We used to have them all the time when they were Silent Friction. My Epiphany from Nashville, Curbside Service, 25 To Life. This is where DIY took over, '*we'll run out of Knights of Columbus.*' We totally broke away, took all their shows, and it ruined that crew. Then you had Axion who did Buddyfest. They had Underoath, Dead To Fall, Aria, Bury Your Dead before they blew up. Axion were introducing two-steps and breakdowns in this area. On the other side the death metal scene are booking Nile back when their guarantee was only $200. This is *Catacombs of Nephran Ka* era. They already had distros, bringing in Jungle Rot, a lot of Relapse bands before they started getting big. They pretty much stuck to their own."

"Are there many Christian hardcore bands in Alabama?"

"There's a ton of Christian bands, which to me perverts the straight-edge notion. Straight-edge is supposed to set you up where you have the clarity of mind to help make the world a just place. It's definitely not an end in itself, only a means to an end. Many Christian bands decide that it goes with their religion. To have that type of attachment to faith, which is belief in something you have no proof of… If you read the Bible word for word, it's a horrible, horrible thing. If we compare that to *Star Wars*, who are we rooting for? We're rooting for Luke and the Rebel Forces. The bad guys are the Imperial Army with the Emperor in charge of everything. He's got his right hand man, the martyr Darth Vader. We've got Storm Troopers in their white Imperial uniforms – the angels fighting for the lord. But who do we root for? The rebels, the one third of the angels that were expelled. If you look how petty that god is in biblical terms, it's horrible to say this is holy when we can look at the witch trials, the Spanish inquisition, the crusades, oppression of women. You can find a verse in the bible to justify any sin you want. My favorite is Ezekiel 23:20 where it talks of two adulterer sisters, something like they '*lusted after lovers whose genitals were that of mules and his emissions were that of horses.*'"

"Is this a prevalent theme in your lyrics?"

"That does play into what our message is politically. We're saying all these nice and beautiful things about god. We're trying to set up a deity who isn't this petty, cruel kid with a magnifying glass to an anthill. God is something that you cannot define. With our human comprehension, this is something we can't grasp. The only thing we can say we're gifted with is our own existence. What we should be dealing with instead of the afterlife is what happens right now. A lot of the Christian bands have a dark and scary image, yet they parade their

Christianity. And when Jesus is supposed to be the prince of peace? It doesn't add up when you think of their logic and their ideals, but when you realize heavy Christian music is the fastest growing music industry in America… Kids are there to throw down, listen to heavy music, and socialize between the sets. They're not leaving there with any more knowledge about Jesus Christ. Then you look at the world situation. If we do let the Christians hold our political power, are they now trying to push a foreign policy that's trying to make Revelations come true? Your foreign policy is making Armageddon happen? Fuck that. They're trying to legitimize prophecy by their policies, and that's a scary fucking thing."

"Where does the band name come from?"

"Back when we were Postal, *The Crashing Falcon* was going to be the next album title. It just sounded cool, like cellar door. This is the same idea for kamikaze pilots. The phoenix rises from the flames. What would be the antithesis of that? The Crashing Falcon. But it also works like 'Fist Of The Lotus,' like a kung fu move.

"Tell me about the music itself."

"As far as heavy goes we're looking for a certain emotion. It is a thing like '*what does madness sound like*?' Not necessarily anger, because speed isn't necessarily power. We can watch the fastest death metal bands play. If they are doing a blast-beat at 270 BPM – if he's barely tapping his snare – if you don't have good triggers or a good PA, it's not going to come off in some underground dive."

"What do you have to say about straight-edge scene?"

"People will say '*it's not for me but I respect it.*' You don't even have to respect it. This is picking abstinence over moderation, because abstinence is either '*I'm not gonna deal with this, 'cause it's going to fuck me up,*' or a dietary choice. Alcoholism runs in my family. They're not nice drunks, their violent drunks. I have that stigma, and I don't need to deal with that. Many of the sXe are right wing conservatives. Especially with people talking about bringing back prohibition, which is a terrible idea. If it were up to me I'd legalize drugs. Certain parts of town should have a red light district. It keeps down violence and crime, just like New Orleans."

"Are there fascistic, violent straight-edge movements here? Like the Salt Lake City kids who were carving X's into peoples backs? What about the Courage Crew? There are quite a few of them in Detroit, or used to be. They actually ripped off some kids' ear at the Bottle Rocket Fest in 2004. I knew a guy that had his leg broken and

half his ribs because he was eating a hamburger at a crustie, vegan, sXe squat."

"Thankfully no. The kids dance hard as hell, but overall they're super nice. There are occasions when you have people from different cities, different crews, or the Ozzfest mentality, and if they get kicked in the face a fight is going to break out. But that's any scene. We started from where you had emo bands playing with ska bands, punk bands playing with heavy bands all in one show. I know where things got divided, when these bands drifted apart. I guess that just happens naturally, but there were personal politics. I'm a little guilty of feuding, but overall I'm trying my best to stay open-minded and keep shows diverse. We've had Dysrhythmia play here, we've had Origin..."

"What are some bullshit aspects within hardcore and tech that need end?"

"The whole macho Ozzfest, *'I'm the alpha male of the bunch, let's join the Marines.'* On the East Coast people started swinging fists to clear space 'cause they were sick of that. But people get very particular about their dancing. They'll make fun of a kid whose two-step isn't as superb as theirs or his spin-kick is too karate-akkata. I think that overall hardcore needs to be more like Don Cornelius' *Soul Train.* That would be awesome. If we look at the evolution of dance – we have punk, the grunge, people getting drunk and not caring about manners. You got your picking up change, two-steps, skanks, windmills, spin-kicks, cartwheels.

"How do we up the female quotient?"

"It's interesting – we still haven't figured out how to make it a couple's dance for hardcore. People will say *'that's gay,'* but when you think about what music is and the role its played in human evolution – whether we want to admit it or not – it's basically mating dances. You look at the male dominated, chauvinistic, *'I'm the silver back of the pack type gorilla dancing.'* Its spiders throwing their legs in the air, *'I'm the crab with the biggest pinchers.'* It would be great if people were more pro-active in evolving that. Let's get hokey with it. Rock and roll is supposed to be freedom. It needs a lack of rules...."

THE ANGELIC PROCESS OVER PEPPER STEAK (TAKE II)
Keep repeating to yourself that it will pass. These shakes aren't permanent; you don't have a developing case of Parkinson's. My hands won't stop trembling, my body is shaking spasmodically. The walls

keep sliding, objects distorting, faces keep breathing. I feel like Keanu Reeves at the end of *A Scanner Darkly*...

Then I realize I haven't had any R.E.M. sleep since the LA Murderfest in April. The body goes under, but the mind keeps buzzing. The second I come to I wake up in an unfamiliar place, never really sure where I am at first or what's going to happen next. Then I recall my lack of water or healthy food, and that all I've been able to drink in Alabama is scotch or whiskey.

It's been relentless party-wise. One second I'm crawling around a sleazy club, the next we're stoned listening to Akitsa or Godless North at the apartment, or Mortigan is on drums and I'm flying through guitar scales in our joke grind band of the week "CHINESE WORK ETHIC."

We've been taping our sessions on a karaoke machine at Profana's shack-turned-HQ, which like a splice between a Stan Winston horror workshop and a down-south haunt of the incarcerated Damian Echols. The mini-home is filled with candles, live-band flag backdrops, pentagrams, splatters of fake blood, Jason Vorhees posters, and thick pieces of leather and spent bullet shells. Profana utilizes it to run his hand-made, BM war-gear online store...

At any moment The Angelic Process will be picking me up for Pepper Steak at a little Chinese joint on Logan Street. These two are driving a 2 ½ hours from the outskirts of Atlanta, and I've had enough difficulty getting musicians to walk a single block.

The duo pull up in a small black hatchback, backseat cluttered with promo boxes. They are both genteels. In Shotgun is K Wood; a sort of quiet, polite, farm-boy gone soundfreak with tribal tattoos on his arm and long black hair. His wife [*and bassist*] M Dragynfly is pure southern charm. Says Wood: "*I started the band in 2001 as a studio project. We always received a good response, but people didn't know what to do with it. I released the debut EP and hooked up with Crucial Blast they were trying to get out of the noise ghetto and we were very ambient.*"

"*We signed for a limited edition cassette. He was pushing us to tour. I tried to get musicians together but it just didn't happen. In Alabama finding musicians is very difficult. A lot of standard rock bands, country stuff. We had drummers come in but they found it was very hard to play, so in the early days we had a drum machine. I recorded the second full length in my own studio. I put it out limited edition, and took time off to go to art school...*

"Where did you grow up?" "I'm an only child; I grew up in the country. We call Athens our hometown. I spent my high school years in garage bands playing Nirvana covers. Alabama had no exposure to the outside world. If it wasn't on major radio or MTV I had no access to it. I didn't even have the internet until I was 18. I'm 28 now, I graduated '97... Back then I had just turned 18 and was in a really bad car accident – broke every bone in my hand, cut the other up real bad. I'm left handed, so I play with my right, and I can't even close it [*tries to squeeze but it only folds halfway in*]. I'd just bought a new Stratocaster the day before and made the decision not to go to college so I could work on music. I ended up laid out for 6 months with amnesia and severe head injuries."

"Damn."

"I'm sitting there thinking I'm never going to play music again. I just sat on the couch, I couldn't get up. I'd just been getting in the more underground strange music, and I put on *Swans Are Dead* for the first time. I listened to it on repeat for 4 hours – the absolute demonic roar, the hugeness of the sound really clicked that chord. I spent the next month listening to that record over and over, getting into My Bloody Valentine, Neurosis. Jarboe's performance made me want to play music again... I spent the next year relearning how to play guitar right handed. My hands were still wrapped up, and I'd tape a quarter to my thumb and sit there learning how to strum again. It was a harsh thing... In '99 my grandmother passed away, left me her house and a little money. I turned it into my own studio and spent the next 3 years recording. In April 2001 I wrote the first Angelic Process songs."

"Tell me about the music."

"We do the Swans thing, the same three chords for 6 minutes, but they're not defined. For instance, one song is 9½ minutes long and has a 4 minute crescendo. It's not a spiky, pointed guitar sound. We kill all the treble – it's very warm and enveloping, the vocals are kind of buried. Very heavy bass sound, very prominent – using feedback for melodies, frequencies, feeling physical aspects of sound. Taking noise and tribal drumming, but writing songs with actual structure... I definitely come from the My Bloody Valentine school of vocals and using them as another instrument. What I'm saying is not as important as how it sounds in the context of everything that's going on. I'm not trying to convey any specific message – I want a definite mood. Our music in joyous & angry, yet melancholy all at once…"

M Dragynfly: *"Our music is about the human condition. You're never just happy – there's always the undercurrents, the worries. All the layers coming in and out, the tribal drumming is almost a racial memory, like a heartbeat. Everything is churning on top of it, little things weaving in and out. It's almost like being alive. Feeling, living… People think metal has to be angry, ugly or violent. But Angelic Process isn't violent. There aren't lyrics and we have textural vocals. It's pure, raw emotion."*

"I think we've incorporated more melody than our contemporaries. Indie people like it, death mettalers, black mettalers, noise people. There's a French acoustic artist who's said we've influenced him… The timings are crazy, the tunings are strange. Now we officially tune down to C. I actually play guitar with a cello bow."

"How do you go about that?"

"I'd been screwing around with an e-bow, it resonates one string. Well what about all the strings? I started to get knives and pieces of metal and trying to bow it… I was a bad insomniac so I wouldn't sleep for days, I'd just hammer on this one idea… It didn't occur to me to just get a cello bow. I bought a violin bow initially, but I didn't know anything about it."

"He's not musically or classically trained at all. I can read music, and I was totally lost. He steps outside the widely accepted rules. He finds great sounds, but he doesn't do them in any way that anyone would dream of doing, even just hooking equipment up."

"What kind of strings do you use with that?"

"Regular old Super Slinkies, 9 gauge – it's more defined at lower tuning. You need to use a block of resin though. Keep the strings clean and it grips just like a cello. Paper towel works the best for cleaning. My style with this has developed over 6 years. I still play with a pick for certain parts that have to be more defined. You have to lower your guitar down far in a horizontal fashion. You have to keep the bow parallel to the guitar. You have to make sure it's not skipping over strings. Sitting down recording is one thing, but standing up and playing live, worrying about vocals and FX pedals and the laptop, it's not a natural motion. You have to build up the muscles in your shoulder. Positioning so you can hit individual strings, that's really hard. Other than that it's like playing a regular guitar… She plays with the biggest size strings I've ever seen in my life, like telephone wires…"

"I found this old, old set of Fender strings in the back of an old music store. I had to dust off the package to even see what it was. Ernie Ball Super Slinkies, the package was sun bleached, and they're huge, just monstrous. I don't know where I'd even find something else like this again."

"Everything is pretty much huge custom made toms and cymbals. We took the focus away from the snare, which gives it way more of a bass-heavy heft. We love ritualistic, tribal drumming. The roots of drone occur in nature – it's old as time itself."

"How many projects have you been in?"

"I was playing in a hardcore band. But you break up 'cause you can only go so far. Let's tour, not just play the same three places in town. The clashing egos and personalities – why are you doing this if everyone's going to fight constantly? You can't decide on what kind of music to make, you sit down and make a list of *'we're going to make these defined rules so that everybody can sort of get along.'* You see bands on tour and they're so unhappy. They're fighting, wasted constantly. What's the point? That's the problem with Athens. In Alabama you get the stereotype of *'you're not as intelligent.'* So we had that working against us.

"Do you find a nice section of people getting into it?

"We're a bridge band. We bring in people from different scenes and link things together. We have a small cult fan base, we're selling records in Japan and Brazil, but it's one here, two there. Every label is *'we love it, but if you can't tour we can't put money behind it.'"*

"Where did you go from there?"

"In 2003 I recorded a concept album about a man who lapses into a coma and finally dies. That was based off my first love. In 2000 she was actually in a car accident and ended up dying. *Weighing Souls With Sand* is the other side of that. It's about the aftermath, the man's wife trying to deal with him dying and not being able to. She commits suicide at the end. That comes directly from my experience. Its not like you have a fight and you break up – you wake up and she's gone. How do you deal with that? I almost didn't... I was very close to killing myself many times because I'm a depressive person by nature. I'd been going through a lot, trying to sort that out, pushing it down. I ended up getting in a bad relationship. I just poured everything into that record. I said *'Fuck it, if I can't do this right, I'm not going to do it.'* We sold 50 copies and I just put it away. I moved to Savannah Georgia and ended up running out of money. It's a college town so only the lowest paying jobs are available, and you're paying $1000 a month for a two-bedroom apartment if you're lucky. That relationship ended, I came home, and held up at the studio trying to figure out what to do. The Angelic Process was just hanging over me, like *'This was something special and important, and you failed.'* I spent a lot of time dealing with things…"

"How have your live shows been going?"

"We've got to have the right volume or it's not going to work. We went to great lengths to try to alleviate that. We had this gig in Atlanta at a place that looked like a crack house. Their monitors weren't working, half the PA didn't work – it was just mud. So we spent a year collecting gear…

"Do soundboard guys butcher it often?"

"We've had a lot of that problem. *'You can't hear the vocals.'* Well you're not supposed to, it's not this separate thing – everything laps on top of each other. Play them the record and they say *'well, that's not right.'* Well it's the record, that's how we do things. We'd send our press kits to bars and they'd say *'people can't drink to this.'*"

"Is that the general consensus of all the clubs in Alabama?"

"Yeah, and Atlanta. You go to Alabama and you're going to be playing a bar where people are drinking & talking. We had such a hard time last year. January 2006 we restarted the band. We got great reviews – WIRE, Terrorizer, Decibel. We've had more interviews and reviews in foreign languages – France, Germany, Portugal, Italy. We've been on magazine comps in Belgium and Portugal, we're on Terrorizer's new comp… The only negative reactions we've ever gotten are from people who don't quite understand production. The only bad review is because the guy said straight-forward he didn't like synths. I was surprised because I thought the more 'true' death metal guys would complain. Instead they've contacted us to say we're taking the best aspects of these bands and putting them into something new. We get everything from *'this is a battle between good & evil'* to *'this is what it sounds like when I'm in my room after my parents had a fight.'*"

"What's the Jarboe connection?"

"Actually Jarboe lives in Atlanta, and we've been lucky enough to become great friends with her. She's coming to New York to support us. She's playing second to us, because it's her town and she wants people to show up. We love her for that. I didn't want to talk about that too much because I didn't want to be name-dropping, but she's talking about us in interviews and it's more widely known that we're friends."

"What's the status of this new album?"

"This is going to be a big record for us. The last was number 34 in Terrorizer's 2006 list, and it was a limited edition release – it got a 9 out of 10. We spent nine months working on this new one. We found out today that Amazon.com, TowerRecords.com and CDuniverse have already sold out in pre-order phase."

"So this is the moment."

"Yeah, it really is… We had a big label come calling, but they offered us a shitty deal. We were going to make zero on the record, they weren't going to provide any tour support. Monika has a child with her ex-husband, so we have a family. Bills have to be paid, child has to be fed. We share custody, she's 4 years old. She's not going to be independent anytime soon. We can't just drop everything and tour."

"Do you have anything smaller planned?"

"We're going to do a European tour booked by fans. We have people buy one CD, they come back and buy everything we've ever put out. These people turn out to either run labels, are booking agents or promoters. One of the guys runs the Roadburn Festival in the Netherlands – which Neurosis and Melvins played last year – and he's bringing us over. The festival has sold out two months in advance. The ZXZW Festival [the premier fest in Belgium] is flying us out and paying for everything. Its a $1000 dollar ticket, we can't afford that. They're taking care of all accommodations."

"It's funny. We're getting airplay all over Europe. We're on the radio, we're in the magazines. At home we can't play a gig. We do everything backwards. Record deal? Sure, fine, all day long. But we can't play down at the corner (laughs)."

"We're headlining every show at the ZXZW festival on our first European tour. *We're headlining*. Who does that? Then we play Georgia and we're support, opening 20 minute sets. Then we're going up to Brooklyn and Jarboe is opening for us. They said no, and she called to say *'I'm coming up there to specifically play this show with them. I'm opening, that's the way it is.'*"

"What's a crazy story that happened to you and when you tell people they think you're a pathological liar?"

"I was in Savannah in this ghetto area. People are getting shot next door to me, it was bad. I was staying in this really weird building that had an indoor courtyard shut in by a square block of buildings. I had a small studio in my apartment and was working late one night. The place didn't have above-head lights so I had to place some, and the light was definitely going in one direction. I see a shadow going the wrong way on the wall about four feet tall. I turned around and no one was there, but there was still this shadow. So I go over to the light, and the shadows' moving all over the place. Then it's gone. I look across the hall. It's a straight hall from my studio to the bedroom, and about 15 feet away, this little girls standing there. She smiles at me and I step back, kind of close my eyes, shake my head and she's gone... That whole time there I'd see weird things, like I'd turn a corner and see a little kid standing there. It had a very strange energy to it, but it wasn't anything malicious. Turns out in the 1920's it was an orphanage and a lot of kids ended up dying there, that's why it shut down. Now my ex-girlfriends apartments, lights would blow constantly. Hers had something awful about it."

"My mom was working with her band in NYC in the 70's. They had a studio they were renting a rehearsal space from & the studio people said 'you guys have to clear out because The Rolling Stones are coming in to record.' So my mom cleans out the studio, fixes everything up, makes it nice and neat. She sets down a vase with a dozen red roses in it and a note that says 'For Mick.' Well The Rolling Stones were delayed a couple weeks, so when they finally arrived, the only thing they found in the studio was a vase of dead flowers & the note. The album they recorded was 'Send Me Dead Flowers'..."

QUINTA ESSENTIA

My last night in Alabama, and I'm looking forward to a world without whiskey. The week has passed in a blur, and I've consumed enough black metal and acrotophelia to keep me grim for another 50 years. Only one last interview remains – Mr. Jason Flippo of Quinta Essentia, another band Lance Wright hammers the skins for.

They are in the vein of a keyboard-less *Equilibrium* Emperor and a faster-paced Gorguts. They are currently finalizing their first USA/Canadian tour. Headlining will be Swedish death metal legends Benediction and the blackened thrash band Nominon, also from Scandinavia. A quick self-description: *"With the initiative to rule the earth with a colossal sound that carries reality and imagination to a dark world, Quinta Essentia, displays this epic summoning with their live performance and recording."*

Jason is on a high note right now because today Megadeth released *United Abominations, "Their first good album since*

'Youthanasia.'" He's excited and waving around a painted portrait of Vic Rattlehead in one hand and a fat, freshly sparked jibber in the other.

This long-haired, combat-booted metal commando and I conduct the following on the back patio, swatting mosquitoes every 20 seconds and sipping Budweiser: "I joined Blood Stained Dusk in 2000 when I was just out of high school. I joined right before the *Dirge of Death's Silence* album on Baphomet Records. We toured with Monstrosity the summer after, about 20 shows. We went from Louisiana, through Texas, Arizona, New Mexico, California, and Colorado. We picked up another guitarist who was doing heroin and shit. He was a fucking maniac, this Russian guy. He and Patrick dove deep into that stuff, and Patrick wasn't really like that. He was into the whole necro-needles-and-creativity shit. Around then I started Quinta Essentia. I wanted to do something more influenced by Bay Area thrash and progressive metal. I wanted to create something dark, technical, ritualistic, magickal with these over-the-top deep concepts. I'm on guitar and vocals. The album is called *Neutrality For Defined Chaos* and it was released on Deathgasm Records. Somewhere in the middle of that I started working with Fleshtized. On 2 weeks notice I played the Baltimore Death Fest on bass. We decided to record and picked up Rob Client from Pessimist on vocals. He was on *Cult of the Initiated.* It's still unreleased, but we're shooting it around."

"What's the message of your art?"

Quinta Essentia is very dark, ethereal, double guitar harmony sections around technical rhythms. There's a song called 'Hidden Constellation,' and it reflects on several concepts regarding Quintessence. Quinta Essentia is Latin for the 'Fifth Essence.' In astrophysics, quintessence is the cosmic microwave diagram that holds the celestial bodies into place. It's basically dark matter or infinite space. 'Hidden Constellation' is an existence on the plane of the dark, seen by no eyes, but felt by the black hole. Like an incantation to the darkness of the cosmic power. It's transcendental magic in a way, but I still take the scientific approach. I'm not a religious person. I do believe in ritual magic to create your intuitive path and your strength. Magic is a simple to me as creating your future by your own willpower and the way you view yourself."

"Do you see your art as a positive, as opposed to society interpreting it as negative? Especially in the Bible Belt..."

"I'm used to it, as far as being alone with our group. It's something negative and positive. I believe if you're going to dwell in negativity than put yourself out of you misery. If you're going to be here than do something, work for something you believe in. There are messages in Quinta Essentia that range from the inevitable human holocaust, to materialism and greed, uncontrollable change that could come at any time. I'm not trying to change anybody. I have hatred for organized religion just like the next metalhead goes, but its not going to control my life. I think hatred is something that takes away from your willpower. To extend control over something is really just extending control over yourself. That's where the message goes into a positive. The negative is towards the inevitable, evil nature of mankind."

We take a break and breathe of sigh of relief. It was Jason's first real interview, and he is nervous that he didn't fair so well. I just laugh at him and spark another joint. Mortigan steps out onto the patio, and all of us are kind of staring at each other in total quiet, sipping beers and enjoying a peaceful slice of night. You can't even hear crickets... As I open my mouth to babble something profound a drunken mob of hicks yell at each other in the parking lot, and all we hear is a sharp *YEEEE-HAW!!!* echoing from the blackened distance...

PART VIII: NEW YORK CITY
(AMERICANA OMEGA)
MAY 24TH-JUNE 4TH 2007

ROOTS

In order to get to Schechter's house I have to walk through downtown West Dearborn, slip Monroe Ave, turn the corner of Outer Drive, and walk the same route I had to 300 times over while he and I were still in high school.

Having marched across strange terrain all year, this stroll was beyond alien. I keep looking over my shoulder for a coked-out platoon of jocks. This was a bad neighborhood for me. Dozens of fights, lots of bad memories. I could never tell who hated me more, the cops or the civilian population…

I had to return here to rediscover an old friend. He was expelled in 9th grade and vanished until 2005. He'd emerged from years of silence with his freshly assembled hardcore punk outfit Street Crime, lineup consisting of 19 year olds he called the "*Junior Punk Rock Mafia.*" There was no time to catch up, and he disappeared quickly thereafter. I'd get occasional sporadic emails tanked with prose he'd been writing – either surrealistic poetry or grody chapters of his hard-boiled junkie cop pulp novel.

Schechter was one of my biggest influences early on. I was a real train wreck, and he was the quiet kid from all over the country with the military dad reading anarchist propaganda in the back of class. He introduced me to an entire host of new material – Leary, Hoffman, Rollins, LaVey; anything mind-bending he'd supreme knowledge of.

Schechter was the first one to ever sit me down and say '*this is what punk rock is all about.*' He really nailed it into my head that there was a fang-bared, fighting subculture that actually existed outside our ignorant, minuscule reality. I already was a nut bag at 14 – I knew the world was corrupt & reality flimsy, but he blasted so much discipline into my head that I was never the same. I just needed a masthead, and he pointed me in the ambiguous direction.

We were nightmares for the staff. We pissed on classroom floors, smoked dope in the building, hijacked chalkboard from instructors and gave our own class lectures. Every homework answer dealt a blow to our teacher's foundation of reality.

Schechter got expelled for showing up wasted on hash brownies, zonked out of his mind. He had been skipping class and stumbled into the basketball court barefoot. He was screaming at the gym teacher to give him his shoes. His father moved them out of state, and in his absence I dived head-first into militant, occult-drenched, metal/punk pan-tribal socialism. I was a crazy fucker, and revolution was the key phrase of the era…

Here I now am, over a decade later, extreme in fanatic triumph of will. And here now is Schechter, who's fulfilled his potential in the most ironic of all twists. Jeff Schechter was a Marine Sniper on the ground wave of the Iraq invasion, among those directly responsible for securing Baghdad block to block in guerrilla warfare. His scores were cream of the crop, and he's trained 55 men for one of the toughest sniping units in the armed forces. His body count is unknown, although hefty.

Schechter describes himself as such: *"I am a blue-collar tramp, a dream chasing scumbag forever compromised and contradicting myself. Since my service in the Middle East I have developed a few debilitating social phobias. However, I yearn to be the center of attention. Having so many inner contradictions has led me into the darker, more introspective years of my life… I claw at the veneer of what people try to force feed me and what has become the desired, acceptable lifestyle. This is what I struggle against and I will suffer until either it, or I, am destroyed."*

We haven't had a real conversation in over 10 years, although one of the first things he related was that he'd kept some post-apocalyptic prose I did in 9th grade taped inside his war journal. Bombs are exploding, machine guns fired, half the city is burning, and Schechter's sitting on the steps of a Mosque, writing poetry in a Wagnerian trance with his assault rifle delicately beside him:

"Sandstorms and tears, Finally appreciating teenage lust, In angst-filled teenage loss… My mothers face is wet, and Screams from inside a family portrait- Hiding from wayward lies… Making peace with the stars, I lay back, atop a machinery of hate- and I know I will never find the solace I have here, now… It is cold around moist feet in the night, And nail heads dig round, wise heads into my sore and solemn back… Soon life will change, and in the silence we will all be children…"

THE LONG U-HAUL EASTWARD

SATURDAY, MAY 26th, 7am; Schechter, Skinhead Eddie & I shove off for Wallington Borough, New Jersey – a Polish grotto so miniscule it doesn't appear on the map. Schechter is expatriating himself from Detroit today and never looking back. He's setting up shop on a new life with his girlfriend who's already secured an apartment. He's restarting his band Street Crime with a new group of players, completing work on his first book, and planning to enjoy the NY life.

Street Crime is definitely going to be a niche-minded sell. Being a Marine and coming back to the hardcore punk underground, fully supporting the war and having a nationalistic punk band is a real hamper, since it's such a viciously recalcitrant world. He's in a good position though because his brother runs Sound Riot Studios and is a manager of some sort for My Chemical Romance. This also means we have free access to a quarter-million dollar studio in Brooklyn.

New York is only a stones through from Wallington Borough, and I have high expectations. No matter how minuscule your day is, every slice of Manhattan is an adventure. I have a list of over 50 bands from the area, many of whom are located in Brooklyn and Queens. It seems all of New York has been stomping like the rows of a hockey game for my arrival. The message I received through Greg of Paragon Records (and black/death act Dimentianon): *'Just fucking get to Duff's Brooklyn – blood, metal, and Satan. What more could you ask?'*

It's a 13 hour drive, and we're halfway there before I even am even able to crack Schechter's ice-hard wall of punctuality. Like so many vets I've known, he has that gung ho attitude of *'get it done, stick to plan, keep moving forward.'* He's a no-bullshit sort of character, drilled into his world. You don't even need to talk about Iraq to tell he's haunted. My manifest presence is only scraping that barrier.

The difference Jeff has with every other vet is that we both grew up in the highest population of Arabs outside the Middle East. Our neighborhood (East Dearborn) is referred to as "Little Lebanon," where 80% of grown adults are Arab, and 65% of the youth are too. Many business signs are in that weird cursive writing, and all high schools are predominantly Arabic.

We both bounced between East and West Dearborn where the cultural lines are rigidly divided, but it is a point of pride to always claim East Dearborn, and that's where I've always considered home.

Greenfield Road juts through East Dearborn. On one side it's Baghdad; the other solidly black.

Growing up in Dearborn, the racism was explosive. It's not that the average person plays into it, and the last thing I want to be accused of is being a racist bigot. If anything, I hung out with more Arabs, black, & Mexicans kids then I ever did the honkies.

What I speak of is a hostile environment propelled by distrust and vile omnipresent stereotypes. Despite so many moderate, sane, respectful Muslim immigrants, there is still a huge percentage that buys into that mainline thread of conservative Islamic culture where they seriously consider non-Muslim people as infidels. To deny this reality is to be naïve. When a large segment of this population consider the infidel to have no soul, as objects to exploit – it's a serious arrogance that is at the bedrock of so many of these folks logic. And it is this attitude and the overall Islamic attitude towards women which, if you ask me, really set the tragic inertia rolling in Dearborn more so then blind idiocy of senseless genetic hatred.

People play into skin color hostility everywhere, stupidly, just as they do economic jealousy – but Dearborn is a special case of communities rubbing each other the wrong way, pathologically, for decades. And this monolithic tension came out especially amongst the youth violently enacting their parents ugly views, angry teenage males fighting each other everywhere, constantly, forever.

Our high school had a divided population; constant threats like a prison courtyard. Everyday there were group brawls or isolated punch-outs. Edsel Ford was featured on the news several times for race riots I'd witnessed firsthand with 300+ students.

There was a long period of tension when the head jocks started going toe to toe with the biggest of them – all these steroid meatheads on both sides making threats like pro wrestlers. There were shootings, jumpings, assaults. You got used to people walking past you saying, *"Hey white boy -- Jihad is coming. Wulla we're going to kill you."* And having to see the other moderate, non-violent, friendly Arab kids roll their eyes, or get dragged into the foolish actions of hot-headed peers.

Then you graduate, you calm it down. You don't talk about it anymore, and the world is oblivious: They want you to go to college, become a man – this white-picket fence deal. You keep reading about al Qaeda's initiatives in the major newspapers and see it coming 10 million miles away. No matter what course you take in life, this is going to shake the world to its very foundations. Then one day planes are flying into The World Trade Center, and the world lives in your paranoid delusion…

That's exactly what's going through Schechter's head when he says, "*Well, you know... One thing I wanted to bring you out here for... Growing up where we did...*"

"How do you deal with it, you mean? How do you even begin to tell people?"

"*How do you deal with that? Then going from who we were as kids and becoming... From anarchist punk to borderline American fascist... Heh, heh... But you see I don't take anything back. I never felt more alive, I was a beast. And now I'm just here, driving in civilian clothes... It's all fucked man...*"

That's all I can pull because his defense mechanism rides high, and he goes right back to spewing lines from *The Big Lebowski*. He explains the enigma of '95 – he never got expelled over hash brownies. Some Arab kid was slamming his own girlfriends' head into a locker. When Jeff stood up for her, 6 backed him into a corner and pulled a switchblade. Security broke it up and his father dragged them to Texas.

When I explain everything that went down until graduation – all the fights, the guns, the drugs, the deaths, suicides and prison terms – he just keeps driving quietly... He lets out a big sigh and pulls into a rest stop in the Pennsylvania Hills. He says hops out the truck and wanders off for 15 minutes. Just observing the environment; looking at the grass, the sky. The world he abandoned and the world he now enters collide like glaciers…

THE EAST COAST Oi FEST

SATURDAY, May 26th; Somewhere in Pennsylvania at the major skinhead event of the summer. The East Coast Oi Fest maintains 4 stages & 60 bands over two days. We came here for Skinhead Eddie, who is going to be my sidekick for the week.

He's so non-threatening it's great. He hates white power, is a traditional SHARP, and is Jeff's best friend. He kind of reminds me of a 5 foot 6 Paul Giamatti. He's another Michigan boy the spins dub reggae downtown Detroit. He's got the burgundy stompers nicely shined, the workpants, the derby cap. He's the sort of fella you want to go fishing with.

The Oi Fest is not my world in the slightest, and I'm not pretending to feign knowledge of the lineup. The only bands I've even heard of are Reagan Youth, Flatfoot 56, and The Templars. It's an intimidating scene. The club is drenched in humidity, walls dripping with sweat and Pabst. There are like 300 bulldog skins in Lonsdale's & suspenders stomping around. The testosterone is so heavy you can taste the mace of a coming riot. These guys are beating the living shit out of each other in the circle pit, and very few who don't look the type.

The night rolls on and the vibe is tedious, all these onstage rah-rah working class declarations. Outside I try to interview the guitarist from Wretched Ones, but he's one of those *"you have to talk to the other guy about that"* guys.

Across the alley are a group of six unclassifiable sort-of punk kids. They hitched from Northern California over 20 states in a two-week mission to come here. Their reward is being trash-talked by a mob of skins for their tye-dye shirts. The main antagonist is this 17 year old black kid skin doing a *'I'm so fucking punk rockkk'* number on them. What a turd, with his white laces & suspenders. He probably drove 20 minutes to come here.

Eddie marches up drunk & jolly, repeating a line I blurted earlier: *'Hey Bartek, you know it's not gay so long as you're jacking each other off to Hatebreed. It's so macho it cancels out the faggotry. HAHAHA!!!'* A voice from the gaggle of dolts rises with an explosion of anger: *"YOU GOT A PROBLEM WITH HATEBREED MOTHERFUCKER?!?"* Just get me out of here…

DRUNKEN NIGHT OUT

The second you hop off the PATH train and hustle your way through The Port Authority, you have to push your way through a swathe of humanity climbing endless flights of stairs. Once you emerge into the thick of Manhattan, it's like being thrown directly into a grueling mushroom trip where you have to keep moving forward at all costs.

The first sight is usually the one that cripples the unprepared. One minute you're in an underground subway that ranks of electrical burnt-rubber like the bumper-car ring of a carnival. The next you're surrounded by a hollow road of mountains far as the eye can see. Everything is 70 stories tall, 100,000 people are rushing in cold, self-centered circles, and every inch of sidewalk hosts a conman or grill cart hustling beef kabobs & roasted peanuts. Welcome to Manhattan, the 21st century bazaar…

The thing with New York is that it doesn't really come alive until 2am. Sure, there is always non-stop action, but a true New York night is accented by those fond occasions when you wander into random people drunker then you are, and find yourself on a bench at 5am chatting with some total creep who's laughing about all the broads he's sodomized. You've no idea who either of each other are, but it really doesn't matter, because at any moment the next hammered freak will join your party, and all three of you will be pissing in public yelling at pedestrians with your cocks in hands.

This is the goal Skinhead Eddie and I intend to reach. We've already killed the flask of vodka, and keep ducking into the alleyways slamming Mickey's 40's and Sparks tall-cans. This is his first visit to NYC, and I'm playing tour guide of the Lower East Side. I was here once before, living briefly with a Rod Stewart record producer in 2004.

Schechter and I form a strange dichotomy for Eddie to be trapped between. On one hand you have the pure Marine, on the other a Gutter Colonel. We both live like we're in a perpetual war, and both are highly militaristic. My boots are polished same as his, my survival skills just as McGyveresque, and we're both as weirdly punctual & disciplined. Eddie feels like a human ping-pong ball.

We are polar opposites in the underground. Eddie's a wool-dyed skin, and I'm as loose as they come. He's christened me 'The Crust King' and keeps knocking "food" out of my hands when I try picking scraps from the trash. *"Dammit Eddie, I eat for entertainment. How else do you expect me to last in this place with $80 to my name?"*

By 6pm we're so drunk that we're running around Central Park trying to find the pigeon lady from *Home Alone 2*. Manhattan feels like a bubble-wrapped, cattle Tokyo gone awry... *Three more Sparks tall cans and Eddie is pissing a river on the sidewalk. A polite upper-class lady in a trench lifts her coat and politely skips the bubbling brook...* Eddie keeps slapping his knee and falling over Puerto Rican Andy: *"So I picked up this bitch at an AIDS walk-a-thon"...* Eddie hollers *'I ain't no fuckin' clown!!!'* and gets nasty with the subway hustler trying to pass off laundry detergent as ya-yo...

Outside the PATH in Jersey City the payphone rings. Nothing the man says I can distinguish, then Eddie jacks the receiver: *"What's that you say?"* He stumbles away claiming he'll be right back, then disappears for 20 minutes... Schechter pulls up and I have no idea what to say. Then we both hear maniacal belly-laughter as Eddie emerges from the darkness, booking like a steam engine towards the car...

MEMORIAL DAY SPECTACULAR

"Did a gay guy really try to get me to blow him for coke?" Eddie puts his face in his hands hung over, trying to weed out the ugly, hazy memory... It's been a lazy day. We're both worked over from last night, but its Memorial Day, which equals Schechter's big night out. Only problem – insofar as the context of band interviews, everyone is on vacation because the holiday. I can't get anyone on the horn, and I feel the creeping pulse of Denver once again.

Later that night at a Sports Bar Schechter proposes a toast to a fellow Marine: *"This is for my good friend. He has no legs."* Up until now, our little U-Haul ride was about all the info I could extract from him. But he is ready now to let his tale spill into my recorder. He leads us back to a sharply illuminated pool table. He downs more shots before slinking into it... But he's pacing around, he's fucking up his billiards game. He keeps looking at me totally haunted as the memories hit a wall. He just keeps chuckling to himself, saying little phrases I can't distinguish. Then he says *"Fuck it, more booze..."*

SLOW MOTION EXPLOSION

I awoke refreshed, shirtless on the kitchen floor next to a trashcan quarter-filled with stomach bile. I'd tried to walk it off, but I'd found myself in the laundry room reading a *Dianetics* book someone left on the dryer and having a conversation with the ghost of "3." Nothing makes you upchuck more cold-bloodedly then the unwelcome mirages of ex-girlfriends...

I finally get to explore Wallington Borough on foot. It maintains the aura of George Romero's *Martin*. Another dead industrial village – buildings rotting apart, barbed-wire fenced industrial factories and semi-truck depots – a mile to the nearest gas station. There are a handful of rusting bridges that echo the 1920's, but all rivers beneath are mud-brown from human waste. Every white person for miles speaks polish, and the only English dialogue I receive is from a Chinese immigrant whilst ordering Pepper Steak.

Back to the sports bar from last night. Things are getting rough. The girlfriend isn't used to two guys just hanging out on the floor, and Jeff is stuck in the middle, kind of wanting to get this over with. Skinhead Eddie is set to leave the same day as me, but we have 5 more days in limbo. The goal was to couch surf around Queens and Brooklyn, but nearly all 50 bands have totally flaked out.

There is a bus that goes from Wallington Borough to Manhattan, but it only runs twice a day – from 7am-2pm & 4pm-7pm, Monday through Friday. For any real NYC adventure to happen, we have to stay there overnight and hope that we get back to the apartment before Jeff or the girl go to work at 9am, because they won't give us a key. And even if we do get an apartment key, we still don't have access to get into the building. I'm not going to push the issue.

All of this comes to a boiling head when Schechter comes to pick us up. Eddie overlooks the time, and Jeff's been waiting in his car for 20 minutes, driving around the block over and over because he can't legally park out front. He gets frustrated pissed because he needs to get up at 5am. When Jeff starts getting hostile with Eddie he blurts something that sends them both into a bickering hurricane. I'm a confused little boy in the backseat of two fighting parents.

In front of the apartment they go at it for a half hour as I'm twirling the grass on the lawn, wondering why I'm not drunk in Long Island or Yonkers with death metal band A or thrash group B. If there isn't a single band in New York hip to my mission, what vague hope do I have for smooth sailing in the remaining four months of the journey?

I've still got at least 6 cities to go, bare minimum, or there will be nothing cohesive to write about in the end. The possibility of a grand finale at this point is utterly hopeless, seeing as that New York <u>WAS</u> the perceived last chapter. I'm only here 'cause the stars aligned correctly and Schechter was in Detroit at the right time.

Jeff storms in his bedroom and Eddie is drunk and pissed on the couch. He stares blankly at the wall for 5 minutes, then without looking up he tells me: *"Fuck this. I'd rather die face-down in the gutter then put up with his insulting shit for one more day. Tomorrow we're going to New York and we're not coming back until my flight takes off…"*

DORO PESCH'S BIRTHDAY PARTY

Eddie and I are up at dawn lacing our boots and preparing for war on New York. We actually have set objectives today – Metal Maniacs World HQ to meet my editor Liz Ciaverella for the first time, then a rendezvous across town with another Detroit Expatriate for a multi-warehouse art gallery.

Then off to The Delancy Lounge for Doro Pesch's birthday party where Dave Brenner (the "Wizard of Oz" of underground metal PR men) will gladly feed us shots of Jaeger. And yes, I did say Doro

Pesch – "the German Lita Ford," formerly of the cult 80's power metal band Warlock.

We're out the door at 9am, stomachs filled with herbal energy pills and black coffee. At the bus corner is an odd polish lady in her late 20's, though her face is hardened by that coal-worker sheen. She's oddly cartoon-like and flirty, although we can't exactly tell if she's hitting on us.

She talks in a foreign tongue we have no way to follow – always in short, manic bursts capped by giggling laughter. Her name is Jana, and she keeps asking questions in whatever polyglot form of English and Slav-talk she's speaking. She goes through our wallets looking at pictures then hands us two free bus passes.

The bus is actually closer to a top-of-the line Greyhound then any generic rider. Its interior resembles a jumbo jet aisle way and the driver actually has a change dispenser hooked to his belt, making NYC the only place in America where you get correct change and aren't gypped stuffing $3 into a machine slot for a $2.25 transfer.

We're pumped out at the Port Authority and wander to a hotel where Jana works. She's an hour late, and we think she might have just gotten fired. She leads us to the outskirts of Central Park Zoo where we watch baby seals slapping beach balls through iron bars.

I'm determined to get through to her, so I keep bringing up Josip Broz Marshall Tito. She giggles, then I bring up LAIBACH which I think insults her. She just kind of gives up and leaves us there when we tell her we have no inclination of going back to Jersey. Regardless, we scribble our cell numbers so Eddie and I might be able to mack on some Warsaw honeys…

We've been singing Dead Boys lyrics & crawling Greenwich Village. It's a perfect sunny day, around 80 degrees; ripe and alive. We're getting kabobs from a street corner grill top when this horrifying bum lady with scaly red alligator legs starts hitting on Eddie. He her a $5 spot just to get rid of her. *"Do you think I could contract that crocodile rash shit from touching her fingers?"* I nod enthusiastically just to freak him out, and he runs into Jet Burger compulsively washing his hands.

It's 2pm when we make it to Metal Maniacs. It's a multi-office business complex on the Lower East Side which reaches 20 stories. The 11th floor is our particular stop, and we head in casually. There are 15 cubicles in the tiny room. Not understanding the set-up I walk to the first lady I see: '*Excuse me, are you Liz the editor?*" "Yeah." "*Oh great, good to finally meet you. I'm Ryan Bartek.*"

She's like, "*great, great*" but is giving me this weird eye. We keep bantering on and on like an ancient reunion, and it takes 10 full minutes to iron out that this is the wrong Liz. She really has no idea who I am, and this is actually the hippie magazine Relix. Slap-happy laughter ensues and I'm lead to another area with 15 more cubicles, each which represent a different magazine under one umbrella corp.

The real Liz Ciaverella is tiny and petit, 5 foot 3 with heavy black mascara under her hypnotic eyes – lots of necklaces and rings, black sort of frilly dress shirt. She looks like the kind of gal that would be running the counter of a New Age book store, burning candles and incense. She sees the two of us standing there, and looks creeped out by my twisted grin and Coroner shirt. "*Hey, I'm that Bartek asshole.*"

She starts laughing. She didn't expect us to come in off the street, and had no idea what I looked like to begin with. Liz feeds us leftover chocolate cake in the break room, and the assistant – who happens to be of the renowned tech/death band Biolich – is one of the first people in America to recognize my Bethlehem back-patch. It's always like a fan-boy reunion when this occurs, and no one ever stops talking about the SUIZID record.

Liz says, "*This is what I deal with every day*" and hands me a chicken-scrawled fan letter. This is a guy who's written every month for the past 11 years, sometimes in crayon & always like a child, demanding that the world needs more power metal.

The Doro Pesch guest-list is squared away and we hit the streets again, resting in Tompkins square, which is the famed crust punk haven of NYC. Anyone of that persuasion is sleeping in the shade, yet that crowd is sparse at best. Jeff calls and apologizes for the episode last night: "*Sorry man, not everyone is trained to live like me. I really have to keep in mind that I'm back in a world with normal people again. It's just tough, you know?*"

I drop into an air raid position because I swear I just witnessed the scariest of crazed ex-girlfriends walking across the street. While I'm on the ground with hands covering my head, Eddie starts freaking out and cursing obscenities. His socks and boots are thrown aside, and he's gripping his bare foot with wide, panic-stricken eyes.

The Ebola virus somehow got into his sock. There are scabs running up and down his foot, this rash from hell cracking & blistering his bleeding skin like a bad case of chiggers. Maybe the alligator lady really did transmit her disease. In any event this spells doom for the next few days, because the infection is so raw that Eddie can barely even walk…

6pm, Times Square. We're in a yellow taxi cab with Amy, who is Eddie's good pal from high school. She's a year into her NYC existence as a Detroit expatriate, attending classes at a high-class art school in uptown Manhattan. You just can't kill the Michigan in the girl. One of the first things she asks is if we want to play euchre.

She kind of sickly wants to move home, totally convinced in the theory that everything great about Detroit blows everywhere else, and everything that sucks about Detroit is marvelous anywhere else you travel. There is no in-between.

Amy doesn't like New York people all too much. *"It's like a glittering paradise for two months. Then all you hear are gun shots, screaming drunks, traffic and noise. It fucking smells bad, there's no room to breathe, everything is ridiculously expensive. I really want to get the hell out of here."*

She's taking us to this multi-warehouse postmodern art exhibit where an armada of free booze is being circulated. The exhibit is spread throughout a half-dozen buildings up and down this old warehouse back street in Greenwich. Outside the galleries are clots of snooty pretentious Warhol types talking loud, obscure bohemian jive so that they'll overhear each other and feel mega-hipster. Inside the snobs are hanging around sipping champagne, acting self-important, eye-balling us like rancid turf people.

Eddie and I push our rumbling way to the heralded alcohol. Tubs and buckets of ice galore, hundreds of long-neck bottles up for grabs – Blue Moons and Heinekens and Guinness and Coronas and imported German whatever-the-fucks; champagne, wine, cocktails…

No one says shit to us as we're openly shoving our backpacks full of glass, jabbering like 17th century pyrates commandeering a yacht cruiser. One preppy guy uneasily looks at me like he's gonna call security, but I just take off my sunglasses and flash him the look of a rabies-infected badger. We're too grizzled looking to fuck with, and we both smell like middle school gym lockers.

Exhibit to exhibit is the same. Slam all the booze we can, keep filling the packs, pretend like we're interested in buying something. Some of these portraits are brilliant, but the majority are like chunks left on the editing room floor of Juxtapoz magazine. Total crap is being passed off from $1,000-$15,000....

All three of us are trashed and wandering around Manhattan. As Amy and I shove McChicken slop in our faces, she requests that I interview her because she's a self-proclaimed cult legend: *"Yeah, I was in Ron of Japan in 1996. We were on Hanson Records; they put out some Andrew WK stuff. We're kind of like The Ramones, except we all had the same first name. I'm Ron Rosuave. Devon was Ron Rosaucey, and our friend was Ron Rosexy."*

"We were a noise band by default, we just didn't know how to play any instruments. I played recorder. I'm a very accomplished recorder player. I learned a lot of distortion and effects on the recorder. We hooked it to an amp and used pedals. We did everything on one track and it was mono. I played in the kitchen while my friend played in the living room, distanced enough so our tiny recorder picked it up just right."

Songs about wanting to be president, why dogs should be allowed in hospitals. Our logo was a three legged gerbil with a saddle, which I think sums it up pretty well. We wrote a lot of Princess Di tributes. Most of those got lost, 'cause Devon's an alcoholic. They were pretty amazing..."

The Delancy Lounge is packed with 200 crammed into an area fit for half of such population. Everyone is shit-faced, metal paparazzi are everywhere, and there are so many decorative plants it mimics the Burmese jungle...

Liz introduces me to Doro, who is super-friendly and has a thick, almost manly Deutschland accent. Liz has befriended her in the past 2 years, which is like a dream come true since she's been a Warlock die-hard since the age of 11.

By the time they pull out the birthday cake, Liz's husband – the mysterious Dave Brenner – appears from the thicket with a complimentary Long Island iced tea in hand. He's got long brown head-banging hair, a goofy, uneven smile, and a shrug-heavy *"everything is fucked, let's get hammered"* vibe.

Dave is like the Wizard of Oz – he's the ultimate underground pr man, a propaganda assailant working unstoppable spam campaigns for over 30 labels. Night after night he hacks away at his keyboard, networking tours in Europe and North America. He's been shipping boxes full of promo CD's to soldiers in Iraq as to fuel the war with his own personal soundtrack – tanks crushing through molten sands blazing Vried, Katharsis, Lecherous Nokturne, Skeleton Witch. He pulls out a zippy hash pipe and we start puffing away, hidden in the quasi-canopy: *"So Dave, the burning question I've asked everyone – what's something remarkably bizarre that's happened to you and when you tell people they think you're a pathological liar?"*

"Ha ha!! Well, back in the day, when I was about 12, I was at this summer camp in Pennsylvania. We had this plan to play Capture The Flag, and once our counselors fell asleep, there were about 10 of us that ran into the woods dressed like ninjas. Right when we were in position, all of us crouched on the ground, we start hearing these footsteps marching towards us, like military style. From out of nowhere, marching across the field in squad formation are like 12 guys in these weird fucking druid hoods, and all of them have army boots and these black suitcases. Like they're just chugging through this field at like 1am, in the middle of nowhere, and they're all in perfect unison. All of us kids, we're just hiding in these bushes watching this. The column keeps marching through the open field – right-left-right-left – and go through the open pasture into the darkness of the woods. Every kid I was with that night, every one of them – we were so fucking freaked out there isn't any real word to describe it. Since then, I've gone through every possible scenario in my head that would make this thing make sense, but I'm still at a total loss. Like, seriously – what the fuck was that about? It still fucks with me ..."

2 hours later, everyone is gone. Eddie and I prowl the streets absolutely blasted. We've killed all the stolen beer and are currently working on Sparks tall cans. Best feature of NYC – booze is sold 24-7. Eddie keeps pissing everywhere, like every 15 minutes, limping around from Ebola foot and talking shit to lampposts.

We bump into a hammered Australian guy on vacation who goes into a soliloquy about surfing. Eddie grabs my shirt and pulls me off mid-conversation. "Dude, I was having fun there." Eddie replies, *"Ah fuck 'em. I hate Australians, all they talk about are the waves in Sydney. Surf surf surf, that's all you fucking hear – ride the fukin' wave mate. Fucking Aussie bastards."*

5am and we're on the steps of an apartment building in a crust/skin collision: *"Dammit Bartek, GG was not a good person! He contributed nothing!"* "No, no, no, he had it all right! You gotta live out of a paper bag. It's the only true freedom left!" "*Fuck that! You gotta work and live and contribute! You just can't run around fighting people, doing heroin, and raping your audience!*' "But it's not about that, it's about…"

Somehow we make it to the Port Authority by near daylight after sneak-attack subway hopping. The skin/crust collision has gotten silly in our duel, and I'm eating stuff out of the garbage just to gross him out. I run to the escalator and stick my tongue on that black handle grip as it rolls upward, slurping ten feet of revolving rubber. "*Oh my fucking god, that's how you get botulism!!!*"

I lose Eddie for a half hour and rediscover him blacked out against the wall, eyes rolling in the back of his head, plopped next to a fresh pool of piss. This time he was urinating in the middle of the Port Authority while commuters were hustling to work & politely ignoring him. Its 6:30 but our bus doesn't even start running until 8am. Eddie says, "*Lucky for us, Jeff slipped me the key to the apartment. But it's only for the actual room. Just don't tell his girl, she'll throw a fit. But we still have to break into the building.*"

Our heads are beating in misery as we get off in Wallington Borough. Two blocks later we're rolled by 4 squad cars. The cops detest us on sight and are full of questions. Supposedly someone called in fear of us because we were strange looking wanderers, which is crap because we've only been on the street for 10 minutes.

They dig through our backpacks, pick through our pockets, frisk us against the cars. All they find is an empty flask but are still determined to haul us into the station anyway. The only thing that gets us out of their misplaced rage is that we're staying with a Marine, and Eddie pitches that whole '*how you boys doin' today?*' rap like a used car salesman. That's the one thing skins have always been best for – pulling the pro-authoritarian fake-out number…

THE 48 HOUR PUSH

Schechter is examining Eddie's foot the same way he'd tend to a comrade hit by a roadside bomb: "*Jesus Eddie, what the fuck did you do to yourself?*" Eddie looks at his bleeding, cracked skin with grit-faced terror, "*It was all that alligator bitch, I swear!!*"

There's no way around it – Eddie is down for the count. He can barely walk and we have three more days until our escape pods launch off. On top of this, Jeff has another grueling 12 hour workday tomorrow and is pre-booked to take his girlfriend out to a fancy dinner, which cuts

272

him completely out of the picture until Sunday when we are to visit Sound Riot Studios in uptown Manhattan. He'll be working on the new Street Crime demo throughout the day with his engineer brother, the same guy on the My Chemical Romance management team.

New York started so epic and somehow every band has flaked out or is otherwise unavailable. I was supposed to hang out with the singer from Biohazard at his home studio, catch a metal opera performance by Ballet Deviare, slink into Jersey to meet GG's brother Merle, possibly a tryst with Frank Miller. All vanished. Then there were the bands, labels, studios, film directors – a list so phenomenal it will only cause the reader grief to reveal the cult namesakes…

The last of the Wallington busses soon cut off, and the route will not resume until Monday morning at 8am. If I accept this mission there will be no escape from New York. The choice is such – give up completely and hang around the apartment watching movies for the next three days, or go it alone like Snake Plissken. Totally cut off from the world, up for 48 straight hours, $70 to my name, enclosed by skyscrapers & a dangerous 1.5 million human carnival in which anything can and will happen…

8pm, back to the Port Authority in Manhattan in the upper levels where it resembles an airport food court/mini-mall. No point in rushing it – just pace yourself for the marathon 'cause the finish line will not be any closer no matter how much steam rages. I'm feeling pretty good about it though. As much as I like Eddie, the truth is I work better alone and a hectic mission like this only brings out that isolated trooper in me.

As much fun as it is running around the country meeting bands, seeing shows, partying and such, what I really get my kicks from is simply being the fly on the wall. Just observing cultures foreign to me, random people in vulnerable, quiet limbo; feeling invisible as if no one is paying attention. Even though they remain speechless, that silence says more then words ever will.

The way they read the newspaper, carry groceries – the look on their faces peering out the subway car in deep thought or no thoughts at all. There are no drama plots going on, no self-centered sitcom. No employment reality babble, romancing or false pretenses…

The highlight of my evening in this respect is at the bagel shop eating a giant pretzel, watching a 20-something brunette. She is reading text messages on her cell phone looking depressed. One of the typed conversations is something special, probably the boy she digs.

Whatever was said swirls around the contours of her soul. She sparks a delicate smile, brushes herself off and disappears back into the endless sea, bright and proud. *She is the most beautiful thing in the world...*

10pm in Brooklyn, eating Pepper Steak at a grungy Chinese diner with hideous looking sun-bleached combo pictures. I had gotten lost on the Subway and ended uptown Manhattan, cursing the indecipherable red/blue/yellow/green train line map on the wall. No one speaks English, and it's a roulette gamble every time... Back to my observation of humanity; those flickering subway lights. A satanic Johnny Cash version of "When The Man Comes Around" popped in my head, and a balding businessman in suit eyeballed me like a lunatic while singing it aloud: *"Broken trumpets sin like vipers/600 billion demons screamin'/Multitudes are marchin' to the genocidal drum/Angels fallin' Hebrews cryin'/Muslims raped & Christians dying/It's Post-Omega's Anti-Kingdom Come..."*

Through the back alleys of a warehouse despoblado & adjoining the river you'll find Duffs Brooklyn, world-renowned as the greatest metal bar in The States. It's like a landing port for any touring band in the extreme metal underground, and the major hub of all activity in the Tri-State area. This is the very birthplace of NYDM (*New York Death Militia*), the extreme metal equivalent of The Hells Angels.

Most NYDM members sport black-leather vests covered in patches, the NYDM logo itself featuring a skull with battle-axes as crossbones. Will Rahmer of Mortician started the organization in the early 90's, and chapters have spread worldwide. Outside of New York, the club transfers to the title USDM (*United States Death Militia*).

The NYDM guys consider it a blood-oath to accept membership, and one must always sport their colors. Most of the members have NYDM tattoos. A breach of contract is a messy occurrence, ending in bloody street fight or disgrace. In any instance, the excommunicated ones patch will be forcibly removed.

Everyone in the fraternity is sworn to uphold its rituals, and if there is any NYDM associated band touring an area the chapters take care of promotion, provide lodging, and salute one another like members of Project Mayhem. There are no screamo, nu-metal or metalcore bands allowed in the paradigm – it's all death, thrash or black, and all commercial trends are stomped.

Duff's Brooklyn reminds me of The Old Miami in Detroit – there is an outdoor patio with a BBQ grill, leather couches and Lazy boy recliners; interior walls covered in bumper stickers and classic tour posters. It's quite possibly the only bar in NYC with $2 PBR.

There is barely anyone here except for a small gathering of Slavs speaking whatever language it is they do. One guy has a Requiem Aeternum shirt, which is an excellent obscure prog metal band from Uruguay that I thought no one else had ever heard of. He turns out to be an immigrant that hung out with those guys and designed their banner.

I get a phone call from the band Bone Crushing Annihilation, who has called off the interview which was about to take place. 48 hours of pure movement is now inevitable & the crowd here is wafer-thin because Emperor are playing their first US gig since 2001. There are only two reunion shows – NYC & LA – and that's where Will Rahmer himself is this evening.

I grab another beer and am relaxing on the patio when a black hearse rolls up. This big fella with a snakeskin cowboy hat pops out; he's at least 6 foot 6 with a scruffy beard and feathered fedora cap. Speak of The Devil – it's the owner & name-sake of the establishment, Jimmy Duff himself: *"This bar originally started in Hells Kitchen as 'Belleview,' which at the time was still gritty. This is back in '99. I'd been working in nightclubs for years and someone needed a partner."*

"It was always a dream of mine to have my own bar. I didn't set out to make a metal bar, just one that I felt comfortable in where I liked the music, the way it looked, the bartenders. It was a very organic thing. It took off because there was nothing else like it in the city… This is where all the bands come, it's a pit stop. You have everyone from Rob Zombie, Pantera, Iron Maiden, the newer death metal bands. We have every genre come out."

"Did you play in any bands yourself?"

Jimmy Duff: "No, I've just always been a die-hard metalhead. I moved to Manhattan in '90. I didn't know any metalheads out here because in Manhattan there's not a whole lot. Back in the day it was hard to network. I met people online, we'd go to shows. When I opened the bar my friends thought it was the place to go before and after shows. That's how it happened."

"Tell me about the NYDM thing."

"From the outside looking in people aren't sure what it is, but it's basically a music club. People think it's a gang or something, but it's just a group of like minded people who're dedicated to the scene, the more extreme side of metal, the death side. It's a small circle. Everyone works together as far as promoting, going to different shows. This guy has a recording studio so we can help you out with this or that. It's like a family and everyone sticks together and supports each other. There's nothing else like it. It is the largest metal club in the world. There are chapters in Ireland, France, all over the US, Puerto Rico. Let's say you're NYDM and there's a festival in Maryland. There'll be people to meet you, pick you up from the airport, crash at their house. It's about sticking together."

"Tell me about your webzine on duffsbrooklyn.com."

"We have so many bands that come though here on a regular basis that it just occurred to me that I can interview these people in a natural environment. Where it's not some publicist involved, it's not over the phone, there's no pulling strings. One metalhead talking to another, bullshitting, having drinks. Not hard hitting journalism or anything of that nature. This place isn't about a marketing strategy. It's not a business, it's a lifestyle. I've been very successful and people have said *'lets open an Irish bar.'* This is real, this is what I like, and I can't fucking fake it. What am I going to open an Irish bar and play a shillelagh while I'm in a leprechaun suit? What the fuck is that? Is it what it is, the real deal, I live it 7 days a week. If I can pay my bills, that's success. Right now I'm talking to you, drinking a cold beer, listening to music, I'm quote-unquote working. No one's telling me what to do. I'm free."

"What are some random musicians you've met here and some of the crazy stories?"

"We have to consider the statute of limitations (laughs). I'll have to call my lawyer for advice... Type O Negative had their DVD release here. I've met a lot of bands not even one tenth as successful as they are and they've had rock star attitudes, been stand-offish. Those guys are just the coolest, no special treatment. Peter Steele bangs out here as a regular on off nights. He knows he can come down here and not get ganged up on by people. He's a very introverted kind of guy. He just wants to hang out, not get on that whole trip of where he's being bothered."

"In NYC are people more open minded?"

"In New York, to not be open minded is a luxury. The population is so diverse, at the end of the day you take the punk rockers, the metalheads, the hardcore people... We're the dying breed. They're trying to get rid of us. The mayor has said he wants to make

New York City a '*luxury product.*' Guy's a fucking billionaire. You put a gun to his head and he couldn't tell you much a carton of milk costs. He's out of touch with the regular people. This is a blue collar town, it always has been. You break your ass and you want to go to a show, you wanna drink some beer, you want to jump around and yell your lungs out – it's a primal thing. I think there's camaraderie. Were the outsiders, we're the tattooed fucking freaks. We're the last of Mohicans in New York City. Anything goes here, it's for the fringe. Just look around, no one here looks like they don't belong. But even if someone is wearing a button up shirt we don't cop attitudes. We don't judge people by the way they look. Every once in awhile you get an asshole but very rarely. I've been at this location over 2 ½ years and I've only had to physically remove one person. That said I'll probably get shot tonight, haha."

"Do cops fuck with you down here?"

"This is the only bar in New York City where you can step outside, legally have a drink in hand or a cigarette, and you won't get a ticket or arrested. The mayor's an ex-smoker. When he was running for reelection he didn't say anything about smoking laws. First thing he did when he got in office was push through the no smoking law, which hurt bars tremendously and the business at large. You got a bar and everyone's inside drinking and smoking, now all of a sudden they have to be outside. They're a little buzzed, they're getting loud, you've got neighbors complaining, you got cops. It's a whole fucking mess. The common-sense approach would have been to pass ventilation laws. I know other ex-smokers that have an axe to grind. '*Fuck it, I can't have my cigarettes anymore, fuck you, you can't have yours either.*' So that's his attitude."

"What's the weirdest thing that happened to you and when you tell people they think you're a pathological liar?

"The funny thing about the lifestyle I lead is I've been doing it for years. Every weekend is crazy in it's own way and when you live it week in and week out, you don't pay much attention. You could be here tonight, it could be something you remember for the rest of your life, and I might not, because I've done it so many times… At the old place, I had friends that were police officers. We were hanging out late and just for kicks we destroyed the place. It wasn't so fun cleaning up the day after, but at the time it was very primal. So we're raging, just fucking raging. There's a couple ceiling fans, I rip one out. The other one was spinning so one of the officer's started trying to shoot it out. Bullets are flying all around, they're going through the wall, and we realized there's a diner on the other side. Everybody shut the fuck up. I get myself together and go get a coffee next door, looking at the wall. Luckily 9mm's aren't that powerful…"

6am, SATURDAY MORNING

I was able to get a few hours of rest on the patio couch before the staff booted everyone. Before leaving a street kid explained to me – in between puffs of M-5 grade government issued marijuana – that smoking or possessing weed in NYC is now a minor felony, which automatically bars anyone from leaving the United States thanks to the Patriot Act.

A quick subway jump and back to the Lower East Side. The streets are depopulated save for lurkers with that meth-zombie swagger. I burn some time at McDonalds, but all the black coffee in the world doesn't help how dead tired I am.

I head into Tompkins Square long before it officially opens hoping to locate some crusties and perhaps a guide to the legendary C-Squat. It's a small warehouse that Leftover Crack bought for the community, and is run as an anarchist co-op. Whoever the main guy is running the show, I was told in San Fran to march right up and say that Frankie Helvis sent me.

But there are no punk rockers to be found. The park is dead except for a few piss-smelling vagrants, and as I walk past the bench tables a Harlem mob start shouting: "*Hey you fucking white bitch! That's right motherfucker, you got a problem? Say something motherfucker, I'll fucking slit your throat!!!*"

I don't bother to acknowledge them, but they're hopped up on something. One guy starts trailing me. I have the blade slid open in my pocket, and the first thought that jumps in my head is to instinctively whip it out, slice open my arm, and start yelling: "*You want AIDS motherfucker? YOU FUCKING WANT AIDS!?!*" I look back and no one is there, stunned by my primal reflex.

Instead of hanging around as a target, I head back to the streets. Since vagrancy is an arrest-worthy offense, I have to camouflage myself. I find a senior apartment complex and plop on the bench, writing some poetry before spreading a newspaper on my lap. So long as my head is down and it appears I'm reading, I should be safe. My theory works, but I can't go under because my neck is killing me, and the bench structure is poking my spine and sending waves of pain…

My eyes burn & my brain is bubbling. I walk 7 blocks trying to find any nook outside view. I come across a black timber wood-box nailed to a brick wall that halfway encloses a dumpster. I curl inside the refugium with backpack as gruff pillow…

CRUST HAVEN

"No coincidences, just an ocean of collision." At least that's what I keep telling myself as I'm passing the 40 oz to Acacia in the shade of Tompkins Square. We're drumming rants in our first reunion since January. I'd only briefly met her once before, yet I feel as if I've know her for aeons.

While waiting in line at the San Diego Greyhound for the Albuquerque bus I spied her out the glass door. She came tumbling out a parked bus with that Marla Singer stomp-and-hustle. She was a 5 foot 3 crustie with dyed red hair that could easily pass for 16. She looked fried and discombobulated as if she'd been sleeping on the bus for hours. She swung like an airplane with a fucked rudder, her coat dangling half-way off in the rain. I could tell this one would be fun, especially after she flashed the 666 tattoo on her butt cheek.

She'd been living at some squat called The Meat Locker in SD that no one had ever heard of. These were the super-secretive pyrate crusts that were just as far underground as The Villa Winona. She had just broken up with her boyfriend and was off to Phoenix to stay with her family, gearing up for a summer of train-hopping, hitch-hiking, multi-state panhandling fun. We knew we'd collide again somewhere, someway…

Now its New York world, and three days ago she got married in Tompkins to her new man-friend Brandon, a short fella with a labrae piercing, stretched ears, and a dread-locked mane. They are like two cartoon characters that've been tooling around the country since Phoenix, and have just been cooling it at Tompkins, which I'm now convinced is the double-negative of Golden Gate Park.

There are no acid-headed hippies or jovial Ulysses. These are the elite East Coast crusts – dirty mean fuckers, hard-boiled from the brutal nature of New York: *"I went back to San Diego for a month. I came there with a kid and we tried to hitchhike from Riverside to Vegas. From Vegas I met up with a friend with a van. Than we went through Arizona, went to Phoenix, broke down 20 miles outside of Tucson. First the tire blew. JP, the old drummer from Leftover Crack –*

he was the only person that stopped. He helped us go buy a tire and put it on."

"So the guy from Leftover Crack randomly appears?"

Acacia: "Yeah, I didn't know he was. He was just the only person that stopped. Nobody else gave a shit. He was *'ah, I saw a bunch of crustie kids with a van, figured I'd stop, blah blah blah.'* So we're on the way to get the tire, and he's like, *'ever listen to Leftover Crack? I used to be their drummer.'* We thought he was bullshitting. Later I went on their MySpace and it actually was him. In the middle of fucking nowhere, Tucson, Arizona. I guess he had family out there so he quit and moved from New York. He's got a kid."

"It's weird when you hear shit like that. I just found out that after the Ministry tour ends, Al Jorgensen is going to retire and be a math teacher at Texas A&M."

"That's crazy. My cousin Rodney Mullen is a professional skater. He's one credit away from his Masters in Physics. When he's done skateboarding he's gonna be a professor at NYT. He can even do that now – he's got so much fucking money its ridiculous... Well, after that, I met up with him [*points to her hubbie*] and some other kids and we went to El Paso. Stayed there for a month, got rid of our scabies, then we headed to Austin. We kept running out of gas. We met the guy from *Devils Rejects* at South By Southwest, Brian Pesain – the guy who gets his head blown off."

"Damn... I'm quite tipsy. I brought some 40's as peace offerings, now look at me. Livin' in the fucking dumpster man... (They show me pictures from their endless trip. In one they sleep in a dumpster, random absurd images of total destruction). Who's this guy? That's the most caveman looking motherfucker I've seen..."

Brandon: "(Laughs) Yeah, he'll be here later. I traveled with him over a year. He's like my best friend. He squatted in Israel for 5 years but got deported."

"Where else did you go?"

"We went to El Paso and then met up with him. We went for South By Southwest but didn't see and bands 'cause we were drunk the whole time. We couldn't make any money 'cause there were 40 other kids in town, and we didn't hang out with any of them. Everybody sucked. We went from Austin to Little Rock."

"Tell me random stories..."

"We rolled into Little Rock, five of us and this dog we got in Detroit, a banjo, the washtub bass, and a mandolin. So we try to catch

out of this rut, and this one kid thinks he knows everything. He's getting us lost the whole way. We take this one train into the yard, we get impatient, and we ride these units. It takes us 75 miles to this Coca Cola facility. This kid's belligerent with a bottle of Evan Williams lighting flares and trying to burn us. Dude, get the fuck out of here. Stop trying to touch every butt and calm the fuck down…"

"He's the one that's supposedly been riding for 10 years and he's doing all this dumb shit."

"We wake up in the morning, we get off, we're trying to hitch back to Newport. This cop stops, runs our names, checks our shit, and this kid lies and says we're a traveling folk band. He's like 'yeah, she dances and I sing. And see we got this harmonica here and this Washburn bass and banjo and mandolin'. The cop crammed into his squad car, all of us with all our shit and he drives us back to where we were. He watches us get on a train and waves goodbye. Then new cops come up 'cause we're drinking and this kid's like 'oh it's a hot day, don't make us pour our beer out.' The cops are 'in that case, fair enough, but go around that corner so it's not in plain view. You can just hang out.' We're waiting for a train, and this idiot gets us lost again. We go to Independence, Arkansas and the conductor puts us off right in front of the news station. They're trying to interview us, taking pictures. They gave us some money, a bunch of food. The conductor's like 'I'm going to give you a ride but I got to drop my truck off at home.' He disconnects the unit from the train. We're all sitting there, all five of us, just on the unit. He's blaring his horn, people are looking at us from traffic like 'what the hell?' He dropped us off, they gave us more money."

"We were trying to go to Memphis. He gave us direction on what train to take."

"So this kid had all the money, and he wouldn't let us get food. He kept trying to buy more beer. So fuck this, this trains going by, let's go, let's go. Grab our shit and there was cement and loose rocks, so I slip off and grab the ladder and got dragged. I came within 13 inches of getting my head cut off."

"It scared the shit out of me. We finally get in and the train stops."

"So we got into this open auto train carrier and took that towards St. Louis."

"Is St. Louis a good town for squatting?"

"No, not at all. People hate it. But we had really good luck. People were driving and they'd stop their car and give us a box of pizza and beer."

"We made a $100 bucks not even trying to get money. It took us 20 minutes if that."

"People were like chasing us down the street, 'here's some money, here's some money.' This weird lady took us to her house 'cause we had scabies. She got rid of our bugs. She washed our shit, we took showers, she fed us..."

"Let us smoke all of her weed...

"She made us fuck in her daughters bed..."

"She was like *'I got you guys robes for the showers.'* First she was like *'oh my god, I'm so glad I found you guys.'* She came up out of nowhere and we were like *'who the fuck are you?'* Alright, we're going to her house to clean up, 'cause he was supposed to work in Iowa City doing piercings and shit. She said she was an old Dead-Head. So she goes around the corner, calls her husband. She says *'ok, here's the deal. We went to a bunch of Dead shows back in the day. You're 27 and you're 30.'* I can't even pass for 22."

"You can't even pass for 12."

"I can't even buy cigarettes, and I'm 22. If I don't have my ID I'm fucked. No one will sell booze to me. *'Go back to high school, its past your bed time'...* This lady was fucking weird, like maybe she's in a cult. Stares off, monotone..."

"Worked for Pepsi for 30 years, doesn't really know anything..."

"We get to her house, the husbands like *'you like the Grateful Dead?'* (Acacia dead pans) Yeah. Love 'em.... Listen to 'em... *ALL THE TIME*."

"Oooooh, and PHISH..."

"I can't even name a song 'cause I fucking hate the Grateful Dead. So you're saying I'm a hippie now (slightly angered)? She's like *'my daughter's not home, she's at work. You can use her room.'* She gave us five towels each for the head, the waist, the feet, everything. So we're in the shower, she keeps knocking on the door, handing us weed, handing us robes. They made us food and watched us eat."

"'Oh we're just gonna watch you eat.'"

"'Keep your robes on, I told my husband that you were gonna eat in your robes.' She purposely left all out clothes in the dryer and

made us wear robes so we'd eat naked. They sat on the couch, drinking their Bud Lights, and watched us eat. "

"Then she hands us more weed, and makes us sleep in her daughters bed, and slips her hand in, and says' 'you guys can do whatever you want' and locks the door on us. We're like 'where the fuck are the cameras?'"

"She makes us have sex in her daughter's bed"

"They're like looking under the door and shit."

"Then she gives us money for some old baseball cards we had. We told her just take them, 'cause her generosity is creeping us out. And she demands five dollars for one baseball card. Then her daughter comes home. The daughter's like '*do you guys want some money? Take my ten dollars, take it.*' Then we're leaving and she's like '*hugs for everyone.*' Alright, thanks for the ten dollars and letting us fuck on your bed."

"Then she goes to her daughter like 'oh you just moved home.' She tells us' yeah, I was staying with my mom's friend, sometimes my parents try to get me involved in things…' Then she looks out the window and starts crying and shit."

"I was like '*oh, you know it happens sometimes.*' She's like, '*Yeah… It does…*' She looks down, then looks out the window, and I could see her eyes well up. I'm just like '*what the fuck is wrong with this family?*'"

"That's St. Louis. So she's like 'I'm gonna walk with you and pick up trash.' She follows us at least ten blocks."

"She didn't say anything, just behind us going '*don't worry about me, just picking up trash.*' Picking up litter on the ground…"

"Then we met some kid that tells us we can crash at his friend's house and they were really cool ex-traveling kids. We're just really glad to be away from the weirdo's. The next day this guy we met prior picks us up and gives us a ride all the way into Iowa and drops us off 80 miles from Iowa City. Stayed at the truck stop overnight, they bought us breakfast in the morning, then a trucker saw her and gave us a ride… Iowa City is the only thing worth going out there for. It's pretty cool, it's a nice little college town. I tried to work at Nemesis Tattoo, but it's all APP shop standard."

"How long have you been on the road for?"

"On and off, 5 years. When I was a little kid, like 8 years old, I rode a bike without a tire for miles away from my grandma's house. And I just slept in an alley. I felt like I was an old person. That's kind of

what started it. I was 15 and panhandling, and this guy walked up to the same spot. Great, another homebum. And I looked real close, and wait, homebums don't wear Crass shirts. So we're talking, the train goes by. He's like 'yeah, I get on those.' I'm a little kid, so I got on, took a short ride with him. Eventually it just clicked. This isn't something I chose, it just chose me. For a lot of kids that's what fucks them up, 'cause they hear or see it and they think it's something cool to do. I did a lot of squatting since I was 14-15. I'm 20. When I was 15 I bounced back and forth from Miami to West Palm. Then I took a couple trips upstate and came back 'cause I was on probation. Then I violated when I was running two tattoo shops at the same time. After that I got a warrant for violating and I split cause I was going to go to prison for a year. I haven't been back in three years. I went out to Colorado for a couple months. Then I went out West, went East, than West, then South, then East. Back and forth – just a constant, solid 2 years man…"

"Here's the main question – I'm pretty street wise cause I had a rough, weird upbringing, but this is the first time I've really traveled living on the streets. You guys have been doing it way longer. I come to certain conclusions, but what are the main rules of the road, and the rules to get around? What are the most important tips for anyone that would run away and go do this sort of thing?"

"I could tell you but you'd have to turn that tape off. It's not one of those things. It's not allowed. You just gotta learn, you gotta meet the right people that know what they're doing. You just gotta go."

"Because everyone has to learn on their own…"

"No, they have to be taught, but they need to learn it on their own while they're being taught. You need to experience it. I can't just blurt out a bunch of the shit that I know 'cause that's just gonna fuck it up for everyone else. This is my lifestyle, this is who I am. I can't just say do this or that, because what works for me doesn't work for other people. What does work for other people and works for me, I'm not allowed to say. It just needs to be figured out. Nobody is allowed to say. It's an unspoken agreement."

"What are the 5 best towns in America?"

"I like Pittsburg, I like Seattle. I really don't like California at all. I hate it, it's a wasteland, there's nothing there."

"Isn't it a felony charge to hop on a train now?"

"Since 9-11, technically, you could do up to 5 years. But generally, if someone wants to be a real asshole, you'll go to county jail for a little while. You might not get out for a year. They never really

do the five year thing. I've gotten lucky. I've only had one ticket, and generally what they give you is trespassing on private property. You go to court, it's a $200 fine. Which you just skip out on and get a warrant. Just don't go back and get caught. Or they'll just pull you off and make you hitchhike. I've met workers that have given me water and cigarettes, buy me food, hang out with me."

"Tell me a crazy story…"

"Well here's one about New York. There's this guy named Steve, everybody knows him. He'll pay you $200 dollars if you go to his house. All you got to do is call him and meet him and he'll buy you really good beer and cigarettes, and you have to talk to him. He tells you these stories, and then this story about how a kid shaved his balls. And he like asks you about it and quizzes you on it. And then he puts a blanket on his lap, and you rub his knee while he jerks off. And then he gives you like $200."

"I'd rub his knee for $200."

"Yeah, everybody has. I need to see him next week (laughs). He does it five or six times a week. Apparently he's got money."

"Any other stories?"

"We rolled with Barnum & Bailey Circus. We're sitting in Cleveland after getting sand-blasted trying to hitchhike there for 8 hours to Toledo. This train goes for a half mile, like Amtrak style cars. 'The Greatest Show On Earth' is painted on the side. There's clowns on this porch smoking cigarettes and I'm like 'you guys ever see a real train rider before?' We find this flat car with lion cages all strapped down. There's a Ford Taurus. We just click the door and it opens. We get in the car, put our gear in the trunk. The keys were in there and everything. We get drunk, eat some chips, wake up in the morning and the windows are all fogged. We were all sloppy."

"Have you been to C-Squat yet? The NYC squat?"

"Yeah, but it's a co-op, and most of those people are assholes."

"If you want to stay there you got to be cool enough apparently and up to their status and fucking pay them rent."

"We used to have a squat here called The Batcave. It was an old abandoned Jewish press. It was built on toxic waste. That's in Brooklyn. My friend lived there the whole year. The big one is Paradise City in Philly. Last year I was involved in the Philly riots. It was nuts. Cops on horse, cops on bike, in helicopters, paddy wagons, cars, on the beat. Just grabbing kids by their packs and throwing them down, mocking them, beating them. I guess Philly PD shut down that squat.

They felt they owed it to us 'cause they're not in control. They beat up some pregnant girl, the front page picture was bike cops with guns pointed at kids. They cracked a girl's face from above her eye all the way down her nose. They pulled this one girl's shirt up and anyone that tried to pull it down they beat with clubs or maced. All I could do was run around and try to get people and get maced. Direct people which way to go down alleys. Philly's fucking..."

"Are we going back there after this?"

"We can if you want..."

"Are you hitchhiking out?"

"No. We have to put the dog in a box, like a TV box or something. Put her on a dolly and carry her on the subway and take the commuter train to Jersey. We don't like it out here. There's too many cops. Hitchhiking is illegal as fuck out here. You get pulled off like that (snaps fingers). There's no need to anyway."

"What's the longest you've ever been stuck trying to hitch?"

"Eight days in Nebraska. I don't think anyone from Nebraska gave us a ride either. We got saved by some punk rock trucker. He drove us to Denver. Then we went to Cheyenne and ended up in Idaho. Hitchhiking sucks, I hate it."

"What do you think of Hollywood?"

"We were just in Hollywood. There was a squat where they actually had some electricity and water. But they just got raided. You can't get away with shit in Hollywood. They got a camera in every corner. You have a fight in Hollywood then cops are going to find you and you're going to jail. It's dirty. LA is fucking nasty."

"You a big Charles Bronson fan?"

"The actor or the band?"

"Brian says he could kick Chuck Norris' ass."

"Brian's an asshole."

"Bronson could kick Norris' ass. I actually met Chuck Norris while I was on the road..."

"No way! Holy shit!"

"Yeah so I got stuck in the middle of Texas on a Greyhound, and across the stop there was a field, and they were shooting 'Walker Texas Ranger.' So there's the film crew all set up, all these people watching, and across the fence there's this cow giving birth to a calf. The calf is dying, it's all weak and sickly. So the TV crew are all sad, and Chuck sees this, and leaps over the fence real quick like lightning. He cuddles with the calf and rubs his beard on it, which

makes it come back to life. So we're all sitting there, and we're all cheering. Chuck stands back up, looks over and waves at us. His face turns to a scowl, and he spin-kicks the calf and breaks its fucking neck. He turns back to us, all shell-shocked, and says 'Chuck giveth, and Chuck taketh away...'"

OTESANEK

It is at that very moment, bombing with a lame Chuck Norris joke, when someone hollers *"Fuck yeah, Bethlehem!"* from beyond the park fence. Another odd fish is gleefully smiling at my back-patch, and he's a creepy looking dude too. I walk over to shake his hand, and he immediately starts talking about black metal, ignoring his girlfriend & baby stroller.

"I like Mayhem, as you can see.' Rudy flashes his knuckles which are pure scar tissue, and lifts his black silk dress shirt to reveal a forearm covered in fresh razor gashes and scarred lines deep in the skin. His eyes are cold and icy blue, his hair jet black and shoulder length.

Rudy looks like a skinny Anton Chigur and is either smacked on heroin or morphine, because he has that floaty, not-far-from-nodding-out swagger. He talks in short little bursts, thinking hard before the next line, hitting a rolled cigarette like a captured spy being questioned by Interpol: *"The new Mayhem is real awkward, but Bethlehem's more suicidal... I put that Bethlehem record on when people come over and I don't even think about it. I just think its something good to listen to. I put it on man, people that don't even listen to metal, and it never crossed my mind that people would get so uncomfortable by it."*

"Yeah, it hurts their brains."

Rudy: "It makes them feel horrible inside... And when they leave the room they leave it changed... Most of them don't even know that music like that exists. It's fucking petrifying."

"After I'm done listening to SUIZID I feel like I watched Blue Velvet 50 times in a row."

"That's proper, that's perfect... Then it's like when they left they got locked in a room with Cannibal Holocaust, and all the in-between scenes got cut out, so you're watching people get raped and cut the fuck up. The whole time you're afraid of what's next... You're not even afraid of cannibals, you're afraid of yourself..."

"Tell me about your band from Philly."

"OTESANEK, I played drums. It was together 6 years. The demo came out February 2001. We did 6-10 live shows a year."

"You have a following at all?"

"Yeah, everywhere... It was mood. Punishing, atmospheric... Like funeral doom, just notes of awkwardness..."

"What was your live show like? You have any visuals?"

"No, fuck that man... No need for it... We made it to be what it is... It evolved into something that I don't think sounds like anything else. It really fucked with people... It created a mood, whether you hate it, love it, or just fuck man, I'm uncomfortable... I don't want to be in the room... I think when we got most reflective we broke up..."

"Got any new projects?"

"I hope. I'm going to kill myself if I don't, haha.

"You live in New York?"

"Yeah, I'm with my girlfriend as you see here. I'm just glad I'm not in Philly. I've moved back and forth about 5 years... If I don't play music I'm going to die. Anything as long as it's honest. Fuck doing songs like White Stripes... All these fucking douche-bags... I don't want to sound like Cannibal Corpse. I don't care if it sounds like Britney Spears man, as long as it's fucking true -- which I would never let happen by the way... I want some noise kid to play some verse, and I'll lap drums over it. Not sound like Eye Hate God, no blues... Awkwardness is devastating..."

BREAKING OUT IS IMPOSSIBLE. BREAKING IN IS INSANE.
1pm now, and Acacia and her hubby jolted for more booze, leaving me with a mob of hardboiled land pyrates. One gets into a fist-fight and is hauled off the police. No one seems to care, save for some everyone-be-devoured dark chuckles.

Drinking this much this early this tired was not a bright idea. I still have another 30 hours to go, and I'm a notoriously sleepy drunk. I've really surprised myself in the past week, but standard nature claims its routine. I'm focusing ever-more-intently on napping, but I botch this plan when I kick up a conversation with a crust named Skum.

Skum says this is *"his park,"* he grew up here, knows everyone, and can relate the greatest interview of this book... but it'll cost me a 40oz. So I split a Mickey's with him but all he does is talk in circles. He's already slurring drunk and obviously lying about being an ex-Marine who fought in Kosovo. He's too young, twig-skinny, half-blind, and his broken glasses are glued together like piecemeal mosaic.

We start getting into a drunken *"no I'm more hardcore"* babble match. It keeps accelerating until I bring up the snorting cremated ashes thing, which is like the ultimate ultra-triple-dog-dare. He starts accusing me of being an undercover cop. I'm laughing as he pats me down seeking a wire, figuring he'll just cool off. But it gets worse.

He jacks my tape player insinuating I'm collecting evidence on him, then he starts galloping through my bag looking for NARC evidence. When he finally settles down I try to brush it off as hammered stupidity, but then he tries to steal the pack of Bugler I lent him to slip a rolly. He says it's his now, claiming *"ground rules."*

I'm ready to jack this guy in the face. He glances over and nods at 4 burly street punks who slowly start closing in on me – even the old shirtless guy that looks like Dee Dee Ramone is ready to rumble. *Fuck you shithead, I'm not gonna scrap over a fucking pack of rollies!"* I snatch them from his hand, snag my backpack and walk. It was bad enough getting harassed by gang-bangers. Now my own people want to jump me. Well, it just goes to show – for every golden-hearted pyrate, there's some fake-ass chump playing East Coast tough-guy...

Back in Manhattan world the street is boiling hot, because the jet-black pavement only incubates more scalding heat which comes at you from above and below. The sky is clear and the sun is blazing, the humidity is death and there are so many people... *no, god no...* a roving pack of Juggalo squatters, 10 of them with faces painted like clowns...

Fuck it, unload the whopping $50 night. Food kills time & Gatorade is entertaining... Devastated, sweltering, stopping every few blocks for kabobs or roasted peanuts... This is so bad. All I can think of is Eddie on a bean bag watching *Gremlins...* It's in the aisles on an air-conditioned porno store that Dave Brenner calls and invites me to Brooklyn for super-hot Chili...

Back through the streets of fire to the subway which is even more molten then the open air. The zag shoots me out and I have to stumble another six blocks to Brenner's pad. The houses are one long grid of old school European housing, buildings short and connected with the same roof height. All those immigrants mushed together. Dave's on the front steps tossing a trash bag as I waddle up, head-spinning with no motor function left. I tell him: *"You know man, try as I might, I can't figure out if I love New York or hate it with a passion."* Dave just chuckles: *"Well, that's how it always is."* I ask: *"How do you do it?"* Says: *"Fuck man, I wanna move to Pennsylvania."*

MAKERS OF THE MUSIC AND DREAMERS OF THE DREAMS

The only real moral of the story is that New York is anything you want it to be. There is so much occurring at every given second with supreme homogenization you can live a thousand different lives while reprimanded in one body. It is the ultimate playground of the human chameleon. Dave said that if you're unsure whether you love or hate NYC that only indicates you're head over heels for The Big Rotten Apple. I'd fancy to court this princess one day, but for the time being, I think I'll root my pastures somewhere less hectic...

As for Jeff and Eddie, there was no grand finale, no monolithic interview, no big-bang. I fell asleep at 7pm and when I woke up everyone was gone. Eddie was packing his bags about to catch a taxi to the airport. He left me with one brilliant story though, something that totally changed my perspective on a fellow Detroiter.

"*You remember that lame Von Bondies band that got signed to a major and then bombed hard? Well that singer, that tight-pants fuck with the emo hair, you know Jack White punched him in the face, right? He gave that fucker a black eye, and the sissy sued him for like a hundred grand... Well, here's why – they were backstage at Magic Stick, and Jack was avoiding him 'cause he could never stand the guy. They had that rivalry forever, you know? Anyway, the Von Bondies guy was in the backroom where everyone parties, and Jack overheard him talking shit on Judas Priest. Everyone thinks it was about money, or about jealousy, or some scenester rock star bullshit. It was about Rob Halford dude -- he socked him for K.K. Downing...*"

PART IX: PURGATORY
(CRUSH & BURN & RISE AGAIN)
JUNE 9TH-AUGUST 8TH 2007

THE NEW PETER VENCMAN

The absolute worst feeling in my life is when I wake at night in a sharp surge of displacement – when I am a stranger to everything and to myself, lost and fragmented, devoid of time and the physical awareness of my own body – and all that is the absurd life that I have created and that has forged me, with all its passions and deficiencies, remains wholly asleep...

For 2 minutes I am someone else, something else, like a soul hinging partially from the body & observing its surroundings in mute panic that isn't panic but a characteristic unexplained. All the circuits flare, and all that was and is floods back in sub-atomic reaction. The memories, humiliating and mad, return like demons with razor sharp talons. I am then a lost child, searching for parents who've long abandoned me if they ever did indeed exist, and a cold wave of terror eclipses like a black nova of ice. *And all I feel is fear...*

This is what stirred me to this pen, to this paper, to this cold bottle of Brand X tropical punch. 6:30am at the Villa Winona, everything as it never was, a new beginning which has eluded me, alone in these thoughts which bind and cripple...

So I purge. Let this ink be my release. Far better than the electric typewriter 'cause its vibrations send every cockroach running towards the shifting ribbon. They are everywhere, as is the curse with San Diego, and no one has money to fumigate. The Wendy's dollar menu is far more important then household hygiene, because everyone is starving. The homegrown remedy is to leave five cups half-filled with Kool-Aid on the kitchen floor. Usually obliterates a dozen roaches overnight. Expect nothing else when you live in a quasi-squat with a bunch of street people.

It's the strangest thing. When the authorities aren't at the helm, the crazies corral themselves together. No one has jobs, all but Brandon are on social security because they are criminally insane. Together we form the nucleus of a commune in which all give their personal share to the collective. Don't think I'm poking fun. I am, of course, one of them, and a vital component of the operation...

One neglected subject thus far is "Ryan The Ghostbuster." This guy was discovered by Mr. Skinner laying face down in a field with purple hair and a black trench-coat that read "EXORCIST" in white painted letters. Ryan is a 59 year old man that never halts perpetual motion. We are unsure if he even sleeps or if it's an otherworldly form of meditation. He might be a closet tweaker, but we've never caught him in the act. Onyx has a theory that the ghosts Ryan sees are actually demons of his past constituted as his fears. He registers his thoughts as evil electrical impulses and tries to contain them.

Before losing his mind Ryan was a master electrician. Years ago he was contracted by the government to complete work on a nearby military instillation. His psychosis bridged over that very day and he started rewiring everything in the base so it would electrically re-route and destroy all its ghosts in his sclf-styled processing grid. For this deemed act of Cold War espionage Ryan was facing life in prison, but was instead deemed criminally insane and institutionalized for a long stretch.

Thereafter he lived on the streets of San Diego for 15 years, becoming strong as an ox by dragging around a cart with a full entertainment center (*TV, Panoramic Stereo & DVD*). He'd power it by rewiring the sides of buildings and have outdoor bashes with all the bums in the neighborhood. He was also arrested and institutionalized for rewiring the electrical grid to 6 city blocks. He is like MacGyver with that little toolbox.

Ryan's birth-date is sometime in December 1947. He is 5 foot 7, the caricature of a worked-to-the-bone Yugoslavian mine worker from a National Geographic photo session following the post-Tito crash. He moved into The Villa Winona shortly after my first visit in 2006. Since then, Ryan has rewired our flophouse.

Everywhere there are chicken wire mesh grades, broken glass, sheets of metal, fans and mirrors strategically placed to deflect and trap ghosts – all of which runs through an opening in the electrical current that reroutes demons into a loop. This loop filters all currents together into the slice-and-dice blade of a master fan which is electrical taped together. It looks like a cross between Egon Spengler's backpack and a stage prop from *Pee Wee's Playhouse*.

Ryan sits in front of it as the air blows the shredded up ghosts inside of him, and his exorcist powers grind up the ghouls and send them right back to hell. Technically he is an "*in- house Exorcist*," and claims he had to become one because he was sick of *"shiesty priests hogging all their abilities for themselves."*

He also waters the house, sprays disinfectant over the walls and couch, leaving a thick, lingering Pine Sol smell which makes us hallucination dizzy. It's so strong it drifts into the alleyway and has made cops show up thinking we were running a meth lab. Ryan's room glows from yellow construction lights and its walls are covered in aluminum foil. He sleeps on the grass outside face down or stretched out in an enclosed cot that's covered in chicken wire and electrified by a car battery.

He spends nearly all his monthly Social Security check on horror and sci-fi DVD's, and our days are spent in film marathons. He buys brand new TV's and Playstations and immediately drills holes in them, gladly installing ghost grids. He also lived in the attic for a week last scorching summer, combating the Aztec demigods and mummies he knows are hiding up there, and we are all terrified to actually pop our heads in the crawlspace to view his grand design.

Whenever Ryan gets too out of hand, Onyx just chases him around with a spray bottle, squirting blasts of water. Other then that he's gentle as a lamb, 'though poised for atonement...

So just imagine going on the road for 6 months, showing back up phenomenally primed for a non-stop blur of manic writing, but not only does your computer keep dying every 20 minutes because of some flawed Windows a methed-out hacker created & can't fix for 3 weeks, you have to deal with this guy in a bike helmet covered in aluminum foil walking around spraying chemicals & babbling: '*What are we sharks? We don't fuck with two dicks.*' Kerouac never dealt with this shit. He just took speed & pissed in mason jars at his aunt's house...

THE GOLDEN SPOTLIGHT SHINES ON ONYX
"Tell me about your bondage theory."

ONYX: "Well I just have this theory when women are brought up by controlling mothers they have a hard time having sex without feeling '*I'm a dirty little girl, mother wouldn't approve.*' So they search for somebody to take the choice away from them. They have to have it where they get hurt otherwise they're unable to come to grips with the fact that '*I have no control over this.*' They have to reach that point where '*this isn't me anymore, this man has control over me. This wonderful orgasm is being pushed upon me. I have no guilt here.*'"

"What's your favorite psychological game as a power master? Or are you like an artist with a palate of colors and you can't choose which shade is the best?"

"That question is hard to answer because I have my favorite positions and my favorite torture devices. My favorite looks, like the look of complete helplessness. Everyone looks down on that, but I have a feeling my grandmother put that there in a kind of off-handed way cause she always used to watch the news and you'd see this pretty woman who got slain, being tortured or whatever. She'd be like *"ah, that poor girl."*"

"Do you feel dirty about that or do you revel in it?"

"I'd say more dirty. It's been a real conflict for me because it's something I truthfully love, I mean LOVE. I had a real hard time with girlfriends doing it. I could tie 'em down, play with them but there was always that after we're done load on my head. Am I doing the wrong thing? But when I charged for it… Well, they really want this. Just flip through the money, its all there."

"What's the most you made in one session?"

"I made $7,000 once. She was whack… I justify it to myself like, '*Well, god would want you to make this person happy. This person is very depressed. This person's begging you to do this.*'"

"So you're a pervert shepherd of your flock?"

"It's been something I've spent a lifetime trying to figure out myself. When I see a woman getting smacked, that's not attractive. When I see a woman crying, that's not attractive. It's when I know that I'm in complete control that they won't get hurt, yet in their mind that fact is gone. That mind is empty of what's going to happen next. I can just… *those eyes…*"

"When did you start doing this, 'cause I know you were a virgin until your early 20's."

"I was 5 or 6 years old. I saw *Return Of Benji*, they had a scene where the kids were caught and tied to a chair. Because it was a children's movie, the kidnapper was nice to them. But the girl, her eyes, the way she couldn't move… The niceness of the kidnapper was all she had. It did something to me. After that I started playing a game with people – 'kidnappers.' We'd tie up somebody, a different person every day. I was like the GM [game master] of it though. It always had to go my way."

"So you were the master of your own torture?"

"Yeah (weird goat laugh). It just kinda followed me."

"When did it really start for you?"

"I went to meet someone at a gay bar and this guy was like '*I got 75 bucks for ya.*' The guy was in a wheelchair. Sounds strange to me now, but I felt like I had to do something. He had this big fucking bag of toys. That thing was loaded with vibrators, dildos, whips. He had some cuffs in there. Some of the things in there I remember saying no to. And he listened like I was important... Now the girls didn't start to happen for a long time, and they started off as girlfriends. Tell the truth I've only had about 3 or 4 actual clients that were not attached by a girlfriend. One was an attorney. She told me every night she went home to get fucked – but in order for that to happen she needed to have the shit whipped out of her for the sins she was about to commit. I had no sex with her whatsoever. She'd come over, strip naked, I'd smack her thighs with a paddle. Pretty much the corporal shit – spankings, slaps. When we met I was scared. '*Well how much do you charge for something like that?*' Well, I don't know. Uh, $500 for a half hour? '*Ok.*' What??? I wasn't expecting anyone to go for that. That was kind of my '*I'm scared but I have to say something*' response."

"What about the midget?"

"The midget was fun. She was more into the sensory depravation and hard bondage. One time I hog tied her and I tossed her in my dresser drawer and locked it. Then I watched *Pinky And The Brain* for half an hour. I grabbed her by the neck and put her on the bed, still hogtied. Started fingering her... I got $750 that time."

"When is going too far going too far?"

"There's some things I can't do. I can't slice somebody. There was one who wanted me to slice her breasts every quarter inch with a razor blade. Just do it all over the place until she passed out... Bleeding, I don't like bleeding. Raping and bleeding – those are my cutoffs. Suffocation, I find it sort of erotic, but I don't want to be the one who does it. I think I'd be carried away. That look just gets better and better..."

"You told me a story about the cops..."

"I was going to meet a client at the park, and the cops stopped me there. Someone called and said I was hitting on kids. You know, I say '*hi*' and stuff. They open my briefcase full of bondage equipment. Figured there'd be no problem 'cause I cater to overweight people. In this case, she was 300 pounds. So there like "*oh you gonna use these on little kids.*' I'm like '*Dude, with the lowest buckle on these things I have to use the ankle restraints for wrist restraints.*" So they take my briefcase, it's gone for 6 months. I got it back and the dildo has been used. The condoms are missing... Two months after that, I'd gotten arrested 'cause a friend of mine – we were drunk and fighting over the bottle and I pushed him into the hedge. When I went in and the female cop that used my dildos comes into the room and freaks me out. She's like *'I hear you like spanking women.'* And that's as far as I can go, 'cause I'll get in trouble..."

CLASH OF THE TITANS

Quite the explosion this morning – Onyx was filling a cup of iced tea when The Ghostbuster strolled by talking to himself. Ryan muttered *'yeah, I know what you're thinking,'* to whatever apparition was trailing him. Onyx flew off the handle into a phenomenal rage. He leapt on the old man's back and put him in a vicious headlock: *'DON'T YOU EVER TELL ME WHAT I'M THINKING!! I'LL FUCKING KILL YOU!! DON'T YOU EVER FUCKING TELL ME WHAT MY THOUGHTS ARE!!!'*

Onyx trembled in a violent, psychotic cold-sweat and wouldn't let go. It took Brandon and I talked him down for 5 minutes, because if we broke them up forcefully, he'd snap Ryan's neck. The look on the exorcists face... those zombified, blue eyes within a minuet hair to reality; *the terror...*

Later that day, walking home from pizza world, I spot a public bus on the side of El Cajon Blvd, freaked pedestrians gasping in horror at the crushed man beneath the wheels. For some reason I keep thinking its Onyx... Funny enough, when I walk through the Winona door, Onyx is standing in the middle of the living room with his arm in a sling and a circular morphine patch on his forehead. He'd been run over by a bus. Just a different one, further down the road...

ALASKAN THUNDERFUCK

$10, no paycheck for 2 weeks, no food but Little Caesars, my kingdom for a beer... $150 journalism check is stolen from the mailbox and cashed at a gas station in Michigan.... *Pork Chop runs off to Portland to crust the streets...* Downtown Brown secures The Van's Warped Tour... *Mr. Skinner knocks up his girlfriend...*

Lennon robbed at gunpoint by crack heads for $5,000 laptop and $1,000 hard cash. The next day he gets attacked by Jo-Jo's father with a baseball bat, is kicked out of that house, and crashes into a parked *car, spending 5 days in lockup... A crippled, schizophrenic, illiterate Jesus freak from Alabama rents the couch. Two days later he has a paranoiac breakdown and calls the police because we're reading his thoughts. The ambulance takes him to the rubber room...* The Angelic Process had to cancel Euro tour because K Wood broke his hand. He doesn't know if he'll be able to play guitar again...

"MR. BARTEK, CAN YOU FORWARD THIS MESSAGE TO ALL :STALAGGH: FANATICS YOU KNOW? LAST WEEKEND ONE OF OUR VOCALISTS (THE ONE WHO KILLED HIS MOTHER AT THE AGE OF 16) WAS KILLED IN A CAR ACCIDENT AT THE AGE OF 29. HE PERFORMED ON SEVERAL OF OUR PROJEKTS. NOW THAT HE IS DEAD, WE CAN FINALLY TELL WHY HE KILLED HIS MOTHER AT SUCH A YOUNG AGE. WHEN HE WAS BETWEEN 6 AND 11 YEARS OLD HE WAS SEXUALLY ABUSED BY HIS UNCLE. HIS MOTHER KNEW ABOUT THIS AND LET IT HAPPEN. BECAUSE OF THIS SUCH A MURDEROUS HATRED TOWARDS HIS MOTHER GREW IN HIS MIND THAT AT THE AGE OF 16 HE KILLED HER WITH OVER 30 KNIFE STAB WOUNDS."

THE HORROR OF MONTEZUMA

Across from the SDSU campus, standing idle for years and randomly discovered by a wandering punk on acid, stood "The Montezuma Squat." Torn down last month, it housed 10 street crusts affiliated with The Villa Winona. It was a dead frat house, a labyrinth of spray-painted corridors only reached by slipping under a barb-wire fence and rolling through an overgrown swathe of weeds and grass, stealthily risking a felony trespassing charge with a max sentence of one year.

We'd only arrive in the dead of night, this pitch black and nightmarish maze traveled by cell phone luminescence. Holes punched in the walls, graffiti caked over everything, abandoned Pabst aluminum crushing beneath our feet. Every room of the 15 lodges a blank abyss, shattered glass spread everywhere. The central squat was deep in the back quadrant, boards over the windows. Only one designated restroom – just another open floor of broken glass that everyone pissed and shat on. It had been festering for months.

My first visit was a candlelit affair, street kids heating ramen over the burning wax. They were planning a riot for Downtown San Diego, an anarchist holiday called "Reclaim The Streets." We were having a merry old time, swapping scumbag stories galore, until we were accidentally maced by an exploding pepper spray bottle that someone had been fidgeting with. A giant cloud of burning death fogged a room the size of a closet...

That was ages ago, the night of the Jakked Rabbits gig. Now The Montezuma is but a sad pile of ruins. The squat was promptly demolished because a random kid was spotted by cops. He wasn't even one of them, and when the police asked what he was doing there, he replied *'just waitin' for weed.'*

One of the strangest stories of this campaign occurred at The Montezuma in my absence. One of the squatter girls was wandering the complex at 2am and began hearing strange noises in the festering shit room. Stoned and confused, she flung open the door and shined a flashlight in the corner – revealing a butt naked 70 year old man crouched in broken glass. He was gimped out with a dog collar & chain muttering to himself masturbating, waiting for his power master to arrive and engage in feces ecstasy rituals...

The girl screamed bloody murder, as did the elderly gimp, and the squatter mob – fearing she was in life threatening danger – boldly ran to the scene. They barged in fearlessly, stomping through landmines of encrusted bowel movements, and lunged at him savagely. The gimp kept apologizing, and they kept kicking and pelting him with beer cans. All of them ripped, some on acid, this Mohawk-laden lynch mob chasing the sobbing, geriatric nude into the blackness of night...

MURDER IN CRUSTLAND

When Acacia and Brandon left Tompkins Square they headed directly to Philadelphia. A few days later, while drinking 40's with a crust mob, a savage fight broke out. One unloaded on another, kicking in his skull into the rooftop until his brain literally bashed out. Everyone fled and his corpse was discovered the next day. In result, Acacia and Brandon were arrested as murder suspects. No charges were filed, and both ran to the anonymous Southwest where Acacia transmitted this message.

It is but another blow of the propagandic damage that has been growing exponentially. The traveling, train-hopping, street punk subculture is gaining inertia to the point where it is inspiring massive crops of newbies who've been pouring onto the road at a larger scale then ever before. Another demonizing witch-hunt appears to be materializing on par with the 'Trenchcoat Mafia' fall-out of the post-

Columbine era, or that of the attack on the rave culture boom circa 2000...

"WEST PHILADELPHIA - June 18, 2007 - Philadelphia Police arrested three people late Monday in the wake of a rooftop murder in West Philadelphia. However, after questioning they were released. Now police are looking for another pair."

"Police apprehended the men at 70th and Cobbs Creek Parkway. They were brought in for questioning in connection with the beating death of a 28-year-old man on the roof of a building near 49th and Locust Streets. The three are described as modern day hobos. Anarchistic vagabonds who travel by train, jumping boxcars when it's time to go. But today the three of them apparently tried to make a getaway by train - but they didn't get very far. The men jumped the train at 70th and Cobbs Creek, but the cops caught up with them and hauled them off in handcuffs. After questioning the men were released, and now police are looking for a man and a woman, possibly with a dog."

"The victim's body was found on the rooftop of an abandoned apartment building in West Philadelphia. Police sources say a group of squatters were drinking on the rooftop last night when a fight broke out. The victim was stomped to death. Police say the squatters are a part of an underground network of young people who reject the norms of society. They travel by train, from town to town, taking over vacant buildings. Neighbors say the group's been in the neighborhood for about three years."

"??? tells [random unnamed media propaganda tyrant], "No sanitation, no running water. There's nowhere to take a bath. They've been here. The tenants and us have been complaining about them. They'll come once a year, they'll clean out the building and then (the squatters will) come right back and move in numbers. Each year the numbers are growing." Police say there are pockets of them throughout West Philadelphia. They raided one house of 48th Street and took seven squatters in for questioning. Police say the squatters are mostly well educated from upper-middle class families, who choose to reject society's values and live on the fringe."

THE CARNAGE OF CARNAGE

Since I'd run around in circles attempting to accomplish the following interview in Denver, I decided if any band deserved an email break (*and to justify my endured migraine*) it would have to be Cephalic Carnage. Among the finest forward-thinking extreme metal acts in the USA, Cephalic Carnage formed in Denver in 1997. Four albums later, they've become a staple of Relapse Records.

Having toured with Dillinger Escape Plan, Mastodon, Shadow's Fall, High On Fire, Origin, Unearth, Strapping Young Lad, and Macabre – along with plenty of activity in the DIY crust/grind world – Cephalic Carnage have rightfully earned their dues. The following text is a whacky hack-n-slash from CC vocalist and former Latvian pit-fighter/death match/ping-pong tournament champion Lenzig Van Strokingoff…

[I begin by relating the tale of the Spongebob Squarepants worshipper from McDonalds, and without even mentioning coordinates, Lenzig Van Strokingoff knows the pinpoint location].

Lenzig Van Strokingoff: "I've been on that same #15 bus you are talking about, eating at the same McDonalds on 16th Street Mall and seen freaky things. What are you to say? Freaks come from everywhere. Like the incident on the bus, it happens all the time. I've seen it in Hollywood, New York, Chicago, etc and a lot crazier as well. I was born here and love it."

"Street crazies aside, I'm sure you've met all sorts of freaks and legends."

"Meeting this one-legged soccer star in Mexico City, whom I told "*break a leg*." He hobbled into the game and scored 6 goals… The singer of ACCEPT was kind of a chode. Saxon were the coolest ever… I met Larry the Cable Guys' uncle. That gets me some weird looks."

"My buddy from Quinta Essentia said you have some sort of underground squat venue in Denver you're doing shows out of. You ever made it to The PWN House in Norman, Oklahoma?"

"Monkey Mania has closed down, but there is The Junkyard and a few other places that Catheter and Clinging To The Trees Of A Forest Fire run here. Always got to stay one step ahead of the law to keep the scene alive… Only been to Oklahoma City and Tulsa, never Norman, but have heard about it though the Exitium cats. I really like the Oklahoma City scene the best. There is a network of bands that exchange shows from OK and CO, so I get to see both sides of the scene. It is weird when you're with bands on Victory or Ferret, but with crusties some have been into us since the beginning, which is cool and weird. It's not as segregated as the hardcore scene, where the band before us could play the exact same music but a lot cheesier and have the place going insane. Then we come on and do a better musical job, and these folks hate it and us. So I love the crust scene, at least the folks that are appreciative and responsive."

"You've done a ton of these D.I.Y. shows out in the middle of nowhere. What are the few overlooked cities you are amazed by that no ones even heard of, where there are the same 50 die-hards will drive a 100 miles just to support?"

"Omaha, Lawrence (Kansas), Des Moines, Iowa City, Des Plaines Illinois – not all are squats or crusties or DIY, but they have amazing scenes… Albuquerque is sort of a second home to us – killer metal like Noiseseer, Manias, Abbaddon, Echoes of the Fallen, Victamas, Word Salad, Logical Nonsense, Veil Of Miscreation…"

"When I was in Denver in February I met one of the Columbine survivors. It was quite intense realizing how there is this aura of people blotting it out. You can't really talk about it on the street. Even asking for a book about it gives librarians a discomforted face. You guys are about the same age as me, I graduated 1999. Did you get police harassment or dirty looks for being weird metal kids? What is your general comment, having grown up in the Denver area?"

"I am a bit older then that, but can relate to what was going on. It depends on what part of town you are asking. In a ghetto they will say that goes on everyday in their neighborhoods. I wrote a song "Driven To Insanity" on *Exploiting Dysfunction* and never had anybody from here ask me about it. The cops really had to make a scapegoat out of somebody. The guy who sold those fools their guns used to go to grind shows and parties, he's probably still a cool guy. I don't think he would have sold those dudes guns had he known they were going to cause mayhem. Since they were dead, and it was in a very prominent part of town, somebody had to pay for their sins. It was him – not their parents – but a metalhead who made a mistake and was fooled by manipulative rich kids."

"Does Chuck Norris' beard cure cancer?"

"Only if it is on thy labia or genetalia. He will rub it with his hockey play-off beard 20 times 'till it bleeds, then kick it repeatedly 'till you are cancer free…"

GIVING THE DEVIL HIS DUE

"So, Mr. Shipley, where do you suggest we begin?"

Lord Mörder: "I was arrested February 6, 2003 in connection with a shooting of a Christian Ministry dormitory that was the home of former comrade and suspected traitor, Berzerk. Initially, my co-defendant Arminius and I faced charges of attempted murder and conspiracy to commit murder, both of which carry life sentences. Eventually we were offered non-life plea-bargains. Due to our overwhelming guilt, we couldn't pass up the 'deal.'"

"Was the action taken more to rattle the nerves as opposed to a true intention to do bodily harm?"

"Basically it was a test to ascertain where our so-called comrade stood in the scheme of things. Unfortunately, our suspicions were all too real because he inevitably set us up. No, doing bodily harm wasn't the goal. Had it resulted, however, I would have taken it as an act of war, rather than a crime."

"Was this action pre-meditated to any great degree, or was it spur of the moment? Were you guys drinking that night?"

"It was absolutely pre-meditated. We considered escape routes, the disposal of evidence, best times to strike, and potential outcomes. Unfortunately, mistakes were made, evidence was left behind, and we underestimated Berzerk's treachery. The alleged drinking was part of our defense, but I didn't drink that particular evening. In fact, I would never take on such an important task while intoxicated. Fighting a charge is like a battle over the truth. In this day and age, while facing multiple life sentences, trying to ask for any type of deal isn't going to happen if they think you shot the place up stone sober. It's indefensible. Unlike the Nazis, who claimed they were '*just following orders,*' we endeavored to come up with a defense someone might believe. That's the dynamic of criminal justice. I always find it funny that people automatically believe what's portrayed in the media. A journalist quoted someone as saying I only made anti-Christian claims to attract fans and to become famous. You wouldn't believe the number of people who accept this as fact, even though my actions say otherwise. If I endeavored to be a rock star, I wouldn't have undertaken the actions of a terrorist."

"What happened to Berzerk and Daishe as a result of this? Are they still active in the California scene or have they pretty much vanished off the face of the earth due to this entire episode?"

"Last I heard, Berzerk had fully embraced his pathetic God, and has more or less gone into hiding. In the 3 years since I've been incarcerated, only once have I heard of an occasion of his appearance anywhere. He quickly left when attitudes turned hostile. As for Daishe, to my knowledge he is still playing the part of the BM warrior. He's tried to deny his cooperation with the cops even though legal documents and recorded testimony of his snitching speak for themselves. It would he in Daishe's best interest to remove himself from the scene and go hang out with his real comrades, the cops."

"Where did this idea of 'The Plague' develop? Was this an invention of the prosecution due to some random statement from a flyer?"

"(Laughs) What's a Plague? I think every scene has a group of like-minded individuals, and sometimes they attach a name to their crew. The prosecution claims The Plague is a Satanic terrorist group, and I'm the alleged leader. Fortunately, they've never been able to substantiate these claims."

"Do you follow the basic tenants constituted by Anton LaVey, or is your philosophy a larger, more complex ideology?"

"Philosophically, I take a lot of cues from LaVey, but my ideology is by no means limited to his published works. I feel LaVey, as well as Crowley, concentrated too much on indulgence when so many other virtues needed equal if not more attention. Indulge all you want, but a weak punk or a dope fiend has no business claiming to be a Satanist. I often hear how it is impossible to attach rules, ethics, or moral guidelines to a belief system based on individuality. But isn't that what LaVey did? He says to indulge, but don't hurt children. Indulge, but don't involve unwilling participants. Treat people well, but if they don't reciprocate then smash them. So, based on some twisted interpretation of LaVey, if an 'individual' is a sick freak who fucks little kids, is that just his way of indulging? Sometimes people don't want to hear the truth – that they overindulge due to a weak character. I advocate strength, honor, and loyalty. Might is right, and a Satanist is a strong person who commands fear and respect. We are wolves among sheep. A Satanist is a soldier."

"Since the death of Anton LaVey, many personalities have come forward in the realm of Satanism, although none have been proclaimed as "the spokesman." You have gained considerable interest in recent history for your fiery rhetoric, especially in the black metal underground due to Sol Evil and your blackly colored

history. Do you see yourself as a spokesman, or more a "drummer boy" for the cause at large?"

"Too often in the past, individuals have come out of the shadows proclaiming their authority over what Satanism is while the examples they set with their lives consist of nothing but weakness, pseudo-intellectualism, and psychodrama. Who are these self-proclaimed experts on Satanism? None of them have possessed the intelligence or charisma of their late leader, nor have they understood the essence of the real experiences, real ordeals, real darkness and real self-effort that is involved in the Satanic way of living. These supposed authority figures have been the 'drummer boys,' banging away on the minuet and unimportant aspects of their tame brand of pseudo-Satanism."

"None of them have truly earned your respect?"

"As spokesmen, as in life, they are all spectacular failures. Satanism is a complete way of living, practical in its application, but difficult and dangerous in such a way as to create a higher being. I have already experienced more in the first quarter century of my life than these poseurs have dared to imagine in their wildest wet dreams. There are many farther along The Way than I, and therefore more 'qualified.' While I am at the beginning of my sojourn, I possess a unique platform from which to propagate the true essence of Satanism. As such my capacity for growth is immeasurable and my capability to act as a spokesperson for Satanism now and in the future is undeniable."

"Are you preparing to put out a book or personal manifesto on the subject?"

"Absolutely. With each new experience and every published essay I am sharpening my abilities to properly articulate my message. There is no telling how long it will take to publish my first lengthy piece of prose, but there is no question that it will be done, and it will merely be the first of many."

"What many don't understand about Satanism is that it is not all-out devil worshipping, sacrificing children and animals – it is the isolation and destruction of a concept by embracing all that concept prevents us from experiencing. In your opinion, how can Satanism revitalize/redefine itself to become more of an all-encompassing counter culture movement, as opposed to a loosely knit fringe organization concentrating exclusively on one symptom of the larger problem, although a rather multi-dimensional concept?"

"Satanists should stand together in defiance of the system as a whole, for it is the system that places on us the manacles of false morality. Satanism is not about just being in opposition to religion. Satanism needs to be redefined as something larger than a mere belief system of hedonism, with no larger goal. Satanism should be based on the code of the warrior. A Satanist is a soldier who embraces strength in a quest to dominate existence. Being both hero and villain, man and beast, he acknowledges his deviance alongside his compassion as all aspects of life are encountered from a position of strength. Not everyone can be a Satanist, as there will always be those who embrace their own imprisonment. Nonetheless, the war must be fought for those who endeavor to transcend the masses."

"Nearly everyone that has come to these views was the product of a strict religious upbringing, or had very bad experiences in relation to it. I am curious about your personal development and especially the cultivation of your radical views. When did your interest in Satanism develop and what was your initial introduction to black metal?"

"My initial interest in Satanism began when I started high school. As a person gets older and begins to develop their views about the world, they either embark on a sojourn of true contemplation or blindly accept the status quo and remain a part of the herd. I chose to shun the herd. I found black metal a short time later when I read an article about Emperor. I found it fascinating that BM was more than just music. The musicians were soldiers as well as Satanists. BM became a way to expand Satanism, and these artists had substance behind their beliefs. I find it lamentable that BM has become so watered down. I laugh at the keyboard commandos who love to hypothecate and analyze what others have done when they are not men of action – and quite frankly, not men at all. In my world, they don't get a vote."

"How does your ideology differ from LaVey?"

"Anton LaVey represents modern Satanism. In theory, his church was the embodiment of sinister Satanic Imperium on earth needed to bring about the new Dark Age. In reality, it was nothing more than a sideshow for occult dabblers, the rebellious, and cowards searching for an excuse to indulge their petty weaknesses without feeling like outcasts. His church presented prime time entertainment for the masses, offering just enough hedonistic atheism and mindless psychodrama to offend the Nazarene majority to remain in the limelight and proclaim themselves the "true authority." LaVey was a showman and a politician: he endeavored to shock audiences sufficiently to keep their attention, but not so much as he wouldn't be acceptable. Peter Gilmore, LaVey's former crony and current know-nothing, is like the inept child who's found his father's gun – too afraid to use it and knowing that if he does he'll probably shoot himself in the foot. Is it any wonder modern Satanism seems to have been laid to rest along with its founder? In contrast to both LaVey and Gilmore, I am a Traditional Satanist. I apply the Septenary Tradition to life and the cosmos in order to bring forth evolutionary change via internal and Aeonic magick. Through my experiences and the seven-fold way, I continue to evolve my own consciousness and that of the cosmos as well as aid the sinister dialectic. Satanism is a practical way of living, and when applied correctly can be a means to self-awareness, evolution, and even immortality. It concerns making conscious our shadow nature through magick and experience. The Satanist believes we are gods already. Satanists are strong, proud, and defiant. They detest all faith-based religions. The Nazarene faith has been the scourge of western civilization for over a thousand years; it has inverted all natural values and set back the course of our conscious evolution. In contrast, Satanism is a natural expression of our 'Promethean' urge to evolve, and Satanic magick and experience are a means to awaken the potential within all humankind."

"Explain the Septenary tradition…"

"In the Septenary tradition there is a belief in magick. Fundamental to this is the belief that all living things possess certain energies. These energies may be said to derive from the 'ACAUSAL,' a parallel universe not limited by our spatial dimensions or linear time. Every living being is a point where these energies manifest, and because of our consciousness, we humans are 'gates' to this realm. We possess the ability to 'open the gate' to the 'acausal' that exists in our psyche. External magick is the use of these energies to bring changes in the causal, while internal magick is the use of 'acausal' energies to bring about psychic, internal change. In ancient Greece Socrates declared the psyche was immortal. Thousands of years later, we still acknowledge it as the source of our humanity. An important part of the psyche is the unconscious, the area which the individual is unaware and where the archetypes may be said to 'reside.' The Septenary teaches the psyche is capable of development. The individual's psyche may be said to be both 'above' and 'below.' There is usually something unconscious as well as the potential for future development toward greater consciousness. The archetypal images, ego, self, and 'immortal' are all part of the psyche. In the past the striving for 'self-hood' was often represented by myth. Another term used is 'individuation' (C. G. Jung). Esoterically, in the Septenary this is Adeptship. However, Adeptship implies a conscious, rational understanding of one's self and others, as well as mastery of certain esoteric arts. It also implies a cosmic or Aeonic perspective to Wyrd and the self. Jung's individuation may be considered a 'natural' stage. In contrast, Adeptship is a goal attained by following a specific esoteric way. Individuation is a stage, not the end of personal development. There is no end to the refinement of the self. The esoteric path followed in the Septenary is the seven-fold way. This is inner-alchemy aimed at creating a higher being capable of immortality. These ideas of alchemy were thought to be developed during the Middle Ages, are actually a continuation of earlier ones, particularly from the mystery schools of ancient Greece. The goal, as always, is both heretic and Satanic: to obtain immortality independent of 'God.' There are no limitations but those that are self-imposed, and even these are meant to be transcended. Physical action, warfare, and the culling of the human herd are all acceptable in disrupting the existing order and aiding evolution. Therefore, although there may be parallels between Traditional and modern Satanism, the differences couldn't be greater."

"Do you dig the Beatles?"

"I'm not much of a Beatles fan, but I dig Frank Zappa – he makes me laugh."

"You are still actively writing music from behind bars. Do they allow musical equipment in the cellblock?"

"Our equipment is shit and the pigs fuck us over every chance they get. Only recently have they begun to allow us to possess guitars in the cells, but the actual music program is a total joke. Sol Evil will go on with me. The music is stronger than any prison impediments."

"What other music do you enjoy outside of BM?"

"I like music that invokes emotion. I'm into death metal, melodic metal, hardcore, punk, electronic, retro, classical, in addition to a myriad of other types of music. I love the Cure, and Billy Corgan is my favorite artist. I also enjoy The Doors, Pink Floyd, Depeche Mode, The Smiths, and Bjork. I enjoy some hardcore/metalcore, particularly bands like Dead to Fall and Heaven Shall Burn."

"Tell me about The Satanic Inquisition."

"The Satanic Inquisition is a publication Eugene Alexander Dey and I created in order to bring forth greater Satanic awareness. The other aspects of the publication (e.g. music, journalism, humor, etc.) are meant to complement the overall message while offering something different. Most publications today concentrate on only a few aspects that concern the Satanist way of life; the *SI* endeavors to encompass the whole through our collective writings. Satanism is a misunderstood belief system. As successful as LaVey was at letting the world know Satanism existed in one form or another, the majority of the population is still ignorant of even the basics. It can't be said enough that Satanism has *nothing* to do with "Devil Worship" and is not based on the inversion of Nazarene beliefs. The concept of Satan as the archetypal accuser or adversary predates Christianity, and in fact the words "Satan" and "Devil" are derived from the ancient Greek *aitia* and *diabole*, that were synonymous in their use of denoting an accusation. Likewise, the Hebrews stole Zoroastrian's concept of an 'evil' deity to oppose the 'good' from the Babylonian gods Ahura Mazda and Ahriman to create an opponent for their YHWH."

"How do you feel about how you've been shown in the press?"

"Originally, the *OC Weekly* ran a series of articles about the crimes and spun them in such a way as to invoke 'sympathy for the devil.' All the 'acceptable' aspects of my life were championed and excuses made for my actions and deeds. Rather than being portrayed as a 'terrorist,' I was depicted as a confused, misguided, even inebriated youth who had done something stupid. On the Internet, among other places, many of the reactions were typical and expected. The average person is dross and easily swayed by popular opinion. Thus, when it was publicized that my actions were 'a stupid thing to do,' and desire for fame was cited as my reasoning, the bandwagon of the mediocre filled rather quickly, and many lined-up to express their condemnation. It's always easy to attack someone in absentia, but the way these character assassinations were executed sounded too much like an internet circle-jerk to be taken seriously. People will believe what they want, but popular opinion doesn't constitute fact. To some I am a 'terrorist,' to others a 'sensitive young man.' Which of these, both or neither are true is subjective."

"Do you have a strong sense of family, or are you a throwaway with a strong sense of street family? I ask this because often when an individual fosters such extreme ideas regarding fringe

movements as concrete reality – and this is not to discredit your views because reality only exists within the minds eye – they are a product of being kicked to the curb by society on a repeated basis. What is your background as an individual? What was your childhood like, your teenage years? Were you a drop out or runaway?? Give us a deeper understanding of who you are as a person."

"Just like anyone, I have disagreements with my family. But they are never irreconcilable. We stick by each other regardless of the circumstances. True, they don't embrace or adopt my Satanic beliefs, but we agree to disagree and acknowledge there are countless other facets of life to consider. I had a relatively normal childhood. As a kid, I got straight A's and had perfect attendance. I played sports and my dad coached my baseball teams. As a teenager things did get wild after a while, but not to the point where I did drugs or got arrested. In high school I joined a party crew 'UNIVERSOUL' and at some point went out looking for trouble. But once the excitement of gang fights and occasional shoot outs dissipated, I backed away and graduated with my class in 1998. After this I worked as a special education teacher, attended college, and had my own place. Aside from my decision to dramatically rise above the herd in the instant matter, I am a friendly, easy going person with a passion for life. As with most revolutionaries, if not for love of self, family, and friend, there would be nothing left for which to fight."

"How has your blood family taken to all of this?"

"Their disappointment is expected. They aren't too happy, and feel I should have found other ways to get my points across. Nonetheless, they do support me, and that's what counts."

"You have stated in no uncertain terms that the mission statement and philosophy of Sol Evil is to spread "violence and terrorism" against the followers of all white-light religions. However, at the same time you have processed a deep personal belief in "freedom from man, God, societies and ideals," particularly in the question of whether or not you subscribed to any neo-Nazi or NSBM ideology. So obviously, a paradox exists. This is not to say hypocrisy, because I believe what you are describing is a view of necessary organized resistance against something you view as inherently detrimental with a lavish history of tyrannical oppression at every socio-political level. You've also spoken regularly of your zealot-like aggression against "puritanical totalitarianism." So what I ask then

– is the practice of fascism to counter fascism something that truly can be embraced as a means to an end?"

"Admittedly, I was more blatant and aggressive in my youth. When I said the goal is to spread violence and terrorism against all white-light religions, it was coming from a younger, wilder, and less experienced version of myself. I don't retract anything I've said; but as an older, more mature Satanist, I acknowledge there is a lot more to Satanism than merely declaring a global war. As a youngster, I was full of piss and vinegar and wanted nothing more than to engage my enemies on the field of battle. Since then I have distinguished myself as someone willing to fight based on ideals. The goal isn't complete annihilation of the herd, or even the herd mentality, but to win the right to apply our virtues of strength and honor, without the mass hysteria of subservient morality condemning us for our vitality. All insurgencies must start somewhere, and revolutions are generally very violent – but political and philosophical resistance are both essential elements in order to wage true warfare. A worldwide Satanic Armageddon is more of a metaphor. I fight for the right to serve as a legitimate adversarial spokesperson against the ultra-influential religious institutions who seduce the world with their intoxicating messages of zealous servitude. There are always going to be rules, norms, and leaders. Every movement must have a set of guidelines. I don't see organized resistance as fascism to counter fascism, since everyone is free to choose where to stand in the fight. But organized resistance can absolutely be a means to an end. As I've said on numerous occasions, one voice spoken among many is nothing compared to many voices spoken as one. Organization among like-minded individuals is the only way to make a difference."

"Where is the line drawn?"

"I draw the line only where the fight against one sort of oppression becomes the fight for another."

"Is there any question of morality involved or is this something to be seen as a symbolic concept, as in more of a mental war to awaken the masses than that of a physical war? That is, should I say, except for the occasional violent outburst such as 1-19-03?"

"A Satanic war should absolutely be both mental and physical. Just look at the power of the Church. They have some of the sharpest tacticians in the world. Through philosophical enlightenment, one can begin to awaken those who have the potential to transcend the herd. By taking a physical stance, one makes the powerful point, such as, 'I mean what I say.' Few people can stomach being a Satanist, and only a small number have what it takes. For the rest, the herd, they are what they are – and I am who I am. It is conceivable to begin an era where strength, honor, and loyalty are virtuous. Anything is possible through the will of the people."

"How has prison altered your view of race/class war?"

"Since California is the most racist prison system in the country, it's inevitable that one develops an intolerance towards others, if not full-on racism. In here everyone's a nigger – we're society's shit. Most of the prison's population deserve the reputation, but there are some good dudes. Every race, class, and attitude is represented, and pieces of shit are in abundance. It's best not to hate someone because of how they were born, but judge them for the choices they make."

"When released, what are your immediate goals?"

"Well, it's been a long time since I last had sex, so I have a lot of making up to do. Dropping the soap just isn't how I imagined it (laughs). I need to spend some time reconnecting with everyone I left behind. A long time away is hard on relationships, and the strength of those soldiering through this ordeal along with me never ceases to confound all expectations. My wife especially has shown strength second to none, and deserves as much attention as possible. Once released I'll need to fully establish myself as the dominant force in Satanic metal and Satanism in general. My triumphant return shall be marked by the release of the new, truly inspired Sol Evil material and the overwhelming presence I shall bring to the world of the sinister. Each day marks another step closer to my release and the inevitable darkness that shall follow. The world should beware."

"What's the weirdest letter you've ever received from a fan (outside my own of course)?"

"I remember receiving odd mail when in county facing multiple life sentences. The letters asked for details about the crimes against which I was fighting, so I naturally didn't bother responding. Whether it was the prosecution looking for a stronger case or just a curious fan is irrelevant; I couldn't admit guilt while claiming innocence. I don't usually receive what you would call 'weird' letters from fans though. The mail I most often receive is from those who wish to show their appreciation for what I've done, or condemnation of it, and occasional inquiries into my personal Satanist beliefs and practices. Actually most messages are through email from people asking if I have Internet access. Unfortunately no, an inmate in the California Correctional system has no Internet access. However, any mail I get via the Internet my wife forwards to me through regular mail, and I respond to all who write. The fact such correspondence takes so much time is rather discouraging, but I welcome any and all mail. Besides, no one is weirder than you (laughs)..."

8 MONTH ANNIVERSERY (7.20.07)

You ask how this has all affected me. What state of mind does one enter after eight full months of living like this? I remember back in 1998 Marvel Comics initiated a campaign to reestablish the roots and origins of all its prominent characters. To revitalize, to clean the slate, to take ancient archetypes & reintroduce them to the generation at hand, to set the stage for what was to come amongst the next 5 year plan.

For some reason this platform has always stayed in my mind, this pointed paragraph of an answer from Joe Quesada. Hitting 17, the messy trail of the prior 4 years being refurbished – back to my roots, reexamining the central core characters, their influence & interwoven complexity of our paths... In lieu of the chaos which later emerged, this loose-screw cocoon morphed into an obsession of deconstruction. I had become a whirlwind of flux, and still am to this day...

This book is my attempt to strip it further bare then I have ever succeeded – to throw away your life, close off your friends entirely; to sacrifice yourself to art, knowing that with every action you are a character in a novel that you are in fact living simultaneously. You become the sacrificial lamb conduit of an unsteady ball of inertia that comes speeding from obscurity that you must cling onto whenever the opportunity emerges. There is no time to think, nor time to breath. Even sleep is sleeplessness...

So what is this affect upon a man? I do not believe I am qualified to give an answer the general public could ever understand. I felt ancient and elderly at 5 years old. The world I live in bares little resemblance to the world you live day to day – I cannot feel it, I cannot connect with it. I can only watch it twitch nervously like a psychiatric patient acutely under my lens, my soul itself the amplified magnifying glass...

But feel it I do not. I analyze your animal mechanisms; I know too much, I've seen too much. The bleached walls, the crystalline sky, the shoddy davenport, tiled floor & loose change on the street – the inert bookshelf, the parked car, the garbage can rolling in heavy wind amidst the oil-stained alleyway...

To me these things are the only things which seem real. You are the clutter & animate inanimate objects, the robots & gears of the machine. No culture, no ideals; no romance, imagination, charisma, talent, structure, community, reliability – you are a culture of spiritual invalids. You are the ghosts haunting my world which run on poltergeist motor function. *Naivety, ingratitude, persecutors, liars, and shams…*

I withdraw and scrutinize the primordial sense of self – no television, no movies, video games, books, comics, automobile; no possessions save what a backpack and duffle-bag can maintain. I stand at a periphery in which I am frozen in time mere moments before falling to the depths of the canyon below. I have nothing to prove to any of you, and I have nothing left to give you. This is my real problem with women. Once they see my truth, they get lost in it. Bad things happen when people listen to me talk. It's my most charming, boyish quality…

So I boil it down to what I'm really made of, and all I'm left with is the permanent impression of the violence that has dominated my life. Violence has been the one consistent variable in everything – art, music, emotion, language. Everything has been colored aggression, revenge, destruction. It is the one personal theme that I have never eclipsed. I am a victim of my environment and a mere reflection of its bruised and scab-picked surface…

I no longer have any great war. All of those I once fought for are far from me – death, prison, worse. I had turned into poor Willy Loman, lost in a world of ghosts. Perhaps there was a truth in this masochistic alienation…

All of that has been wiped clean. There are no more phantasms. There are no more flashbacks. The memories are fading if not permanently gone; I am something else now, something of pure energy; *elemental*. To even call me human seems absurd, as absurd as that statement is within itself…

I choose to accept the absurd notion and place myself as a peripheral visitor. I'm a tourist. I'm bored, I want to go home, but home there is not. Death seems the only return, but that is never to be romanticized. I have no ideology. I no longer have a great message or cause. I don't know what to believe because to summarize a view of life you would need definition of the self yet this is a lapse because there is nothing to compare myself to in order to mold a solid cohesion.

It is my final decision at this moment in time that I am a nihilist, albeit with an acute and poetic sense of humor. Every strategy to decode the cosmos ultimately showcases a frailty which unravels it. But it does not stifle the absolute humor of the grand punch-line – *it's just that the joke itself that remains a mind-clawing enigma…*

No morality truly exists. Nothing governs us save the flimsy laws of science and survival. Beyond that is a gap filled by religion, propaganda, television, marketing, merchandising, immediate hedonism, collective populism and its self-sustaining herd mentality nucleus. We are not a race, nor a nation. We are lumps of putty molded by our immediate environments and the models we assume from systematic human interaction – clumps of tribes assuming an interconnected identity by technology far advanced then we are compatible for, in a world moving at lightning speed towards homogenization & endless confusion. This is the core, and it looks and feels like Manhattan as Armageddon…

BATTLE MOUNTAIN

To purge every ghost of the past and burn every lasting piece of spiritual or mental baggage of The Old World to a cinder has become the immediate obsession. 2 months have rolled by, and this purgatory has caused deep, unrelenting analyzation of every adventure …

When it began I was still soft. I still threw around money & comforted myself with safety nets. SoCal was a cakewalk. Albuquerque got me going. Denver was a frozen disaster that put me through the ringer. My penniless return to San Diego was rocky, but low-rent economics sailed me through just fine...

San Francisco was a shaky, unprepared situation created through my own good faith in absolute strangers. When every safety net fell through, for the first time it was just me versus the street. I stayed positive throughout those first grueling days, although I was ultimately on edge and fighting panic veiled below the surface. It was The Eagles Nest that finally broke me – or shall I say made me *blossom.*

After a week on the street with no shower, grizzled and wastoid, I never wanted to leave. Golden Gate Park was a glowing paradise and my one true home. It was with that transformation that this book truly ignited, and it was that very adventure which broke the cocoon. That was the beginning of whatever it is I now am today…

It rolled onto an immediate tour that shot me across America, cutting my teeth on the art of the spoken word. I landed like a falling comet in Detroit as a crazed pyrate lord – a reborn stranger wandering the haunts of my past. It was the scenery to a life so distant it seemed I never lived. I'd been gone 5 months and it felt like a decade…

Huntsville was an entirely different head-trip; it was heavy metal world in the strictest sense. Detroit Part II was a pit-stop as fleeting as any of those on the Greyhound circuit. New York came next, and I stormed in like a Marine whilst living with a Marine. But San Fran it was not. There was no joy to this urban wasteland. Just a cut-throat blur of hectic, non-stop humanity.

With every image I ingested, I only became more rock solid. There was no fear of anything, and I crept through the shadows like an invincible alien, defying every danger that Brooklyn, Manhattan, and New Jersey had to offer...

Now I stand at the periphery having clawed tooth and nail through two months of misery to fund this final trek. Two giant adventures are lined up before me. The first target is the final frontier – *Seattle, Washington*. I've saved it for last because I know this will be the most grueling of all. I have no personal ties, I have but a handful of connections, and I am prepared for the absolute worst.

I am filled with euphoria about this. I don't even look forward to meeting a single band – I'm on the edge of my seat waiting to live out San Fran Part II. It will be freezing, it will rain constantly, I will sleep under viaducts, eat out of trashcans, hang out with bums & there will be a zero forecast of romance. I'll actually have a sizable budget for the week and a half I roam the mysterious city, yet no idea where I'm going or what to expect in terms of environment.

For the grand finale I've somehow pulled Spoken Word Tour #2 out of my ass – *"The Spread The Disease Tour."* Downtown Brown is back having freshly been the first band in years to be kicked off the Van's Warped Tour, and it will be both of our biggest.

This is a 6 week extravaganza hitting every nook & cranny of the United States aided by a solid booking agent & pro PR. Posters have been sent to every venue, the guarantee's in place, the opening band with a video on MTV -- a weirdo industrial-metal act from Minneapolis called Screaming Mechanical Brain. They have a built-in draw, having toured with Mindless Self Indulgence. Then there's my contribution. This book has goddamn heat on it – bands contacting from all over & I've contacted every group I've been speaking with this entire time & said when/where their cities show is. For once, I'm letting them come to me... *Now comes the final voyage...*

PART X: SEATTLE
(1997 ETERNAL)
AUGUST 9TH-AUGUST 19TH 2007

THE LAST GREAT FRONTIER

The most predominant characteristic for a first time traveler going this deep into the Northwest are the humongous jungle-like canopies of skinny pine trees that make you feel as if you've strolled into a National Geographic special on the mythical existence of Sasquatch.

The Greyhound roars through high-altitude mountain forests and jutting tunnels carved through solid rock, yellow lights whizzing by like a successive transport of indoor roller coasters. The fog is heavy, the blotted sun seams larger, the high-altitude brings a clarity of mind unbreached by any other area of the United States.

Then BAM, you're in Portland, which is a firm genetic splice between Andy Griffith's Mayberry and a New England fisherman town. Outside the bus terminal you can see a long stretch of downtown, which captures the Market Street essence of San Francisco. The air is clean, the people appear happy, and it seems to be a world without bloodthirsty street-crime and grim misery.

I was supposed to stay in Portland for the weekend with yet another Detroit Expatriate who is a stop-motion animator on the new Neil Gaiman film. The same company that did *Nightmare Before Christmas* and *James & The Giant Peach* base their operations here, and I had a tour of the studio lined up and an interview with one of the producers. Then I was to swing over and meet Odin Thompson from Moribund Records on Saturday, and enjoy Sunday with Pork Chop from The Villa Winona before jetting out to Seattle, who's been living on the streets with a mob of crusties.

Well the animator happens to have taken a flight to Detroit for the weekend, and even though her boyfriend was going to show me around, Odin has disappeared, and Pork Chop is an hour Southwest in Lebanon with no cell phone. Therefore, Seattle has gained an extra three days of mayhem.

I know this will be the most devastating of all. There are no Detroit refugees to back me up, I have only 4 or 5 band numbers, and I am totally ignorant of the cities layout. I also expect it to stereo-typically rain non-stop. It will be San Fran Part II, and more quixotically vicious then the 48 hour push of NYC. Think that was gruesome? Try a 224 hour 12 straight-day marathon – I'm going out with a bang, just for you, dear audience…

I'm so hardened by this year that what I would've considered a cataclysmic situation only 8 months ago is now but a fleeting inconvenience. I was a wobbly cup of Jello when I left Michigan. Now I'm the T-1000, even though I can't form arm knives with liquid metal.

I'm prepared for the absolute worst, but I have some money to play with – $300 for the week and a half expedition. After living on $15 a week for the past year, this is a jackpot. I'll be able to kill time with plenty of grub and not have to walk three miles to the next checkpoint because that $2 bus fare is my food budget for the entire day…

It's another 4 hours before we roll into Seattle, which explodes on the horizon after a sharp turn of the mountains. Its foundation is compactly based in a valley, squeezed together like a shining jewel. The Space Needle rides high like the Eiffel Tower, calling all the ships to port. The landscape recalls a miniature San Fran, as if the center of the Bay Area were instead based on Mackinaw Island.

Hi-rise freeways run the length of the Puget Sound, the lake-like water basin that is something between the coast of an ocean and a Scottish loch. Its coast is dominated by gigantic white and orange cranes that lift train-car sized hunks of steel onto cargo ships. They look like abstract giraffes, or Imperial Walkers from *Empire Strikes Back*. In the distance are multiple islands with mountainous peaks, as if King Kong lurks discreetly.

The freeways themselves are architected with a postmodern, futuristic flare – three stacked directly on top of one another, like triple-stacked wafer crackers, vehicles hauling where the chocolate filling would be sludged. Bridges everywhere, the town's center surrounded by hills and lakes that shine in the glistening sun. Luscious green vines crawl up every viaduct and many of the buildings, like the Charlton Heston New York of *The Omega Man*. This is without a doubt one of the most physically beautiful cities in America. Even the Greyhound station is phenomenal, housing its own hi-grade Thai Restaurant.

Standing on the street-corner for 30 minutes I've already been approached by a handful of crusts and middle-aged heady liberals for no real reason other then I looked interesting. That distinct *Andy of Mayberry* Portland vibe is amplified, and it is obvious that the seething mass of 1960's radicals who flocked North of Frisco over the years have wholly terraformed this city. I can just feel a rumbling artistic capitol shaking the earth…

LORD NIXON

It's Friday, August 10th, 2pm when the white cargo van rolls up. It usually doesn't run this smooth. Only an hour into this and I have my first interviewee, whom is a living legend. His name is Kyle Nixon, he runs the high-traffic site Seattle Punk Rock (dot com), and was the vocalist of SOLGER, the first-ever hardcore punk band from Seattle (circa 1979).

Kyle's a calm speaking manic-depressive in his mid-40's; medium build, short black hair, one iota under 6 feet tall. He swings us by Dick's, which is the famous punk rock hamburger joint. It's sort of a cross between a high-grade White Castle and Daly's: *"I used to take every touring band that would come through up here. Black Flag ate here, Poison Idea. It's kind of a ritual. In the old days you could feed an entire band for $10."*

Bellies full we zoom onward to The Funhouse, which is the major punk/metal bar. It is easily distinguished by the giant evil clown head on top of the building. Its location is fitting, being stationed directly across the street from the Space Needle its neighboring kiddy carnival. It's so abruptly perfectionist – this haunting, John Wayne Gacy, booze ridden hangout of tattooed and mohawked freaks that the children gaze upon while riding miniature Big Wheels and Pyrate Ships. *"Is that my future mommy? That clown is scawe-wing me."*

Inside The Funhouse it is a conglomeration between Burt's Tiki Lounge (ABQ) and The Old Miami (Detroit). Cheap drinks, small "4 inches off the ground with a two speaker PA" stage, comfortable leather booths alongside the walls, skinny collectible concert posters galore, band bumper stickers slapped everywhere, and a privacy-fenced open area out back complete with a BBQ tent and a basketball hoop for drunken subculturals to play HORSE:

Kyle Nixon: *"I'm a native. I started off as a promoter, got into punk rock November of '77. I was of the first group putting up flyers for the Dead Kennedys, their first Seattle show. That was '79. By 1980 I threw my first show and right after that we played with Black Flag. We played with The Neoboys from Portland. You might of heard of Poison Idea from Portland. Before they were Poison Idea, a couple members were in a band called The Stand and actually broke up at my apartment. They had a big fight with some rockers that night."*

"Where does the name SOLGER originate from?"

"It's soldier, it's a misspelling. If you look at the Civil War, you read these letters of guys writing their loved ones and they spell soldier 'SOLGER.' Because they were very illiterate, and that's how it sounds."

"Your albums still have a cult fan base…"

"If you look up the band on the internet, and you read the reviews of the first record [1980], you'll find it goes about a $100 on EBay. The last one sold for $115."

"Was it a self pressing?"

"Yeah. I didn't believe in labels and I didn't believe in quality either. The songs are great but I transferred the master to a K-mart tape. So just fuckin' super crustie. People listen and they're '*holy fuck, this is so bad but so good.*' But then I had Jack Endino, the guy who did Nirvana's *Bleach* remaster everything, and put it on CD in 2003. In 2002 I also sang for The Fartz, before they broke up for the last time. "

"What year did SOLGER break up?"

"We broke up October '80. We played with Black Flag…"

"Was that when they had Keith Morris?"

"No, Keith never toured. The first tour up here was February 15th & 16th, 1980. They crashed at my house. I tried to sneak in, couldn't get in. I was 17. I met up with them the next day and got to sing 'Nervous Breakdown.' I had the only copy at that point of their EP. I got it from the promoter 'cause it was nothing to him. I walked around with this like '*fucking god*'… I booked them to come back for an all ages show in May."

"What was Black Flag's guarantee back in the day?"

"There was no such thing as guarantees back then. The Subhumans got a $100 but didn't play 'cause the place turned into a miniature riot. A guy tried to commit suicide onstage, this all out brawl happened… That was the beginning of hardcore in Seattle. That show was Seattle's first taste of what hardcore punk was all about. Some people got it, some people didn't."

"Were you in any bands after SOLGER?"

"I did a fuck band, one called Shit. Our guitar player joined The Fartz and I played with The Fags. There was another, like a ska type band called The Niceboys. It was with Tommy from The Fartz… Our first show was opening for Neoboys. In August we got Black Flag up here again, then we played Portland with them the next night for a whopping $25. Afterwards I went back to promoting. Did another

Black Flag show in '83. I had booked Circle Jerks, we sent them $600 dollars. They didn't show. We had an insane bill for them too. We had Husker Du and Malfunction, which later became Mother Love Bone... We'd play the Russian Hall on Beacon Hill and cops would come and start beating on kids with batons, tell them to get out of the building. We're trying to get out but we'd have to go through a gauntlet of batons. Why don't you just let the kids leave the building? They didn't understand punk rock back then. And now they pose no threat at all. They've seen a 1000 Mohawks. They know it now – just kids, teenagers doing their thing.... So I just did a lot of oddball shows. Black Flag was giving out my number on the East Coast so I was getting a lot of phone calls. I quit promoting in '83. Just took a vacation from punk rock. It was pretty much dead in Seattle."

"What was the main thing that killed it?"

"The lack of imagination; creativity severely lacking... The thing about punk rock – the exciting part is white hot passion. When you're really into it it's your world, it's fuckin' everything. And then once you've been on all sides of being a promoter the passion just goes. The acts that come up are far and between that excite you. The good thing about punk is anybody can do it, the bad thing is you can suck and start a punk rock band. There's a few great bands, a bunch of good bands, a ton of shitty bands. Once you lose that passion its time to take a break. Punk died '84, '85. It really reached its peak. Hardcore in '84 was probably its last push, then everything started sounding the same. Very chunky styled riffs, Discharge, GBH... The English explosion in the late 70's was fantastic. New York had it's scene with The Ramones and Blondie. When LA had their scene a lot of people had the same attitude – '*Fuck the English.*' In the same way, they were saying '*Fuck New York.*' The hardcore style, the attitude was you make your own scene. Make your own music that's a little more intense and vivid. And then it just got so shitty."

"Did you get into any of the grind stuff?"

"One of the things I didn't like was the speed. You can play really fast and hide all your mistakes. So the whole speedcore, the whole grindcore – where there's no melody, no structure, no songwriting, and it comes down to shouting... Darby had his own singing style. Jello had his. Even Dez from Black Flag, he was different then Keith and Henry. It got to the point where all the bands were sounding way too much alike and it got boring. Originally, when new wave and punk were the same, you'd see the weirdest shit. It was

Halloween every night. And now a bunch of people wear Misfits clothing. The whole cool factor was that we made our own shirts. If you dug Crass you'd make a stencil on a shirt. There was no stickers, there were no shirts. I'll buy a shirt, but I support pretty much only the little guys, like some local out of Portland or Oakland. If I don't know you, I'm not wearing your fuckin' shirt. I don't go for uniforms, the studs and all that stuff. To me that's the 1982-84 type look. People should be more creative then that... I like personal lyrics in a more thought provoking way. It's easy to jump on a band wagon and bash the administration. Right now for punk it's good 'cause we have Bush. Reagan was great for punk... There was a time where you could wear a swastika. People don't get why Sid Vicious or anybody back then would. The whole oxymoron is that if you were a punk rocker in Nazi Germany, if you are a deviant, you would've been killed along with the mentally ill, the weak, the life unworthy of life. They took artists that did weird art, they killed them and destroyed their art. And people still have their head so far up their political ass they don't understand sacred little things like that. I like to see a guy up their singing with a goddamn swastika. Singing about the most fucked up shit in the world. It doesn't mean you support Hitler. That swastika literally goes back thousands of years meaning good life and positive things to Indian cultures. Fucking all over the planet it meant great things. It never had a negative connotation until 1933. Now punks just preach a direct message instead of something indirect. We had a song called 'Raping Dead Nuns.' It got attacked by feminists. It wasn't about fucking raping women. The song was about fucking with the church. We were an anarchist political band. Part of this, its anti-authority but no state and no god. So in the no god attack aspect, 'Raping Dead Nuns' means this dead old church. People can't get over any form of shock symbol. And we got these new skinheads which are supposedly anti-racist but they're just as fucked up as the racists. Back when it started in Seattle, a good portion of us, myself included, had sexual experiences with the same sex. We were open minded as you could fucking get. We didn't let that kind of crap get in our way. We just took any mind-fuck that came up to fuck with people's heads. The punks either got it or they didn't. Now most of the lyrics are fairly direct. They just spout out their philosophy. It's like politics – it's just another preacher."

"You mentioned being an anarchist band..."

"I was a purist when I was a kid. When you get older you kind of loosen up your attitude. Your so hardcore you fuckin' focus on little things. When I was in a punk rock band I was about destroying punk rock. I was about destroying music, destroying everything. Now I look back and I think all of it was great back then. I think it was so much better when it was all mixed together. Everybody was there at the show. You'd see the same people. Scenesters, the gay crowd, the art people, the new wavers, the poseurs, the real punks – they were all there. It's just nice to see all the assholes. This is your town, this is your scene, and you're the ones to show the prestige of it. And the bands, even if they weren't great, at least you'd get to network and talk."

"Do you think Black Flag went in the shitter when Rollins came up or do you dig that stuff?"

"I kind of bailed on them before the experimental shit happened. Henry brought in more of a macho, masculine posturing to the band, whereas Dez was the fuckin' nicest guy in the world, Ron was really cool. They were like regular folk. And the crowd, they weren't football players that turned into punk rockers. The pits were still wild, you could still get your ass kicked or a fight could break out. But it wasn't against a bunch of fuckin' huge ass strong dudes that just got into punk rock. Henry's crowd turned that way... Maybe it was just bad luck on his part. There were a lot of assholes who came into punk rock late, like punk is all about beating people up or something."

"Is that when it died? Was that a main reason?"

"Yeah, pretty much fucked. I'd say it was really over in '83. People started doing a lot of hard drugs, coke started getting real big. People were doing speed. We had a couple guys shooting speed during practice and it was like '*what the fuck is this?*'... I'm into mind-fucks, anything that would just blow my mind. I used to do a shit-load of mushrooms, I used to do a shit-load of LSD. I used to do 7 hits of acid at a time, that was my regular."

"What about GG Allin? Ever run into him?"

"I was out of it when he came in, but I think he was actually good for punk rock. His songs are nicely moronic and stupid and I think punk had gotten away from being stupid and obscene and, you know, eating shit and drinking piss. That stuff I did. And so..."

"You ate shit and drank piss live?"

"No, but I have pissed myself playing guitar. People have done that but... You know when I'm on my own time I do that stuff and... So I think it was good they had something back that was shocking crowds and being banned. If someone were to do that now, it'd be like telling a joke twice. It wouldn't be significant."

"What's something remarkably bizarre that happened to you and when you tell people they think you're lying?"

"I was a manic depressive, my moods would be all over the fuckin' place. I tried to commit suicide in '83 and one of the questions they ask when you're strapped down in a chair at the hospital – '*do you want to kill anybody?*' Yeah, the president, Reagan. So they called the Secret Service. They come to interview me and I have like four cigarette burns on my head. I have a whole pack all the way up my arm from that particular night. Just getting drunk, getting myself psyched up trying to feel something other than being numb. '*Yeah, I want to kill the president just to be famous, like Boothe. No reason, I don't give a shit about his politics.*' So they send in this guy, agent Steve Waters. He takes pictures of me, asks if I have a bomb and all these other things. And he had me tell him all the different ways I'd kill him. Whenever presidents came to Seattle they'd land at Boeing Field. I said I'd come in with a gyrocopter and blast way, kind of like *Mad Max*. I said these are all just creative thoughts. They'd make a great book or a movie. It doesn't mean I'm gonna do 'em. You can't put people in prison for thoughts… So they got me on file. They won't release the documents, and I really dug those pictures with the four cigarette burns… The Ignorant – the band I manage now – they wrote a song about that called 'Dancing On Your Grave.' I took them up to Hendrix's grave last year, so they mixed the killing of the president in with me smashing all this shit that was on Hendrix grave. All this fucking bullcrap – smashing it, dancing…"

"How do you feel about Andy Kaufman?"

"He was just fucking over the top as far as opening his head and whatever happens… I didn't start eating shit & drinking piss till Andy Kaufman…"

"How does The Funhouse rank as far as punk bars?"

"I think The Funhouse is the best punk rock bar period. El Corazon, they put on a lot of the bigger shit. Hells Kitchen down in Tacoma is great. Studio 7, I put shows on there."

"Does the punk scene have a real bug up their ass about Kurt Cobain? I know he always considered nirvana a punk band. He grew up hearing about the music without actually hearing it and just figured that's probably what it sounded like."

"He actually was friends with The Melvins. His first real punk experience was supposed to be watching The Melvins behind a Safeway in Aberdeen. The whole grunge scene were former punk rockers. They took part of that attitude… Like I was telling you about the thrash. If you're not talented you can get away with speed, but if you start throwing some melody and some great lyrics and slow it down a bit, you can really go to town."

"What do you think of the accusation that Courtney Love killed El Duce because she'd contacted him about murdering Cobain so she could collect the insurance and estate? Is that just a big, overblown, baseless conspiracy?"

"I'm pretty sure El Duce killed himself. You could tell by Cobain's writing and the way his life was, that he was a manic depressive. And she is too. It's really hard to live with people like that. I'm a manic depressive. I've been taking medication since '86. When I'm in my spiritual zone, I am fuckin' manic as hell, I am so fuckin' out there. I'm fuckin' absolutely useless as a husband, dad, or anything. My wife has put up with it for all this time. I've been with her for 21 years, she's the only woman that could ever put up with me… Jack Endino, he had to deal with both Courtney Love and Cobain. He just straight up calls Courtney a bitch. Jack is like the sweetest fucking guy on the fuckin' planet. And to hear him say anybody's a bitch is like, '*Holy Christ, she must've been a bitch to get under Jack's skin.*' That just speaks volumes to me…"

…I excuse myself to use the little boys room and staggering through the club I realize how superbly hammered I am. Nixon is so bowled over in his rant that he's fed my cocktail after cocktail, and I'm having trouble staggering back to him, nearly crashing into the half dozen wasted punkers playing basketball while Judas Priests "Painkiller" is raging through the outdoor P.A. system. I've only been in this city for 3 hours, and I have no real plan. But I'm not paranoid. No, I'm too drunk for that, and besides, it's a clear blue sky. Once I make it back to Nixon, who is also smiling happy drunk, I recall him mentioning that people refer to him as "Lord Kyle," and that he was in some sort of fringe religious sect…

"So tell me about the cult you were in."

"There's this guy Gary Mailer. One of the things he's gonna try to do is run for president but he's also – he claims to be the 12th apostle. Paul was not the 12th apostle… Christians who are upset with Christianity, they read this and they just can't fuckin' believe the truth. I've sat with this guy, and I was the first one to come to him… And this guy used to just talk to me years ago. He'd just tell me stuff – the mantra, what his church was teaching. And I went to a ministry school and the dean pulled me in because my views were contrary to the church fathers. Revelations would just come to me 'cause god would show me the stuff. I would tell him exactly what god told me... So I'd gather with Gary Mailer, and that was in Salem, Missouri. He's a prophet. I used to be a prophet until I fell. One of my major falls was getting involved with punk rock. He kept trying to get me to quit and I would not give up. There's actually a document where I signed over the 12th apostleship, because I was the 12th apostle – Satan. As Satan I signed over the apostleship that Judas Iscariot... Satan had entered into me. So I had a right to hand that over, 'cause Paul never had that right. People think of him as the 12th but he was never the 12th. The 12th actually has to be connected to the 1st. The only way to do that is for a man to live from the time of Christ until now. The only one that could do that is Satan himself. And I embodied Satan. So I signed over on this bridge, where the two eagles come together or whatever... Signed this agreement that I'm handing over the 12th apostleship to Gary Mailer. When we sat there, the holy spirit had come to us, and revelation would just come out of our mouths out of nowhere.... And I had this thing, just like in the punk rock days, where fire would just come out of my mouth. We'd have people show, get all excited about gold dust and fuckin' all this other shit had meanings. And I would just fuckin... Flames. Like I would just burn these people to toast. Totally just destroy them..."

"*Where's Gary now?*"

"He's in Salem, Missouri. Last time I was there, I made sure on my first day before everyone gathered, I said 'I *wanna go fishing with you. I haven't fished since I was a little boy.*' And Missouri's got all these springs. I mean rivers come right straight out of the ground, right out the side of the mountain. Then you fucking throw your fishing pole in there and you got a 14 inch rainbow trout... So we caught all these fish, and I knew I was gonna get the boot because of my involvement with punk rock. There's three prongs that destroyed America. The Women's Rights Movement, Jazz, rock n' roll, punk, rap, metal – kids rebelling. You don't have to be a fuckin' genius to know it's the devils music. And Euthanasia. All these sins came about in the 1920's... I rely on my own friendship with Christ. I didn't go to Christ, Christ came to me and that was back in '91. He came to me with a big sign right in front of my face that said the word TRUTH... Then he came to me in a dream I was really upset about the bible translations and how wicked they were. There was actually Wiccan language slung into the translations. I even gave them to my pastor. I gave him a bumper sticker of a moving translation in one of the bibles he used. He said if it wasn't for the 18 versus that had been missing from the bible there's be no repentance. And I started bawling in my dream and I woke up just crying my brains out… It's not that these verses are missing – they've been twisted in such a way that the grace of god has been so misrepresented. But he had to do this in order to save. Because the level of responsibility… We're spiritually blind people. They aren't in touch with god. Christians especially aren't in touch with god. People who don't pretend to be Christians, it's not even their issue. But Christians particularly are so blind that if there wasn't such a mix up of mercy and grace, we'd be totally responsible… So by the fact that we're blind and don't know, is a grace. And these verses… 18 is the number for bondage. He speaks in a language of numbers. I'm a numbers man. 8's my number."

"How did 8 become your number?"

"8 is a bridge number, I'm a bridge between… Spiritually, this goes with Aliester Crowley as well. Crowley knows some stuff that the Christians don't acknowledge, because it's a cult supposedly. I believed he received his stuff prophetically. Whether it was Satanic or God doesn't matter, that information had to be there for a reason. But the truth is 8 is a bridge number. There's a book called 72 names of God, and one of them is Ohm, the chant they use in India. What it means is the beginning, which is the fool, which is me, who walks out of nothingness into everything. And that's what god did. And then he becomes the hierophant, which is really the bridge between the spiritual and the natural world that we know…"

"The Astral Plane?"

"Right, it's the middle. It bridges the two… The 3rd part of my name, it's the Hebrew letter which they use in the 72 names of god. It's the man hanging from his foot, laughing. So on one hand you have the man who comes out of nothingness into something, he becomes the bridge, the hierophant... And then there's my wife, a total bi-polar, manic depressive type of person… And I've been a prophet in this group since 2000. And uh… A lot of people call me on the verge of suicide. You know… I talk 'em out of it… The phones are ringing dry… I have problems… I'm a fuck up, you know… My thing is whatever I fear I hear…"

"So that you won't fear it anymore?"

"Exactly. Eating shit, drinking piss – I drank piss for 40 straight days."

"That's an accomplishment."

"That's one of the reasons I'm The Ignorant's manager. At last years party, my 44th birthday party and the guitar players 16th birthday party... So I piss in the sink first, all over the fuckin' dishes dude, at this kids 60 year old mom's house. We're fuckin' wasted. The Slashers just played, great show. And I'm fuckin' drunk off my gourd, I piss all over the dishes, go outside and I fuckin piss in this little kids cup. Diego, The Ignorant's singer, he's taking pictures of me. I drank most of it. The last bit I spit out on The Ignorant. Fuckin hits Deigo, most of them. Two of the guys quit the fuckin' band. And Diego fuckin' loved it. He started calling me "Lord." Punk rock had already called me lord, all the punk rockers call me 'Lord Kyle' or 'Lord Nixon.' He considered it Baptism. And the person that used to book them all the time, she smelled that hat and she puked, just from the fuckin' thought of it. It's all mental you know? Like I was saying – Andy Kaufman, outside the box. I was shoving fuckin' meat up my ass when I was 12 years old. Hot dogs, fuckin' pieces of cubed meat from stew, and jacking... I was doing GG Allin before there ever was a GG Allin. I've always been fuckin' out there. And so for me to fuckin' put shit in my mouth or fuckin' drink piss, that ain't nothing. Actually Jim Morrison, John Lennon, they both drank their own piss. The prime minister or whatever the fuck he was in India, he lived to 101 years old. Every morning, because it has the most melatonin. Millions of people across the planet drink their urine everyday. Jesus said, '*Out of the innermost being of the belly comes living water.*' You take that figuratively, not spiritually – its urine. Urine contains all the minerals you lose, it's sterile. Gary Mailer was a lab tech. He knows that stuff's there. I told him I'm gonna start drinking my urine for 40 straight days, and I'll do it with you... You might meet some fucked up people on the road, but you won't meet people this fucked up."

"You'd be surprised..."

"What Gary Mailer would do to this fuckin' country is change it back to the way the founding fathers had it. This country has gone downhill. I'm a part of that downhill. Because I'm Satan. So are you, Ryan. We all are."

"Yes yes, I aspire to be..."

"It's easy. What's hard is right. I know the spirit of Christ. He came to me. I wasn't looking for Christ, I wasn't seeking Christ. Christ came to me and spoke to me many times, showed me things I didn't want to do. People were like, '*Why you doin' this?*' I'd be like, '*I have to fuckin' do this, because I've been shown to do this.*' And people couldn't believe I would fuckin' pull bullshit like this off. Weirder then fucking anything ever done in punk rock... In fact I fasted 40 days on the judgment of America. I saw in a brick in my kitchen one time, I walked into my kitchen and all of a sudden a brick appeared in front of my eyes and it had the end of the world and all the death and destruction, even the death of my infant son, and I fell to the floor and cried out '*How can I stop this?*' So I fasted 40 days without eating, and then I met Gary, and we started talking... There is no wraith. He's gonna do the work, God himself is gonna do the work. And it starts off with The Man... It's so true. If people would just be honest, they would agree. Because people are so into self-interest, they fight it. But to me that's the revolution. And when people call into the talk show – and this is 250 stations across the country – Gary's the 27th biggest talk show in the market in America... If you go to the remnantbride.com [Mailer's website] all those writings involve my input. There's also a yahoo site that has my writings on there. And thecurseof1920.com – that's the book that just came out. It's strictly about the curse upon America... I'm the Elijah to Gary Mailer, and Gary Mailer is the Elijah to Christ. I talk to him all the time. He's my best friend..."

INTO THE ARMS OF THE GALWAY ARMS

Kyle and I are exceedingly drunk, heading to El Corazon to drop off Zeke's merch guy Bobby. He has a grinding jaw & talks a mile a minute. He'd been friends with Kurt Cobain since high school, and is giving this long-winded tale about huffing rubber cement with him in the back of a Frito Lay delivery truck. As usual I ask the golden question: "*So was Kurt a big Marx Brothers fan?*" "Without a doubt."

Bobby's convinced me to hang out at the show tonight, which is the after party for the largest tattoo convention in the Northwest. El Corazon is hosting the full three-day official concert series. Tonight it's Zeke, The Jet City Fix and Drown Mary. Tomorrow it's In Memorium, Owen Hart, Claymore and HIMSA. Sunday is being referred to as "Joe Fest," where unrelenting drummer Joe Grindo will be playing four sets in a row with all of his bands – Book Of Black Earth, Lair of The White Worm, Splatterhouse & SKARP.

Another hour passes, and Kyle has taken me to the other main punk bar The Galway Arms in the University District. The "U-Dub" is packed full of squatters, crusts, panhandlers, street artists, metalheads. Capitol Hill is seen as the indie, tight-pants, college kid hipster spot – plus it's the main nerve of the gay community.

The Galway Arms is _the_ definitive seedy Irish punk bar of Seattle with a 4-inch, 2 PA stage. The wooden floor reeks of alcohol like varnish. Everything is dark with red lights – giant black skull & crossbones flag hammered to the wall. I'm introduced to bartender Adam Houghton, this tattooed beast of a loudmouth with a mangy red beard. Houghton helps run Beer Metal Records and is the throat-screamer of grindpunk band Deathlist 5.

Kyle slaps a PBR in my hand and siks me on fellow Beer Metal henchmen Justin Hofmann, whose father was the bassist of The Fartz. Justin has red hair and a red beard, and is quite jovial and sharp: *"I'm 24, I'm in Two Jerks & A Squirt, and I do booking here at The Galway. We're the production side of Beer Metal Records, which is a local family of musicians here. Deathlist 5, Last 1 Out, The Dingbatz, The Hollowpoints, Super Happy Story Time Land, 7 Year Old Blind Girl. It's a pretty hefty list."*

"Things have been going well. Seattle's kind of aching for a comeback. My band actually just started out recently. Myself on bass, and Carly Monster from The Dingbatz singing. Puked On and Vito from The Plankton Beat play with us. We have two major influential elements – the new school punk/grindcore, and the old school hardcore…"

So what are the pot laws here like? Lax as California?

Justin Hofmann: *"its pretty low-yield. It is officially the cities lowest priority. They'll just take your pot and throw it away, pretty much. Usually they'll make you break your pipe. If you're a dick to them they'll write you a ticket. You'll never get arrested, ever. You'd have to really piss them off to get that far (chuckles)."*

How do you feel about Jimmy Hoffa?

"I think he lives. I don't think he's anywhere. I think he's part of witness protection."

Probably, maybe… What's something just totally weird that happened to you?

"Actually one time I convinced a number of people out in Tacoma that there's a new STD called 'Scrotum Turtles.' And upon contracting it they only remedy would be to dip your balls in bleach."

How many people did dip their balls in bleach?

"Unfortunately none because none of them had the symptoms of Scrotum Turtles. As far as physical symptoms it's quite the same as crabs, except upon magnification you would see a bunch of spiky turtles, like 'Teenage Mutant Ninja Turtles 2.'

What is 'The Secret Of The Ooze?'

"It turns people into mutants. That is the secret. It's just a biomass by-product of a pharmaceutical nightmare program. There's no real secret dude..."

It took little effort to sell myself whilst passing a bowl in his parked vehicle. We listen to various Power Metal selections and the local band Toe Tag as Justin scrolls through his cell phone, and laying out a half-dozen bands for me to speak with. He has the blueprint on every squatter house in Seattle.

I'm a little saddened to be honest, because I've been spying every possible viaduct to sleep under. Maybe I won't need to sleep in these black trash bags for rain protection. For the first time in the history of this book it appears as if my master plan might actually work. All it took was 11 fucked missions to get it right.

More booze at Kyle Nixon's house. After he tells me Stone Gossart from Pearl Jam considers SOLGER a prime influence, Nixon hands me a DIY poetry book from Mark Bruback and two SOLGER vinyls. One of the 45's cover photos is of Cobain with a shotgun in his mouth, splattering his brains through the air.

Kyle introduces me to his son who plays in a band he manages called The Slashers. They are a good-time offensive hard-edged punk band, all long-hair high school drop-outs between the ages of 16/17, and I contribute to the delinquency of these minors whilst passing a joint on the patio table: *"We're down to three chords and a bad attitude. It's just us getting fucked up and writing shit... Our message is destroy, get fucked up... Skateboarding, we're influenced by that. Captain Morgan's, GG Allin... We like to have band orgies... Sasquatch is real. We play poker with him on Thursdays..."*

THE JET CITY FIX

10pm now, Nixon's long gone. I'm at El Corazon, a mid-level concert venue that feels less like home and more like a booze corral. The floor is lengthy, packed & sweaty. All the walls are painted black; it's a concrete-cell slab of a heavy metal slaughterhouse.

I'm outside hanging in the Camel Cigarette tent, glowing neon and plush with art deco padded chairs. Tons of boozehounds, many with that fresh-tattoo plastic wrap on their skin. Joe Camel fronts me two free packs & freebie flask. Some Italian guy in a white dress shirt with spiky metrosexual hair is on vacation, partying it up. I tap him on the shoulder and give a raised fist: "*Gabrielle D'Annunzio, Fiume or death!*" He busts out laughing "*Yes, yes, D'Annunzio, ha ha ha!*"

I don't even care about the show because I'm more interested in being a bum. It's a sick addiction, honestly. Lucky for me there is a viaduct a half block away. The drifter in the sleeping bag said that the cops don't care, so long as you're gone once commuters begin the 9 to 5 shakedown.

Turns out he's from my old neighborhood in East Dearborn. Same with me – working for Ford Motor Company drove him insane. '*Man, if you're from Greenfield and Warren, then trust me, Seattle is paradise.*" And just like everyone else from East D, he stereotypically starts ranting about how much he detests Arabs.

Back at the venue there is an all-female rock band blazing away, total AC/DC goes Turbonegro. They are all beautiful, and a long night with homebum loses its appeal to succubus nature. They agree to an interview, and but up first is The Jet City Fix, their first performance in over 2 years. They have energy, but it's pretty average rock stuff, big on the 80's guitar rock – AC/DC with a punk edge, but tight solos nonetheless. Says Shane Flauding: "*We're a bunch of fucked up individuals, we've been around 2001. This is our first time back in the scene. We've had a 2 year hiatus.*"

"Tell me about Seattle."

Shane Flauding: "Best city in the world. New York has nothing on it as far as music goes. We're about the rock. But we also have a bunch of Weezer sweater rock, but what can you do?"

"You've toured quite a bit…"

Ty McDonald: "Toured the US 5 times. We've been to Canada, we've been to Europe…"

SF: "We've played in Spain with Danzig…"

TM: "In 2003 we did 200 shows. This year we've been easing back into it."

"What are the worst cities in America to play?"

SF: "Detroit is horrible. We had a great show at The Magic Stick. We played with Link Wray. He's 74 years old, he's the guy who created guitar distortion. It was packed. The White Stripes and Von Bondies were there too."

"Tell me about the new record…"

TM: "We recorded it with Jack Endino. He did it all – Nirvana, Soundgarden, Mudhoney, Murder City Devils… He's a master of the sliding scale. He gets major label jobs and he'll bill major label rates, and he'll do a punk band from Seattle over the weekend for peanuts."

SF: "We wanted to make a dirty rock album and he did it perfect. He wanted us, so that was cool. He likes our band."

"What's the difference between Portland and Seattle?"

TN: "Portland is what Seattle was 10 years ago, more organic and less snooty. They like rock down there. Here it's more indie sweater stuff. Down there per capita it's the highest adult attendance live entertainment rate in the world. There's a lot of strippers and dirty rock dudes."

"What's the message?"

SF: "The message of our band is do some drugs, drink some beer, fuck some pussy, have fun. Drugs, sex, and rock n' roll."

"What are some bullshit attitudes in the underground you can do without?"

SF: "Racism. The problem is a generalization. We see it at our shows. We're a fuckin' AC/DC type rock band, so we have skinheads at our shows. It's not what we're about, but we have it all the time…"

KISW STORMHARBOR

Zeke comes strutting out in peak element. With hometown advantage, ZEKE tears the roof off with their revamped Motorhead goes Discharge speed-rock stamp that is as unique as it is devastating. The only other time I'd seen them is opening for Superjoint Ritual at Harpo's Detroit. Then they looked petrified of the audience (*for good reason*). Tonight they are white hot and stab a crushing blow that's so pulverizing the walls are shaking.

They filter off and one of the chick band chicks nabs my sleeve and starts tugging me down the street: "*Come on, we're going to the studio.*" We pass homebum and I just shrug, but he checks out the five girls I'm with, smiles, and gives the big thumbs up. We walk another two blocks to a corporate high-rise. When they said "*studio,*" I figured a rehearsal space – not KISW, the biggest rock station in Seattle.

We zoom up the elevators, all of us wobbling drunk, and next you know we're in the sound booth of DJ Steve Rock, being interviewed live. I keep leaning into the mic speaking hushed subliminal messages: "*GhostNomad owns your soul, live for Satan, kill for Gandhi...*"

The mob of rock n' roll honeys moves into the corridor, and I explain my ordeal to Steve Rock, who is amazed by the ferocity of this project. He's a big metalhead, very friendly, and demands I fill my backpack up with energy drinks from the stations freezer: "*KISW, the rock of Seattle for 35 years. My name is Steve Rock, I'm on Friday, Saturday, Sunday. Friday night I do 'The Grindhouse,' which is pretty much our main Nirvana/Metallica type deal, but I end up doing a bunch of DIO, Maiden, Pantera. Saturday nights is 'Metal Shop' from 11pm-2am. I program the three hours going from Red Chord to Suffocation to Iced Earth and Symphony X. Metal, all kinds.*"

"*Tell me about Seattle.*"

Steve Rock: "Seattle is probably my favorite city in the nation, there are hardly any cons. It's hard to get anywhere once you have something like grunge hit your city. What can you do after that? So it looks like nothing, but honestly I see more bands rising up. We do have our fair share of metal. There's still a lot of bands keeping it rock."

"*A lot of major radio stations have a play list. What's the ratio of unadulterated airplay and what do you spin when it occurs?*"

"There are a few really large companies in America running the show. I'm pretty stoked that this is an Intercom company and not Clear Channel. Those guys are pretty much governed by one book. My boss who's brought this station to number one in ratings, he used to run Q101 in Chicago. He gives more leeway than other people do. It's for the good of the people how we have it programmed – old song, new song, middle song. From grunge to metal to somewhere in the middle. I've gone way off the map on a few occasions and all he'll do is raise an eyebrow. On Saturday nights I get my three hours to do literally everything I want. I'll do NASUM into Hatebreed into Killers."

"*What are some bands you're pushing?*"

"I like bands that keep it fresh and push technicality. The Red Chord, I love those guys. Gunface, The Faceless, Napalm Death, Sepultura, Carcass... I'm an advocate for music in every sense. Never judge a band before you see them live. It's good to know there's more melding of subgenres with 16 year old guitarists playing far more advanced than any of us ever will."

"What needs to change about major radio?"

"The FCC. Like the people who are rating movies – it's just a tiny speck of sand in the ocean trying to command the entire ocean, and that's ridiculous."

"What's just a bizarre story you have?"

"My friends don't see me as much these days. When I tell them a story like Phil Anselmo asked to see me after the last DOWN show and played me all his new side projects on his IPOD... That's the hugest deal to me. My friends are like *'yeah, yeah, you're Steve Rock, big whoop.'* So no one gets excited with me anymore. I'm like *'I hung out with Slash!'* They're like *'Yeah. Cool.'* As far as unbelievable feats, I ate 9 Arby's sandwiches in a row. I'm pretty proud of that."

"Did you shit blood?"

"No, just Arby's. For a long, long time..."

As I'm hustling to give my number to the gals the elevator door closes shut. One of them just winks and waves goodbye, the slip of paper still in my palm. Stranded again...

Two of the other station guys grab me, flash this bag of purple and orange kryptonite, and we head up to the roof. One of the two is Pat Fry, guitarist of a local death metal act christened Churchburner. He's this big dude with long blonde hair and a scruffy beard that reminds me so much of Dusty from Severed Savior. He exhales a toke: "*Man, if you dig this shit, your mind is gonna be totally blown on Sunday.*"

"*What's going on?*" I ask, naïve as a Sunday lamb.

"*Fuck, you're kidding me. I thought that's why'd you be here in the first place. You just happened to show up randomly when the biggest free pot festival in the world is going on. It happens every year, it's called The Seattle Hempfest. There are like 100,000 stoners who show up from all over the world. Everyone s just tossing around pot like its rice at a wedding. They got two stages of bands, all these speakers. Woody Harrelson was there last year, and he was so stoned he could barely perform his speech. He kept fucking up and laughing, he was so fucking beyond baked dude. And this year Ed Rosenthal is gonna be there. He's like the biggest grower of pot in North America...*"

From on top of the high-rise you can see all of Seattle stretched below. It is magical beyond description. This is all too perfect. Barely here 12 hours and I've left such a corrosive dent that the ball will keep rolling unrelentingly for the next 11 days...

Rolling in Pat's truck scoping a park to sleep in, he gives a confused look and says: 'Do you just wanna crash at my house? *"Sure. Great."* "Why didn't you just ask?" *"'Cause that's not how I roll. I'm like a vampire – you gotta invite me in..."*

A NIHILIST AND NIHLISTIK TERRORIST, NO CONNECTION

Oh MySpace, you clever little devil. One quick peruse at the Seattle Public Library and the last-ditch email campaign worked elite. I now possess the cell numbers to over 40 local bands, and Steve Rock will also be promoting me on air, telling people what I look like and that I'll be lurking in the shadows.

First up is an Iraq vet named Draygen from a black/death metal band called Nihilistik Terrorist. He's security at Hempfest this year, and has pledged to get me backstage access. We shoot the breeze as he gives me a lift to The Funhouse, which I have declared as my official bum post for the week: *"The demo I'm working on now, the majority of the songs are 7-9 minutes long. The song names are 'Dethrone The False Messiah,' 'Hierarchy Of Heretics,' 'Preaching Nihilistik Terror' and 'Systematic Annihilation... The lyrics revolve around atheism, nihilism, terrorism, war. Not necessarily satanic, maybe more an atheist point of view. I just recruited the drummer from Morbidism. The stuff that generally influenced me is Excommunion, Angel Corpse, Destroyer 666 – the more cult underground. I got here about 2002 from LA to see what death metal was available, started getting into black metal. Not much of a scene here for that... I did some time in the army, went to Iraq in 2004."*

"Were you the clean up crew?"

Draygen: "The beginning crew... Overseas I started getting into booking and promoting bands all through my computer – Infernal Legion, Drawn And Quartered, Winds Of Pestilence, Unsanctified, Intestinal Strangulation. I think the biggest con in Seattle are the ego trips and the whole rock star attitude that kills the possibly great bands."

"What do you do for work?"

"The army gave me an opportunity to come up here. I work as a DOD contractor. My actual job term is 'Mutilation Specialist.' A lot of people are jealous when they hear that. Basically I go to different scrap yards, look at scrap metal and decide if its mutilated to DOD standards. Stand around with my arms crossed, look and say '*Yep... It's mutilated.*'"

"*Is the nu metal thing completely dead out here?*"

"The nu-metal wave is dead as far as your Korn and Slipknot type bands. The younger kids are just going to feed into what's popular. Piss on the commercial scene, they don't need our help. The radio friendly bands don't need our help, the people trying to make an easy buck out here, all those local metalcore bands – piss on them. They don't give a shit about people"

"*Do you want to comment on the Iraq thing? Do you think it's a hopeless situation?*"

"I can go on forever... To some extent you might find it hopeless, but it's a lot of democrats trying to screw it up for everybody. America's the type of country that doesn't like losing and that's where it could be heading if they get their way. For the year that I'd been out there – a year of hell obviously – there's a lot of shit that you go through. You come back, you're changed. All you can do is hope it doesn't come back and bite you in the ass."

"*Do you think that if they do get a government stabilized it will last? Do the people there actually want what we're trying to do, or do you think it's headed for civil war?*"

"I think the government might have a chance, but until the Sunni's and Shiites get their shit organized, I don't think its gonna happen. It could wind up like Israel and Palestine where they're just fighting each other for decades so long as you've got al Sadr, supposedly al Qaeda. And Bush probably won't leave until he gets all the oil he wants, but that'll never happen."

"*I heard they haven't even been able to get the pipelines up for more than eight hours, because militants keep blowing them up every time they look away.*"

"The main line is out in Basra, so they're just gonna keep on blowing it up..."

11pm at El Corazon, second day of the Tattoo series. I've been hanging out with Nihilist, the singer from In Memorium, who looks like a death metal Steve Buscemi. We pull tokes off his mock-cigarette one-hitter under that same viaduct, but homebum is nowhere to be found.

Nihilist is a minor legend in extreme metal folklore. Every band he's ever been in you will find burned amongst the CD collections of die-hards – Abazagorath, Lordgore, Hatefuckers, Engorged, Wraithen, and Stahlmantel, which is a side project of the main guy in Bethlehem, whom you all know I am a big fan of.

In Memorium are on the roster of the premier US black metal label Moribund Records, who have the elite graphic design/satanic propaganda attack hype-machine market cornered. Moribund is the undisputable king of the flavor-of-the-month BM club, packaged so ingeniously it's irresistible, and In Memorium's stock has been rising alongside labelmates Leviathan, Xasthur, Azaghal, Hacavitz, Azrael...

Nihilist is slapping on the corpse-paint and fixing his shredded, blood-caked white dress shit while the head of El Corazon's security keeps eyeballing me. *"What's up?"* I ask. Hey looks me over again, squinting: *"You look so fucking familiar..."* Same on my part, which is strange, because I feel like I've known this guy forever.

Turns out to be Johnny Pettibone, the vocalist of HIMSA, which are one of the major metalcore pigeon-holed bands today. They recently toured with Danzig, Behemoth, Chiamara and Mortiis on the Misfits reunion circuit, been getting airplay on MTV, and have been on the road 4 years.

This is the first show they've done since declaring hiatus a year ago, and it is THE moment for them. Their first major record is about to be released by Century Media, and soon they will be off to Europe for a six-week tour with As I Lay Dying, Darkest Hour & Maroon...

HIMSA

Johnny Pettibone: "I grew up outside Seattle in a small logging community 40 minutes away. We were all in hardcore bands in the 90's and we always played together... The great thing about Seattle hardcore is we never pigeonholed ourselves with that, we always loved metal too. The band actually started in 1997 out of the ashes of a hardcore band called TRIAL. It was all completely different members, the only original left is Derrick the bass player. I came in 2000 after moving from New York. I was working for Sick Of It All, I was a guitar tech.

"How'd you land that gig?"

"Again, just Seattle hardcore. Them coming through here, becoming friends, my old band playing with them. My old drummer went to New York before I did and said they needed someone to work cheap, string guitars on the road. I'd always looked up to those guys..."

"Tell me about the new album."

"It's called *Summon In Thunder*, it's our first for Century Media. We didn't think we'd make it this far, our third record being accepted by a label like that. They took us on at a really good point. The new record is about inspiration, being where I am today, living in this city. Being surrounded by great musicians and great influences. Seattle's always kind of done things on their own, even with the huge blowup in the 90's. It's kept its honesty and organic mentality. We're just so far off in the corner a lot of times we get missed. Like tonight, it's all heavy bands, but all different genres. We like playing shows like that. That's what *Summon In Thunder* is – it's a metaphor for what has made me who I am and what has made this band. We come from the ethics of the DIY punk and hardcore scene. We kept evolving, went out on the road and made people see what HIMSA was really about. We stayed on the road 4 years, pounding out 'Courting Tragedy & Disaster' and 'Hail Horror' on Prosthetic Records. We just had a year off writing and recording the new record.

"How was the Danzig tour?"

"It was fuckin' probably the best month of my life. As a young kid I was a Misfits fan, as is everyone from this background. He was one of my main influences – not as vocal sounding but the way he does things. Yes, he is a businessman, and he has a long history behind him. But he always takes care of his own things. He picks the bands he wants for his tour, he does his own art direction, he does all his recordings. He's very hands on... But for us to do that tour, and for him to do that Misfits set on it was just momentous. Every night I felt like I was a 13 year old kid."

"The metalcore tag – you guys were around long before it became trendy...

"I think we got pigeonholed because of bands we toured with. In the structure of what mainstream thinks metalcore is – an At The Gates riff with a Hatebreed breakdown. We don't write like that. I see us as more of a thrash metal band. We grew up on Integrity, Cro-Mags – hardcore bands that had a crossover sound. The 90's hardcore scene here, that was the sound. It was a heavier, chunkier sound then the straight-up fast punk riffs. But metalcore, it's just another tag that the mainstream gives to categorize something. Granted, that scene is really big right now, but its kind of like nu-metal where its going slowly away. When I see Hatebreed, that's what I want to hear. When it's The Haunted, that's what I want to see. I don't mesh those two together. These kids think hardcore bands, that breakdown – well Slayer wrote the first breakdown on *Reign In Blood*. Kids don't get that. Young kids, you know, you're striving for an identity. I've seen it come and go. It was the hot thing for a minute."

"What do you think is the next big thing? It seems that a lot of these metalcore bands are starting to jump ship to play doom and experimental."

"I totally agree. I think its young kids finding who they are and growing out of it because so many bands playing it has gotten watered down and monotonous. A lot of bands are going heavier and I think that 80's thrash throw-back is hitting, bands like Municipal Waste."

"You like Toxic Holocaust?"

"Yeah, all those bands. There is so much music that fucking people don't even know about. I hope it remains that way because I don't want another form of music that I love kind of fuckin' ruined. But I'm not an elitist. I'd rather have people on my side then listening to Fallout Boy, Godsmack or something. We're out to survive, but we're out for some longevity and something we're still passionate about. We got to tour with Danzig and we got to tour with Cradle Of Filth, but it hasn't changed us at all. We're still humble, we'll still play basement shows. That's where we come from and that's where I'm comfortable. I'm not comfortable on a huge stage with a barrier. I need kids diving on me and crawling and shit."

"Who do you think are the best in Seattle?"

"Downstairs the next band playing is In Memorium. They've never got the recognition I thought they deserved. I'm bummed out kids don't give them a chance or haven't been able to see them. Claymore is an awesome tech band, just fucking brilliant. A lot of crust bands, kind of pissed hardcore bands like Owen Hart. They're fucking so pissed. Seattle has gone through this transition – a lot of kids are taking it back and doing hall shows again and not relying on clubs and promoters. DIY is so important because a lot of bands come through and don't have the potential to play a big club because the overhead. You gotta survive on the road."

"Well, basics covered, do you got something weird and totally off topic to tell me about yourself?

"Well I have this huge fear… Actually this is the first time ever talking about it, 'cause I always felt weird talking about it... I have a huge phobia of little people."

"Like dwarves?

"It's nothing personal."

"Like you have nightmares of midgets coming after you?"

"Yeah dude, I can't watch *Wizard Of Oz*, I can't watch *Time Bandits*. It stems from being 3 years old at the circus. I thought it was another kid like me, and I approached it turned around with clown makeup and this deep voice. Just scared the shit out of me. Ever since this traumatic experience… Honestly, you ask anyone that works here, I get shakes. I feel bad 'cause it's not their fault. You know, just part of life, how they were born. I get fucking clammy hands, I freak out. What sucks is there's a fella in Buffalo that is a fan of ours and he's always up front singing along. I make it through the set but he's always there singing every word and just like FUCKIN A' man. I need to get over this fucking thing. 35 years old and it's like get a hold of yourself. And I try, it's just…"

"I'm terrified of whales."

"Of whales? Wow."

\   *"I used to have these nightmares of being underwater in this black sea and these things rubbing up against me and I'm under the water enough where I can't get to the surface no matter what and just… Whales. Fucking freaks me out…"*

"Yeah, I'm afraid of the ocean."

"And manatees freak me out."

"They're like the most curious, mellow creatures"

"Yeah, but they're like big and gray and shit… Well… um… nightmare tour story?"

"When I was in Undertow we were on tour in Southern California, and we were so running out of gas. Pulled over in Compton and this guy comes running across the street in front of our van. All of a sudden three other dudes are chasing him, like 40 feet behind, and blast him with a fucking shotgun. The guy went down. I never seen anyone killed like that before. We hit it and ended up running out of gas a couple miles down the freeway. It was so insane to see something like that. They shot him and just knew he was dead. I mean it hit him directly and he just flew. They turned around like it was no business. Holy shit you know, holding that much power in your hand. That's life to them, this struggle to survive. That was just insanely brutal…"

SOLIVAGANT HAZE

Outside the venue the show has cleared out and I'm enjoying my night as a bum. I'm listening to the Charles Manson *White Album* on my headphones with shoes and socks, pressed against the side of the building. Johnny is the last one out and before he jumps into his car he looks like he's about to ask if I need a place to crash. I just keep singing "Sick City" and salute him military style. He nods and drives off in his black Firebird. No partying with rock stars is going to spoil my fun.

Now what? *Final Fantasy Mode: Deluxe Edition.* It still hasn't rained, and it's perfect 70 degrees. I'm wide awake a little after midnight, and its time to explore. That one magical viaduct aside, it looks like Seattle was intentionally built to fuck over the homeless population. There are no real natural shelters, no accessible bridges to hide like a troll under, lest you hop a 20 foot freeway wall.

Yet the streets are pleasant and compact, life still buzzes everywhere – coffee shops and hipster teriyaki joints, quasi-Coney Islands and burger franchises. A few blocks from El Corazon a movie theatre has a half dozen crusties passed out beneath the marquee; around the corner is another bum-crawling alley. Everyone passed out, bodies lying motionless like a Mongolian slaughter campaign.

I try sleeping with my duffel bag as a pillow on the patio of a yuppie bistro, underneath a glass table with green umbrella. No good, no comfort – an arrest waiting to happen, and its awfully cold. Tack on a third pair of pants, another shirt… A few more inconvenient stops and I find a warehouse garage door opening dug into a 10 story building. There is a blue port-a-potty with a small hiding space out of sight and encircled by nitrous tanks. Hopefully I don't flop around in my sleep too much, 'cause my legs might get crushed by a semi truck…

* * * * *

It was so cold behind that port-a-potty I dreamt of being handed a blanket that actually physically warmed me by its mental apparition. It was like a subconscious defense mechanism my body created. In dreamland I was living in a world that resembled *Street Trash,* and had a 63 year old oil-stained hag for a wife.

I awoke not far from that manifestation; freezing, 4:30am Sunday. No point in dragging this out – just find a franchise, get some coffee, warm my bones. I push Starbucks for two hours on a single decaf. The customers look unnerved & the staff wants me to split, but they are scared to confront me. The Drawn and Quartered record was so loud on my headphones that it drowned out the Kenny G serenades emitting from the 'Bucks plasma-screen jukebox.

As I prepare to leave I use the restroom. I turn the corner and find that I've essentially been in the snack lobby of the Hyatt Hotel. Luckily bum-o-flauge works many ways. I cruise by the security guard with my duffel bag and backpack, faking him out easy. He bats no eye, convinced I belong there. The bathroom is so high class that the toilet stalls have full wooden doors instead of that swinging metal hinge where you can tell if someone's inside.

A free makeshift hotel room, and truly high class. I close myself inside and curl up on the emasculate floor. I'm about to go under when I realize – *just like the Bistro* – I'm definitely going to get arrested if they catch me. Paranoia rules out serious rest so I initiate Plan B, which is generally Plan A in all other such previous scenarios...

I linger in the hallway awaiting a renter who has the security card as to swish open the elevator door. *30 seconds, check*; *4ᵗʰ floor, check – last obstacle?* Security card needed to enter the gym & jacuzzi. As I reach the door I see the murky silhouette of a woman through the thick white glass. *Right place, right time – BAM...* I'm in, and I'm totally alone...

The only issue the security cameras. I slide on my shorts and pretend like I'm working out to appease the Electric Eye, then deftly hop into the sauna. It kills my sore throat, then I happily cannonball into the Jacuzzi on its hottest, bubble frenzy setting.

I milk it for an hour before I'm interrupted by a graying couple in white towels. I look like a demon with my mohawk dripping spider-legs, middle fingers painted black, fresh tattoo of a skull on my chest which reads 313 EXPATRIATE. I let them have it lest security hamper my H2O fetish, and soak in the shower for another 25. Wrapped in towels I nod off for a half hour on the locker room bench, my skin more prune-like then Submariners forearm...

Downtown there are now thousands rushing around. I'm determined to get some actual sleep, and have stolen a crisply white Hyatt towel for a blanket. I push it as far as I can to the library before discovering the jutting glass window display of a tuxedo store. I crawl underneath and it reeks like piss; everywhere there's crusted up green & white pigeon gifts like Kandahar landmines. *The slumber of champions...*

I'm dead under for two hours until some idiot keeps poking me to ask if I'm alright: "I'M *A FUCKING BUM YOU PIECE OF SHIT! LET ME FUCKING SLEEP!!!*" The tuxedo store employee smoking a

Newport spots me and kicks me out and I head towards the library for an internet rampage.

I've never seen a metropolis so well laid out, efficient and clean. Every denizen that whizzes past me has a laptop slung around their shoulders. Some are of the wall-street lot, but many have outlandish, retro-rock amalgams going on – like that grunge look of 1993 but primered with an earthy, futurist shell. You spot hobnail boots & zany Koopa-world haircuts from the Dennis Hopper *Mario Bros.* Even the sewer caps have carved Mayan-like engravings…

Busses everywhere, bicyclists gliding – more public transport then independent automobiles. This is because it is impossible to park downtown unless you have $10 for a garage, secondly because the eco-friendly mindset believes in environmental responsibility over lightning quick automation.

Every four stores is a coffee shop, and every other building is a high-rise apartment or dwarf skyscraper… *Wi-Fi bleeds through every pour of concrete, talking trash-cans with artificial intelligence…* SF-like hills paved with concrete, businesses dug into the side of slopes…

Pike Place Market is the main tourist hub, a fisherman's village turned mini-mall running down the edge of First Avenue. Huge sea creatures sold wholesale, men with rubber goulashes and yellow rain-hats pawning prawn & sea bass like auctioneers.

The library is a futuristic Willy Wonka castle of information with Kubrick-esque architectural design. It borders between futurist utopia and superb Haunted House attraction. Every turn is a mind-altering new twist of the literature universe. The massive glass overhang is like a glacial cliff, neon-yellow walls of pure steel; ten levels of oddly shaped corridors & computer rooms. Elevators that speak, an escalator with floating eyeballs & talking projected lips blabbing incoherent jabber…

With all the pizzazz the Central Branch has to offer, ironically there's nowhere to just comfortably read a book. Areas are supposedly designated for that, but that's where you find the stinking hobo mobs warming from the street. You can't just zone out and read a page – you're devoured by the perpetual splash of loud colors, movement & intensity surrounding you. It is hopeless as a cry in deep space…

SINDIOS AND THE AZTEC APPARITION

3pm, the Osaka Grill; being introduced to teriyaki. Eddy Rock (*real name, scouts honor*) has bought me this gargantuan plate of chicken & rice that's unbeatable at $5 a combo. Eddy's from Mexico City – this short, cartoon-character of a hyper-kinetic with a thick accent and intense blue eyes...

He is the puppet-master of Sindios, a local thrash/black crossover that has this sort of KMFDM Brute, fascist empire graphic design obsession with a black Squid symbol inside red & white arm bands. All of Sindios' imagery runs the lines of police state brutality, illuminati control, governmental subversion...

"What's minimum wage out here? Eddy Rock: "I think its $7.35. *"In Michigan it's like $5.20.* "Can people live with that? *"No. But that's what everybody works apparently. Detroit's like... Michigan's destroyed. The entire economy's shot, it was all auto and now it's all gone. Ford's such a terrible company anyway... You're from Mexico City right? What's the economy like?*

"Pretty fun, biggest city in the world. There's always something to do any hour of the day. I could say that it used to be one of the greatest places on earth until the late 80's.

"What changed it?

"I don't know. I guess the United States decided to invade everything with McDonalds. So let's put it this way: A combo is like $5, $6 dollars right? The money conversion, the same $6 will be like 70 pesos. You pay the same to eat there for the same thing, The only difference is that here your gonna get $5 an hour paid working there, and then your going to get $5 a day working there. So who's making profit? Who's going broke?

"Ever eat mushrooms and go to the top of the Aztec pyramids?

"I did that last year.

"Oh wow... I've asked that randomly to people for the past 10 years and you're the first. What kind of hallucinations did you get?"

"I thought it was entertaining but then again when I was climbing back down it was like '*fuck I don't wanna do this.*' When the pyramids were built no one was allowed to look at the king, so they designed a way that you could not walk straight forward while looking up. The steps were like half the size of your foot, way too steep. And you have to walk like a primate."

"So it's like groveling to the king all the way up... Do you think they were built by aliens?"

"I don't know if they were built by them but maybe their architects were. Down in the south, one of the scriptures on the wall has this perfect portrait of an astronaut. But that's from the Mayan culture."

"And that shit directly says 'space people came down and taught us this' on their hieroglyphs."

"Most of the research tends to be buried because most of those things now are just tourist attractions. Last year there was this huge thing because they were building a Walmart next to one."

"Yeah, it is sacrilege, but wouldn't the Mayans appreciate a Walmart next to their tribe?"

"(Laughs) I don't think so... People did well without cell phones and VCR's. I don't watch TV so I don't know. I get mad when I watch TV. I'd rather just read a book."

"Why did you move to Seattle?"

"It started as a vacation. I have a friend from Mexico City that lives here. At that moment I was working for a record label NEMS, we weren't doing that good. We only used to license things, so we'd press Mexican versions of The Gathering or whatever hip thing metal-wise. And just throw in a few extra tracks to make a more attractive domestic version instead of the import. Supposedly make them cheaper. The original company was based in Argentina, they opened up a branch in Chili, Bolivia, Beirut, and one in Mexico. Thing is we didn't do too good. If we did we didn't know where the money was so that was a bad thing for me."

"When did that end?"

"Around 2000. So I was without a job and my friend told me to stay a few weeks. My friend had his own band. They had this guitar player that later went on to Nightrage and then later Dissection."

"Does that guy live out here?"

"He was from France but lived here a few years. That was Sol Negro. Doomish black metal, the slow pace. I'm 37 so I'm more into the old school thrash/death thing. People say we're black, I say we're not. We're just one band doing our thing. I play guitar and scream, we're a three piece. I go for the high-pitch. Three years after hear we are. We have one record and we're working on the second."

"What's the first?"

"*Modern Plagues*. There's a Mexican version with a tiny label but we haven't really heard from them."

"Is it true that there are more Sepultura t-shirts in Mexico then Metallica?"

"Close. Maybe since those countries live in a less populous way, obviously their concept of heavy music is heavier. It involves the way you live. Here you know... hard, metallic, all those things. Yeah, but come on, you ask your parents *'hey can I get money to go to the mall?'* That doesn't happen in places like that. So mostly you're going to a flea market and buying a bootlegged tape from some strange band you've never heard of because it has blood and death all over the cover."

"People are more religious too."

"That's one of the reasons because when you go *'ah fuck this, fuck that,'* it is actually insulting. Here, nobody cares. Even Christians don't care. Look at our preachers – *'Someone has to go shoot Hugo Chavez.'* There religion is taken seriously... I have a funny story. I was probably 17, this was in '87. My first band was sort of a black metal band, but we were singing in Spanish. Everybody tends to speak in English for sound reasons. When will they ever 'make it' in Spanish? On the radio you hear it in English and it's just noise. But in Spanish they hear exactly what you're saying. So we had songs you know, titles 'Spitting On The Bible,' 'Ejaculating Blood On Christ's Face.' People started liking it and making kind of big just for doing it in Spanish. We got invited to this radio show where they also invited a Catholic priest to help us leave our life of sin and blasphemy."

"So it was like a talk show?"

"Yeah, that was great. Especially when you're young and you don't know why you're saying what you're saying (laughs). So according to that priest we were abused when we were kids so we're taking it out on god. That was funny."

"Tell me about the power metal band you have going on."

"It's called Calvaria. I've been friends with the singer since I'm like 15. He's always been into the Helloween, Primal Fear sort of thing. That band's been around 10 years. They play big shows. They did the Monteray music festival with Twisted Sister and DIO. This last tour we did was with Symphony X. Every time a band from another country goes to Mexico there's never a shitty show. Maybe the band would be shitty but the support would be there. There's always a 1000+ people for whatever band. I went to see Satyricon down there. Here they'll probably play for 300, there 1500. Going to shows like that is an experience. They tend to become tiny festivals, so there's booths with all labels selling shirts and magazines and posters. There's also this flea market every Saturday for the past 30 years and it only involves music. They only sell records, shirts, DVD's, and everything rock related. You walk and there's like 5 stands of death metal, then one is black metal, one is power metal, punk rock. You'll go crazy. You'll walk outside and there's the punk bar, there's the metal bar. It's always packed."

"What's just something remarkably bizarre and when you tell people they think you're a pathological liar?"

"I thought I saw this ghost and to this day nobody believes me. I remember it very well because that comet Haley that comes every 70 something years, it landed on '87. My mother took us to this place half a mile from the pyramids to go camping and watch that comet at night. I was with my brother and some friend from school. We walked from our campsite, we were gathering small pieces of wood for our fire, and then I hear my brother and friend '*Hey Eddy, stand still.*' The first thing I thought, this is a tiger or something dumb like a dog. I turn around and I see both of them running. Yeah, great joke… Now I see why they're running. There's like this lady, like a foot off the ground walking. But she wasn't attacking us or nothing. She's just like a transient, just passing by. Obviously I started running…"

"Was she misty white?"

"A little bit, and glowy. When we got back to our tent it was like '*what did you see?*' I saw this this this this that. We all saw the same thing. I don't believe in collective hallucinations, I don't."

"I had a bunch of friends, they snorted a bunch of K and were on liquid LSD, and they were on ecstasy too, and there was about 20 kids in this small room after a rave in Detroit. They're all out of their minds, staring at the wall in K-holes and playing video games at 4am, and then out of nowhere everyone in the room freaks out and starts screaming because all of them saw a gremlin. Like a demon rip out of the wall, BLARG at them and then jump back in the wall. All of them saw this at the same time and ran out of the house. Neighbors were freaking out, there's like 20 kids running through the streets."

"Yeah, how come you gonna see the same thing?"

"So anyway, what's the message of your band?"

"Lyrically I tend to be paranoid… There is no al Qaeda, there is no Osama bin Laden… You're being watched, you're being spied upon. Right before your eyes there are things that are happening and we just sit down and don't do anything. We cannot start a revolution obviously but we can still learn, and inform, and preach."

"Do you think it's a hopeless situation?"

"It's not hopeless, but we're lazy. In my optimistic belief there's gotta be 1 in 5 other people here that know what's going on. That we're being lied to, that taxes are not used for what we think. Our federal reserve is actually a bank in the UN. We're not even legally supposed to pay taxes. Then our tax money is used to pay the internal debt of the country. It's not for building roads. Fine, we're going to conquer the whole planet. What are we going to get in return? 'Cause I'm not going to support you 'cause '*wow I love the flag.*' Fuck that. I'm not getting an education. I'm not getting anything. The only way I think this will change in when you see 30 million Americans in the street."

"Do you think Bush would leave office even for that?"

"He would leave his office and they'd be more conscious of their actions. They're free to do anything they want because nobody can say anything. And if you say anything '*well go move to Puerto Rico.*' Come on man. The ones that are saying that the most are the ones that aren't getting anything. Especially education because our government wants us to be stupid because that way we're going to believe that Iraq had something with the 9/11 bombings."

"What I'm surprised by is that the US government just didn't plant weapons in Iraq after the fact so they could say there was our proof. Why would they not even bother? Why be that lazy?"

"You remember when they were trying to get us into that mess there was this huge ad going across the nation that said '*lets support our president*' and said things about Hussein like '*oh, he spends too much money on the military, he's an evil tyrant.*' Wait a minute. We had an embargo that went from 1991 until the day we invaded. With that embargo, that involved no countries helping them. And if you went and helped them, you're gonna be part of the embargo too. How is he gonna spend money on the military? How's he going to support his troops? That invasion was well planned. Ok, lets starve him to death, invade him, 2 or 3 days that country is ours. The second biggest oil reserve on the planet."

"I have a USA Today printed right before the invasion listing the best/worst case scenarios. Worst case scenario was 6 months of more of continued fighting with a 6 billion dollar price tag. We're up to a projected 3 trillion long-term and nearly 5 years in."

"If we stay ignorant, they're going to take advantage of us. It's not about going in the street and starting a war. Just be educated. Yes, we're all gonna die, but why do it with that humiliation? You died a dumbass. It's not supposed to be like that. Everyone looks to America like WOW. Everyone wants to move up here.

"But it's a Big Shiny Prison."

"There you go… You really think this thing about immigration? Let's blame it on these people from Latin America."

"The guest worker program is just legal slave labor."

"'*Thanks, the apple picking season is over, go back to your country and do whatever. You're not allowed to come back by the way.*' Because you're not allowed to have it again."

"It's a one time only thing?"

"'*Thanks for feeding my people, now go starve somewhere.*' People that come here, they don't want to slack off. Nobody wants to live off welfare. I don't think there's a single person that likes that. And here, this job is designed for Mexicans. This one is for Arabs. It becomes this oppressed monopoly of things. I'm destined to work in a kitchen all my life just because my skin is like this? Automatically I'm stupid? I don't like that."

"What's the feud between Northern and Southern Mexicans? I know someone in prison in California, which is a really racist prison system. Everyone is segregated to color, and he says the Northern and Southern Mexicans hate each other for some reason…"

"It's like this conflict of identity, more or less. The people that live on this side of the border that are Mexicans, most of them are here very young so there is no nostalgic feeling about their country. So Southern Mexicans don't think they're Mexicans. They think they're Americans. And these people are Americans no matter what their color is. Well they're gonna identify with people from their native roots. Because you cannot identify with white people."

"I can't identify with white people."

"(Laughs) Then there's this ingestion of '*can you people live in this neighborhood?*' You been to Chicago right? The South, predominantly black and Hispanic. Seattle, go to the south – black and Hispanic people. Why is it always the south? I think cities are planned that way maybe. LA, Southwest. I was reading that – this only belonged to Seattle – that only that side of the city was destined for the non-white. Supposedly that law is gone, but the settlement has been there for a hundred years. If they are coincidences they are very deep ones…"

SCORCHED EARTH AND THRASH HOLOCAUST

As appealing as Joe Grindo Fest sounds, I'm inclined to hit The Funhouse for the Sunday night thrash show. Hatchet and Fog of War are on tour from the Bay Area, and local band Scorched Earth is headlining. I've been in communication with Scorched Earth guitarist/screamer Terry McCorriston for the past few months, who also happens to be Nihilist's roommate.

I find Terry in the BBQ area after he recognizes the old Bethlehem back-patch. He's a classic metal guy with a PBR – tall, long black hair, leather biker jacket, sweet Lemmy facial hair tribute shaved especially for the show. He is originally from Alaska, and talks in a slow, monotone fashion that makes you think he might be a bore, but he has a surprising knack for gut-busting pop culture references: *"It used to be a pretty big scene here back in the day, before grunge. B.C. – 'Before Cobain.' That's my saying, copyright 2007 McCorriston Industries."*

"There was a pretty big metal scene here a long time ago. A lot of bands like Queensryche, Metal Church, Forced Entry, The Accused, Bitter End. There was a pretty big thrash scene but when grunge came along, everyone traded in their big Reebok high-tops for Doc Martins and shit. The grunge scene here, I never liked it in the first place. I've been totally into metal this whole time. There were virtually no shows throughout the 90's."

"How old were you when the grunge thing hit?"

Terry: "I was about 17. I'm 32 years old now."

"It just got totally overwhelmed?"

"Pretty much. There was also the 'teen dance ordinance' which didn't allow all ages shows for the most part. Like you needed a million dollars worth of insurance. They repealed the ordinance in 2000. As a result you see more all age's kids at the bigger shows. Around here people generally will come out to support you if they perceive that you've been popular somewhere else. Tonight I don't know what to expect. It's Sunday night, it's a total thrash show. Fog of War and Hatchet are from the Bay."

"When did Scorched Earth form?"

"It goes back a long way. It started as a one-man band in 1994. We were called Nazgul at the time. We have three albums now. They're all self-released on our label Conqueror Worm Records. A lot of bands don't seem to get recognition out here by national press. We get letters from all over the world, but we've never been signed to a decent label.

Part of that is because we read the contract and a lot of those you get totally fucked on. We've done it the DIY route, very punk rock although I haven't followed punk in decades. That's what actually got me started playing music."

What's the big metal bar?

"King Cora, Linda's... The metal scene here's weird now because you have a lot of guys who come from the hipster aspect of it. Then there's the guys that have been doing it all this time. Then of course there's guys who claim that they play thrash metal and it's like dude, come on. You said you sound like Sodom and you're punk rock."

"What do you think of Carlos The Jackyl?"

"He's a fat guy languishing in France and he's irrelevant..."

Terry excuses himself to grab another brew, and Scorched Earth drummer Josh Hanenburg immediately sits down. He's a jolly spazz with a shaved head & glasses, talking with his hands like a frantic opera conductor: *"The other day at practice we were talking about the good old days. In Bremerton we had this really shitty club called Natasha's. Everyone in Seattle was forced to go. Slayer played there, GBH, Accused, Forced Entry"*...

"We were also remarking on how things were much more dangerous. Back then you see a guy in an Iron Maiden shirt and you knew they were on something or they wanted to kick your ass for money. Less then 10 years later everyone with a metal shirt is really cool, really mellow, no one really dangerous. Back then it was a subculture that allowed them to pursue whatever fucked up activities they were after. Natasha's is now a junkyard. So I had to wait 13 years before there was a scene again, before we had people we could relate."

"What other bands were you in?"

Josh Hanenburg: "I was in a really awful band called Suicide Culture in the 90's. Like the worst time ever to be in a metal band. It was impossible to bring people to shows and get them interested. And you were always playing with the next Korn wannabe band, the next fuckin' Limp Bizkit band. Everyone wanted to be Pantera back then."

"Got any random, funny stories for me?"

"Ted's a teacher in grade school. Asshole Ted will not sell our stuff to the kids who ask for it 'cause he's worried about his job. We had these kids downloading his band, and they were asking if I was the crazy one. I was joking around in one interview about being molested by my uncle in front of the camera. I thought I made it obvious that I was joking but the kids blasted him, it's all they talked about. Kids will write on their homework *'oh by the way Mr. Kohn, I got $50, can I buy a shirt?'* He doesn't want to hand out t-shirts with upside down crosses on them, you know? It'll piss off the wrong parent. We got a crop there, a lot of kids, just money waiting to be had. Fucking let us play an assembly or something."

"What you need to do is get a big choir of elementary kids like Therion."

"I'm the proggy pretentious nerd, and they've trashed every idea I had about making things bigger and more interesting. If it were up to me I'd have orchestras. Actual cannons firing off. I like MANOWAR, but I also like YES."

"What about ABBA?"

"ABBA is truly the devils music. As much as I profess to hate them, one second of their music is firmly implanted in my brain for weeks. 70's prog rock or modern black metal, that's what I'm into."

"I love Seattle, I seriously want to relocate here and bring a bunch of people."

"The guys in Skelator, their squat is called 'Snake Mountain.' They keep bringing up people all over the place to live here. So we're slowly getting this young crop of European power metal guys. It's really weird. They love Primal Fear, any band with a sword on their cover. I love Rhapsody. See, that's pretentious big-scope music. It's the most idiotic fantasy stories I've ever read, but when put to music with that kind of drive you're like *'YEAH, FUCK YEAH! THE CRYSTAL SWORD!! THE WHITE EAGLE!! FUCK YEAH, AWESOME!!!'* And if you have Christopher Lee narrating, anything that comes out his mouth is fucking cool…"

FUNERAL AGE OVER PEPPER STEAK (TAKE III)

Monday, wake up covered in cat hair at the Scorched Earth guy's apartment. Last thing I clearly remember is them destroying the place with a vociferous Bathory/Motorhead/Destroyer 666 assault, and Terry goofily stroking his "regenerating beard" onstage which had everyone rolling: *"It's what gives me my metal power."*

Nihilist is absent, Terry is at work, Halloween masks & Lovecraft paraphernalia are everywhere. I take advantage of the house line and call every band on my list. Whoever responds first is the lottery winner of the afternoon… *And the lucky contestant is…*

Mr. Kevin Bedra, of the death metal band Funeral Age. Ironically, it's the same group that formed from the ashes of Hanenburg's "*awful 90's band*" Suicide Culture. Bedra picks me up at the West Seattle library and by 3pm we're gouging Pepper Steak at a Chinese restaurant called HO-WIN: "*I started listening to metal in 1983 when I was in 6th grade. The first album I ever bought was Defenders of the Faith. In '85 I started to get into Metallica, Slayer, Possessed, Venom. In the 90's I was listening to Morgoth, a little Morbid Angel. You have to understand I was raised in a home where if I didn't go to church twice a month I couldn't live there, and I came home and all my metal albums were burnt.*"

"*What is your message as an individual?*"

"I'm 25. I have a job, the music is what I do because that's what's in my heart. I think when it all comes down to it – heaven, hell, whatever – there's gonna be a time in everybody's life when they're gonna look back and they're gonna ask themselves '*did I do what I really wanted to do?*' That's the driving force. It isn't me pushing something along that really isn't gonna happen. I've been fortunate enough to work with guys who are genuine people. It's more so that relationship I'm concerned with, because of that the music is borne. If you're playing in a band where you feel like you're dragging someone along, let them go. It costs friendships, it costs relationships. I've broken up with women that wanted me to become this domestic person. I don't have regrets as far as decisions of that nature. All you have is your vision and your heart – going against them causes spiritual pain, like you don't know what's wrong. A lot of people, it drives them to suicide. It might not look like we are successful, but right now its better than ever. I think the people that have gone away and done their own thing, its all been for the best. I played with a couple people in Scorched Earth and they've done something great with it. I think it's turned out to be better than they could've expected. At the end of the day, at the end of my life, that's what it's going to come down to. If anybody in this world tries to tell you to go anywhere that isn't in your heart, I think that they're lying to you… My dad calls and asks if I want a job at the shipyard. He's asked me that for years. In his mind he has my best interest, but it's not where my heart is. I think that money is an illusion and people get wrapped up in it. It can take people away if they give it that power. They kind of lie to themselves. Terry from Scorched Earth, he's about my age, and he's in the same boat. When I see him play – all these guys that have been in these bands for years – it inspires me because I know they are just going with their heart. It's because of that that this form of music transcends age and generation gaps. I'm 35, our new drummer is 18, our guitar player is 21. There's no separation. I think in that way that's how this type of music has lasted. You can go to any part of the world and ask these same types of questions and they'll have the same types of answers."

"How do you feel about 'Metalocaplypse?'"

"I think it's fucking stupid. I think they're trying to make a cartoon out of the person they think I am, and trying to sell it to me. They're trying to sell me to me…"

BEER METAL WORLD HEADQUARTERS

8pm now, getting dark. Kevin dropped me off at The Funhouse checkpoint, but once again my hobo fun is spoiled by punk rock legends. When Justin Hofmann (*from Galway Arms*) said everything would be taken care of, he wasn't pissing around. Every single band in their network has been notified, and all are raring to ride the propaganda train.

Justin scoops me up and plops me off at the Beer Metal house, where the bartender from the Galway (Adam Houghton) resides. One step in the door and the funk of a thousand burned joints coats every shred of furniture & carpet threading as if a herd of skunks were frightened by a galloping surge of rambunctious minotaur…

The punks emerge from their hiding spots like Aliens swarming on Colonial Marines. They fill my arms with a dozen records + a bundle of flyers & bumper stickers – bands like 7 Year Old Blind Girl, Potty Mouth Society, Kill The Precedent, Dingbatz & The Greedies…

The studio downstairs is pro, computer equipment everywhere. You'd think they were Office Max gnomes stealing shit at night like the buggers do your socks: *"This is the Beer Metal studio where we record all our bands. We do the production here ourselves – CD burners, CD printers, the works. We all bust our asses so we can do this."*

"In the three years that I've doing Beer Metal Records I've probably invested close to $50,000 of my own money. I seriously think we've put close to $100,000 in this label over the past 3 years and seen no return whatsoever. That's why we're broke all the time, because we put everything into this. Most would've given up by now. All of this gear, all these CD's, these are other bands records that Jeff and I paid for. Shawn paid for all of his own studio equipment."

"I work 36 hours a week at the bar, and I easily put another 40 in front of my computer booking bands, trying to keep things updated on our website, trying to write new songs, and on top of that trying to keep a relationship with my girlfriend. If it ever came down to this or my girlfriend, it'd be this. That's no joke."

"That's my problem with women too. The revolution always comes first…"

Adam Houghton: "As much as I wish to have a staff and delegate authority, when all is said and done, I <u>HAVE</u> to do this 'cause no one else is going to do it, and its worth every single penny that I'm never, ever going to see again. If I wanted to make money, I would've gone to college."

"Tell me about Seattle."

"The Seattle music scene is fucking retarded and hasn't meant anything since 1997. You ever get a zit in the middle of your back and you try to pop it and it hurts really, really bad? And then one day you can finally squeeze all that little bit out? That's kind of where we're at right now – the second you can squeeze that little bit of goo shit out."

"Why 1997? What was the downfall?"

"TRIAL broke up. TRIAL was the greatest band this town has ever seen, I don't care what anyone says."

Jeff Little: "Who the fuck is TRIAL?"

"Exactly, that's what I'm saying. There's like 4 people who know who TRIAL is. In 95, 96, there were only three local bands that meant anything to me – Blotch, TRIAL, and Harkening. Nowadays no one cares. People are more concerned with making sure each one of their hair follicles is in place and staring at what kind of shoes the other guy is wearing. It's all about the fashion, not the thrashin."

"But you still have plenty of hope?"

"There's a lot of bullshit, but a quarter of the bands are pretty good. There's like 900 bands though. Everybody and their mom is in a band, that's why the scene sucks. That and local government killing All Ages shows."

"Mayor Nichols and his predecessor Lowry – those guys fucked it up with the Teen Dance Ordinance. It basically made it impossible for All Ages shows to happen so it went completely underground. Then all these kids were forced to wear their hair over their eyes and girl pants. All the old rad clubs like The Rock Candy and The Deviate and The Off Ramp and The Velvet Elvis – they catered to All Ages. Kids would come home with twisted ankles and a black eye and the parents would complain... 14 years later and I don't regret any of the things I did. It was people like my contemporaries whose parents were much, much older. Their kid comes home with a little scrape on his arm and they hold the clubs accountable when the kids are willingly beating the shit out of each other. So for 10 years kids have stood around staring at each others Adidas and Nikes... I remember the first time I ever heard about a mosh pit I was like 11, it was this kids older brother, he'd talk about buying tickets to the mosh pit at a Metallica concert. He made it seem like there were a 1000 guys wearing 5 foot tall Christmas tree spikes on their jackets trying to kill each other. It scared the crap out of me. When I was 12 I saw my first mosh pit and was like, *'Well this isn't so bad. In fact this is a lot of fun.'* The pits used to be violent and now kids are afraid of getting elbows. Any show that's associated with Beer Metal Records is usually a violent, thrashing show. Not violent in a negative way, but in a fun, physical way. We're the last generation of people who aren't teenagers who actually give a fuck about thrashing. All the kids between the ages of 15-19 are pussies. It's coming back now 'cause all these kids see how fun it is to thrash around and hate everything. Its fun to hate everything..."

"I heard you bitching about skinheads at the bar, you said some brilliant things..."

"The skinhead movement in this town hasn't meant a goddamn thing. There's a few really rad traditional skinhead guys and then there's the washed up old guys who 10 years ago thought it was cool to hate niggers and they realized that Seattle really wasn't the place to say chink and spick and kyke. Once they realized that the punk rock kids around here were politically correct they didn't want to deal with that. I agree a lot with the working class traditional skinheads. I hate the Nazi skinheads. I hope they all burn in hell, every fucking one of them."

"Tell me about the origins of Beer Metal."

"It started with Jesse Frederickson, guitarist from Anti-Everything. His father passed, he inherited a bunch of money and bought a recording studio. We pretty much inherited it."

"He moved back to Port Townsend. So Jeff and I inherited Beer Metal and have spent the last 3 years and all our money running around this town meeting kids like The Plankton Beat and Clean Cut Lie. We're all in bands you know – Deathlist 5, Last 1 Out, Kill The Precedent, North Pole Society, The Hollowpoints, Road To Ruin, Pottymouth Society, The Dingbats, Three Found Dead. The Greedies were the band that had the chance of making Seattle cool again but there was too much internal conflict. I will defend everything they ever recorded. They are probably my favorite band that has ever been on Beer Metal."

"They presented the idea of getting this all together. Really uniting the bands, getting us together and playing shows, really supporting each other. That's what it's all about.

"It's not legitimately a record label at all. There was a business license and we never paid taxes on it, and every 3 months or so I get a call from the Washington State Department of Revenue asking me where there money is. I hang up on them every time... It's just a bunch of bands who give a fuck about music. It's a big slop of rock and roll. The name Beer Metal is kind of misleading cause we've only recently acquired one metal band, and they are metal in the most epic sense."

"They're called Super Happy Story Time Land."

"They're a bunch of kids from this town called Sequim, which is about as big as the lip of this beer bottle right here. The only thing to ever come out of it besides this beer is that band. It's a bunch of kids who have nothing better to do then thrash."

"We want to promote variety more than anything else. We've put out somewhere between 15-18 records, and by the end of this summer we'll have about 20. This new comp we're putting out is like 30 songs from 30 bands."

"Well, we're in Seattle. I thought you might like to comment on the grunge thing..."

"The term grunge was coined by Vanity Fair. Grunge was never something that any Seattle band called themselves. Vanity Fair and Calvin Klein did a fashion show in 1991 where they were wearing flannel because a bunch of Seattle bands were. Well, it's fucking freezing ass cold here and The Melvins and Nirvana came from logger towns where there's a bunch of rednecks. Versace would take these $12 flannels, cut the tags off them, sew their own on, and sell them for 4 times as much. Now – if you wanna label bands from 1991-1994 in Seattle as grunge, cool. There was only one good one, and that was Nirvana. I like The Melvins, I like one or two Soundgarden songs. Given the opportunity I would pee all over Eddie Vedder, and not in a sexual way. I've peed on a lot of people in a sexual way, but Eddie Vedder..."

"He's given the worst name to any style of music here".

"I blame the fall of music and the fact that people associate Seattle as grunge town on Pearl Jam. Like almost every bit of it. When

Soundgarden put out *Superunknown* it just died man. That was terrible – it was so unbelievable what was representing my town. I'm sitting here dying, going to punk rock shows, listening to local bands like TRIAL and Whipped and Bristle, Murder City Devils. The guitar player from Murder City Devils – one of the greatest fucking rock n' roll bands to ever come out of this town – now plays guitar for Modest Mouse."

"Do you hope one day Eddie Vedder hates you too?"

"I'd rather have somebody hate me than love me. When someone hates you they tend to talk more about you. Tell everybody how much you hate me and you're gonna make your kids love me. Case in point – Marilyn Manson. All he did was make parents hate him to the point where the kids loved him because they knew it'd piss their parents off... I was always a metal, punk, and hardcore kid. In '93 when punk broke – Green Day, Offspring, NOFX – I didn't really listen to that. I was more into Dead Kennedys, The Fartz, Total Chaos, GBH, Exploited. But more than that I was into Sepultura, Metallica, Megadeth. I was steeped in that shit. I discovered bands like Rancid and MXPX years after they had done their cool stuff. Rancid in '93, I didn't listen to that record until I was 25. I didn't listen to any NOFX record until 2002. It was so shoved in my face that I couldn't stand it. All the jocks, all the meatheads were wearing NOFX and Green Day t-shirts. These were the kids that pitched me shit my whole life.

"What's up with the knuckle tattoos?"

"That's Bork's name [guitarist in Deathlist 5]. Someone said I wouldn't do it, so I did just to spite them, 'cause when someone tells me I can't do something that's exactly what I'll do. This other one is OUCH. I used to get in a lot of fights and the last thing I wanted someone to see before I knocked them out was the word OUCH coming at their face. Coincidentally the day after I got this I punched some dude in the mouth and it fucked the tattoo up, which pissed me off. "

"What are your plans with Deathlist 5?"

"We're going on tour in October and we actually got turned down by the Double Down, the most prolific punk rock bar in Vegas, because we were 'too hardcore.' Like seriously, I'm going to save this email for the rest of my life: '*Honestly man, your music is way too hardcore for our little room.*' That made me happy. If you're gonna get shot down, I'd rather have someone tell me that my music is way too intense for them."

"Do the different cliques in the punk scene get along?"

"In Seattle I'd say there's like 4 or 5 different groups of punk rockers, like tribes. We all intermingle with one another, we're civil most the time. But then there's the cowboys that wear white belts – The Capitol Hill Cocaine Cowboys (laughs). That's gonna be a song title right there... These kids are the ones concerned with the fashion. The idea of going to a place to be seen as opposed to being part of a scene. We want to throw away the whole idea of '*my clothes are blacker then yours.*' Its like communism, it works on paper. Everyone is equal until there are some who are more equal. Punk rock is the perfect metaphor for communism. That's what we're trying to eliminate..."

CHURCHBURNER & THE BEAT ON PLANKTON

"*Um, Mr. Bartek?*" Puked On is poking me with a stick, kind of distanced with this sort of intimidated respect because he's a huge fan of Aaron Comctbus. "*I'm taking off to work. Feel free to hangout long as you need.*" In between grumbled dialogue he bolts, and I'm left alone in the massive three-story flop-house from 1904 they claim is haunted.

Whatever ghost inhabits it keeps throwing glass bongs off the shelves, shattering them on the floor. Six in the past four months actually, and you always hear the footsteps of an apparition clomping up & down the basement stairs in the night.

His nickname is "Puked On" 'cause some twin of a sister he dated barfed all over him while passed out on a floor. Puke is 21 but can barely pass for 17. He has this sort of child actor thing going on, like he could play a teenager well into his 30's. He is the singer/guitarist of Beer Metal band The Plankton Beat who describe themselves "Porch Thrash," because they literally write all of their tunes on acoustic guitars while drinking 40's on the front porch. They rip hardcore punk the medieval way before caking it with distortion.

Justin Hofmann dumped me off here last night after the Beer Metal house turned into a raging turbine of Gas-Mask bongs and steam-rollers. A full interview was attempted, but we were so hammered from 30 can PBR cases that we all kept trailing off in-between monster clouds of herb. They are the first in America to call it "*chiefing.*"

But we did make plans for the weekend – I'll be scooting off to Portland with them for a 2 day mini-tour. Bar gig on Friday and a house party Saturday, both with headliner Embrace The Kill. It will be thrashpunk act ETK's first two shows ever, and interesting because the main guy runs Crash Assailant records. He's released material by Leftover Crack, Time Again, Citizen Fish, Millions of Dead Cops.

The Plankton Beat kitchen table is a charcoal-like mess of spent resin balls that looks like the aftermath of St. Helen. I scoop some up with an Old Royal playing card, then kick back to read the *Cometbus Omnibus* that Puke left me, which I'd never even heard of until last night. Apparently the guy from Operation Ivy went on the Greyhound circuit too, and pumped out a legendary 'zine of such adventures lasting from '82-'92. *Whooptie doo – if it wasn't bad enough having to deal with Thompson & Kerouac accusations…*

3pm now, across town & by Mercer Park; I'm reunited with Pat Fry, who rescued me from the KISW radio station. We're hanging at Sound Asylum Studios, a two-floor rehearsal spot in the process of being built, and the entire structure is nailed together with unpainted timber wood.

You can't smoke inside, because it'd be like tossing a cigarette butt into a gerbil tank with all that shredded pine at the bottom. You keep sneezing 'cause the wood chips are float up your nose, and the vibrations from Churchburner only send more adrift.

Churchburner are like Dismember meets Six Feet Under if they were actually good. Straight-forward mosh riffs, real chunky riff-heavy stuff without too much unnecessary pizzazz. They have the low-end cookie monster vocals, the anti-religious sound samples, the bottom-heavy bass and guitar tones. Says Pat: *"Our lyrics are about history, brutal events that have shaped today. Nobody has the right to say that they know anything about any god, because religion is the root of all evil. The lyrics reflect all the problems that have arisen from people feeling the need to stand up for nothing."*

"The name Churchburner – how do you feel about the Norwegian thing?"

Tim Butterfield: "To get an army that'll…"

Pat Fry: "Carve X's in peoples heads?"

"That'd be cool as long as there's no legal repercussions for us, ha ha ha…"

"We're not telling anyone to do that, but if all of a sudden some cult originates from our ideas and burns shit down that's all on them. But you can't get in trouble for implying so… The bottom line is that it's a brutal fucking name. It's more symbolic."

"But if you knew you could get away with it…"

"It would have to be a new church 'cause some of the old churches are pretty cool…"

"I would burn a lot of shit down if I could get away…"

A PROUD MOMENT OF FANBOY SUPREMECY

Tuesday night, 11th & Pike – The Chophouse practice studio L7 made famous. I'm in the middle of an intoxicating moment. From day one the main priority of this Seattle mission has always been Drawn And Quartered, one of my favorite death metal bands of all time. Not many people seem to know about them because they've never toured much or been granted many big-name zine interviews. Still, they have a die-hard cult following, being the premier DM band on the ultra-satanic Moribund Records.

Their style has a unique bent with this phenomenally serpentine undercurrent. It's hard to define, but when I hear the roaring guitars, the gritty production of their albums – I feel the same awful vibe that gripped me when force-fed catechism classes in youth. That BC Rich shreds and I visualize all those storybook paintings of Christ being beaten & tortured, those old school Italian depictions of brimstone.

I had for some time been communicating with guitarist Kelly Kuciemba, who is the mastermind behind this unearthly horror. I'd set up the Greyhound ticket specifically to catch a battle of the bands performance they were playing on Friday, which then got moved to Sunday, which then got wiped out completely.

I explained how dire it was to get them in this project and how much I dig all of their records. In response Kelly went out of his way to set up a special practice. They haven't really jammed in over 3 months, but tonight its all for me. So in short, one of my favorite death metal bands of all time thought enough of my quest as to schedule my own private performance.

3 hours in the jam room, every awesome track one after another. Vocalist Herb picked up some special hydro just for the moment which we've been smoking nonstop between each song. Excuse me for sounding like a mutant ninja, but fuckin' *shredtastic…*

When all is said and done, we're high as kites, and when they are tossing me a stack of bumper stickers/CD's, I find out the drummer Dario also happens to be KROHM, the mysterious one-man transcendental black metal prodigy also on Moribund who I've highly respected for years. I expected him to be in a dungeon somewhere caked in corpse paint slicing himself for Baphomet.

Instead, he's just a laid back guy in blue jeans and white t-shirt, black hair styled in a short crew cut. When I dig a little deeper they're all in these cult bands I've been into for years – Kelly in Plaguebearer, Herb in Blood Ritual, Dario from Infester; Greg from Pervert/The

Meatshits, and all three of Herb, Greg and Kelly in Winds of Pestilence…

We attempt to get into the interview, but its tough pulling anything out of them. At that moment its obvious why no one's ever really heard of this band – they are quiet guys and all sort of socially backwards, with no real hardcore grasp on fanatic self-promotion. They don't do their own album release PR or graphic design – Odin at Moribund handles all that. They just kind of record and send it to him, and most the time Odin books their short occasional tours.

The world-class champion flag-waivers of extreme metal during the all-consuming grunge current have been forever ignored by the local press. They have no Seattle following outside guys like Terry from Scorched Earth or their immediate friends. In sum, they are just a bunch of stoned miscreants in their mid to late 30's and play death metal 'cause that's what's in them, which in my opinion makes them even that much more spectacular.

They aren't really convinced of any legendary cult status, despite the Moribund hype machine. It's kind of like hanging out with Saprogenic from Detroit. Yeah, they'll go play the West Coast or Japan and a dozen people will drive 3 hours to drool, but in reality they are some brutal, underdog death band with no gimmicks, playing the same dives over & over...

Before Kelly hobbles out the door with his bum hip, he sums it up perfectly: "*It's hard to rant into that tape player because my ranting was the 3 hours of jamming. That's my ritual... I don't want anyone to know what I do. I make a living at Drawn And Quartered for all they know. My life is dedicated to this attempt, and everything else is half-assed. I could have a good career making a lot more money, but I don't want to be tied down. I smoke weed and I play the guitar. And if I don't do that at least a couple times a week I start getting jittery and cranky. I'd probably kill people. I'd probably be a serial killer if I didn't have this outlet... Nah, I'd probably just have some boring job...*"

HUNAB KU

Wednesday afternoon now, back at The Funhouse waiting for Mike Gilmore, the vocalist of experimental/tech band Hunab Ku, who's band bio declares: "*Fathered by the likes of groundbreaking artists such as Fantomas, Aphex Twin, Meshuggah and The Dillinger Escape Plan, the music of Hunab Ku paints a calculated and vivid picture of modern, avant-garde metal. One that is undeniably original, and one that is impossible to ignore..."*

Last night Drawn And Quartered dumped me off here, leaving a trail of clam-baked clouds fogging out their Nissan window as they drove away smiling. Before they left the greatest death metal band in the world even bought me an ice cream cone...

 I'd lingered around The Funhouse anticipating my next adventure when it appears that word has gotten around about who I am. In the BBQ tent this Betty Page looking chick approached me. *"Are you that guy doing that book?"* "Yeah, I guess you could say that. You a big *Mad Max* fan?"

 Her face turned to a scowl. *"Did you just say Max Hardcore? What the fuck is wrong with you, you sick fuck?"* "No, no, I mean like Mel Gibson, the apocalypse..." She lightens up for one second, then I finish, *"But that creepy old man with the cowboy hat does some pretty sexy shit, don't ya think?"* Killed that one pretty fast...

 Luckily I got a ride back to the Plankton house from some guy in a Slipknot hoodie whose girlfriend was the bar's co-owner. Otherwise I'd been sleeping in the bushes of the Space Needle, which kind of resembles green pubic hair in the right abstract lighting...

Back to the current moment. Mike Gilmore approaches with a curt handshake, and buys us a pitcher of PBR. He's about 5 foot 10 with a medium build and short black hair. Friendly demeanor, and a jeans and t-shirt guy all the way.

 "So tell the me the usual for starters – Seattle, Hunab Ku, who you are and what you do, blah blah blah."

 Mike Gilmore: "Where to begin? Well... I was in a band called Tub Ring."

 "You were in Tub Ring?!?"

 "I was in Tub Ring from '93 to 2001, I was the drummer. I'm the singer in Hunab Ku now. I thought as a drummer, you know how you feel overlooked as a composer and whatnot... I broke off with another dude who played guitar and we wrote a record. Pretty much did a lot of the instruments for lack of musicians. So we assembled a record, sort of put it out here to get members for the live band. That really caught a lot of people's ears. Surprisingly enough, Dillinger Escape Plan – that's how I met them. I started going back and forth with Between The Buried And Me, The Red Chord. It was really promising to get that feedback... We're still in Chicago at that point and it just wasn't happening. I couldn't even tell you how many drummers we tried out. So we head out here at the end of 2003, just picked up and left – a bass player, a guitar player and myself. After two years of searching – and I mean *searching* – we put a reward poster up: '*Anyone who can play one Hunab Ku song to the tee within five takes gets $300.*' We had so many takers and it never happened. No one... It is very complex. There's just not many people who can pull it off perfect."

"How would you describe the music?"

"Very progressive. It's always easy to compare bands, and I know no one wants to, but the fact is you gotta relate to people what they've already heard... Tech metal, like if Dillinger Escape Plan, Fantomas, and Meshuggah had a big baby. A big, weird, fucking baby... It's got like umpteen tempo changes, soundscape-wise its all Mike Patton stuff. Its just out of left field, you don't know what's coming. Meshuggah heavy ass-kicking type groove stuff..."

"What about the message, the lyrics, the presentation..."

"We're very untypical. We don't really look like metal guys, half of us are jazz guys & lovers of all kinds of music... You know, I'm 33. When you go through your 20's a lot of shit happens – becoming an adult, traveling, moving away from your family. Art is supposed to reflect life, and what could be more reflective? I'm not all about partying, I just don't feel like that. It's no girlfriend stuff, none of that crap. Just real, true life stuff."

"The Tech thing..."

"We got a drummer after two years of moving here, and then it took about a year to get him up to speed, 'cause he was a straight-up fusion drummer, like a jazz drummer. But he was always a big metalhead, into Necrophagist and shit. We've played about 13, 14 shows since last summer. All winter we didn't play, took some time off to get this record out... Music like this, you don't sort-of just practice. It's all the time or it's nothing. We practice 4 times a week, at least..."

"Do you have a distributor yet?"

"No, it is independent. We are having some help from a local label called Black Sheep Records. It's just cool for someone to latch on and say '*I believe in what you're doing*' and honestly help. Granted, it's not tons of money – they're just helping with the street team, helping get our disc in local press, sending out 100's of press kits and absorbing the cost for that. It may sound like a little bit, but that's a lot of work...

We're so happy to get this out. I know its gonna turn heads, 'cause even if we were on a bill with those bands I'd mentioned, it'd be like, '*whoa, those guys are aliens.*' The core of what we do is pretty much metal, but we're way on the outskirts of that. Metal crowds can relate, but some purists would be like, '*what the hell are they doing?*' I'm all for the fusion of different styles, that's how music evolves."

"Was it the same way with Tub Ring? Because that was heavy, way out there, really weird, but it's a different kind of heavy. Did the straight-forward metal guys really hate Tub Ring because you guys were more whacky and fun?"

"The last one I was on was *Drake Equation*. That was produced by Trey from Mr. Bungle and Secret Chiefs 3. Since then, they've changed drastically. I wouldn't want to say pop but… There's more actual songwriting and tons of catchy melody. I seriously love it. It's like they became one of my favorite bands after I left, which is funny… Hunab sort of has that thing, but we're not as misfit-ish because we are very heavy, and live it's very brutal, even though there's these strange-o, whacked out breakdowns and weird sounds, samples, effects & electronics. The core of it is metal and I think that's going to catch people. I don't want to be a faceless band. I'd rather have people be '*I hate that, I know I hate that*' then '*Wow they were good, what's their name?*' Blah. People just latch onto what they know."

"Well you understand where I'm coming from. Do you think Seattle is the best city in America for people such as us?"

"Man that is a great thing you brought up because this city is very accommodating of people like ourselves. It just drew me out here – that was the most major thing. It's not '*go to high school, go to college, job, car payment, blah blah,*' that thing. Here there's people in their 50's and 60's doing art. Maybe they do have a day job. Sure, everyone's gotta live, but seeing painters on the sidewalk – I think that says something about the city. It is very liberal too, and not very accepting of this cookie cutter lifestyle. It's a huge weight off my shoulders. Coming out here, it made me realize, '*What the fuck? Why does the number of years that I'm on this planet dictate how I have to live or when I have to stop doing my art?*' The only thing it does mean is that I'm honing and sharpening my tools. I'm not a regular guy. I work but it's all in the name of what I do. I don't go there for one moment because of anything else but music."

"Got any good acid stories?"

"Now we're going there? I used to be huge into Grateful Dead, I traveled with them a little bit. That was... I'd never shied away, especially being quote-unquote 'metal.' I'm a very non-typical 'metal guy,' 'cause I think its so played out. Any stereotype gets annoying, and there's narrow-mindedness in every subculture. I've never been a scene person. I don't care about what people 'have' to look like. That shit has no bearing – I just want to make innovative music. I think people get so caught up in that, and metal – it's just so cheesy. I don't have any ill feelings towards anyone, its just like *'shit man, that sucks for you.'* Music to me is supposed to evoke emotion. Life, at the end, is all about the emotions you've had, and it's important to get that from a broad spectrum of art. But it's extra funny when we're opening up for a larger metal band and the crowd is just stereotypical metal. We get these looks, like *'these non-metal guys.'* I grew up in the early 80's, I have tattoos. I idolized motherfuckers like Slayer with leather & spikes, but I don't feel like I'm a part of that. I feel comfortable just being comfortable. Maybe it's just over-analyzing on my part, but I think people are like *'you don't fit here,'* and then we get up there and we're insanely violent and fucking crazy and weird. Then people come up to you like, *'whoa man, that was fuckin' killer, so heavy and just nuts.'* Just drop the pre-conceived stereotype shit man..."

SO METAL WE SHIT BOLT THROWER RECORDS

Capitol Hill with In Memorium vocalist Nihilist, who's has just ordered our second pitcher of beer. It's been a long day of drinking. By the time Mike Gilmore left, we'd ran through two pitchers of beer and some vodka & cranberry. I spent the next two hours outside Nihilist's work, slobbering like a buffoon and forcibly singing Dragonforce to yuppie onlookers...

Its metal discussion tonight, and we have quite the fantastic kvlt metal character on deck. Nihilist is a minor legend, having parlayed between a half dozen groups and launching a dozen albums – In Memorium, Stahlmantel, Hatefuckers, Abazagorath, Thy Infernal...

One quick lick of the In Memorium bio tells all: *"Spawned amidst the grim bedeviled hinterlands of the Pacific Northwest in the vernal months of 1997, In Memorium was invoked to channel the spirit of utter darkness and distill it into a musical avatar. The result was an aural holocaust that has not merely continued to this day but has deepened, descended further and further down into the stygian bowels of sheerest morbidity."*

"Well the predominant thing I've come to realize about Seattle is that it's forever 1997."

Nihilist: "It's funny you say that 'cause I was walking down the street a month ago with shorts on and combat boots and somebody yelled out their window '*IT'S NOT 1997 ANYMORE ASSHOLE!!*' So yeah, I guess you could see that. There's a lot here that reminded me of the 90's in general. It kind of never went away. They still play Weezer like there's no tomorrow, they still play Guns N' Roses, all that shit."

"Take that as a free license to rant…"

"To me the origins of Seattle comes from The Accused, Metal Church, Queensryche, stuff like that. I've never understood the fascination with Nevermore being huge. Power metal is pretty popular here, a lot of people asking if I like Blind Guardian, Stratovarius, Iron Savior. To me its all Iron Maiden, Helloween, MANOWAR…"

"Weren't you in Engorged?"

"Here's how it all started. I grew up in Illinois 21 years, my sister lived south side of Portland, so growing up we'd always visit. When I moved to Portland I was living with a bunch of crust punks and made friends with Agalloch. Bunch of bands like Detestation, Resist, Landfill, Starving Delirious. I met this guy from Murdergod, which to me was the be all end all culmination of Bestial Warlust and grindcore. Three of the members, we started doing a band called Hatefuckers which was a grind kind of funk – weird culmination of stuff with two vocals, a guy doing noise, samples, crazy stuff. Hatefuckers kind of morphed into Thy Infernal and Engorged. I got kicked out of Thy Infernal in 97, right as we were signing to Moribund. Then I got asked to move up here and join In Memorium."

"What's the Bethlehem/Juergen Bartsch connection? I heard he just got out of the mental institution."

"I work with him on a project called Stahlmantel. I was in Wraithen and my band mate got an email from one of the guys in Bethlehem saying he really liked our demo, it got around to Juergen too. I asked if they wanted to do a split 7" inch. So we did the split, we paid the rights to the Bethlehem song – $250. We did the covers ourselves, did the layout, pressed it ourselves. Magic had control of all the stuff, had all the stuff sent to him in Alaska where he's married to the ex-keyboardist from In Memorium. No one has been in contact since their wedding… I basically got 25 copies, took them to Europe when Abazagorath went on tour. Then I moved out to Jersey to do the Abazagortah album. Juergen asked if I wanted to sing on 2 songs for a new Bethlehem album. Sent me the songs, I recorded one but he didn't receive it in time for the *Mein Weg* album. You know 'Dr. Meezo?' He says he's going to use it someday. So now I'm doing Stahlmantel with him. He sends me all the music, I do all the vocals at my band mates house, but there are a lot of times where I won't hear from him for weeks, and then he'll email me saying he's having problems. There's a time I went 5 months without from hearing from him."

"What do you think of Michael Jackson?"

"I like the *Thriller* video. Every time I hear this song now I think of *Seinfeld*, which I'm a total fucking devotee of."

"I recently realized that George Costanza is always going to take a shit, or coming into the shot pulling up his pants."

"The first time he meets the girl he really likes the interesting conversation they have is how toilet paper has never changed and may never change throughout their lifetime. It's the girl he says '*I love you*' to. I think the best white comedian ever besides Lenny Bruce would be Bill Hicks."

"Got any random weird stories just for the hell of it?"

"I saw a ghost, the lady who babysat me when I was 11. That really fucked with me. Made me really understand there are ghosts out there. I wasn't stoned, I wasn't drunk, I was 11 years old, I didn't go to her funeral. She babysat me for 11 years, she was murdered, she was suffocated and they cut her finger off to get the ring."

"Is this what launched your fascination with death?"

"I've always had a total morbid fascination with death."

"Do you also agree that scene in 'Return Of The Living Dead' where Linnea Quigley dances naked on the tombstone…"

"One of the hottest scenes ever. Definitely up there with Phoebe Kates coming out of the pool in *Fast Times At Ridgemont High*."

"Well here's a more serious question. Your in a well-known black metal band, extreme metal is your realm – how do you feel about fanaticism in black metal in general. Varg Vikernes for example, NSBM, USBM. What do you think is too far and how do you feel about all the European chaos?

"The black metal scene in Norway, that to me changed metal. The other day there was this couple with us and '*oh what happened in Norway?*' The guy started telling the woman, I'm listening in, it's like, '*Oh my gosh, how urban legend has twisted and turned and made this snowball effect*.' The black metal scene in Norway achieved what they set out to do. They thought death metal was becoming trend metal and life metal. No mosh pit core and no fun. And they took it to that level. We're gonna fight, we're gonna be these evil fucks and fucking burn churches, we're gonna do these arsons. To me it makes certain sense. The way I got into black metal was my friend Steve-O from Impetigo, he turned me onto Burzum and Mayhem. Once the murder happened, it was kind of like this guy murdered my friend. He was the leader of this group. Apparently there's all sorts of reasons and money and jealousy. All of that stuff can take control of people."

"When is going too far going too far?"

"The worst case scenario is the Dimebag incident. To me you're onstage, your just in your world, you're not thinking that anyone is coming to stab or shoot you..."

"Well how do you feel about occultism in black metal?"

"To each their personal own. I used to be into the occult when I was younger. To be quite honest where I'm at is kind of at a nihilistic, going out and getting obliterated... My personal philosophy is to try and do as much with my music and art I can in the time I have. Religion to me is something that has no meaning. I know there's something out there. I'm kind of a cross between agnosticism and nihilism. I'm definitely a nihilist with a sense of humor. I don't have an answer. I don't like to put a definite tag on anything. I have certain weird beliefs... Fuck, I hope Cthulu will someday come to life. But it's not... I'm two pitchers full of beer and stoned. This is usually me. My whole world is *'what's my next project?'* I love to quote GG Allin – *'stay one step ahead of the law.'* Do my own thing, not get arrested, have fun, indulge in as much female flesh, alcohol, and drugs as I can, and watch film. That's all I really care about. And cooking, cause I'm a chef."

"Who are the real deal as far as the dead-serious occult guys in black metal?"

"Mezedrous, the main guy from BloodStorm. He seems like he's pretty hardcore into the occult. And of course Crosscrypter from ABSU. My buddy Daryl from Abazagorath. Most people I meet are more street crazy or just kind of weird, demented in certain senses. One of the strangest people I know is Rob Fornicator. He was in Disciples of Hate, Nailed, WHORE, Murderbasket, and Fornicator. I've known him since I was 17. He's like 6 foot 7 and skinny as a rail. Rob likes to dress in drag onstage and sing about beating the fuck out of women. Completely drag, with a short PVC skirt, 20 high boots and fuckin' full-on wig. He'll sit there singing about murdering women and whatnot. But he does it very humorous..."

WEIRDEST MOMENT OF THE YEAR

After stomping around Downtown with Nihilist being obnoxious assholes, he sets me off with a complex map of three bus changes. These huge busses are not good for a wobbling drunk about to barf everywhere. They have two cars connected with a rubber split and high-rise styled stadium seating...

At The Galway I meet up with Houghton & Hofmann, but I'm so drunk I'm falling asleep at the table. One of the staff tells me I have to be a social butterfly or I gotta scram... Fuck it – just take a nap outside and wear some of it off real quick-like, lumber back in and chill at the Beer Metal house tonight...

I woke in a severe twitch that shot me upwards, scrambling to hunt down my ride before the bar cleared out. I poked my head from the shadowy corner, and no one was in the gated area. There was no music, no ruckus. Flip open the cell, gaug bearings – 4:12 am, 39 degrees...

At least I'm rested, if only slightly. I gather my belongings as the first bus of the morn luckily pulls around the corner. I dust myself off and as I sluggishly move towards the bus stop, some black guy comes running out of his apartment and hands me a grocery bag full of microwavable Chef Boyardee cups. *Bum-o-flauge works many ways...*

9am, yuppies en route to work, Downtown street bustling – cool, perfect, sunny blue, and still it hasn't rained. I feel so amazing right now just singing Charles Manson songs, those pretty girls smiling at me for it without the slightest connotation of reference. My shoes and socks are off, I'm leaning against a blue mailbox, my backpack & duffel surround me.

People aren't sure if they should be flipping me change. After all these years I've finally succeeded – *TOTAL ROCK BOTTOM*. Just the clothes on my back and no care in the world – no fear of death, no fear of human interference – every city in America none other then my own personal playground, every metropolis from sea to shining sea...

I never so purely felt the reward of this year-long cathartic caesura. I looked into the sky, and I felt fate gazing downward. *"Fuck it, why not? I'll ask god for a miracle."*

See, when I was a little kid I was brainwashed to be a good Catholic boy, I used to talk to God all the time, always felt this deep-seated connection. When I lost my faith I turned hard, and went headfirst into utter havoc... Many years passed, deeper and deeper into the abyss of sin, feeding off that gut-instinct of *"wrong, bad, immoral,*

Satan" like a stone-crazed junkie. Basically, I had to go *Pink Flamingos* style and become the filthiest man on earth. It wasn't until 6 years ago that I actually decided to talk directly to God again for the first time since I was a kid, just for the hell of it.

It was an ugly moment. I'd a few friends that died or went to prison, and midst midnight I'd gotten a call from the love of my life (*of another era*) admitting her secret heroin addiction. I freaked and ran onto the back porch chain-smoking. The moon was huge; a strange cloudy mist covered the lining of the sky. It was like all of existence was staring me in the face, and every other human on earth asleep.

So I looked into that moon and said, "*God, if you're up there, if you're real, I want you to prove it to me right now. I want my miracle. Bring on the Apocalypse. Flush this entire world down the toilet. I want the skies to burn, I want chaos and hell. Show me what a pair of balls you got you cock-straddling, AIDS infected pussy.*" When I woke up planes were flying into the World Trade Center...

So today, on that street corner in Seattle leaning against that blue mailbox, I looked into the clear blue sky and said, "*Hey God, it's me again. All of this is too weird to ignore, and it seems like destiny is putting things in my path. So I want* <u>*Miracle # 2*</u>*. I need a prognostication of the future. All my old enemies are long gone, and it's a new world. Where is this going? Who will be my great arch nemesis? What one person so perfectly defines all that the future will symbolically hold? If you pull this one off, I'll no longer doubt the endless wheel of karma... But you're still a cocksucker.*"

I went to the Seattle Public Library and hung around for an hour until they opened, bums pacing around like Indian snake-dancers doing the pooh-pooh dance. You'll find them here every morning; the second the revolving doors are unlocked the toilet becomes a makeshift locker room. Dozens of them all waiting to shit, shave, power-wash in the sink, blow off their scrotums in the air-jet hand dryers. It reeks like a thick fog of ass the next 3 hours.

This is why I wait for it to clear out before I even attempt to urinate. When I finally lurch inside it looks like Vikings ransacked the men's room – toilet paper over the floor, muddy footprints, facial hair shavings that look like grody insects floating in splotches of water. It was totally empty except for one guy in the toilet stall taking the loudest, bloodiest, most vicious caveman-grunting shit I'd ever heard in my life. *It was savage...*

I chose to ignore the terrible ruckus and brush my teeth in the Hades sink when the stall door swings open and the guy walks up behind me. As he's coming up I get this Spidey Sense tingle that travelers get when they meet really intense, displaced people.

But still I don't look up. This guy just stands at the sink next to me, not washing his hands, just hovering there, looking at me. I keep brushing hoping he'll go away 'cause I'm not feeling all too friendly.

"*Hey there young man.*" Great, another creep trying to get me to blow him. I give in and look over. He's giving me this big silly grin, kind of nodding his head. I look back down at the sink, look back, look at the sink, tracing the water spiraling down the drain. Then I realize what's happening…

HOLY SHIT – it's BARACK OBAMA… _

Obama just stands there in jogging pants and a hoodie, like he slipped out of his campaign trail for a stroll, and had to take a monster beefer. No Secret Service, no media, no fan boys. Just Barack and myself, and he has this twinkle in his eye – this sickly weird glance like he knows me. He just stands there expecting me to say something.

A brilliant line struggles to twirl in my skull, but instead I just go, "*Oh… You.*" with this "*It's really strange for YOU to meet ME here*" delivery. He starts laughing his ass off, holds open the door, hangs for a second, glares back, laughs some more, then slips off…

I stand in the bathroom for five minutes trying to process the cosmic ramifications. I exit through the revolving glass doors, look into the sky and holler, "*CAN IT GET ANY FUCKING WEIRDER!!!*" Pedestrians give startled glances and a taxi driver screeches his breaks, nearly rear-ending a bus...

It was undeniably a Barack sighting, which is even less plausible in the Washington area then a glimpse of Sasquatch. Three downtown blocks have been cordoned off by police and news media, as Barack's speech is now underway…

Nap in the local squatter park of Capitol Hill. Some travelers from Phoenix are a tall white guy with dreads and this sort of raver looking black chick. They are absolutely obnoxious together, he's mouth farting her belly and they can't keep their hands off each other. The public restroom is filthy, and the guy in the stall asks, "*Hey man, can you be my eyes?*" The plastic needle cap pops off & rolls, tapping the rim of my shoe…

BEST BAND NAME EVER

I can't believe how smooth this week has run. I've been a human pinball all week – one person drops me off, another takes me into custody almost immediately. This time I'm at another pro-rehearsal space drinking beer and getting a fantastic blast of avant-doom.

These guys are called LESBIAN. Like seriously, that's their band name "*We all grew up in the same area. I was in Jan Michael Vincent Car Crash. Ben and I played in The Abodox, Arran and Dan played in Golgothan Sunrise. There was a show that Golgothan Sunrise couldn't do at The Funhouse, so Dan asked if we wanted to throw some shit together. We fucked around for 5 days... We have 2 basses, one guitar.*"

"This is a pretty PC city, lots of gays and lesbians. Are people offended by your name?"

Dorando Hodou: "Nobody in town, especially Lesbians. It's not supposed to be offensive. People who are straight have more of a problem with it."

Arran McInnis: "It was a kick-ass name for one night. But we're still doing it 3 years later."

"We started to think about the name. It's really funny, we're sticking with it. People are telling us to change it. We got a lot of pressure. Every time that came up, here's another rad reason to keep us going on the name."

"It's not metal enough for some people, so we couldn't get on shows with bigger bands. What the fuck is that? People who write reviews too, they try to make a connection to the name and the sound. I remember reading one review for Pelican, and 'yeah, they're music is like a bird soaring through the clouds, like a pelican would do.' What the fuck is that?"

"So they think your romantic doom, like a bunch of lesbians having an orgy in an ancient castle... Do you call your fans les-beings or something of the sort?"

"Well call ourselves Lesbro's. We had an interview in Seattle Weekly and I was just joking around with the guy. He said, 'hey, can I get you lesbians for an interview?' Yeah, we'd love to, but by the way we refer to ourselves as 'lesbros.' He took it literally and put it in the article."

"You guys went to Texas?"

"We got hooked up with a shitty show. 'We see you guys are going to SXSW, wanna swing by San Antonio?' It was at this place

called 'Club Crystal.' We looked a their website and it's all black chicks in thongs with big booties. It was a total blues place in this strip-mall. We were stoked, and then it got moved to this other venue."

"Like this TJ Maxx…"

"It was this abandoned Kmart or something. Huge unmarked building, huge empty parking lot. 4 or 5 stages, semi-professional wrestling; you could only mosh in the ring. There were like 5 bars, but it was all 18 year old kids in metal bands. They tried to get us to share gear and all this. So we played in this middle room with all the bands playing at the same time."

"We got busted toking in the parking lot. We're standing outside the van drinking beers, and these guys pull up on a golf cart. *'Empty your pockets, I know what that shit smells like.'* Zero tolerance in Texas. Luckily they couldn't find anything."

"But we did find Exit 420 to Baker Road in Texas. Fucking deer, fuckin' fog…"

"What's your next album about?"

"'Inner Space' kind of shit."

"Like Rick Moranis?"

"Yeah, it's based on the Rick Moranis movie. You play the record and it actually synchs up with Martin Sheen…"

"Like Pink Floyd and 'Wizard of Oz?'"

"Yeah."

"When are you gonna make the 'Short Circuit' album?"

"I'm all about 'Short Circuit Part 2'…"

MILLIONS OF DEAD COPS

Portland, Day Two. Last nights gig was another high octane performance at The Jolly Jill – The Plankton Beat, Larry And His Flask, and thrashpunk act Embrace The Kill's worldwide debut. I awake in yet another squat with band members littering the floor, a creepy older man pacing angrily because I'd hijacked his couch. He's burnt from hard road & missing a few teeth, giving the spliced amalgam vibe of a dock worker & carny. Flipping through some WWII books in black coffee clarity, we discuss literature. When I notice the giant MDC tattoo on his forearm, it hits me – *I actually stole Al Schvitz bed…*

20 years ago I would've been set on fire, but these days, he's quite friendly. Al is a tough-n-gruff East Coast bastard with a heavy Jersey accent, and is the drummer of one of the longest running REAL punk bands in the genre's history. Millions of Dead Cops formed in

Texas in 1978 and are notable as one of the most politically extreme bands in hardcore. Dropping their legendary debut at the peak of the 80's punk explosion, MDC trampled American & European audiences touring with all the greats in their prime – Dead Kennedys, Bad Brains, DRI, Black Flag…

Initially, MDC was clasped onto by skinhead thugs, but the whole palate changed when they realized that vocalist Dave Dictor – then the perfect visual refrain of a testosterone fueled bulldog – was openly gay. And he *loved* aggressively freaking them out with it. Thus begat a fine line drawn in the sand, and nearly 30 years into their career, they are still as viciously anti-fascist.

We clog the diner across the street for scramble-cakes, then enclose Al on the outdoor picnic table like punk rock grandpas story time. He's so New York it's inexplicable, the kind of character you'd discover in Tompkins Square bickering & playing chess with cranky old Jewish men: "*I play drums on all but one or two records, because during those periods of time I was… Well… On a vacation I didn't want to be on. Be that as it may, I do have probably the most reason to dislike the cops more than any other person in the band.*"

"Tell me about Portland."

Al Schvitz: "Portland is a weird place. They put up with no-cause evictions. You're a second class citizen more than anywhere."

"Where'd you grow up?"

"My family is from Queens. If I watch *The Sopranos* when all the ladies talk, it makes me a little reminiscent of my mom and her 6 sisters just yakking away with those twangy Jersey and Queens accents. But I can tell you this – what they're saying about families, those whop families. It's different out on the East Coast. These people rob each other and it's unbelievable. And there's a bunch of them. I have a huge family. It's thicker than water. Here it's not."

"Did you use to hang out at CBGB's?"

"CB's was around 30 years. All these entertainers, Billy Joel is protesting this and that and whatever. Fucking write a check asshole, just shut the fuck up. I mean, you know, buy the fucking place. Why do we need to get the government involved? I don't understand why The Rolling Stones need to affiliate with fuckin' Budweiser or anyone else to do their fuckin' shit. Those guys used to mean something, they used to be bad. I'm 53 years old. My parents used to dislike The Beatles, then The Stones came along, and it made The Beatles look better. I don't get some things."

"Well I assume you got a billion crazy stories for me."

"Well let me tell you, I played 1200 shows in 30 or so countries, over a 150 cities. Which is kind of like a show every night for 4 years."

"Got any good Amsterdam tales?"

"That's an interesting place... I'll tell you one thing – take 25% of the money that we spent on smokables over a quarter century. If early enough I'd said I want 25%, I'll keep the records, at the end that's mine. Right then I could have easily sent my three children to college. But no, I was a dumbass hippie or something. No regrets, but yeah there's regrets..."

"Your book is called 'The Politics Of The Front' right?"

"Yeah, it's about my wicked ways. Its also about seduction. Because you're in MDC people tend to believe you're not the police. So you're cool in town, they make themselves available to you. Well before you know it, heh heh... It happens pretty quick... I would've made somewhere in the area of $200,000 bucks tax free the year they caught me. By the time everything fell apart I paid $32,000 for an attorney. The shit I lost, the time I lost, supporting my kids when I was in... If I didn't prepare I would've done a lot more than the chickenshit 6 months I did. Pretty much didn't have anything left. It's a very debatable thing people will say – there's no victimless crimes and blah blah. But I can say I never solicited to anybody, I never called when it got in. One thing I did do, half a dozen people back in the 80's we knew had AIDS. They really needed drugs to take away the sickness. I'd take a loss on it. I don't know if it was a good thing to do to save my soul... But you look back on everything. If you're gonna do illegal shit, you're gonna wind up paying your taxes at H&R West Block Sam Quentin. You don't want to be there. It's really a very, very scary, bigger than you can imagine kind of place. South Block of Quentin is the largest cell block in the world. It's so far down in every direction– five tiers up, tiny little cells. It's like the biggest pet store with bird cages and you look up and you're like, '*Oh my fucking god, what have I...*' The cells, you can touch the ceiling, two people are in there and it's tiny. You don't get any space. But you learn, you don't have a choice. That's just reception, they sort you out and send you to more of a humane place. But it's quite a shock. I can't imagine anyone that inside they don't cry a bit. It's something to be considered, especially in California, 'cause they love to send people to prison. They love to violate people on parole. My crimes were in '94, '95, so we're talking 12-13 years. That's how long they came and got me, after 8 years."

"Is California still the biggest prison state in the USA?"

"I know it's a state that spends more on locking people up then on education. Point is they came and got me. I couldn't fucking believe it. My parole officer told me California could have an active warrant, somebody just running and not going to court for anything but a violent crime from Oregon. If you're arrested in California, they're not gonna come get 'em. We're talking about anything but a strikable offense. But California will come and get your sorry ass on a first-term dope case from 1994. Just your lucky day. They'll come get you in Guam. They'll come get you in Florida. They'll get you in Canada. I don't know why but they do."

"Is Texas the same way?"

"Texas is scary in another way. Texas is scary before you get in the system. The Ku Klux Klan is marching in Austin."

"You spent time in San Fran with the band."

"We lived in Texas and went on tour from Austin to San Francisco because I talked to Biafra for hours and hours. He talked me into coming up a week and a half, to play this last Dead Kennedy's gig before they were going to record. So we go up there, it appealed to us so much. This is '82. It probably would've been wiser to move to Southern California, but then again I didn't like the heat. It was hard, it took months to all transfer up here. No joke, it was compact."

"What's just a weird place you woke up on tour going 'Where the fuck am I?'"

"The squat in Florence, Italy. What they think is ok may not be ok to everybody. Their buildings are fucking a 1000 years old, some old castle or whatever. This guy leads me through a hole in the wall, through a hole in another wall, so I'm between these two walls and in-between two squatters there's room for you. Italy was pretty Wild West you know?"

"How deep east in Europe have you toured?"

"Belarus, Moscow, Leningrad…"

"Did you play in Slovenia?"

"We played there a few times. When I think of Slovenia I think of crossing the border from Croatia and one of those cocksuckers stealing my passport. Going to the American embassy and spending all day trying to get a passport and at the end finding out the gig was blown. These people have some suspicion that I sold my passport for drugs. I was so freaked out, we were all freaked out. We're Americans, we're in a fucking consulate. We got working papers, the hells wrong with you?"

"What was the network like in those days?"

"In '82 you'd go to England and they'll set up a PA system and that PA will tour with you. That whole backline will be there, top to bottom it'll be the same. Then you go to Germany, that's a different PA for all of the country."

"What was Germany like?"

"We took a train first time. It was terrifying, the fucking Germans come in and, *'Hubbuh huhbuh huh'* screaming at us. Searched our shit, searched it again, then oh my god they found it. They found this little disc of Desket, the kind that absorbs moisture in an acoustic guitar, *'Ho ho, they have the Desket!'* I'm sitting in the back of the train like, *'What the fuck is going on?'* We go to the gig with the Dead Kennedys and there's 45 little busses marked POLICIA. Fucking parking lot's full of police. And they're all dressed like fuckin' military. They're all green. It was not England. England is what you'd expect – it was kicked back, it was over the war."

"You got to Moscow in '92 after the Cold War. What was that like, watching the sociological aspects of it?"

"Well I'll tell you this. Germany reunified a year after the wall. We were the last band to ever play in East Germany. We weren't the only last band. Hells Kitchen played in Leipzig, and we both weren't getting off the stage until midnight. We were onstage playing in East Germany, when we left we were in Germany."

"Were people insane in the crowd?"

"Truth is East Germany had it better than most of these countries. But it's a lot of desperation. Money was all fucked up. People were not that thrilled to have their whole economic thing just changed. When I went to Moscow I'd never seen so much desperation. Begging you… It was scary, very disturbing. I'd notice thing like kids with polio. First I'm thinking, *'Fuckin' Russian government.'* You're thinking wrong. Couldn't America do something about kids with polio? Are they worried about what, them growing up and riding a missile? Its all such bullshit. We were the ones that were brainwashed, they weren't. 1 out of 5 Russians dies in WWII. Think we'd be all gung ho to jump in some fucking war if we had 1 out of 5 dead, some fucking unbeatable… It was all so clear to me. How could I be so fucking stupid? The bloc countries didn't hate us, they didn't hate Russia. It was a political necessity. It's not our fault or their fault that they don't have oceans around their capitals. We were the ones that profited from that arms race, not them. We made the first move with the Bay of Pigs. We showed them what the chess court would look like, and a lot of people suffered for it."

"What do you think of Castro?"

"I was in Cuba when Castro took over…"

"Really?"

"That's right. Me and Fidel were hanging out, I was about 4 years old. No, heh heh, actually my parents – mom, dad and me were on vacation on Veradera Beach near Havana when all the shit start to get really dicey. It took us a couple weeks to get out. We met soldiers on both sides – Batistas' soldiers and communist rebels. I only know this from 8MM fuckin' movies…

"Do you think he was in the right to begin with but turned into a tyrant by the end?"

"I don't know that much about it. I know what somebody wants me to know, or whatever. I think Fidel was probably the best thing that ever happened to Cuba. Unless you thought some guy that fuckin' supports the mob and torture... I know people live longer there. I know people are educated. And I know we don't have the right to tell anyone where to have missiles."

"Tell me about El Duce."

"Well El Duce, that's a character. It's weird, people project what they're band is, this and that. That's not always what they are. Sometimes it is, and to a certain extent you represent what it's about. It's hard to go out onstage. If you're a singer… You know I stay away from Henry Rollins before he's going on. I'm fine with Henry, but I know Henry is becoming something else. It's like actors do. Now and El Duce, or a Lee Ving, Lee Ving will go out of his way to show you that he's not as knuckle-headed as a lot of his shit. He's not that sexist, that's a lot of his shtick. El Duce is the real article. I remember the first time I saw him. We're playing in the Metro in Atlanta and this old Chevy comes screeching up, back door opens, this old bearded fuckin' guy that looks 45 years old kind of falls out looking for a beer, kinda sits on the ground. I've only seen him in a hood. That was El Duce. We didn't play with him that much. But I know I wouldn't want to go on tour with him because he's famous for getting fed up with somebody in a band and all of a sudden you go to take a piss – and they'll pick the right place – you know, Wyler Texas, and they'd be gone. Cry now buddy…"

MILLIONS OF DEAD COPS (REPRISE)

Back to the house and Plankton Beat is gearing up for the later house party. For the time being I'm actually going to hang out at MDC's practice, where they are putting the final touches on their set list before the tour begins next week.

The space is above a used car dealership where you actually have to go through the showroom to gain access. That's where I meet vocalist Dave Dictor, who's another grizzled 50-something New York guy. He's got this Hawaiian shirt tucked into faded black denim jeans, and is notably irritated. It doesn't help that I ignorantly chose to sit in "his chair." Never a good thing really. This just sets off a domino of other issues and I'm stuck in the crossfire of a band bitch-fest...

They hustle into it and roll through 15 songs pissed songs to get out the frustration before Dave tells me he's ready: "*Sorry for getting a little goofy on you back there. We've got the first gig Thursday and want it to be perfect. We've been around 27 years and want to be perfect.*"

"*Where's the tour going?*"

Dave Dictor: "It's just up and down the west coast – Tacoma, Seattle Bremerton, then Chico, Eugene. San Diego, LA 2 or 3 times, Victorville. Bay area, Gilman Street. Then back up and we're gonna play Portland then Richland. So it's like 16, 17 dates."

"*How do you feel about Portland and why did you choose this as your headquarters?*"

"I really love Portland, it's a cool city. I chose Portland because my ex-girlfriend – the mother of my child – she moved up here and got married to a really shitty guy – real crazy guy, ex military guy. Sure enough they broke up. He had a kid with her, he was threatening to take all the kids to Canada or Idaho. I got her and the children away from him, put them on a train to New Orleans. At that point she was like, '*Why don't you raise Jesse?*' I was a single dad, and Jesse's a real Oregon kid, so I came back here… It's a real punk rock town. I don't want to use the word unity but… Any night there could be eight punk shows going on with about a 100 people, and you kind of wish '*Wouldn't it be cool if it was one big punk rock show?*' And not just like NOFX or goofy ass name bands, like Bad Religion playing Warped Tour, but bands like Tragedy, Poison Idea, MDC, Defiance. We could have 700 people at a show but that never happens. So you got Tragedy playing against Riot Cop playing against MDC playing against Flipper all on the same night. It's not like CBGB's was in New York."

"You were around when that place blew up in the 70's?"

"Yeah, I grew up in New York but I didn't really hang in New York. I went there a couple times in '80, '81, '82, but I was living in Austin from '77-'82. I was part of the Big Boys/Dicks scene with The Offenders and The Boy Problems, and The Necks. DRI came out of Houston, Butthole Surfers came out of San Antonio. Eventually Lower Class Brats, but I was gone by that time. I moved to San Francisco in '82, I loved it. It was punk rock paradise between '82 and '92. The rents were low, there were abandoned warehouses, squatting, big political scene through the 80's..."

"What do you think kind of ended it?"

"Things can't sustain themselves forever. The mayor Feinstein, who went onto become senator, declared war on punk rock. He didn't want all those demonstrators and punk rockers making democrats seem like they were tolerant. Demonstrators got beaten to a pulp, squats got raided. It was like a war on the scene. Then gentrification started happening, more artists came in. The rents went up, the dot com thing took over in the 90's. The apartment that I lived in 1985 for $540 – 3 bedroom flat that turned into a 4 easy, that goes for $2200. I got friends with nice flats that are paying $3000 – 3 or 4 people all paying $750 each... No one in Portland is paying $750. There's a lot of punk rock houses where people will pay $150, $225 a month. You can afford being an artist. You can get a job working part time and you get a little practice space. A San Francisco practice space is an arm and a leg. It's just the nature of people moving where they perceive it being cool, and now Manhattan is the same way. West Village condos are $5000 a month. To live there it's half a million for a tiny ass fucking place."

"Tell me about some random legends you've met..."

"I will say I miss and really love Tom Roberts. I created an album with him called The Submissives. It never got much notice, it sold 3 or 4000. He was the most creative guy I ever hung out with. It's where the rubber met the road. Like when we recorded that first MDC album in a course of 6 months and the next thing you know the Dead Kennedys are taking us to Europe. Tom Roberts and I were both reclusive, living just 8 blocks from here on top of a club called Suburbia. We lived there free as janitors and night watchmen. When things fall into place, when a guy hums you a song and you start singing a lyric... In two weekends you got 15 songs, then your sending a demo to Fat Mike who falls in love with it. Here's $5000, go into a studio. Here's another $10,000..."

"What about cop stories?"

"I was in LA a long time ago. They pretty much knew we were MDC and they came into this little 300 people Foreign Legion Hall. I was upstage and they were '*cops are outside.*' I go '*fuck the police, the police are the klan, the mafia man. I'm saying one thing to you guys – I don't know how much longer this shows gonna go on but I'm just gonna say one thing – DEAD MOTHERFUCKING COPS!*' And I turn around and there's like a row of policeman. They take me outside, beat me down with a stick, got their knee in my chest, in my head. The guy looked at me and I said '*sir, you know, I just said something really stupid.*' And he goes '*you bet you fucking did.*' Then they held me there, and they arrested like 30 people. Two paddy wagons pulled up and threw in about 8 people in each van. There was still about 15 of us there. The cops waited about a half hour and they're calling up the paddy wagons '*we still got 15.*' Something else must have been going on – you know, real crime. And all of a sudden the cop looks at me and says '*Where you from?*' I go '*I live in San Francisco.*' He goes '*get in your van and just drive straight there,*' HA HA HA."

"Any other rough ones?"

"There's other moments where we got pulled over and they found the Millions Of Dead Cops button on the visor. One Houston cop crossed out the DEAD with a magic marker. Said '*That's better.*' Another guy in Michigan said '*See that field? One of these days you might get marched out there and you're not gonna come back.*' There was one time in Zanesville, Ohio. We got busted and went to jail and our roadie's saying, '*we're on your side. Millions Of Dead Cops is like supporting you guys 'cause all the bad laws like in apartheid South Africa.*' And the cops like '*Shut up.*' He's trying to explain to him MDC is really pro-cops."

"How do you feel about this stage of your career?"

"It's been an enchanting fucking cool space ride. Here the band is going 28 years later – original drummer Al, original guitar player Ron and myself. And still people show up. I couldn't imagine 28 years ago being here in Portland doing this interview with you. Reagan years you thought the world was just gonna blow up. Maybe that's just the follies of being young, but I never could see what the year 1990 was gonna be like, the year 2000. I didn't know if I'd be dead, I didn't know what to think. Now I kind of get philosophical about it. I think punk's gonna be there a 100 years from now. There's gonna be funny haircuts, except its going to be new-school punk rockers like 9 year olds and 10 year olds going '*I hate my dad, it's cool*,' you know?"

"*Any closing thoughts?*"

Peace, love, bliss. I'm trying to envision the world that I wanna live in and make it happen. I think that's where the true thing's going. Not to compare us to Ghandi, MLK or anything like that, but in that vein I'm trying to create the world I wanna see created. You've got to be the example of what's going on. And that's what's challenging and fun in punk rock, bumping into 15-16 year olds. Just to share with them what I feel. I'm trying to heal myself and become a better person all the time. Love life, appreciate it. I don't live like this angry, dead cop, boiling over rage kind of person. I still am upset by the Multi Death Corporation run by these damned Christians hell-bent on pursuing Armageddon and this rapture that's going to destroy the world and microwave the planet. That does upset me, but I'm trying to infuse love energy into it because all the hate would just kind of consume me...

A BRIEF, SHINING MOMENT

"You know, one story I like to tell – I got dropped off in Detroit, it was at a bar. We had been in the van for 4 hours and I was tired. I go in and have a beer. All of a sudden this guy comes up to me, like 6 foot 2 skinhead, he's got these white power tattoos – 'kill niggers' on his arm. I'm just thinking 'Holy shit, what's this guy all about?'

I go, 'Hey man, what's up?' He goes, 'Yeah, I'm waiting for my friends, we're gonna fucking kick this fucking band – this commie fag band called MDC – we're gonna kick their fuckin ass tonight.' I'm like, 'Ah what's going on with that?' And he goes 'Yeah, their just commie fags, they just don't get it, buh buh buh – fuckin' sick of people like that telling me what to do buh-gruh-gruh.'

Starts talking about his Irish grandfather, how they always hated niggers in their family. You know, I got an Irish grandfather. He was always like accepting of people, he never used 'niggers.' He was just trying to get along and realized not everyone's perfect."

And he's like 'Yeah buh buh buh.' I go 'You know, I feel bad 'cause you got a lot of hate and anger.' And he's like 'Yeah they stole all our jobs,' that typical kind of skinhead thing. And I just kind of like hung with him. And he said he prays there'll be something for everyone in this life. And that's kind of what I want, and he's like, 'Yeah it's easy for you buh buh.'"

He's waiting around, looking at his watch, wastes a half hour, then he splits and never came back. Some skinheads did come that night and there was some shit, but he walked. It was like one of these enchanting moments where you're just with someone in this little bubble and your talking to 'em and somehow you dissipate just a little of their hatred. It doesn't always work that way."

"We both come from Irish grandfathers but you got this twist on life and I got this twist on life. But I've got hope in my twist and I'm just wishing you luck. I didn't tell him I'm Dave from MDC. He just backed off his hatred, got tired of waiting around for his friends. Never saw him again. I wrote a song about it called 'Something For Everyone.' And that happened in Detroit City..."

SEATTLE HEMPFEST 2007

Sunday morning now, the Plankton house again. Somehow this has been going on for 11 days, and it's the final one. From here on out, I'll be riding in a van with Downtown Brown 6 straight weeks. Fate has plopped me out at the hard-fought goal line and I now receive finest post-Championship reception imaginable – today is the 15th annual Hempfest/3rd Annual Seattle Zombie March.

In one hour I will smoke for free every strain of marijuana in North America in front of the police nonstop in a celebration of every fringe subculture combined. The roll-call will be dynamic – multi-ethnic crowds of punks, ravers, hippies, goths, metalheads, juggalos, gangstas & even preps. Many have traveled worldwide for the opportunity, all uniting in a magical, impromptu Golden Gate whilst intermingling with gore-caked zombies who are more interested in toking hashish then devouring flesh. The peace pipe bridges all ethnic and deceased barriers...

At the security tent I greet Kevin Black, who's been the head of Hempfest security for the past 6 years. He's a longhair with a snakeskin cowboy hat, jolly as Saint Nick after a December 26th nightcap: *"The Hempfest we call a pro-testival; it's the most successful and largest hemp festival in the world. We work with our police; we haven't had an arrest in 5 years. The police are here to make sure we're safe, not arrest people for pot."*

"We have about 70 speakers, all the top drug reform people form around the world show up here. We have the founder of NORML, the founders of the Marijuana Policy Project. We've got Rick Steves who hosts 'Travels Through Europe' on PBS. We've had Mark Steponowsky from the Dallas Cowboys speak. Our former police chief Norm Stamper, Woody Harrelson's been here a few times. Ed Rosenthal's here every year."

"Oh yeah, by the way, welcome to Seattle." Black scrunches his index finger into a pack of Marlboro Reds and slings out a fat joint, smiling as he tosses it towards me. It spins in the air ever so epic, as if Excalibur, before landing in my greasy mitts…

"…WE GOT OUR BROTHERS AND SISTERS DYING IN IRAQ, AND WE HAVE THE GOVERNMENT PUSHING THE FAILED DRUG WAR ON ALL OF US? THE BEST PART OF HEMPFEST IS THAT IT MAKES IT A POLITICAL STATEMENT. IT DOESN'T MATTER IF YOU'RE YOUNG OR OLD, YOU ARE THEM MOST LIKELY DEMOGRAPHIC TO BE ARRESTED FOR MARIJUANA. OVER 10 BILLION DOLLARS A YEAR FOR OVER 700,000 MARIJUANA ARRESTS. A STUDY CAME OUT THIS WEEK THAT SAID DRUGS ARE MORE PREVALENT IN AMERICAN SCHOOLS THEN EVER BEFORE AND PARENTS ARE IN DENIAL ABOUT IT? WE SAY SCREW THE FEDERAL GOVERNMENT! WE NEED TO REBUILD THE COMPASSION FOR SICK AND DYING PEOPLE WHO ARE USING MEDICAL MARIJUANA TO TREAT CHEMOTHERAPY, AND GLAUCOMA, AND HIV, AND MULTIPLE SCLEROSIS BECAUSE THE FEDERAL GOVERNMENT SAYS THE MEDICINE THAT GIVES THEM HEALING AND RESPITE FROM THEIR CONDITION IS ILLEGAL AND HAS NO MEDICAL VALUE…"

The bullhorn guy rages on from the stage, spouting off an endless brigade of factoids. A white-dressed lady with fairy wings skips by us, tossing around rolled joints like flower pedals. People are handing out hash butter lumps, and so many clouds are poofing it looks like the smoky aftermath of Gettysburg.

In about two seconds this Jersey guy who looks like George Carlin is gonna come in here and say some funny shit: *"My name is Rick Cusick and I'm the associate publisher of High Times magazine. I have the honor every year of coming to the Seattle Hempfest and talking to about a 10,000 people. It's been around for 16 years, this is my 3rd year in a row. It is by far the best marijuana law reform event in the country. They have an extreme organizational integrity and it shows. The West Coast has a great marijuana culture."*

"What's the Cannibus Cup like?"

Rick Cusick: "It happens in Amsterdam every year before thanksgiving. 2,000 plus Americans visit Amsterdam and it's like Mardi Gras. A thousand judges get to judge the best pot in the world. Wonderful experience, but I highly recommend taking a massage half-way through just to get back to normal."

"You're from New Jersey. My experience in New York and the area is that post 9-11 it's become somewhat of a police state"...

"New Jersey's a tough nut to crack. It's the worst place in the world for drug testing solutions. You go to jail 3-4 years every time you get tapped for a solution out of a drug test. New York since Bloomberg has gotten a lot better, but under Rudy Giuliani they'd run you through the system for smoking a joint on the street. It sure as hell ain't California. As I said in my speech it's war. Families are being destroyed, people are having their lives destroyed at too young an age. I'm not saying there isn't a drug problem in this country. I'm saying the problem is the way they are conducting it. They're aggression is totally misinformed and ineffective. That's what's really going on. We all want to stop drug addiction in its worst forms. We all want to make sure drunk drivers don't kill anybody. That's in everyone's best interest. But they focus on marijuana. There wouldn't be a drug war if there wasn't marijuana. It does more good than it does harm. I don't think it does any harm at all."

"What's something remarkably bizarre that happened to you during this fest?"

"Yesterday I was talking to a local activist in this southern drawl about how he wants to open a cannabis ministry and he wants to start a daycare center. Then he reaches down and says '*hey check this out,*' hikes up his pant leg, and he has a titanium leg. He reached down, unhooks it and hands it to me. I'm holding the guys leg, examining it, like someone just handed me their needlework."

More sluggish hours creep by whilst casually viewing live performances & baked speakers. The headliners of the fest were a lazy Disturbed meets Rob Zombie ordeal with bad industrial programming, and a hair-metal cover band with corpse-paint & hot Japanese chick bass player. Other than that it was a third rate Pearl Jam clone-a-palooza.

8pm, growing dark. The park is clearing out and I'm staring into the dim sunset over the lightly glistening river body. The obnoxious black girl from junkie park is no longer with the dreadlocked guy. She is hobbling with a cane alongside a group of squatters, talking differently – a total chameleon, becoming whatever she wants day by day, breezing with the wind…

Watching this baked mass of people – all the docile, half-slumbering individuals clomping quietly out the park – for once I look at it through the eyes of a Jack Webb. Yes, marijuana has all these great uses. Yes, I will smoke pot until the day I die. But everyone here is a zombie, flaccid as lambs, fighting tooth & nail for the right to be red-eyed and sleepy.

The cops aren't right, but they are correct about the nickname "dope." That zany 7th grade *Cheech & Chong* view of things – all it really boils down to is confusion, giggling, and a hamper on any real spunk. It may be an artificial paradise, but it's our right to embody…

TOPEKA KANSAS, TWO DAYS LATER

Old guy on the bus, kind of senile with a cane, blinks a lot, not too bright. Asks what I'm writing. I kind of dodge the book. I ask about his life, he dodges it too. Indirectly we get on the subject of music...

Turns out to be a guy called George Gleason. You know how ASCAP has a network of songwriters and lyricists whom people like Ricky Martin and Lindsay Lohan buy material from and don't credit? Fucker wrote the lyrics for "Purple Rain." His words were covertly picked up by Led Zepplin, Guns N Roses, James Taylor, Kid Rock, Uncle Kracker, Santana (*"Spanish Harlem Mona Lisa"*)…

He goes on to tell me all this shit about Sonny Barger, and how he owes George a favor, and one day he'll be calling out the Hells Angels on the sleaze-ball Hollywood douches who've fucked him: *"Those fucks at ASCAP, they haven't paid me shit in 15 years. They owe me $250,000. The things been dragging in court forever… But I'd still recommend you try it. All you gotta do is come up with something catchy and send it c/o Yoko Ono. She'll get it. She always does…"*

PART XI: GHOSTNOMAD VS AMERIKA
(THE SPREAD THE DISEASE TOUR)
AUGUST 31ST-OCTOBER 13TH 2007

TO SHATTER EVERY MYTH

People seem to have this impression that touring in a band is this glamorous thing where flocks of women throw themselves at you and money rains effortlessly. If you are on tour therefore you are a celebrity, and therefore you are rich of greenbacks.

Nothing could be further from the truth. Although I am fairly accomplished in my own right, I am horridly destitute, because every dime of profit goes right back into the war machine. It's poverty or quits, and Murphy's Law triumphs all.

You've read first-hand how impossible it is for a rock n' roll journalist of some repute to get around completely solo, but a full band with anywhere from 3 to 6 members plus a merch guy? It is economically impossible unless you are amazingly talented, can authentically work an audience, and successfully plant the seeds that will benefit you the second time around.

As an independent act you will never make money on your first three tours because you will rarely get a guarantee, and every profit will be burned in the process. You will always play for free until you have the fan base established and can actually draw heads, or have been visible enough to where you are respected and have strong personal contacts in a handful of key cities. Gas prices are horrendous, food costs are insane, and motels are for suckers. You will freeze, starve, be filthy, sexless, uncomfortable, and constantly want to jump off a bridge.

To initiate a professional, successful tour is to cough up $1,000-$10,000 for a decent van, throw down $1,000-$3,000 in shirts/patches, have a top-notch album to promote ($1,000-$20,000 to record and master properly + $1,500-$3,000 to press). Money in the bank for gas ($500 is cutting it close), gotta raid the dollar store for ramen noodles/spaghettio's to subsist ($100), print and mail high-quality tour posters to all venues ($300).

If you are lacking contacts or otherwise inept at bullshitting your foot into the door, you'll have to pay a well-connected booking agent to schedule the entire thing (anywhere from $300-$10,000). If you can't handle this, don't convince yourself for one second that you can push a tour more than two weeks. Stick to regional, short-burst outings or be devoured by your half-ass unprofessionalism.

You must launch a crushing propaganda offensive. There are two avenues to this – either D.I.Y. or Press Relations. If you go D.I.Y. then be prepared to aggressively take on monster email lists, guerrilla advertising, street teams, diplomatic channels, back-alley deals, countless internet hours, and the crown jewel of brainwashing every niche media outlet that you mean business.

Your album has to coincide with your tour or you will get no press. They need your record at least 2-3 months in advance of its release or you get no press. If you get a push from a label that runs advertising in that magazine, or if you buy ads yourself, its usually a case of one hand washing another – *so long as you're good, professional, and you deserve it*. However, you don't always need to grease the wheels. If one of the writers or the editor digs you enough you'll get away with it.

If you have stretched all possible limits, or are just utterly inept to this business lingo, it is in your best interest to hire a PR Man (*anywhere from $500-$10,000 + mailing and postage at your personal expense*). You have to hawk-eye the PR Guy and the Booking Man to make sure they don't bumble it. Even if they come through with flying colors you still have to investigate the venues you've been scheduled for. Make sure some fool promoter hasn't booked ONLY you. No one will come, the bar will fart, and you will never be booked again. You must take things into your hands, consult the promoter, and book local acts to ensure people there.

DROP THE IDEOLOGICAL SHIT – bars throw concerts so people will spend money on their booze. If no one shows up and there are five bands stuffed in a room playing for each other, this still equals out to about 30 people drinking, which is the usual small bar quota. The bar makes money then you make money.

You have to be wise enough to be part traveling salesman, part carnival barker, and all propagandist. The merch table is a garage sale, and you have to convince random drunks to buy a CD instead of that next Jaeger shot for the wasted chick in the corner he's trying to lure into the backseat of his pickup. You have to give a 110% legendary performance. Don't get shit-faced before you play and try to hack it. Make the local bands respect you, because they are the only one's that really count, not the drunk chick with the Jaeger bomb whose fiddling with your man-sack. The musicians are the repeat audience, not the wasted guy with the sparkly birthday hat dancing around the jukebox.

Every one of the band members should be assigned to a specific task – one guy schmoozes with the promoter, one guy collects all the local papers for contacts, one guy wanders around with the email list, one guy does the merch, and another MUST remain sober. One drunk driving arrest and its curtains. You're all in lock up for the night + the van and all the gear will cost at least a $1,000 to get out.

Secondly, if you are outside the bar circuit, you have three other main options here – big concert venue, house show, or All Ages gig (i.e. skate park, youth center, squat, coffee shop, sewer show). House shows are essential because that's where the networking Goliath lies. You don't make any money, you just give into the party bug and lay down inter-personal connections. If you play an All Ages venue this is where disposable income flows, and it will all be towards your merch. Don't expect door or gas money.

All Ages shows are the most fertile ground for repeat audiences. The problem is that in most cities they can't get into the bars. This forges a careful balancing act, and you might consider two dates in the city – one bar, one All Ages. Just don't let any promoter find out because they are stupid and do not understand the concept of a separate audience. In a hot-headed panic they will cancel the gig just to spite you for their "loss of money," even though you've no guarantee/audience.

A) <u>MAINTAIN THE ILLUSION AT ALL COSTS</u>: The random individual automatically assumes you are bigger then you actually are because you're on tour. Let them believe what they will. Even at such a base career level, you must understand that 90% of America will never get to the point you are at. The average Joe works a shitty dead-end job, probably has kids, pays way too much for an apartment, and this show is his one little Friday night escape from the banalities of existence.

Your unspoken job is to live their dream. They all want to run away with the circus but know they're fucked. Be that thing to them, help nurse that imagination, and leave a lasting impression. Treating these people like they are in fact the rock stars is what propagates a self-sustaining inertia that will continue to blossom. They are also your best chance outside of local bands for getting a place to crash or meal.

Even though you know you're a shit-head, they think you're Captain Cool, and it will all be worth it in the end when they call their friends up the next day and say, *"Holy shit! Guess who slept on my floor last night? Never heard of 'em? Well blah blah blah...'* You become a mini-legend in their saga, and karma boomerangs.

B) <u>TREAT ALL "GROUPIES" WITH RESPECT</u>: Unless, of course, you're GG Allin. But if you desire a long-lasting, healthy relationship, there are a few solid rules. These people are here because they dig your music. They think you're on the level, they are there to support you. Don't hide backstage and refuse to speak to anyone like a rock star asshole (*unless you have some mysterious King Diamond vibe*).

   Try to be friendly, if only a nod of the head or a quick handshake. Don't act "*hardercore-than-thou*," don't try to fuck their girlfriends, and don't insult them because they are wearing the t-shirt of a band you think is bunk. You can still be a class act without feeling obligated to owe them a night out on the town.

C) <u>SEX</u>: Don't kid yourself – you will rarely ever get laid. Punk is way too high-fallutin', and heavy metal crowds are 90% male. Weird bands attract isolated, awkward, asexual geeks, and industrial shows coagulate prude, flirtatious melodramatics and way too many STD's. Guys in bands are ugly, smelly people and the beautiful, intelligent girls that you'd romance in a heartbeat will never stoop to a cheap screw with a trashed band guy. If they do decide to embrace the one night fling scenario, while you'll think you're ape-shit lucky, in reality what's happening is that God hates you. She's in heat 'cause she's ovulating and nature demands coitus and pregnancy. ALWAYS WEAR A CONDOM & NEVER GO DOWN ON HER. Remember – she's gonna leave comments all over your MySpace page and your REAL girlfriend will find out. Plus you'll brew a monster stigma in whatever town that might've been, with jealous ex-boyfriends, whatever. In fucking them, you're only really fucking yourself.

**In the end, if you break even, you are a fucking champ. Going a grand in the red is still marvelous. If you have what it takes, whooptie whoop. Go get 'em tiger. Just don't be surprised when you learn exactly why some swallow that double barrel...

DETROIT (8/31)

It seems fitting that The Magic Stick (*crown venue/bowling alley of the Nuthugger Mafia*) is the first assault of both my and Downtown Brown's biggest campaign ever. The staff hates both of us with a passion as do the majority of scenesters, but DTB always makes them so much cash they let it fly.

It's perpetually a crowd of 400 non-scenesters, kids driving in from the suburbs who would never do so otherwise. The uptight punk uniform people with the tight black pants and converse sneakers go hide in their corners, and the garage rockers bolt out the door. Then there is myself, whom they won't even look at.

I find it rather amusing that the poster from *The Silent Burning's* release party is framed on the wall now. Of course my name isn't listed on it, and if it was they'd just cross it out with magic marker. What a magnificent night it was – Amino Acids CD release party, Bump N Uglies CD release party, MAN INC's first show before European tour, and The Slats from Iowa...

It was the peak of all those bands playing that night. I was off in the corner with my own stand watching people flipping through *The Silent Burning*'s pages with disgusted scowls. I had no illusions – it was my final night as The Golden Boy and I was riding the mortgage on that game of craps. The love of my life (*of another era*) floated in, having disappeared to Tennessee with no contact for over a year. This is long after she caused the World Trade Center bombings, as you may know.

But what a xenial night it was – I got the girl back, my first book had come out after so many years of struggle, the absolute tippy-top of the Detroit era. I was so filled with happy juice that my brain couldn't handle the chemical rush and kept puking all morning.

Two weeks later she was gone and my entire base had turned on me. I didn't understand it – the way fate hands you a fairy tale ending, then just shits on your face the moment you allow yourself to feel it. The highest-speed career suicide campaign in the cities history was definitely underway. I knew I'd alienate people, just not the ones I did. It was the equivalent of Hitler dropping *Mein Kampf* and in response every German abandons him while for some odd reason the Jews turn it into a bestseller...

And here we are today, the place that started it all, nearly 3 years later. It's my first spoken word gig in Detroit in nearly a year, and my first official performance since I left for California. No one I contacted showed up, and the scenesters still won't look at me. Yeah, it's ok when GG Allin does anything, but I'm an asshole.

Nearing midnight and the floor is packed & sweaty. There are about 400 people all stomping their feet for Downtown Brown, because it's their first show since getting kicked off the Van's Warped Tour. While on the road with that massive carnival Swisher (DTB's saxophonist) got into an all-out brawl with security, and then 5 minutes later Glover fell off a three-story roof wearing nothing but a Superman Speedo and cape. Drunk, he bounced off a parked car and was presumed dead by onlookers. One concussion and a $2,700 cat-scan bill later, he's right back up to par.

Counter Cosby warmed up the audience, Salt Lick got them going, Screaming Mechanical Brain pushed them hard, now DTB will destroy. They want the mullet power. Instead, they get me, which just prolongs the explosion. Neil and the boys are sitting down onstage, and none of these people are in the mood for comedy.

When Neil says "*I introduce to you, Mr. Ryan Bartek,*" a crowd of people in the back start chanting "*FUCK RYAN BARTEK, FUCK RYAN BARTEK!!!*" At first I'm thrown off because I perceive it as an insult, but then I remember that's what I've always had them shout when supporting me.

I grab the mic and get into it. I'm keeping it short and sweet – *the Barack Obama poop story.* But I decided to prolong it a little with the whole Catholic explanation, which is wearing thin. They are restless and not having it. A gaggle of 4 up front keep yelling "*DTB, DTB!!!*" over my words, then stop, then start again with "*YOU HATE BLACK PEOPLE, YOU HATE BLACK PEOPLE!!!*" I break my routine and stop the hecklers with a "*NOT TRUE.*

When I finally get to the part where I meet Obama, the crowd has turned to a hushed silence. So I drop the punch line. No one laughs, but they look whimsical. Then I go, "*You know what Barack said to me? He said Ryan Bartek, you're going on tour with the craziest, moistest, most ludicrous band ever from Detroit. You're gonna fuckin' eat hot dogs and battle luchadores with the sweatiest, man-hairiest, hot-rocking band in the world, motherfucking Downtown motherfuckin' Brown!!!*" The place explodes. "*Can I get a hallelujah my brothers and sisters!!!*" "HALLELUJAH!!!"

Place goes wild and I dodge out back stage. The Screaming Mechanical Brain guys pop up immediately, Reverend John Wheeler with his dreadlocks and bifocals. They totally dug it and are psyched to be featured in the last half of the book. The positive reception feels good, but I can't shake the *"YOU HATE BLACK PEOPLE"* thing. *Where the fuck did that come from??*

CHICAGO (9/1)

"What's the big deal? It was a CD release party. That's the key word – PARTY. Even my mom bitched at me." Neil is still piecing together last night, when after three free shots too many, he blacked out and couldn't remember how to play the last few songs. People were walking out, the staff were shaking their heads. They got through an hour of material before Neil started making up new songs off the top of his head and farted all the way off stage.

It was total chaos. They had their live horn section of Benny and Swisher, with tiny Benny in an over-sized rubber Smiegel mask complete with the little brown loincloth. Swisher was hammered in a wrestling leotard, and ran into the backstage waking me up by pissing all over the wall. So nonchalant with his penis in his hand while all these groupie girls are drinking, and all he wants to do is talk about *Trailer Boys*.

Neil was in drunken retard strength mode, laughing & dry humping Swisher on the floor of the former mosh pit in plain view of all their fans. It took all our combined efforts to get him to pay the opening bands and shove him in the van, because he was an unstoppable belligerent juggernaut Commented Neil: *"It's my party and I'll black out if I want to."*

We hear a lurching clomp the stairs, and a solanum-infected Glover dredges from the basement, quivering in shakes of white-ghost alcohol poisoning. He's soaked in shit water because the freezing basement had flooded overnight. For hours he'd incubated in a piss-soaked, feces ravaged sleeping bag…

MINNEAPOLIS (9/2)

It's a 6 hour drive from Chicago to Minnesota, "The Star of the North." Minneapolis – Screaming Mechanical Brain's hometown. Last night's gig was at the Oasis Café, a quaint all-ages Coffee House. There were 150 kids for DTB, and they kept feeding us chocolate cake & Scotch stolen from their liquor cabinets.

For this tour I'm resigned to tales specifically pulled from the city in which I'm appearing. Better way of connecting with the crowd, and a good way to cut my teeth. Problem is I'm going in with totally untested scripts. I had a moderately receptive performance, ranting about hobos from Chicago like the "Blankman" bum with the garbage can accessorized superhero tool belt and aluminum foil cape; the chain-smoking Jesus in the purple robe slinging a massive wooden crucifix.

The big-set ender – *besides Obama, which I'll be dropping for every finale* – was the Grant Park tale where my friends smoked a *"wicky stick"* of PCP with the homeless. One was aced out his mind and kept telling me of the Bum King in the subway tunnels, a hushed mythical character known only as "Red Dragon" (*"Red Dragon know all... Red Dragon gunn get you!!!"*).

We've been killing time during our Minneapolis haul with a Billy Jack marathon, since no one was aware of the spin-kicking, hippie protecting, kung-fu Indian. Billy is to be our symbolic guide throughout this journey. We've a lot to learn from his nomadic ways, especially me, since I've only $180 bucks left for the next 6 weeks.

Outside the Triple Rock Social club the first band to visit me is a local called THEY LIVE; a black-haired piss-n-vinegar guitarist named Casey Boyd takes the controls: *"We're really influenced by Samhain, 80's stuff like The Cure, doomier goth stuff. Goth these days is for the most part a cartoonish fashion show. We are goth more in the timeless cosmic horror sense of an author like H.P.Lovecraft, where if you are considering suicide it's because of some great cosmic terror and not because the girl that works at hot topic broke your heart. We just played in Iowa last night with some hate-core sXe band called Total War. That was interesting, ha..."*

"What do you have to say about Minneapolis?"

"The music scene here's alright. I'm into The Falls, Corpse Show Creeps, The Funeral and the Twilight, Full Moon Massacre, Blue Ox and anyone else that's not all about total cookie-cutter conformity. I think a lot of the bands are lazy, don't make any money off it, so they just quit. We're kind of like those old rappers like Easy E. They put out those CD's with criminal activity money. We do things very illegitimately. Like our shirts, we just go out and steal them from Michaels Arts & Crafts, silkscreen them ourselves. Even if we sell them for a $1 we're making a profit. Last night we just gave them all out."

"How do you feel about the Minnesota punk scene?

"The punk scene in general is pretty stale. I like high school punk bands, where it's just 3 chords and angry, nihilistic lyrics. When I see alcoholic punks in their mid to late 20s who blame all of their problems on the government it really brings me down. Most of the crust punks that I have encountered live in mansions in financially affluent areas. I'd imagine that their whole crust image is not much more than a rebellion phase against their rich college educated parents. I myself am into cleanliness and order."

"I take it you got your band name from..." "That John Carpenter movie. The aliens that run everything but no one really knows"... *"Do you think that could possibly be real?"* "Oh definitely; all the successful people pray to the lizards. They really run things." *"Multidimensional cheese faces..."* "Crabs for eyes..."

STEVENS POINT (9/3)

"Killswitch Engage is so heterosexual they ought to be lifting weights onstage!" The thin, Labor Day weekend crowd roared at Neil's latest hit single, and my rant for last evening was the nature girl CVS photo story c/o Denis Wilson/Brenner's quasi-pagan campsite march. Tonight carries the holiday weekend tradition further with another dead gig in Wisconsin and no local support.

We're playing a little coffee/booze hut called Mission Café, and Main Street looks like the humble town from *The Blob* remake. An obnoxious 40 something guy named "Morphine Mike" keeps trying to grab Neil's microphone. He's dancing around like fruitcake, shouting anecdotes about booting up. He's audible on the recording as I chat with Sandi Plaza, the promoter of the evening.

She's a middle-aged old school metalhead biker with tats running up and down her arms. She played bass for ONIS, Eternal Silence, and Legion. Amusingly she also has that Francis McDormand *Fargo* accent: *"Legion was my self-proclaimed death metal project in the early 90's, and I promoted a lot of shows here in Stevens Point. Legion was a message of things that people didn't want to face - death, dying, religion, the hypocrisy – rape, grotesque rape, just crazy shit. Eternal Silence was pretty much the same, kind of like the old Carcass days. ONIS was about suicide, the realities of life, an ugly side to everything. Sadly I'm no longer in either band – the drama thing, which I want no part of."*

"We're in kind of a desolate small town in Wisconsin here. Do the locals stare you down for having all the tattoos and the scary demon shirts or have they relaxed over the years?"

"Wisconsin used to be 10 years behind, maybe even 15. Back in the early 90's extreme metal was not seen here at all. People would look at me like '*Oh my god, she's a Satanist. She's evil, she's terrible, she's marked.*' People are accepting it now. Parents are starting to say this is a good thing. The kids are supervised."

"How do you feel about extremist actions in underground metal?"

"To each his own, but I just recently lost a friend who took his life. I've seen this happen a lot in the extremist metal, like the black metal. I personally draw the line with cutting yourself onstage. I'm not a fan of that. I don't even want to watch it to be honest. I can see people pouring fake blood... To me it's like I'm an actress putting on a play. I had the gauntlets. Sometimes I'd corpse-out. We weren't making a mockery of it, we were just being fun."

"What do you think of Glen Benton? Do you know Will Rahmer?"

"I love Glen. I've known him since '91, we've been good friends... Will is a good friend of mine. He started NYDM. He's a biker, so am I. So I know what it's about to be a brother and a sister. A good friend of mine, Don Decker, he's the regional NYDM president for the 5 states in this area. I'm not a member, but I'm a supporter. My plate is full, but I still reach out to help."

"Is it true that Will Rahmer never smiles?"

"No, he smiles a lot, ha ha. He'll kick my ass, but he smiles. And Glen smiles too. And he does have an inverted cross very deep into his forehead. It's about that same thing – brotherhood, sticking to the music. That's we he's got a mark. I have my marks too..."

ALLEGEN (9/4)

Swinging back through Michigan for a show in Allegen, a town I've never even heard of. Last night we ended up at the house of a guy who played in a band with one of the other guys from American Headcharge. Everyone got trashed and shaved their heads. SMB vocalist Reverend John Wheeler now has bricks like Vanilla Ice, and Glover has a zigzagged, sideways Mohawk.

We did get a free breakfast though, through a 17 year old high school girl that worships SMB. She threw down $120 on grub, which I thought was raw. I had to scold everyone into paying the tip out of courtesy. Regardless of ethics, the table across the dining room was filled with her jocko classmates and she was so happy rubbing it in their faces, flipping them off, feeling oh so super-cool to be hanging out with rock stars she idolized. That one breakfast tab made her Senior year. *She is the most beautiful thing in the world right now...*

Allegen: the Groundsphere Rhythm Café. It's Labor Day and not far from Kalamazoo – we are playing an old barn silo turned into a coffee shop/booze-stocked multi-purpose venue. I'd have killed to have an all ages spot like this when I was a kid. Instead there are only 7 people here, and it's the venues last show ever due to lack of attendance. Terrible, but what else can you expect hooking up a monster venue like that when nothing surrounds you for 30 miles but pure farmland?

CLEVELAND (9/5)

Peabodies in Cleveland. I'm on one knee with my hand reaching towards the sky epically, spotlight shining intensely on me. What a dramatic way to get across Battle Mountain. It's a pretty hammered show, and no one really gets why I'd want to fly an airplane into a hilltop to score a record contract.

Onward to the after party, the three-level house of a Betty Page type. There are Boris Karloff posters all over the walls, and the nice straight-edge Jewish girl who Glover and I chased around all night saying, "*Billy Jack isn't real...BUT TOM LAUGHLIN IS!*" happens to be drinking tequila and smoking bong loads. Turf from SMB drags her off somewhere, and SMB's merch guy Skode and I keep drinking Everclear.

Lord we are so wasted. Peabodies gave us endless drink tickets and this house has so much vodka lying around that everyone turns Barney Gumble. It's my first time alone with the SMB caravan, 'cause DTB took off with some guy that looks like Rick Moranis for a night of strip club hijinks.

Skode ups the ante by stripping naked. He's got green hair, sort of looks like a young, scruffy Brad Pitt with muttonchops, and is trying to woo the Betty Page girl. She spreads Skodes buttcheeks wide open and shaves his asshole in front of a roaring, obliterated household... Another shot of Tequila and I too am wandering around butt naked. I usually don't go skinny dipping at 3am, but Betty shaved a pentagram in my chest and it seemed appropriate...

BUFFALO (9/6)
"How do you feel about the tour so far?"

Reverend John Wheeler: "It's been more fun than our last. We didn't have a merch guy, it was just the four of us floating through the blankness of space."

"Any harsh Bible Belt experiences?"

"We didn't run across any angry yokels. In Iowa we tried to turn around off this weird road, and this guy that had this haircut from the 70's, Napoleon Dynamite glasses and a mustache came running off his porch yelling something at us. But I just rolled up the window up and drove away. I think he was just sitting there doing drugs all day waiting to attack someone on his property. I almost ran him over. I figured that was probably best."

"Tell me what awaits us in Nashville."

"Well not the pussy of lore. None that you'd be interested in anyway... Nashville's kind of stinky. It's a dirty, bummy town. Last time we stayed with Turfs' uncle. It was this storage space and everyone got covered in these weird bug bites everybody thought was an STD for awhile."

Turf: "I was convinced I'd had AIDS for 12 hours..."

"Chiggers, I think chiggers. These little black bugs that dig into your skin..."

Turf: "I had lime sized wounds covering my entire groin..."

"See they started on his groin, and there's no one who's ever been happier in history that a rash spread all over their entire body. '*Well it's probably not an STD since its on my face now.*' Or it's the worst one ever and you just discovered it."

"Good Reverend, you have a story published in this book here – 'Tour Smart And Break The Band' by Martin Atkins. Right when you open this book up he declares you have to be a propagandist, you have to be the dictator of your own enterprise, and you need to be an underground diplomat. You think he's dead on?"

Turf: "When my mom told me it was a good idea that I started playing music, she didn't tell me that I'd also have to learn web design, graphic design, interpersonal relations, psychology, vehicle maintenance, equipment maintenance..."

"It's a surprisingly blue collar enterprise for something that's supposed to be so artsy. Atkins is pretty much right about everything in there. Him and I talk on and off, there's been rocky patches and good patches. I do agree with everything he says. Would I want to be on his label? Probably not. Do I think he's right about how he runs things? Yeah."

"Where is the scumbag line drawn? I mean we are running around openly telling these girls that we are in fact complete scumbags..."

"Well I am a total scumbag. But you don't necessarily advertise that... Maybe we're the true nihilists. We throw garbage everywhere, we don't care about anything. *'Well what are your opinions on like veganism and like war and stuff?'* I think it's all a big smoke-screen, it's this hive of scum and villainy. Everything's a big crazy control system. I think beliefs are doled out to people to polarize them and keep them busy. We're kind of just destructive and wasteful and all we do is watch our bottom line so we can continue making art."

Turf: "You can't get into this game expecting to make money. Music is one of the most ridiculously competitive fields in America. If you look at the top three dream professions, musician is the number one thing. Everyone wants to do this, everyone thinks they can do this. The president wants to be a rock star... By proxy the only people that are able to do it are the ones that are the absolute most cut-throat, most diabolical, most business like. It sucks 'cause there's such a fine balancing act. You have to wear your artist cap while you're writing the stuff, but as soon as you walk out of the practice space you have to flip into evil business guy mode. You have to be smarmier and smarter then everyone else out on the road that's trying to screw you over too."

"If you think you're gonna be a long-haired pothead rather than a coked up Wallstreet tycoon from the 80's you're sorely mistaken. Maybe that's why coke-heads get so much done. I just have a natural inclination to act like a person on meth amphetamines."

"What else is on your mind?"

"Our goal with this – and this is either cliché or delusional – we want to be like punk in 1977 or grunge in 1988. We might get fucked – someone will do it better, someone living in California with rich parents. Maybe we'll find a way to bottle it and market better than anybody else, be the one sell-out new crazy experimental band on magazine covers with leather pants on... One of the goals I have for the new record is to give a soul to the machine. I want to bring warmth to two things that are notoriously cold and metallic – any kind of real heavy metal and any kind of industrial, electro music."

"What are your lyrics mainly about?"

"It tends to be social stuff. Big sweeping political problems will function in the same way as your bullshit little drama problems. Its funny the weird parallels between a conquering nation and some girl that fucks too many people you know. I believe in the cyclical nature of history and I believe in watching patterns. I have a theory that all alchemists and wizards that kings would keep around were just people that were very learned and good at recognizing patterns."

"Do you have a theory about ghosts?"

"The one thing I've heard is the ghosts that you see are imprints. It doesn't even have to be someone that's dead. Like if someone used to live in a house, and you know they just moved, and you know their still alive but you see them out of the corner of your eye. It's because they used to inhabit that house and leave some sort of prestige material behind. That could be it. When you fall asleep or take a hallucinogenic drug, you might be walking through a forest made of snakes but that's not necessarily real but it seems so at the time. I know when I'm on enough acid that a snake's really not coming out of the ground, but it sure looks like it."

"Do you have any intense inward goal?"

"One of my big goals is to just live totally like *Fight Club*, or at least where I could if I wanted. I enjoy living somewhere that's not disgusting, because life is short and little things make you happy. At the same time I want to be free to do whatever I want at any given time. I don't believe that rock and roll should have rules. You have to wear these pants, you have to structure your breakdowns just so, you have to be a vegan, you have to be a skinhead, you have to do something. I don't have to do anything. Someone's got a real bad taste of the 'supposed to's' here. I got enough of that spending however many years in public school…"

"You know, it's really strange this European style housing from the 1800's. All these houses squeezed together like London because they didn't grasp the concept that so much land was out West." This is Turf's rumination as we walk these historic neighborhoods where all homes are 4 level complexes with 15 rooms each. The gig tonight is at Merlin's with a Zappa-esque, funk-heavy act called Anal Pudding.

DTB had a minor night at the strip-club, then Heavy Metal Karoake at another bar where Rick Moranis put a cigar out on his testicles. They were so intoxicated they left all of Glover's cymbals in Cleveland. Either we need them air-freighted to Columbus 6 days later, or burn a tank of gas swinging by Cleveland before the show…

ALBANY (9/7)

We wake up at Anal Puddings house, another one of those massive European-styled 4 level buildings. It reeks of dogs, and the carpet hasn't been vacuumed for at least a year. On the coffee table is an autographed photo of The Human Enigma – the Jim Rose Circus Sideshow guy that's covered in jigsaw puzzle tattoos. He hangs with those guys whenever he's in town and not busy eating live, raw trout.

Last night here was kind of scary. One of the AP guys said, *"It's cool with us that you're here, but our roommate is kind of crazy, and he's been freaking out when we've been letting bands crash, so just stay out of his way. He's pretty ruthless."*

We get lit on herb, and as we're tuckering out, the vicious roommate comes in. He's been walking the streets all night barefoot and shirtless, reeks like sweat-stained humidity, and he has these faded black denim jeans on plus a curly brown afro-puff. He slowly comes in and notices us, then, snake-like, moves to the dining room where he proceeds to stand there menacingly eating an apple.

This guy has petrifying charisma while he asks us questions, like a satanic Bob Ross gazing into your soul with Luciferic eyes, leaning against a piano and ceramic bust of Mozart. *Just slowly eating the apple, munching ever-so-delicately.* Glover and I were so freaked we'd sunk into the couches and soon fell asleep from his penance stare, like a hyperbolic reaction in trying to convince a grizzly you are dead.

In one big snake-caravan we head to Niagara Fall. SMB have been talking up Tesla's statue, which I for some reason thought was a monument to the hair-metal band. The waterfall an intense sight, there are so many rainbows jutting from the mist. Problem is you stand next to the railing and as the condensation hits, all that raw sewage dumped into the river clings to you like a sticky film. You walk out smelling like dead fish and a hint of piss...

Albany, New York. Same deal with the European houses. The venue is called Valentine's, a packed house of sporadically dressed robots & mad scientists. It's the perfect vibe for my monologue, which is about acupuncture at the San Diego bum corral. The Mathematicians are tonight's headliners, converging on tour as well for one evening.

They are another band I've been talking to all year about an interview. From Rochester, NY, they are like a cross between Beastie Boys, Chromeo, and Christopher Lloyd in *Back to the Future*. They all have pocket protectors and 50's atomic age scientist get-ups, and their show is theatrical and high-energy with tons of sound samples and visuals from projectors.

I walk up to Pete Pythagoras and stare a hole into his head until he stops his conversation. He looks at me, smiling with crazy eyes, totally creeping him out: "*I'm that GhostNomad guy. Told you we'd cross paths somehow – I just didn't think it'd be opening for you…*"

Outside the venue Skode, Glover and I eat delicious Pepper Steak. This big football-player looking black guy stares down at our funny hair: "*You lucky you ain't in no black neighborhood, othawise yo ass idd be up against tha wall.*"

Douchebag leaves postprandial, and this cutie-pie little 4 foot 9 street-girl with humongous breasts – like bigger then her head – solicits us liquid mushroom extract. Danny pulls a bright line from *The Born Losers* and asks if she wants to be "*A Downtown Brown Momma.*" "What's that?" "*Well when one of our members is feeling lonely, the momma comes right in and fixes him up see?*" "Do I get to go on tour?" Danny scumbaggedly lies to her. "Sure" she says, and jumps in his lap.

The guy she'd been tooling around with for the past week says "*Let's cut-out,*" angry and jealous. She tells him to piss off, dropping him on the spot. "*You're just gonna take off on tour with this band you don't even know the names of, just like that?!?*" She doesn't bother to answer him, just ogling at Danny's tentigo eyes. He wanders off into the night cursing obscenities…

"Explain to me the genesis of Mathematicians."

Pete Pythagoras: "Mathematicians started when I met Albert Gorithm IV on a Portland bus while we were both on a road trip. We had a former lab partner in the Northeast named Dewi Decimal and we thought he'd be the best possible option to complete the band. We write about math mostly as a metaphor, but it is usually a little deeper than merely numbers and formulas."

"You kidnapped yourselves for a live performance, correct?"

"Kidnapped ourselves? You must mean Halloween 2006 when we got kidnapped by 'The Terrorists' and they tortured and killed us as they played our songs at a live show. Following that event we were resurrected and made partially bionic. We had a year of cybernetic jams until we found out our friend Dr. Jonathan Phelps was possessed by an intergalactic creature that was trying to control us for its dubious scheme. Luckily Jonathan was aware enough to summon two-dimensional travelers who thwarted the creature possessing the good doctor. Just before that we had thwarted control from the micro chips placed in our bodies and were again ourselves, although we luckily maintained the super hero powers. And that happened Halloween 2007."

"If you had a mogwai would you feed it after midnight?"

"I would probably forget to feed the mogwai and it would either get pissed and leave or die. Actually, after the first day you have that mogwai, it will always be after midnight in a sense. So if you only feed it before midnight on the first day, shouldn't it be alright?"

"Damn, that is a brilliant point... What are the most important rules of the road as far as touring goes?"

"Bring plenty of socks and undies – the rest is negotiable. You will leave your towel somewhere and have to use your t shirt or a ground score towel. Be thankful to the promoter or bartender or kid who hooked you up with the show for any free beer or food or place to sleep. Make sure you figure out who is driving after the show before anyone starts drinking. Avoid McDonald's even though the dollar menu is economical. It will make you smell bad, like piss. You will also be hungry soon after... & after a month and a half on the road, home sometimes feels like the strangest place on Earth."

"How do we fight THE MAN?"

"That depends on what man. Is he an athlete? Does he know martial arts? Does he carry a shank? For that I guess you just have to follow your instincts. If you mean 'THE MAN' as in the powers that be or COINTELPRO then I would say take a long look at how you live. What do you buy? What do you say in public to other people? How do you treat other people? Notice the good but also pay attention to the stuff that might not be so good and think how it affects those around you and how that can all tie into why you are so pissed at 'THE MAN.' Then change your behavior to reflect what you have realized about yourself and your community..."

"Is Joe Vs. The Volcano a minor classic in your eyes?"

"Not too familiar. Saw it a long time ago. I guess it was funny. *Coming to America* is a legend. I know the whole script pretty much..."

MANHATTAN (9/8)

Back at another three-level European house with no sleep, about 10am. Skode, Glover, The Midget and I wandered Albany all morning. Ghetto place, trash bags flowing through empty streets, gang graffiti everywhere. he Midget is so into the momma thing it's twisted, and

Glover's been lying to her all night. She's absolutely convinced she's doing the whole tour with us.

"*She soooo wants to be our hooker Bob, she soooooooo wants it.*" "No, never, uh-uh." "*At least let's take her to New York and dump her off there. She has friends and will just stay there.*" "No, no, this is a terrible idea Bartek." "*But think of all the gas money we'll save selling her at rest stops dude, she's all about it. We can dress her up like a mime or a plumber, she can do all this specialty shit...*"

Sadly, we are forced to leave The Midget behind 'cause of Hairy Bob's party-pooper morality. She's pretty upset, but doesn't want to go off on us and spoil Glover's promise of "*Next time, uh huh, for sure baby.*" We are all such terrible people.

We get into the Manhattan after a long drive. Tonight we play The Delancy Lounge, same bar from Doro Pesch's birthday party. No German legends tonight – just us, promoter Frank Wood (*who talks like Harvey Feinstein*), and an 8 band bill that goes on until 4am.

It's downstairs though, and we have to shove all our equipment and merch bins through packed New York drunkards tossing around beads like Mardi Gras. The stage is the size of a hopscotch cube, and everyone is resigned to use a drum/amp back-line which are in extreme shambles. No time for comedy tonight, because every band starts 10 minutes after the other.

Outside both caravans are hanging out on porch steps drinking 40's. It's everyone's first time in NYC except for Neil and myself, and we're all having a blast. Just boys from The Bowery, obnoxiously hollering at any pretty lady walking by like construction workers, harassing bums for spare change and cigarettes. One gentlewoman got so pissed it took her boyfriend to hold her back, and CASS from SMB was sexually propositioned by a homeless women.

Midst the rabble I get a phone call from NYC band My Uncle The Wolf who were in New Orleans recording with one of the guys from DOWN last May while I was roaming with Skinhead Eddie. Well let's set this plotline right: "*New York is home, more then anything. Sometimes I wake up and I love being here, sometimes I want out,*" says Zach, the vocalist. "*George and I in particular, we used to deal with a lot of the new hardcore bands. After hanging out in that scene for a summer or so, we just got really sick of it because all its about is fighting and all that shit. We have our own clique – the four of us.*"

"Do you think the New York hardcore thing is just kind of jumped on because it's a tag that sells?" George the drummer takes this one. He's got a super mafia accent that just screams the purity of the Brooklyn: *"I don't even know if it sells, because the hardcore shows – nobody ever got paid for 'em. But it's kind of like a status. I don't wanna talk too much shit, but its kind of a high school thing all over again. People kind of disregard the music and pay more attention to the actions, like who knocked the shit outta who. We just wanted to jam man, go dancin'. We're rock and roll with the idea that anything goes. We've played sets where it's heavy as balls, but I wouldn't consider it metal. And we've played sets where we do a lot of quieter stuff, a lot of improv. The last show fuckin' Zach threw his mic down and got off the stage and we just jammed for 10 minutes."*

"How was your New Orleans adventure?" Joey takes this one: *"They were friends with Jimmy from DOWN a little while before I joined the band. He decided to bring us down there and cut our first record with him producing it. So we went to a studio in the middle of the woods for three weeks. We hammered out the tunes, rearranged them. Everyday consisted of waking up, driving to the studio, staying locked in there all day, coming home."*

George: *"This is like the weirdest fucking time for us. We had to get out of here, isolate ourselves in the woods, make this record, and I think we all were surprised by the quality of the work. And now we're talking about, feasibly – I don't wanna say anything 'cause its not in stone yet – but we're supposed to be getting out of New York for a long time."*

We all pause the interview because of an ambulance screaming buy, horns blaring. As it whizzes by us, there is a giant star of David painted on its side. *"Hasidic Jewish Ambulance, that's probably the only place you're ever gonna see that,"* remarks Zach. *Is it like their own ambulance service?* Joey says, "They have like little communities where they have their own police. They can't arrest you, but they can detain you."

"Is Harlem as dangerous as they say?"

"No, but the Bronx is," Joey adds.

George jumps in to defend it: *"If you go walking around like an asshole people are gonna fuck with you. But if you're cool…"*

Zach: *"The only thing you would see is a hooker at the corner. It's normal, that can happen in any part of New York."*

George: *"10-15 years ago the fuckin' city was a mess. Being from Brooklyn you never go to Times Square, EVER. And now different mayors..."*

Zach: *"There's a couple of movies you could watch, I'm talking 80's movies, where you can really see how bad the city looked. I'm talking that Tom Hanks movie, 'BIG.' You can see how shitty New York looked. I didn't go to Times Square until I was 15. When you're from here, that's one of those places that's a big Red X. You're not supposed to go there by yourself especially."*

"How do you feel about the NYDM thing?"

Zach: *"I know some of those guys and those types of cliques don't really bother me. Most of those guys are cool. The hardcore kids, they're gangs basically. You fuck with one of them, you're gonna have to fight them. The death metal guys are more open. All these kids, they just dress all thugged out and walk around with guns."*

George: *"When I got into hardcore like Black Flag and Bad Brains, what I understood about the underground hardcore scene in New York was that if you weren't accepted at home or school you'd go to Lamours or any one of those clubs, you made friends..."*

"Is Agnostic Front the only band that gets away with it?"

Zach: *"Well, they're one of the first. They're not starting fights with kids. What's going on now, these bands that claim they're influenced by Agnostic Front and Cro-Mags – when you go to different places, there's one scene that dominates. I personally was scared to death to play our type of music in New York at first. We were in a couple metal bands, hardcore bands, and so forth. It's acceptable. When we started playing this type of music, I thought people would think 'Oh, they're trying to get ladies.' No, this is what we listen to... Just read Charles Bukowski. Reads his books and you know us. If you know him, that's how we live out lives."*

George: *"We talk a lot of shit on New York, but we still love it. Since we got back from New Orleans, we threw out a lot of shit we were doing. After we did that record, we became who we really are. We've been getting a greater acceptance. We played two shows since we came back, and there was more people at those two then all our others combined, in New York at least."*

"This is the golden question..."

"The Jeff Goldblum question?"

"What's something remarkably weird and bizarre that happened to you and when you tell people they think you're a pathological liar?"

Zach: *"When I was 17 or 18, me and a bunch of guys used to fuck around with an Ouija board. We'd see things in my friend's attic. One day we saw a little girl up there, and started walking towards her, and she disappeared. So we're fucking around with this Ouija board, asking it who's the girl. And all this freaky shit starts happening... Basically the little girl tells us through the Ouija board that she's come for my friends' father. So we're like 'Fuck this, we're gonna put this thing away.' We play with it one more time, kick it over, come back and it's set up again [his voice grows shaky and unnerved]... We throw it out, the next day there's a dead bird laying there, and then a week later this kid's father dropped dead in their kitchen. He had medical problems, but he was probably – in those last 10 years of his life – at his healthiest point. He just got up, looked at his younger brother, stared into his eyes and dropped dead. And the kids little brother wouldn't talk for a year..."*

After I present the boys the restroom which is like a gigantic human urinal – *steel walls dripping H2O from atop and you just whizz on the wall into a pit of marbles and ice* – the gig loses all magic. Every band is Good Charlotte, Drowning Pool or Nickelback oriented, and the second they finish all their friends clear out. By the time DTB goes on there are 4 people left, and no one gives a shit. I pass out in the van.

I awake to a pissed, hammered Neil freaking out 'cause I didn't help load the van, even though Hairy Bob told me to get some rest 'cause I'd been up over 30 hours. Neil is swerving through the surprisingly empty Manhattan streets, frantic, and we pull off on a roadside who knows where, too drunk to care if it's even legal. Neil attempts to sleep on the street, and there is this big hassle of me shoving him back inside the van because he's in retard strength mode, barreling forth in pinguescent lumber...

MANHATTAN (9/9)

"911 WAS AN INSIDE JOB!!! 911 WAS AN INSIDE JOB!!!" There are 300 demonstrators in the middle of Times Square screaming this at police, chanting loud enough to be heard for a quarter mile. Everywhere you turn propaganda is doled out frantically. This is only one of a multi-urban effort – the universal "Street Action" day. No point getting

into a conspiracy rant. We'll just let it slide with an understatedly quaint: *"'fishy' seems a prude assessment."*

I was the first one up in that steaming caprylic van, a funk-permeated sauna of four sweaty dudes who hadn't bathed in days, so much sweat having poured overnight it was dew on the ceiling. We were legally parked not far from city hall, and every building I passed on my stroll was used in the filming of *Ghostbusters*.

Tonight's show is at The Knitting Factory, which is a renovated industrial complex with three levels. We get fucked with the bottom rung, and have to carry all our equipment down a three-story flight of stairs. Get to nap in the air conditioning though, and the tiny bar has this Sinatra vibe to it, with that red-curtained lounge singer stage.

There are three shows going on here tonight, all of which are lame screamo bands with tight-pants & quaffed hair. Once again, no one has come for us. Weren't expecting much really, but SMB seem disappointed even though they are the lucky winners, having one kid with a spiked bi-hawk show up.

His name is Zach Ameeko, and he heads up the industrial act Din Glorious: *"I go to NYU for film. Last year I came out with 'Schizoid Sluts From Planet Fucktard,' which is my sci-fi sexploitation piece. I'm currently in the middle of 'Schizoid Sluts II: Frankensluts.' We're shooting in a couple weeks with people receiving training from Tom Savini."*

"Din Glorious is a New York industrial synth punk band. We started as tribal industrial, very avant-gadre. A very Aus Gang sound, a lot of Native American imagery and performance art. Now we're definitely in the style of late 70's LA synth punk bands like Nervous Gender or The Screamers. We actually bring scrap metal onstage."

"Do you go to the junkyard and pick up scrap metal and bang the fuck out of them?"

Zach Ameeko: "Absolutely. Our main drum piece is a 20 gallon oil drum. We will not bring that out with us on tour, so we'll drive around whatever city it is we're playing until we find a junkyard of construction site. We'll get lucky and have people bring us stuff. As far as New York industrial, it's a lot of kids in bondage pants trying to speak German. Goth clubs are the most boring thing in the world."

"Tell me all about New York."

"The New York music scene is highly overrated by people who are not from here. You would expect a ton to be going on, but every venue seems to be closing up. Rent gets higher, the venues keep closing, and you need more and more of a draw. To start a band right now is incredibly difficult to get booked anywhere where people can see you. It's very hard to get people to leave their borough. But it's absolutely a joy to live here. Sometimes you feel like Bob Hoskins walking around 'Toon Town.' It's insane all the time, and I love every second of it."

"Are there any ultra-sleazy BDSM freak bars?"

"They all suck and the music is like The Genitorturers and a bunch of bullshit that makes you want to blow your brains out. There was a club called Albion where there was always people with fangs biting each other, all that shit. Drinks were way too expensive, and nobody liked the crazy punk people coming in and slam dancing. Bands weren't really playing anyway, it was all drum machine bullshit... If I have to meet one more fat girl who comes up to me with colored contacts and fangs I'm just gonna kick her in the cunt. Vampires and all that bullshit. That's what people think of when they think of goth music when its actually just really fun punk. We got a bad name from all these kids *AND* their shit is boring."

"What is something remarkably bizarre that happened to you ad when you tell people they think you're a pathological liar?"

"Washington DC was our first road gig. It was a total hipster fest – tight pants and black rimmed glasses all around. I had a backpack full of PBR for liquid rehearsal, and we wound up doing this really bizarre, avant-garde set. Halfway through the second song – I play keytar – I shatter my knuckle and it moved to another part of my hand. I play the set, we walk off stage, and I'm completely naked for some reason. I have this massive ham with just nub fingers. I got $15 dollars, I'm not going to the hospital. So the owner of the bar is like '*well, can I get you drunk then?*' So this bottle of Jack Daniels comes off the shelf... I passed out in the kitchen of this club in DC and woke up in China Town with no recollection. I was completely covered in black dirt makeup, a broken hand, huge fist marks all over me 'cause apparently I'd been challenging people to punch me in the chest. And my dick was out. I don't know why. Apparently I'd chased a Chinese food delivery guy down the street trying to tackle him. And I apparently was exposing myself to strangers…"

WILMINGTON (9/10)

We'd spent the night in Jersey with one of Hairy Bob's high school buddies, who is a now an accomplished jazz musician. Once upon a time he was the drummer of HAPPINESS, a "*so obscure their not even kvlt*" weirdo slap-bass grind band. On that old demo the vocals could go head to head with Landfermann in their pained quality. Not because of aesthetic, but because the 16 year vocalist didn't know how to scream and was obviously murdering himself.

Somewhere in Delaware now, just as grim & industrial as Jersey. Their state motto is "*Liberty and Independence.*" Tagged with a magnetic-strip ticket from the highway state line, they digitally know every mile you've crossed when you approach the rather frequent checkpoints which nickel and dime you.

Similarly, any time you exit the freeway from here until the end of Pennsylvania you have to pay a scalping road charge. If you pretend to have lost the ticket, you may be ticketed $100 by the state police with drug dogs standing guard at every check posts. By law, losing the onramp pass gives them probable cause to search you. In result, this unforeseen scam will cost an unfactored $200 to cross the state.

Not good – we're running low on everything, and all we have to eat are shrink-wrapped granola bars. I'm down to a $50 personally, but my multi-talented uses award me a $5 a day food budget out of the band fund (*depending*).

We overshoot the freeway for miles, and the dreary little bar is another Nascar crowd plus a few old women with big 80's hair. At the liquor store the desk-jockey cons me out of a $5 "slip up" I'd waited too long to call out. When redneck Ali Baba asks where we're playing, we answer The Good Shot. "*It's a little dark in there, don't you think?*"

"I don't know, I thought it had adequate lighting." I say, oblivious to the sarcasm. In 2 hours we find out what he meant. The promoters are three black guys that only book hip hop shows and were hustled into this one by the lame DTB bookie Neil paid way too much for nothing in return. Douschebag had passed them off as a funk act, and in 45 minutes the grim watering hole is blacker then Compton.

No openers, no guarantee. SMB stands no chance but they roll through their set anyway, not bothering to slap on the old color-coded uniforms. DTB goes into a huddle, brainstorming. Out of the genius playbook, they pull out the rarely used tactic – "BLACK HOUR." Only the funk-laced tunes, the widely known covers plus allowing the promoters to come onstage and freestyle… Crowd loves it, DTB are all smiles, and a female Baptist choir singer belted out some Motown soul. SMB went away empty handed, and we walk out with $80 in merch…

PITTSBURG (9/11)

TUESDAY, 9/11 2007, six years after the desolation. The headline of USA Today is "HIGHEST GENERAL DEMANDS TROOP WITHDRAWALS."

I've been driving 5 straight hours through mountains in the rain, KROHM the overriding soundtrack. Everyone is passed out, but I don't bother waking them to take wheel duties no matter how exhausted I am. We started at exit 360, and we don't change course until #57. For some reason I felt the need to drive all the way there.

As we approach the off-ramp, I see the billboard – MONROEVILLE MALL, EXIT 57. Ho ho ho. Of course Downtown Brown had no idea why I was driving like a fanatic to get to an indoor mall, and I didn't bother to explain until we were a few blocks away. That's where my favorite horror film of all time was shot – the 1978 epic gargantuan of underground filmmaking *Dawn of the Dead*.

This has been a checklist item since I was 11. Every twist of the shopping center is like Deja Vu. Its way smaller then I'd expected, and the only store that remains is JC Penny, but you can still see the metal grating that's long been painted over where the glass doors used to swing shut.

The goldfish pond and little bridge were still there, the "*don't lead 'em up there*" hallway with the same wavy-metal payphones – *the boiler room corridor, the Flyboy death elevator, the escalator that Roger slides down yelping "whoo-whee!"* It's so surreal, even though there are no Hare Krishnas...

The giant orange clock is gone, the fountain has disappeared, but you can still cruise through the ex-ice skating rink area which has been turned into a corporate food court. There isn't a single plaque or movie poster encased on the wall. I guess they have enough problems with stoned gore-hounds showing up and causing trouble as it is. But that giant billboard was definitely a wink-wink tourist attraction.

We are in Pittsburg for 15 minutes before getting attacked. Not by zombies, but by 20 black guys because we'd interrupted their street football game. They were kicking the van and calling us "*white pigs.*"

The venue is an artsy co-op in the middle of the ghetto called Garfield Artworks. The owner won't let us inside the building for an hour after the show has already supposed to have begun. He comes out like a bolt of unfriendly lightning. He's a short, rude little Jewish guy with red hair that looks and talks like Woody Allen. He tells us not to even bother unpacking 'cause no one will be there, then when he changes his mind and has us unload, the other band shows up who are 3 fat guys with banjos.

It's obviously an uppity indie kid collective, amateurish surrealistic paintings line the interior walls. They won't come out to support our sort of thing – another great move by the shit bookie. The fate of all hangs on SMB, but that shot is ruined because Mindless Self Indulgence is playing down the street, consuming whatever crowd they'd possibly have. Woody tells them *"Well, if you're friends with them, why don't you go play that show? Why would you think to book a gig with us on the same night?"* We don't even tell him we're leaving.

Heading back to Cincinnati to grab those forgotten cymbals, the tire blows out at 70 MPH as we're in-between two semi trucks. Bob braces the wheel, and Neil freezes cold, because he's in the Top Shelf bed. If we hit anything he's going to torpedo out the front windshield...

Bob makes it to the shoulder like a pro, grinding the rim. We were bad on money before, but now we're fucked. To make matters worse I can feel the dragon of a viral infection creeping up. Everyone in DTB is coughing & we all have sore throats...

COLUMBUS (9/12)

Back to Ohio, whose motto is *"With God, All Things Are Possible."* No, only with Moranis...

Cleveland, definitely Fall now, another band rehearsal complex with Rick himself. We'd spent an hour trying to get what little of the tire remained from the rim, but it just wouldn't budge. We had to call AAA for a tow truck driver who got out, took a gander, spit, then came back with a 4X4. One mighty caveman whack and it came plopping off.

Man we felt stupid. The driver saw Glover and I splitting a Bugler and said *"Man, I'd keep that down if I were you."* "Ah it's just a rolly." *"Shit man, I'm a tow truck driver, not a cop. I was kinda hopin' to hit that, har har har."* We parted ways as he drove off smiling with a bundle of CD's, bumper stickers and complimentary t-shirt. He didn't even bother to bill us.

Rick Moranis has been aiding us with van maintenance all morning, and is full of ancient Buddhist wisdom: *"Cleveland is a lot of faggy death metal and I hate it – bunch of kids that watch too much cookie monster. I like the riffs, but the vocals don't do it for me. It's either that or fuckin' emo. Emo makes you want to make love to a man, and death metal makes you want to hate-fuck a guy... The mission of my band is to be sweet and try to get laid. Try to not ever have a job. I'm 26, I live at home, it rules... We were tongue in cheek when we started, now we're taking ourselves seriously. Songs like 'Barfight,' 'Gay Stripper,' 'Hot Chick Police.' We really had to look within ourselves to find our musical voice..."*

"What are some crazy experiences playing biker bars?"

Rick Moranis: "Fucking a chick in a bathroom somewhere like Peabodies. That's pretty much the jist of rock 'n roll. It's lying to people, telling them that you're cool. They start believing it and you get sex and drugs out of it..."

"What's the best way to get sex out of people?"

"You say, *'Hey I'm in a band.'* It sounds cheesy, but it works. You almost look at 'em like you're lying and you know you're lying but they're not sure you're lying but you are lying. And you start believing your own bullshit... I prefer always to fuck a fat chick over a skinny chick. They're easier and they'll lick your butt... My buddy was in town and we went to heavy metal karaoke. He takes this chick – this huge, huge chick – takes her out to the car and gets a blowjob and makes her lick his butt. He tells her to start making out with me, then I went in the bathroom and fucked her. She was on the rag too, which was awesome... Then I fuck her, it's a real small bathroom. Like putting her face near the toilet seat, she wouldn't put it in there. So I banged her and came on her clothes then I went back outside. That was cool. She was huge, like if Neil P and Hairy Bob combined bodies. She did have upper lip hair..."

"Ever get hot chicks?"

"We played an after-party for Sebastian Bach when he came through with Guns 'N Roses. Sebastian never showed up. He signed a contract and they were paying him a couple grand. We promoted the shit out of it so it was packed, and we were supposed to go on at midnight. Axel Rose was being a dick and they went on late, so he never made it. I just went up to this retardedly hot blonde. In 5 minutes we went back to the motel room, there's a couple fucking next to us. She's doing a bunch of drugs, then she's like, *'I came up there to fuck a real rock star.'* And I just lied and was like, *'yeah, I'm in this sweet band.'* She didn't know. She takes a bottle vodka and is like *'come in the bathroom and watch me shit.'* So she's shitting, and she starts sucking my dick, drinking vodka and shit. I fucked her like a chump too cause I was drunk and on all sorts of shit. It was the hottest chick ever and I'm talking to my limp dick like *'why can't I fuck this chick right now? You're not working'...*"

"Did you put it in her mouth while she was pooping?"

"Yeah. She was on the toilet shitting while she was blowing me. She said it real dirty too, like *'come in here and watch me shit.'* She was drinking vodka on the toilet with her panties around her legs. I was into it..."

"What's the weirdest place you've ever woken up after blacking out drunk?"

"I was driving a beer truck so I had to be at work at 5 in the morning. Somehow I left the bar and I'm all fucked up – I didn't know what was going on. I had this TV in the car 'cause I was moving. Somehow I wake up in Akron at a BP station. Its like 9 in the morning, I got 5 calls from my boss on my phone. I look outside and TV's fucking broke right in front of BP, right by the fucking doors. I guess I'd been sleeping there for 5 hours, my pants were down, I had my cock in my hand. People are going to work and shit... The other one was just bad. That same job, I was on a bunch of pain pills 'cause I threw my back out and was just getting fucked up. I was living at my band space, I was kind of depressed. I was in a real bad neighborhood. You don't just walk around that neighborhood at night. I just got annihilated, shit-faced drunk retarded. Just sad drunk. It was the winter... I wake up with no shirt on in someone's front yard. I fuckin' got bite marks on my arm and I look like I got the shit beat out of me. My face was all fucked up. Then there's this dead dog laying in a bush down the road..."

"You killed a dog?"

"I may have. It looked like it was trying to kill me. And I got the shit kicked out of me, I'm sure of that. I know the dog didn't punch me in the face like 30 times. I just woke up this bloody mess, bite marks on my arm... It was a big dog. I don't know if I killed it or what. There was blood all over the snow. And nobody calls the cop, 'cause its this super Hispanic part of town. Everyone's poor. It actually probably happens a lot... Yeah, I think I may have killed a dog. That was pretty much bottom of the barrel for me. That's rock bottom..."

"What's some weird shit you've seen in Columbus?"

"There was like a Swedish black metal band at Peabodies, or one of them fucked up countries. They were so metal they'd kill things and bring them onstage, whatever that means. You know, 'cause they have to be more metal than other metal bands or whatever those guys do. They went out to get blood. They had to go to West Side Market too. They didn't even kill the chickens themselves. They had like a severed animal head, I think it was a goat head, and they took a bunch of underage chicks into the basement of the club and just smeared blood all over the walls, blood all over the chicks n' fucked 'em. Management wasn't too happy with that. That's like an international crime on multi-levels. There were blood hand prints all over the walls..."

"What's something remarkably bizarre that happened to you and when you tell people they think you're a pathological liar?"

"We did a show with Ron Jeremy. We ended up hanging out with him at a strip club and got VIP treatment. He was there with his girlfriend, she was kind of overweight. She was cute, but not hot. There's just thousands of women shoving their pussy in his face and he could care less. He just wanted to drink his one rum and coke and get back to the hotel. Back at the hotel everybody wants to party and he keeps taking chicks in the bathroom and showing them his cock. He wouldn't show us his cock either, which we are all kind of pissed about. He keeps taking chicks in the bathroom. If they didn't blow him he'd kick 'em out. And if they did blow him, well then he'd kick 'em out anyway. Everybody is getting all drunk in 5 different hotel rooms and nobody can find Ron. We go to my room and Ron Jeremy is passed out on the bed next to Joe my bass player. They're watching Discovery Channel at 5 in the morning, and Ron's girlfriend is on the other bed. Ron's snoring and they're like laying on each other. So that was pretty weird..."

CINCINATTI (9/13)

Last nights show at Bernie's was another gambrinous, bombed out mess. Too sick to perform, too worked over. The Betty Page chick who shaved Skode's ass was there, which really baffled me because I didn't register how close she lived to Columbus. Glover got stranded after taking his 30 something school teacher love-interest home, and walked around all morning talking to bums outside the library...

It'll be much easier once SMB drops off the tour in two days, because we have no possible contender as far as disposable audience income towards merch. That van problem chalked up $400 for new tire + alignment & completely wiped out the band fund. We're in the red, and everyone is pulling from their bank accounts. I too am down to a bare economic thread with $20 cash in hand and $15 scrapings on the debit. The new DVD's aren't selling, and we're rapidly running out of CD's. Unless things start turnin' round, we might never make it to LA.

The whole tour has been scheduled around The Viper Room, which is the co-owners birthday party booked earlier this year. It's promised to be rock star land galore, with record executives and celebrities' a-go-go.

LA is blindly spreading its legs, and we are preparing total war – a punk assault so catastrophic we'll be blackballed by Hollywood forever. *Orson Welles, eat your heart out…*

At the moment we're still in Columbus, all of us sick, watching Dan Aykroyd's forgotten masterpiece *Nothing But Trouble*. We're in Alex Price's living room, the drummer of Psychostick. They are a comedic metal band along the lines of Green Jelly, and they've had a minor hit radio single aptly titled "BEER." The SMB guys are going over logistics with him, because they'll be touring together soon…

We're all huddled together begrudgingly watching this lame, paint-by-numbers rock band called American Bang from Nashville. This is their first tour ever, having just signed to Warner Brothers, and they're getting a flat guarantee of $250.

All of us have been killing ourselves on this tour, and these weak fucks have stolen all our door money. DTB brought the entire audience, and all American Bang brought were their own portable fans so their long Hollywood hair magically blows onstage the way a real rockers should: "*Hey guys, this next song is about girls. And we all love them right? Ha ha. Hope you all go home and get laid tonight. This one's a Guns N Roses cover…*"

LOUISVILLE (9/14)

I wake up filthy, starving, horridly ill and in the backyard of last night's opener The Eat A Fetus Trio, even though there's four of them. I slept in the dirt outside because the house had so many crusty loads of dog shit all over the carpet there wasn't a safe place to lay down. At least in this minefield there is fresh air.

Flashes of last nights chaos filters through my brain like jagged rocks: "*We branded our old drummer with a crucifix in this kitchen. We put this crucifix on the stove for like 15 minutes, and it actually burned the Jesus off it. It was iron hot, red hot. The flesh just seared, the smell was ridiculous. He was like, 'Don't take it off, I want a giant scar.' All the girls were freaking out. I guess that's what it smelled like in 'Nam.*"

"*If midgets are incorporated into our act, we'd make them perform tambourine solos. Midget porn would be the best, just have them fucking onstage. Or like putting a midget on a grill and slapping it around with a spatula... Our message is wear spandex in public. Let dogs fight. We like showing our smiles. We're dead serious about all of it. We're dead serious about Usher"*

Back up the porch steps and past the sign listing the sacred EATAFETA BETA rules: #1 WE DRINK FOR CHRIST, #2 TREAT HER LIKE A PROSTITUTE, #3 EMBRACE THY FATTITUDE, #4 MINIMUM WEIGHT IS 227 LBS, #5 NEVER TRUST A BIG BUTT & A SMILE. Everyone is still passed out in the massive 3-level flop that is sort of like the Cincinnati equivalent of The PWN House, but with 6 dogs and 4 chubby guys.

Last night the bartender thought American Bang sucked and was just as hardboiled over the money situation. He flipped Neil $80 out of pocket and gave us 3 free cases of Budweiser to make up the discrepancy. On top of that we did $100 in merch, so Point B is achieved... I drive all the way to Louisville trying to come out of the funk. A full six hours of yellow blurring lines grips my head with the ultimate spoken word dialogue. Tonight I'm back with a vengeance.

Yet by the time DTB goes on at 3rd Street Dive the flu has swooped back up and knocked me on my ass. I can't muster it, and I'd rather remain silent then bomb again. Neil's throat is so tore up from infection he can barely sing. It's all so terrible. Nashville is our last night with SMB, and I'm bringing the hammer down with Nagasaki-like precision...

NASHVILLE (9/15)

"I saw a UFO in China, actually 7 of them. There's this place in Beijing – 'Rockstar Gonsung,' its obscure as hell. This guy's kind of garage sized pad. Its got all these carpets and stones, like ancient Chinese where you have to sit on the ground when you hang out. There were these guys from this Western Chinese province, but they looked Arab because they're descended from Turks."

"They bring out this stuff called 'mugwart.' I don't know if you've ever smoked this stuff, it's a trancy kind of herb. We're watching these Michael Jackson videos, and my friend speaks a little Mandarin, so he's trying to explain what the lyrics to 'Billie Jean' mean."

"So we're in this trance and as we're leaving – we've been drinking beer pretty subtlety for the past 9 hours – all 5 people with us see these glowing orange lights that are flying 10,000 feet up. Just these kind of tiny, glowing hazes, floating in the same direction. Apparently moving pretty fast, but wavering in their path. Kind of

doing this drunken driver swervey thing. They were just forming these intricate patterns and a few trailed behind. There was no sound like an airplane or anything. It didn't move like an airplane..."

These are the words of Buhao Ting guitarist Shawn Gardner. We're still in Louisville, amusingly 8 blocks away from Hunter Thompson's high school. Gardner's lady friend saved us last night with special tea and a massive assortment of replenishing herbal pills. Didn't seem to do much though, 'cause the flu is still lingering, and even now Bob is sick. *Our remedy?* All you can eat pizza at CiCi's.

Nashville, a venue called The Muse. SMB have had an insanely rough night themselves: *"We were looking for somewhere to stay. This guy, this army guy was there with his weird girlfriend. They were like, 'we live on base, but that's ok.' I get in their car and the van follows me, and he slowly starts revealing more things to me like 'well, its Fort Knox. I'll tell them you're with me. Just give them your id's.' The closer we got the more he was like 'well sometimes they search vehicles, I guess you guys have a trailer and a big van, they probably will. You don't have anything bad in there right?' Well... I guess all we really have is a couple knives, bats, a sword, guns, booze, fireworks, drugs and stuff. Is that ok?"*

"Apparently it was, 'cause they searched everything. They found pot, they found my gun. Everyone turned out ok. Point of the story is the only made us throw away the empty booze bottles and fireworks. It wasn't that bad. I pass out drunk at 4 or 5am, I just hear banging on the door like 'is there a girl in there with you?' And yes, plus five weird dudes that shouldn't be there."

"It was like before noon, and they just oust us all. He's just getting his ass chewed out and we're running over to the van so we can take off. We go to get gas on base and I'm like 'can I get gas or will it be weird?' He's like 'yeah, its fine,' then they yelled at me for that too. They're like 'where's your military ID?' Do I look like I'm in the army? Not only do I not have a buzz-cut but you've probably never even seen this haircut before in your life. Yeah, I'm a refugee from punkrocksylvania. We got out of there and everyone's nerves were shredded but mine."

"Was that the most intense experience you've had trying to crash on the road?"

Reverend John Wheeler: "Yes. There's been a couple things like there's some boyfriend of whatever girl will kick the door in at 10 in the morning. *'I thought you loved me, you whore!'* We're like '*whoops, I was just stopping by.*' Usually there's lots of us and we're scarier than some guy in a white baseball hat so it doesn't really matter. There's plenty of shitty things, but never quite as dangerous or harrowing as trying to break into Fort Knox, which rather famously is supposed to be pretty difficult."

"So what's the new record going to be all about?"

"The theme of the new record is going to be some propaganda thing. We've been making new logos – we're going for a total fascist, imperialist thing. The guy that invented the concept of marketing was the same guy that did WWI propaganda for America. This guy is literally the way American life is right now. They would ask him '*how do we get people to buy more clothes from us?*' Back in the day there was no such thing as style or fashion. He was basically '*well you change them a little bit every year, give people too many options, and call it self-expression.*' So the reason people wear a t-shirt and think it makes them cool is literally a concept invented by this one dude that used to do war propaganda. I've always been kind of a conspiracy guy but it's on such a human, every day level. It's not like a '*oh they're hiding something out in space.*' My plan is to read more of his book and use it to sell the record which is actually making fun of that stuff, which I think would be a fantastic irony."

"What do you want to add to our twisted tale here?"

"You're writing a book about crazy stuff. I almost feel bad, like more crazy stuff should've happened. The whole ass shaving thing in Cleveland was pretty cool. You guys got kind of sick and that caused us to keep our distance… When we slept in that place in Cincinnati, you slept outside in the dirt because there was so much dog poop in the house. I think people take for granted how weird being an underground band is. If we were ever in hotel rooms and had a bus I think we'd miss squalid feces and being chased around by military police. I guess that's part of the whole thing. You start playing guitar thinking you're gonna get pussy – and you will – but at an amazing cost."

"Here's the golden question – how long before the Iraq thing totally falls apart?"

"It's hard to say. The problem is '*what really works, what convinces people that we're doing the right thing?*' The same thing we've been doing here forever – you want the puppet on the right or the puppet on the left? All of a sudden people have a choice, it polarizes them so they have something to argue about, and it's the total illusion of who's in charge. The Simpsons made fun of it with '*you want to vote for Kodos or Kang?'* Choose the form of your destructor. They're using the same model and the Iraqis are reacting so badly to it. They're like, *'we get to choose between two dictators?'* So they're blowing things up and killing the candidates, which to me seems like a perfectly reasonable reaction. So I don't know. It might actually work or it could just remain this big, messy, never-ending 1984 war, or it's going to blow up in everyone's face real soon. They have such a crazy hold on it it's hard to say."

> ***"Any words of wisdom?"***

"The old saying 'good will always triumph over evil' is a myth perpetuated by the truly evil and they're masquerading as good..."

The moment has arrived – no holds barred catarolysis. I've been stringing 'em along with silly little tales and a smorgasbord of previous material: *"So, Nashville... We were just at that porn store around the block, and they had the hugest selection of dildos I'd ever seen. Like massive – up and down the walls, every butt-bead, vibrator, strap-on and blow-up lamb doll. It was pretty fierce what some of these people use on themselves and others. To be honest I'm more a hand-cuff and chokehold guy. Ha, ha, just kidding. I'm far worse then all that shit."*

"So anyway, there was the most terrifying vibrator I've ever seen in my life. It was like a Klingon death weapon. It had all these flashing lights and extensions and shit. Monstrous. Anyway, as I'm looking at this thing, I notice the quaint little sticker on the package that reads 'preferred by 3 out of 4 customers'... So the real question is... What the fuck was that mall survey like? [insert Glover's rim-shot here]."

"Hee hee. Tee ho ho. Yeah, sex. Fuckin' and stuff. Well Nashville, let me tell you, I fucking hate cops. Like bad. I don't give a shit about 'oh they're just doing they're jobs, they're not all that bad.' Doesn't phase me. I know why they exist, I get the overall necessity. But it doesn't change the fact that their all self-righteous meathead bastards. Oh, do we have a cop in the audience? Someone's Dad? Even better."

"Anyway, I used to work at Dunkin Donuts. Man, cops love those things. I love those things. I loved making 'em. See, when you slap together those jelly donuts with the white powder, how it starts is you have a plain husk with a tiny hole in it. And you take that husk and you INSERT something into that hole. It's not too big of an opening, but you can fit A LOT of things in that hole. And then you CRANK that

jelly rod, and you SQUEEZE all that filling inside, EVERY last drop… Yeah. Sold it to a cop. Ha ha ha."

"But that's just for starters. You see Nashville, before I was a journalist, before I was a comedian, I hung around a lot of really bad people doing really illegal shit. Anyway, there was this house we'd hang out at, kind of like this epicenter. I'm not gonna say what we were moving, but, you know, if the cops raided it we'd all stand to do at least 25 years in a federal penitentiary."

"So we're outside, and there's this homeboy making a big scene 'cause he went to the pet store, bought a gerbil, doused it with gasoline and lit it up on the porch just to watch it run around. Not too cool. The guys like 'You have a Michael Myers t-shirt that says 'Guns Are For Pussies' and you're angry at me for setting an animal on fire?' Well duh, people deserve to die, not furry little woodland creatures for no reason, especially over some douche in-joke. That's weaker then being slaughtered by Joan of Ark over the crusades."

"Anyway, as this gerbil's running around in circles like a roman candle, we hear someone sneeze in the tree out front, like hidden up in the branches, camouflaged by foliage. So all these bad dudes come out of the house. I'm just stoned, but everyone else is triple-balling it on ecstasy, Special K and Yay-o. So they're all fucked up, and kind of drunk too. We surround the tree and there's this cop up there, like this ninja cop dressed all in black."

"The guys clinging onto the branch for dear life, pretending he doesn't exist, because he's in the middle of setting up video feed. Which is totally illegal of course, and he can't call for backup lest there be some huge scandal and a bunch of suspensions."

"So this cop is at our mercy. We all start laughing, we're all so happy. 'Hey pig, fuck you pig! Oink oink motherfucker!!' We're like throwing pine-combs at him and shit, telling him we're gonna kill his children. I pull out a bag of skittles and start pelting him with every color of the rainbow. We just decimate this guy for like 20 minutes straight, and he's breathing heavy and totally panicked, 'cause he thinks we're gonna shoot him or something. Funny enough, everyone is so fucked up they soon lose interest and roll back inside."

"I stay out there, saying all these awful things. I'm dancing around the tree backwards chanting 'sausage links, sausage links' over and over But then I realize fuck man, this is a crime on multi-international levels – I'm gonna do 10 years easy if I'm caught. So I start backing off. I tell the guy, 'Hey asshole! Yeah you, pig faggot!

Since you don't know who I am, I'm just gonna skedaddle. Good luck trying to read my license plate bitch.'"

"I walk off laughing and go to my car which I drive in reverse the entire block-length so he can't read my plate. I jet off onto the freeway, scot-free. Well, sure enough, the house got raided the next day. But they never found anything, because they moved all the shit later that night."

"Funny part is once I drove home I totally forgot about it for like 3 years. When it popped in my head randomly, I was like, 'Did that actually fuckin' happen?' Sure enough, a few phone calls later, I had all the testimony I needed. The real question here is what other insane shit have I done that I've just totally forgotten about? Have I like killed prostitutes and shit? I can remember every Pepper Steak combo for the past 15 years, but something like that slips my mind? So yeah, Ha ha. Like I said, I fucking hate cops man..."

HUNTSVILLE (9/16)

SMB is now long gone, and the real tour has begun. Down to $50 for gas, all other finances wiped out by Neil's exploding guitar head which cost $200 to repair. It's out first day off. We were supposed to hang out in Nashville with some burlesque girls I'd met at TABU in Huntsville but that didn't pan out. Instead, we're on Mortigan's couch drinking Budweiser and watching *Fart Seduction* & Max Hardcore.

I thought this convergence could possibly be a bad thing, Mortigan being ultra-black metal and DTB the silliest nerd band on earth, but Old Uncle Morty stated *'Any friend of Bartek's is a pal o' mine.'* My last $15 on the beer hustle – just get 'em drunk and rage through lest any politics get in the way.

Glover and Mortigan have been super-buddy all night, ranting about terrible ass sex and society's imperial damnation. By 5am they both resemble the sleepy-eyed Homer Simpson dragging ass at Moe's Tavern, and I'm not far behind. Between the 3 of us we've literally killed a 5th of whisky and 50 cans of beer *(& yes, I counted)*.

"So what's on your mind Mr. Mortigan?"

Mortigan: "I think the fact that I'm still alive shows that I've gone as far as you can go without a curtain call. 27 years of the beast and still fighting the machine. I think in the past year I've learned more about the world and myself than I ever had. It all comes down to experience."

"How's the new Octagon material going?"

"Before there were minute-long songs with two riffs, now there's songs that are to the upwards of 8 1/2 minutes with 14 riffs. There's a little of the simple for the dullards, but technical, yet not to the point of Dream Theater. It's just more interesting. We're also releasing a split with Gravewurm on Regimental Records and an unreleased Octagon album called *Death Fetish* will be coming out on Regimental as well. RU-486 will be doing tons of splits. One with Zweizz, doing a split with Dravorium. I'm doing a project with him called Cult of the Swine. Tons of little one-off cassettes. Two songs, ten minutes, chrome cassettes, that's all you get. Limited to 66-100 copies."

"You gonna split from Huntsville?"

"Probably New England when the lease is up. I'm too damn nomadic to stay in one spot. I want bright lights and big titties, not Joe's Crab Shack and a hangover."

"You mentioned traveling since I've been gone"...

"DC was one of the most interesting. I tend to forget the sleaze. It's just cool to walk out of a five star restaurant and there's bums on cardboard right there. It's the perfect dichotomy – you can have culture and wholesomeness, then you walk outside and are surrounded in filth. It keeps it real and earthly..."

LITTLE ROCK (9/17)

Today it's all about W.A.S.P. and Stratovarius as we roar through Mississippi into Arkansas. The haul through Alabama had been astonishingly desolate. People riding horseback, cars pieced together like that old Johnny Cash song. Dilapidated houses. weird bridges, industrial silos – a poverty beyond mere description. Even the interstate is a dirt road.

We pull into Little Rock an hour before we're supposed to start – an Italian food joint called Vito's with a full concert hall. Casey Jones is again at the helm, and I stand behind him creepily during his pinball fix until he notices me. Squinted eye confused response: *"Oh... You're back."* Man I love doing that.

No one is there, 2 bands cancel, but we get free pop and 50% off our meals. One artsy-indie band called Cinema Herd struggles through a set of faulty, dying equipment. DTB gets a huge response from the 10 people hanging out and sell $60 in merch. One girl actually drove 3 hours to see them from Southern Indiana, and she knew the word to every song...

LITTLE ROCK (9/18)

I wake up totally insane, whacked by insomnia and humidity, still no REM sleep. Casey's new house is this giant three-level art commune that's been doled out only to specialty cases since the mid 70's. I spend the sleepless morning chatting with his room-mate about these corrosive spiders in Arkansas that with one bite'll melt your appendages right off.

Daddy Long-legs are also more poisonous then Black Widow's, although they can't harm you because their fangs are too soft to puncture human skin. However, if you boil a few in tea, a single cup will kill someone instant as cyanide.

Another day off, and Casey doesn't mind us hanging around. Off to Sonic Burger and the $1 theater where the family-friendly cartoon mascot is an alley cat puffing a cigarette. *Live Fee Or Die Hard* is our selection. Decent, but it's still a PG-13 John McClain... We score a Random gig at White Water Tavern after haggling the promoter. Casey again shows up utterly perplexed, surprised that Neil is ripping a solo onstage. We walk out with a lucky $65.

Back at the art-commune there is a guy in boxers & red devil horns aggressively trying to get us to throw down on cocaine. Some band called Sleeping in the Aviary from Wisconsin is on tour and crashing on the couch. They're these snobby tight-pants indie kids huffing rubber cement and painting mustaches on each other. They won't let me interview them, but demand the tape to roll naturally: "*It's great, it's really great. Gum it, you know. Dip your finger in it and put it on your gums...*"

HOUSTON (9/19)

Humid as hell, mosquito bitten legs – unsuccessfully tried to sleep on the porch but switched to the van. While I was rolling cigarettes a Blood gang-banger walked up in full red outfit trying to bum one... *Sweating, trying to sleep, 100 degrees in the van...* Long ass drive to Houston, and we've been cranking Hall & Oates and the new William Shatner. Texas is even more desolate then Alabama and the economy seems based around 10-wheelers and fake orange-cone construction zones which are obvious speed-traps...

The second you get to Houston everything is HUGE. Giant 8 lane freeways, Walmart's that stretch for miles, and the most terrifying jet runway in America – "The George Bush International Airport." We've crossed into the heart of "THEIR WORLD."

The venue is another art-kid commune called Super Happy Fun Land that's surrounded by industrial factories on a back street off the freeway exit ramp. It looks like Captain Spaulding's Chicken Shack from the outside & Billy Jack's Freedom School on the interior. Walls painted in murals, thousands of books lying around – bongos, pipe organs. Gargantuan mosquitoes cause us to itch profusely alongside the sweltering humidity soup combo.

The black-rimmed glasses artsy chick that let us inside quickly disappears into the backroom & locks the door. There are a few here all have that Pittsburg vibe, hiding & avoiding us. But there are couches everywhere, and we've been allowed free shelter. Still, no one can sleep because the asphyxiating heat...

HOUSTON (9/20)

The state motto of Texas is *"Friendship."* Saturday morning, bright & cheery; Houston's epicenter looks like Fascist Italy. All the buildings are stark-black or a single color, squares & quadrants of a perfect grid. There is no character, just neocolonialist tombs surrounded by desert.

11am, eating breakfast burritos with a local tech/grind act called We Both Know. Both bands dominate the length of the table, DTB just in the background observing like National Geographic videographers.

Ryan Mitchell of WBK starts us off: *"The difference between the two cities is that Dallas is filled with people from Up North who move because they wanna be Texans and wear cowboy hats like hicks. Houston is where all the Native Texas people go to do crime."*

"Are cops evil here?"

Tyler Irvine chimes in: "Absolutely. They tazered a singer over a noise complaint at a real, established venue."

"Anything you go to jail for. Pot laws around here are really strict."

"Don't ever do anything wrong to a cop or attempt running. The cops here are different then the cops up North. Down here they're like shaved bull dogs. They all do judo and shit."

"Have you heard of this Super Happy Fun Land place before?"

"They own the Southmore House too, or their friends. Southmore, it's basically the crustie house. Houston has people who think there is a punk scene but they're ridiculous. Houston doesn't know anything about punk. There's a bunch of old dudes that think they're the tough because they beat up teenagers at shows."

"The music scene's changed a lot this past year especially 'cause this younger crowd is really into death metal. Screamo was really popular here, now you're seeing death metal, grind styles. Most of the metal scene is more of the nu-metal type stuff still, because that's what the older generation is into."

"I was gone for a year in Seattle. I came back here and death metal exploded... Houston has this hardcore scene with like role model dudes. That's the bad deal about Texas, especially the South. Everybody's a badass... It's so irritating. I tried to explain to my little sister who was wearing a confederate flag shirt – why do you wear shit like that? *'It's about my heritage.'* What, ignorance and racism? Why do they even sell things like this? Fuck southern pride... As a band our goal is to destroy the entire world and rebuild it in our own image."

"Are the hardcore bands like straight-up gangs then?"

"We have crews. What is it... the..."

"Grown ass..."

The 'GROWN ASS MAN CREW'"

"Did you just... The Grown Ass... hee hee hee BWA HA HA HA HA!!!"

"They go to all the hardcore shows, do their whole Gorilla Biscuit thing. Again, that's a small sect. It's not a good representation of Houston."

"They're like Nazi's, but at least Nazi's believed in something. It went from role models to *'fuck everyone else we're the shit'* to 20-30 year olds beating up teenagers at shows. It's all fine when they knock kids out in the pit, but when one of those kids punches them in the face accidentally then 20 of them jump the kid outside."

"Tyler, you mentioned Seattle."

"I lived there for a year and filled in for a drummer in a band called CLR. They were a crust punk band. I took a greyhound back here, it took like 3 days. Just when you think your back couldn't possibly hurt worse some fat dude with night terrors sits in front of you. He like screams in his sleep. That really happened too, he's got like a bike helmet with bubbles..."

"Oh you have no idea... I heard that some congressman passed a bill where all the kids in school have to pledge allegiance to Texas. There's a Texas pledge after the classic pledge..."

"They added "Under God" to the Texas pledge of allegiance."

Texas in general – you love it or you hate it. As soon as you leave it you miss it, soon as you get back you're like *'why did I ever come back to this sweltering hellhole?'"*

"Got any good acid stories?"

"One time I took acid and I realized everything was connected to Mother Earth and then I decided that I was going to find Mother Earth and I was going to fuck her. And then I got really thirsty and fell asleep."

"I don't know where I heard it, but its an amazing story. These kids all took 'shrooms I guess, they went out in the woods and started tripping balls. They were like 'guys, lets catch something!' So they take a trash bag out there and catch something. 'Oh my god, we got a gnome!' So they got like a gnome in a trash bag and they take it home and stick it in their closet. They're like, 'Dude, we got to check it in the morning when we're sober.' They all go to work and then see on the news a little 4 year old girl's gone missing. They go back home and look in their closet and there's just this 4 year old girl standing there crying... They went and turned themselves in. The so-called liberals on the West Coast would've nailed their balls to the wall."

"Any crazy show stories?"

"There was this battle of the bands and a girl crossing the street got hit by 2 cars. Hit and run, split her in half. Sucks. Everyone went outside crying and puking. We won, and we're like "yeah, we won" and everybody's still kind of crying, like puking and stuff. She got hit, went up, then got hit by another car. It was BA-BUHM. Her arms back here, her legs up here, her torso... I couldn't recognize the face. We were outside and I heard THUMP and I turn and see feet in the air and I hear THUMP and then the ground. So my band were the first up there. I was cool with it... Not cool with it, but..."

Determined to explore the alien habitat, we make the abominable mistake of going to the world's largest IKEA blown out on the most powerful grass we've smoked all tour. I've never entered such a thing. These Texas people have turned furniture buying into a family-extravaganza activity.

It's got it's own food court; this menacing labyrinth of $5000 davenports and bedroom sets. You have to keep following these yellow lines that don't actually lead you to any exit, just deeper into the belly of the beast.

Neil gets a cell call and paces around a fake kitchen talking to the guy as if he's at a party late at night trying to have a moment of clarity. I see him get lost in the apparition, and the fear in his eyes as he snaps out of it. We're trapped in this goliath of other people's fake lives, with false family portraits in glass cases, cardboard TV's, toilets with no plumbing. "Your" humble life and memories, all easily selectable, lay out before the sterile consumer lens.

Running in circles seeking the exit everyone keeps looking at us funny. By the time we finally spy the glass doors, it's an hour later, and I hear a security siren going off. When I look back we're being trailed by 3 security officers – the *"king-size mattress Gestapo."*

The hyper-obesity of Houston continues as we finish the roach and enter a Sams Club that is just as monolithic and horrid. The aisles of frozen food are locked inside giant bank-styled vaults, like Dachau chambers. As we pass the grocery baggers one radios his manager "10-12 on aisle 13," and again the boys don't notice as we're trailed by security.

There is no way around it – this is where the lizard people will lock us after Bush Clan ignites Revelations. That's why everything in Houston is vault-like – it must house the post-apocalyptic survivors…

DALLAS (9/21)

Reading *Ishmael* at the apartment of yet another Detroit Expatriate, from Neil's high school. He's a hardcore punker turned 27 year old mild-mannered accountant. The aftermath of Super Happy Fun Land was no door money, no merch sales, a band opening with banjo's.

The ride to Dallas is lengthy, and no oil fields to be spotted. Ulysses The Scumfuck calls out of the blue, wondering where I was during the Summer of Love. It was the 40th anniversary spectacular at Golden Gate, and an unrivaled psychedelic explosion.

Tonight's show is at Fat Daddies in the Dallas Suburb of Lewisville. It's another death-trap with a big sign on the door that exclaims, *"Attention Touring Bands: You get no money unless you draw more then 30 people, and then we pay you $1 per head after that. Take it or leave it. Crybabies go home."* Crumbling parking lot, 20 tight-pants kids with quaffed hair & a Battle of the Bands contest to open for Drop Dead Gorgeous…

After a decent Lamb of God type metal band named INBRYO finishes, DTB go full blast, talking mad amounts of shit on screamo culture. You'd think they'd be insulted, but we sell a stupendous $120 in merch. Gets us far from Demon Texas and into the crust cradle – Oklahoma, where *"Labor Conquers All Things…"*

THE PWN HOUSE VOL. II (9/22)

"Tell me about the Oklahoma music scene."

Matt Jim: "It's a very strange creature. The very top of the creature that everyone knows about [insert weenie voice] *"The Flaming Lips, oh man there's Hinder and there's like fuckin' the All American Rejects."* Then there's like the horrible dark underbelly where all the genetalia and nipples of the music scene are. We're like the furry crotch of the Oklahoma music scene. We don't want that nu metal crap, we don't want Hinder fans or anything like that near our shit. What we try to do – Norman, Tulsa, some OKC bands is have a little network. It used to go far southwest as Laughton. It's this huge strip connected by Highway 44."

"I was looking at the Oklahoma free weekly and the cover story is why Oklahoma hates Hinder."

"God, those motherfuckers. Hinder must die because aside from being the worst band fucking ever to come out of this state, their fans are obnoxious, they're obnoxious, nobody wants to play with them 'cause they're fuckin' dicks. They act like rock stars, they're pretentious for nothing, they're music sounds like a keg party on repeat. You sound like Alpha Beta Tao horrible fuckin…"

"Tell me about Snotrokitz."

"Snotrokitz started ten years ago. We were like 15 at the time. We started listening to shit like Capitalist Causalities and Spazz and Man Is The Bastard. We started experimenting with speed, with abrasiveness and got engulfed by it. We still have lots of blasts, lots of screaming. Our songs have a socio-political stance but we're not above being immature with poop songs."

"Plenty of fun encounters with the police out here then?"

"We used to go to Arkansas City, the shittiest, horrible town in Kansas. There's this bar called The Mule Barn and they had those big blue plastic containers with the white rope handles. They're like 20 gallons, packed with ice and 80 beers. So we'd get in the back of my buddies Bronco, throw it in the back and leave. I tell my friend that if we do get caught, we're just gonna drop our pants and start jacking off. There's no way they'll get us in trouble. We can just plead insanity. We grab the container and it was smooth sailing until we were a block away. Who shows up but Arkansas City police department? We're sweating, kinda out of breath, and he's like '*whatcha boys got there?*' We just looked at each other and shrugged, put down the fucking thing of ice and beer, and pulled down our pants and just started yanking on our flaccid penises. The cop goes '*Oh Mary mother of god!*' and gets in his car and leaves. That night I had just felt that we won somehow."

"Have you done a lot of psychedelic drugs?"

"I've done way too many psychedelic drugs. We had this shit, back when you could order it from the internet under the guise of research chemicals. It was called 5 methoxydimethyltryptamine – 5MEODMT. It was like psychedelic crack, a crystalline powder that you had to smoke out of a glass dick. But you take one huge hit and it's like everything disappears and becomes something else. Voices start speeding up and slowing down. Time becomes distorted. Everything is just too much. It's like a big psychedelic elephant sitting on your head. I freaked out because I snorted a whole bunch. You smoke it lasts 20 minutes. You snort it lasts an hour. 1 saw Bill Clinton on *The Daily Show* talking about his memoirs and he started getting these big purple spots on his face. He turned into this giant, insectoid, lizard creature with human limbs, like he had an exoskeleton with hundreds of eyes on his eyes. I had never, ever done anything like that before. I did it a few more times after that and then I had to quit psychedelic drugs altogether. I haven't done them since. Well… I got drunk and took bites out of my San Pedro cactus. It makes you puke, you will throw up, no matter what. Once you ingest it, soon as you throw up your puking all the bat alkaloids and funky shit and then the mescaline kicks in. It is heaven, it is bliss. It's one of the most beautiful visions. Everything's like kind of pastel, kind of dusty."

"Have you done Peyote?"

"Yeah, a long time ago. It's the sacrament of, you know, my people. I grew up with that shit. My grand grandpa was a peyoteist. We had a certain reverence for the guys on peyote. They have to fast for a few days before they're even pure enough to touch it. They say their prayers, they sing their peyote songs. They have all these weird visions which they tell everybody. After they have a huge feast, everyone gets to eat. I've never partook in the ritual. That's the elders, those are the old guys that get to do it."

"What do you think of Billy Jack?"

"Billy Jack? Fuckin' Reds hero man. My mom, that's her hero. He's the type of guy where you take off your cowboy boots, take off your socks, and go whoop some ass. Beneath Billy Jack's nut sack isn't a tank, but just another foot (laughs)."

"I know you mentioned people say derogatory things towards you. You watch a movie like Billy Jack and see how it was in the 60's…"

"Back in the 60's a lot of hotbed shit was going on. That's not to say a lot of those ethnically bound institutions are that strong in this day and age. The institutions still exist but not that bad, especially when you go to an inner city area. The thing that pisses me off is whenever people – under the guise of equality – wanna say *'hey, you should give up your ethnic identity so we could all be one homogenized society.'* Fuck assimilation."

"In Albuquerque I was told of these Native American pagan black metal bands that only play on the reservations. Like they don't allow outsiders in, white people are not allowed close, and their band names aren't even spoken outside the inner, clandestine circles…"

"There was one a long time ago, they were Navajo guys. They were singing through the perspective of the Navajo skin-walkers. The skin-walkers could put themselves in any animal, they could change themselves into any animal, they could turn into any human. They were shapeshifters but more malevolent, kind of the equivalent of vampires. I'm not even sure if I'm getting that legend right, we don't have that in my culture, the Aponi culture. There's also a couple of stink-ass pop punk bands that did. They just didn't want to play outside reservations at all. A lot of the Indians in the Southwest are like that. In Phoenix they're more crusty type punks, willing to play outside…"

PLAINVIEW (9/23)

Great show last night, all the mayhem to be expected. No tornado's, yet Matt still got naked. Exitium have also happily reformed with the drummer from Devourment, and we'd walked out with $150 in door money and another $80 merch. We're going to make it to LA after all.

Tonight's gig is of my own hand. The lame bookie left gaping wounds in the itinerary, and at the last minute was able to score a show in Plainview, just outside Amarillo, thanks to Chris Olibarez [*who runs Hymns of the Needlefreak fanzine*].

I'd been contributing surplus album reviews to him for awhile, and he was pleased to assist. I just didn't think it'd be to this level. In 3 days they booked 4 bands, printed 3,000 flyers, contacted local press, and bought radio ads for my spoken word performance. Now every band in West Texas is flocking to Club Zodiac for a chance to meet the famous metal journalist guy.

Along the way an O-BOMB is about to explode in my intestine. Those damned Indian tacos of Matt Jim sent me flying into a gas station restroom in the middle of nowhere, for miles nothing but open fields and two *Chainsaw Massacre* houses spread miles apart. When I return Hairy Bob is appropriately talking to a guy in a "NAILSHITTER" t-shirt.

I'm at a loss for words. It's the guitarist from Crematorium, and the vocalist – Dan Dismal who threw the LA Murderfest – is in shotgun of the van next to ours. I was supposed to interview him in April but could never finger him amongst the crowds. Now the most bizarre convergence of all time is taking place…

"So I heard that you're in the middle of a nightmare tour."

Dan Dismal: "Put $700 into the van for a diagnostic check to make sure nothing would go wrong. On the way to Seattle we get a crack in radiator, $450. They've got to bypass the HC, another $200. The knuckle on the front passenger wheel disintegrated, that was $1700. After that the transmission takes a shit, that was $2500. Been babying it all the way home cause it keeps spitting fire and smoke and bullshit…"

"I was supposed to interview for this book someway, somehow. We're here by fate. What's on your mind?"

"This is the longest tour we've done in three years. We've broke down so many times we remember why we don't do tours this long anymore."

"Tell me about LA. Is it hell on earth?"

"Where we're at now, this is kind of hell on earth."

"LA has that kind of plastic stigma of Hollywood…"

"The problem is that a lot of the people who're anti-Hollywood are almost Hollywood in their own ways. Problem with the metal scene in LA is that there's no actual scene. It's like three bands who know each other. There's a lot of separation going on. If you go to black metal shows, you don't go to death metal shows. Punk band, vice versa. No one goes out there just for the music. It's kind of ridiculous, doing this and revolting against Hollywood. It's like being anti-racist and going to a Klan rally. People just need to remember that no one was ever born a metalhead. Anybody that says they were, it's fucking bullshit. *'Oh I used to listen to MC Hammer, then I go into Slayer.'*"

"How many shows you've thrown in LA?"

"At least over 250. I started because promoters are scum usually. That was back in 2002. At this point I'm at 10-20 shows per month. It's pretty ridiculous to tell you the truth. I'm not a rocket scientist, I just stepped up to the plate."

"What's the single crowning show you've ever done?"

"This year's Muderfest. Even before it happened people were like '*this is bigger than the Maryland Deathfest.*' For me to pull this off on my 3rd year."

"I know most of those bands have big guarantees. Did you break even?"

"Yeah, I made $400."

"Wow, I thought you would've been slammed..."

"That's what I was stoked on. The second one we lost $8,500."

"Were people negotiable with their price-tags?"

"A lot of them were cool because I told them, '*this is a fest, it only holds 900 people.*' Repulsion cut their guarantee down, Obituary cut their guarantee down. Deceased played for plane tickets. Waco Jesus flew themselves out. A lot of bands didn't even ask for much because there's no fest in LA. There's no fest on the West Coast really besides Oregon..."

Club Zodiac is near impossible to find, accessible only by an unmarked dirt road. It's in between an open field, a slaughterhouse, and the Hale County Penitentiary, which is pronounced *"HELL"* in their thick southern drawls.

The second I hopped out there were a gathering of metalheads sizing me up with that spittoon, Texas grandeur. They really looked at me funny because of the painted black middle fingers, and generally nervous of talking to me.

Chris Olibarez cordially greets me – a very friendly Mexican guy in his early 30's and limping with a cane. He destroyed his ankle but it's not stopping his set tonight as the drummer from NIHILISTIC OUTLAW: CRIMINAL ORDER.

His grind vocalist Paul, who also spearheads the long-running Death By Metal fanzine, is just as freaked out by me as were the bands. Literally, everyone is in cold-sweats when I talk to them. I know it got weird in Detroit, but for me to have that sort of power somewhere this remote? How many Plainview's exist in America? Then it dawns on me – they all read *"The Mabusvanian Conspiracy."* Shit, I'd be freaked out too...

"Is Plainview a scene made up of about 20 core guys?"

Chris Olibarez: "Plainview is actually only us and Gates of Sodom. We're the only two bands. The population is only 20,000 I think. We're kind of one of the most hated bands from around here. I really don't know why. I think they hate us because they're busting their heads doing shows and we're just sitting back getting drunk, giving free shirts out. Hank IIIrd wore our shirts in Hustler Magazine, Tattoo Savage."

"Your shirts and bumper stickers are very anti-republican, very anti-illuminati. We're here in Bush Country…"

"I think that's another reason why people don't like us. The last time we did shows all the Christians and Christian bands were tearing down flyers. Throwing them down, protesting. There were Christians at the venue asking people *'why are you coming to this show?'* Giving bibles and Christian CD's, stuff like that."

"Do they do that at a lot of metal shows?"

"We're the only ones doing metal shows. They don't do that over there in Lubbock or Amarillo. I think here it's so rare they can attack it more. We promote it so much, put it everywhere so much that they have time to actually know what's going on. They don't start shit, they just do it at a distance. Like my wife, she works at a slaughterhouse. Everybody knows everyone that works there, and they're coming in and saying *'you asked for the day off just to go to this show? Well here's a CD of some Christian music, you should listen to this, blah blah blah.'* We have a 10 year old son, and he was wearing a HIM shirt. There was this guy going *'that's satanic, why are you teaching your kids to be satanic?'* You don't even know what you're saying. Is that what you're religion teaches? To go and be dramatic in front of people you don't know? It's crazy dude…"

The totally weird vibe rolls on, and Downtown Brown thinks they'll be killed. The fest is called "Unholy Sunday," and the bill is Freak Havik, NIHILISTIC OUTLAW, and Gates of Sodom. For one thing, this is the first show Chris Olibarez has ever thrown, and the first DIY metal concert EVER in this town. All shows in this area are either in Amarillo or Lubbock, both 45 minutes South and North.

The yokels in back – all these pissed biker & cowboy guys – they've never seen anything like this. None of this crowd has, and there's a big attendance ratio. There are fold-out wall tables everywhere like a high school cafeteria, and all these old people are sitting down just kind of watching, as well as a bunch of totally innocent teens.

The first band up is Freak Havik. They do some covers and play a mish-mash of Pantera meets Hatebreed meets some nu-metalish modern rock with singing melodic breakdowns. Nothing earth-shattering, but it is to the audience, and the band is having a blast. You can actually see the DIY spirit growing, like one of those dinosaur sponges you soak and grows huge overnight.

Everyone sitting down again cafeteria style, and it's my turn to say something. Chris talks me up through the crackling and blown out PA speakers, and I walk up to the microphone that's duct-taped to a cymbal stand. I'm entering the world of Conway Twitty. All these middle aged people and rag-tag metalheads, all these 14 year olds just waiting, like I'm some politician the Union 386 booked to say I'm fighting to keep their stamping plant alive.

I do my usual intro, then hit it off with some silly tales about working for ESPN and meeting Bruce Campbell & Chi Chi Rodriguez. Keep it simple, keep it marketable – no jacking off in donuts and feeding them to cops. But then I get to the core of it: *"Plainview, Texas. This is incredible. I want to thank every single one of you for coming out tonight. Give it up for all the bands, really [huge applause]."*

"You know, it is true that I'm a writer for this big-shot magazine. I've been all over the place. I've partied with rock stars, I've hung out with celebrities. But none of that compares to being here at this very moment. Truth is I could be anywhere right now, hanging out in Los Angeles or New York living the supposed high life, being buddy-buddy with all those plastic surgery people."

"But those people are fucking fake. Those people don't care about anything. That world isn't real, and you shouldn't give it any power in your life. This is where's it's real. This is true metal, this is true rock n' roll, this is punk rock at its finest. And I tell you no lie that I'd rather be on stage here right now in this little nothing bar in the middle of nowhere Texas then gabbing away at Madison Square Garden in front of 20,000 people. This is where it's happening, this is where it's real, don't let that fucking TV fool you for one second. That much said, give it up for the greatest rock n' roll band ever from Detroit, Downtown-muthafuckin-Brown!!!"

The crowd explodes, and Neil looks like he's about to as well. DTB rages through the hardest rocking jams they have, and the crowd has never seen or heard anything like this. Chris is laughing hysterically

and grabs my shirt: "*I wanna do it all man, I wanna do it all!!!*"
Everyone's is digging it until Neil brings back the rant about Jesus
wiping his butt, which promptly kills off all the old people. But even
the gritty old cowboys are dancing up front, lifting their beers. We go
on to sell $80 in merch and $70 from the doors.

Now it is time for NIHILISTIC OUTLAW: CRIMINAL
ORDER, who've been handing out free shirts all night. Young and old
are sporting pentagrams. The singer Paul is nervously pacing around
stage. It's N.O.C.O.'s big moment to play for the famous rock n' roll
journalist guy, but once they start the PA farts out. The microphone
won't work. Paul rushes in spastic circles for 15 minutes trying to get it
going, panicking. Armageddon is unfurling…

But then we have ignition, and N.O.C.O. blow the roof off the
place. They thrash around, LOUD, pouring sweat, Paul screaming his
twisted soul into the screeching PA of total sonic destruction – jumping
around, rolling on the ground, throwing himself into the mini circle pit.
Right now he's the greatest vocalist in the world…

ALBUQUERQUE (9/24)

Next morning, still in Plainview eating weird miuendo chili soup.
We're at the home of B McNuts, one of Olibarez' friends. He's this
short, odd Mexican guy that led us to his crib as a crash spot, but
neither he nor his little 3 year old boy with a mohawk would let us
sleep. Every 15 minutes B McNuts wife would come out and yell
"*WHAT THE FUCK ARE YOU KIDS STILL DOING UP?!? GET THE
FUCK TO BED!!! NOW!!! I GOTTA WORK IN 3 HOURS NOW
FUCKING SLEEP!!! GODAMMIT!!!!*"

The guy was far too much to explain. After I nodded off he took
Glover on a hectic 2 hour tour of all the real estate for sale in his
neighborhood, then attempted to teach him the science of levitation. He
was intent on having all 5 of his children put their fingers under Glover,
causing him to float with their mental concentration beams.

I woke up prematurely around 3am and found B McNuts
dancing over my sleeping bag, coked up with a party hat and taking
Polaroid photos of me passed out on the floor. Yeah, one of those foil
ones with the tinsel on top and that little elastic string for the chin…

Albuquerque now, on the Vertigo Venus porch, and Ken
Cornell is in a fog of deep contemplation. The entire cast of characters
from my ABQ mission are all here tonight, sipping booze and passing
the peace pipe.

Nothing stifles the war-mode of Jeff MacCannon though. When I ask about the importance of filth in American society, he goes: "*I'm gonna go on the accordance of gay filth. Homo's today think we're like everyone else. That is not true. We're different – we're dirty, we're perverts, we're all these horrible things and that's good. No matter how many times you go to church on Sunday, no matter how many marriage rights you stand for, or Asian babies you adopt, you're still a product of a society that loves fisting. And there's no way you're ever going to be normal.*"

"*You should just accept it and move on. Because all these people that are like [twinkie weezer voice] 'I'm gonna go hang out at the straight bars and drink beer with guys and maybe one will be curious about men and come home with me.' These guys end up in dumpsters on fire. They seem to think that they're safe. They would be safe if gay men were more like they were in the 70's – i.e. leather clad with guns. Now they're chicks. They go to high school until they're 40, they wear glitter, they flounce about, and get beat up and die. And rightly so 'cause that's just stupid and if that is the popular personality in our society, than fine – kill it. I quit, I'm done. I am about ready to go out gay-bashing.*"

"*I used to live almost exclusively with drag-queens for 3 years. If anything that taught me is that glitter is made of pain. Drag-queens, they're horrible people. They take on all the aspects of femininity like having lots of clothes and accessories and make up and shit and they keep this whole frat boy, manly thing and they don't clean up anything. They'll clean their wigs by leaving it in the sink for a week and then hanging it up above a heater. And they wonder why it turns green and smells like them.*"

"*Gay society now has turned into this horrible amalgamation of stupid. It's either you're a filthy, drugged out drag-queen, or you're filthy drugged out guy whose trying to be 16 for the rest of his life, or you're a dirty old man whose just made of leather. Not wearing it, made of it. It a product of this IPOD nation where everyone has their own little subculture that comes with its own satellite radio & t-shirt…*"

ALBUQUERQUE (9/25)

Early morning, everyone asleep. Just Neil Patterson Esquire the IIIrd and myself on the front porch. Calm, reflective. He sees me pull out the tape recorder and hit record, and he just kind of smiles and leans back in his chair, setting down the acoustic guitar. *"Finally huh? So is this the definitive interview then Bartek?"*

"No, but it's a start. Tell me about the tour thus far."

Neil P: "Well… It's a test of a man's will to do what he loves every day. When you're given obstacles, to just void them when you have no money, no food… Fuckin' dogs with scabies… It's way better than working."

"Were you disappointed by New York?"

"No, I knew what we were going into. New York's a tough fucking town. When you're on tour with a band nobody knows about, and nobody knows about you either, you can't really expect to draw people in a huge city. It's kind of like Detroit where people are going to go to The Knitting Factory only to see a band they really want to see. Even that band that was on tour with all that money and those huge cargo vans, there wasn't that many watching them… Punk rock man. They had that emo skull on their tour van. It was like a skull and crossbones except they had quaffed hair going over the right eye of the skull. We're like dangerous, but fashionably dangerous, heh heh…"

"Do you think there's any hope for Detroit?"

"I don't think there's ever going to be unity in Detroit. The only unity that's involved is with the indie garage rock scene. It's a big coalition of people who are into something because they're told to be into something. Why are the tight-pants shoegazing bands who can't play their instruments considered indie? I consider Downtown Brown an indie band. We put out our own records, we tour with our own money. But all these terms get put on all this shit. If we were The Black Lips and we got naked onstage would Rolling Stone say we put on one of the best live shows in America? I think we do. I haven't seen one band besides Gil Mantera's Party Dream that can even touch what we do. To just get up in front of a bunch of people who have never heard us and no matter what – emo kids, punk kids, some guy named Rooster with a fucking mullet in the middle of Texas – what we do translates. It's universal. But Rolling Stone is never going to say shit about us because we're not cool. We'll always be considered a novelty act because you can't smile in rock and roll. You can't write goofy lyrics. I'm sure any notable, crappy huge magazine that everyone reads – Mr. Bungle never got an article in that. Frank Zappa is still kind of dismissed. There's no light at the end of the tunnel, there isn't some huge paycheck"

"Never give in though…"

"As long as you feel you're contributing something that has worth and weight to society, even if it's a song about poop. If it puts a smile on someone's face, if people are entertained by that I'm doing my job. I'm here to act like an idiot and make people smile. That makes me smile, that's why I do what I do."

"What are you expecting in LA?"

"Well, you were there. The guy really liked us a lot and invited us to play his birthday party and that's this Friday. He said there's gonna be a lot of industry people in the audience, but I don't know... We're fat. LA's a beautiful town. At least Hollywood, it seems that everyone is hot. Dudes, chicks, hermaphrodites, whatever... Everyone's eyes in the entire world are focused on beautiful people that aren't even really talented who live in that town because they're postered on billboards and plastered on the cover of every magazine that every fat Midwestern housewife picks up and reads because they're life is so boring they have to adhere to someone that's hot. Not even someone whose talented, not even like a Jimi Hendrix. Someone that could play the guitar, someone who could sing really well. Someone like Jennifer Lopez, someone that really doesn't do anything but she has a hot ass so I want to buy her perfume. That makes me want to throw up. I think we're the antidote for Hollywood. I think if we go in there being fat, being boisterous, complete assholes... They never saw anything like that. They're used to everyone licking their ass. We got in there and we were talking about snorting coke of Johnny Depps' cock and everyone fucking loved it. Hollywood's a big ass licking contest. I'm not about to do any of that shit..."

PRESCOTT (9/26)

Beefcake Steve was so cool he gave us all their door money, and arranged for us to crash at his band mates house, who ironically has a long brown beard, dresses completely Amish, and is, of course, the solo artist of the noise-core project AMISH NOISE.

$85 later in gas we arrive in the mountainous region of Prescott, Arizona penniless and late for the gig at Sundance's. We're screwed – both openers have long played beforehand, and it isn't until 1am when DTB hit the stage to play for 8 people in a dead bar.

Somehow, someway – we walk out with $120 in merch. The rockabilly bartender – overjoyed we know Twistin' Tarantula's – gives us free CD's of his band The High Rollers and fed us $70 in complimentary liquor...

SAN DIEGO (9/27)

We'd awoken somewhere in Arizona at the manager from Psychostick's house where glass bowls filled with condoms laid on every table surface. *"So are there any mint flavored ones?"* I ask. 'Well no. But there might be a banana." *"Yes, perhaps. But I only seek mint."* "Why?" *"So you can offer me a condiment"* [insert rim-shot + laugh track here]...

Onward to The Villa Winona. Just one last interstate through the mountains, road ending at the Pacific crest... We're stopped at a draconian checkpoint so farcical it couldn't be authentic. There are American border control foot-soldiers with AK-47's manning a roadblock, snooping through cars looking for illegal immigrants or Muslim jihadists.

There is a giant green sign that reads "HOMELAND SECURITY TERROR THREAT LEVEL: ORANGE." It's got all the five colors and this little magnet pointing an arrow which indicates how afraid we should be. This isn't my high school in 1996. This is real, this is happening. Welcome to THE BIG SHINY PRISON.

The show is on Ocean Beach at The Dream Street café. The crew comes roaring out – Dr. Santiago, Mr. Skinner, Brandon, Panda, Jo-Jo. DTB gets Wax & Herbal T (*the best identical twin white rappers in America*) to join onstage for a freestyle session...

Long walk on the beach, too many tall cans and painkillers. We find ourselves at an after party hosted by Donnie L. Carter from The Fabulous Rudies, an independent ska band the boys made pals with on Warped Tour this year: *"We're a little more rude than we are fabulous. To quickly sum it up, we are a Southern California ska band. We did the entire Warped Tour in 2007, did some dates in 2006, 2005... This year we were the BBQ band. Warped Tour is almost a circus. The bigger bands will have their tour bus, booking agent, manager. We rented our own RV – our tour managers were just Tom and myself. It's definitely DIY. If anything goes wrong, you're to blame."*

"What's the message of The Fabulous Rudies?"

"We're a ska band trying to bring fun music back to the public. The other half is kind of politically conscious, socially conscious. The fun music, the dance music – but there's also lyrics about the wars, suicide... Ska was kind of a bad word in the record industry so we started to branch out, but we always had that as our roots. Everything came together these last 2 years. Southern California is starting to accept it again, other areas in the United States as well. There's another crest of the wave right now."

"*Where does ska go over best?*"

"There are some crowds that don't get it. Not so much this year, cause we were definitely going up the wave. We've done the whole southwest, we've done Northern parts in California, Vegas. We have seen some crowds that don't accept it. Right now there is a big acceptance, especially here, LA & New York. Those are the two big ska movements – Southern California and New York. After the third wave which produced bands like Reel Big Fish, Save Ferris, The Bosstones, those have been the hotbeds of ska activity in US."

"*You're in other projects too?*"

"In San Diego it's hard to avoid reggae. Me and the sax player have Stranger. For us it's a side project, but they've been in it 6 years. They're in South Bay area San Diego, which is close to the border of Tijuana. They have a bit of that Mexican influence, which is kind of the heart of music in Chula Vista and East LA. They kind of epitomize the reggae aspect of that area; the horn section is a beautiful thing. I play trombone. The horn section for Rudies is tenor sax and trombone. When we record I play trumpet. For stranger, that's generally what we stick to. Side One Dummy was looking at signing them, maybe even taking them on Warped next year. If we do go on tour this summer, we hope Stranger gets on half the Warped Tour…"

"*What is the strangest thing that happened on tour?*"

"We actually hit a mounties in Canada with the RV. We had gotten into an accident in Vancouver and kind of bent the tail end of our RV. So when we passed we scraped the side of this Mounties…"

THE VIPER ROOM (9/28)

As we pull into the Hollywood strip I ceremonially Frisbee the new promo disc of Critical Bill's debut record into the gutter. Just another one of those encoded *"if this leaks on the internet we're suing the pants off you"* albums sent for review. *Floccinaucinihilipilification…*

Our rage has never been so fever-pitch. For another useless Detroit band like that to get a major label deal – for that much money to be invested in a Godsmackey, rapcore hangover with the word "Detroit Underground" plastered all over the press release when all they do is play the fucking Emerald Theatre in Mt. Clemens? Our blood is boiling, and it's time to demolish The Viper Room.

This is Downtown Brown's finest moment. The venue lets us have the prime parking space in front (*doesn't happen*), allows us to bring ALL the merch we want inside (*against the rules*), give us free reign to shoot all the video and photos we want (*normally it costs $250 for video and $100 for photo*), give us a limitless free full bar all night (*pushing $500 easy*), a 20 person guest list (*$15 per ticket*), and the co-owner paid a sound-man $300 to record the DAT mix for his own personal live album. *Merry Christmas assholes...*

3 hours later, the big moment, sober & razor-sharp. The red curtain opens, the Detroit Expatriate packed floor goes wild, and Neil's eyes are glowing with the satanic thunder of Loki: "*We are Downtown Brown from Detroit, Michigan!!! FUCKING BURN IN HELL LA!!!*"

* * * * *

2 hours after Hiroshima. The Viper Room has become the Double O Pub from Redford, Michigan. 400 people are so drunk they are writhing on the floor like snakes, falling over one another like panicked sheep charging down the high-rise stairwell of *The Towering Inferno...*

Painted up plastic surgery dolls with artificial tits are heckling Orange Bitches as they walk down the strip. People are pissing everywhere, vomit pools, abasia – the interior walls drip with booze and perspiration. $365 in merch sales are wadded in my pocket, another $200 is flowing in from the doors and we didn't even sell one ticket.

I'm the only sober one here, and I'm walking around with a coffee cup full of piss to throw at the doorman who's the biggest, fakest, Hollywood asshole prick in all of Los Angeles (*long story*). Hairy Bob has cut loose for the first time ever. Eyore is dead, and he's charging around like a muppet from hell licking call-girl's faces. He has literally pissed himself laughing. As the black security guard tries to maneuver him into the street, Bob hugs him joyfully: "*You don't understand, you don't understand. We do this thing called Black Hour. You'll love it, you'll fucking love it!!*"

Glover and I try to corral Bob into the van, but he won't stay inside. It's drunken retard strength to the furthermost degree. He keeps flinging out the side door, rolling around the ground laughing, rubbing puke puddles all over his clothes. I take him in back parking lot 'cause he needs to piss, and while I'm searching for the door guy's car so I can dump the love-filled grande container into his dashboard air vents, Bob pisses all over himself again. I have to put back on his pants like an elderly care worker.

Back in front Neil has his arm around a probable stripper: *"No, you don't understand, it's all about Toxic Holocaust. Come with me to Norman and we'll listen to vinyl. Baby, you'll love it, you'll fucking love it."* The bar has fed him at least 25 shots of Jaeger by now.

I look for support, but Glover is out of his mind as well, dancing around singing with his arms around LA rocker guys with pretty-boy blonde dyed streaks. The last band – another ass licking Viper Room usual – are having the time of their lives ripping apart the weak, wormy little doorman onstage. The whole crowd roars in response, *"Yeah, fuck that doorman faggot!"*

Outside it's even more havoc. Neil has a line of 4 guys and they're all pissing in the middle of the street belly-laughing as Ferraris and Jaguars swerve by, trying not to run them down...

LAST TANGO IN LOS ANGELES (9/29)

SATURDAY, September 29th, Amoeba Records in Hollywood. In a moment I'll be meeting up with Matt Olivo from Repulsion. I have a four-band date tonight – Charles Elliot, guitarist of death metal act Abysmal Dawn and PR guy for Nuclear Blast Records USA. His girlfriend Liz Schall of LA thrash band Dreaming Dead (*formerly Manslaughter*). Sascha Dunable from the grind/death/tech beast Intronaut...

No one has ever heard of Repulsion it seems, especially in Michigan. Detroit may have given birth to the first true punk band, but Flint gave the world its first grind band. In 1985 a handful of 15 year old kids recorded an album called *Horrified* and changed metal history.

For years they were virtually unknown except to a few die-hard tape-traders – among them some guys in England who were thus inspired to start Napalm Death (*plagiarism or inspiration, that is the question of the century*).

Repulsion were also one of the first metal acts to use horror/gore-oriented lyrics, which led an endless succession of bands attempting to *"out hardcore"* one another, that zenith lyrical battlefield inertia existing to this day.

22 years later has *Horrified* gained true recognition when Relapse Records pushed a heavy re-issue campaign, and numerous books like Albert Mudrian's *Choosing Death* added substantial fire to the legend. These days, a lengthy resume of underground notables

champion Repulsion a major influence – Carcass, John Zorn, Napalm Death, Exhumed, Cattle Decapitation, Pig Destroyer, Agoraphobic Nosebleed...

Says Matt Olivo: "You know that Repulsion only does occasional shows..."

"Yeah, I saw the first one in Flint, and I was at the LA Murderfest this year. I think 'Horrified' is great, I still have a beat up old t-shirt I've been sporting for years... What did you come up here for today?"

"I look for classic rock, whatever strikes my fancy. I like jazz, I like blues, film scores... The other day I bought Iron Maiden's *Number of the Beast* on vinyl. It's not that I ever stopped listening to stuff like that, but I just like to mix it up."

"What are you getting today?"

"Wes Montgomery's 3rd album. I'm not a big jazz collector. There's just certain artists that I like and he's definitely one of them."

"So are you guys ever going to record the ultimate follow up?"

"Chances are very slim. For one thing we probably couldn't produce the ultimate follow up in terms of songwriting. We just moved on – emotionally, musically, creatively. It was a very, very short period of time from a long time ago."

"What are you working on now? Do you have another band?"

"Not really. I'm a sound editor, I work on TV shows. It keeps me very busy, so I don't have time. I'd love to do a band. Scott is involved with Death Breath, which is Nikea Anderson formerly of Entombed and Hellacopters. Death Breath is basically his return to death metal. It's an all star lineup kind of band. They're getting ready to do a tour of Scandinavia next month."

"Are you big on the kung fu flicks?"

"I like some kung fu flicks. [Flips a DVD cover at me] This is one of my favorite movies of all time, *Shogun Assassin*. It's actually a compilation of a series of films called the *Lone Wolf And Cub* series in Japan. This film was basically the idea of an American distributor to take sections of this series, put them into one, and see if it'll sell."

"What television shows have you worked on?"

"I started out working on *Dawson's Creek* and *Strange Medicine*. Now I'm doing a lot of reality TV. *Top Chef*, shows like that."

"Coming from Michigan, all of us grew up with kind of that 'blah get a job' working class attitude. And it's a different kind of environment here. LA is its own country. I'm just curious a bit of your perception coming from that and ending up here."

"It's actually something that comes up quite a bit in the back of my mind. You grow up in Michigan and everybody is… your parents are very pragmatic. You talk about a career in the arts, and they're like, *'Are there medical benefits? What about the 401k plan?'* So that stuff gets drilled into you at a very early age. It does make some of your decision making kind of conservative. But my personality can't be held back. I'm glad I don't think that way. I'm glad I got out."

"When did you move to California?"

"'95."

"Did you go to sound editing school?"

"When I was a senior in college I was awarded a scholarship to the television academy to do music composing. I hung out with composers that were doing TV shows out here. And then I got started on that path and doing independent film scores. Which was going well, but I got really burned out on it 'cause it's a very solitary occupation. You spend a lot of time alone in front of your computer and ultimately it turned me off. It's probably what a lot of serious writers go through. The way you're writing is different – you're going out, gaining experience and interviews. But those writers that basically go to the library, do research, come home and type… That life just isn't for me. I like to talk to people, I like to be sociable. I learned the craft of sound editing and eventually got hooked up with people and got into the biz."

"How did you feel about the LA Murderfest? You got to play with a lot of bands that you probably wanted to back in the day."

"Yeah, it was great. We've always been one of those bands that didn't really have the kind of contemporary metal sound. We still sound very weird, I think. The only thing we were going for when we wrote those songs was extreme music. Along the way we were sort of able to make it our own. Playing with these other bands that have that real sort of straight forward classic metal sound… Most of the bands don't get us. And we don't really get most of the bands, but it's not stand-offish or anything. Yeah we've always wanted to play a show with Obituary, but it was important for us to play for our fans in the area. We were so excited to see the turnout and the response. In fact Scott and I both want to go on record saying that that was the best show we ever did."

"Did you guys hang at Negative Approach shows?"

"We sort of missed that particular era of Detroit hardcore, but we were lucky enough to meet early on a motivated group of people in Flint that were promoting shows for national touring punk acts. We were very influenced by punk...We'd always go to the shows – DRI, COC. We played at that show – Animosity and Dealing With It. We were called Genocide at the time. That was a dream gig for us. But we watched a lot of hardcore bands in those days."

"Do you have any random stories of punk legends?"

"I remember the first time I met Henry Rollins. Black flag played a show, the 'Slip It In' tour in flint. He showed up at 1 in the afternoon, they started setting up, and we're helping out. I just remember he came in, sat against the wall, and just was writing in his notebook for hours. Didn't talk to anybody, hardly even looked up. He did the show, he was very intense. It was somewhere between Jim Morrison and Rob Halford in a way. He was kind of metal, he had long hair in those days. He wasn't muscley – he was wiry & skinny & crazy & tatted out. And then after the show he was very friendly and open and meeting everybody. There was a big sink in that back of the venue, like a sink where a person could sit there and do dishes with giant pots and pans. And he just sat in it and turned the water on and was like dousing himself. This was my first experience with somebody who had a very intense sort of extreme personality. It wasn't faking it."

"What about LA these days, that reputation as a very plastic, fake kind of place. Do you feel that is an overblown stereotype?"

"I definitely think it's true. There are a lot of people here who go to clubs and dress a certain way because they want people to look at them. Or they hang out and become friends with people because they want to be seen with them. I'm not really a club type of person. When I do go out it's usually to see a show and have a few beers with my friends. I can see it all around me, to answer your question. It's everywhere. It doesn't really bother me that much. I've got my own little world and the people I know are real."

"How many dates have you done since Flint?"

"Under 10. We played in France, we played in Spain with Extreme Noise Terror. We played the Maryland Deathfest, the Milwaukee Metalfest..."

"Are you going to do any short tours for the hell of it?"

"We talk about that, but its not serious talk. If the stars lined up properly and it wasn't gonna kill anybody financially or time-wise we'd probably do it. But its not a big time priority."

"What's just a crazy story you have that no one seems to believe when you tell them?"

"I got a funny story… Let's put it this way – I personally know what it's like to be caught with drugs in your clothes at a major international airport. Let's just leave it as that (laughs)."

"Have you met any random legend?"

"Steve Railsback. Most people remember him for the portrayal he did as Charles Manson in *Helter Skelter*. He went on to do a bunch of shows, most recently he played Ed Gein. I actually hung out with him, we worked on a short film that he directed. He plays madmen very well and I think there's a reason for that."

"When you look back at this moment 20 years from now, would you say you are pretty content?"

"Yeah, I feel fine actually. I meet people, friends of mine that are still in bands that started around the time we did. And if you can still tour and still make money and still have fun, I think that's great. I certainly wish that Repulsion could have had a career like that, absolutely. But I moved on. I wasn't one of those people that sort of got bitter. So now I'm in a position where when stuff does happen with Repulsion it's a really, really nice surprise and a really fun thing to experience as opposed to '*I never really moved on and I'm desperate to taste it again.*' It's not like that. Something happens and it's like, '*Wow, they want to re-release the Repulsion album? Somebody wants to put it out on vinyl?*' That's crazy. Scott and I just continue to be completely blown away and humbled. It's not something we take for granted. For something that you did a year or two as a kid and it's still lingering in your life in a really cool positive way… So I'm happy…"

"Main question– what do you think of Billy Jack?"

"(Laughs) I thought it was pretty pimp…"

I cordially disperse my ways from Mr. Olivo and wander over to the black metal vinyl section where Charles Elliot (Abysmal Dawn) and his girlfriend Liz Schall (Dreaming Dead) are flipping through German obscurity.

They're ready to drink, and the second the car ignition is cranked, the first charming notes of the latest Akercocke are soon pummeling our eardrums: "*Well I started at Century Media in their warehouse, kind of worked my way up 'till I was doing A&R and publicity for Olympic Records. When they merged I was doing A&R for*

Century. I don't know why (laughs). My musical tastes aren't really what sells."

"Who did you sign?"

Charles Elliot: "Aborted from Belgium. That was the only band I signed. I licensed Swallow The Sun for Olympic. They were going through a time where they didn't want to sign too much and cut their roster down. Kinda focus on their bands instead of 50 more and shitting out six per month. So I went on tour with my band last fall and when I came back I'd lost my job. I worked at the Key Club as a loader for awhile, then I got a job at a warehouse selling fitness supplements. Then I got offered the job to do publicity for Nuclear Blast last May."

"Do they pay you well for that? Do you just sit around writing emails all day?"

"It's alright. For the most part, emails and on the phone all day. Writing bios, sending out press releases. Calling people and harassing them about the latest whatever. It's a cool gig though."

"Where did you tour when you went out?"

"All across the US for a month and a half with Six Feet Under, Krisiun and Decapitated. Krisiun are like what every band should be, like if the scene would unite and act like brothers."

"Do they ever take off their bullet-belts? They seem like they're the type of guys that would even shower with them on cause they're that metal."

"When they're not onstage the singers wearing like exercise shorts (laughs). Krisiun are the coolest guys in metal I think. They're really true, down to earth people. They're all about the music for all the right reasons. They really have that sense of community and look out for other bands. I can't stress how cool those guys are, they are like the coolest metal band ever."

"Is The Viper Room the epitome of plastic crap?"

"Yeah, you played the center of it all. Well that strip there. Like the Whiskey A Go-Go, the worst fuckin' venue on the face of the planet. It's fuckin' terrible. If you're a new band here, you know the Whiskey. That's the place to play by reputation. So everyone wants to play there cause they can sell tickets. As a result there's no quality control and you end up with a bill of 8-10 bands. The local LA music scene is a really competitive one. A lot of bands, especially now, I sometimes get the feeling that not all bands really like us. I don't know why. I think it's just the competitive aspect. We fill up venues pretty quick. I think some people hate us and would like to see us fail based on that. But whatever."

"Ever see Lorenzo Lamas walking around downtown?"

"No, but driving by some Cajun seafood place on Sunset Boulevard Fabio was like dead center, doors open, the table right in front where he could be seen while driving by. We made a u-turn and started yelling *'HEY FABIO, FUCK YEAH!'*"

**It's not long before we're in Echo Park, sipping Black & Tan's in a musty old bar that seems more like a veterans club from Arkansas then an LA night-spot: *"I'm in Dreaming Dead, I sing and play guitar. It's a death, black, thrash thing – there's a lot of mixture. I also played in Iron Maidens. It was an all female tribute band to Iron Maiden. I was in that for a year."*

"So do you play accordion?"

Liz Schall: "Yeah, I do. I just know like polka, like *'duh-duh-da-duh-duh-da-da-da-da-da'*…" *"Ha ha…"* "We toured with Decapitated. When they came back through a couple months ago we invited all the guys to our place and kind of had a little jam section. Liz brought out the accordion and was jamming with Votek and Vahn."

"So you mentioned earlier something about being kidnapped in Columbia? This guy had a buck knife in his hand or something."

"Yeah, it was fucking oh my god. I started screaming but nothing came out. I turned and he was like *'shut the fuck up, shut the fuck up'* in Spanish. Give me all your shit, give me what you got. I just give him my little fanny pack, my headphones and my money, and then like we just sat down for the next five hours. Talking about how he's homeless and all he ate was chocolate all day long. He slept in this abandoned house on a mattress and his life was totally fucked up."

"So he robbed you and hung out and talked to you?"

"Yeah, but he had the knife in his hand, was pointing it at me. All of a sudden he would withdraw and get all crazy 'cause I would look in the distance 'cause I wanted to run. I was just talking to him cause maybe we could become friends or something. Than he would be like *'you're looking to run away aren't you?'* I'm like 16 years old, I'm just fucking scared shit-less and smoking cigarette after cigarette. He's like *'well go ahead run, 'cause it'll be funner to kill you.'* And he's got like a ski mask on, he's got gloves… 5 hours in he's like *'fuck this, you're just trying to trick me into killing you.'* He grabbed me by the arm and dragged me somewhere else. We're in the middle of nowhere.

No one can hear me, nobody can help me, no cell phones. He puts the knife to my throat and '*I'm gonna kill you, do you got anything to say?*' I'm like... It's so fucking horrible. He puts his arm around me and starts dragging the knife down my neck, like between my breasts and puts it straight on my stomach then he grabs my fat like he's gonna thrust. And I'm '*no, no,*' freaking out. It's raining, its cold and wet, I have blood all over me. 'If *you're gonna kill me just cut the throat 'cause I'm pregnant.*' That threw him off. Then I started giving my sob story. But I wasn't pregnant."

"Smart move – maybe I'll use that one sometime..."

"I had syringes 'cause my friend was actually pregnant and I was at her house giving her natural liquid shots to see if she would have an abortion. He's like '*give me a good reason why I shouldn't kill you*' and I'm like '*cause I love you (laughs).*' Then he takes his ski mask off, puts his knife away, and gives me my shit back. And he starts kissing me. Fuck dude, now I'm in trouble. So then he gives me money, takes me out to the street, flags down a cab, and sends me off. That was that. That was terrible. I couldn't tell my parents 'cause I was afraid my mom wouldn't let me out anymore..."

***Somewhere between a bathroom pit stop and another Budweiser Sascha Dunable from lauded grind/death merchants INTRONAUT walks in. "*Is that actually a Bethlehem back-patch?*" He's a tall blonde guy in his late 20's that lives in Echo Park. He also is apparently a huge fan of *Troll 2*...

Intronaut are currently gearing up for their first European expedition: "*We're just jamming right now. We have a new guitar player and a European tour in a month. The headliner is The Ocean form Germany, they're on Metal Blade. The support is Nehemah from Sweden and War From A Harlots Mouth, which is kind of a metalcore band from Germany. So we're all just saving our money.*"

"Did you get plane tickets paid for or is it pay your own way?"

Sascha Dunable: "Yeah, we have to pay for our own tickets. But we had enough in our band fund to pay for all of it. It'll be 5 weeks. We're going everywhere in Western Europe – Germany, Italy, Spain, Switzerland, Portugal, France, UK, Austria. The last show we're being flown into Athens."

"Is this the moment for you then?"

"Yeah. Not the biggest tour, but the biggest adventure for sure. A lot of planning and stress... We've done 3 US tours and 1 West

Coast tour. We did an 8 week tour with Misery Index, the last week was with Yakuza."

"Where does the name INTRONAUT come from?"

"Like an astronaut would travel in outer space, an Intronaut would travel in inner space. So you're like the stoner who stays home on Friday nights, totally baked, you post on an internet message board. Play riffs and record them on your 4 track. I am an intronaut…"

"What fuels you?"

"I was thinking about that. I wish you could see my place 'cause I live in a shit one bedroom apartment with my bassist. It's cheap and it sucks – the walls are super-thin and we have loud ass neighbors, cockroaches and shit. I don't know why that makes sense to me. I don't know why I choose to live like that so I can tour and not make any money at all. I work at a smoothie and coffee place, we have a lot of raw vegan food. It's in West Hollywood so a lot of celebrities come in."

"What's the weirdest celebrity you've met at the store?"

"Mike Tyson. I rang him up, I didn't say anything. I'll tell you what he bought though – some sort of sexual aid, like a supplement. I guess his fists weren't as big of a sexual aid as he needed…"

RENO (9/30)

At Sascha's apartment I'd become Grandpa Bartek, frenetically relating Detroit stories to the rock stars sitting Indian style before me like wide-eyed kids at a campfire. We later ended up in Hollywood Hills partying at the sleek condo of Danny Walker, world-class drummer of Phobia/Intronaut, Phobia being one of the most highly-regarded American grind bands outside Repulsion themselves.

With a high ranking portfolio that lists ex-Impaled & ex-Exhumed tours/recordings. He just kept on pouring the tequila, shot after shot, happy to shoot the shit with the first *"real spoken word artist"* that's ever graced his homestead: *"I scored the Phobia gig when my old band Uphill Battle played with them in Goleta, I think in 2002. They hit me up to do some session work a couple years later, which turned into a more full time gig. I grew up listening to Phobia as a kid, and I've been playing with them now for over 4 years. I'm like the 11th drummer in their career."*

"These guys like to drink a lot. We party down and play a lot of shit holes. One time in New York our vocalist Shane was so drunk I looked over and he was lying flat on his face with both his arms at his

side. The microphone wasn't even near him. It was just funny to see him standing one minute and on the ground then next..."

The general consensus is that LA was the equivalent of us busting our nut for this tour. Nothing can top it except for 2 long days in Denver. We'll be crashing with the chicken-suit mascot of iamsickandtiredofwhitegirls.com. My own personal highlight will be returning to Seattle – Adam Houghton has us set for a Galway Arms extravaganza, and that whole cast of characters will be showing up.

 For all the money we made in Los Angeles, its still skin of our teeth, because from LA to Reno is literally a quarter of the country (*thank you shit bookie*). It takes us 11 hours to get there, and Neil keeps calling the promoter to make sure everything is set if we're late. He keeps egging us on...

 Once we do show up, he tells us we can't play because there's only 6 people & he's tired and wants to go home. Everyone is notably pissed, and the next gig is Blackfoot Idaho, wherever the fuck that is, and then we have a full day off. Unless we score a miracle, its Plan B sperm bank action, and I hate needles.

 I'm dreaming that we're flying in the Econoline, high above the clouds, just cruising. As the van begins to descend and crash to the ground – *the very moment of impact* – my legs go flying out the van in the real world, because in reality, Hairy Bob just swung open the door my feet were resting upon. He could take no more guff and booked our first motel...

BLACKFOOT (10/1)

The motel was definitely a bad idea. We just put the last $100 in the tank and we'll be lucky to make it to Idaho on fumes. No food, no money, no cigarettes. Glover is pissed, Bob is back to grumbling Eyore, Neil is cranky, and I'm getting sick again with a throbbing wisdom tooth ripping out my jaw. I just want to get this done. I've been trapped in *The Big Shiny Prison* for nearly 11 months and I want my life back.

 We're at a quarter of a tank when we roll into Blackfoot, which is a small town in the mountains cut off from the world. The venue is Tony's Billiards, an old pool hall turned into a bar/venue, and there are no cars parked out front. We accept our doom and head inside where there are 5 old men drinking. That's it, we're finished... Then we turn the corner. 55 tight-pants screamo kids are standing there, waiting: "*We checked out your shit on MySpace. We've been waiting all month...*"

BLACKFOOT (10/2)

Some basement in Idaho, whose state motto is *"It Is Perpetual."* The opener Acardia fed us everything in their fridge and gave us the door money ($65). We also scored $105 in sales. Absolute miracle and we need every penny for the massive 16 hour backtrack to Portland. Thanks again shit bookie.

Checking the tire at a Burger King the sharp metal of the rubber's mesh interior jut out. We take off the bolts yet it won't budge. Pittsburg is first on our minds and we take the tow truckers hint. I find an old 4X4 rummaging through an open yellow field and we take turns whacking it off, yelping like clodhoppers. Mexican families gaze at us bizarrely as they feed their children, 6 year olds with tiny fingers pressed against the glass. Glover beats the rim screaming *"COCKSUCKER"* over & over.

I drive all night, a straight 7 hours through sinister black mountains, wind raging & rain pouring, Noise Unit and Primordial dominating the stereo. Finally hit the clearing and can go no more. 3am and we park in a large gas station on the outskirts of Echo, Oregon... *20 degrees, freezing to death in shotgun – no blanket, no pillow, wrapping sweaty old shirts 'round my face to savor the heat. 4 pairs of pants still doesn't do the trick.*

A twisted, one-raised lid half-sleep. I peer out the windshield and the gas station shed is green, the larger shed is red, and both are illuminated by neon lighting – for a moment I'm fully convinced I'm trapped in the Monopoly game board...

PORTLAND (10/3)

Best cultural thing about the Northwest: *Halloween actually means something.* Only October 3rd and pumpkins are everywhere, the station attendant is wearing a pointy witch hat...

We filled the tank with our last $100 and 35 minutes later we realize Hairy Bob went the wrong way. We backtrack to Monopoly shed land and realized we've burned a quarter tank of gas, and have not a dime left.

A long ride of Zappa & *Devil In Miss Jones*; a high-altitude swathe of forests and mountains – the backwoods quotient of Skull Island; the lakes, the fog, the accordant pristine... Raining, autumn leaves about the ground, fallen. Tonic nightclub, the first time I've seen my name on a huge glowing marquee. They thought we were two separate bands and didn't bother to book any local support except for the dirge-punk Dartgun who draws 10 people.

The singer is gangly in a black skirt and looks a cross between Lurch & Billy Corgan. They have three goth "*dudettes*" singing backup, banging tambourines – a far cry from Rod Torpelson's Armada [*featuring Herman Nenderchuck*].

I do an extended set tonight, a full 25 minutes. I'm on target but the crowd is lost. Neil, Glover and I split three 10.5% Camo & Evil Eye tall cans which worked us over pretty bad, and when I finally jump off stage, DTB goes right into it.

Problem is Glover fell asleep at his kit while I was rambling, and woke up into the first song having forgotten how to play drums. The tune crashes in 30 seconds. They go to an easy one which also just doesn't happen. The hour-long set is reduced to 15 minutes of extreme slop-degradation, and Bob just smacks his forehead and says "*Oh Jesus…*" into the microphone.

No money, food or crash spot – 30 degrees at the rest area 2 hours from Seattle. Just pretend it never happened. The same frozen, rancid night of yesterday with sweaty shirts wrapped around my face…

SEATTLE (10/4)

"*And you know what Barack Obama said to me? You know what Barack said?!?*" Nihilist, Adam Houghton, Terry McCorriston, Justin Hofmann, all of Plankton Beat as well as a dozen others look onward, waiting for the final punch line of my best spoken word gig ever: "*He said, Barack said… My name is Ryan Bartek. Fuck the rest of the United States. The second this tour is done I'm moving to Seattle.*" I drop the microphone, crash on the floor like a puppet with cut strings, & the place goes wild with applause...

MISSOULA (10/5)

We spent last night taking epic metal photos outside Galway Arms with Sol Negro, In Memorium and Scorched Earth, capping it off with a bong party at the Plankton house.

In Idaho the ground is covered in snow, like it's been there for weeks. When we left Michigan it was still summer… How long has this… *31 straight days…*

Tonight's show is the "Kill Your Clit 10,000 Festival" in Missoula, Montana. It's a gig from one of Hairy Bob's high school pals, and there are two kegs, four 30 cases of Budweiser, 5 punk bands and

30 Skinhead SHARPs in a punk-rock bicycle shop called "The Bike Doctor." I've never seen a circle pit surrounded by walls of BMX's.

It's a rowdy crowd but they're all age 18-22, so no bulldogs. Just good time punk, all the bands trashed and LOUD, no faulty Viper Room glitz concerns. It feels like home… No one gets the spoken word set. People are too drunk to listen, even if it's about MDC, DWARVES and GG Allin. So I make it quick for the three guys up front hanging out of respect, even though some heckler turd is yelling for me to get off the stage…

SLC (10/6)

Another night spent freezing in the van, this time outside the promoter's house. She's actually dating the heckler turd, and he ducked me all night at the after party. Even though I slept in the frost-bitten van, I was kept warm by thoughts of *Detroit Rock City,* which I'd never seen. Neil and Glover were defending it and flipped it on just to school me. Then as the blunt kicked in for all of us, as the opening montage started, a still photo shot of Billy Jack appears with the mythical grace of a leprechaun.

Addicted Café in Salt Lake City, Utah, whose state motto is *"Industry."* What a monstrous town – all the houses have this utopian architectural design somewhere between Ron Hubbard and the Aztecs. The gig is at a vegan coffee house where they feed us tofu burgers. I went for the MDC thing again but it didn't really go over. Amusing stories, but there's no real punch lines. *Punch is the key to all routines…*

Outside more Lewisville and Blackfoot type kids tell us: *"We're definitely the ones you're talking shit on, but we love it anyway."* We walk out with $50 and the lone interesting character lurking in the background offers that we crash at his apartment. He's kind of a crust, although pro-hygiene, and has massively stretched ears with monster plugs & knuckle tats the read LOST BOY with the symbol of Hook on his pinky: *"My first names Brody, last name is Hollow. That's what everyone knows me as. Salt Lake City, I'm only here for one reason – this beautiful lady beside me. Other than that this place is a fucking shithole. I really don't like it. I enjoy my job, I do help run the Addicted Café."*
"Tell me about the environment here."

Mr. Hollow: "Well, for one thing I'm not a smoker, but I think its pretty ridiculous that they move it up to 19 to smoke. They have the weird membership laws or a ridiculous door fee to get into bars."

"How much per month to drink here?"

"$30. It's up to $10 per time to go into a bar. One thing I've noticed about people here, they have the mentality of being power strong, like you would say you're in some rip-off version of New York. Everyone's walking around with a bad attitude, no hospitality whatsoever. Everyone is a fucking dick."

"I've noticed a lot of bums, but the bums can't drink. Kind of defeats the purpose…"

"You go to the French quarter in New Orleans where I'm from, and every bum out there's a wino or chasing some 40 oz.."

"So you grew up in New Orleans and hit the road when you were 13?"

"Yes. My mother died of a massive heart attack. At the time I was a fucking night owl and a half. I woke up when the sun went down, stayed up all night playing video games eating, 'cause I really didn't have a life. When I was 13 I was a recovering drug addict. I spent my days and nights away from the people I took that shit with… Just fuckin' bad news. Anything you'd put in front of me I was going to do. So I wasted my time in a loft I built myself above my parents' mobile home – a full legitimate, giant studio apartment basically."

"So you were orphaned at the age of 13?"

"I was actually orphaned at the age of 2. I was adopted. Both my biological parents were pretty young. My biological mother was 17, my father was 21 years old, a high school drop out selling cocaine. And my mom's kind of a loose cannon, very cooped up as a child. When she became of age she just fuckin' blew up. Funny thing was most in my shoes were accidental kids. I was fully planned for an entire year. A year later they were '*oh we don't want this anymore.*' The woman that adopted me was amazing, the greatest fucking woman I've ever met in my life. She actually got my first piercings and backed me up when I wanted to become a body piercer and do body modifications."

"Can you give a Prince Albert?"

"Yeah."

"What's the weirdest genital piercing you've ever seen or given?"

"I haven't done many genital piercings. Probably the weirdest thing I've seen that most people would freak out about besides a full nullification – that's when you completely take off your entire genitalia, and if you're a male that means scrotum, testicles, shaft, the whole nine yards…"

"To become a trannie or…"

"No, like fully taken off."

"Like the Heavens Gate people with the Reebok sneakers?"

"The craziest genital thing I've ever seen is probably castrations that sometimes are replaced with silicone beads to make it look like they have testicles still. And actual penis splitting."

"Like having two snakes?"

"Yeah, usually they have an erection and they come together. You'll see where it's severed, kind of like a split tongue."

"How do you pee?"

"It just shoots out. You have to sit down to pee."

"When you went on the road where did you first go? Did you go train-hopping?"

"I actually never did train-hopping 'cause they weren't that big in the south. I did jump around on a lot on 18 wheelers. My first big adventure was when I was 14. It was only a few months after my mom had died. I was a sponsored inline skater so I grabbed my skates, my pair of shoes, and I jumped on an 18 wheeler. I got dropped off in north Houston, skated down an interstate for a couple of miles, jumped on a Greyhound bus. My destination was San Antonio and I arrived there to see a girl I had a really big thing for. 4 days later I was arrested on school property for trespassing. The original law was they were only going to give me a warning because I'd never been there before. But they arrested me saying I was a runaway. It's kind of hard to be a runaway when you don't have parents. They put me on the banned list for ever going back to Sperricks County, Texas."

"Where did you go from there?"

"I moved back to New Orleans. I ended up in south Florida twice in the next year. I was not in school because I had to work to support myself… After Florida I stayed in Louisiana awhile. I opened up two skate parks and helped run both for the next 2 years. Then I moved to Homa, Louisiana, a small Indian town, and started working for the Journey shoe company. I stayed there 'cause I was with a girl for 2 years. She was a handful… I spent 6 months in a tree house living like I was straight out of Peter Pan. That's why I got 'LOST BOY' tattooed on my knuckles. My pinky has a Captain Hook pyrate hook."

"That's brilliant."

"I lived like that my entire life. I never had nothing, so I had to make something up for myself. I'm actually from a super small swamp town named Rose, Louisiana. It's three main roads, and in between two of them is a giant bayou. There were shrimp boats all the time. Everyone was into fisherman work. We were right in the Gulf of Mexico – a total Cajun hick town where everyone thrived on sports, hunting and beer. I wasn't exactly down for much any of that."

"Ever been attacked by a crocodile?"

"Actually when I was 8 years old we had a cabin on a small strip of land between a marsh field and a river. There was actually an alligator swimming in the canal behind us and I was just a really wild kid. I had this weird obsession with cutlery, and I get the bright idea to run and jump off of a tree into the canal and try to swim and catch the alligator."

"So you had a knife between your teeth like Rambo?"

"Yeah, but it swam off. My older brother actually came in, grabbed me, and whopped me upside the fuckin' head... There was another alligator that had been in that area forever. My dad saw it when he was a boy, his dad... This gator must've been 80 years old. It was the size of a boat."

"How long do those things live for?"

"Over a 100 years. There was a time when some of my family was coming over to the cabin and the gator actually came right up under the boat and flipped it. No one got hurt, but still that's a scary ass factor. There's a gator bigger than the boat you were traveling that can swallow you whole... Back when I was living in that tree house, we had this water factory – where the levees ran and purified the water – and it ran into this lake. We'd all go swimming and jump off the building, high dive, little swamp kids running around with nothing better to do. There were two gators swimming around, and one of my friends wilds out and runs and jumps off the building and straight-up drop-kicks the alligator. Like full on ran, jump, dive, dropkick... Alligators are pretty intimidating creatures, but if you fuckin' come at them enough they're kind of like dogs. If you let a dog know you're not gonna let it fuck with you, it's not gonna fuck with you. Kind of the same thing. Pretty much water dogs."

"What about sharks?"

"I almost lost my right hand to a shark. We were out crabbing and I was in the water getting some traps out. I turned my head back for a second to grab an ice hook. When I look back there was just a big fucking mouth coming straight out of the water. I moved my hand just in time. I was only 11 years old."

"Where was this?"

"This was almost the Gulf of Mexico. We were in a marsh that led to the gulf, so sharks would come in like it's nothing."

"What's just some crazy shit that happened to you?"

"Most people think I'm a liar when I say I'm 18 years old. A lot of people don't believe me when I say I got my tongue pierced at the age of 11 with a nail. Which I don't have anymore, because I decided to upgrade to a split tongue [Mr. Hollow sticks out his snake tongue and we all scream in return]."

"What about weird ghost stories?"

"My older sister was heavily into black magick and witchcraft. One night when I was 8 she had friends over and they had previously done something in her room, some sort of ritual. She always tried to keep it away from me 'cause she didn't want me to get wrapped up in it. I was walking through her room to get to my room, and the guy that was on her floor grabbed my leg and when I looked down at him... There was something wrong with him. He wasn't on drugs. There was something else going on. Like his eyes were not fucking right. And at the time you couldn't get contacts to throw your eyes all crazy. He couldn't have afforded them anyway. This dude was a fucking dirt bag, from hell... I mean literally at that point. So my assumption was that the guy was literally fucking possessed. I'm not even joking on that. He grabbed me and I fucking screamed bloody murder. That was the scariest shit ever."

"Any other stories?"

"Recently I was living in Indianapolis. We drove to an abandoned tuberculosis hospital in Kentucky where there was a giant paranormal thing. It was a typical haunted attraction. You pay them however much and you stay from 10 at night until 6 in the morning. You just get locked in the building. You just walk around, they tell you all the hot spots. For about an hour of the night we actually played ball with a dead little boy – not even joking. You bring any toys, preferably balls, and you go in this part of the building and roll the ball down the hall. There is a little boy – they've named him Timmy – that died in the tuberculosis hospital. His apparition comes back around if you bring toys. It's basically him reliving it over and over again. Like how some people have that theory where it's an imprint."

"So you roll a ball, you turn around and it rolls back at you?"

"We didn't turn around. We rolled the ball down the fucking hall. This was in the dark. People are gonna say '*blah blah blah, there could've been someone there*.' The thing was we rolled the ball down – no flashlights, we were super-quiet – you could hear it echo. It was gone way down the hall. We turned the light back on and it was maybe 8 feet in front of us. We were throwing these balls pretty hard to make sure they went way down."

"And they just silently reappear before you?"

"Right fucking by us, every time. One time that we threw the ball and it was mid-air, just like flying, and it hit and went chuh-chuh-chuh, then just a thud. And then footsteps. Turned the light back on and it was back to us halfway. And there was this one graffiti mural painted on the wall, most of the time that's where it stopped."

"Oh wait, that's that same place that was on 'Celebrity Paranormal!' Gary Busey was walking around all grizzled and pissed like Busey does, and he stopped dead in his tracks. He started saying under his breath in that Busey way, 'STOP... Do you hear that? It sounds like a... mechanical tiger'…"

"Yeah, and they had this thing called 'The Death Tunnel.' It was a chute where when the patients died, they'd secretly throw the bodies down the fucking drop and the morgue would come pick them up at the bottom. It's a long, steep ass tunnel. All sorts of dirt and debris…"

AURORA (10/7)

"Oh yeah, another funny story, ha ha. I slit a guys throat with an aluminum can in a bar fight. He might be dead, I don't know. I just left like it was no business. Anyway, have a great trip guys!" Mr. Hollow waves innocently as we exit Mormon paradigm…

8 hours to Denver, and en route our second day gig is cancelled by a flaky promoter who panics over us playing a 21+ bar the night before, as if we were to steal his All Ages audience and cause a whopping financial loss. It's just a cheap excuse so he doesn't have to pay that $150 guarantee. Somewhat of a mood killer, but not for Neil – his girlfriend whose been calling non-stop all tour has taken a jet flight to Denver for a weekend of debauchery….

3:30am in Aurora, a quaint suburb of Denver… We're hanging out with kittens. Like literally. Canadian Greg has a kitten farm where he is breeding EBay pets, and the backroom is infested with Siamese babies like rats in a Bronx sewer main…

Neil and Glover are so twisted drunk they keep slamming shut the door: *"No, you can't come in, we're hanging out with kittens – KITT-TENS."* Neil's totally lost his mind. The girl never showed up or bothered to call. No answer, no nothing…

AURORA (10/8)
$170 last night, and the little sports bar has brought us back for an encore gig. Bad for Neil though, since he's in a nervous collapse living out Day II of the *"TWILIGHT ZONE BITCHFIST."* We pull up to the venue and it's the same cars parked in identical spots. Same opening band, same set-list. The chalk board writing mirrors that of yesterday – same crowd, bartenders, same freezing cold chill and *AAAAHHH…*

LINCOLN (10/9)
So tired & sick again. Neil ill. Glover irate, Bob out of steam. We all just want to get this over with. Crazy venue called Box Awesome, stationed in the historic district near Nebraska State University. The gig is empty, but the owner gives us an eighth, two packs of Marlboro Reds, and a 24 of Schlitz for our troubles… Another freezing night of sweaty man-juice towels wrapped around my face – rest area off the freeway, wisdom tooth ripping out my face, spinal vertebrae volcanic… *Panzerfaust*, 10 Schlitz & a mountain of pain…

CEDAR FALLS (10/10)
Huge ride through Iowa, heat blazing from my forehead; everything is vertigo. Would comment on the venue but I snoozed through the performance. 103 degrees, in and out all day, a coprolithic state of vertiginous blah…

OTTUMWA (10/11)
After The Casbah gig, drinking tall-drafts with a guy dressed as Hunter S Thompson who tells me how I should write my book… Casbah's second to last show ever having sunk three mortgages into the place, and the only in attendance were Raoul Duke and some jocko creeps who got into a fight in the gas station parking lot, causing a big scene with the police… After industrial-metal opener Tree Of Man bolted with all their friends, DTB played for 3 little kids age 7-12 who were running around the open floor playing catch with a Nerf football…

LAKE COUNTY (10/12)

I wake up in the middle of Iowa in a plastic red racecar bed. Misfits posters, 8 Bit NES cartridges... For 5 seconds I forget when I am, and assume that it's 1995 and I have a science test today... *No, no – it belongs to the promoter's 11 year old son, and I was so drunk that I stole his mattress & made him sleep on the couch.*

I shake it off and head upstairs where I say hello to the bartender from Denver at the kitchen table. I huddle the toilet and urinate in a half-world... *Wait a minute, this can't be right. Why is the bartender from Colorado here?* The eyes focus and its Hunter Thompson, minus the fisherman's hat. I need REM sleep so bad...

Last show of the tour, and its *Rock N' Roll High School* (a.k.a. Wade's Halloween party). Wade is a die-hard 15 year old DTB fan that has every album and t-shirt. He wrote them and asked innocently "*Do you guys wanna come and rock my parent's house?*" thinking nothing would come of it. No problemo kiddo. This is on par with KISS coming to hang out with Eddie Furlong.

But THE MAN is trying to keep us down. Oh yeah – just like a zany, light-hearted teen comedy, the principal has gotten wind of this big old party. He crumpled up the flyer in front of Wade "*This won't happen young man, if it's the last thing I ever do!!!*"

Mr. Rooney is trying to stop Aerosmith from playing Waynestock. He called all the parents, he called the cops. Wade's parents are on the defense with noise & block-party permits, but the square haters of rock and roll persist. *Damn you Jeffrey Jones!!!*

Late at night, the big moment. The cops have come twice already, declaring Marshall Law superiority over our legally binding documents. The swine told us if we curse on the loud speaker it's over. This means I'm muzzled, my tour ending in Colorado. I look over and give Neil the raised finger, like the broken quarterback to his reeling squadron with 30 seconds on the clock and only the miracle play remaining...

DTB can do it though, the ultimate mega-jam. A hundred teenage freaks uniting against the L7 witch-hunt scarfing hot dogs, dressed like witches & trannies. I'm running in place, getting revved up while dressed as the Burger King – humongous smiling mask, fuzzy royal cape of velvet, metal-tastic fist goat-horned in the air...

AND YES!!! DTB rocks the garage a good 25 minutes before we're shut down. Everyone is dancing like Ewok's at the end of *Return of the Jedi*, shouting insults at the cops, howling and loving the night: *"Rock rock rock rock Rock-N-Roll High School..."*

THE DEATH OF THE ROAD (10/13)

It feels so anti-climactic; this fizzled, burnt up, spurting out of a whirlwind. No time to think, no time to piece it together... On a balcony in Chicago, not far from Downtown. 12am, contemplating jumping the fence and running back to the streets, one last chapter...

But I'm exhausted. Plus the book has to end somewhere, lest it be Sisyphean. So we now conclude this head-spinning journey with the final interview – Downtown Brown, who's reputation precedes them. Just the 4 of us at a Denny's in Illinois, contemplating the long haul. After we leave this place, the adventure of 2007 comes to a close...

"$1 on the tip. It's the last of everything."
Hairy Bob: "You had the last of it every week Bartek."
"No, ha ha. This is the last of it, like literally... So how'd you feel about the tour?"

Neil P: "Essentially we got DVD's, lit them on fire, and put them in our gas tank. I really don't care. I'm going to go back to my $9 an hour job. I'm gonna try to bang this girl that has a fat ass. I'm gonna tell her my girlfriend's dead. '*She fell off a cliff and died on impact.*' Yeah, my girlfriends dead. She died in a bizarre gardening accident."

"How would you describe how you're feeling at this very moment?"

"I'm not dead yet, and that's a good thing. I thought the tour was fun man. We made a shit-load of contacts. Booking the next tour... it's just going to get easier. When people get to know us and we start drawing crowds, will get flat guarantees. And then sooner or later we'll be self-sufficient. Enough to at least keep our shit stocked."

"Everything is organic here. You've impressed fans and therefore the fans want to throw the shows themselves which is far more important than getting any booking agent. Do you agree?"

"Like last night?"

"Yeah, like a million Wade's that spawn out from the initial blast of madness that you've wreaked across America."

"The young kids are way more passionate about music than people who are over 21. When you're over 21, you wanna go to the bar and try to get laid. That's basically about it for most people. It's not going to make an impact on your life. Especially the shit we do."

"What year do you think the magic dies? How old?"

"When Wolf [DTB's bassist from 2002-2005] was still in the band, there were 300 who paid to get in Alvin's [a notorious Detroit venue]. I would say 50% of the people who were there are now 24, 25, have shitty jobs, hate their lives, and don't go out and have fun anymore at all. I think it dies once responsibility kicks in. When you're a kid you can do whatever. You live with your parents, you have disposable income... Once you grow up and people are like '*you need to do this, you need to do that*' you do it. I say fuck that. I'm like Peter Pan..."

"So what's the next step in the saga?"

"It's all about connects, finding a way to get our shit on Adult Swim or something. *Robots Vs. Dragons* [a cartoon Neil wrote the theme for], that's owned by Cartoon Network. It's like a flash cartoon site. It's been advertised on Adult Swim for 8 months... Very soon the web and the TV will be the same thing. That's when kids aren't even going to leave the house anymore. I remember when I was a kid, I rode my fucking bike around, and we'd go steal shit from Arbor Drugs and light fireworks. Kids nowadays, they fuckin' sit on their ass and do nothing. Because of the whole terrorist shit, everyone is so afraid of just everything. Halloween is dying. People don't even trick-or-treat. No one even came up to the door last year... But there is hope. There are people like Wade, people everywhere that are sick of everything.

"Tell me about your next album."

"Its gonna be the album that no matter how goofy the lyrics are, people aren't going to be able to deny the fact that we can jam. There's gonna be instrumentals, it's gonna be 78 minutes. And people do need to see us live to know what we're about."

"You have a phenomenal amount of scenesters that hate your guts back home. Have you found that is the case on the road?"

"We end up rubbing everyone the wrong way. I don't think we carry ourselves like assholes. I get up onstage and that's kind of my persona, but most people who play with us know us offstage. So why we rub them the wrong way if we're just doing what we do? Tony Clifton was a character, you know? We're all kind of supposed to be larger than life. I'm definitely a big pussy in real life, but when you get up onstage and you have a microphone, it's like theatre."

"What's your favorite memory of the tour?"

"I think my favorite memory... Did I puke at all during this tour? Oh, in Arizona. I puked in my mouth, that's the only time... Yeah, I'm pretty sure..."

"How can you drink like that and not die all the time?"
"I don't drink that much…"
HB: "Oh yes you do…"
"Do I?"
"But you still get everything done, so I guess that's ok. Your job is to be the drunken party guy."

"I like being alive man. I find that things are a little more lubricated when I have a few drinks in me. The other thing too… I don't know. Its hard for me to turn it off. I'm not the type of dude that's gonna be *'no I don't want that shot of alcohol you're buying me.'* Like when we were in Iowa and they took us out to the bar. I tried to be sly about it, but what am I going to do? I'm in the middle of Iowa with this dude dressed up like Hunter S Thompson and this weird lady who keeps apologizing for getting drunk… When I get home I don't party that much… Glover, do you think I drink a lot?"

<u>"Danny Glover: Yeah…"</u>
"You're built to drink and shit."
"Really?"

<u>DG: "The thing is you can take down a lot, you can drink A LOT, yet you can still be somewhat… Once you cross a certain line though, you are intolerable, you are just a beast."</u>

"You get pretty vindictive too. Then there are times I think you're grabbing the handle to jump out the van onto the freeway…"

"Yeah, well… First of all I way 230 lbs. I'm lame when I'm home 'cause I get up for work at 4:30 in the morning every… Man, you guys make me feel like an asshole. You guys do drugs man."

"Oh I'm not denying the fact that I'm a human wrecking ball. Shit, I start drinking vodka and I snort human ashes. I'm just commenting on your ability to consume alcohol. When I drink beer it just makes me fall asleep. I don't know how people can drink and drink and drink all day and just be wired."

"Different drugs affect people differently. I never have it on my plate. I never predetermine… I'm in the type of business, the type of lifestyle where people want to have a good time."

"In the grand scheme of the rock and roll revolution – banding together in certain areas, like if one were to invade a city and make a little underground railroad of freaks that gave a fuck…"

"I think there's potential for that in every city… It's gonna be very, very tough to do. There's not a network like there was in the 80's. Every punk band, no matter how weird they were, just because they were punk they had a place to play in every city. All the bands were friends. Like when Social Distortion first toured with Youth Brigade, they stayed at Minor Threat's house out in DC... There's just over-saturation of everything – anyone can afford a crappy little mixer and get a MySpace. So there's all these shitty bands and there's really no sense of community. Everything is labeled to the point... They tell us we can't play with a grindcore band. We used to try and get My Friend Rudra on our Lansing shows, and this booking agent was like, '*we can't have you guys play with a band like that, it just wouldn't work.*' Why the fuck not? You claim to be into rock and roll, but instead of picking up an instrument and actually learning anything about music, you just fuckin' take money from bands. Promoters are scumbags' dude, all of 'em. Except the ones that have DIY ethos. That's why the dude in Cedar Rapids gave me a bunch of drinks. He paid us $40 and there was no one at the show."

"You think Theatre Bizarre is the best venue in America?"
"Yes."
"What do you think Glover?"
DG: "This meat-lover's breakfast is awesome... We shouldn't have been pussies with Turf man, we should have seriously made him smoke opium..."
"Dose him with some acid..."
DG: "And just watch him go. Like just wind him up and watch him go."
"I wouldn't want to deal with him on acid though. He'd be on some weird god trip. He'd turn into Stephen Hawking and talk about science and shit. Go crazy and attack someone with a knife thinking he's Marquis de Sade or something... Hey Neil, I'll trade you a sausage for a pancake..."
"Yeah... That was fun as hell, hanging out with Wade's family, all his friends. That guy had just one really big testicle that he showed to everyone."
"What was his name?"
"BIG NUT." Probably the most random thing I've ever seen in a nice looking house where the parents were right there. This dude's just showing his nuts to everyone."
"And the parents didn't even care."
"No, they were totally cool. That's how you raise good kids. You just do drugs around them all the time... All I gotta say is when

this band gets to the point… We're gonna be the most retarded traveling circus of retards ever. Warped Tour was just a taste."

"We were talking if you actually had a budget, would you get a second bus and just fill it up with all the random weird characters you've met across America? Like a party bus, they'd all be on guest-list at every show."

"And they essentially would come to every show just to stir things up and fuck with people, creating total chaos. If B McNuts was at every show… The midget would make her rounds. Then we can videotape all of it and make money on the side. We'd have the midget porno tape. I like chicks that have a kind of nonchalant attitude about sex. It's just fucking and its dumb. That's what Swisher realized. He can sniff out the slut anywhere. Swisher's the ultimate scumbag. But he's got game dude. He has a 'slut sensor.'"

"Do you think…"

"Back to the whole drinking, I'm the party guy thing. We gotta create ourselves as memorable characters. If we just showed up at everyone's house and they're like *'hey man, you guys wanna hang out?'* 'No, we're just going to sleep.' Those people aren't gonna come to your show again. They're gonna be like *'those guys are kinda lame.'"*

"Any final words? It's the last question in the book Neil."

"Everything's fucked. You might as well have fun before everything goes to shit and this entire country's a police state and we're not even able to make music. Shit's gonna suck really bad really soon, so we might as well just be complete bums and drive around the country and do what we love and hopefully people are hip to it. Merry Christmas, that's what it's all about."

"How long' till that happens?"

"You tell me, you're the conspiracy theorist…"

Just Neil and I, rolling back to his home. Everyone else has departed, and as Mr. P parks his Escort, I open the passenger door, take three steps, and collapse on the front lawn… I did it. *Just sit – breathe…* It's over, it's done… Staring upwards at the bare tree appendages curling through the Michigan blackness, brightly illuminated moon in the upper corner … I'm just gonna sit here forever. Nothing, no terrorist attack or zombie Armageddon can shake me from this hard-fought pinnacle of Zen… *"Hey Bartek,"* the voice calls from inside the house. *"Hey Bartek."*

"Yeah?"

"Smackdown's on."

EPILOGUE

For the wide-ranging counterculture in all its splintered forms – *in every artistic, sociopolitical, and common day life-&-love-&-career sense* – here is the road map of the future: The best overall city in America is Seattle. The best metropolitan environment is The Bay Area. The most potential for growth is Detroit.

The two best locations for a serious touring band to base their operations on the West Coast are divided between two regional hemispheres – either Portland/Seattle in the Northwest, or West Oakland, which is primly located smack-dab in the middle of California. The third possible West Coast location is Los Angeles, particularly a low-ball satellite city thereof.

However, apart from the pristine climate and high-grade connections you will inevitably make, SoCal is an altogether rancid stinker. I say this unrepentant as my firm conviction – alongside New York, Los Angeles is bar-none the worst city for a band attempting to relocate and break it big. It's a fairy tale – *the greatest prank ever pulled* – and you will be eaten alive. It's only real usefulness is as a strategic tour-routing location for the hit-and-run band living like Roma out a van & low-rent sympathizer safe houses.

The best relocation spot in the Southwest is a definite toss-up between Austin (TX)/Albuquerque (NM). The finest Mid-Western area is Metropolitan Chicago (IL), Tampa (FL) in the Deep South, and Denver (CO) in the Great Plains. The strongest East Coast colonization target is somewhere wisely selected within the Tri-State area, not far from the stretch of NYC. In this you have a handful of major cities – Boston, Jersey City, Philadelphia, Rochester, etc.

On an ironic note, the two best overall cities for a writer, artist, or filmmaker of any kind are both New York and Los Angeles. Accumulating experience for convincing literature or casting actors are one thing, sweating it out in dive bars and pay-to-play gigs a totally separate realm…

The best venue in the USA is the Theatre Bizarre (Detroit). The greatest punk hangouts are the unholy trinity of Burt's Tiki Lounge (ABQ), The Funhouse (Seattle), and the 2500 Club (Detroit).

The milestone goth/industrial nightclub for pure dirgy, darkened filth is The Leland City Club (Detroit), and the classiest is Mephisto's Detroit (Hamtramck, MI). The best metal bar is Duff's Brooklyn (NYC). The scummiest, most dangerous, and greatest metal venue in the USA is Harpo's Concert Theatre (Detroit), which no good local band will ever open, but every amazing crowd-drawing headliner will pack to the rafters. If you are a metal band of any sort and can't win over that crowd then throw in the towel, because you are worthless and stand no chance of longevity.

The best park in America is Golden Gate (San Francisco). The strongest record stores for pure vinyl and the widest underground selection are Amoeba (Los Angeles), Amoeba (Hashbury, Frisco), and Rock of Ages (Westland, MI). The highest-echelon annual marijuana "protest-ival" is The Seattle Hempfest.

The comic book store that feels most like home is Green Brain (East Dearborn, MI). The scummiest motel in the United States is Dr. Fun's (Inkster, MI), open "25 hours a day, 8 days a week," and sells whip-its at the front counter. The greatest milk-shake in the world is the Chocolate Blast from Baskin Robbins. The best coffee house is still The Zone in East Dearborn (MI), and it closed down in 1997. The greatest breakfast burrito in the world is Si Senor on 48th & El Cajon Blvd, San Diego CA 92115.

On a gross $3,500 dollars I traveled through 35 states, lived on the streets of a dozen major cities, spent roughly 606 hours on Greyhounds, traveled over 20,000 miles, recorded two EP's & a full-length LP, and somehow pulled off two spoken word tours...

I lived among bums, mixed it with con men, drug dealers, strippers, skinheads and prostitutes; panhandled with crusties, chilled with rock legends, movie stars, politicians, intercontinental businessmen, and 'In-House Exorcists'...

Having analyzed society to a great extent amidst this voyage, my final opinion is that *there is no country*. It's the same piecemeal mosaic that exists in all political spectrum, that *Truman Show* vibe I'd encountered as a Hollywood newbie. This is why I now relate a long-dead and absurd catch phrase: "*Il Duce Ha Sempre Ragione,*" translated, "*The Duce is always right.*" And he was, but not in any direct sense.

During the course of this book I found myself reading lengthy studies about Fascist Italy as a propaganda state. Mussolini was definitely an impostor, an actor, not a good man and anything but *"the greatest statesman of the 20ᵗʰ century."* Yet Benito understood propaganda and as the first modern political stage-actor, he'd built his Corporate State on the charismatic pizzazz of a huckster prank that was borne equally of desperation and media manipulation. Fascism was an ambiguous political faith and was so loose in its application that it could mean anything to anyone.

In WWII, that abstract Italy crumbled to ruin and all the major catchphrases and images of the iron-hard state were found totally empty. In the end, Mussolini was revealed to his countrymen as the sort of Wizard of Oz that he always was – just a tired old man in a drained little body, a gruesome hangover from another era.

Even though a "Duce" is a non-entity in the United States, the Wizard of Oz is still very real. Ours is not a single individual, but rather a multi-headed hydra of Corporate CEO's, CIA puppet masters, Senators, Power Elite, and Pentagon Brass. We've had it drilled into our skulls that America is this indivisible Union guided beneath an iron-eagle which adheres to the declaration of independence as a definitive moral compass – FBI, CIA, MIB, Homeland Security, Coast Guard, National Guard, Navy, Army, Marine Corp; local fire and policemen, teachers, principals, crossing guards, hall monitors. *The omniscience and uniformed omnipresence of the great Electric Eye...*

But that's just not the case. It only exists on paper. America is essentially a propaganda state that only takes its form by virtue of its population's instinctive morality and sense of reality. True democracy in the form which we pay lip service to only materializes when the people themselves take the initiative.

Radicalism is generally a non-entity outside of major cities, and in average America the backbone social-fabric mentality is that of those *"this is my hometown forever"* people who never travel anywhere.

Take for instance The Bible Belt versus The Pacific Northwest, or Southern California contra The East Coast – totally different mainframes, massively different ethics both politically and in the justice system. Where some poor schmucks like the West Memphis 3 would be burned at the stakes as satanic, child-killing monsters in rural Tennessee, this would never happen in a place like Seattle, where DNA evidence would be collected, sincere research would be collaborated at all official levels, and the jury would view them simply as harmless weird kids in metal t-shirts at the wrong place and the wrong time.

The only real thing holding America together outside the vast apparatus of authority is this social/cultural homogenization derived from television, radio, media, "national values," religion, and the infrequent backlash waves of patriotism that stem from disasters such as 911, Pearl Harbor, or Hurricane Katrina.

The USA is essentially a loosely connected mess of consumer-dependent Walmart tribes, and in many cases solidified only on terms of religion and patriotism, familial tradition, or compulsory entertainment addiction. The iron-fisted nuts and bolts of the operation are the universal fear of prison, domestic militarization, and the spin persuasion of public opinion in the interest of mass crowd control.

What are we moving towards then, if the homogenization is ever actually completed? Well, Manhattan of course – a total meltdown of all cultures into one boiling pot, where no answer is ever the answer, and there is no room for severe concern about how weird the guy next door really is, and no real environment that would foster religious fundamentalism over the long course of human history & evolution…

Much in the same way that there is no true, unified form of nationalism within the context of American sociology, the counterculture is just as entirely flimsy and malleable. Take for instance black metal, which is but one subculture (*splinter movement*) within the greater design of the overall counterculture (*all subcultures as one mass entity*).

Although you can trace black metal's origins to Venom and Bathory, the main context assumed these days' roots back to what happened in Norway. The music and imagery of Mayhem/Burzum/Darkthrone/Immortal were transmitted worldwide, and have therefore become the unavoidable bedrock of the foundation. That solid bedrock – devoid of any precise ideology except that it was dark, extreme, and pro-heathen/anti-Christian – became an "up-for-grabs" manifestation that assumed its form by whatever personal impression its audience adjusted.

Black metal then became (*for lack of a better analogy*) a sort of non-corporate McDonald's franchise – international, with it's own basic "menu," but no direct rules on implementing the menu, advertising, food preparation, store hours, etc. Something up for grabs that could mean anything to anyone, and this is what creates the general disparity best summarized between a character like Nihilist from In Memorium or Edwin from Kettle Cadaver.

Whereas Nihilist is the sort of open-minded, jovial guy addicted to dark art & heavy music, you have an Armageddon-pursuing fanatic like Eddie – an Odinist ne plus ultra side-show freak from hell. It is the same disparity in punk rock, whereas a Jello Biafra rests on one side and a GG Allin resides on the other, line firmly drawn in the sand...

What it comes down to is being impressionable at an early age, what the music means to you, and the people with whom you associate that ultimately colors your understanding of it. And because there are so many people pushing for individuality at all costs, this creates the inability of a coherent line. To have a coherent line would just create another uniform, and the deep-seated, gut-propulsion to escape conformity is why the counterculture exists in the first place.

So what is the solution? If a coherent line is unattainable, can there be any real continuity in the underground? What masthead would have to be utilized to create a sort of quasi-nationalism? And could it ever bridge over into a viable form of *"Pan-Tribalism,"* as in a sort of non-hierarchical, apolitical, ambiguous socialism within the counterculture?

My only answer is perhaps a universally shared code of respect. Brotherhood, utopia – that's just taking things too far. It failed in the 60's, and flower-power radicalism is dead. All hope in terms of underground unity today rests squarely upon the shoulders of respect for one another's own identity, a general emphasis on communication instead of competition, and a repulsion for violent control over others.

We all got into this to get away from the bullies, the ones trying to control our lives and tell us how to think, how to look, how to act. That's where the emphasis should primarily lay, and in order to harvest the grain you've got to cut the weeds...

* * * * *

2008 now, not all that far from the coming decade. Many people ask me, as a professional big-shot journalist guy, my ultimate opinion of what the next big thing is in music, or in terms of the counterculture. I honestly don't have the slightest clue. It will remain as always I'd assume – a deepening obsession with individuality at all costs, which will only create a higher manufacturing-line procession of unique nut jobs that will inevitably create more subcultural splinters through the cult of personality.

Personally I'm going to rely on the real star of this book, who'd actually only made a slight cameo, which in the end I'm sure he will always deny and no one will ever believe, because its authenticity is just as remote as a 90-year-old Elvis Presley flipping your waffles at IHOP. I'm talking about Barack Hussein Obama...

As it stands, he's still duking it out with Hillary Clinton, and McCain has all but mutilated Mike Huckabee. Going back to the "*no country, Wizard of Oz hydra*" thing – true, the president has only classically been a smokescreen. Previously the pres has only been a figurehead with limited power, more a mascot then anything – a bone thrown to the public to make them feel as if they have a real voice. The only one since Lincoln to assume dictatorial powers was FDR (*although one could prime a case against Nixon*).

And then came George W. Bush. No, Dubya isn't a totalitarian dictator in the Stalinist or Hitlerian sense, but with The P.A.T.R.I.O.T. Act Bush curtailed civil liberties and erased federal boundaries to the point where Executive Office now has final veto power over every branch of legislature, even the Supreme Court. In wake of the blind rage Post-911, the White House has become something out of George Orwell's *1984*, or perhaps even worse – John Carpenter's *1997*.

Anyone with political common sense or belief in liberal democracy struggled wholeheartedly in the bleakest hours of 2001-2003. We watched them pull every horrendous trick out of the book, and it crushed the spirits of many.

In retrospect, it was all necessary. Because of the god-like power Bush has wormily created, somehow, miraculously, the conditions have been appropriated where the first non-Skull and Bones, ultra-liberal mulatto mut from way out in the left field of Hawaii will most likely assume absolute control over the second strongest military and economic power of planet earth (*sorry kids, but Red China is our sugar daddy*).

Every vestibule of power in "The Free World" will be delivered into the hands of a guy who went out of his way to grab the attention of some punk-rock bum brushing his teeth in a library restroom to say loud and clear: "***Yes, it was I – Barack Hussein Obama – mysterious candidate of elemental force who was taking the most hideous, caveman grunting shit you've ever heard in your life. And no, I'm not even going to ask for your vote. I just wanted to say 'hello' you strange, filthy street crustie who is most likely jacked out on heroin due to your grizzled, hard-boiled, and neurotic appearance. And by*** *the way, have a great day my good chap. Awfully lovely outside, don'tcha think?"*

Still, no matter how amazing he is (*or is not*), you know the whole world is going to blow up immediately after he takes office. Every Rush Limbaugh and Bill O'Reilly will blame him for everything, and everyone with common sense for progress and decency will stand their ground. He'll have classified access to all those Top Secret reports involving 911, and all the sneaky, horrendous power-plays and outright criminal actions of the Bush regime. In any instance, it'll be 1969 all over again – a giant line right down the middle of American society, and for once tilted towards the freaks…

* * * * *

I find it incredibly ironic that I now write these final lines in the exact same Michigan trailer park that incubated this entire fiasco to begin with. Call me a superstitious old coot, but what landed me here is the same churning wheel of karma that placed Dan Dismal at that gas station in Texas, crossed my path with Dennis Wilson in Albuquerque, had Acacia flowing through Tompkins Square NYC, dropped me nerve-shot at the Kerouac exhibit in Denver, fucked every safety net in San Fran until that saprophyte tomb of a sleeping bag at The Eagles Nest baptized me in fire… It's the exact same force that linked everyone – *no matter how random, scattershot, and insignificant* – into an interwoven tapestry beyond mere reasoning…

As for myself, I'm looking for a world without walls, without all the hang-ups and degradation and fear, hatred & paranoia that has given America the very title of this book. When I started this voyage I was still in the mind frame of revenge, bitter and raging over my fall from grace in the Detroit underworld. One year later and I'm poking the bloated carcass of whoever that guy was with a stick.

Of all the characters in this book, Raul spoke the wisest line: *"Fuck living in a prison in your own mind."* Thank you o-buddy o-pal, because whenever I close my eyes I'm still in Golden Gate Park playing acoustic in the shade, not the slightest care in the world. I don't want to take over the world. I just want to share it with someone… And that's exactly what I'm about to do. See, what brought me back to Michigan to finish this thing is exactly what set me off in the first place…

After I'd finished the book tour I was given a choice – comfortably set myself up in San Diego or go for broke & head to Seattle on a whim. I chose my poison, and went to Washington with $160 in my pocket in hopes of a new life. When I actually got off the bus, with the reality of post book-world finally caving in, I had no idea what my plan was.

My first instinct was to go to the Plankton Beat house, and luckily Puked On allowed me to sleep 16 hours straight. when I woke up in that surge of clarity, I headed downtown to an When park and unraveled like Rambo at the end of *First Blood*...

I had to get out; I needed the comfort of The Villa Winona. I called Greyhound and learned the next bus didn't leave for another 5 days... There I was, wanting nothing more then to hibernate, forced to wander the rapidly freezing Seattle landscape for another week. By chance Acacia and Brandon were in town, and all the friends I made during my August excursion kept me high & dry.

Three months later The Villa Winona had become the equivalent of Colonel Kurtz' last stand. There were now 10 people living in a two-bedroom house the size of an average Michigan basement. Skinner, Panda, Onyx & his wife, (*the non-Acacia*) Brandon, Chuck The Homey, Emerson, Dr. Santiago, and my no good brutha-from-anotha-mutha who was kicking the habit for good. And that doesn't even include the 20 plus other characters who'd materialize in random intervals.

By the middle of January every one with a job worked at that same pizza shop, which was now overrun by Mexicans. There was no privacy, the bad vibes kept enlarging, the roach situation had shot to unfathomable degrees... *No money, no food; the fights kept raging, the drugs and booze kept escalating, the madhouse had grown to inexplicable bounds. We all felt the coming doomsday...*

I was paralyzed by a growing depression and couldn't look beyond the immediate situation. I had sought in my journey the romance to end all romances, and came up empty-handed. Early November my quasi ex-wife called, ready to leave Michigan at the drop of a hat. I told her this was not the path she wanted to go down. I hung up, having broken her heart.

When I swallowed my uncertainty, I called back in jubilant euphoria. She was sobbing in the back of a squad car on her way to prison. 2 months of probation left, and a single noise complaint – *her first offense* –and the courts to strip from her the paternal rights to her son. She was en route to a year long sentence over nothing. I limberly dropped the phone, laughing horrendously...

The walls were closing in, the book kept dragging. Getting back to Seattle seemed hopeless, and no one wanted to leave SoCal... *Then I finally hit the mark*. I had $900 in the bank, dropped to 3 days a week at work, and was determined to complete this manuscript with all my free time. I came home brimming with sunshine, checked my email, and after 2 years of silence, "3" had emerged from obscurity.

Three phone conversations later I'd booked her a one-way ticket to San Diego. We were soon reunited forever & fang-bared to take over the world... Yet within a week it had deteriorated to catastrophe. It's a multi-layered shit-storm, but in brief, doomsday occurred. Santiago fled to Ohio, 3 went to MI, and I evacuated the next day...

So she's in Washington now, setting us up some roots, patiently tapping her foot & waiting on my lame ass to finish this thing... In the beginning I set out to reclaim all that I'd lost & in the end I succeeded brilliantly. The tragic irony is that in doing so, I'd lost all I'd become...

I tried to go back to what I once was. I set up shop, started a new band, saved money. I was determined to rent a house, get a car, a better job, some kind of certification. Push the journalism career, get the PR company rolling – network tours, book bands, all that high-fallutin' jazz... But who the fuck am I kidding? I'm GhostNomad, and my soul is no more than the blurring lines of the wide open road...

Anyone that wants to look me up, come to Seattle. I'm hoisting The Black Flag & calling all the wayward ships to port – then I'm heading back into the thick of America like the scumbag, bottom-feeding, ruthless land pyrate that I am. Fuck it man, live like Skynard or die tryin'... Anyway, I'd love to stay and chat, but my ride leaves in an hour. Siamo contenti? *Son dio ho fatto questa caricatura...*

Well, that's my story & I'm stickin' to it.

– GhostNomad –
(3.3.08; 1:40 pm; Greyhound Reference #26273180)

THE BIG SHINY PRISON
(*HISTORY OF A YEAR: 12.20.06-10.13.07*)
c/o Ryan Bartek, GhostNomad & Benedict Badoglio

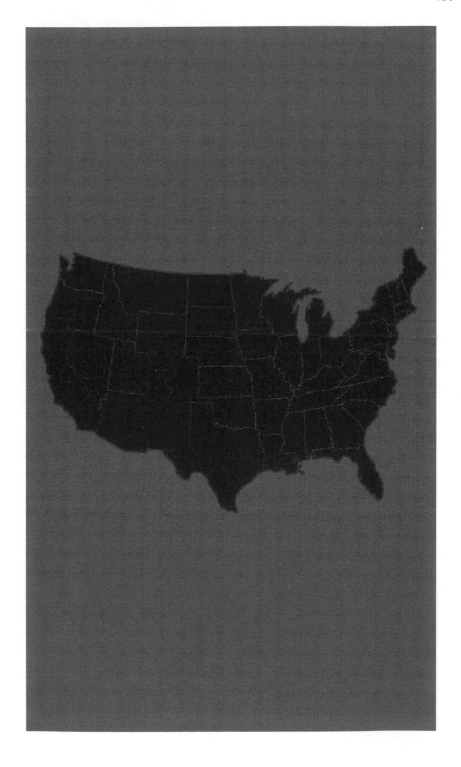

Guilty Parties

Brutal Truth, DWARVES, Pig Destroyer, Repulsion, Anal Cunt, MDC, Psyopus, Cephalic Carnage, Downtown Brown, Kylesa, Ludicra, STALAGGH, Lesbian, HIMSA, Atheist, Sol Evil, Impaled, Kettle Cadaver, Scorched Earth, Light This City, Foxy Shazam, In Memorium, Duff's Brooklyn, EXITIUM, Angelic Process, Blood Stained Dusk, Screaming Mechanical Brain, Genghis Tron, Intronaut, Abysmal Dawn, Solger, PHALLUS, Melechesh, OCTAGON, My Uncle The Wolf, The Gracchi, Salt Lick, Amish Noise, 7000 Dying Rats, Waco Jesus, Vertigo Venus, Severed Savior, Kill The Client, Dreaming Dead, They Live, Quinta Essentia, Whorehouse of Representatives, The Mathematicians, Anal Pudding, Disgorge & A.K.A. MABUS.

thank you all & please don't sue me, haha

Dr. Ryan Bartek

Ryan Bartek is a writer and musician from Detroit, now living in Portland Oregon. He is author of six books: "Anticlimax Leviathan," "The Big Shiny Prison (Volume One)," "Fortress Europe (The Big Shiny Prison Vol. II)," "Return To Fortress Europe (BSP Vol. III)," "The Silent Burning," and "To Live & Die On Zug Island"

He is guitarist/vocalist of the extreme metal band SKULLMASTER, the decimating grindcore act VULTURE LOCUST, grind squadron SASQUATCH AGNOSTIC, and punk act LURKING STRANGERS.

Bartek also performs acoustic/antifolk/folkpunk as The REAL Man In Black as well as public book readings and spoken word performances.

Primarily known for his journalism in the metal/punk undergrounds due to his counterculture travel books and long-term output for mass-market magazines, webzines & respected fanzines, R. Bartek is also the shadowy figure behind the press relations firm Anomie PR which services propaganda to thousands of media outlets globally.

All albums & books have been released under Anomie INC / Anomie Press, as FREE digital downloads

* * * * *

Ryan Bartek's book collection & music discography 100% FREE

www.BIGSHINYPRISON.COM

Inspired by the legendary works of Henry Miller, Jack Kerouac and Hunter S. Thompson, Detroit writer Ryan Bartek traveled the USA to create his own metal/punk road saga of extreme journalism. 1 year, 35 States, 600+ hours on Greyhounds & 1000 cities later, *"The Big Shiny Prison (Volume One)"* was released – a unique travel book featuring hundreds of face-to-face interviews with legends in the metal/punk undergrounds, as well as other fringe & alternative cultures in America today.

Less a "music book" and more a tribute to the Beat Generation, this genre-defying work combines the classic autobiographical road novel with the modern state of the underground. The result is an epic of monumental scope that has amassed a cult following since its release as a Free PDF in November 2009.

"The Big Shiny Prison (Volume One)" features appearances/interviews with members of Brutal Truth, DWARVES, Pig Destroyer, Repulsion, AxCx, MDC, Psyopus, Abysmal Dawn, Kylesa, Ludicra, Cephalic Carnage, Atheist, Impaled, HIMSA, Melechesh, Severed Savior, In Memorium, STALAGGH, Kettle Cadaver, Otesanek, The Angelic Process, 7000 Dying Rats, Screaming Mechanical Brain, EXITIUM, Light This City, Genghis Tron, Blood Stained Dusk, Solger, VILE, Sol Evil, SINDIOS, Kill The Client, OCTAGON, The Gracchi, My Uncle The Wolf, Apocryph, Salt Lick, Amish Noise, Lesbian, Churchburner, Fre-Ne-Tik, Alchemical Burn, Crematorium, Waco Jesus, Snotrokitz, Vertigo Venus, Kill The Precedent, Beefcake In Chains,, Dreaming Dead, They Live, Brian Botkiller, Diverje, Scorched Earth, Quinta Essentia, Alternative Tentacles, Whorehouse of Representatives, RU-486, Mathematicians, Anal Pudding, A.K.A. MABUS, Disgorge, Nihilistik Terrorist, Lysia Gori, The Crashing Falcon, Stormdrain, Bu Hao Ting, Potty Mouth Society, Stahlmantel, Uranium Death Crow, Hammers of Misfortune, Ron of Japan, Sasquatch Agnostic, Jakked Rabbits, We Both Know + Hunab Ku.

For more info & books from Anomie Press visit us online @

www.BigShinyPrison.com

Made in the USA
Columbia, SC
16 November 2018